ELGAR HANDBOOK OF CIVIL WAR AND FRAGILE STATES

Elgar Handbook of Civil War and Fragile States

Edited by

Graham K. Brown

Director, Centre for Development Studies and Senior Lecturer in International Development, University of Bath, UK

Arnim Langer

Director, Centre for Research on Peace and Development (CRPD) and University Lecturer in International Relations, University of Leuven, Belgium

Edward Elgar
Cheltenham, UK • Northampton, MA, USA

Published by
Edward Elgar Publishing Limited
The Lypiatts
15 Lansdown Road
Cheltenham
Glos GL50 2JA
UK

Edward Elgar Publishing, Inc.
William Pratt House
9 Dewey Court
Northampton
Massachusetts 01060
USA

A catalogue record for this book
is available from the British Library

Library of Congress Control Number: 2012938053

ISBN 978 1 84844 842 1 (cased)

Typeset by Servis Filmsetting Ltd, Stockport, Cheshire
Printed and bound by MPG Books Group, UK

Contents

Contributors

Pamela Aall is Provost of the Academy for International Conflict Management and Peacebuilding, United States Institute of Peace (USIP), Washington, DC, USA.

Tony Addison is Chief Economist and Deputy Director at the United Nations University World Institute for Development Economics Research (UNU-WIDER), Helsinki, Finland.

Pauline H. Baker is President of the Fund for Peace, Washington, DC, USA.

Robert H. Bates is Eaton Professor in the Department of Government at Harvard University, Cambridge, MA, USA.

Jacob Bercovitch was Professor of International Relations at the University in Canterbury, Christchurch, New Zealand.

Graham K. Brown is Director of the Centre for Development Studies and Senior Lecturer in International Development at the University of Bath, UK.

Halvard Buhaug is Research Professor at the Centre for the Study of Civil War, Peace Research Institute Oslo (PRIO), Norway.

Phil Clark is Lecturer in the Department of Politics and International Studies, School of Oriental and African Studies (SOAS), London, UK.

Chester A. Crocker is the James R. Schlesinger Professor of Strategic Studies at the Walsh School of Foreign Service, Georgetown University, Washington, DC, USA.

Han Dorussen is Professor in the Department of Government, University of Essex, Colchester, UK.

Virginia Page Fortna is Associate Professor in the Department of Political Science, Columbia University, New York, USA.

Sakiko Fukuda-Parr is Professor of International Affairs at the Graduate Program in International Affairs, New School University, New York, USA.

Kristian Skrede Gleditsch is Professor in the Department of Government, University of Essex, Colchester, UK.

Nils Petter Gleditsch is Research Professor at the Centre for the Study of Civil War, Peace Research Institute Oslo (PRIO), Norway.

Yvan Guichaoua is Lecturer in Politics and International Development at the University of East Anglia (UEA), Norwich, UK.

Fen Osler Hampson is Chancellor's Professor and Director of the Norman Paterson School of International Affairs, Carleton University, Ottawa, Canada.

Caroline A. Hartzell is Professor of Political Science in the Department of Political Science, Gettysburg College, Gettysburg, PA, USA.

Håvard Hegre is Professor in the Department of Political Science at the University of Oslo, Norway and Research Professor, Centre for the Study of Civil War, Peace Research Institute Oslo (PRIO), Norway.

Helge Holtermann is a PhD Candidate at the Centre for the Study of Civil War, Peace Research Institute Oslo (PRIO), Norway.

Lise Morjé Howard is Assistant Professor in the Department of Government, Georgetown University, Washington, DC, USA.

Patricia Justino is a Fellow of the Institute of Development Studies (IDS), Brighton, Sussex, UK.

Arnim Langer is Director of the Centre for Research on Peace and Development (CRPD) and University Lecturer in International Relations, University of Leuven, Belgium.

Roy Licklider is Professor of Political Science in the Department of Political Science, Rutgers, the State University of New Jersey, USA.

Katy Long is Lecturer in International Development at the London School of Economics and Political Science (LSE), UK.

Carmela Lutmar is affiliated to the Division of International Relations, School of Political Sciences, University of Haifa, Israel.

David M. Malone is President of the International Development Research Centre, Ottawa, Canada.

John McGarry is Professor of Political Studies and Canada Research Chair in Nationalism and Democracy in the Department of Political Studies, Queen's University, Kingston, Canada.

Carol Messineo is an independent consultant, New York, USA.

Nils W. Metternich is Postdoctoral Associate in Political Science, Duke University, Durham, NC, USA.

Robert Muggah is Fellow at the Institute of International Relations, Pontifícia Universidade Católica do Rio de Janeiro, Brazil.

Syed Mansoob Murshed is Professor of the Economics of Conflict and Peace at the Institute of Social Studies, The Hague, Netherlands and Professor of Economics, Coventry University, UK.

Heiko Nitzschke is First Secretary in the Security Council team at the German Mission to the United Nations in New York, USA.

Brendan O'Leary is Lauder Professor of Political Science in the Political Science Department, University of Pennsylvania, Philadelphia, PA, USA.

John Ohiorhenuan is a former Deputy Director of the Bureau for Crisis Prevention and Recovery, UNDP and Adjunct Professor at the Graduate Programme in International Affairs, New School University, New York, USA.

Andrea Ruggeri is Assistant Professor of International Relations in the Department of Political Science, University of Amsterdam, Netherlands.

Birgitte Refslund Sørensen is Associate Professor in the Department of Anthropology, University of Copenhagen, Denmark.

Frances Stewart is Emeritus Professor of International Development at Oxford Department of International Development, University of Oxford, UK.

Mohammad Zulfan Tadjoeddin is Lecturer in Development Studies at the University of Western Sydney (UWS), Australia.

Ole Magnus Theisen is a doctoral researcher in political science at the Norwegian University of Science and Technology (NTNU), Trondheim, Norway.

Henrik Urdal is Senior Researcher at the Centre for the Study of Civil War, Peace Research Institute Oslo (PRIO), Norway.

Peter Vermeersch is Professor of Political Science at the Institute for International and European Policy, University of Leuven, Belgium.

Stefan Wolff is Professor of International Security at the University of Birmingham, UK.

Preface

The *Elgar Handbook of Civil War and Fragile States* brings together contributions of a multidisciplinary group of internationally renowned scholars with the aim of providing the state of the art on such important issues as the causes of violent conflicts and state fragility, the challenges of conflict resolution and mediation, and the obstacles to post-conflict reconstruction and durable peacebuilding. This Handbook should be an extremely useful resource for both scholars and students of violent conflict and fragile states, and can give practitioners and policy makers some useful guidance and direction through the academic jungle of the latest research on these issues. While other companion volumes exists, this volume brings together a wider range of disciplinary perspectives, including development economists, quantitative and qualitative political scientists, sociologists and anthropologists, as well as peace practitioners. All contributions are written in a non-specialist way, however, and should be accessible to all readers.

While the compilation of the Handbook has been a thoroughly rewarding project, it was with great sadness that we learned of the death of one of our best respected contributors, Professor Jacob Bercovitch, on 10 June 2011. He was one of the leading experts in the field of conflict resolution, international negotiation and mediation. During his impressive career, Prof. Bercovitch not only contributed numerous publications to this field and established the widely used International Conflict Management dataset, but he was instrumental in shaping the field and directing the research into areas of great international importance. Many contributors in this Handbook will have been influenced and inspired by his work in one way or another. This is definitely the case for both of us.

Acknowledgements

Some of the chapters in this volume have appeared previously in different editions. Chapter 9 is a shortened and updated version of a chapter published in Robin Mearns and Andrew P. Norton (eds), *Social Dimensions of Climate Change: Equity and Vulnerability in a Warming World* (Washington, DC: The World Bank, 2010). An earlier version of Chapter 11 was published as a UNHCR Policy Development and Evaluation Service paper in March 2010. Chapter 20 was previously published in Chester A. Crocker, Fenn Osler Hampson and Pamela Aall (eds), *Turbulent Peace: The Challenge of Managing International Conflict* (Washington, DC: United States Institute of Peace Press, 2001). Chapter 21 was previously published in the *Annual Review of Political Science* **11** (2008). Chapter 23 was previously published in *International Affairs* **87** (1) (2011). We are grateful to the publishers for permission to reprint here.

1 Conflict, post-conflict, and state fragility: conceptual and methodological issues
Arnim Langer and Graham K. Brown

1.1 INTRODUCTION

In this chapter we explore the concepts of 'conflict', 'post-conflict' and state 'fragility'. The objective is to disentangle the conceptual confusion and overlap that exists between these concepts that complicates their use both in academic research and in policy making. After discussing definitional issues relating to conflict and fragility in the next section, we then analyse empirically the global evolution of the incidence and nature of violent conflict and its links with state fragility. In Section 1.4 we then consider issues involved in defining and identifying a 'post-conflict' situation and again relate this back to issues of state 'fragility'. Section 1.5 concludes.

1.2 CONFLICT AND FRAGILITY: CONCEPTUAL DISTINCTION AND OVERLAP

Let us start by exploring the concept of 'conflict'. Conflict is one of the most widely studied concepts and empirical phenomena in the social and human sciences. In 1960, Anatol Rapoport wryly observed that 'conflict is a theme that has occupied the thinking of men more than any other, save only God and love' (quoted in Bercovitch et al. 2009, p. 3; Rapoport 1960, p. 12). Moreover, in the contemporary post-9/11 security environment, it is no longer clear that these three concepts are as distinct as Rapoport appeared to assume.

Consequently, one can find 'conflict researchers' in such diverse disciplines as politics, psychology, anthropology, sociology, economics, philosophy and theology. And it is clearly the central theme within the 'conflict resolution' or 'peace studies' discipline, which developed as an independent field of study in North America and Europe from the 1950s (Ramsbotham et al. 2010). Given the multidisciplinary breadth of the pool of conflict researchers, it is not surprising that there is no agreement over the exact definition of what constitutes conflict. However, in general, the concept refers to an incompatibility of positions, a serious disagreement between different people, groups or countries, a violent dispute and/or a period of fighting between different parties (see, for instance, Bercovitch et al. 2009; Cramer 2006; Horowitz 1985; Lederach 1997; Ramsbotham et al. 2010). While conflicts usually have a negative connotation, it is an intrinsic and inevitable aspect of social life and interaction between individuals, groups and countries. As Bercovitch et al. (2009, p. 3) note in this respect 'conflict is normal, ubiquitous, and unavoidable. It is an inherent feature of human existence. It is even useful on occasion. It is difficult to conceive of a situation which is conflict-free. Indeed, the very presence of conflict is at the heart of all societies'.

While conflicts can occur between a range of social actors and on different levels of interaction, in this volume we are concerned with intra-state violent conflicts. The issues and parties involved in these conflicts differ widely. Moreover, as noted by Bercovitch et al. (ibid., p. 5), because conflict parties 'differ so widely in terms of their values, beliefs and goals, it is expected that they will differ with respect to their perception of the issues in conflict. In fact, conflict parties often disagree on the issues in conflict'. Within the conflict literature there are also widely divergent views on the causes of violent conflicts. Different causes and factors have been associated with the emergence of violent conflicts and other forms of intra-state violence, including youth bulges (see Chapter 10), weak institutions and corruption, climate change (Chapter 9), high levels of poverty (Chapter 4), an abundance of natural resources (Chapter 8), the presence of horizontal inequalities (Chapter 7), and individual economic motives and agendas (Chapter 6). Moreover, these different factors and associated causal linkages are often interrelated and mutually reinforcing.

Academic disputes over the 'causes' of violent conflict often align, albeit imperfectly, with methodological and epistemological positions. The dominance of quantitative econometric methods for identifying variables that predispose towards conflict, while highly influential in policy environments such as the World Bank and Western development agencies such as USAID (United States Agency for International Development) and DFID (UK Department for International Development), is heavily contested by other scholars who see such methods as at best a crude oversimplification of complex theoretical concepts such as 'ethnicity', and at worst as contributing towards the reification of particular identities and behaviours that, these scholars hold, are at the root of most violent conflicts. In this chapter we do not deal explicitly with these methodological debates (but see Brown and Langer 2010, 2011 for discussion of these issues). But we are convinced that understanding the emergence of violent conflicts and designing appropriate policy responses requires bringing together and integrating insights and knowledge from across these disciplinary and methodological divides.

Whether or not one subscribes to econometric methods in the analysis of conflict, some form of quantification is important for tracking the evolution of the incidence and nature of violent conflicts over time and across regions. In order to systematically collect the necessary data to track conflicts over time, we need to operationalize the concept of conflict. Different datasets (for example, Uppsala Conflict Data Program, University of Michigan Correlates of War (COW) Project, Heidelberg Institute on International Conflict Research COSIMO dataset) use different ways of operationalizing conflict, and this in turn may have important implications for any quantitative research based on these datasets. In a meta-analysis, Sambanis (2004b) compares the correlates of conflict across 12 different datasets and finds that very few variables are robust to different definitions, GDP per capita being the notable exception.

Christopher Cramer has noted in this respect that '[d]efinitional frames are often more than purely descriptive: they shape *what* is viewed and *how* it is interpreted' (Cramer 2006, p. 51, emphasis in original). But there are a number of other limitations and shortcomings with the way different datasets tend to operationalize violent conflict. We illustrate this by looking at the Uppsala Conflict Data Program (UCDP). The UCDP is arguably the most widely used conflict dataset, which operationalizes violent conflict as follows: 'An armed conflict is a contested incompatibility that concerns government and/or territory where the use of armed force between two parties, of which at least one is the government of a state, results in at least 25 battle-related deaths in one calendar year' (UCDP 2011). Again Cramer (2006) is very useful in highlighting two problems with this type of conflict operationalization. First, the casualty threshold is clearly a very arbitrary number. Second, the focus on battle-related deaths means that no consideration is given to other casualties and deaths that are indirectly the result of the violence. In most contemporary violent conflicts in the developing world the indirect deaths toll (through, for example, violence-induced famines or other forms of deprivation) by far outnumbers the battle-related death toll (see Chapter 27). While these are indeed important shortcomings of most existing conflict datasets which are often insufficiently taken into account in a substantial part of quantitative conflict research, it is equally true that the tracking of violent conflicts (with all its flaws and limitations) remains a necessary and extremely valuable research activity which can provide a wealth of information and can improve (in combination with other research) our understanding of the causes and dynamics of violent conflicts, and can also provide essential information for policy makers. Before exploring and analysing a number of important conflict trends in the next section, we shall turn to the concept of fragility or fragile states and its overlap with the concept of conflict.[1]

The concept of fragility is predominantly used within the international development policy community where it was introduced around a decade ago. It is therefore helpful to look at some of existing definitions of fragility within that community. The UK's DFID and the Organisation for Economic Co-operation and Development (OECD) have similar definitions of fragile states, which focus on service entitlements. DFID defines fragile states as occurring where 'the government cannot or will not deliver core functions to the majority of its people, including the poor', where core functions include service entitlements, justice and security (DFID 2005, p. 7). In as much, DFID explicitly notes that it does not restrict its definition of fragility to conflict or immediate post-conflict countries; non-conflict countries which are failing to ensure service entitlements constitute fragile states under DFID's definition (for example, Guyana). Similarly, countries in conflict but which are nonetheless providing an acceptable level of service entitlements to the majority of the population would not constitute fragile states under DFID's definition – this might apply to many countries with ongoing, but contained, separatist struggles such as Thailand. The OECD definition is similar, but emphasizes the 'lack of political commitment and insufficient capacity to develop and implement pro-poor policies' (Morcos 2005).

Canada's Country Indicators for Foreign Policy project (CIFP) uses a definition of fragile states that extends beyond service entitlements to include those states that 'lack the functional authority to provide basic security within their borders, the institutional capacity to provide basic social needs for their populations, and/or the political legitimacy to effectively represent their citizens at home or abroad' (CIFP 2006, p. 3). The USAID approach is similar, but differentiates between states 'in crisis' and those that are 'vulnerable'. 'USAID uses the term fragile states to refer generally to a broad range of failed, failing and recovering states ... the strategy distinguishes between fragile states that are vulnerable from those that are already in crisis'. Vulnerable states are defined as 'unable or unwilling to adequately assure the provision of security and basic services to significant portions of their populations and where the legitimacy of the government is in question'; while states in 'crisis' are defined as ones where the 'central government does not exert significant control over its own territory or is unable or unwilling to

---

[1]   This section draws on Stewart and Brown (2009).

assure the provision of vital services to significant parts of its territory where legitimacy of the government is weak or non-existent, and where violent conflict is a reality or a great risk' (USAID 2005b, p. 1).

Finally, the World Bank identifies fragile states with 'low-income countries under stress' (LICUS). 'LICUS are fragile states characterised by a debilitating combination of weak governance, policies and institutions, indicated by ranking among the lowest (<3) on the Country Policies and Institutional Performance Assessment (CPIA)'. Such states 'share a common fragility, in two particular respects: weak state policies and institutions: undermining the countries' capacity to deliver services to their citizens, control corruption, or provide for sufficient voice and accountability'; and are at 'risk of conflict and political instability: between 1992 and 2002, 21 out of 26 countries with intermediate or worse civil conflicts were also LICUS' (World Bank 2005a, p. 1).

While the definitions of conflict and fragility suggest that these are clearly distinguishable concepts, in practice, it appears that there is a significant overlap between conflict and fragile states. This empirical overlap is illustrated in Table 1.1, which relates World Bank designated fragile states to their conflict history over the last two decades. Only four of the World Bank fragile states – Kiribati, São Tomé and Príncipe, the Solomon Islands and Zimbabwe – have not experienced any violent conflict according to the UCDP dataset. However, both Zimbabwe and the Solomon Islands have experienced significant political violence, albeit not within the definitional parameters of the UCDP dataset.

While many definitions of fragility purport to be based on characteristics other than violent conflict, then, it is clear that the empirical overlap is considerable. The causal direction here arguably runs both ways: while conditions of fragility are often identified as a important cause of conflict, conflict itself can in turn create those conditions associated with state 'fragility' (see, for example, Chapters 3 and 24).

1.3   GLOBAL TRENDS IN VIOLENT CONFLICT

In the early 1990s, Western observers such as Robert Kaplan feared that the world was on the brink of a 'coming anarchy' as the end of the Cold War appeared to have unleashed long-suppressed conflicts in Sub-Saharan Africa, Central Asia, and even on the doorstep of Western Europe in the Balkans (Kaplan 1994). While the multitude of conflicts envisaged in these doom-laden scenarios largely failed to emerge, the post-9/11 security environment has given rise to new fears of 'unending war' on a global scale (Duffield 2007). In this section we review global trends in violent conflict

Table 1.1   Conflict and state fragility since 1991

World Bank List of Fragile States	Years of peace in 2010	Countries that have seen conflict since:			
		1991+	1996+	2001+	2006+
Afghanistan	0	*	*	*	*
Angola	0	*	*	*	*
Bosnia & Herzegovina	14	*			
Burundi	1	*	*	*	*
CAR	0	*	*	*	*
Chad	0	*	*	*	*
Comoros	12	*	*		
Côte d'Ivoire	5	*	*	*	
DRC	1	*	*	*	*
Eritrea	6	*	*	*	
Georgia	1	*	*	*	*
Guinea	8	*	*	*	
Guinea-Bissau	10	*	*		
Haiti	5	*	*	*	
Iraq	0	*	*	*	*
Kiribati	–				
Kosovo	10	*	*		
Liberia	6	*	*	*	
Myanmar	0	*	*	*	*
Nepal	3	*	*	*	*
Rep. of Congo	7	*	*	*	
São Tomé and Príncipe	–				
Sierra Leone	9	*	*		
Solomon Islands	–				
Somalia	0	*	*	*	*
Sudan	0	*	*	*	*
Tajikistan	11	*	*		
Timor-Leste	10	*	*		
Togo	23				
West Bank & Gaza	0	*	*	*	*
Western Sahara	20				
Yemen	0	*	*	*	*
Zimbabwe	–				

Source: Authors' calculations from UCDP (2011) and World Bank (2005a).

Source: Authors' calculations from UCDP, CSP and AKUF datasets.

Figure 1.1 Global incidence of violent conflict, 1946–2010

since the end of the Second World War to unpick these claims and identify important dynamics.

Despite definitional difficulties, particularly when it comes to coding conflicts for the construction of quantitative datasets, for much of the post-Second World War era, the broad global trend in conflict incidence was clear. Figure 1.1 shows the total number of ongoing conflicts each year according to three different datasets: the well-known, and oft-used, Uppsala/PRIO Armed Conflict Dataset; the Center for Systemic Peace dataset, maintained by Monty Marshall; and the less well-known AKUF (Arbeitsgemeinschaft Kriegsursachenforschung) dataset maintained by the Institute of Political Science at the University of Hamburg. Both the absolute number and the trend in conflicts reported by these three datasets are largely the same between 1946 and the mid-1990s, showing a clear and steady upward trend peaking around 1990, and then falling away rapidly. But after 1995, the datasets show divergent trends: AKUF dataset records around 40–50 conflicts for every year since 1995; CSP records a continuing downward trend from 1995, bottoming out at around 32 ongoing conflicts at the end of the twentieth century; and Uppsala/PRIO shows a steep drop like the AKUF dataset towards the end of the 1990s, but then there appears to be evidence of a return upwards trend from 2001.

These divergent trends post-1995 suggest at least that the category 'conflict' has become harder to operationalize over the past two decades. This could, in part, be explained within the context of Mary Kaldor's (1999) influential assertion that this era saw the emergence of 'new' types of warfare that were characterized by, *inter alia*: greater criminality and ethnic manipulation than in earlier 'old' wars, which she sees as more ideologically driven; greater targeting of civilian populations and a con-comitant inversion of the combatant–civilian casualty ratios over the past decades; and higher levels of intra-state conflict than inter-state conflict. Each of these characteristics make it more difficult to define the bounda-ries of 'conflict'. For instance, while the Abu Sayyaf group in the southern Philippines emerged in the context of a long secessionist struggle and declares itself to be a political organization fighting for independence, most analysts see it as a criminal group undertaking extortion and ransoming activities under a banner of political separatism. Of course, some theories of civil war – notably that associated with the work of Paul Collier (2000a) – see all conflict as such self-serving activities disguised to varying extents (see Chapter 6). But in so far as we need operationalizable rules for coding conflict, the activities of groups such as Abu Sayyaf's become extremely problematic.

While the historical validity of the clear distinction that Mary Kaldor draws between 'new' and 'old' wars has been heavily contested (Kalyvas 2001), there have nonetheless been clear trends in the changing nature of conflict and warfare globally over the past half century. We can get a glimpse at this by disaggregating the datasets in various ways. We can begin by examining the changing intensity of ongoing conflicts. Both the Uppsala/PRIO and CSP datasets distinguish between different levels of conflict. Uppsala/PRIO has two levels of intensity coded for entirely on the basis of the number of battle-related deaths: 'War', where a conflict has at least 1,000 battle-related deaths in a given year; and 'Minor', where a conflict has between 25 and 999 deaths in a given year. CSP codes for intensity on a 10-point scale of 'Magnitude' which takes into account battle deaths, but also other human costs (displacement, diminished quality of life, and so forth) and socioeconomic costs, such as infrastruc-tural damage and environmental degradation. Figure 1.2 shows the trend in these two measures of intensity since 1946. Between 1950 and 1990, both intensity variables are broadly flat despite, as we noted above, the steady increase in the incidence conflict over this time. In the post-1990 era, however, there is a clear decline in the intensity of conflict. It is worth noting here that the Uppsala/PRIO dataset codes intensity for each con-flict on an annual basis, while the CSP magnitude score is attached to the entire duration of the conflict; this may explain the greater short-term fluctuations in the Uppsala/PRIO trend.

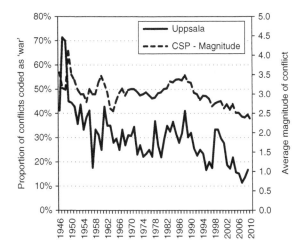

Source: Authors' calculations from UCDP and CSP datasets.

Figure 1.2   Global trends in conflict magnitude, 1946–2010

While conflicts have, in broad terms, become less common and less intense over the past couple of decades, however, they have also become much more heavily ethnicized, as Kaldor asserts. The CSP dataset codes for three different types of conflict: 'International' conflicts, including international wars but also 'internationalized' domestic conflicts such as decolonization struggles and Western intervention in Afghanistan and Iraq; 'Ethnic' conflicts that involve the state and 'a distinct ethnic group'; and, a residual category of 'Civil' conflict. Figure 1.3 shows the trend in these three types of conflict. In the immediate aftermath of the Second World War, around three-quarters of conflicts were either International or Civil; by the 1990s, however, around half of all conflicts were fought along ethnic lines, and this remains so to date. It should be noted here that these data do not impute any causal mechanism to ethnicity – which is a subject of intense theoretical and empirical debate (see Chapters 2, 7 and 16). Rather, this represents a simple coding of the main visible dividing line in any given conflict.

Geographically, conflict in the post-1945 era has been concentrated in two main regions. First, a long band of conflict-prone countries stretches down from Turkey and Israel through the Middle East, South Asia and into Southeast Asia. The second region is around the Great Lakes region of Africa, stretching also southwest towards Angola and northeast towards Sudan, Ethiopia and Somalia. Two other regions have also seen a high level of conflict: West Africa and Central America.

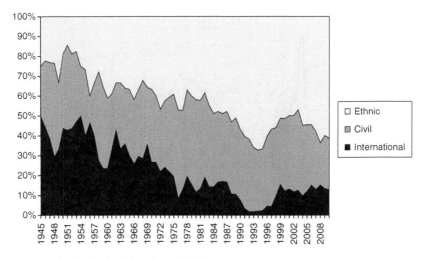

Source: Authors' calculations from CSP dataset.

Figure 1.3   Global trends in conflict type, 1946–2010

These geographical patterns have shifted over time (see Figure 1.4). Between 1970 and 1990, for instance, the West Africa region accounted for around 2 per cent of the conflict years globally, but by the turn of the century it accounted for around 10 per cent, with long-running civil wars in Sierra Leone, Liberia and Côte d'Ivoire and intermittent insurgency in a number of other countries, including Niger, Mali and Senegal (see Chapter 15).

A final transformation in global conflict patterns worth observing is the extent to which recent decades have increasingly seen global conflict dominated by recurrence of previous wars rather than the outbreak of 'new' wars (see Figure 1.5). Since 1995, more than three-quarters of the conflict onsets in the Uppsala/PRIO dataset are recurrences of previous conflicts. In part this can be attributed to the problematic nature of coding for the 'end' of a conflict. In Senegal, for instance, the Uppsala/PRIO dataset records six conflict 'onsets' related to the secessionist movement in Casamance between 1990 and 2003 with only one year of 'peace' between the termination of each phase and the onset of the next. It is not clear how far we should really be treating these as distinct 'onsets'. But it also points to the difficulty of establishing lasting peace in post-conflict societies.

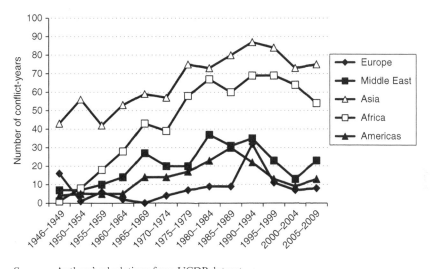

Source: Authors' calculations from UCDP dataset.

Figure 1.4 Geographical trends in global conflict incidence, 1946–2009

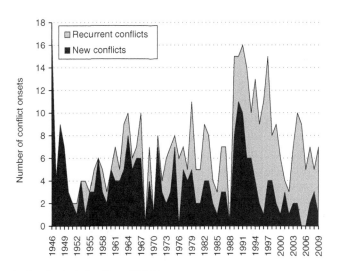

Source: Authors' calculation from UCDP.

Figure 1.5 Onset of new and recurrent conflicts, 1946–2010

1.4   FROM 'POST-CONFLICT' TO 'FRAGILITY'

The 'post-conflict' situation is not as easy to define as it sounds.[2] In major international conflicts, a formal surrender, a negotiated cessation of hostilities, and/or peace talks followed by a peace treaty mark possible 'ends' to conflicts. But in the intra-state conflicts that we are concerned with in this volume, it is not so simple. Hostilities do not normally end abruptly, after which there is complete peace. There may be an agreed 'peace' but fighting often continues at a low level or sporadically, and frequently resumes after a short period. Genuine attempts at reaching peace can frequently be derailed by 'spoilers' – that often turn out to be breakaway insurgent groups that are not yet ready or willing to give up armed conflict.

Rather than pick one or other condition to define the beginning and end of 'post-conflict', an alternative approach is conceptualizing the post-conflict scenario not as a period bounded by a single specific event, but as a process that involves the achievement of a range of peace 'milestones'. Taking a process-oriented approach means that 'post-conflict' countries should be seen as lying along a transition continuum (in which they sometimes move backwards), rather than placed in more or less arbitrary boxes, of being 'in conflict' or 'at peace'. An indicative list of peace milestones and possible indicators is given in Table 1.2.

Although we term these peace 'milestones', they are themselves processes, and may experience regress. For instance, for about five years following the initial peace agreement in 1998, the transition to peace in Northern Ireland was threatened by a number of spoiler groups both on the Catholic side (the Real IRA) and on the Protestant side (the Ulster Volunteer Force: UVF). In this sense, 'cessation of hostilities and violence' in the province could not really be said to have been completely achieved at that time, yet it would also seem to be wrong to deny that Northern Ireland did indeed enter into a post-conflict phase following the signing of the Good Friday Agreement in 1998. Hence, taking a process-oriented approach seems best.

While the achievement of some of these milestones may to some degree be contingent upon the prior achievement of other milestones, there is no conceptual necessity to impose a strict sequential order upon their achievement. For instance, refugee repatriation often commences soon after the cessation of violence and hostilities, even when there are no formal political agreements or when conflict parties are still in the process of negotiating a settlement. Most of these milestones are self-evident and require little further explanation. Moreover, while they represent the

---

[2]   This section draws on Brown et al. (2011).

Table 1.2   Peace milestones and indicators of progress

Peace milestones	Possible indicators of progress
Cessation of hostilities and violence	Reduction in the number of conflict fatalities Reduction in the number of violent attacks Time passed since major fighting stopped
Signing of political/peace agreements	Signing of and adherence to ceasefire agreements Signing and implementation of a comprehensive political agreement which addresses the causes of the conflict Endorsement of peace/political agreement by all major factions and parties to the conflict
Demobilization, disarmament and reintegration	No. of weapons handed in No./proportion of combatants released from military duty and returned to civilian life No./proportion of combatants released from active duty and returned to barracks No. of military barracks closed Successfulness of reinsertion programmes for ex-combatants Reduction in total number of active soldiers/ combatants Spending cuts on military procurements
Refugee repatriation	No./proportion of displaced persons and refugees that have returned home voluntarily No. of displaced persons and refugees still living involuntarily in refugees centres within a conflict country or abroad
Establishing a functioning state	The extent to which impunity and lawlessness has been reduced The extent to which the rule of law is introduced and maintained The extent to which corruption has been reduced Tax revenue as a proportion of GDP
Achieving reconciliation and societal integration	Number of violent incidents between groups Perceptions of 'others' via surveys Extent of trust (via surveys)
Economic recovery	Economic growth recovery Increased revenue mobilization Restoring of economic infrastructure Increased foreign direct investment

ideal progression, about half the cases of 'post-conflict' countries revert to conflict within a decade, and many more continue to suffer sporadic outbursts of violence.

Finally, a brief note on what constitutes the end of 'post-conflict' and a return to 'normalcy'. It is not possible to develop a precise definition of what constitutes the end of post-conflict; thresholds imposed would necessarily be arbitrary. This can be illustrated by considering possible economic indicators for assessing economic recovery. One indicator might be a return to the economic status quo ante – for example, a country's prior GDP per capita or human indicators, or rates of change of these indicators. Yet some economies grow throughout conflict (for example, Guatemala), so this is clearly an inappropriate criterion, while even in these economies certain parts of the economy may generally suffer damage which is to be measured not only by worse indicators of achievement than at the beginning of the conflict, but also by their lagging behind the rest of the economy and region.

On the other hand, severe conflict can inflict socioeconomic impacts that may take generations to remedy – or may not be remediable at all. Conflict-related increases in AIDS and HIV infection rates and major population displacements are examples. From this perspective, requiring that the economy returns to the pre-war status could be too ambitious.

Conceptualizing 'post-conflict' scenarios as a continuum characterized by multiple criteria rather than a single temporal characteristic (that is, years since the end of conflict) clearly brings it closer to the conceptualizations of state fragility discussed above. It is also much more reflective of reality: many countries in conflict emerge slowly out of conflict with a state that is often unwilling or unable to deliver services to large segments of society, but some emerge with their institutions largely unscathed. That these latter countries should be seen as having transcended 'post-conflict' status more rapidly is intuitive both analytically and from a policy-making perspective.

1.5   CONCLUSION

In this chapter, we have considered the relationship between concepts of 'conflict', 'state fragility', and 'post-conflict' and their operationalization. It is clear from this discussion that there are significant conceptual overlaps between these phenomena and that none of them is tightly definable. According to the World Bank definition of fragility, for instance, only two out of 33 fragile states were neither conflict nor post-conflict countries. The amorphous and overlapping nature of these concepts, while presenting problems for quantitative operationalization, is reflective of a fuzzy reality. Nonetheless, quantitative operationalization is important both for tracking trends over time and for econometric analysis. What this analysis of the concepts demonstrates, however, is that we need to remain critically engaged with the nature of our concepts around conflict even as we use them for analysis.

2 Ethnicity
Robert H. Bates

2.1 INTRODUCTION

Ethnicity poses major challenges to our understanding. How is the good polity to deal with cultural differences? Is it to insist that each individual be treated 'equally'? Or is it to take official note of cultural variation and ethnic diversity? These questions pose challenges for normative theorists. Equally compelling are the challenges posed to students of development, a subfield in which the study of ethnicity looms large.

Among the many things that 'development' can denote, I refer to two: economic prosperity and political security. Ethnicity plays an ambivalent role with respect to each, it would appear, promoting private accumulation but inhibiting public investment and multiplying opportunities for peaceful bargaining while also provoking bloodshed and violence. Even within a discussion so narrowly framed, the relationship between ethnicity and development emerges as complex.

2.2 PROSPERITY

The formation of capital underpins the growth of prosperity. When people form capital, they refrain from consumption and set a portion of their earnings aside; by investing that portion, they seek to secure a higher level of consumption tomorrow. When the gains from the investment outweigh the losses from the initial sacrifice, then the result is an increase in welfare for the individual and economic growth for the society.

When we speak of investment, we are speaking of capital formation. Families play a major role in capital formation and, in particular, in the formation of human capital. They do so by structuring relationships between generations such that the older generation, rather than consuming all its income, instead devotes a portion of its resources to the younger, who in turn will prosper and, while doing so, offer support to the older generation in return.

This intergenerational flow of funds underpins two forms of capital formation and ethnic groups play a major role in both. One is education; another, migration. The two are closely related, of course, as by educating their children, parents seek to prepare them to compete in urban labour markets.

To illustrate, consider Victor Uchendu, a noted anthropologist, who writes of his childhood in Eastern Nigeria (Uchendu 1965). Uchendu recalls the pride he felt as a child as his academic abilities became apparent. He writes too of the sacrifices his parents made to pay for his schooling and of the contributions collected by his community to send him to be educated abroad. Each step of the way – from village school room, to secondary school, and thence to the university – opened up a broader range of opportunities. Uchendu also writes of the burden of his success; for those who made it possible then looked to him for leadership, hoping that he, as an 'Ibo son abroad' would facilitate their own transition from a villager to a member of the global community (see also Hanna 2008; Hershfield 1969; Mgbeafulu 2003).

The pressures placed upon Uchendu find their parallel in other upwardly mobile communities. The Kikuyu of Kenya, the Chinese of Malaysia, the Jews in Europe, and the Bengali in India: these and other ethnic groups have pursued a strategy of collective improvement, based upon the transfer of resources between generations and the formation of human capital (Chua 2003).

Already suggested is the close link between education and migration: investments in the former are often made to assure success in the latter, as the skills acquired in school translate into better prospects in urban labour markets. Migration, it has been found, like education, represents a strategy formulated by families rather than a decision made by individuals. With globalization, moreover, the urban destination need not be an adjacent city or the national capital, but rather Houston, London, or Paris (Bates 1976; Stark and Bloom 1985). Reflecting the investment-like character of the process, the northern flow of people is mirrored by a southern flow of remittances. But why do these assume an ethnic character?

One reason is that as educated people from the countryside flow into labour markets in town, their skills confer a competitive advantage. Locals often respond by demanding that they be reserved places in the classroom and that the government guarantee them a 'fair share' of the jobs. As 'sons of the soil', they demand preferential treatment (Weiner 1978). Such responses characterize those of the Yoruba, in the face of Ibo immigration; the Malays, in response to the Chinese; the local population of Assam, when challenged by the Bengali – the list is long.

Less apparent but no less powerful is the role of ethnicity in strengthening the expectations that shape the relationships between generations. It is the adults who sacrifice and invest; the youths who benefit and repay. The sacrifice is immediate; the repayment necessarily delayed. While both parents and offspring should benefit from the investment, it is the parents who bear the risk; and the pact between generations will break down should they fear the youths' defection. The role of the ethnic group is to reduce such fears.

One way is by strengthening the family bonds. The groups celebrate the blood their members share and the ties of kinship that bind them. They honour the contributions of previous generations and the debt that is owed. By inculcating such values, they make it possible for the elders to believe that the young will fulfil their part of the intergenerational contract. In addition, in some settings, ethnic groups possess power. If a group possesses a homeland, the elders are likely to dominate its political and religious offices. Being in a position to sanction youths who abscond, the elders may then have reason to believe that few will actually do so (Bates and Yackolev 2002).

2.3   PUBLIC GOODS

While ethnic groups may thus contribute to prosperity by promoting the formation of human capital, they also appear to impede it. They do so when the diversity of preferences among ethnic groups reduces a community's ability to supply public goods or to share in the costs of their provision. A transport system; the supply of electricity or water; a harbour or airport – each requires large public investments. And the costs per capita – that is, the tax burden – will be lower the larger the size of the community that provides them. But as the size of the population increases, so too will the heterogeneity of preferences (Alesina and Spolare 2003). One group might prefer that a road run through its territory, rather than elsewhere; another that the airport not be located in 'its backyard'. The ability to apportion the costs and benefits declines as the number and intensity of such disagreements rises, making it more difficult for multi-ethnic societies to contract for the supply of public services. Ethnic diversity is an important source of such heterogeneity. A great deal of research has been devoted to its impact. To quote Banerjee et al. (2005, p. 639), the relationship between diversity and public goods provision is 'one of the most powerful hypotheses in political economy'.

Ethnicity is thus Janus-like. Ethnic groups provide governance structures that promote private investments in education and migration. For individual families, then, they strengthen the prospects for prosperity; and for societies, they strengthen the forces of modernization. On the other hand, where there is ethnic diversity, this tends to weaken the ability of the state to extract public revenues or to supply public goods. In so far as these services are themselves valuable or underpin private production, then, ethnic prosperity lowers the level of prosperity and thus the level of development.

2.4 CONFLICT

In addition to raising the costs of providing public goods, ethnic diversity – it is held – poses an additional threat: the prospect of conflict. While intuitively appealing, there is little systematic evidence to support this claim. Rather, once again, a more nuanced view emerges from the literature.

The equation of ethnic diversity and conflict stems from an obvious reality: in much of the developing world, where there is conflict, ethnic groups are likely to be involved (Kaplan 1994). But, as noted by Bates and Yackolev (2002) and Fearon and Laitin (1996), while ethnic diversity may characterize developing polities, conflict remains a rare event: even where there is a high level of ethnic diversity, there is often little fighting. The implication is clear: as a rule, ethnic groups cohabit peacefully. And, indeed, cross-national regressions find no systematic relationship between measures of ethnic diversity and the likelihood of civil conflict.

In general, ethnic politics in the developing world resembles that in the major metropolitan areas in the developed. Politicians draw upon ethnic blocs of voters; extract enough resources to offer enough patronage to retain their positions and bargain with others similarly positioned.

Having set aside the conventional wisdom and clarified the basic reality, the fact remains that ethnic groups do fight each other and that ethnic conflict is among the most deadly form of conflict (Fearon and Laitin, 2003). It is important to determine, then, the conditions under which ethnic politics turns violent.

An important case is when a group faces the prospect of political exclusion. When in 1962 politicians from the Northern Region of Nigeria allied with those in the Western Region, for example, the Ibo in the Eastern Region then 'Stood Alone', in the words of the West African Pilot; their isolation marked an important step towards the civil war that resulted from their attempted succession. More systematic are data from India where (Wilkinson 2004) finds a systematic relationship between the threat of exclusion and political violence in municipal elections. In constituencies that offer multiple ways of forming majority coalitions, he finds, politicians face incentives to bargain in order to construct a majority coalition and the composition of that coalition may alter between elections; when the constituency is evenly divided and the divisions likely to be longstanding, however, then political leaders may seek to provoke incidents that will politicize and rally their backers. The expected value of the risky outcome from violence may exceed the losses certain to follow from the exclusion from power.

Politicians may also provoke ethnic violence when the loss of office would leave them vulnerable to reprisals. This is particularly true, of course, of those who have themselves employed violence while in office. Examples can be taken from the period of re-democratization in Africa. Some, such as Samuel Doe of Nigeria (Huband 2003), purposively attacked the traditional rivals of his own ethnic group so that the latter would be unable to defect from his coalition and thus lose the protection he, as president, could offer. A similar account is offered for Rwanda, when the Hutu elites appears to have provoked retaliatory attacks by Tutsi in an effort to obviate the formation of a cross-ethnic coalition that would have threatened their rule (Strauss 2006). Statistical support is offered by Collier and Bates (2008), who find that when rulers have employed violence to consolidate their power, then ethnic diversity increases the likelihood of conflict.

2.5 CONCLUSION

Recent work has thus deepened our understanding of the relationship between ethnicity and development. In light of this work, the sweeping claims of earlier scholars (Apter 1963) and contemporary commentators (Kaplan 1994) give way to a more nuanced assessment. We now know that ethnicity can both help and hinder the process of development and the conditions under which it will do the one or the other.

The next steps in this research are suggested by Habyarimana et al. (2009), who isolate the specific pathways by which ethnic group membership promotes – or fails to promote – the provision of public goods. Using experimental methods in a field setting, they probe the micro-level linkages that underlie the macro-level patterns described in this chapter. While, in the judgement of this writer, Habyarimana et al. fail to probe behaviour under conditions of threat – conditions commonly associated with ethnic politics – they brilliantly illustrate the kind of research that can – and should – be conducted. Advances in this field have been marked by the increased precision of measurement and the refinement of argument. By furthering both, Habyarimana et al. provide an important stepping stone for further progress.

3 Human security
Sakiko Fukuda-Parr and Carol Messineo

3.1 INTRODUCTION

Human security is a concept that identifies the security of human lives as the central objective of national and international security policy. It contrasts with, and grew out of increasing dissatisfaction with, the state-centred concept of security as an adequate conceptual framework for understanding human vulnerabilities in the contemporary world and military interventions as adequate responses to them. As Mary Kaldor (2007) explains in her introduction to her volume *Human Security*, human vulnerability is pervasive, threatened by 'new wars' where actors are no longer states, that do not follow the rules of conduct of 'old wars', and that cannot be won by the means of old wars. Moreover, these new wars are intertwined with other global threats including disease, natural disasters, poverty and homelessness. 'Yet our security conceptions, drawn from the dominant experience of the Second World War, do not reduce that insecurity; rather they make it worse' (ibid., p. 10). Similarly, Mahbub ul-Haq proposes human security as a new paradigm of security:

> [T]he world is entering a new era in which the very concept of security will change – and change dramatically. Security will be interpreted as: security of people, not just territory. Security of individuals, not just nations. Security through development, not through arms. Security of all the people everywhere – in their homes, in their jobs, in their streets, in their communities, in their environment. (ul-Haq 1995, p. 115)

The concept has become increasingly widely used since the mid-1990s (Gasper 2010a). While initially used primarily with reference to state policies and the search for new international security and development agendas after the end of the Cold War, it is increasingly being used in policy advocacy by civil society groups on a broader range of contemporary issues from civil war to migration to climate change (Gasper 2010a; O'Brien et al. 2010; Truong and Gasper 2010).

Academic institutions have developed research programs and degree programs in human security. Yet human security is a contested concept. There are multiple formulations of its definition and divergent efforts to evolve associated global agendas. Efforts to promote human security for foreign policy of states and institutionalize it at the UN have generated controversies. A large literature has emerged challenging, defending, or explaining the meaning and the added value of the concept. Many practitioners in international affairs, in both security and development fields, remain sceptical of its practical usefulness and political relevance. Often criticized as ambiguous, and subject to as many interpretations, questions remain as to exactly what function it is serving. Is it a full-scale conceptual paradigm, a doctrine for a new global security policy, a norm, or just a term, as Roland Paris (2001) asks? A rich literature aiming to answer these questions has emerged, as later sections of this chapter will review.

In this chapter we review the concept, its use in policy debates and the academic literature on the concept as an idea in international relations. We argue that in spite of the controversy, human security is an important concept not to be ignored as a significant discourse in contemporary debates about the world order. It opens up new lines of analysis, gives voice to new actors. Its value added in the security field is that it focuses attention on human beings and integrates non-military mechanisms as means to security. Its value added in the development field is to focus attention on downside risks. We consider human security to be an idea that is part of the capability approach. For that reason, human security is closely related to human development and to human rights.

This chapter reviews the concept and its applications, focusing on those areas most relevant to violent conflicts and fragile states. Section 3.2 reviews human security as a concept, exploring alternative definitions currently in circulation and their historical antecedents. Section 3.3 identifies the major policy applications to promote 'human security' and their diverse objectives and mechanisms. Section 3.4 surveys the critical debates, particularly in the academic literature. The final section concludes with commentary on its relevance for violent conflicts and fragile states.

3.2   THE CONCEPT

While human security is now used as a general term with a wide range of meanings in many contexts from domestic violence to migration, it originated in the many debates about 'collective security' around the end of the Cold War. The central idea is the primacy of human life as the objective of security policy – or the referent object. This is a claim that has major implications for almost all aspects of thinking and acting on security which had for decades been built around the primacy of the state. The concept of human security expands the scope of analysis and policy in multiple directions. According to Rothschild, it extends downwards 'to the security of groups and individuals'; upward, 'to the security of international systems'; horizontally, from military security 'to political, economic, social, environmental, or "human security"'; and in all directions 'upwards to international institutions, downwards to regional or local government, sideways to nongovernmental organizations, to public opinion and the press, and to the abstract forces of nature or of the market' (Rothschild 1995, p. 55).

By focusing on the individual, the concept must necessarily include all aspects of human rights including the need for meeting basic needs and the demands of political and social freedom – both 'freedom from fear' and 'freedom from want'. According to the South African political leader Frene Ginwala,

> Thinking about security broadened from an exclusive concern with the security of the state to a concern with the security of people. Along with this shift came the notion that states ought not to be the sole or main referent of security. People's interests or the interests of humanity, as a collective, become the focus. In this way, security becomes an all-encompassing condition in which individual citizens live in freedom, peace and safety and participate fully in the process of governance. They enjoy the protection of fundamental rights, have access to resources and the basic necessities of life, including health and education, and inhabit an environment that is not injurious to their health and wellbeing. Eradication of poverty is thus central to ensuring the security of all people, as well as the security of the state. (Ginwala in Commission on Human Security 2003, p. 3)

A departure from the realist, state-centered concept of security that has dominated academic research as well as foreign policy thinking of major powers, this conceptual reframing of security has important policy implications. It brings new issues or vulnerabilities and measures or actions as priorities for global security that were not on the international and collective security agendas:

- vulnerability to oppression and physical violence due to deliberate action and neglect by the state to its own citizens that results in mass displacement of people both within and across national borders, and the responsibility of the international community to protect people in these situations;
- vulnerability to poverty and destitution as a factor interconnected with threats of violence, and the need to recognize the interrelationship between conflict and poverty as cause, consequence, and policy response to civil wars;
- development and ending poverty as important means to achieve human security, and international cooperation for development as a priority;

- vulnerability to downside risks from multiple sources including natural disasters, economic downturns and climate change as priority concerns for a wide range of public policy areas. Downside risks were neglected in dominant thinking about poverty and development which focused on progress, inequality and deprivation;
- actors other than the state as sources of threat and as holders of obligations to protect; and
- global interconnectedness of security threats (such as terrorist networks, global financial crises and global diseases) and necessary responses.

3.2.1   The State and Individual in the Conception of Security in Historical Perspective

The idea of the individual as the referent of security is not new. The twentieth-century conception of the state as the referent of security was not crystallized until the eighteenth century when, following the French Revolution and the Napoleonic Wars, threats to the state emerged as most important security issue; 'the reification of the state was the product of specific historical circumstances' (MacFarlane and Khong 2006, p. 246). Previously, the concept of security was broader, referring to both the state and the individual (Rothschild 1995). For the Greeks, the city-state provided the order and protection prerequisite for human endeavors and well-being (MacFarlane and Khong 2006). For the Romans, *securitas* denoted an inner state of tranquility and freedom from care (Rothschild 1995, p. 61).

Although the term was not used, human security is at the heart of the purpose of the United Nations. In the aftermath of the horrors of the Second World War, the framers of the 1945 United Nations' Charter were motivated by the need for nations to act collectively to protect freedom and dignity of individuals and recognized the tension between the individual and the state, and required states to respect human dignity and fundamental freedoms as human rights. The international conventions on human rights established these norms. Collectively, these agreements accord international legal recognition to the rights of individuals and provide individuals with a legal basis for challenging 'unjust state law or oppressive customary practice' (Michael Ignatieff, quoted in MacFarlane and Khong 2006, p. 18). The Charter also recognizes the link between development and peace, seeing the social and economic turmoil following the First World War as a factor behind the rise of Nazism. The Charter articulated concern for economic and social progress alongside peace, security and human rights. These have since served as the central objectives of the United Nations.

In the 1970s and 1980s several commissions produced reports that challenged traditional notions of state-centred national security and served as precursors to an idea of human security (Bajpai 2003). For example, in 1972, the Club of Rome Group issued *The Limits to Growth* and asserted that 'men of all nations' face threats from economic disruptions, environmental degradation, and erosion of traditional values (ibid.). In 1982, the Independent Commission on Disarmament and Security Issues chaired by Olof Palme issued *Common Security: A Blueprint for Survival* which called for cooperative approaches to the threat posed by nuclear weapons and discussed how security involves not just military but also economic and political cooperation (Rothschild 1995).

3.2.2   Contemporary Definitions of Human Security

A multiplicity of actors (governments, international organizations, researchers, non-governmental organizations: NGOs), use the term for different purposes (agenda setting, advocacy, analysis) and in diverse contexts (foreign policy, international diplomacy, analytical framework for evaluating the state of the world and proposing appropriate policy priorities, as a field of study and research in international relations). There is no single consensus definition of human security, which in itself is a source of criticism of the concept as lacking a common definition and therefore ambiguous. The competing definitions are broadly categorized into two groups – broad and narrow – around each of which two parallel discourses have evolved.

The 'broad' formulation
The broad conception is concerned with human vulnerability overall, and therefore encompasses all forms of threats from all sources. This includes, in addition to organized political violence recognized in the narrow concept, other forms of violence, as well as threats of natural disasters, disease, environmental degradation, hunger, unemployment and economic downturn.

The broad formulation has been proposed by a number of authors, including UN documents on human security since 1994, the 1994 UNDP *Human Development Report* (HDR), the European Council and the Barcelona Group, the Commission on Human Security, the Government of Japan, as well as academics such as Beebe and Kaldor (2010), Chen and Narasimhan (2003), King and Murray (2001), Tadjbakhsh and Chenoy (2007), Thomas (2000) and several others. While some take a more reductionist approach to focus on threats from disease and natural disasters (King and Murray 2001), others take a broader approach to include all threats and vulnerabilities to human freedom and dignity including threats of hunger, disease, natural disasters, economic downturns and political repression. In UN documents and debates, human security is often characterized as incorporating the two pillars of the UN Charter which are the foundations of human rights instruments: 'freedom from want' and 'freedom from fear' (Annan 2000; Frechette 1999; Ogata 1998; Thakur 1997).

The 1994 HDR (UNDP 1994), often credited as the source of the contemporary use of the term, notes that it is difficult to formulate a rigorous definition of human security because 'like other fundamental concepts, such as human freedom, human security is more easily identified through its absence than its presence, and most people instinctively understand what security means'. It offered the following definition: 'Human security can be said to have two main aspects. It means first safety from such chronic threats as hunger, disease and repression. And second, it means protection from sudden and hurtful disruptions in the patterns of daily life – whether in homes, jobs or in communities'. In this conception of security, the threats or causes of insecurity can be from the forces of nature or manmade, from wrong policy choices. It identified seven important dimensions of human security:

(i)   economic security (an assured basic livelihood derived from work, public and environmental resources, or reliable social safety nets);
(ii)   food security (physical and economic access to basic food);
(iii) health security (access to personal healthcare and protective public health regimens),
(iv)   environmental security (safety from natural disasters and resource scarcity attendant upon environmental degradation);
(v)   personal security (physical safety from violent conflict, human rights abuses, domestic violence, crime, child abuse, and self-inflicted violence as in drug abuse);
(vi)   community security (safety from oppressive community practices and from ethnic conflict); and
(vii) political security (freedom from state oppression and abuses of human rights).

In its 2003 report, 'Security Now: Protecting and Empowering People', the Commission on Human Security (CHS), offered a definition that overlaps considerably with the 1994 HDR, but also attempted to bridge the gap between the 'narrow' and 'broad' versions. It refrained from itemizing threats to human security, referring instead to a broad set of 'elementary rights and freedoms people enjoy' forming a 'vital core'. Nonetheless, it gives examples of important 'menaces' from environmental pollution, transnational terrorism, massive population movements, infectious diseases, and long-term conditions of oppression and deprivation (Commission on Human Security 2003, p. 24). It emphasizes the involvement of multiple actors beyond the state – NGOs, regional organizations, civil society in managing human security, and empowerment of people as an important condition of human security and emphasize that state security and human security are 'mutually reinforcing and dependent on each other' (ibid., p. 6). And the report devotes chapters to people who are vulnerable to threats of violent conflict, poverty and economic security, health, knowledge; areas that overlap with the seven areas enumerated in the 1994 HDR.

The broad conception is closely related to, and reflects the intellectual roots in, the theories of capabilities and of human rights. Not surprisingly, the articulation of human security in the 1994 HDR and in the 2003 CHS report conceptualizes human security in terms of Sen's capabilities approach (Sen, 1999). According to this approach, human freedoms are the ability of individuals to be and do the things they value, and the choices they have to lead their lives accordingly. The concept of human security considers the downside risks: 'human security means people can exercise these choices freely – and that they can be relatively confident that the opportunities they have today will not be lost tomorrow' (UNDP 1994, p. 23).

Other authors who use the broad human security concept do not draw so explicitly from the theory of capabilities but nonetheless come to human security as a necessary element of a life with dignity and freedom. Leaning and Arie (2000) emphasize the psychological sense of well-being that is attendant upon material aspects of human security. Their concern is not merely for access to reliable shelter, but also for 'a sustainable sense of home'; not merely for political freedom and lack of repression but also for 'constructive group attachment'; not merely for safety from sudden downward dislocations but also for 'an acceptance of the past and a positive grasp of the future' (ibid., p. 38). Caroline Thomas writes about 'personal autonomy, control over one's life and unhindered participation in the life of the community' (2000, pp. 6–7). Using these broad criteria, human security encompasses a life lived with dignity as well as one free from fear.

The 'narrow' formulation

The narrow formulation focuses on threats of violence, particularly organized political violence, and is used by the Human Security Network at the UN, the annual Human Security Reports, and academics such as MacFarlane and Khong (2006). They specify human security as 'freedom from organized violence', that is (i) committed by an identifiable perpetrator and (ii) is not random but rather is organized in a way that 'makes that violence potent' (ibid., p. 245).

The proponents of the narrow definition criticize the broad definition as being too broad to be useful (MacFarlane and Khong 2006; Mack 2002). They defend the narrow definition for the reverse reason: 'This narrower focus on human security emphasizes the more immediate necessity for intervention capability rather than long-term strategic planning and investing for sustainable and secure development' (Liotta and Owen 2006, p. 43).

3.3   INTERNATIONAL POLICY DEBATES

Since the mid-1990s, a number of policy debates have revolved around human security in several contexts. First, Japan and Canada took political initiatives to promote the concept and to institutionalize it within the UN. Second, it has been used as part of the European Union's effort to rethink and redefine its common security policy. Third, it has sometimes been adopted as official government policy. Fourth, it has been used in policy analysis and advocacy as a normative and conceptual framework over a number of issues – particularly climate change in recent years.

3.3.1   Diplomatic Initiatives to Promote the Human Security Concept and Its Institutionalization in the UN

The 1994 HDR stimulated new debates within the UN and related fora around human security as a new paradigm of development and security. Canada, Japan and Norway in particular took initiatives to promote the concept, which developed along two separate, parallel trajectories. Canada and Norway created the Human Security Network of foreign ministers in 1999 to meet annually to dialogue over priorities for common security. The group includes Austria, Canada, Costa Rica, Greece, Ireland, Jordan, Mali, the Netherlands, Norway, Slovenia, South Africa (observer), Switzerland and Thailand. Their vision aligns with the narrow definition of human security, emphasizing threats of violence, repression and human rights abuses; they have championed some specific initiatives, such as: the international ban on anti-personnel mines; the international criminal court; the control of small arms and light weapons; the protection of children and women from violence; climate change; the promotion of women, peace and security; human rights education; and some poverty-related issues.

Japan took up human security as a broad concept, and has championed the use of development cooperation as an instrument to promote it through country-level activities. In 2001 the Ministry of Foreign Affairs set up an independent Commission on Human Security, an international panel of high level personages co-chaired by Sadako Ogata and Amartya Sen, and in 2005 created the Friends of Human Security. Japan has also led diplomatic efforts to introduce debates about human security in the General Assembly. Other members of the Commission from different parts of the world have taken the initiative to promote the concept in their own regions. In 1999, Japan established the United Nations Trust Fund for Human Security (UNTFHS) with the UN Secretariat to promote a human security agenda as something that can be operational and implemented on the ground, and to finance community development in health, education and agriculture; landmine removal; and post-conflict reconstruction and peacebuilding (Atanassove-Cornelis 2006; United Nations 2010b). This strand of initiative contrasts with the Human Security Network in the formulation of the concept, definition of threats, and policy response. While the Human Security Network promotes global policy initiatives, this initiative promotes national development programs supported by development cooperation.

In 2008, the United Nations General Assembly embarked on a thematic debate on human security and its implications for member states and the United Nations. In April 2010, Secretary-General Ban Ki-moon presented to the General Assembly the first official report on the concept. Titled 'Human Security', the report broadly defined the concept as 'freedom from fear, freedom from want and freedom to live in dignity' (United Nations 2010b, p. 2). In May 2010, UN General Assembly held its first formal debate on human security as presented in Ban Ki-moon's report and in July the General Assembly passed its first resolution on human security, which was to continue debate.

Throughout the last decade and a half, these diplomatic efforts to promote human security in the UN have met with political resistance and controversy. From the very start when the concept entered international debates, many states reacted to human security as a potential challenge to the principle of state sovereignty. If adopted as a doctrine for international security, it could build a culture of intervention. Thus, for example, in 1994 several developing countries protested at the launch of the HDR. They reacted particularly to the idea that early warning of human security crises could be mounted by monitoring such indicators as inequality, human rights abuses, poverty, ethnic conflict and military spending, and if that were done, countries such as Afghanistan, Haiti, Sudan, and Zaire would raise the alarm. Human security debates have continued to raise questions from delegations about the role of the state and the potential conflict with sovereignty. Each debate on human security raises questions from several G77 countries about the implications of human security and sovereignty. The negotiated language on human security emphasizes human security as a comprehensive framework for preventing and mitigating vulnerabilities faced by both people and governments. But this has been complicated as this approach was being negotiated simultaneously with the debate of the Responsibility to Protect (R2P) which calls for international interventions, limited specifically to cases of genocide, war crimes, ethnic cleansing and gross violations of human rights. The human security concept has been separated from the R2P agenda. The G77 has not supported human security, even though the concept could be helpful for their interests, especially in promoting development as priority UN agendas (Tadjbakhsh and Chenoy 2007). Lacking strong support, the initiatives to institutionalize human security as a framework for international security in the UN and elsewhere have not flourished; the resolution adopted in 2010 was to continue the debate, the Trust Fund has not attracted many donors other than Japan, and the membership of the Human Security Network set up by Canada and Norway has not grown. The UN debate has focused on addressing two questions: the need to continue the debate, and the need to clarify the concept.

Nonetheless, despite the controversy, the core normative principles of the human security concept are entrenched in the UN's key policy documents since the 1990s on post-Cold War common global security agendas. The 2004 report of the Secretary-General's *High Level Panel on Threats, Challenges, and Change* articulated a new vision of collective security framed around the human security concept. It asserts that human beings bear the burden of security failures but states bear the responsibility of preventing and responding to security threats. The report called for UN member nations to arrive at a new consensus that recognizes the globalized nature of contemporary threats and accepts vigorous cooperative solutions. 'Today's threats recognize no national boundaries, are connected, and must be addressed at the global and regional as well as the national levels' (United Nations 2004a, p. 1). The report calls for strengthening funding mechanisms and collective security institutions and instruments. These are analytical documents of the Secretary-General, however, and not hard resolutions passed by member states.

3.3.2   The Responsibility to Protect

In 2000 the then Canadian Foreign Minister Lloyd Axworthy launched an International Commission on Intervention and State Sovereignty

(ICISS) to 'promote a comprehensive debate on the relationship between intervention and sovereignty, with a view to fostering global political consensus on how to move from polemics towards action within the international system'. It articulated the 'right of humanitarian intervention' or the responsibility to protect R2P individuals from large-scale and systematic violations of their human rights, committed by their own governments. A responsibility to protect shifts the focus from state sovereignty to the human rights of people residing in those states. Under R2P, a state's sovereignty is no longer absolute but rather is contingent on whether residents are protected from gross human rights abuses; the international community has a legitimate duty to intervene in the domestic affairs of states to contain dire threats to human safety. According to the ICISS, 'the protection of human security, including human rights and human dignity, must be one of the fundamental objectives of international institutions' (ICISS 2001, p. 6). The ICISS developed a three-part framework that emphasizes responsibility to prevent the outbreak of violence as well as to provide support for rebuilding and reconciliation after intervention (Jolly et al. 2009, p. 175). Because states that govern under rule of law and human rights norms are best positioned to guarantee the safety of their citizens, implicit in R2P is the need to address the development dimension of human security with assistance to strengthen state governance and address economic and social inequalities (ibid). This articulation was endorsed by the 2005 World Summit, and by the UN Security Council Resolution 1674, and a GA resolution in 2009 (United Nations 2005, 2006b).

3.3.3 European Union 'Doctrine'

While UN-related diplomatic initiatives promoted human security as a concept, with its policy implications left ambiguous, open to interpretation, they do not go as far as proposing human security as a 'doctrine' for international security policy. However the Study Group on Europe's Security Capabilities, known as the Barcelona Group (independent group created by the then EU High Representative Javier Solana) proposed human security as a doctrine for European security policy. This initiative builds on the new European Security Strategy adopted by the European Council (2003) in 2003 that identifies terrorism, proliferation of weapons of mass destruction, regional conflicts, state failure and organized crime as the key threats facing Europe. The Barcelona Group's 2004 report articulates a doctrine, especially concerned with the humanitarian emergencies and human rights crises related to these threats. For the Barcelona Group, 'Human security refers to freedom for individuals from basic insecurities caused by gross human rights violations' (Study Group on Europe's Security Capabilities 2004). The doctrine proposes:

(i)   seven principles: the primacy of human rights, clear political authority, multilateralism, a bottom-up approach, regional focus, the use of legal instruments, and the appropriate use of force. The report puts particular emphasis on the bottom-up approach: on communication, consultation, dialogue and partnership with the local population in order to improve early warning, intelligence gathering, mobilization of local support, implementation and sustainability;

(ii)   a 'Human Security Response Force', composed of 15,000 men and women, of whom at least one-third would be civilian (police, human rights monitors, development and humanitarian specialists, administrators and so on). The Force would be drawn from dedicated troops and civilian capabilities already made available by member states as well as a proposed 'Human Security Volunteer Service'; and

(iii) a new legal framework to govern both the decision to intervene and operations on the ground. This would build on the domestic law of host states, the domestic law of sending states, international criminal law, international human rights law and international humanitarian law.

3.3.4   Foreign Policy of Governments

Japan and Canada each embedded human security within its foreign security (Debiel and Werthes 2006). Propelled by a 1998 speech by Prime Minister Keizo Obuchi that articulated human security as a pillar of Japan's foreign policy, Japan's Ministry of Foreign Affairs adopted human security as a framework for their development cooperation.

Canada took up the narrow formulation of human security emphasizing the protection of individuals from violence (Department of Foreign Affairs and International Trade 1999). Canada permits the use of military force for humanitarian intervention to protect civilians, and engages in peacekeeping operations, in conflict prevention and peacebuilding, in strengthening governance and accountability to foster democracy and human rights, and in countering transnational organized crime. Canada has been instrumental in establishing an International Criminal Court and in advancing the protection of children in conflict.

3.3.5 Human Security Perspectives on Diverse Global Challenges

Human security has been applied to a number of thematic issues as an evaluative framework for assessing the state of affairs, and for critiquing and designing public policy. It can be useful for social, economic and environmental themes in focusing on the downside risks, complementing conventional analyses which focus on progress, deprivation or disparities.

Downside risks associated with globalization pose new types of challenges in the twenty-first century that require international cooperation to prevent or mitigate. Among these threats are: financial volatility associated with the rapid cross-border transfers of money; job and income insecurity due to global competition; pandemic disease; international migration as a result of violent conflict, political repression, poverty and resource scarcity; environmental degradation and global warming; organized crime and illegal trafficking; and transnational terrorism. Threats may exist at all levels of national income and, in an interconnected world, can ramify across borders to involve other countries and their populations (MacLean 2006; UNDP 1994, 1999). Glasius and Kaldor (2006, p.62) assert that in a globalized, interdependent world, 'it is no longer possible to defend the interests of a particular nation or region unilaterally'. In an integrated world, mutual vulnerability exists for all nations, groups and individuals (Nef 2006). Systems are only as strong as their weakest link, creating shared and reciprocal vulnerability among all actors (ibid.). This mutual vulnerability not only increases the risks to which all are exposed but also serves as a catalyst for challenges from below to repressive regimes, unjust regimens, and the orthodoxy that has guided trade and financial liberalization. The process of global integration creates winners and losers, particularly as the world market dominates local economies and resources (Hettne 2010).

The people-centred framework of human security provides a means of assessing globalization's social, economic and environmental sustainability. This activism on a range of issues extends security sideways to non-governmental organizations (NGOs), to public opinion, and to the press (Rothschild 1995).

3.4 ACADEMIC DEBATES

Human security has fostered a large and growing academic literature. Interestingly, much of this literature is concerned with contesting and defending the concept itself, rather than its theoretical coherence or associated policy agendas.

3.4.1   Concept Lacking Precision

One common theme among the critics of the concept is that it is ambiguous and vague, lacking the necessary precision for a useful theoretical construct, encapsulated in the title of a paper by Roland Paris 'Human security: paradigm shift or hot air?' (Paris 2001). Paris and other authors are particularly critical of the breadth of the concept and argue that it lacks the analytical and descriptive power of a robust theoretical construct to identify causal relationships, and define appropriate responses. As already discussed in the section on definitions, proponents of the narrow formulation argue that the broad formulation is an exercise in conceptual overstretch that diminishes its use as a policy tool (MacFarlane and Khong 2006; Mack 2002). Although security threats typically command top priority in the allocation of attention and resources, policy makers cannot prioritize and allocate scarce resources among competing claims that are all tagged as equally compelling security threats, and historically 'simply declaring that something is a vital security issue' has not led governments to fund it (Mack 2002, p. 6). Mack finds little analytical or practical utility in the laundry lists that characterize broad conceptions of human security, finding them mere 'exercises in re-labeling phenomena that have perfectly good names: hunger, disease, environmental degradation, etc.' (p. 6). Moreover, the all-encompassing formulation does not help understand the causes of threats, the mechanisms whereby they operate, and the means by which they may be remedied.

These critics further argue that the broad concept could have a perverse effect and encourage, inappropriately, the application of military solutions or the illegitimate use of force to political, social and economic problems (Liotta 2002; MacFarlane and Khong 2006). For example, the United States' drug interdiction program in South America is a militarized solution to narco-trafficking, one that has been both ineffective and disruptive to lives and livelihoods (ibid.).

For the proponents of human security in its broad formulation, human security is not a policy tool but a 'foundational concept' (UNDP 1994), a paradigm (ul-Haq 1995) that brings values and ethical norms to security debates (Tadjbakhsh and Chenoy 2007) – or at least an 'organizing concept' (King and Murray 2001). As explained in the HDR 1994 and the CHS Report, such concepts are intangible and difficult to define in concrete terms since threats and vulnerabilities depend on context. For these reasons, the HDR 1994 enumerated seven components of human security with the proviso that this was only an indicative list while the CHS Report resisted specifying them at all. Like other foundational concepts, human security can only become a useful policy tool once it develops its toolkit – the battery of concepts, measures, and empirical and theoretical research.

In fact, a nascent literature already exists. Jolly and Ray (2007) found evidence in the recent National Human Development Reports of 13 countries, that the concept of human security is already framing both analysis and policy making. The very breadth of the concept is its strength, allowing policy makers to adapt people-centered approaches that reflect their country's specific context, creating 'national sub-sets of human security.' Priorities are identified 'after exploring the concerns of people in specific situations rather than before' (ibid, 457). Furthermore, human security's methodology, based upon analysis of causal processes, permits policy makers to establish linkages among traditional military threats, non-traditional human security threats, and human development and to create coherent policy responses that simultaneously mitigate insecurity and promote sustainable development. Policies developed in a human security framework may better reflect the insecurities of the post-Cold War world, where safety, health and livelihoods are threatened by crime, global pandemics and environmental challenges, while at the same time permitting a range of priorities based upon country context.

3.4.2 Politics and the Trajectory of Human Security

Struck by the multiplicity of definitions and the ambiguity in its meaning and implications, some authors have analyzed the political dynamics behind the use of the term. The term is in fact a site of contestation (Tadjbakhsh and Chenoy 2007). Several see human security as a concept deployed by the 'middle powers' (notably Canada and Japan) primarily as a diplomatic tool to promote their foreign policy goals (Suhrke 1999; Tadjbakhsh and Chenoy 2007). Thus within these countries, it was the Foreign Ministry that championed the term, and it did not penetrate further. Suhrke (1999, 2004) and Woodward (2010) argue that these middle powers attempted to take a lead in the debates about institutional rearrangements in the post-Cold War era and to challenge the US position. Woodward argues that the window of opportunity to recast global debates about security closed with the 9/11 terrorist attack that brought state-centric thinking back to the fore.

It is the use of the term for diplomatic, rather than analytical purposes, combined with the intuitive appeal of the term that has led to the proliferation of meanings attributed to it (Farer 2011). Dubbing human security 'a rogue term' like 'self-determination', Farer notes:

> [T]he lack of uniform definition or use stems . . . not from intrinsic incoherence but from the way in which, from their first appearance, the phrases seemed to challenge the views, values and interests of the practitioners of traditional diplomacy, powerful actors who then had a choice: resist them absolutely as rogue concepts threatening the very structure of international relations or neuter their revolutionary potential through an interpretation rendering them compatible with, even a reinforcement of, the basic structure of the status quo. (p. 43)

Calling human security 'the dog that doesn't bark' David Chandler (2008) claims that despite its widespread use in international policy discourse, the human security paradigm has had little impact on policy outcomes because it has 'reinforced, rather than challenged, existing policy frameworks'. He contends: 'in the post-Cold War world, human security approaches have been easily – and willingly – integrated into the mainstream because they have sought to (1) exaggerate new post-Cold War security threats, (2) locate these threats in the developing world, and (3) facilitate short-term policymaking in the absence of clear strategic foreign policy visions' (p. 428).

On the other hand, Gasper (2010b) argues that it is short-sighted to see states as the only actors utilizing the human security concept. He shows that although human security was primarily a discourse used by states in the UN and associated fora, NGOs and other civil society actors have begun to use the concept. While the G77 has been resistant to the concept, the civil society of the Global South has not. The concept is gaining traction in debates about a wide range of development and security issues, both local and global.

3.5   CONCLUSIONS

Paradoxically, despite being frequently criticized in both academic and political debates, the use of human security is increasingly widespread. This 'rogue term' has been harnessed in intergovernmental debates and has not been free to drive the revolutionary change that Mahbub ul Haq predicted in 1994 in launching the HDR. Yet its influence on the discourse and practice of foreign policy has not been insignificant. MacFarlane and Khong cite four conceptual innovations:

1. it has placed human beings at the core of security and the state is no longer privileged over the individual;
2. it has provided a vocabulary for understanding the human consequences of violent conflict;

3. some state and regional organizations have incorporated human security concerns into their foreign policy; and,
4. securitizing such issues as health and the environment has resulted in more policy attention and resources for these issues (2006, pp. 228–30).

The foreign policy of Japan and Canada, the International Criminal Court, the International Campaign to Ban Land Mines, and the ICISS and the Responsibility to Protect are solid achievements indicating that since 1994, human security has played a significant role in foreign policy (Werthes and Bosold 2006). In 2010, Ban Ki-moon reported to the UN General Assembly (United Nations 2010b) that the human security agenda had gained ground as reflected in statements released by the Association of South East Asian Nations (ASEAN) defense ministers, the Asia–Pacific Economic Cooperation forum (APEC), and the Organization of American States (OAS). In January 2011, the UNTFHS and the Inter-American Institute for Human Rights launched a website, Human Security in Latin America, to promote and foster human security research and initiatives (United Nations 2010b). The Barcelona Report has proposed human security as a doctrine for European security policy. An incipient concept of human security may be emerging in the United States; the Quadrennial Diplomacy and Development Review, refers to a mandate to promote human security, which the document does not define, and calls for the creation of a new under secretary to oversee 'all major operational bureaus that support the State Department's mandate to promote human security' (United States Department of State 2010, pp. 42–3). And as noted above, the core normative principles of human security are firmly reflected in the UN approach to security and development, and the attempt to integrate the two objectives into a more coherent, human-centered framework.

Paradoxically, the very ambiguity and breadth of this concept is a target of criticism yet is in fact a source of its strength and appeal (Atanassove-Cornelis 2006; Werthes and Bosold 2006). Critics see human security as a policy agenda. This is a misinterpretation of the concept which its proponents propose as a definition of ends, not means, of an international security agenda. Like other broad agendas based on ethical values, human security is not amenable to an unambiguous action plan. Policy strategies need to adapt to the specific challenges of a given time and place, as the CHS report and the 1994 HDR explain. So, as Gasper (2010b) concludes, civil society finds the term useful because it can play five roles, namely: to provide a shared language to highlight a new focus in investigation; to guide evaluations; to guide positive analysis; to focus attention in policy design; and to motivate action.

Debates about human security have been mired in confusion over what it is – a concept? A paradigm? A doctrine? A theory? An ideology? We understand it as a concept that is normative, describing what kind of security for which the world should strive. As Tadjbakhsh and Chenoy (2007) ask 'It works in ethics, does it work in theory?'. The normative concept opens up questions about causative ideas – what are the threats, from whom, and how can they be defended against? But these are questions for a rich research agenda that has only begun to be tackled.

4 Poverty and conflict
Håvard Hegre and Helge Holtermann

4.1 INTRODUCTION

When Hobbes (1651 [1968]) wrote *Leviathan*, civil war was a constant threat in Western Europe. Since then, it has become extremely unlikely. This is not the case in the poor countries of the world, in many of which there is still 'continualle feare, and danger of violent death; And the life of man, solitary, poore, nasty, brutish, and short' (ibid., p.186). In this chapter, we look at some reasons why poor countries are conflict prone, and how conflicts contribute to retaining countries in poverty. As Hobbes did, we shall concentrate on internal conflicts, since these conflicts are predominantly fought in poor countries, and since inter-state conflicts often have less devastating consequences. Some of our arguments apply to inter-state conflicts too, however.

4.2 POVERTY LEADS TO CONFLICT

The spread of internal armed conflicts in the world displays a striking relationship with countries' level of economic development: civil wars are heavily concentrated in low- and lower-middle-income countries. Figure 4.1 shows the number of direct battle deaths as a share of the population as a function of each country's poverty level in 1965.[1] We use infant mortality rates (IMRs) as our measure of poverty, define internal armed conflicts as in Harbom and Wallensteen (2010), and take data on battle deaths from Lacina and Gleditsch (2005). (We use IMRs rather than average income or GDP per capita because the IMR covers more countries and reflects the poverty of the median citizen better than GDP per capita, the most common alternative measure. The two measures are highly correlated, though.)

The descending line in the graph is the average number of battle deaths

---

[1] We include only countries that were independent in 1965. For simplicity, we have divided the total number of battle deaths over the 44-year period by the population in 1995. We also include fatalities in inter-state conflict (they account for about 17 per cent of the total number of fatalities).

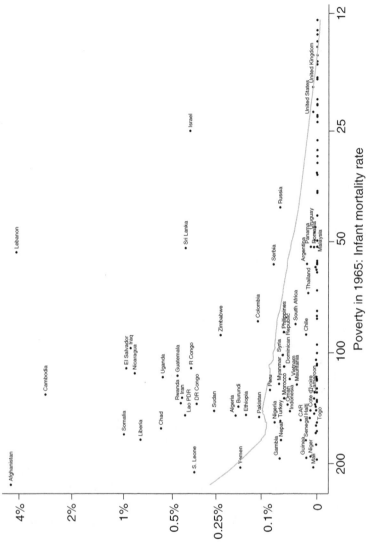

Figure 4.1   Proportion of population killed in battle, 1965–2009 as a proportion of 1995 population, by infant mortality rate in 1965

as a percentage of countries' populations, estimated as a function of countries' poverty level in 1965. This measure of conflict intensity decreases steadily with poverty. Over the past 20 years (1989–2009), only 2 per cent of the world's country-years with civil war have taken place in upper-middle- or high-income countries, although these constitute more than a third of the world's countries and contain a quarter of the world's population. Low-income countries experienced civil armed conflicts at about five times the rate of upper-middle- and high-income countries.

This bivariate relationship between poverty and conflict cannot easily be explained by other factors. Multivariate large-N analysis has shown that the level of economic development is a strong predictor of civil war when controlling for a range of other explanatory variables (Collier and Hoeffler 2004b; Fearon and Laitin 2003; Hegre and Sambanis 2006). The relationship also holds when looking at more disaggregated geographical units than the country (Rustad et al. 2011; Buhaug et al. 2011).

4.3   WHY POVERTY LEADS TO CONFLICT

The empirical correlation between poverty and conflict is unambiguous, but there is no clear consensus as to why. Leaving the issue of reciprocal causation to Section 4.4, we here briefly review the literature discussing why poor countries have more internal conflicts than wealthier ones.

4.3.1   Stakes of the Contest

For internal conflicts to occur, the organizers of the insurgency must perceive that something is to be gained for the rebel group. What motivates rebel leaders is not easily ascertained (Collier 2000a), but most likely involves overthrowing the central government or achieving some form of regional autonomy. The purpose of overthrowing the government may be to promote a public good in the form of democracy or justice of some sort, or the private good of replacing the existing government with themselves. Likewise, regional autonomy may be sought in order to grant social groups political autonomy or to secure the group's right to extract resources in a region.

The stakes of such contests are typically high in poor countries. A large share of productive assets in poor countries are immobile and therefore easily taxable (Accmoglu and Robinson 2006; Boix 2003; Rosecrance 1986). Actors who control the apparatus of coercion – centrally or regionally – are able to obtain returns to their investments that vastly exceed any other economic activities. Where a larger fraction of assets are mobile, the use of force is less profitable. This is a powerful motivation for authoritarian rule, and hence creates incentives for the opposition to use force either to remove or to replace the autocrats. Likewise, the incentives for incumbent rulers to silence the opposition by means of force are much larger in poor countries where a disproportionate share of the wealth is locked in land or natural resources. Similar mechanisms apply at a smaller scale in contests over regional autonomy. In richer societies, both the elites and the middle class have better opportunities to withhold their assets from taxation or other forms of coercive extraction, and the stakes of the political contest are lower.

The fact that poverty creates incentives to use political office for private gain, adversely affects governance of countries. Poor countries are rarely democratic (Lipset 1959; Przeworski et al. 2000) and tend to be plagued with corruption, intense repression, poor economic policies, and other ills (Treisman 2000). Rulers often secure support through granting ethnic kin favors and political positions because they can commit more credibly through traditional networks in poor countries with weak administrative institutions (Keefer 2007). Such ethnic politics, in turn, often creates inter-group distributional conflicts (Cederman et al. 2010).

4.3.2   Military Opportunity

Large-scale armed rebellion is not feasible in countries where the state has great military capacity and a strong presence in all populated areas (Fearon and Laitin 2003). In poor countries, the government's capacity and reach is typically limited. This is partly due to a lack of financial and human resources, partly to a scattered settlement structure and poor communication infrastructure that increases the cost of local intelligence (Herbst 2000b; Leites and Wolf 1970; Lichbach 1995). Under such conditions, it becomes possible to launch large-scale insurgencies from the periphery of the state.

4.3.3   Ease of Mobilization

Armed rebellion is highly resource demanding. To build and sustain a guerrilla band or army, the rebels need recruits, arms, money and food (Weinstein 2006). To hide from the government – which is usually militarily superior, at least at the outset – rebels must control information flows (Fearon and Laitin 2003). Although some resources – for example, initial financing and a core of skilled cadres – may be externally provided, rebel organizations are dependent on local populations for obtaining vital resources such as food, shelter, information and recruits (Leites and Wolf 1970, p. 33). Much of the civil war literature consequently focuses on how the economic, political, or social conditions of low-income countries impact on the feasibility of insurgent resource mobilization. Why do people contribute resources to rebel organizations? We look at three types of reasons or 'mechanisms' – economic incentives, security incentives, and social, emotional and moral impetuses – and discuss how these may be linked to typical characteristics of poor countries. Part of the explanation may be found in other processes and structures, although lack of space prevents us from discussing them. For accounts focusing on the historical dynamics of developing countries, see Ayoob (1996), Cohen et al. (1981) and Cramer (2006). See North et al. (2009) for an account linking both violence and economic development to broad 'social orders'.

4.3.4   Economic Incentives

Economists studying violent conflict focus in particular on individual potential recruits' economic incentives. A common assumption is that people are rational and attach great value to individual economic outcomes. Consequently, economic opportunity costs of becoming a rebel soldier are emphasized in such explanations of rebellion. Clearly, poverty makes the alternative to rebelling less attractive in absolute terms. In the words of Collier and Hoeffler (2004b, p. 659), '[r]ecruits must be paid, and their cost may be related to the income foregone by enlisting as a rebel'.

Whether conditions in low-income countries are generally conducive to generating income for rebels is less clear. If the entire society is poor, there is little household income to tax, and governments also have access to low-wage soldiers. On the other hand, landed property, a typical asset in low-income countries, is favorable to taxation by stationary rebels, just as they are for governments (Acemoglu and Robinson 2006; Boix 2003). Governments in low-income countries, moreover, typically have poor control of their own territories (Herbst 2000b). This is vital for rebel economic activities that require high rebel territorial control, such as taxation of natural resource production or household incomes (Fearon and Laitin 2003). In sum, low-income opportunities in parts of the population, taxable wealth in the form of rich natural resources or a segment of rich landowners, and state weakness would seem to be ideal local conditions for financing rebellion.

For contributions short of full-time participation, selective economic incentives are unlikely to explain local populations' willingness to support rebels. Part-time rebels, working for example as local informants, organizers, or militias, have no significant economic opportunity costs, since their ordinary economic activities are usually not disrupted. It would also be very costly for rebel organizations to reward every single contribution. If rebel organizations can make such contributions either the most socially or morally desirable or the safest choice for local populations, they may not have to pay for them. This logic appears to be followed by the many insurgent organizations relying predominantly on coercion (Kriger 1992, pp. 181–6; Weinstein 2006) or some combination of persuasion and public-goods provision (Popkin 1988; Viterna 2006; Wood 2003; Young 1998) for eliciting part-time collaboration. Offering public or club goods, such as protection against criminals or provision of land, conditional on collective cooperation may be cheaper than buying single contributions (Berman and Laitin 2008; Popkin 1988). However, such goods may be more important for generating sympathies and making promises credible than for shaping economic incentives to contribute. If people are profit-maximizing and monitoring mechanisms are poor, such methods are vulnerable to free-riding.

Economic incentives can more plausibly play a role in the choice of full-time commitment. The few existing studies using systematic data on rebel combatant backgrounds suggest that the poor tend to be overrepresented among rebel as well as government forces (Arjona and Kalyvas 2006; Humphreys and Weinstein 2008; Viterna 2006). Rebels' own statements, on the other hand, tend to emphasize other reasons for joining (Humphreys and Weinstein 2008; Kriger 1992; Viterna 2006; Wood 2003); in a notable exception, Arjona and Kalyvas (2006) report that one-fifth of Colombian guerrillas said they joined due to the promise of material goods. Some dismiss such evidence, however, since rebels may conceal selfish motivations in order to maintain popular support (Collier 2000a). Payment of full-time combatants may also be feasible and effective for well-endowed rebel groups, since the number of full-timers required for waging irregular war is not very large (Leites and Wolf 1970, pp. 9–12). There is evidence that economic benefits are offered to rebel combatants in some conflicts (Humphreys and Weinstein 2008, p. 111; Weinstein 2006, p. 125). However, many insurgent groups provide few or no economic benefits to their combatants (Graham 2007; Stoll 1993; Weinstein 2006). Even a successful money-maker such as the FARC (Revolutionary Armed Forces of Colombia) does not pay its soldiers. This may suggest that there are adverse selection effects of using economic incentives in recruitment and/or that there are cheaper means available to rebel leaders (Gutierrez Sanin 2004; Weinstein 2006).

4.3.5 Security Incentives

In war, death looms large. Consequently, several scholars focus on the role of coercion and survival for rebel and government resource mobilization (see, for example, Fearon and Laitin 2003; Kalyvas and Kocher 2007; Leites and Wolf 1970). They hold that most people do not have strong, unbending political preferences; or they do, but are unwilling to die for them. Therefore, power grows 'out of the barrel of a gun' – armed organizations that effectively punish defection or provide protection to collaborators succeed in mobilization. Notably, the ability to do so may depend less on aggregate military capabilities than on local intelligence-gathering abilities (Kalyvas 2006; Maranto and Tuchman 1992).

Several conditions characteristic of poor countries facilitate shaping local civilians' security incentives in favour of insurgent groups. In regions where the government is militarily weak, rebels may establish control and mould incentives through sanctions (Kalyvas 2006). Incompetent counter-insurgency efforts with widespread use of indiscriminate violence, typical of many developing-country governments, also create incentives in the rebels' favour (Mason and Krane 1989). The local farmer may become as vulnerable to counter-insurgency activities as the local guerrilla, leaving no security disincentive for joining the rebels (Kalyvas and Kocher 2007). Indiscriminate violence may have some advantageous effects for the government, however, like making people flee from rebel-held to government-held areas, as seen during US bombing of villages in South Vietnam (Lyall 2009, p. 336).

Those lacking strong political preferences rationally contribute the minimum resources required from the most threatening organization to stay out of harm's way. Several studies point to the importance of security incentives for civilian contribution of resources such as information, food or part-time labour to armed parties in civil wars (see, for example, Kalyvas 2006; Kriger 1992; Stoll 1993). Shaping security incentives can be a cost-effective way of mobilizing such resources for the organization controlling an area, and are probably more important than economic factors. To obtain resources that require universal compliance, such as control of information, it is less costly to punish a few defectors than to pay all compliers (Olivier 1980, pp. 1363–4). Insurgents may also promise protection to civilians in return for their cooperation (Mason 2004, p. 156).

Security incentives also matter for recruitment. In areas under firm government control, few will be daring enough to join the rebels. Recruits tend to come from areas of substantial rebel presence (Arjona and Kalyvas 2006), and are often already in a situation of threat from government violence (Goodwin 2011; Stoll 1993; Viterna 2006). Still, becoming a rebel is seldom likely to be the safest option available. Flight will usually be a better option for those fearing for their security (Lyall 2009, p. 336).

Some are forced to join by rebel groups themselves (Humphreys and Weinstein 2008). Although forced recruitment has frequently been used by some groups, such as the Revolutionary United Front (RUF) in Sierra Leone and Renamo in Mozambique, it seems to be a strategy of last resort, opted for in hard-pressed situations (Eck 2010, ch. 3; Weinstein 2006, pp. 111–16). A likely reason is that coercive recruitment has considerable disadvantages. In particular, it does not yield highly motivated and disciplined recruits (Gutierrez Sanin 2004; Weinstein 2006).

4.3.6   Social, Emotional and Moral impetuses

People do not only consider the personal security and economic consequences of their choices (Petersen 2001; Taylor 1988; Wood 2003). They are embedded in social structures where people around them – neighbours, friends, colleagues – may sanction or reward their actions. Moreover, people sometimes act on emotional impulses or out of moral convictions. These are all related to the beliefs and values of communities.

Ethnic in-group solidarity and monitoring mechanisms (Gates 2002) coupled with between-group competition or animosity (Horowitz 1985; Petersen 2002) may create social and emotional reasons for participating in ethnicity-based rebellions. Obviously, as the Balkan wars showed, ethnicity is not only salient in developing countries. Another fundamental characteristic of poor countries, however, is their dense rural social structures. Strong village communities may be particularly conducive to collective action. Since their social relations are many-sided and direct, they have powerful monitoring and sanctioning mechanisms (Taylor 1988, p. 67). If insurgents can take control over such communities, or gain their voluntary cooperation, they may utilize these structures for resource mobilization (Petersen 1993; Popkin 1988).

Emotional and moral impetuses for contributing to rebellion may also find fertile soil in poor countries. Most poor countries display many common sources of anger and frustration towards the government and the prevailing sociopolitical order: lack of formal political institutions (Hegre et al. 2001); ethnopolitical exclusion (Cederman et al. 2010; Gurr 1970); government corruption and predation (Shleifer and Vishny 1993); lacking provision of public goods such as security and education (Bates 2008; Fjelde and de Soysa 2009); indiscriminate and brutal state responses to violent, and sometimes also non-violent, opposition (Mason 2004), and traditional social structures obstructing opportunities for groups such as youth and women (Kriger 1992; Richards 2005), to mention a few.

Social and emotional impetuses may help explain rebel contributions short of full-time participation. (Viterna 2006; Weinstein 2006; Wood 2003). There are limits, however, to how much the majority of people will sacrifice to stand up for their beliefs. Wood (2003) finds that where the government had a strong presence, people were highly unlikely to contribute to the rebellion, even if they supported it.

Beliefs, moral values and social dynamics may be even more important for understanding full-time participation. 'First movers' usually face extraordinary risks, and often have both deep commitment to the cause as well as high risk tolerance (Petersen 2001, pp. 272–95). In war, future developments are difficult to predict, making people uncertain about the consequences of their actions. In such situations, emotional and social pressures may well determine behaviour. Several studies find that a significant proportion of insurgents enlisted out of political conviction (Arjona and Kalyvas 2006; Viterna 2006; Wood 2003). The extent to which these mechanisms are linked to structural conditions in developing countries is less clear, however. Village structures, for example, may facilitate collective action, but for the rebels to exploit this, they must first immerse themselves in these societies and gain the support of the majority (Berejikian 1992, pp. 650–51). The reasons for participating in rebellion are multiple and varied. For many, they are probably quite personal and local (Gutierrez Sanin 2004; Richards 2005). Rebellion might thrive on such 'small' motivations – presumably present in most societies – if the opportunities are ample.

4.4   CONFLICT LEADS TO POVERTY

Armed conflicts, in turn, exacerbate poverty, and adversely affect the poverty-related conditions that facilitate conflict. This was certainly recognized by Hobbes (1651 [1968], p. 186): 'In such condition, there is no place for Industry, because the fruit thereof is uncertain'. Figure 4.2 indicates the magnitude of the relationship. It shows the infant mortality rate (IMR) in 2009 plotted at the y-axis against IMR in 1965. Countries are represented with circles with sizes proportional to the percentage of the population killed in battle.

The figure shows again the predominance of armed conflicts in poor countries – most of the large circles are in the left half of the figure. All countries have reduced infant mortality over the 1965–2009 period. Some countries have made spectacular improvements – Chile, Portugal, South Korea and Cuba had rates over 50 per 1,000 in 1965, and now have rates under 10. The ascending line in the plot shows mean IMR in 2008 as a

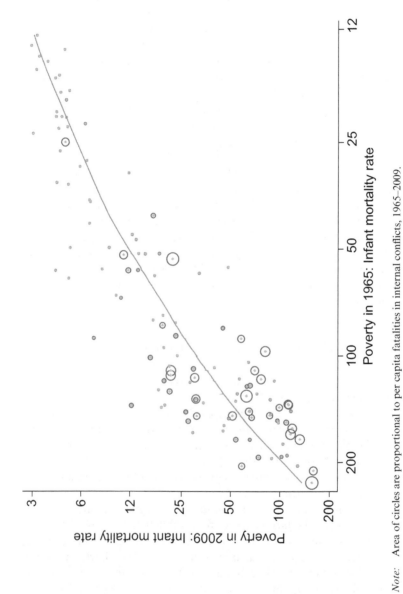

Note: Area of circles are proportional to per capita fatalities in internal conflicts, 1965–2009.

Figure 4.2 Poverty and conflict fatalities between 1965 and 2009

function of IMR in 1965. Countries above this line have done better than the average at a similar initial level, countries under it worse. A large cluster of countries under the line to the left of the plot are 'conflict trapped' – they have had serious conflicts and only weak poverty reduction. Examples are Sierra Leone, Iraq, Zimbabwe, Uganda and Liberia. A few middle-income countries have also suffered from conflict. Lebanon, for instance, had infant mortality levels at the level of Malaysia in 1965, but Malaysia has reduced its IMR more than twice as much over the 1965–2009 period.

Conflicts affect poverty through several pathways, and exacerbate the conditions that facilitate conflict – high stakes of the political contest, military opportunity for challenging the state, and ample opportunities for rebel resource mobilization. The adverse effects occur through macro-economic effects, through reduced public spending, and other societal changes.

4.4.1   Effects on Economic Growth

An important effect of conflict is a strong adverse effect on growth in the economy as measured by GDP per capita. Collier (1999) estimated that economic growth is reduced by 2.2 per cent annually during conflict. Later studies obtain similar results (Chen et al. 2008; Gupta et al. 2004; Gates et al. 2012) (see Bozzoli et al. 2010 for a review of the literature on the economic costs of conflict). Adverse effects are not restricted to the conflict country. Murdoch and Sandler (2004) and De Groot (2010) find that the neighbour-hood of a civil war country also suffers from the disruptions. These studies find clear effects using country-level data, and certainly underestimate the local effects in regions where fighting is particularly intense.

Conflicts affect several of the factors important for growth. First, there is direct destruction of productive capital and infrastructure such as work-shops, storing facilities and roads. The increased risk of destruction or appropriation by rebel groups (or less accountable governments) creates a strong disincentive to invest. Internal conflicts often bring capital flight and disruption of trade flows (Bayer and Rupert 2004; Collier 1999; Long 2008). When capital and trade opportunities disappear, unemployment necessarily mounts.

Figure 4.3 illustrates the magnitude of the growth losses. It shows average GDP per capita for the 1970–2002 period for countries starting out at 1,100 dollars per capita in 1970[2]. The dotted lines represent countries without conflict. The dashed lines indicate the growth trajectory for

---

[2]   The estimates are based on a statistical model of the relationship between conflict and growth (see Gates et al. 2012).

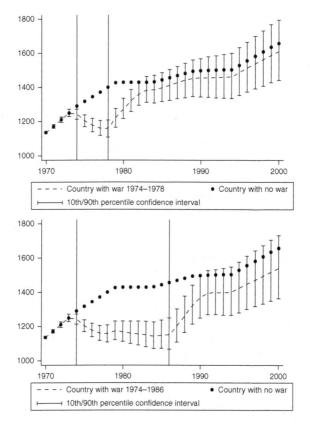

Note: Simulation above for short war (1974–78) and below for long war (1974–86).

Source: Gates et al. (2010a).

Figure 4.3   *Simulated change in GDP per capita 1970–2000, for conflict and non-conflict country*

otherwise similar countries with conflict. The upper panel shows expected GDP per capita for a country with war (more than 1,000 battle deaths per year) that broke out in 1974 and ended in 1978. The growth losses over these five years of conflict are very large – about 20 per cent relative to the non-conflict country. The estimates indicate that countries see an immediate pick-up in growth after conflicts of this duration, however. The lower panel simulates a country that saw outbreak of a war in 1974 that lasted for 13 years, up to 1986. After the conflict, parts of the war losses are recovered. Five years after the conflict ended, we cannot discern further pick-up growth in either of the scenarios. The aggregate pick-up growth up to then is, on average, not sufficient to close the gap caused by the conflict. The typical conflict country is almost 10 per cent below the trajectory it would have followed without the conflict.

4.4.2 Effects on Public-goods Provision

Civil wars also affect governments' willingness and ability to provide poverty-reducing public goods. Widespread violence and physical destruction disrupt transport and cut off rural populations from health and education facilities. Civil war leads to diversion and dis-saving effects (Collier 1999): Military expenditures invariably increase during war, reducing funds available to promote public health, education, poverty alleviation and so on (Gleditsch et al. 1996; Knight et al. 1996). Local expenditure effects, again, can be much more severe than national effects: when territorially concentrated groups are perceived as the rebels' social support base, governments will often be tempted to cut off public spending in their territory. The population in the area will then be hit twofold, as the military contest is also likely to be most intense there.

The detrimental effects of conflict, then, are not restricted to the economic sphere. Several recent studies have looked into the effects on some aspects of poverty. Public-health outcomes, in particular, have received considerable scrutiny (see, for example, 2012; Ghobarah et al. 2003; Iqbal 2010). Conflicts increase the prevalence of poverty and hunger, slow the reduction of child mortality, and hinder access to safe water and primary education. For example, five years of sustained conflict with only a moderate number of direct fatalities push on average 3–4 per cent of the population into undernourishment (Gates et al. 2012). Gates et al. also find that conflicts generate surplus infant mortality at the same level as the direct deaths – for every soldier killed in battle, one infant dies that would otherwise have survived the indirect effects of conflict.

Figure 4.4 and 4.5 shows the trends in two development indicators: Infant mortality rates (per 1,000 live births), and percentage of population with access to safe water[3]. The figures report separate trends for developing countries experiencing no conflict between 1980 and 2008 ('Non-conflict'), countries experiencing at least one year of conflict in the 1981–90 period but no conflicts thereafter ('Post-conflict'), and countries seeing conflict during the entire 1991–2008 period ('Conflict'). Globally, there has been improvement on all these indicators over the last couple of decades. Conflict countries were initially much poorer than non-conflict countries.

---

[3] The figures are taken from Gates et al. 2010a.

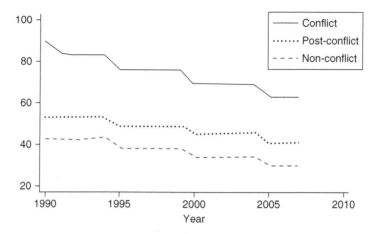

*Figure 4.4   Trend in average infant mortality rates by conflict status,
1990–2008*

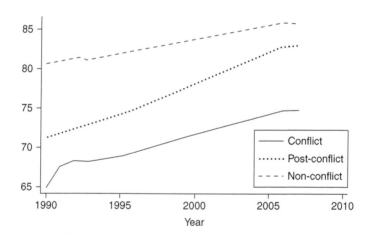

*Figure 4.5   Trend in average access to safe water by conflict status,
1990–2008*

Even though conflict countries have improved on all these indicators, they
have not been able to close the gap up to the non-conflict countries. This is
in contrast to the post-conflict countries, which have improved at a faster
pace than non-conflict countries, at least for access to water.

Some of the detrimental effects of conflict is due to the direct violence.
Mortality increases through deaths incurred as a direct consequence of

fighting. By and large, however, the indirect effects of conflict – internal or interstate – are likely to be much greater than the direct effects. Degomme and Guha-Sapir (2010, p. 297) argue in a study of Darfur that 'more than 80% of excess deaths were not a result of [the] violence. . . . but the main cause of mortality during the stabilization period were diseases such as diarrhoea'. Civil wars also often displace large populations, and the temporary accommodations often expose them to new risk factors. As noted by Ghobarah et al. (2003, p. 192), 'epidemic diseases – tuberculosis, measles, pneumonia, cholera, typhoid, paratyphoid, and dysentery – are likely to emerge from crowding, bad water, and poor sanitation in camps, while malnutrition and stress compromise people's immune systems'.

Even without displacement, conflict can destroy pre-existing local health facilities, as well as block access to proximate facilities because of the risks involved in traveling through conflict zones. The increased spread of disease may be caused by the inability of states to provide health services for their population during wartime, or to conditions, such as in refugee camps, that increase the transmission of disease. Ghobarah et al. further note that other forms of violence often escalate in the aftermath of war, adding to the mortality and disability rates.

Finally, conflict reduces the efficiency of the public health resources that are allocated. Again in the words of Ghobarah et al., 'Wartime destruction and disruption of the transportation infrastructure (roads, bridges, railroad systems; communications and electricity) weakens the ability to distribute clean water, food, medicine, and relief supplies, both to refugees and to others who stay in place' (p. 193). Medical personnel tend to leave conflict zones if they can, leaving the poorest and least mobile behind. Ghobarah et al. note that military forces often deliberately target health facilities and transportation infrastructure to weaken the opposition.

Armed conflicts, moreover, do have political consequences. Most seriously, government repression increases sharply during conflict (Carey 2010; Gates et al. 2010b; Moore 1998; Zanger 2000). This may explain why democracy rarely follows in the wake of armed conflicts, despite the fact that many insurgent groups declare democratization to be the goal of the insurgency. Still, on average, conflict does not reduce the 'democraticness' of formal political institutions either, possibly because increased government repression in some instances is countered by concessions in others.

4.4.3 Direction of Causality

Estimating the magnitude of the causal effect from poverty to conflict is difficult when conflict also affects poverty. A few studies have looked into the problem. Blomberg and Hess (2002) show strong evidence for causal effects in both directions. Miguel et al. (2004) use an exogenous instrument – variations in rainfall – to show that low or negative growth rates lead to civil war. Ciccone (2010) questions the robustness of this analysis, however. More radically, Djankov and Reynal-Querol (2010) argue that the relationship between GDP per capita and civil war is due to unobserved heterogeneity between countries – there are some omitted variables that explain both poverty and conflict. Unfortunately, their analysis does not indicate what these variables might be.

4.4.4   Effects on Subsequent Conflict Risk

All the direct and indirect effects of conflict discussed above increase the risk of renewed conflict. Capital flight leaves only immobile and capturable capital such as mineral resources and agricultural production. Along with the economic capital, moreover, often flies large proportions of countries' human capital. Long conflicts, then, make societies more prone to attempts at gaining political influence through use of force.

Despite the increased repression during conflicts, governments are rarely militarily strengthened by them. Rebel groups that succeed in sustaining insurgencies are allowed to build financial and organizational capital that may be drawn upon in a future conflict. Armies may be weakened both militarily and morally, particularly in cases where social groups opposing the government are also represented in the army.

Past civil conflict typically also raises the incentives for local populations to support insurgencies in the future. The detrimental economic effects of war mean lower economic opportunity costs as unemployment increases and wages drop. The security incentives to support rebel groups discussed above may also be strengthened by past conflict. Local populations that have supported rebel groups in the past are likely to be targets for government repression if conflict re-erupts, forcing them to flee or support the rebels anew. Repression, the failure of governments to provide poverty-reducing public goods during conflict, and other polarizing processes also affect the social, emotional and moral impetuses to support rebel groups if conflict breaks out again. All these legacies of past conflict increase the risk that conflict restarts after few years of peace.

4.5   THE CONFLICT TRAP

The evidence reviewed so far points to a conflict trap (Collier et al. 2003): countries become stuck in a vicious circle where poverty facilitates

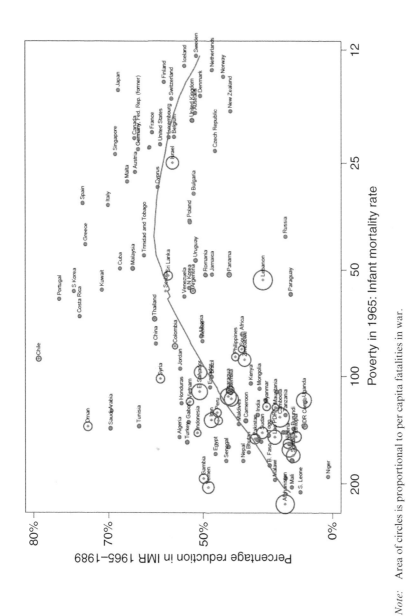

Note: Area of circles is proportional to per capita fatalities in war.

Figure 4.6 Reduction in infant mortality rate 1965–1989 against infant mortality in 1965

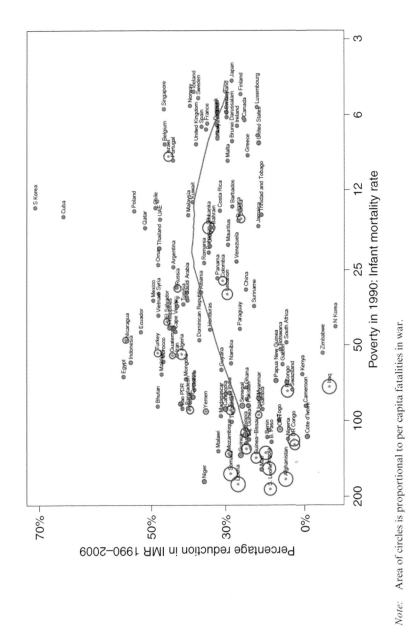

Note: Area of circles is proportional to per capita fatalities in war.

Figure 4.7 Reduction in infant mortality rate 1990–2009 against infant mortality in 2009

56

conflict, and conflict in turn exacerbates poverty. Figures 4.6 and 4.7 further illustrate the conflict trap. Figure 4.6 shows the *reduction* in infant mortality from 1965 to 1989 plotted against the initial IMR in 1965. Figure 4.7 shows the same for the 1990–2009 period. In both figures, the line shows the mean improvement given the initial level. Countries with large circles located under the mean-improvement line are trapped in the conflict–poverty vicious circle. Examples in the 1965–89 period are Ethiopia, Laos, Cambodia, Uganda and Somalia. Also the more developed Zimbabwe, South Africa and Lebanon have severe conflict and weak IMR improvement. In the 1990–2009 period, Somalia, Zimbabwe and Lebanon remain in the poverty–conflict trap. Laos and Cambodia, on the other hand, have ended their conflicts and show considerable improvements in development.

Some conflict countries show considerable improvement despite relatively intense conflict – Iran, Yemen and El Salvador, for instance, during the first period, and Nepal and Algeria during the second. Conversely, some non-conflict countries show dismal improvements in IMR despite their ability to avoid conflict. This is the case for Niger and Burundi in the 1965–89 period, and Kenya, Zimbabwe and North Korea in the second period.

4.6   CONCLUSION: HOW TO BREAK THE CONFLICT TRAP?

This chapter has discussed how some conditions typically present in poor countries make internal armed conflicts more likely to break out and be sustained – poverty is associated with high stakes in inter-group conflict, military feasibility of armed challenge to the state, and ample opportunity for rebel groups to mobilize resources from local populations. Conflicts, in turn, exacerbate all of these conditions, giving rise to a poverty–conflict trap that some countries fail to break out of.

Herein lies a serious challenge for actors such as UN peacekeeping operations that seek to prevent the human suffering due to conflict. Attempts at changing the situation through poverty reduction are hampered by the poverty-increasing effects of ongoing or recent conflicts. However, vicious circles may also be turned into virtuous circles, where improvements in one field lead to improvements in another. This has been possible in many parts of the world, such as in Southeast Asia (see Figures 4.6 and 4.7). To break a vicious circle of this type, changes must be supported by improvements in facilitating conditions *outside* the feedback system. Such exogenous factors do exist.

One important condition is *external sources of economic growth*. Economic growth suffers from domestic conflict, but fortunately also has external sources. This is increasingly true in a globalizing world. Increasing demand for goods and services in other economies are likely to increase opportunities even in poor countries. Trade and investment created by continued healthy growth in the developed world as well as in Brazil, China, India and other emerging economies is likely to continue to have a positive impact on growth, which in turn leads to less conflict. Such trade-driven growth is one likely reason why Portugal, Vietnam and Turkey have managed to escape the conflict trap.

Another factor is *external political influence*. Domestic conflict–governance interactions may be altered by policy changes of important external actors. External intervention is an important part of the reason why Afghanistan, Vietnam and Lebanon became entangled in the conflict trap in the first place. Less external influence may also be a partial explanation why Vietnam later succeeded in escaping it. All external influence, however, is not negative. International pressure was important to end apartheid in South Africa (although IMRs have not improved much as a result), and EU policies may push Turkey in a positive direction. UN peacekeeping operations, moreover, are effective tools the international community may use to break vicious circles (Collier et al. 2009; Doyle and Sambanis 2000), in particular when they have robust mandates.

A third factor is *neighbourhoods*. Several studies show that conflicts tend to spill over (Gleditsch 2007). Effective prevention of conflict in individual countries is important for breaking the vicious circle also in the immediate neighbourhood. Likewise, neighbouring governance is important. Several studies show that economic growth and peace thrive best in countries that have rich and democratic neighbourhoods (Frankel and Romer 1999; Gleditsch and Ward 2006; Hegre and Sambanis 2006). Rivalry and foreign policy is also central, given that many rebel groups are funded and hosted by neighbouring governments (Salehyan 2010). Nonetheless, the structural force of economic development and integration may not only dampen internal rivalry between groups, but also between countries (Rosecrance 1986). It therefore holds the potential to bring not only civil peace, but also more peaceful relations at the regional, and even global, level.

5 Conflict and the social contract
Syed Mansoob Murshed

5.1 INTRODUCTION

The rational choice approach has put forward two competing hypotheses that explain civil war in developing countries: greed and grievance; see Murshed (2010, ch. 3) for a survey where it is suggested that although these may be necessary conditions for the outbreak of large-scale violence, they are not, however, sufficient. There must be other factors at work, related to the institutional failure to resolve conflict peacefully. Addison and Murshed (2006) label these mechanisms as the 'social contract'. Thus, even when capturable resource rents constitute a sizeable prize (greed), violent conflict is unlikely to take hold in states with a framework of widely agreed rules, formal and informal, that govern resource allocation and the peaceful settlement of grievances. Such a viable social contract can be sufficient to restrain conflict, and following its collapse on the road to war, reconstructing a new social contract is key to long-term conflict resolution.

Turning to the history of notions of the social contract in political philosophy, Thomas Hobbes characterized the state of nature as anarchical, akin to perpetual war, with each man taking what he could and no legal basis for right or wrong (Sabine 1961). Consequently, it was in the interest of individuals to collectively surrender their personal freedom of action to a ruler (absolute monarch) in return for personal security and rule-based interactions in society. This type of social contract may be described as vertical. If Hobbes regarded war as the natural state of man, John Locke had a more felicitous view of the state of nature. Locke regarded the right to life and property (often access to common resources) as a natural right, which existed in the state of nature. These rights could not be properly enforced in the state of nature, except through mutual self-help. In civil society, it was the duty of the sovereign to enforce these natural rights; rule ought to be based on consent; society should have the right to oust a tyrant or failing ruler. Hence, Locke advocates what might be termed a 'horizontal' social contract. In general, political theories of the social contract base authority and the exercise of power on rational self-interest, as well as consent, and as such their aim is the avoidance of large-scale violence in a well-ordered society (ibid.).

Contemporary civil wars are more closely linked to the breakdown of explicit or implicit mechanisms to share power and resources, rather than the complete absence of an agreement that governs these. Among the various issues in question, two domestic factors may be highlighted. The first is to do with breakdowns in agreements to share resources and finance public goods, often in the context of economic decline, and the second refers to malfunctioning political institutions. Both of these factors produce what Ghani and Lockhart (2008) describe as the 'sovereignty gap' (the wedge between the state's de jure legal status and its de facto ability to provide public goods such as security so essential to the social contract), and the accountability gap (when it is unaccountable to the people).

The first point refers to the economic factors underlying the social contract, specifically the resource-sharing agreements the state, or those in power, have with various stakeholders, and the breakdown of these arrangements can produce greed and/or grievance. Within nation-states, the fiscal system will secure a workable social contract if the allocation of public expenditures and the apportionment of taxes are judged to be fair, or at least not so unfair that some groups judge resorting to force the better option. Disputes over the apportionment of revenues from natural resources are especially common and, as in Nigeria or Indonesia, these take on ethnic and regional dimensions. One reason why a contract to share revenues encounters difficulties is the imperfect credibility with which the side that controls the 'pot' honours its commitment.

Second, there is the political dimension to the social contract. Hegre et al. (2001) point out that the risk of conflict is lower in both well-established democracies and autocracies. This suggests that conflict risk is at its greatest during transitions to and away from democracy, when state capacity is weak, and also in fledgling and imperfect democracies (anocracies). This is when the violent expression of grievance is most likely. Autocracies are adept at suppressing dissent, and established democracies deal with the same problem in a more peaceful fashion. Also, state capacity (its ability to both police citizens and provide public goods) is greater in established autocratic or democratic societies, rather than in societies undergoing transition. The functions of the state are important in maintaining the cohesiveness of society, which in turn is central to a functioning social contract. Besides its legitimate 'Weberian' monopoly over violence, a functioning state must be able to enforce laws, property rights and contracts, as well as have the fiscal capacity to raise revenues and provide public goods (Mill 1848 [1998]). The list grows longer as economic prosperity and complexity advances; more-affluent nations have bigger governments (as measured by the share of government consumption in national income). Economic decline in 'failing' states severely undermines the state's fiscal capacity, something which makes it aid dependent (Ghani and Lockhart 2008). Aid dependence, in turn, further diminishes state capacity. Furthermore, a 'failing' state's ability to guarantee personal security, property rights and laws is often limited, leading to the gradual privatization of violence between predatory and defensive elements within society. All of these circumstances combine to produce a degenerating social contract, where individuals rely on kinship groups and local warlords for security and public good provision; this heightens the risk of civil war as society descends towards an anarchical (Hobbesian) state of nature.

This rest of this chapter is organized as follows: Section 5.2 deals with economic issues related to fair division, fiscal federalism and the social contract that are crucial for solutions to the material basis for greed and/or grievance motivations for conflict; Section 5.3 is concerned with political matters surrounding federalism and the difficulties of maintaining power-sharing agreements that end civil wars which may require power-dividing structures; finally, Section 5.4 provides a brief synthesis of the diverse issues discussed.

5.2   FAIR DIVISION AND FISCAL FEDERALISM

The economic pie needs to be fairly divided among potential antagonists if the social contract is to be sustainable. Similarly, a necessary condition for the viability of a peace treaty may lie in meeting the participation constraints of those involved, and ensuring that its stipulations are enforced. But it will never fulfil incentive compatibility constraints, which are to do with the exercise of effort to ensure that the accord lasts, unless it is perceived to be just, fair and equitable. If a peace agreement, and the divisions and compromises it entails are perceived to be unfair then the deal itself will not be robust. The social choice theory literature on mechanisms for sharing and division offers us several insights into how to sustain social contracts and peace agreements. For example, Brams (2006) points out several allocation rules for a single divisible good, many divisible goods and several indivisible goods. Sharing in this regard must be equitable as well as efficient, which is why envy-free allocations are so important. In an envy-free outcome each participant does not regard the allocation of another participant to be superior to what he/she has achieved.

Fiscal federalism means decentralized government expenditure decisions and/or revenue-raising powers to subnational entities. The revenue aspect may be important, particularly for regions with natural resources as in Indonesia or Nigeria, as it appeases local discontent about regionally generated revenues being siphoned off to central government. Other regional governments may be better able to raise local revenues, or even conduct their own borrowing. Decentralization may also increase the utility of regions that can take their own decisions about local public expenditure. It is important, therefore, to distinguish between the revenue and expenditure side of fiscal decentralization and its relation to conflict, although the two are always connected in practice.

On the expenditure side, a citizen is normally indifferent to who (federal, state or city government) provides public goods, as long as provision is adequate. Citizens may care about the type of provision in some instances, say about what languages are taught in school, which might vary over different education authorities. Nevertheless, many expenditure priorities are subject to political processes and the formation of public policy. Then, it may matter which executive authority (regional or national) or what legislature (regional or national) decides on public finance and spending priorities.

Related to this is the theory of club goods (see Cornes and Sandler 1996 for a succinct survey). As the name suggests, club goods are excludable and voluntary. Only members can benefit from the club good, and membership is voluntary. The provision of club goods does not always require state intervention, as members' incentives do not lead to under-provisioning. As with a public good, members of a club do share something, so the rule for the optimal provision for public goods based on the vertical summation of individual preferences for the common good or service applies. But here, there is an additional requirement, related to membership. This is to do with the fact that on the one hand increased membership can reduce per unit costs (because of economies of scale or scope); but on the other hand, more people sharing leads to congestion and may crowd out benefits. So, both of these factors need to be taken into account in the pricing and provision of club goods. The important point here is that many government services are closer to the characteristics of club goods (or at least they are impure public goods) compared to pure public goods, particularly at the local level. Furthermore, an outcome closer to the club goods optimum may be achieved with greater local control over public expenditure. Since this implies volition, it may be conflict reducing.

What role does fiscal federalism have for ethnic conflict resolution? Besides outright war involving the state, ethnic violence can also take the form of peaceful protest by ethnic groups, or sectarian violence that is not targeting the state or rebellion against the state. Tranchant (2007) points out that fiscal federalism, by decentralizing public expenditure decisions, is in principle violence reducing if different ethnicities are concentrated in different geographical entities of the federation. In other words, if each group is the majority in one of the subnational units that make up the federation, the likelihood of peace is increased. This still leaves the problem of their conflict with the remaining minorities inside the subnational unit and the risk of violence increases with the number of minorities. Fiscal federalism, however, will not reduce conflict if minorities are spread out across the whole country; these minorities are not a majority anywhere. More generally, there are other problems as well: fiscal federalism can cement ethnic cleavages, it can act as a method of appeasement only for resource-rich regions, and fiscal federalism can generate veto-player functions where blocking by a region does not abate conflict.

Tranchant's (2007) empirical strategy looks at the risk of conflict onset, and also its intensity, once there is onset. Fiscal decentralization increases the intensity of protest, but not the risk of protest onset for dispersed groups. As far as rebellion is concerned, decentralization reduces the risk as well as the intensity of this phenomenon when minorities are a majority in some jurisdictions of the federation, and even reduces rebellion in some dispersed cases. Sectarian violence is also reduced by fiscal decentralization. By contrast, Alemán and Treisman (2005) in their case studies of four countries (India, Pakistan, Nigeria and Yugoslavia) find no systematic evidence to support that fiscal decentralization lowered the risk of secessionist violence, but fiscal appeasement (which allows some regions more resources or to keep more locally generated revenues) may help in conflict abatement. Fiscal appeasement may have more to do with the revenue or income side compared to decentralized expenditure decision making. Murshed et al. (2009) find that fiscal decentralization dampens 'routine' violence in the Indonesian island of Java.

Badly conceived fiscal federalism, or the failure to adapt federalist rules to new and emerging situations (such as natural resource discoveries or debt burdens) can exacerbate latent conflictual tendencies in federations. In countries where minorities are dispersed, other forms of functional federalism or power dividing mechanisms are necessary in addition to fiscal federalism. Fiscal decentralization might work better in middle-income countries with greater revenues to spend on public goods, and in countries where resource-rich regions demand financial autonomy. Indeed, Tranchant (2008) empirically demonstrates that fiscal federalism is more successful at reducing conflict risk in countries with superior institutions, better governance and more durable political institutions. In particular, nations with malfunctioning institutions often have weak central governments, which encourages violent challenges, and fiscal decentralization may fail to mollify potential rebels.

5.3   FEDERALISM, POWER SHARING AND POWER DIVISION

The term 'federalism' usually denotes a system of government in which sovereignty is constitutionally divided between a central governing authority and constituent political units such as states or provinces.

Classical liberals argued that federalism could prevent internecine warfare within the federation; Mill (1861 [1962]), for example, argued that federations created stronger states, reducing the temptation towards aggression, and allowed for the maximization of the gains from trade within the federation. He, too, favoured allowing the centre sufficient power to secure the benefits of union, particularly powers to prevent internal cross-border duties that could diminish interregional trade. His necessary conditions for a successful federation include overlapping characteristics in race, language, religion, political institutions and rough parity among subunits to prevent excessive domination by any. Following his logic, modern-day ethnically fragmented federations in developing countries should encounter difficulties on account of their seemingly irreconcilable ethnic diversity, and the vested economic interests of some subunits (locally generated resource rents or apprehensions of its industries being eliminated by larger competition) might make it wish not to join a federation. Tackling these problems will require judiciously designed fiscal federalism and resource sharing when forming federations. It should be pointed out that free trade and financial flows can produce highly integrated economies (globalization) without political union, however, it is difficult to imagine political federation without a degree of greater economic integration.

More recently, three processes of federalism have been identified by Stepan (1999): (i) independent states may 'come together' by ceding or pooling sovereign powers in certain domains for the sake of benefits otherwise unattainable, such as security or economic prosperity; (ii) 'holding together' federations developed from unitary states, as governments respond to alleviate threats of secession; and (iii) 'put together' federations by a strong centre such as the former Soviet Union. The coming together federations are typically arranged to constrain the centre and prevent majorities from overriding a subunit, as in the United States, Switzerland and Australia. These may be more relevant to developed countries. Coming together federations are largely irrelevant in poor developing countries where the gain from shared sovereignty seems limited. Holding together federations often grant particular subunits particular domains of sovereignty over language and cultural rights in an asymmetric federation, while maintaining broad scope of action for the central government and majorities (India, Indonesia and Spain). They may be regarded as cases where the object is to appease certain minorities and prevent secession in an otherwise powerful centre, with relevance for most contemporary developing country situations. Put together federations are also of importance to post-conflict countries, where external powers interested in the peace often behave like the powerful centre, devising federal arrangements (Iraq, Afghanistan) that become unstable over time because of the absence of sufficient power dividing mechanisms and the general paucity of public goods, which intensifies the competition over scarce resources.

Federalism implies decentralization of powers and functions of the state; the degree of decentralization may be at issue (a strong centre in holding together federations or a weaker centre in coming together constructions), but its salience in ensuring lasting peace through power sharing and dividing is almost indisputable. This is not to deny that flawed federations cannot implode, as the recent examples of the disintegration of Yugoslavia and the USSR painfully demonstrate. Certain federal constructions can become very unstable, if territorial (local) majorities have interests in undermining federal government, in the absence of stable dividing mechanisms.

The linking of decentralization to conflict is a fairly new area of research, with the international donor and policy community strongly in favour. From an academic viewpoint, Brancati (2006) summarizes two contrasting political arguments about the effects of decentralization in general on secessionist ethnic conflict. On the one hand, decentralization may curtail ethnic tensions and secessionism by bringing the government closer to the people, increasing opportunities to participate in government, and ultimately giving groups control over their political, social and economic affairs. On the other hand, decentralization may exacerbate ethnic conflict and secessionism for the following reasons. First, decentralization reinforces ethnic identities by recognizing certain groups in countries, and giving them a sense of legitimacy. Second, it enables groups to enact legislation that discriminates against regional minorities. And third, it provides regions with mechanisms, such as regional legislatures, local media and regional police forces that make engaging in ethnic conflict and secessionism easier. Brancati conducts a cross-country statistical analysis and concludes that decentralization is a useful device for reducing both ethnic conflict and secessionism, but the effect is undermined by the growth or emergence of regional parties. Roeder (2005) also points out that the risk of conflict escalation (from ethno-politics to national crises) is not diminished in territorial federations. One interpretation of this phenomenon is to say that these situations imply that some minority voices are insufficiently included in federal constructions. What is missing in many of these studies is the economic dimension as discussed in the previous section, specifically the fiscal devolution of powers to local authorities, which can be argued to be of greater significance than the mere creation of democratically elected subnational legislatures where greater local competencies are meaningless without economic teeth.

Turning to post-conflict societies, power sharing is an important part of framing any peace agreement that ends civil war. Peace is incentive incompatible if leaders of warring groups do not get positions of power in the settlement that follows. Power sharing can take several forms (political, territorial, military and fiscal). It is a way of reassuring weaker parties after a conflict via a signal of inclusiveness (Rothchild 2008). A lot of thought and attention goes into designing post-war power-sharing mechanisms, where the principles behind fair division can be applied. A successful mechanism brings about a balance of power among former belligerents. At first a transitional government and legislature is devised, with shared cabinet positions and even rotating presidencies on occasion, as was the case in South Africa. Its success or failure rests on the individual parties' commitment to the stipulations and mechanisms of power sharing (the rules of the game), as well as the presence of external mediation and guarantees for these. A road map is usually prepared with mechanisms that devise a more lasting political and governance structure. The ultimate aims are democratization and economic reconstruction. Is it a good idea that power-sharing agreements remain in place in the longer-term political dispensation, particularly in ethnically fractionalized societies?

In the longer run, power sharing by being inclusive (or 'consociationalist' in the terminology of Lijphart 1999), may be a preferable form of workable democracy to majoritarianism, which is a system where the winner takes all. Power sharing is not only inclusive, as minorities are part of government, but may dampen harmful and potentially conflict-producing elite competition. It has been argued to be a superior mode of government (with proportional representation in elections) to the more traditional Westminster-style majoritarian systems, as the majority has to accommodate the minority. This is certainly relevant to ethnically fragmented developing countries.

While power sharing is necessary for the peace agreement initially, there may be a trade-off between short-term power sharing and long-term institution-building which leads to a stable peaceful democracy. This has been described by Rothchild and Roeder (2005) as the power sharing dilemma. Rothchild (2008) cogently demonstrated that while power-sharing may constitute a convenient short-term mechanism for achieving a peace accord that ends hostilities, it may become a source of long-term tensions. Power-sharing arrangements crafted together with the best of intentions may go through an uneasy post-war phase, eventually descending to a stage where it is only partially inclusive (as is the case in the Sudan with the Darfur dispute unresolved at the same time as there is a North–South peace accord; or in Rwanda prior to the genocide of 1994 with Habyarimana playing a mixed strategy of simultaneously working with Hutu moderates as well as pandering to extremist elements). The ultimate denouement could be the collapse of power sharing and a return to violence (for instance, in Côte d'Ivoire in 2003).

The factors that contribute to the demise of power-sharing formulas include first, the problem of asymmetric information in the peace accord. Each side to the peace treaty may have private information regarding their own strengths, the presence or absence of spoiler groups within, as well as its own military capabilities; information that is unknown to other parties and external guarantors of the agreement. This includes some groups or militias attempting to retain an outside option of returning to war by only partially disarming. Second, there may be an imperfect commitment to the treaty, because of the paucity of domestic and international anchors to the peace. To this list we may add the all-pervading atmosphere of mutual mistrust and suspicion that characterizes many fragmented societies. Third, we have the underproduction of external sanctions and guarantees of the peace accord, including inadequate external assistance to augment the peace dividend in war-torn societies where the economic pie has shrunk considerably as a consequence of war. Power sharing may also break down if external guarantors are biased, and show excessive favour to one group (the French in Côte d'Ivoire or erstwhile Zaire). Fourth, the power-sharing deal may be incomplete and not include all relevant groups. Power sharing may not, therefore, prevent the formation of splinter groups which act as spoilers towards the peace process.

Fifth, Roeder (2005) argues that leaders of certain ethnicities have an incentive to escalate the tensions and disputes along ethnic lines that are bound to reappear at some future juncture, thereby undermining the federal government. Various parties to a power-sharing deal could try to act as veto players, thereby undermining the system. The stability of power sharing relies on a delicate balance of power. Each side must be deterred from using violence by the belief that it will bring about retaliation or through a cost–benefit calculus which informs their minds that the costs of violence exceed potential gains.

Sixth, power sharing based on ethnicity is bad for long-term democratization because all issues risk becoming 'ethnicized', and it produces incentives to make demands in favour of ethnic groups, particularly when there are resource rents at stake. Power-sharing formulas may even become obsolete if the population's ethnic compositions change over time (Jarstad

2006). Most societies are dynamic, and the ethnic mix is subject to change. For example, in the Lebanon the allocation of seats in Parliament reflects an obsolete ethnic composition dating back to the 1920s.

Finally, power-sharing formulas may give too much weight to those enamoured of violence, and place too little emphasis on moderate voices. This not only endangers the peace accord, but may also retard the future evolution of democracy.

For all these reasons, power-sharing formulas need to be carefully designed. One way forward is to have temporary power-sharing mechanisms that are dismantled later as democracy takes root. Second, mechanisms to prevent opportunistic behaviour by one party or the formation of violent splinter groups have to be considered. Third, the voice accorded to moderate elements has to be increased. Cognizance also needs to be taken of the fact that a future democratic system may have to take on a different configuration from an immediate post-war power-sharing agreement.

The long-term solution, according to Roeder (2005) lies in 'power dividing' institutions. Its characteristics include first, certain limitations on the powers of government. So, for example, the United States has a Bill of Rights which the state cannot tamper with, and Europe has a Human Rights Convention. Second, it is important to devise multiple majorities. This means separated decision making at various levels. This may include a federated form of governance. But power division can take place even without a politically federal structure in smaller nations. For example, even in city government, one committee decides on finance, another on education policy, another on police and yet another on street lighting. Power division occurs if the composition of each of these bodies is different, leading to varying decisive majority configurations, so in one committee one group may have a majority, but not at all levels. Power division also means the separation of powers between the executive, legislative and judicial branches, as first discussed by Montesquieu (Sabine 1961), and later by Madison in his Federalist papers (Cooke 1961). Third, none of the multiple majorities should have veto powers. This means checks and balances (also proposed by Madison) and constraints on executive power. The saliency of an independent judiciary in this regard cannot be overemphasized.

One interpretation of the above idea is that there should be more layers of political and economic decision making than there are ethnicities. This is likely to lead to more cooperative behaviour and several overlapping coalitions between groups. Decentralization of the decision-making processes may be relevant here. A federalist construction with provinces or states, rather than a unitary system with a bicameral legislature may be desirable. The electoral system whether proportional or majoritarian, should succeed in representing different ethnicities.

Crucially, Roeder (2005) argues that the very long-term survival of power-sharing mechanisms in ethnically divided societies requires the construction of power-dividing rules, as described above. Only then will it be stable in the long run. So, power division is essential to the sustainability of power sharing.

5.4   SYNTHESIS AND CONCLUSION

The preceding sections have identified three factors that contribute to long-term peace and a viable social contract. The first is an equity consideration, or a dimension of distributive justice. Here we can draw on the social choice literature on fair division. Without it, any social contract is unlikely to endure.

The second aspect concerns decentralization in the allocation of public expenditure and revenues, fiscal decentralization. Revenue sharing can be important to many societies, particularly when there are valuable local resource rents at stake, and certain groups are disaffected by their inability to effectively control what they regard as rightfully theirs. Equally, expenditures may be important, and decentralized decision making about public expenditure may yield greater utility to local communities. So, potentially we have two issues here concerning the social contract. The first is to do with appeasing potentially disaffected groups about controlling locally generated revenues; giving these groups greater fiscal powers over revenue amounts to fiscal appeasement via increased regional public sector income, and this may be necessary to avoid conflict. Second, there is local control on the nature of public expenditure in ethnically divided societies. This is, broadly speaking, conflict reducing if each fiscal subunit has a substantial and different majority ethnic group. If ethnic minorities are thinly spread across the federation, other means of addressing potential public expenditure grievances have to be devised by the central government, leading to a broad-based and inclusive provision of public goods with the special needs of certain groups (language, say) met. Decentralized decision making about public expenditure may be more relevant for middle-income developing countries, as there the share of government in national income (GDP) is greater than in low-income countries.

Third, we have more realist notions about the balance of power which maintains peace among potential protagonists. In ethnically divided societies, power sharing may be insufficient to sustain peace if the leaders of different ethnicities have incentives to escalate conflicts, or 'ethnicize' future conflicts. In some cases, power sharing may become the source of future conflict. In these circumstances, power-dividing formulas that devise multiple decision-making layers, with no single veto player, may be necessary. These arrangements point to a federal system, although federalism is not essential to power division. In the end, multiple sources of power (power division) may facilitate and stabilize power sharing among different ethnicities. Many federalist constructs are imposed by outside powers or donors following a conflict. These arrangements may not hold together, unless they are domestically incentive compatible. A similar argument applies to agendas for democratic development. Unless democratization and power-sharing (dividing) formulas are *sui generis* (or endogenous), they are unlikely to withstand the test of time.

Finally, the social contract is between citizens with the state or sovereign authority. Consequently, the failure of the state to fulfil its functions leads to the breakdown of the social contract, and in many instances civil war. Once an uneasy peace is established, besides the restoration or reconstruction of the social contract, state capacity needs to be rebuilt. Of the functions of the state, four areas may be highlighted, the first two of which constitute the primary functions of the state in classical liberalism.

First, the state must be able to enforce laws and contracts and ensure the personal security of its citizens. Otherwise, violence tends to become privatized. In many failing states, people are compelled to rely on informal kinship ties to fill the sovereignty gaps left behind by a declining state. Second, the state must have fiscal capacity, both at the central and decentralized levels, to raise revenue and provide public goods (this list grows longer with economic progress). In states which are at a post-conflict reconstruction phase, this hugely important task of rebuilding state capacity is often thwarted by the manner in which external assistance is provided (Ghani and Lockhart 2008). The state's role is often supplanted by donor provision of public goods (including particularist procurement practices), and the presence of financial aid stunts the development and need for domestic resource mobilization. Besides official aid donors, the activities of development non-governmental organizations (NGOs), both domestic and foreign, can retard the development of state capacity.

Third, the state has to provide the framework within which long-term economic growth is facilitated. Long-term growth may depend on institutional quality, but more immediately the right policies have to be followed. The issues include inadequate infrastructure, the paucity of capital, trade policies and macroeconomic management.

Finally, the state needs to be able to regulate the market. Just as the market can provide the basis for prosperity that ultimately diminishes the chances of conflict, the unregulated activities of the market not only produce major economic downswings, but the workings of *laissez-faire* can even enhance conflict risk. Thus, the government needs to ensure that growth needs to be broad based in order for it not to ignite conflict. Despite the fact that growth ultimately reduces conflict risk, the road to prosperity carries along its path the increased risk of conflict, unless measures are taken to address poverty and inequality, which in turn breed the greed and grievances that produce conflict. The inevitable structural changes to the economy that emerge in the wake of growth inevitably produce winners and losers. For conflict to be avoided, the losers must not be allowed to fall too far. Thus, the current donor focus on poverty reduction is simply not enough; the presence of conflict risk-enhancing inequalities, particularly group-based horizontal inequalities (Stewart 2008a), also need addressing.

6 Economic dimensions of civil war*
Heiko Nitzschke† and David M. Malone‡

6.1 INTRODUCTION

The political economy of civil wars has acquired unprecedented relevance for scholars and policy makers as important to preventing and mitigating armed intra-state conflict. The issue surfaced in the international agenda since the mid-1990s due to a convergence of political factors, policy concerns and academic interests at that time. Given the important role of natural resources as a source of combatant financing in numerous civil wars, the term 'resource wars' soon gained currency (Cilliers 2000; Klare 2001; Renner 2002). Advocacy campaigns against so-called 'blood diamonds' found particular traction, reflected also in United Nations Security Council resolutions, Hollywood movies and, more recently, international media coverage of former super-model Naomi Campbell's appearance at the Sierra Leone War Crimes Tribunal in The Hague. Yet the issue of 'war economies' has much broader research and policy implications. Analysing the economic agendas in civil wars provides important insights into the onset, duration and mutation of armed conflict, the linkages that exist between local conflicts and world markets for both legal and illegal trade and finance, and what challenges these dynamics create for peacemaking and peacebuilding. By now, these issues and their policy consequences are under scrutiny by non-governmental organizations (NGOs), research institutes, humanitarian and aid organizations, governments, international financial organizations (IFIs), and, importantly, the United Nations (UN)

This chapter provides a *tour d'horizon* of this field, based in part on the research findings and policy debates that have emerged from the International Peace Academy's (now International Peace Institute's)

* The views expressed in this chapter are the authors' alone.
† Heiko Nitzschke, a member of the German Delegation to the United Nations and recently both a UN staff member and then a German Embassy officer in Sudan, was earlier a senior programme officer in the International Peace Academy.
‡ David M. Malone is a former Canadian Ambassador to the UN and High Commissioner to India and former President of the International Peace Academy in New York. Today he serves as President of Canada's International Development Research Centre.

project on Economic Agendas in Civil Wars (2001–04), as well as a growing body of research, policy and advocacy elsewhere. We first present an overview of the policy and research factors that brought the political economy of civil wars onto the international agenda, followed by key findings and their policy implications. We then analyse some policy options before offering aspects for further research and policy action in the concluding section.[1]

6.2 RESEARCH AND POLICY ON THE ECONOMIC DIMENSIONS OF CIVIL WAR

Against the significant shifts in the post-Cold War global and economic order, some analysts had come to speak of qualitatively distinct, 'new wars' characterized by economic predation and increasing civilian casualties (Berdal 2003; Duffield 2001; Kaldor 1999). 'Perhaps more than any single factor, [the] new focus on the economics of intrastate conflicts was prompted by an observable increase in the *self-financing* nature of combatant activities' (Ballentine and Sherman 2003a, p.1, original italics). Faced with a decline in superpower support, both government and rebel combatants sought alternative sources of revenue to sustain their military campaigns, often through trade in legally or illegally exploited natural resources, smuggling of contraband and drugs, and the capture of diaspora remittances. The resulting 'war economies' thrive on links with arms brokers, transnational criminal networks, corrupt governments, and certain corporations, reaching well beyond war zones to the world's commodity markets and major financial centres (Duffield 1999; Jean and Rufin 1996).

As argued in academic case studies and NGO reports, these dynamics pertained to numerous conflict areas around the globe: during Cambodia's civil war, for instance, both the government and the Khmer Rouge sold rubies and high-grade tropical timber on world markets to finance their respective military campaigns (Le Billon 2000a). Liberia's warlord-turned-president Charles Taylor was able to export large quantities of rubber, timber and diamonds to finance his violent rebellion and subsequent incursion into Sierra Leone – for which he recently faced trial in the Sierra Leone War Crimes Tribunal in The Hague (Ellis 1999; Global

---

[1] This chapter builds on the 2005 UNU–WIDER Working Paper No. 7 'Economic Agendas in Civil War: What We Know, What We Need to Know', reprinted in Addison, T. and T. Brück (eds) (2009): *Making Peace Work: The Challenges of Social and Economic Reconstruction*. Basingstoke: Palgrave Macmillan, pp. 31–50.

Witness 2002). In Colombia, guerrillas and paramilitaries have increasingly engaged in the production and trafficking of drugs (Richani 2002). And in the eastern regions of the Democratic Republic of Congo (DRC), exploitation of and cross-border trade in illegally mined natural resources generated income for conflict profiteers both within and beyond the country (Nest et al. 2006).

Within the policy community, the Canadian Foreign Ministry developed an early interest in the role of economic factors in civil wars. With its election to the UN Security Council for a term in 1999–2000, the government in Ottawa focused on the reform of UN sanctions, which had proliferated during the 1990s. In January 1999, Canada took over the chairmanship of the Council's somnolent Angola Sanctions Committee, responsible for the monitoring of 'targeted' sanctions against the rebels of the National Union for the Total Independence of Angola (UNITA) led by Jonas Savimbi (Angell 2004). In their pioneering investigative work, the NGOs Partnership Africa–Canada and Global Witness documented that revenue from oil and diamond exploitation generated huge profits for the government and UNITA rebels but contributed to enormous loss of life and crippling poverty for most Angolans (Global Witness 1998; Smillie et al. 2000). In May 1999, Canada's Ambassador to the UN, Robert Fowler, commissioned an in-depth independent study by a panel of experts on the taxonomy of sanctions-busting in Angola. Borrowing well-honed tactics of advocacy organizations, the resulting report 'named and shamed' international businessmen, arms traffickers and government officials in the region for their involvement in the trafficking of diamonds and weapons in violation of the sanctions (United Nations 2000a). For the UN, these shock tactics were novel and, to many, unwelcome. But expert panels established for subsequent monitoring of sanctions regimes and related economic strategies were to make ample use of such instruments, drawing on NGO, academic and forensic financial and economic research (Vines 2004).

During the same period, a body of academic studies illuminating the economic 'drivers' of contemporary civil wars was emerging from the UK (Berdal and Keen 1997; Keen 1998). Until then, most scholarly writing on civil conflict after the Cold War tended to concentrate on the costs of conflict and to treat civil war as a disruption of 'normal' social, economic and political patterns within society. 'Peace' and 'war' had been understood as distinct categories, the latter being viewed as inherently dysfunctional. This dichotomy has a long tradition in Western thinking and influenced the way international organizations approached civil wars. Scholars such as David Keen by contrast demonstrated that far from being irrational, violence often serves both political and economic functions for combatants, civilians and external actors. Keen saw many of these conflicts as 'the continuation of economics by other means' (Keen 1998, p. 11; 2001).[2] Where there is more to war than winning, those benefiting from violence may often have a vested economic interest in the conflict's perpetuation, posing major challenges to international peacemaking and peacebuilding efforts (Berdal 1996; Collier 1994).

Against this background, several think-tanks and academic institutes undertook to improve the understanding of the political economy of armed conflict. In particular, they examined the economic motivations and commercial agendas of contending factions; assessed how globalization creates new opportunities for these elites; and examined the policy responses available to external actors, including governments, international organizations, NGOs and the private sector, to shift the economic agendas of elites in civil wars towards peace. The International Peace Academy (International Peace Institute) in New York, for instance, established a three-year research and policy development project on Economic Agendas in Civil Wars (EACW), which brought together leading academics and practitioners and set an agenda for further research and policy action (Berdal and Malone 2000).[3]

Influenced by works of scholars such as Paul Collier, David Keen, Mark Duffield and William Reno, early research on the political economy of civil war focused on four questions: whether economic factors are consequential to combatants' decision to pursue war or seek peace; whether economic 'greed' of rebels is the major cause of conflict, not socioeconomic or political 'grievances'; whether resource-rich countries are more prone to armed conflict than others; and how local war economies and conflict dynamics are affected by their linkages with global commodity and financial markets.

6.2.1 Beyond Greed and Grievance: Findings from Research

Of the early writing on the economic dimensions of violence and armed intra-state conflict, none was more influential, if controversial, than the

---

[2] For similar functionalist perspectives, see also Chabal and Daloz (1999), Reno (1995, 1998).

[3] The EACW project evolved in parallel with and was informed by other research projects, including the World Bank's work on 'The Economics of Civil War, Crime and Violence', UNU-WIDER's research on the 'Origins of Humanitarian Emergencies' in partnership with Queen Elizabeth House at Oxford University, as well as its research project on 'Why Some Countries Avoid Conflict While Others Fail', and the Fafo Institute's 'Economies of Conflict' project on the role of private sector actors in war economies. Numerous research and advocacy organizations have since added a 'war economy dimension' to their agendas.

'greed thesis' by Paul Collier and Anke Hoeffler.[4] Much of the academic debate became polarized around the *greed* versus *grievance* dichotomy in explaining civil war put forward in their articles.[5] According to Fearon (2004), 'the study's main finding and the author's interpretation of it may be the most widely reported result of any cross-national statistical study of civil war, *ever*' (original italics). Among the many important findings of their econometric work, the most widely reported was that natural resource dependence (measured in terms of primary commodity exports as part of GDP) is correlated with a higher risk of conflict (Collier and Hoeffler 1998, 2004b). This was interpreted to suggest that resources provide the motivation or opportunity for rebels to finance their military campaigns through resource predation. That rebels can 'do well out of war' was advanced as better explaining the onset of conflict than socio-political grievances, such as income inequalities, ethnicity, or lack of political participation (Collier 2000a).

The greed thesis had a tremendous impact on policy discourse. Collier's findings were particularly appealing to policy makers discouraged by the complexity and seeming intractability of 'ethnic' and religious conflicts of the early 1990s. If many contemporary conflicts are driven by contests over economic resources, these 'resource wars' might be more amenable to resolution than conflicts over such identity issues as ethnicity, religion, or ideology (see. Ballentine 2003, p. 274). Among academics, however, Collier's findings met with more scepticism. Several other quantitative studies pointed to methodological questions over the natural resource dependency–conflict correlation (de Soysa 2002; Ross 2004c; Sambanis 2002). The dataset used in Collier's work, for instance, did not include diamonds and narcotic crops (Fearon 2004), which were often cited in the 'war economies' literature as the loot of greedy rebels. Michael Ross concluded that 'the claim that primary commodity exports are linked to civil war appears fragile and should be treated with caution' (Ross 2004c, p. 342).

Among country experts and comparative scholars, particularly from the developing world, there was uneasiness over Collier's dismissal of political, social and other grievances as 'rebel discourse' not to be trusted (Addison and Murshed 2003b; Alao and Olonisakin 2001; Cramer 2002; Herbst 2000a; Hutchful and Aning 2004; Porto 2002). Country case studies found economic motivation or opportunity of rebel groups not to

---

[4]   This section draws on Ballentine and Nitzschke (2003) and Ballentine and Sherman (2003b).

[5]   For a review of the 'greed vs. grievance' debate, see Berdal (2005) and Wennmann (2008).

be the main factor for the onset of the conflicts analysed. Rather, the onset of violent conflict was triggered by the interaction of economic motives with longstanding grievances over the mismanagement or inequitable distribution of resource wealth, exclusionary and repressive political systems, inter-group disputes, and security dilemmas exacerbated by unaccountable and ineffective states (Ballentine and Sherman 2003b; Nafziger and Auvinen 2003).

The studies also highlighted the explanatory limits and a worrying degree of state-bias of 'rebel-centric' studies on the economic dimensions of conflicts. The correlation between natural resource dependency and conflict risk is not a direct relationship; nor is the opportunity for rebellion merely a function of the presence of such resources in a given country (Ballentine 2003, pp. 261–7). Both qualitative and quantitative studies confirm that critical governance failure by the state appears to be the mediating variable between resource abundance and the risk of armed conflict. Systemic corruption and economic mismanagement, patrimonial rule, and the political and socioeconomic exclusion of ethnic or other minority groups ('horizontal inequalities'), are permissive factors conducive to the onset of both separatist and non-separatist conflicts (Cater 2003; Fearon and Laitin 2003; Nafziger and Auvinen 2003; Sachs and Warner 2001; Stewart 2002a).

Research confirmed, however, two key relationships between resource wealth and armed conflict, posited by studies on the so-called 'resource curse' (Ascher 1999; Gary and Karl 2003; Gelb and Associates 1988; Karl 1997; Leite and Weidmann 1999; Ross 1999, 2001a). First, mismanagement of resource wealth may create grievances that – particularly when fused with a history of ethno-secessionist tendencies – may become permissive factors for armed conflict. The inequitable sharing of revenues from natural resources (or the perception thereof) is a major factor in separatist conflicts such as in Papua New Guinea and Nigeria (Alao and Olonisakin 2001; Herbst 2001). Second, the resource curse can corrode state institutions, with important implications for armed conflict. 'Unearned' resource rents that allow elites to buy security through corrupt patrimonial networks, rather than through the establishment of a 'social contract' based on the tax-financed provision of public goods and services, may in the long run undermine the regime's legitimacy and relative military, political, and economic strength, rendering it vulnerable to rebellion (Addison and Murshed 2002; Le Billon 2003; Reno 2000, 2002; Rosser 2006). The weaker the state, such as in Sierra Leone, Nepal and Zaire/DRC, the more feasible becomes rebellion – whether to reform the kleptocratic patrimonial system or simply to grab a slice of the pie.

While research does not support a direct causal relationship between economic motives and opportunities and the *onset* of armed conflict, it confirms that economic factors, including access to natural resources and other sources of finance, can have important consequences for the *character* and *duration* of conflicts, as well as on efforts to end war (Ballentine 2003). Studies that analysed the types of natural resources, their modes of exploitation, the way their benefits accrued to conflict stakeholders, and the distinct impacts of these issues on conflict dynamics and types of conflict are particularly useful in this regard (Le Billon 2001a; Ross 2003, 2004c; Snyder 2006).

Furthermore, conflicts that start as political rebellions can mutate over time as economic considerations become as important to some combatants as political aspirations, or even more so. The Angolan conflict, the quintessential 'resource war', for instance, had its roots in an anti-colonial struggle and resource predation became relevant only in the latter stages of the conflict. Similarly, gemstones or drugs became a prominent source of rebel self-financing in the grievance-driven conflicts in Burma, Cambodia, Afghanistan, Colombia, Peru and the DRC only *after* fighting there had broken out (Ross 2004a). In the Sudan, the civil war had raged for decades before oil was found in the border areas between the North and the South, yet it influenced the dynamics of the war by providing Khartoum with income to finance its military campaign and by increasing the strategic importance of the oilfield areas (International Crisis Group 2002a).

Many contemporary conflicts have become systemically criminalized, particularly where access to lucrative assets exists. Today's combatants (both rebels and governments) often engage in illegal economic activities either directly or through links with international criminal networks engaged in the trafficking of arms and drugs, smuggling and money laundering (Ballentine and Nitzschke 2003, pp. 16–17). The degree to which combatants move in and out of criminality varies. In Colombia both the guerrilla groups and paramilitaries engage in narco-trafficking and money laundering, as well as kidnapping and extortion. In African conflicts, such as the DRC, Sierra Leone, Liberia and Angola, rebel groups have tended to work with shadowy 'conflict entrepreneurs' attracted by the high profit margins and the lack of regulation and law enforcement in these conflict zones.

Case study research furthermore highlights the importance of business actors as intermediaries between local war economies and global commodity and financial markets (Global Witness 2002; Le Billon 2001b; Raeymaekers and Cuvalier 2002; Swanson 2002). Companies, especially in the extractive industries, can willingly or unintentionally contribute to conflict dynamics by fuelling local grievances, by hiring repressive private security companies, or simply by providing host governments with financial resources to conduct war. The anarchic environment of conflict zones also opens up business opportunities for 'rogue companies', those usually small firms that use conflict as a cover for operations and that in some cases actively supply combatants (Taylor 2002). As discussed further below, the regulation of business actors may thus be an important tool for conflict prevention and resolution (Ballentine 2007; Ballentine and Nitzschke 2004; Global Witness 2010c).

Importantly, studies highlight that 'war economies' in fact serve different functions for different conflict stakeholders. In addition to combatant elites, war economies can provide benefits for civilian populations where the informal economy is widespread and where traditional livelihoods are destroyed during conflict (Collinson 2003; Goodhand 2004; Mwanasali 2000; Pugh 2002). Artisanal diamond mining activities in Sierra Leone, coca and poppy cultivation in Colombia and Afghanistan, as well as diaspora remittances in Sri Lanka, Kosovo and Nepal have become critical sources of survival for the civilian population. While often under predatory control of rebel forces, civilian incomes from these activities sustain livelihoods and compensate for the state's failure to provide basic services.

Lastly, the economic activities of belligerents may become powerful barriers to war termination for several reasons. Income from the exploitation of lucrative resources and combatant remuneration in the form of licence to loot and pillage may be important factors in the fragmentation of both militaries and rebel groups (Ballentine 2003, p. 270). In the DRC, the number of rebel groups – financed in part through the exploitation of coltan and alluvial gold in the Kivu provinces – increased steadily throughout the conflict and its ongoing violent afterlife (Grignon 2006). Resource predation can also create command and control problems among combatant groups. An example is the oft-cited 'sobel' phenomenon ('soldiers by day, rebels by night') witnessed in Angola and Sierra Leone where soldiers frequently colluded with rebels for personal gain in the diamond-rich areas, with negative consequences for military discipline and the civilian population (Adebajo 2002; Keen 1998; Reno 1998; Sherman 2003). In such circumstances, it can be harder for leaders to impose peace agreements on their rank-and-file followers.

Revenues generated through resource predation and shadow economies can also exacerbate what Stedman (1997) has termed the 'spoiler' problem (see also Zahar 2003). Spoilers have a range of motives for opposing peace agreements – from unmet political aspirations, to personal grudges, to ideological or religious convictions. However, spoilers operate most effectively where sources of self-financing (or outside support) are readily available. A comparative study of 16 peace settlements between 1980 and 1997 confirmed that two of the main factors in failed peace implementation were the proliferation of combatant parties and the continued availability of valuable natural resources (Downs and Stedman 2003).[6]

6.2.2   Policy Implications

At a minimum, empirical research cautions against extensive reliance on econometric modelling or 'resource reductionist' approaches to explaining contemporary armed conflict (Cater 2003). While many economic activities, and particularly the exploitation of natural resources, contribute to hostilities, they do so in a diffuse and indirect way. In addition, policy makers need be wary of a state bias. Resource predation can benefit governments as well as rebel groups. Bringing state motives and behaviour back into the equation highlights the importance of transparent, equitable and accountable resource management for conflict prevention and peacebuilding (Nitzschke and Studdard 2005).

The increasing criminality of today's conflicts presents policy makers with a dilemma. For some observers, contemporary insurgent groups are comparable, at least in theory, to criminal organizations (Collier 2000c). However, even if insurgency and criminality often overlap, they are not the same phenomenon and produce different societal consequences. Whereas criminal organizations employ violence in the sole pursuit of profit, combatant groups engage in illicit trade and economic predation at least in part to pursue military and political goals (Williams and Picarelli 2005). Casting rebellions simply as a criminal endeavour rather than a political phenomenon obscures legitimate grievances and forecloses opportunities for negotiated resolution of the conflict if strategies of prosecution or military defeat are preferred over mediation (Ballentine 2003, pp. 270–71; Gutierrez Sanin 2004).

Policy also needs to be sensitive to the different functions that war economies may serve to their participants. Some engage in the war economy to finance the war effort, others for personal enrichment. Yet others are forced to participate to secure their survival. It is important to address the functions of the shadow economy that benefit the enemies of peace and

---

[6]   Similarly, Doyle and Sambanis (2000) find in their quantitative study that primary commodity exports are negatively associated with the success of peacebuilding efforts in 124 wars that occurred between 1945 and 1997.

stability, but also those aspects socially beneficial to civilian dependants (Keen 2005; Pugh 2002; Woodward 2002).

6.3 POLICY DEVELOPMENT: MANAGING THE RESOURCE DIMENSION OF ARMED CONFLICT

The self-financing nature of many contemporary civil wars has drawn attention to the connection between the trade in natural resources, the role of private companies in conflict areas, global financial flows, and armed conflict.[7] Consequently, curtailing and managing these resource flows through 'control regimes' – be they policy, legal or market based – has become a matter of increasing interest (Ballentine and Nitzschke 2005; Bannon and Collier 2004; Cooper 2002, 2006; Sherman 2002; Wennmann 2007b). The rationale underlying resource and finance control regimes is fairly straightforward: if conflicts thrive on the trade in 'conflict goods', then curtailing these resource flows may help prevent or resolve conflict. The same, then, should hold true for efforts aimed at attacking organized and 'white-collar' crime, and the financial lifelines of combatants – all closely linked to local war economies in the form of arms and drugs trafficking, diaspora remittances, money laundering, corruption and, possibly, terrorist finance.

In addition, policy instruments to minimize the negative role of private sector actors in zones of conflict have become a matter of increased international attention (Banfield et al. 2003). Policy development in this field can build on a range of policy, regulatory and legal instruments on the national, regional and global levels that can address war economies (and their fallout) in order to enhance conflict prevention and conflict resolution (Ballentine and Nitzschke 2005; Bannon and Collier 2004; Le Billon et al. 2002).

6.3.1 Regulating War Economies?

Perhaps the single most robust instrument specifically deployed to curtail the flows of finances, natural resources, and arms to and from combatants is targeted sanctions (that is, arms and commodity embargoes and financial freezes) imposed by the UN Security Council. An innovative mechanism to improve sanctions regimes has been the establishment of *ad hoc* panels of experts, mandated by the Security Council to monitor

---

[7] This section draws in part on Ballentine (2004) and Nitzschke (2003).

sanctions against the Revolutionary United Front (RUF) in Sierra Leone, the regime of Charles Taylor in Liberia, the Taliban and, later, al-Qaeda, and, more recently, to monitor the arms embargoes in Somalia and in eastern DRC. Starting with the groundbreaking Angola Monitoring Mechanism in 2000, expert panels and their investigative reports to the Security Council have by now become a routine instrument of 'non-coercive diplomacy' (Boucher and Holt 2009). The Panel of Experts on the Illegal Exploitation of Natural Resources and Other Forms of Wealth in the Democratic Republic of Congo represented a unique case in that the Security Council did not establish it in relation to a sanctions regime, but to investigate in more general terms the illicit economic activities of key actors to the DRC conflict (United Nations 2001). While the Panel of Experts' mandate ended in 2003, much of its work was taken on by the Group of Experts established the next year to support the work of the Sanctions Committee established to oversee the comprehensive DRC sanctions regime imposed in 2004.

As to whether sanctions have contributed to conflict resolution, the jury is still out. Clearly, weapons and commodity embargoes raise the opportunity costs for those targeted; commodity sanctions and the reports by the expert panels have raised awareness of the economic dimensions of conflict; expert panel investigations have also provided important insights into the range of actors who continue to engage in sanctions-busting and into the role of natural resources in fuelling war economies. However, there is increasing agreement on the technical and political limits of sanctions (even in their targeted form) as a policy instrument (Wallensteen et al. 2003). They are undermined by a demonstrated unwillingness of the Security Council and UN member states to enforce them effectively and to follow up on the findings from the expert panels. For instance, secondary sanctions against neighbouring states implicated in sanctions-busting are hardly ever imposed. And even well-known sanctions-busters often enjoy practically unrestrained impunity, as best personified by Victor Bout, the notorious arms-trafficker featured in several UN expert panel reports and inspiration for the Hollywood movie *Lord of War*. Bout, against whom an Interpol arrest warrant was issued in 2002, has been quoted in a *New York Times* Magazine interview as saying 'maybe I should start an arms-trafficking university and teach a course on UN sanctions-busting' (Landesman 2003). Bout was finally arrested in March 2008 in a US-led sting operation in Bangkok while allegedly attempting to buy weapons for the FARC (Revolutionary Armed Forces of Colombia) rebels (Johnston and Mydans 2008). He was extradited to the USA in 2010 and is currently awaiting trial.

The commercial or geopolitical interests of Security Council members may provide additional obstacles. In the case of Liberia, France and China initially resisted the imposition of timber sanctions against Liberia given their important interests in the tropical timber trade. Allegedly, 'diplomatic' pressure was exerted by several capitals on the UN Secretariat and members of the DRC Panel of Experts to clear certain companies of allegations made in the panel's final report, resulting in a much weaker text (RAID 2004). In 2010, the Rwandan government allegedly threatened to pull out its troops from all UN peacekeeping operations if the final report of the DRC Expert Group implicated the Rwandan army in illicit activities in the DRC.

Important lessons can also be learned from the Kimberley Process Certification Scheme (KPCS) aimed at controlling the trade in 'conflict diamonds', defined as 'rough diamonds used by rebel movements to finance wars against legitimate governments'. Designed as the first certification system that in a detailed manner deals with the trade in conflict goods, the Kimberley regime utilizes a combination of legal norms and market forces to encourage countries to join given that they would otherwise not be allowed to trade legally in diamonds with KPCS member states (Grant and Taylor 2004; Smillie 2005). Initiated in May 2000 under the chairmanship of the South African government to deny 'conflict diamonds' access to international markets, the Kimberley Process was the outcome of commercial, reputational and humanitarian concerns among its government, industry and civil society participants. The KPCS came into effect in January 2003 and was soon hailed as a success story. More recently, however, the limitations of the KPCS have become evident. For NGOs and activists, the KPCS is a mechanism that can help address the wider trade in 'illegal diamonds', which has contributed to systemic corruption, human rights abuses and, ultimately, violent state collapse in several countries. Company representatives and diamond-producing governments, however, prefer the narrow definition of 'conflict diamonds', which is the working definition for the KPCS and relevant UN Security Council resolutions. This dichotomy brought the KPCS to the brink of collapse in 2010 when NGOs opposed that Zimbabwe would be allowed to export diamonds from its Matamba field under the KPCS regime. One of its 'founding fathers', Ian Smillie of Partnership Africa–Canada, resigned his Chairmanship of the KPCS NGO Steering Committee. According to Global Witness,

> [The KPCS] has had a positive impact in a number of African diamond-producing countries, and brought a degree of transparency to the notoriously murky global diamond industry. However, it has not fulfilled its potential as a vehicle for change because too many member governments continue to prioritise political and economic interests rather than making serious efforts to end diamond-related abuses. (Global Witness 2010a, p. 3)

Other regulatory frameworks – including on the suppression of money laundering, narcotics trafficking, international organized crime and high-level corruption, as well as efforts to control terrorist finance – have evolved rapidly in recent years, though not necessarily in response to civil wars. Following the September 11 terrorist attacks, these issues gained additional policy profile as part of the global fight against terrorism. Reports that al-Qaeda had laundered money by buying diamonds in West Africa establish a link between terrorism, conflict trade and money laundering in civil war contexts (Eckert 2004; Farah 2004; Global Witness 2003). Targeting the finances of combatants may be a cost-effective means of influencing the behaviour of combatant elites in civil wars. Relevant technology and expertise are already available in relation to drug traffickers and terrorists groups and could be directed against belligerents. On money laundering, the OECD's Financial Action Task Force on Money Laundering (FATF) has become the most effective international instrument and, as Winer (2005) argues, there could even be a direct application of the FATF's mechanisms to conflict commodities. Yet this potential remains to be tested. Nevertheless, regulatory approaches to organized crime, especially those against drug traffickers, have a history of failure, which cautions against overreliance on such instruments.

6.3.2   Business and Armed Conflict

The regulation of private sector activities in zones of conflict has emerged as a controversial but timely issue, raising the questions of whether, how, and by whom companies operating in war zones should be regulated (Banfield et al. 2003; Lilly and le Billon 2002).[8] Recent years have seen a growing convergence among research and advocacy agendas focusing on corporate social responsibility (CSR), human rights and conflict management around the broader issue of business in armed conflict. To produce coherent and effective policy responses, however, there is a need to recognize that these partly overlapping agendas have different objectives and priorities, which may well be at cross-purposes.

Much of the debate on corporate regulation is centred on the 'voluntary versus mandatory' dichotomy, with companies, industry organizations and governments stressing the importance of voluntary self-regulation, and NGOs, activists and legal experts arguing for mandatory regulation.

Voluntary initiatives, such as the UN Global Compact or the

---

[8]   This section draws on Ballentine and Nitzschke 2004.

Extractive Industry Transparency Initiative (EITI), can be relatively easily adopted by companies, and in the long run may promote changes in the corporate culture and internal practices. The 'weapons of choice' for such initiatives are legally non-binding guidelines and codes of conduct such as the 2006 OECD Risk Awareness Tool for Multinational Enterprises in Weak Governance Zones, or the recently adopted 'OECD Due Diligence Guidance for Responsible Supply Chains of Minerals from Conflict-Affected and High-Risk Areas' Yet, a significant obstacle to voluntarism is the 'collective action problem' exposing more progressive companies to possible loss of competitive advantage. Importantly, extractive companies from developed countries often face different domestic pressures from those often government-owned competitors from the developing world. When in 2002 – partly, at least, due to public pressure and shareholder activism – the Canadian company Talisman Energy and the UK company Premier Oil disinvested from Sudan and Burma, respectively, they were replaced by companies from India and Malaysia. While the withdrawal was hailed a success for NGO campaigns and shareholder action, the situation on the ground remained unaffected. Thus, no kind of voluntary code will alter the incentives or the behaviour of companies that do not value reputation or fear shareholder and activist campaigns.

This highlights the need, in some circumstances, for mandatory regulation as a complementary mechanism to voluntary self-regulation. The potential for a legal framework that would regulate corporate activities in conflict zones has become the subject of increased interest. The robust OECD Anti-Bribery Convention, diverse human rights instruments, as well as international human rights and humanitarian law are relevant in this connection. Recent years have seen increased efforts among NGOs, academics and legal experts to reach consensus on what business activities could or should be subject to legal regulation (Global Witness 2010b; IPA/Fafo 2005; Schabas 2005). The Special Representative of the UN Secretary-General on the Issue of Human Rights and Transnational Corporations and Other Business Enterprises, John Ruggie, also contributed to the discussion (United Nations 2008b, 2010a).

6.3.3 Limitations of Regulation

However, international regulation faces potential shortcomings of its own. By definition, it can only address activities that are prohibited by law. As such, legal remedies cannot address conflict-promoting or conflict-exacerbating activities by private actors that are nevertheless legal, however counterproductive they may prove to be. Policy development thus needs to take place along a continuum ranging from voluntary codes of conduct to corporate regulation under national and international law, rather than addressing a dichotomy.

This underlines further that the creation of a robust international regulatory framework to address war economies will be insufficient on its own. Control and interdiction efforts to curtail resource and financial flows to combatants face several challenges that need to be overcome.

Conflict-prone or war-torn countries typically lack the law enforcement, intelligence and border policing capacities that are required for effective enforcement of interdiction and control regimes. There is thus an urgent need for more targeted capacity-building, possibly also as part of technical development assistance. The Kimberley Process, and the FATF regimes may provide important lessons learned in this field.

Interdiction and control regimes may also have unintended consequences for conflict dynamics and key stakeholders. Interdiction tends to raise the prices of the goods it seeks to interdict – and thus also potential profit margins for conflict entrepreneurs. An obvious example is the half-hearted effort to interdict poppy cultivation in Afghanistan, a main source of income for local warlords (Burnett 2003; Rubin 2004). In Bosnia, local strongmen benefited significantly from smuggling activities in circumvention of sanctions, strengthening their influence over the country's fragile political and economic post-war institutions (Andreas 2004; Pugh 2002). In order to minimize the harm regulatory approaches may cause to the most vulnerable conflict stakeholders, sensitivity to their plight should be the *sine qua non* conditioning factor for any policy action (Ballentine and Nitzschke 2003; Jackson 2005).

Even the most robust policies to curtail resource flows to combatants may produce diminishing returns as new illicit activities and networks and means to evade detection develop. Regulation tends to be responsive rather than pre-emptive. Ultimately, in the absence of efforts to address the causes of conflict, regulatory efforts will primarily address the symptoms of conflicts and not their causes.

6.3.4   War Economies, Peacemaking and Peacebuilding

Many of the research findings generated in recent years challenge core assumptions of policy makers. The notion of a 'comprehensive political settlement', used to describe many of the peace agreements brokered by the UN during the past decade, suggests that the formal end of armed hostilities marks a definite break with past patterns of conflict and violence.

This has rarely been the case. The formal end of conflict in countries such as Sierra Leone, Angola, Afghanistan and the DRC, did not bring an end to the predatory economic relationships fostered during wartime. If left unattended, these relationships can fatally undermine subsequent efforts at peacebuilding and leave lasting developmental distortions.

Until recently, the main focus of both conflict analysis and policy action remained on the national level. Yet, in most conflict theatres, regional factors are crucial to the onset and the character of warfare, and, consequently, for conflict resolution. Cross-border dynamics (such as invasion, refugee flows, loss of trade for neighbouring states, cross-border raids, inflows of small arms) were often treated as 'spillover' phenomena (Brown 1996b; Wallensteen and Sollenberg 1998). Yet cross-border dimensions of today's conflicts are usually more extensive and sometimes systematic than previously recognized (Rubin et al. 2001). The war economies sustaining conflicts in Sierra Leone, Afghanistan and Bosnia and Herzegovina, for instance, thrived on deeply embedded political, military, economic and social linkages with neighbouring state elites, informal trading networks, regional kinship and ethnic groups, arms traffickers, mercenaries and commercial entities, who all may have had a vested economic interest in the prolongation of conflict and instability (Cooper et al. 2004; Studdard 2004).

Those brokering peace agreements and planning peace operations (today mostly focused on medium-term peacebuilding rather than merely short-term stabilization) within the UN and the world's capitals have become increasingly interested in the operational implications of these dynamics to increase the odds of successful peacemaking and peacekeeping (de Vries 2009; Nitzschke 2003; Wennmann 2007a).

Assessing the economic endowments and activities of combatants and their sponsors will help third-party mediators to identify possible spoilers. Where politically feasible, they should seek to foster provisions for resource sharing in peace agreements, such as in the 2005 Comprehensive Peace Agreement in Sudan, which incorporates an agreement on wealth sharing (including the sharing of oil revenues) alongside a power-sharing agreement. This requires not only mediators who are knowledgeable about the political economy of the given conflict. It also requires the same of resource persons and consultants advising the parties to the peace process on the often-complex legal, social and macroeconomic issues related to resource sharing (Tellnes 2005; Wennmann 2010). Closer consultation and cooperation with IFI representatives during the peace process must also take place to ensure complementarity of UN and IFI strategies, as famously was not the case in El Salvador (de Soto and del Castillo 1994). This may well mean challenging some core assumptions and approaches of contemporary peacebuilding orthodoxy (Paris 2004; Pugh 2002; Woodward 2002).

The process of demobilization, disarmament and reintegration (DDR) of former combatants has become a standard tool of UN missions and donors in countries emerging from armed conflict. A difficult and expensive process in Afghanistan, Sierra Leone and Liberia suggests serious challenges. Where fighters have been remunerated in the form of natural resource exploitation or civilian predation, their proclivity to voluntarily disarm and return to civilian life may depend on their expectations for socioeconomic reintegration in the form of access to land, education, or other income and employment opportunities (Date-Bah 2003; Humphreys and Weinstein 2004; Spear 2006). Reintegration assistance needs to be introduced early on to undercut the temptations for continued participation in the war economy. In Sierra Leone, for instance, many ex-combatants not reached by the UN's reintegration programme became a serious security threat, mobilizing for protest and moving to the diamond areas where they challenged local youth groups or were recruited as mercenaries for the war in Liberia (Durch et al. 2003, p. 30). For UN peacekeeping missions, renewed focus on reintegration programmes may require more coordination with humanitarian and development actors, and must be met with up-front provision of funds for 'quick impact' reintegration projects, involving job provision.

Criminal networks relating to the shadow economy are a major challenge in many post-conflict contexts (Pugh 2002; Williams and Picarelli 2005). A primary task must be strengthening law enforcement and the judicial sector as part of security sector reforms. Outside cooperation on law enforcement and mutual legal assistance, as well as direct policing by UN peace missions, can provide encouragement (TraCCC 2001). But increased attention needs to be paid to creating incentives and alternative income-generating activities for entrepreneurs and others engaged in the shadow economy to 'turn legal'. To tackle the regional shadow trade and smuggling in countries with weak border policing capacities, structural incentives for licit cross-border trade need to be created. Improved cooperation within regional and subregional organizations or through multilateral agreements is thus, in principle, very useful (Cooper et al. 2004, pp. 219–38).

Where the illegal exploitation or corrupt and inequitable management of natural resources has been central to conflict dynamics, the early restoration of transparent and accountable resource governance in the post-conflict period is crucial (Auty and Le Billon 2007). This requires in-depth transformation of predatory state institutions that promote kleptocratic rent seeking rather than socially beneficial economic activity. Clear donor strategies are needed so that increased technical assistance for public administration, particularly in the areas of financial oversight, budgeting, accounting and public expenditure reviews, become an integral part of post-conflict programmes. As experience with the Chad–Cameroon pipeline project highlights, even well-intentioned programmes may fall victim to host-state politics. The issue of resource management thus deserves further systematic scrutiny by development and security practitioners.

Loan agreements and technical aid should also feature provisions for effective legal and administrative regulation for corporate engagement in natural resource industries. The World Bank's private sector arm, the International Finance Corporation (IFC), can play an important role in designing extractive industry codes and mining policies that help minimize the risk of corruption and corporate malfeasance, by, for instance, integrating transparency provisions for corporations and host governments.

6.4 CONCLUSION: THE WAY AHEAD

Where economic factors are dominant in conflict, greater challenges for conflict prevention, peacemaking and peacebuilding will exist. Several issues for further research and policy action are offered as concluding thoughts.

First, research findings on how economic factors impact on the causes, characteristics and duration of conflict have been useful. Quantitative studies that test theories by academics are important, yet they are likely to have only limited policy impact given their often contradictory conclusions. More systematic field-based research is needed on the political economy of armed conflict, particularly on those dynamics that suggest entry points for more effective policy action. As Ross (2004c) indicates, 'statistical correlations can only take us so far'. Whether addressing the so-called root causes of conflict, providing capacity-building for transparent and accountable resource management schemes, providing technical assistance for the establishment of a transparent financial sector, or providing alternative livelihoods to former combatants, the synergy effects between aid and security need to be more systematically analysed and reflected in policy development (Addison 2003; Boyce and O'Donnell 2007; Carbonnier 1998; Collier et al. 2003; Collinson 2003; Le Billon 2000b). An important issue for more systematic research is the political economy of security sector reform, including DDR (Brömmelhörster and Paes 2003; Hendrickson and Ball 2002).

Second, a strong case has now been made for continued support by donors and other governments of policy development on the economic dimensions of conflict. The role of governments is crucial in achieving an effective, fair and workable framework of global governance that stands a chance of effectively addressing the linkages between local war economies and the global consumer markets for conflict goods, be they diamonds, timber or drugs. Governments and multilateral agencies need to improve cooperation to strengthen the conventions against transnational organized crime, terrorist funding, and the mechanisms against money laundering and corruption. In addition to corporate self-regulation, mandatory and even legal frameworks are required to effectively address corporate engagement in conflict zones. Yet, in terms of driving the agenda forward, some degree of realism is needed. Even the best-intentioned ideas can fall victim to the types of trade-offs that policy makers must make to accommodate diverse constituencies. Real interests – and big money – are often at stake. NGO, academic and media advocates need to be aware of these factors and design strategies to overcome them that acknowledge the costs as well as the benefits of action. Here, the role of the private financial markets as a lever for change in business practice deserves further scrutiny (Mansley 2005).

Lastly, one cannot overemphasize the role of the UN system in driving the policy agenda forward (Global Witness 2010b; Guaqueta 2002). The UN Secretariat and the Security Council became engaged in issues of illicit economic behaviour during armed conflict in part serendipitously, largely through the Council's imposition of targeted commodity and financial sanctions in the 1990s. By now, the detrimental role of conflict trade for collective security and conflict prevention is generally recognized, not least due to the investigative reports by the various expert panels on sanctions (Boucher and Holt 2009). The UN High Level Panel on Threats, Challenges, and Change recommended in 2004 that 'the United Nations should work with national authorities, international financial institutions, civil society organizations and the private sector to develop norms governing the management of natural resources for countries emerging from or at risk of conflict' (United Nations 2004a, p. 35). The UN Secretariat also has a strong interest in these issues, given its responsibility for designing and implementing mediation efforts and post-conflict strategies on the ground that need to take economic factors into greater consideration.

The attention that the Security Council now pays to sanctions-busting, natural resource exploitation and the role of private sector activity in conflict zones, marks a recognition of the relevance of these issues to the maintenance of international peace and security. Some of this action was sparked by the above-mentioned research and advocacy organizations, which have enjoyed increasing access to the Council (Paul 2004); Individual council members were also instrumental in driving the agenda further: the Canadian and Norwegian governments championed the issue within the UN, making use of their tenure as elected members of the Security Council in 1989–90 and 1991–92, respectively (Guaqueta 2002). The German government convened a meeting during its April 2004 Council presidency on 'The Role of Business in Conflict Prevention, Peacekeeping and Post-conflict Peacebuilding' (United Nations 2004b). The Belgian presidency in June 2007 called for an open debate on the nexus between natural resources and conflict. In its official Statement, the Council then 'recognize[d] the role that natural resources can play in armed conflict and post-conflict situations' and underlined the importance of a range of policy mechanisms also addressed in this article: sanctions and expert panels, commodity monitoring and certification schemes, transparent revenue management, the role of private business and regional organizations, as well as UN peacekeeping operations, in helping prevent the illegal exploitation of natural resources from further fuelling conflicts (United Nations 2007). This was an important step, indeed. However, reactions among the permanent Council members and the broader UN membership to placing the issue on the Council's agenda have ranged from the supportive to the sceptical (for example, Russia, China and some of the G77 members).

The Security Council has a crucial role to play in future policy development, not only by crafting strategies to control illicit economic behaviour in civil wars, but – not least due to its 'Chapter VII power' – by establishing through its case-by-case decisions new global norms concerning such behaviour. The Security Council has thus far mandated three peacekeeping missions – UNMIL in Liberia, UNAMSIL in Sierra Leone and MONUC in the DRC – to perform tasks related to the control of natural resource management in the respective host country. More recently, the Council took pioneering action in response to the anarchic and predatory resource exploitation in the eastern regions of the DRC. Starting with the establishment in 2007 of the Group of Experts on the Illegal Exploitation of Natural Resources, the Council has subsequently pressed forward by endorsing in its Resolution 1952 (2010) the Experts' proposal to establish due diligence guidelines for importers, processing industries and consumers of Congolese mineral products to mitigate the risk of furthering the conflict in that region. As a consequence, the Sanctions Committee may list not only those directly involved in illegal activities, but also those individuals or entities supporting the illegal armed groups through the illicit trade of natural resources, including as a consequence of not having exercised due diligence consistent with the steps set out in Resolution 1952 (2010). This shows how far efforts have come to 'mainstream' consideration of economic agendas in civil wars in the UN system's policy responses. Whether this will lead to changes on the ground, however, remains to be seen.

7 Horizontal inequalities and conflict
Frances Stewart

7.1 INTRODUCTION

This chapter advances the view that horizontal inequalities, or inequalities among identity groups, are an important cause of violent conflict in multi-ethnic or multi-religious societies. It follows that horizontal inequalities need to be monitored in multi-ethnic societies; and where they are found to be large, corrective policies are needed.

Violent conflict within countries is, unfortunately fairly common, especially among the poorest countries. It causes immense human suffering and has heavy socioeconomic costs, many indirect as a result of the economic disruptions caused by war (Collier et al. 2003; Stewart, Fitzgerald and Associates 2001). In multi-ethnic or multi-religious societies conflicts are increasingly seen as being between ethnic or religious groups. For some, this has led to the conclusion that there is an unavoidable clash between cultures (Huntington 1996) and that separating groups is the only long-run solution. Yet this view is clearly incorrect given the fact that the vast majority of different ethnic/religious groups live peacefully side by side (Fearon and Laitin 1996). Moreover, since identities are socially constructed and not intrinsic or primordial, understanding how and why these identities are constructed and become salient at some points in time but not others is essential for understanding why there is conflict between such groups.

A completely contrasting view is that group identities are irrelevant to the determination of conflict and that it is a matter of individual economic motives – notably of maximizing welfare – and constraints that cause conflict (Collier and Hoeffler 2004b; Keen 1998). Group identities may be created and used instrumentally, but they have no independent influence according to this view. Yet such an individualistic and economistic view cannot explain why group identities are so important to people that they die for the cause, or indeed kill people for very little personal reward. As Turton has noted the 'very effectiveness [of ethnicity] as a means of advancing group interests depends upon its being seen as "primordial" by those who make claims in its name' (Turton 1997, p. 82).

The view that horizontal inequalities cause conflict falls between these two extreme views. According to the horizontal inequalities hypothesis, a

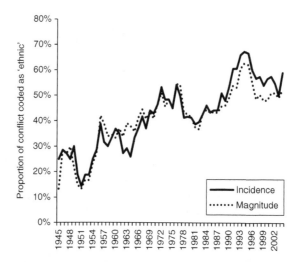

Figure 7.1   Trends in ethnic conflict as a proportion of total conflict,
1945–2005

combination of cultural or identity difference and socioeconomic or political inequalities can give rise to intense group resentments which may lead
to violent inter-group conflict.

7.2   GROUPS, HORIZONTAL INEQUALITIES AND CONFLICTS

Horizontal inequalities (HIs) are inequalities between groups of people
who share a common identity. Relevant inequalities include economic,
social, political and cultural status dimensions. HIs are different from 'vertical' inequality (VI) because vertical inequality is a measure of inequality
among individuals or households, not groups. In addition, measurement
of VI is often confined to income or consumption.

The identity basis of conflicts has become much more explicit since the
end of the Cold War, as ideological differences have diminished and socialism no longer seems a serious alternative. Data show a major increase in the
proportion of all conflicts that are labelled as 'ethnic' over half a century:
from 15 per cent in 1953 to nearly 60 per cent by 2005 (see Figure 7.1).

Today, mobilization along group identity lines has become the single
most important source of violent conflict. This leads us to a critical question: why do the majority of groups live peacefully together, but some
multi-ethnic societies break out into serious violent conflict?

The central hypothesis developed here is that it is where a group sharing a salient identity faces severe inequalities of various kinds that violent mobilization is most likely.

HIs encompass economic, social, political and cultural status dimensions:

- economic HIs include inequalities in ownership of assets – financial, natural resource based, human and social – and of incomes and employment opportunities that depend on these assets and the general conditions of the economy;
- social HIs include access to a range of services – education, health and housing – and inequalities in achievements in health and educational outcomes;
- political HIs consist in inequalities in the group distribution of political opportunities and power, including control over the presidency, the cabinet, parliamentary assemblies, the army, police and regional and local governments; and
- cultural status HIs refer to differences in recognition and (de facto) hierarchical status of different groups' cultural norms, customs and practices.

Although HIs in any dimension can provide an incentive for political mobilization, group leaders may be primarily motivated to lead rebellion by political inequalities (that is, political exclusion), as can be seen for example in the recent case of Kenya, while the mass of people may be more readily mobilized to fight because of the existence of severe socioeconomic and/or cultural status inequalities.

The relevance of any element depends on whether it forms an important source of incomes or well-being in a particular society. For instance, the distribution of housing (a key source of discord between Protestant and Catholics in Northern Ireland in the 1970s) is likely to be more relevant to industrialized countries than to a country where people still build their own homes. Land on the other hand is of huge importance where agriculture accounts for most output and employment, but becomes less important as development proceeds. Each of the dimensions is important in itself, but most are also instrumental for achieving others. For instance, political power is both an end and a means as inequalities in political power often lead to similar social and economic inequalities. Similarly, there are causal connections between educational access and incomes, as lack of access to education leads to poor economic opportunities, while low incomes tend to lead to poor educational access and achievements in a vicious cycle of deprivation.

There are clear synergies between the concept of horizontal inequalities and other approaches to understanding inequalities and the dynamics of mobilization in multi-ethnic countries. For example, Charles Tilly's (1998) concept of 'categorical inequalities' describes similar group inequalities while Ted Gurr's concept of 'relative deprivation' as a cause of minority rebellion (Gurr 1993) represents a similar view, though in contrast to relative deprivation, the horizontal inequality hypothesis points to the fact that it can be the relatively rich, not only the relatively poor, who initiate conflict – it is by no means always that socioeconomically disadvantaged groups initiate violent conflict (Holsti 2000). For example, in Burundi, the Tutsis have attacked the poorer Hutus; and the relatively rich area of Biafra initiated the Nigerian civil war. Such attacks seem to be motivated by a fear that the situation is not sustainable without force and that the relative prosperity of the group is or may be subject to attack.

7.3   EVIDENCE OF A CONNECTION BETWEEN HORIZONTAL INEQUALITIES AND VIOLENT CONFLICT

Empirical evidence of an association between HIs and political conflict comes from both case studies and econometric analysis.

7.3.1   Case Studies

A wide range of studies has shown high HIs in countries in conflict, often with participants making a quite specific connection between the HIs and mobilization for violence. Stewart (2002b) provides evidence on HIs for a range of cases, including Brazil, Chiapas, Mexico, Fiji, Sri Lanka, South Africa, the USA, Malaysia and Northern Ireland. In seven, the HIs were associated with conflict (riots in the case of the US). In one – Brazil – there was no conflict, but a very high crime rate; in three, corrective action made a major contribution to the peaceful resolution of the situation. Brown (2008) provides evidence for HIs in a number of separatist conflicts in Southeast Asia. Other case studies undertaken are for Nepal (Murshed and Gates 2005), Nigeria (Ukiwo 2008), Côte d'Ivoire (Langer 2005), Burundi (Nkurunziza 2011), and Bolivia, Peru and Guatemala (Caumartin et al. 2008).

The case of Chiapas in Mexico is one such example, where comprehensive deprivations among the indigenous population of Chiapas in Mexico underlay the violent protests of the 1990s. For example, the proportion of people in Chiapas on incomes below the minimum wage was nearly three times greater than in Mexico as a whole, and the illiteracy rate more than twice the Mexican rate. The indigenous population were almost entirely marginalized on poor and ecologically vulnerable land. These conditions underlay the violent rebellion of the Ejericito Zapatisto de Liberacion Nacional (EZLN) in 1994, in which indigenous collective leadership took control of four municipalities initiating an armed struggle against the Mexican state. The demands of the EZLN were for improvements in economic and social conditions, as well as greater autonomy for the Indigenous communities and the protection of their cultural heritage.

Côte d'Ivoire represents an example of particular interest since quite severe socioeconomic North–South inequalities were compensated for by political inclusion and some compensatory economic and social policies for a lengthy period under Houphouet-Boigny. But his successors displayed much more favouritism to their own group in both economic and political terms. General Guei in particular began to adopt the language of Ivoirité; he was followed by Laurent Gbagbo, who denied many northerners the vote or right to be presidential candidate while introducing a highly exclusionary cabinet and aiming to change the ethnic composition of the military as well. These actions were undoubtedly behind the rebellion, particularly the exclusion of northerner Alassane Ouattara from being a candidate for the presidency. The Charte du Grand Nord summarized the grievances and demands of northerners, pointing to the prevalent HIs: it 'called for fuller recognition of the Muslim religion . . . more efforts to reduce regional inequalities' (Crook 1997, p. 171, cited in Langer 2005, p. 31).

The cases of Malaysia and Northern Ireland are interesting as in both cases action to correct HIs appears to have helped to create and sustain peace. In Northern Ireland, Darby noted that 'There is no doubt that Catholic relative deprivation is a cause of alienation and discontent' (Darby 1999, p. 149). Systematic inequalities persisted for the first three-quarters of the twentieth century. For example, a study of occupational mobility in Belfast between 1901 and 1951 shows no narrowing of the gap, with the Catholics disfavoured at every level (Hepburn 1983), with fewer Catholics moving upwards from manual to non-manual occupations from 1901 to 1951 than Protestants, and more Catholics than Protestants moving downwards. For the 1970s, Miller (1983) found that the initial disadvantage of Catholics worsened further across generations. The unemployment rate among Catholics remained consistently above that of Protestants during most of the twentieth century.

The Catholics were consistently underrepresented in the higher echelons of the civil service and in the police force (the Royal Ulster Constabulary, RUC), accounting for only 17 per cent of the police force in 1936, 12 per cent in 1961 and 11 per cent in 1969. There were also inequalities in educational achievements, incomes and housing conditions. In 1971, for example, 29.3 per cent of Catholics had a housing density of more than one person per room compared with 9.8 per cent of Protestants. There were also sharp political inequalities. One of the first changes made after the partition of Ireland in 1924 was to abolish the proportional representation system, followed by the redrawing of boundaries. Buckland (1979) shows that, The 'sole concern' of the Ministry of Home Affairs was 'how to give effect to the views of the Unionist [Protestant] rank and file' (quoted in Whyte 1983, p. 233).

Systematic corrective action was taken from around 1970, and by the turn of the century many of the inequalities had been eliminated. For example, the Catholic proportion of top civil service jobs had increased from 8.2 per cent (1970s) to 32 per cent in the 2000s and the proportion of people with a higher degree who were Catholic had risen from 27.4 per cent in the 1970s to 46.2 per cent in the 2000s. Housing differences had virtually disappeared and the unemployment differential between Catholics and protestants had fallen. Perhaps most important, perceptions among Catholics that they were discriminated against had fallen from three-quarters to just 15 per cent. These changes, brought about by anti-discrimination policies, undoubtedly helped create conditions for peace, with the Good Friday Agreement of 1997 representing an important breakthrough (Ruane and Todd 2010).

A similar story can be told with respect to the Bumiputera and Chinese in Malaysia. The Bumiputera (an umbrella term for indigenous groups), who account for the majority of Malaysia's population, were at a severe economic disadvantage *vis-à-vis* the Chinese when the country became independent in 1957, leading to a potentially explosive situation with violent riots in the late 1960s. But systematic affirmative action has successfully diffused this tension. At independence, household incomes of the Bumiputera were less than half those of the Chinese and although they formed over 60 per cent of the population, they accounted for only 8 per cent of registered professionals, less than 2 per cent of ownership of capital on the stock exchange and their educational enrolment rates were lower at each level of education.

After the ethnic rioting occasioned by the May 1969 general election, the government identified the severe economic inequalities between the Malays and Chinese as the major cause and introduced an ambitious and comprehensive redistribution policy, the New Economic Policy (NEP). The NEP was aimed at creating 'the socioeconomic conditions for national unity through reducing poverty and interethnic economic disparities, especially between the indigenous Bumiputeras (mainly Malays, especially in peninsular Malaysia) and non-Bumiputeras (mainly Chinese and Indian Malaysians)' (Jomo 1990, p. 469).

The NEP is arguably the most successful ethnic-inequality-reducing programme implemented by a developing country. Policies that followed included quotas, targets and affirmative action with respect to education, land ownership, public service employment and ownership of quoted companies. The policies were undoubtedly successful. The proportion of Bumiputera professionals rose from 8 to 54 per cent; Bumiputera students in tertiary education increased from 43 to 54 per cent of the total, and there was a similar improvement at other levels of education. The share of corporate stock ownership rose from 1.5 per cent in 1969 to 20.6 per cent in 1995. While Bumiputeras retained their dominant position in agriculture, there was an economy-wide switch out of agriculture into manufacturing and services, and the Bumiputera position in these sectors improved significantly. Nonetheless, although the NEP led to a drastic reduction in the Malay–Chinese income inequalities, severe income differences persist and the policies have also roused fierce opposition from the non-Bumiputera population.

7.3.2   Econometric Evidence

Case studies are illuminating. They show that in many cases of violent conflict there are severe HIs and often these are explicitly appealed to when people are being mobilized to fight. They also suggest that HIs are likely to be most provocative of conflict if political inequalities accompany socioeconomic ones. However, there are exceptions – where there are HIs but no conflict, as for example in Brazil; and cases like Colombia where there is conflict, yet no particularly clear-cut HIs. Econometric evidence is therefore important in order to investigate these issues more systematically.

A variety of types of econometric investigation have been undertaken; cross-country studies of socioeconomic HIs; cross-country studies of political HIs; and similar studies looking at both socioeconomic and political HIs. In addition, there are some regional and within-country econometric investigations. In general, the studies find a positive and significant relationship between socioeconomic HIs and conflict; and also between political HIs and conflict with a particularly high risk of conflict where there are both socioeconomic and political HIs in the same direction, confirming the insights from case studies.

Gudrun Østby has conducted a number of cross-country investigations, using data from the Demographic and Health Surveys (DHS). She shows a significant rise in the probability of the onset of conflict across countries, for countries with severe social and economic HIs, for 1986–2003 (Østby 2008a). She defines groups alternatively by ethnicity, religion and region and finds a significant relationship between HIs and the onset of violent conflict for each definition. Social HIs are measured by average years of education and economic HIs by average household assets. The effect of HIs is quite high: the probability of conflict increases threefold when comparing the expected conflict onset at mean values of all the explanatory variables to a situation where the extent of horizontal inequality of assets among ethnic groups is at the 95th percentile. She also provides econometric support for the hypothesis that conflict risk is worse where there is consistency between socioeconomic and political HIs. She develops a measure of political exclusion and shows that while this measure of political exclusion as an independent variable does not affect the probability of conflict, it has a strong interactive affect with interregional asset inequality. That is to say, asset inequality has a stronger effect in increasing the probability of conflict in the presence of political HIs. The measure of political HIs used by Østby is the nature of the political system, that is, whether a country has proportional representation or a federal system, both of which are argued to be associated with lower political HIs than majoritarian voting and a centralized political system.

More direct evidence on political HIs and conflict propensity is provided by Wimmer et al. (2009) who compiled a global database for political exclusion, defined as exclusion from political power of major groups, for 1946–2005, and show that countries with high degrees of political exclusion are more likely to experience armed conflict. Using the same cross-country data for political HIs and the G-Econ dataset for 1991 to 2005, Cederman et al., 2010, show that 'groups with wealth levels far from the country average are indeed more likely to experience civil war' (p. 104). This is found whether the group is wealthier or poorer than the average. They also show that political HIs add to economic HIs in raising the risk of conflict.

Investigations at the regional level include Brown's (2010) study of the determinants of separatist conflicts. He covers 31 countries, from East and West Europe, North and South America and South and East Asia. He finds that the likelihood of a separatist conflict increases the richer or poorer a region is in terms of GDP per capita, compared with the national average. Another regional study is that of Barrows (1976), who investigates Sub-Saharan African countries in the 1960s and finds consistently positive correlation between HIs and political instability across 32 Sub-Saharan African countries in the 1960s, with measures of inequality including share of political power and socioeconomic variables.

In addition, several intra-country studies demonstrate a positive relationship between the level of HIs and the incidence (or intensity) of conflict. Mancini (2008) uses district-level data to examine the connection between HIs and the incidence of conflict in districts of Indonesia. After controlling for a number of intervening factors, including economic development, ethnic diversity and population size, he finds that horizontal inequality in child mortality rates and its change over time are positively (and significantly) associated with the occurrence of deadly ethno-communal violence. Other measures of HI, in civil service employment, education, landless agricultural labour and unemployment, were also related to incidence of conflict, but the effects were less pronounced than those of child mortality. The Indonesian results suggest, too, that violent conflict is more likely to occur in areas with relatively low levels of economic development and greater religious polarization. In contrast, standard measures of (vertical) income inequality as well as other purely demographic indicators of ethnic diversity were found to have no significant impact on the likelihood of communal violence. A study at the village level in Indonesia, however, found no association between HIs within a village and violence at the village level, contradicting the Mancini finding at the district level, which may indicate that group grievances and the precise location of mobilization and violence occur with respect to larger geographical units than the village (Barron et al. 2009). There have also been studies in the Philippines and Nepal. With respect to the Moro rebellion in the southern Philippines, Magdalena (1977) records a strong link between the relative deprivation of Muslims, measured in terms of differential returns to education, and conflict intensity. In Nepal, Murshed and Gates (2005), using a 'gap' measure of human development, note strong econometric support for a relationship between regional deprivation and the intensity of the Maoist rebellion across districts of Nepal. A later study by Do and Iyer (2005) replicates the finding that conflict intensity is related to regional deprivation, in this case measured by the regional poverty rate and the literacy rate. They also indicate that caste polarization affects conflict intensity.

It is, of course, perceptions which motivate people to action. Kirwin and Cho investigating perceptions in 17 African countries covered by the Afrobarometer surveys found that, among other factors, 'group grievances are strongly associated with both popular acceptability of political violence and higher levels of participation in demonstrations' (Kirwin and Cho 2009, p. 1), where group grievances are defined as how often a respondent's ethnic group is seen to be treated unfairly by the government.

While higher HIs are thus shown to be correlated with a higher risk of conflict, not all violent mobilization in high-HI countries is primarily identity driven, at least in terms of discourse. For example, in Peru and Guatemala the rebellions were presented in ideological terms and prominent leaders of the movements came from outside the deprived indigenous groups, motivated by ideology not ethnicity. In these societies 'race/ethnicity' and 'class' are virtually coterminous, that is they are ethnically 'ranked systems' (Horowitz 1985, p. 22). In such societies, mobilization by class may alternate or substitute for mobilization by ethnicity. Nonetheless, there was a strong ethnic dimension to the conflicts – indicated by the willingness among indigenous people to be mobilized against the state and the victimization – indeed, the almost genocidal targeting – of indigenous peoples by the non-indigenous-dominated governments. For example, Francisco Bianchi, a government adviser in the early 1980s, openly declared that 'for the most part the Indians are subversives; and how can one counter this? Obviously by killing the Indians' (cited in CEH 1999, p. 182). The commission which investigated the historical origins of the Guatemalan conflict in the Guatemalan case found that its roots lay in the 'exclusionary, racist, authoritarian and centralist' characteristics of the Guatemalan state, economy and society (Ibid., p. 81).

It should be emphasized that empirical investigations have found that probabilities of the incidence of conflict rise as HIs increase. Not all countries with high HIs experience conflict. For example, both Ghana and Bolivia have high socioeconomic HIs, yet have avoided substantial conflict. It is therefore important to investigate when high HIs lead to conflict and when they do not. Among the relevant factors are:

- As above noted, an important factor raising the risk of conflict in the presence of socioeconomic HIs is whether there are also consistent HIs in the political dimension as well as in terms of cultural recognition and status.
- The relative size of groups. Very small groups may not mobilize violently because they lack the numbers to have any significant impact (Bangura 2006; Reynal-Querol 2002). Where there are a few largish groups, violent mobilization appears most likely.
- The nature of the state, particularly in three respects. First, whether the state tries to solve incipient problems and makes concessions if needed. For example, Brown has suggested that this is why protests in Sabah, Malaysia, have not become violent, in contrast to state treatment of protests in Thailand and Indonesia during the new order (Brown 2008). Second, whether the state makes some efforts to correct HIs – for example, the Ghanaian government has invested in Northern Ghana in an attempt to reduce North–South disparities, while the Brazilian government has introduced some affirmative action for blacks (Osorio 2008). And third, the strength of the repressive apparatus of the state is undoubtedly a factor determining whether violent mobilization occurs.
- The state of the economy. Much research has shown that conflict is more likely in low-income countries, where there is much under- and unemployed youth, and where natural resources not only create HIs but also help finance

rebellions (Collier et al. 2003; Humphreys 2005; Nafziger and Auvinen 2000).

7.4 POLICY IMPLICATIONS

These findings have important implications for development policy. They suggest that policies to correct economic, social and political HIs should be prioritized in multi-ethnic societies – as part of general development policies. Yet the international policy community too often is blind to the issue of horizontal inequality. None of the issues dominant on the global development agenda – notably, poverty reduction, promotion of economic growth and structural adjustment – incorporates consideration of HIs. The major international datasets – the World Development Indicators and the statistics of the UNDP's Human Development Reports – do not include data on HIs.

As far as political systems and initiatives are concerned, the main recommendations of Westerners are for multi-party democracy and governance reforms, such as improved accountability and transparency. In practice, though, multi-party democracy can lead to exclusionary politics in heterogeneous societies and consequently elections can provoke violence.

With respect to socioeconomic policies, the issue is increasingly acknowledged in post-conflict environments, although actual policies tend to be confined to a narrow range of issues and have limited impact, in most cases in practice (DFID 2005; Fukuda-Parr 2012; Langer et al. 2012). The need for power sharing is also acknowledged more frequently in post-conflict societies, such as Bosnia and Herzegovina, Iraq and Lebanon, but awareness of the need to reassess the design of democratic systems in multi-ethnic settings generally remains rare. Yet from a preventive perspective, there is a need to tackle socioeconomic, political and cultural status HIs in all multi-ethnic societies, not only those that have already suffered violent conflict. Moreover, policies to correct HIs are needed not only in order to prevent conflict, but also from the perspective of efficiency, justice and well-being.

There is a much higher level of consciousness of the importance of HIs in the national policies of some heterogeneous countries, such as Malaysia, India or Brazil, and these states have adopted a range of different policy approaches. The policy recommendations presented below are derived from experience of national policies aimed at reducing such inequalities. However, in developing policies, three caveats are in order. First, obviously, these are not the only policies needed. Policies to correct HIs should, wherever possible, complement other development policies towards growth, employment and poverty reduction; sometimes there may be trade-offs, and then priorities will need to be determined. Second, there is no one-size-fits-all approach to HIs. Understanding the nature and extent of HIs is essential to the design of appropriate and effective policies and requires the gathering and analysis of data. Finally, it is important that policy makers be conscious of and sensitive to the tensions and controversies that might arise from the implementation of policies aimed at redistributing resources across groups. The policies can arouse resentment and opposition among losing groups; and targeting specific groups may entrench perceived differences between groups. Both these effects can potentially increase the propensity to mobilize along group lines. Policies can be designed to reduce these risks, but possibly at the expense of reducing their effectiveness. Consequently, policies need to be introduced cautiously and sensitively.

There are three distinct approaches to managing HIs:

- *Direct approaches* Groups are targeted directly through quotas for the allocation of jobs, distribution of assets or educational access, for example. These can be effective, but they risk increasing the salience of identity difference and antagonizing those who do not benefit from the policy initiative. Generally, direct approaches should be of limited duration to avoid mounting opposition and the corruption that is often associated with their execution.
- *Indirect approaches*   These are general policies that have the effect of reducing group disparities, such as anti-discrimination policies, policies to decentralize power, progressive taxation or regional expenditure policies. Such measures are less likely to increase the significance of identity, but they may be less effective in reducing HIs.
- *'Integrationist' approaches*   These aim to diminish the salience of group boundaries by, for instance, promoting national identity and shared activities across groups. These policies decrease the significance of group differences, but they can conceal rather than reduce inequalities. In general, they are important as supplements to other types of policy, especially direct policies, so that the latter do not lead to national stratification by group.

These are illustrated in Table 7.1.

7.4.1   Policies towards Socioeconomic HIs

A direct approach to reducing socioeconomic HIs has been adopted in a number of countries both in the North (such as the US, New Zealand

Table 7.1 Policy approaches to horizontal inequalities

Dimension	Policy approach		
	Direct HI-reducing	Indirect HI-reducing	Integrationist
Political	Group quotas; seat reservations; consociational constitution; 'list' PR	Voting system designed to require power sharing across groups (for instance, two-thirds voting requirements in an assembly); specification of boundaries and seat numbers to ensure adequate representation of all groups; human rights legislation and enforcement	Geographical voting spread requirements; ban on ethnic/ religious political parties (national party stipulations)
Socioeconomic	Quotas for employment or education; special investment or credit programmes for particular groups	Anti-discrimination legislation; progressive taxation; regional development programmes; sectoral support programmes (for example, Stabex)	Incentives for cross-group economic activities; requirement that schools are multi-cultural; promotion of multi-cultural civic institutions
Cultural status	Minority language recognition and education; symbolic recognition (for example, public holidays and attendance at state functions)	Freedom of religious observance; no state religion	Civic citizenship education; promotion of an overarching national identity

Source: Stewart et al. (2008).

and Northern Ireland) and the South (such as in Fiji, India, Malaysia, South Africa and Sri Lanka). Some of the programmes have been introduced by disadvantaged majorities – for example in Fiji, Malaysia, Namibia, South Africa and Sri Lanka – and some by advantaged majorities for disadvantaged minorities – for example in Brazil, India, Northern Ireland and the US. The latter show that such policies can be introduced even where the political situation appears unfavourable. In some cases these policies were introduced while conflict was ongoing (Northern Ireland) or following episodes of violent conflict (Malaysia, South Africa).

Indirect policies that may lead to a reduction in socioeconomic HIs include progressive tax policies and general antipoverty programmes which *ipso facto* benefit deprived groups relative to privileged ones. They also include regional and district tax and expenditure policies where groups are spatially concentrated. Other indirect measures use the legal system, for example, through the recognition and enforcement of economic and social human rights and through strong and well-enforced antidiscrimination legislation. Where regional disparities overlap with group identities, regional development policies can be a useful way of addressing horizontal inequalities indirectly. Yet, in many countries the regional distribution of infrastructure actually accentuates existing imbalances rather than correcting them.

Integrationist policies aimed at reducing socioeconomic HIs include fiscal or other incentives to encourage inter-group economic activities and engagement. For instance, in Malaysia, a share of capital of companies was apportioned to Bumiputera (native Malay) shareholders.

7.4.2 Policies towards Political HIs

Here it is essential to recognize that such power sharing does not happen automatically irrespective of whether a political system is democratic, authoritarian or dictatorial. Major aspects that require attention in tackling political HIs include the definition of citizenship, the design of the electoral system and rules of political competition and the participation of various groups in key state and non-state political institutions (including political parties, central and local governments, legislature, judiciary, security forces and state bureaucracies).

Debates about direct versus indirect and integrationist approaches are prevalent in the political science literature concerned with the design of political arrangements in multi-cultural societies. On the one hand, Lijphart's consociationalism, which corresponds to a 'direct' approach, advocates 'grand coalitions' which ensures that all groups be guaranteed some form of access and/or representation in all major political institutions and arrangements (Lijphart 1977). Donald Horowitz (1985), on the other hand, argues that the priority in multi-ethnic contexts is to seek mechanisms that will reduce the incentives for group mobilization rather than consociational mechanisms which encourage them.

Electoral mechanisms designed to ensure balanced group representation in parliament, government and the executive form an important way of reducing political HIs, either adopting direct methods – for example, through separate electoral rolls for each group, as has been implemented in Cyprus and New Zealand or indirect. Proportional representation (PR) is an indirect mechanism likely to achieve a greater degree of group balance than first-past-the-post systems, in which minorities 'tend to be severely underrepresented or excluded' (Lijphart 1986, p. 113). However, PR may not bring about shared power since government composition need not reflect parliamentary composition.

Diffusion of power can be another important indirect mechanism for addressing political HIs, with decentralization or federalism as instruments of such diffusion. Where groups are geographically concentrated, a federal constitution can empower groups by allowing them control over many areas of decision making. Decentralization can contribute to power sharing in a similar way. Econometric analysis has shown that decentralization is associated with lower levels of communal and secessionist violence. But much depends on which powers are given to the decentralized units and whether finance is also devolved. There are many cases of apparent decentralization with little effective devolution.

The group background of the executive itself – especially the head of the executive, but also the cabinet – is of crucial importance for decision making. Power sharing at this level can be encouraged through both formal and informal provisions for a fair share of political posts at each level. In many post-conflict societies, formal mechanisms are introduced to 'share' the top governmental positions among cultural groups. For example, in Lebanon, the top three political offices are reserved for members of the three main ethno-religious groups. In Cyprus, Greek Cypriots vote for the president while Turkish Cypriots vote for the vice-president. In other settings, informal mechanisms dominate. In Ghana, a country with impressive peaceful cohabitation practices, the issue of power sharing is addressed largely informally.

Integrationist policies in the political sphere include policies towards political parties. In both Ghana and Nigeria, for example, political parties are required to involve participation throughout the country. The design of the electoral system can also encourage more broad-based 'integrated' coalitional parties, for instance through the adoption of 'list' PR, or a single transferable vote in multi-member districts (adopted, for example, in Malta and Ireland).

7.4.3   Policies towards Cultural Status Inequalities

Cultural status inequalities, unlike those towards political or socioeconomic inequalities, are often a matter of recognition rather than redistribution. Relevant policies relate to the three main areas of cultural status: religious practices, language policy and ethno-cultural practices.

Appropriate policies to bring about cultural equality across religions depend on the nature of the inequalities – whether they derive, for example, from one religion being officially recognized as a state religion, or from more informal sources of inequality. Policies to promote equality in religious recognition include ensuring equal opportunity to construct places of worship and burial grounds; recognition of religious festivals and public holidays to commemorate them; inclusive laws regarding marriage and inheritance; and representation of all major religions at official state functions.

Language policy raises complex questions. Designating one language as the national language is often seen as a means of promoting a cohesive and overarching national identity and possibly generating economic benefits, but it can also cause resentment and economic disadvantage among minority-language speakers. Recognition of several languages has been successful in some multilingual societies. For example in Singapore, 'official' recognition is given to all four widely spoken languages – Malay, Mandarin Chinese, Tamil and English; while government business is conducted in English, Malay is designated the 'national' language and used for ceremonial occasions.

One important area in many societies is that of customary law practices. Acceptance and recognition of legal plurality can increase the access of minorities to legal systems as well as their overall sense of being respected. In Nigeria, for instance, the introduction of Islamic shari'a in many of the country's northern states has contributed to a sense of public recognition and acknowledgement among Muslims (Suberu 2009).

Policies towards cultural status inequalities must take into account the country-specific histories, politics and demographies of cultural interaction. In general, though, state recognition and support for religious festivities, the study of different languages and public holidays all contribute to reducing cultural status inequalities.

In summary, it is clear that while policies to correct HIs are desirable to maintain peace and to generate a just society, the policies need to be introduced sensitively to avoid provoking strong opposition. The Malaysian case also suggests that the policies may best be time limited, as while they received national support in the early years, opposition has mounted, as have corrupt practices associated with their execution.

7.5   CONCLUSIONS

HIs are unjust. Moreover, this chapter has reviewed evidence showing that they raise the risk of conflict. Consequently, they should be monitored in all multi-ethnic and multi-religious societies, and policies introduced to reduce them, with sensitivity to local conditions and to the opposition that such policies may provoke. There is increasing recognition of the need to take HIs into account in post-conflict situations, although generally action has been rather limited. However, there is much less recognition of their importance in general development policies in multi-ethnic societies.

8 Conflict, natural resources and development
Mohammad Zulfan Tadjoeddin

8.1 INTRODUCTION

The study of the link between natural resources and conflict results from the fact that many countries with an abundance of natural resource endowments have experienced violent internal conflict, in which severe civil war occurs, although this is not the case for all resource-abundance countries. For example, 'conflict diamond' has become a well-known terminology referring to a diamond mined in a (civil) war zone and internationally sold to finance an insurgency, as in Sierra Leone, Angola and Democratic Republic of Congo (DRC); while in contrast, diamond abundance in Botswana does not lead to any civil war. Oil in countries such as Nigeria and Sudan fuelled secessionist civil wars, while oil in Norway and Malaysia does not. Such variations in terms of the presence of natural resource endowments and the presence/absence of civil conflict have led to investigation (systematic large-sample or in-depth case studies) of why the presence of natural resources might create a context for, be an underlying cause of, or act as a trigger for conflict. However such a discourse has to be placed within the previously established literature on the natural resource curse hypothesis that draws links between natural resource dependence/abundance, on one hand, and bad macroeconomic outcomes, on the other.

This chapter discusses the link between natural resources and conflict within the broader context of socioeconomic development. It starts from the well-known resource curse hypothesis relating natural resource abundance and growth failure. Then it proceeds with the discussion on the possible relationship between natural resource and conflict, by which the hypothesized resource curse mechanism is embedded in it. The process has also been popularly viewed from the framework of greed and grievance (and their inter-linkage) complemented by the breakdown of social contract as ultimately an enabling environment for conflict to take place.

8.2   THE RESOURCE CURSE HYPOTHESIS

To begin with, we shall briefly review the literature on the resource curse hypothesis. The development economics literature prior to the late 1980s is often referred to for its claims that natural resources are good ingredients for development. However, later research demonstrated that rich natural resource endowments are more likely to result in a curse – rather than a blessing – in the form of negative development outcomes including poor economic performance, non-democracy and civil war. The initial resource curse hypothesis, which was coined by Auty (1993), concerns only growth failure, as Auty suggests, 'a growing body of evidence suggests that a favourable natural resource endowment may be less beneficial to countries at low and mid-income levels of development than the conventional wisdom might suppose' (p. 1). Pioneering cross-country empirical evidence on that was put forward by Sachs and Warner (1995) who found that resource-rich countries, measured by ratio of natural resource exports to GDP, tended to grow relatively slowly. More recent empirical work on this by Mavrotas et al. (2011) suggests that a point source type natural resource endowment retards institutional development measured by both governance and democracy, which in turn hampers growth prospects. Accounts of the natural resource curse phenomenon are available for many countries, with Nigeria providing possibly the most dramatic example (Bevan et al. 1999; Sala-i-Martin and Subramanian 2003). Within the resource curse framework, the central investigation is into the relationship between resource abundance, as one of the independent variables, and macro-development outcomes (in particular, growth failure) as the dependent variable. Adopting a similar framework, the central focus on growth consequences of resource abundance has been expanded into other socio-politico development consequences, such as lack of democracy (Ross 2001a) and civil war (Collier and Hoeffler 2004b).

The literature has established several channelling mechanisms connecting resource abundance with growth failure. Figure 8.1 depicts, in a simplified manner, all the possible mechanisms identified in the literature. Persistent growth failure, which is the crudest measurement of bad economic outcomes, is on the right side and resource abundance is on the left. Arrows connect the two through at least three transmission mechanisms presented in boxes in the middle part of the figure. Conflict is only one of them, while others are economic disruption and institutional failure. Under each mechanism, several processes are at work. One should be aware that there might be inter-dependencies among them and reverse causality between (i) dependent and independent variables, (ii) the channelling mechanisms and the dependent variable, and (iii) the channelling

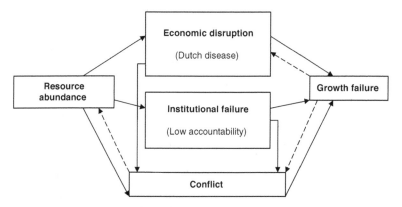

Figure 8.1   An augmented resource curse framework

mechanism and the independent variable. Theoretically speaking, every causal direction seems possible. Arrows indicate all the possibilities.

The initial resource curse literature considered only economic disruption as the channelling mechanism. However, later developments in the literature on the subject have emphasized institution failure and conflict in addition to economic disruption. Therefore, I would call the simplified framework of resource dependence and growth failure presented below an 'augmented' resource curse (inspired by the famous terminology of 'augmented Washington consensus' by Rodrik 2002).

The first channelling mechanism linking resource dependence and growth failure is through economic disruptions, which consists of at least two economic processes, namely Dutch disease and sectoral imbalance/disincentive to entrepreneurship. Dutch disease refers to economic disruption in the form of de-industrialization or de-agriculturalization (in accordance with what is the tradable sector in the economy) originating from the large inflow of foreign currencies from natural resource exports. A substantial increase in the price of minerals can cause resource misallocation via the mechanism of relative prices. The exchange rate may appreciate, crowding out traditional agricultural or manufacturing sector exports. Domestic price changes encourage output and investment in non-traded activities. There is a switch from internationally traded goods to non-traded goods (Neary and van Wijnbergen 1986; Sachs and Warner 1999, 2001). Over time the economy's productive sectors weaken and skills as well as experience in those areas are permanently lost (Krugman 1987). Rent-seeking types of economic activity, fostered by the high rents derived from natural resources-related economic activities, create a disincentive for economic agents to engage in more productive types of economic activities, and since a resource boom lowers returns to entrepreneurship relative to rent-seeking, entrepreneurship falls. Hence there would be a change in the allocation of human capital with a boom and the loss of productive human capital or talent through the rent-seeking process (Baland and Francois 2000).

The second channel concerns institutional failure. Mavrotas et al. (2011) find that a point-source type natural resource endowment impedes institutional development measured by both governance quality and democracy level, which in turn hinders growth. Resource-rich countries that impose low taxes tend to have less representative and accountable governments through the logic of no representation without taxation (Ross 2004b). Their polities are also more likely to be less democratic (Ross 2001a). Furthermore, Ross (2001b) argues that there tends to be institutional breakdown due to negative government responses to the resource boom's positive revenue shocks.

Then research in the late 1990s and early 2000s has added the third channel, conflict, into the broader picture of the resource curse hypothesis (Collier and Hoeffler 1998, 2004b). In this regard, two seemingly competing arguments, greed and grievance, have been widely used to explain the mechanism by which resource abundance leads to conflict; however, later on they seem to be complementary (see Murshed and Tadjoeddin 2009 for a review). Greed is a loot-seeking motivation such as an acquisitive desire similar to that motivating crime, although in the case of civil war often on a much larger scale. Natural resource abundance offers the potential for riches among individuals and groups, and consequently it is likely to increase the salience of the greed motive. Grievance is a justice-seeking motivation based on a sense of unfairness in the way a social group is treated, often with a strong historical dimension. Such motivation potentially appears when a group of indigenous people are denied the benefit of their region's resource wealth. Conflict, in turn, results in growth failure (Collier 1999; Murdoch and Sandler 2002).

Returning to the central theme of the resource curse hypothesis, however, the systematic relationship between resource dependence/ abundance and macroeconomic outcomes remains inconclusive (McNeish 2010; Rosser 2006) and the debate has shifted to identify factors that help countries to avoid the curse by emphasizing the role of institutions.

The inconclusiveness of the relationship is mainly due to the measurement issue. The highly popular empirical finding of Sachs and Warner (1995) and the subsequent studies are challenged by Brunnschweiler and Bulte (2008) and Eric Ng (2006) by offering a clear differentiation between resource dependence and resource abundance. They use the per capita measure of resource rents as the measure of resource abundance instead of Sachs and Warner's (1995) measure of the share of primary commodity export relative to GDP that better reflects resource dependence. They reject the resource curse hypothesis. Ng finds that natural resource abundance *per se* is not a 'curse' for either the level or growth of GDP: resource abundance is insignificantly related to the growth rate of GDP but positively correlated to the level of GDP. Brunnschweiler and Bulte find that resource dependence, when it is treated as endogenous, does not affect growth, while resource abundance (assumed to be exogenous) positively and directly affects growth. They also find that there is no evidence that resource abundance negatively affects institutional quality, contradicting the hypothesis of an indirect natural resource curse implied by Mavrotas et al. (2011).

Later studies have also found that institutions are the key factor to avoid the resource curse. In line with the latest quest for the deep determinants of growth and prosperity, it is argued that everything depends ultimately on institutions. Whether resource abundance might result in a blessing or a curse depends on what kinds of institution are in place: good or bad. Mehlum et al. (2006a, 2006b) theoretically and empirically argue that natural resource-abundant countries include both growth losers and growth winners, and the main difference between the successful cases and the cases of failure lies in the quality of their institutions. In polities with 'grabber-friendly' institutions, more natural resources push aggregate income down, while in those with producer-friendly institutions more natural resources increase income. Other scholars have also emphasized good institutions (Arezki and van der Ploeg 2007; Boschini et al. 2007; Humphreys et al. 2007). These studies emphasize the institutional quality factor as the main channel through which natural resource abundance affects economic growth.

The conclusion arising from these studies is 'to abandon the stylised fact that natural resource abundance is bad for growth' (Lederman and Maloney, 2007, p. 33) and, instead, to understand under what circumstances the resource curse does or does not hold. Within this spirit, Kolstad (2009) goes one step further by differentiating between institutions governing the public sector (democracy) and those governing the private sector (rule of law) and argues that it is the latter (private sector governing institutions) that ameliorate the resource curse. Empirical findings of Bakwena et al. (2010) elaborate, in more detail, types of institutions that help to avoid the resource curse, which includes a focus on the quality of the institutional setting, such as corruption levels, law and order, and bureaucracy, being more democratic (as opposed to more authoritarian), adopting a majoritarian rather than a proportional electoral system; and adopting a parliamentary rather than a presidential regime. However, such emphasis on institutions as a way to overcome the resource curse should take into account the issue of political feasibility, and the explanation of the link between resource abundance and development outcomes should carefully consider social forces and or external political and economic environments in shaping the development outcomes of resource-abundant countries (Rosser 2006).

8.3   FROM NATURAL RESOURCES TO CONFLICT

The simplified resource curse picture presented above can be modified or rearranged, as shown in Figure 8.2, again in a very simple framework. Instead of treating conflict as an additional identified mechanism by which resource abundance is linked to growth failure, we place conflict as a continuation of the original resource curse scenario, where growth failure can lead to conflict. In fact this is a well-established logic within the widely available literature on the economic determinants of conflict. Furthermore, in empirical work, the most robust predictor of the danger of conflict breaking out is low per capita income, implying low growth (Hegre and Sambanis 2006; Ross 2004c). As already highlighted in the previous section, it should be noted that all variables listed in the model are linked to each other to different degrees and often with causal relationships working in both directions; therefore, one should be aware that endogeneity is present.

Institutional failure deserves special attention as it could be directly related to conflict. Institutional failure may result from resource dependence as a result of various processes, such as lack of accountability (Ross 2004b), lack of democracy, high reliance of patronage politics (Ross 2001a) and the presence of rent-seeking and rent-seizing behaviour (Ross 2001b). Yet strong and well-functioning institutions are required by a country or a society to be able to manage conflict peacefully. For example, it has been commonly suggested that democracy is an important mechanism of non-violent conflict resolution.

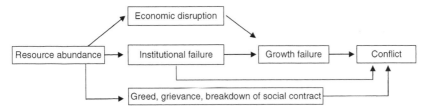

Figure 8.2   Natural resources and conflict

With respect to the political economy of resource rents, capturable resource rents can lead to rent-seeking behaviour. Revenues and royalties from oil or mineral resources are much more readily appropriable than the income flows from agricultural commodities. Increases in the availability of resource rents following a boom in their world prices can increase the appetite for resource rents among certain individuals or groups within society. This is known as a 'voracity' effect (Lane and Tornell 1996), or the 'rentier' effect (Ross 2001a, 2009), and it can instigate serious diversion from normal productive activities. Entrepreneurs may choose to become corrupt rent-seekers rather than engage in the ordinary business of production (Mehlum et al. 2006b; Murphy et al. 1991; Torvik 2002). This itself constitutes a conflict-prone situation leading to institutional damage which in turn leads to conflict.

However, the above story tells only of an indirect relationship between resource abundance and conflict through growth and institutional failures, which is embedded in the original resource curse mechanism. The more direct relationship connecting resource abundance to conflict is best viewed through the famous frameworks of greed and grievance, and the breakdown of social contract as an enabling environment for conflict to occur.

8.4   NATURAL RESOURCES: GREED

The manner in which resource abundance may lead to growth failure has been explained in the previous subsection. As argued in Collier and Hoeffler's (2004b) model, growth failure itself, together with low income and dominance of primary commodities in the economy – all taken together as proxies for greed – better explains the onset of civil war. The primary commodity variable reflecting natural resource abundance is central to the greed hypothesis of conflict.

From the greed perspective, conflict reflects elite competition over valuable point-sourced natural resource rents, concealed by the figleaf of collective grievance (ibid.). Rebellions need to be financially viable: civil wars are more likely to occur when they are supported by natural resource-based rents such as blood diamonds or oil. These resources are best regarded as a non-produced 'prize' (which apart from extraction costs are like manna from heaven), whose ownership is violently contested. The presence of readily capturable natural resource-based rents may make conflict more attractive when compared to peaceful production

The greed motivation behind civil war has been disseminated and popularized by mainly empirical studies, where a cross-section of conflicts in different nations is analysed econometrically, and greed is proxied by the availability or abundance of capturable natural resource rents (ibid.). Greed is about opportunities faced by the rebel group. The opportunities can be classified into three components: financing, recruitment and geography. The most common sources of rebel finance are the appropriation of natural resources, donations from sympathetic diasporas and contributions from either foreign states hostile to the government or multinational companies interested in the region. Natural resource wealth is the chief among the three in terms of relative importance.

Collier and Hoeffler find resource dependence, measured as the share of primary commodity export to GDP, to have a strong explanatory power in their conflict onset model, and they argue for the greedy rebel mechanism, linking natural resources and conflict. However, this finding and interpretation have generated fierce controversy based on questions about the saliency of measurement issues, the problem of reverse causality, possible mechanisms between natural resource rents and conflict, and the choice of estimation techniques.

On the matter of measurement, two broad sets of issues need to be considered. First is the measure of natural resource abundance (wealth) and resource dependence. While Collier and Hoeffler use the primary commodity export share in GDP to measure resource wealth, different proxies have been used by other studies, including (a) specific measures of oil dependence/wealth focusing on per capita oil rents/production/reserves (Humphreys 2005; Ross 2006), offshore or onshore types of exploitation (Lujala et al. 2007; Ross 2006), an oil exporter dummy where oil exceeds one-third of total exports (Fearon and Laitin 2003), and oil exports as a percentage of total exports (Fearon 2005); and (b) diamond wealth measures expressed in diamond production per capita (Humphreys 2005), further disaggregated into primary and secondary diamonds (Ross 2006), and a dummy for the presence of diamonds, disaggregated into primary and secondary types (Lujala et al. 2005). These proxies have led to different, conflicting results.

These conflate resource dependence and resource abundance, a methodology criticized by Brunnschweiler and Bulte (2009), who clearly differentiate between resource dependence and abundance, and use them simultaneously in their cross-country conflict regressions. They take the share of primary commodity exports in GDP as their measure of resource dependence and the aggregate measure of the net present value of rents (in US$ per capita) of a country's total natural capital stock as their measure of resource abundance; and they focus on two disaggregated measures: subsoil mineral resources and land (crop and pastureland, protected areas and forest resources).

The second issue is the selection of the relevant conflict dependent variable in econometric analyses; it can be either the onset or the duration of civil war. With regard to onset, the question is whether natural resource wealth increases or decreases the risk or likelihood of civil war; and with duration, whether or not it prolongs civil war. Collier and Hoeffler (1998, 2004b) claim that resource dependence, measured by primary commodity exports share in GDP, in increasing the likelihood of civil war onset, is both significant and robust; others deny that it is significant (Brunnschweiler and Bulte 2009; Fearon 2005; Fearon and Laitin 2003; Montalvo and Reynal-Querol 2005) or robust (Ross 2004c). On duration, the results are clearly contradictory: Collier et al. (2004) find that the presence of primary commodities has no significant effect on the duration of conflict; but that decreases in primary commodity prices do shorten conflict since they squeeze rebel finances when the level of dependence upon primary commodity exports is high. Using contraband dummy measures, Fearon (2005) and Ross (2006) find that natural resources lengthen civil war duration; while using diamond production per capita, Humphreys (2005) finds that this reduces war duration.

Any measure of natural resource dependence may be endogenous to conflict, and this has two implications: (a) that there is a reverse causality, in which civil wars might cause resource dependence by reducing the size of a country's non-resource sector (for example, manufacturing); and (b) that there is a spurious correlation where both civil war and resource dependence may be independently caused by an unmeasured third variable, such as poor property rights or the weak rule of law.

Brunnschweiler and Bulte (2009) consider reverse causality by treating resource dependence, together with per capita income, as endogenous independent variables in their conflict regression; previous studies had assumed resource dependence to be truly exogenous. The set of instruments they use to measure both resource dependence and income includes resource abundance, trade openness, the constitution (presidential versus parliamentarian systems), absolute latitude, percentage of land in the tropics and distance from the nearest coast or navigable river. They find that when it is treated as endogenous, resource dependence loses its significance. Resource abundance, however, has a negative indirect effect on conflict through income. Based on these findings, they reject previous arguments for fingering natural resource wealth or dependence as the principal culprit in civil war. They speculate that resource dependence (a reliance on primary goods exports) may be a manifestation of the failure to grow and diversify as a consequence of conflict, but does not contribute directly to conflict. In a related paper, Brunnschweiler and Bulte (2008) argue that resource abundance may actually promote good institutional development. Similarly, Rigterink (2010) re-estimates the Collier and Hoeffler model using the exogenous measure of resource abundance and finds that the positive effect of natural resource on conflict vanishes.

Humphreys (2005), who investigated the mechanisms of the relationship between conflict and resource dependence, argues that other factors may also be present. First is the greedy outsider mechanism: the existence of natural resources may be an incentive for third parties – states and corporations – to engage in or indeed foster civil conflict. Second is the grievance mechanism: natural resource dependence may in fact be associated with grievance rather than greed. There are at least four variants of the relationship between conflict and resource dependence: (a) countries with middle levels of dependence on natural resources may be experiencing transitory inequality as part of the development process; (b) economies that are dependent on natural resources may be more vulnerable to trade shocks; (c) the process of extraction may produce grievances – for example, through forced migration; and (d) natural resources wealth may be seen as more unjustly distributed compared to other forms of wealth. Third is the weak state mechanism, also emphasized by Fearon and Laitin (2003). Natural resource-dependent economies may have weaker states, stemming from dependence on resource rents. In these states, untaxed citizens have less ability or incentive to monitor state activity while the governments, relying on natural resource rents more than taxation, have weak incentives to create strong and accountable bureaucratic structures.

On estimation techniques, Fearon (2005) provides the strongest challenge to Collier and Hoeffler's empirical findings on the links between primary commodity exports and civil war. Fearon, who re-estimates Collier and Hoeffler's model using country-year observations, as opposed to the country-five-year observations employed by Collier and Hoeffler, finds that the significance of statistical associations between primary commodity exports and civil war onset vanishes in the country-year regression, meaning that the previous claim of such a relationship is not robust. In other words, this cross-country result will not withstand variation in sample and data coverage. More recently, in their cross-country conflict regression, Brunnschweiler and Bulte (2009) also find that the primary commodity export loses its significance when treated as an endogenous variable – a view shared by Ross (2004c), who reviews 14 cross-country empirical studies on natural resource and civil war, complemented with many qualitative study reports.

These studies varied in terms of time coverage, estimation procedures, resource measure, dependent variable construction (different conflict databases and thresholds) and sets of independent variables used, yielding varying results. Thus Ross (ibid.) concludes that the claim that primary commodities are associated with the onset of civil war does not appear to be robust: oil dependence appears to be linked to the initiation of conflict but not its duration, and illicit gemstones and drugs seem to lengthen pre-existing wars. Fearon (2005) shows that the effect of primary commodity exports is confined to oil, by adding the variable (oil exports to total exports) into the country-year regression. Humphreys (2005) checks the effect of past oil exploitation (oil production per capita) on the onset of civil war and finds it positively significant. However, he asserts that such a relationship works through the weak state mechanism; he reaches this conclusion by adding interaction terms between measures of natural resource wealth and state strength. In a similar vein, Fearon (2005) interprets the oil effect as a weak state mechanism rather than a greedy rebel hypothesis.

Following the critique of Mehlum et al. (2006a, 2006b) regarding the role of institution, Rigterink (2010) finds that natural resource abundance decreases conflict occurrence in countries with 'good' institutions, while increasing it in countries with 'bad' institutions. Although the finding is said to be inconclusive, this points to the ultimately key role played by institutions in determining how natural resource abundance affects conflict, as in the case of how resource abundance affects growth.

8.5   NATURAL RESOURCES: GRIEVANCE

Another way to see the relationship between natural resource and conflict is through the societal grievances over the management of resource rents. The grievance explanation for conflict, which is more attuned to group motivation, is the feeling of a group or groups – sharing a similar identity – that they are being unjustly treated; this can be referred to as a justice-seeking motivation. Central to such grievances are identity and group formation. An individual's utility may be related to his/her identity, specifically the relative position of the group he/she identifies with in the social pecking order (Akerlof and Kranton 2000). In this regard, grievance is mainly rooted in relative deprivation and marginalization felt by certain groups resulting primarily from unfair distribution of resource rents in the absence of a mutually agreed resource-sharing mechanism.

The notion of relative deprivation dates back to the work of Ted Gurr (1970), who defines it as the discrepancy between what people think they deserve and what they actually believe they can get; in short, the disparity between aspiration and achievement. It is not the same as a state of absolute deprivation, which occurs in situations characterized by endemic poverty and where no group may feel relatively deprived, so the forces of rebellion may be more muted. Gurr (ibid., p. 24) puts forward the hypothesis that 'the potential for collective violence varies strongly with the intensity and scope of relative deprivation among members of a collectivity'. This lays down the notion of relative deprivation as the micro foundation for conflict and relative deprivation is considered to be a major cause of civil war, as well as other types of conflict, since it can stimulate general frustration or be used by conflict entrepreneurs as a unifying tool or as a means for group mobilization for collective action. Marginalization refers to a situation where a usually minority group has been protractedly denied access to enjoy resource rents generated from their localities and to some extent they have been excluded from benefiting from the resources they feel that they deserve and alienated from the mainstream policy. It is closely related to the notion of relative deprivation since a marginalized group would certainly feel that they are so relatively deprived, even absolutely deprived. As argued by Aspinall (2007), what determines conflict (or rebellion) is not simply the presence of a natural resource *per se*, but rather how it is interpreted by local actors and people. Therefore it is important to think of grievance, not as an objective measure and treated in isolation, but rather as a socially constructed value that arises and may be understood only within a particular historical, cultural, political context.

Relative deprivation and marginalization types of grievance are usually the outcomes of widening horizontal inequalities between groups fuelling grievances of the deprived group against the competing group(s) or the state, which is often claimed to be responsible for the process of widening inequality to happen (Stewart 2008a). Horizontal inequality refers to inequality between culturally different groups, and should be distinguished from vertical inequality, which is the inequality within an otherwise homogeneous population. It should be noted, however, that relative deprivation might also be acutely felt even under the supposedly more favourable situation of converging horizontal inequality as shown by the cases of secessionist and ethnic conflicts in Indonesia (Tadjoeddin 2011). Although convergence is a desirable outcome of the development process, it may create problems if it is achieved through a non-democratic process.

In contrast to the debates on the natural resource-greed hypothesis, which are found mainly in the terrain of cross-country studies, the natural resource-grievance argument is argued mainly in country-level studies: Aceh and Papua in Indonesia, Bougainville in Papua New Guinea, the Niger Delta in Nigeria and southern Sudan are cases in point.

In Indonesia, the three-decade-long civil war in the westernmost province of Aceh (rich in natural gas) and the less severe secessionist violence in the easternmost province of Papua (rich in oil, gas and minerals), were rooted in regional grievances against the distribution of natural resource rents generated from their regions (Aspinall 2007; International Crisis Group 2002b; Tadjoeddin et al. 2001). Without proper consent from the resource-producing localities, Suharto's three-decade-long centralistic New Order regime collected the resource rents, mainly from hydrocarbons, minerals and timber, and used them to subsidize resource-poor regions. A similar situation can be found in the mineral-rich Bougainville island of Papua New Guinea, where local grievances over the sharing of resource revenue derived from the massive Panguna copper and gold mine located in the centre of the island, the alleged devastating environmental consequences of the mine for the island, and the social effects arising from the influx of outsiders due to the mining business (Banks 2005; Linnett 2009; Regan 2003).

It is a similar story in the case of the oil-rich Niger Delta region in Nigeria, which accounts for 93 per cent of the country's export earnings and provides financing to sustain the Nigerian state. However, despite the region's economic contributions, the region and its local people are disadvantaged in terms of socioeconomic development and continuously suffered from environmental degradation due to oil activities, while the non-oil-producing areas are relatively more developed in terms of infrastructures. Nigeria has been a rentier state for the last half a century since almost all federal government earning derived from oil revenue (Ikelegbe 2006; Nwokolo 2009). In Sudan, in addition to the longstanding political grievance due to cultural and religious divides, natural resource (oil) was the next important factor, although it came later, contributing to the already acute grievances of people in Christian-Animist dominated southern Sudan against the ruling Muslims in the north during the second civil war (1983–2005) in the country (Ali et al. 2005; UNEP 2007b).

8.6   CONCLUSION

Pure versions of the greed or grievance hypothesis are, on their own, unsatisfactory explanations for the causes of conflict. Addison, Le Billon and Murshed (2002), and Addison and Murshed (2003b) construct a game-theoretic model of contemporary conflict involving the competition for resources combined with historical grievances, and a possible transfer from those in power that assuages the grievances of the excluded. In addition to resource rents or greed, grievances also play their part in fuelling conflict by fostering inter-group non-cooperation and lowering the cost of participation in conflict. Conflict can increase because of heightened intrinsic grievances, or because there are more lootable natural resources. Similarly, conflict may decline if historical grievances are assuaged by transfers from the party in power to potential rebel groups. In short, greed and grievances may exist simultaneously. Even if a conflict is initially based on grievance, it can acquire greedy characteristics; and the converse is also true. For example, a civil war originating in demands for land reform (Colombia, Nepal) can acquire greed-based characteristics once the rebels begin to enjoy 'narco-rents' or taxes from the peasantry. Nwokolo (2009) argues for how conflict in the Niger Delta region of Nigeria started with grievance and has been prolonged for decades by greed in the absence of a newly agreed social contract among interested parties. Conversely, a civil war based on a desire to control lootable revenue rents may generate grievances as people are killed.

In reality, competing greed versus grievance hypotheses may be complementary explanations for conflict. Indonesia's resource-rich regions that have had separatist conflicts with the federal government offer us striking contrasts when we try to gauge the relative explanatory power of greed versus grievance. When viewed via the lens of a detailed quantitative case study, grievance explanations dominate any greed motivation; yet when looked at through the prism of a cross-country study, these regions display a modified form of the greed theory (resources helping to prolong the duration of conflict and encouraging secession). It would appear, therefore, that the greed explanation for conflict duration and secessionist wars works better in cross-country studies, but has to make way for grievance-based arguments in quantitative country-based case studies. It appears that grievance may be better at explaining why conflicts begin, but it does not necessarily explain why they persist. Greed and grievance can and do coexist; because one breeds the other, a model of their simultaneous determination is required. Moreover, neither greed nor grievance alone is sufficient to initiate conflict: that requires institutional breakdown, or a failure of the social contract.

With regard to the role of natural resource in conflict, a social contract can be understood as a mutually agreed rule of how resource rent is shared across different parties (for example, centre versus region, across regions and ethnic groups). Such a social contract will address the grievance of the disadvantage regions and control any possible greed to control a particular resource rent. The recent political reform in Indonesia consisting of a new law on fiscal decentralization and the provision of special autonomy to the resource-rich provinces of Aceh and Papua have been largely successful in addressing secessionist challenges the country faced, in particular the civil war in Aceh (Tadjoeddin 2011). In contrast, the absence of such an agreed resource-sharing mechanism explains the protracted resource conflict in the oil-rich Niger Delta region of Nigeria. The Indonesian case can be treated as an example on how good institutions may break the positive association between natural resource and conflict as argued by Rigterink (2010).

9 Climate change and armed conflict

*Ole Magnus Theisen, Nils Petter Gleditsch and Halvard Buhaug**

9.1 INTRODUCTION

A number of high-profile individuals, non-governmental organizations (NGOs), and policy reports have put forward alarmist claims about the impact of climate change on human security. For example, US President Barack Obama (2009) has declared that '[t]here is little scientific dispute that if we do nothing, we will face more drought, more famine, more mass displacement – all of which will fuel more conflict for decades'. Yet, the empirical foundation for a general relationship between resource scarcity and armed conflict is indicative at best and numerous questions regarding proposed associations between climate change and conflict remain unanswered (Nordås and Gleditsch 2007; Gleditsch 2012). Major limitations in data and research designs make it difficult to conclude firmly one way or the other. In this chapter, we assess how factors such as political and economic instability, inequality, poverty, social fragmentation, migration as well as inappropriate responses may affect the link between climate change and conflict. Then, we review the empirical literature. We conclude with some recommendations for future research.

9.2 ENVIRONMENTAL CHANGE

Global warming is expected to bring about a number of significant changes to the environment.[1] Among the many projected impacts highlighted by

* Our work has been supported by the Research Council of Norway and the World Bank. This chapter is a revised, shortened, and updated version of Buhaug et al. (2008b, 2010). We are grateful to the Social Development Department of the World Bank for permission to use material from the earlier publications. The authors are listed in reverse alphabetical order; equal authorship implied.
[1] For the sake of consistency we base our discussion of the physical effects of climate change on the IPCC's Fourth Assessment Report (IPCC 2007) except where other sources are specified.

the Intergovernmental Panel on Climate Change (IPCC), we identify and discuss three that could have substantial security implications.[2]

The first is that renewable resources such as freshwater and fertile soil may become increasingly scarce. Although some regions may benefit from future climate change, increasing temperature, changing precipitation patterns, and an overall reduction in annual rainfall will reduce crucial subsistence resources in most regions (IPCC 2007). This may lead to over-consumption and contamination of groundwater, thus further reducing the supply of freshwater. A warmer climate will increase evapotranspiration and result in the melting of glaciers. More extreme precipitation could also increase topsoil erosion, in turn leading to less fertile soil.

Second, a rising sea level could lead to massive population displacement. Sea-level rise is most threatening to small island states, although people in low-lying urban areas will also become more exposed to seasonal flooding and extreme weather in coming decades. Unlike other anticipated climate-induced environmental changes, however, sea-level rise will occur relatively uniformly across the globe, and it is a gradual and predictable process.

A third physical consequence of climate change is an increase in extreme weather events. The twentieth century saw a dramatic increase in the number of reported climatic disasters (see CRED 2009, p. 3 for definitions and details). This is often interpreted as a symptom of global warming, although most of the increase is driven by population growth, shifting settlement patterns and improved reporting.[3] In 2009, there were 328 disasters accounting for 10,443 fatalities (average figures for 2000–08 are 392 and 85,541, respectively), most of them in Asia (CRED 2010). Climate-related disasters generate more victims overall, but geological events are slightly more deadly. Flooding is the most prevalent disaster type, followed by drought.

9.3   COPING STRATEGIES

In the face of a dramatically changing climate, groups and societies can choose between several coping strategies. First, they may seek to adapt to the new challenges. Adaptation may range from conservation pro-grammes and efforts at reducing consumption to the pursuit of alternative

---

[2]   We use a traditional definition of security as the absence of armed conflict and use the terms 'conflict' and 'armed conflict' interchangeably.

[3]   The severity of disasters, measured as the number of casualties, varies enormously between years and shows no evident time trend.

modes of livelihood. A society that is unable to adjust to the new challenges may lapse into conflict with one group trying to secure an increasing share of the diminishing resources by force (Homer-Dixon 1999, pp. 74f.). For instance, many have prophesized large-scale wars over water (Klare 2001). A third alternative is to move to more attractive locations.[4]

Whether an increasingly exposed society seeks adaptation, conflict, or exit depends on the nature of the changing environment, the vulnerability of the population, and contextual factors (Barnett and Adger 2007). Gradual changes, such as dessication and sea-level rise, are generally suitable for a gradual response. By contrast, intensifying climate variability and natural hazards may occur more suddenly, ranging from mere minutes (landslides) to months (drought). Thus, some environmental challenges will require immediate action. In the absence of rapid adaptive measures, resource competition or migration become more plausible outcomes. The inability to adapt is captured in the environmental security literature's concept of an 'ingenuity gap' (Homer-Dixon 1999, 2000), which may explain why developing countries are more prone to instability and conflict.

9.4   ARMED CONFLICT

Figure 9.1 shows that the number of armed conflicts increased during the Cold War and peaked in the early 1990s. Conflict frequency then dropped significantly, followed by a smaller rise in the most recent five-year period. The severity of armed conflict, measured as annual battle-related deaths, has generally declined since the Second World War. These trends correspond poorly with aggregate trends in climate change and offer little support for simplistic claims that warming breeds civil war. Figure 9.2 demonstrates that most armed conflicts today occur in developing countries and that almost all conflict-ridden countries have at least one neighbour in conflict.

9.5   A SYNTHESIZED CAUSAL MODEL

Most scholarly assessments between resource scarcity and conflict sketch a causal story where scarcity fuels conflict only in poor societies already suffering from a multitude of other ills, thus adding another stone to the

---

[4]   We do not pursue further the possibility that a society fails to respond to worsening environmental conditions, as it is not an active coping strategy.

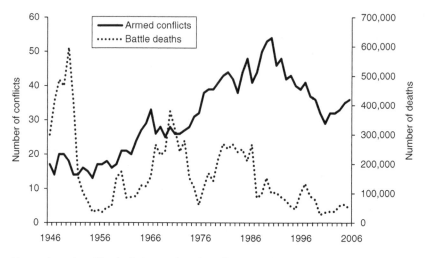

Note: Armed conflicts include state-based conflicts with 25 or more battle-related deaths annually. Battle deaths include only casualties directly caused by fighting.

Sources: See UCDP/PRIO Armed Conflict Dataset (Gleditsch et al. 2002) and PRIO Battle Deaths Dataset, v. 3.0 (Lacina and Gleditsch 2005). Data available from: http://www.prio.no/cscw/armedconflict.

Figure 9.1   Frequency and severity of armed conflict, 1946–2008

burden (Homer-Dixon 1999, p. 16). Five main climate change-induced catalysts of organized violence have been suggested. First, increasing scarcity of renewable resources in subsistence-economy societies may reduce public goods and political legitimacy (Homer-Dixon 1999). Second, in heterogeneous societies increasing resource scarcity may attract opportunistic elites who radicalize the population by intensifying social and ethnic cleavages (Kahl 2006). Third, increasing scarcity may cause unemployment, loss of livelihood, and loss of economic activity (Ohlsson 2003), thus also decreasing state income (Homer-Dixon 1999). Fourth, efforts to adjust to a changing climate – or to remove the causes of global warming – may have unforeseen side-effects that could stimulate tension. Finally, deteriorating environmental conditions may force people to migrate in large numbers, possibly increasing environmental stress in the receiving area (Reuveny 2007). Whether adverse climatic change generates any of these effects depends largely on the characteristics of the affected area – whether they are able to adapt to unusual environmental conditions. Thus, poor and unstable countries with poor governance, large polarized subgroups, social inequalities, a violent neighbourhood, and a history of

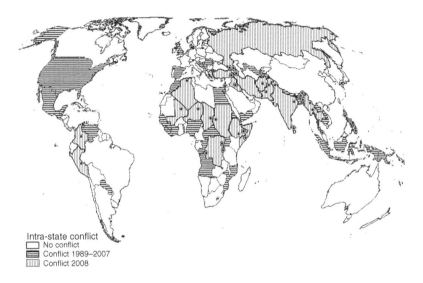

Note: Many territorial conflicts, such as those in Russia and India, affect only a small part of the country. The dots denote the approximate geographic centre of the conflicts.

Figure 9.2   Intra-state armed conflicts, 1989–2008

violence, are plausible candidates for climate-induced conflict (Hegre and Sambanis 2006). Figure 9.3 provides a synthesized causal model. The following sections expand on the five suggested mechanisms.

9.6   POLITICAL INSTABILITY

Many scarcity-based accounts of armed conflict point to the weakening of the state as an important intermediate development (Homer-Dixon 1999, pp. 98ff.), and weak states generally have an increased risk of instability (Fearon and Laitin 1996). Responding to soil degradation, crop failure, or drought is costly, and poor and institutionally weak regimes may not afford the necessary measures. Increasing climatic variations may also affect the redistributive capacity of governments and drain attention and capital away from other important functions. A weak state may give rise to opportunistic challengers who do not themselves suffer from the deteriorated environment and the regime may also opportunistically play social groups against each other. Kahl (2006) argues that such 'state exploitation' is characteristic of election-related violence in Kenya in 1991–93 and the genocide in Rwanda in 1994.

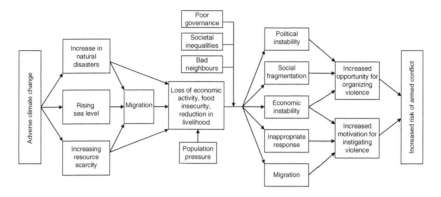

Note: For the sake of clarity, complex patterns (interactions and feedback loops) are kept at a minimum.

Figure 9.3   Possible pathways from climate change to conflict

Political instability is among the relatively few robust correlates of civil war (Hegre and Sambanis 2006). A number of studies on the relationship between civil war and level of democracy find support for a curvilinear relationship (Hegre et al. 2001), reflecting greater instability of regimes between full democracy and full autocracy (Gleditsch et al. 2009; Vreeland 2008). Democratic systems avoid public unrest primarily through justice, responsiveness and protection of minority rights, whereas autocratic states deter organized violence primarily by denying the formation of effective opposition groups and repression. Rulers of in-between regimes are also too weak to gain the control needed to become autocrats, leading to some democratic concessions (Fearon and Laitin 2003).

9.7   POVERTY, INEQUALITY, AND ECONOMIC INSTABILITY

A second plausible climate-induced catalyst of social friction and armed conflict is economic instability and stagnation. Food insecurity and loss of livelihood are possible consequences of adverse climatic changes in many parts of the world, resulting in poverty at the national as well as at the individual level (Barnett and Adger 2007). Poverty, typically defined as low per capita income, is a well-established and substantively important cause of civil war (Collier et al. 2003; Hegre and Sambanis 2006).

Political economists usually attribute this finding to factors that increase individual criminal behaviour relative to normal economic activity (Collier and Hoeffler 2004b; Grossmann 1991). Low wages and high unemployment rates lower the threshold for joining a rebellion. Loss of income may also force people to migrate, potentially leading to new population pressure, resource competition and rebel recruitment (Raleigh and Jordan 2010). A more traditional motivational explanation stresses the importance of relative deprivation, where marginalized segments of society take up arms to alter the status quo (for example, Gurr 1970). While vertical social inequality (systematic differences measured across all individuals) appear to have only a limited or no influence on civil war (Collier and Hoeffler 2004b; Hegre et al. 2003), horizontal inequality (systematic differences between groups) is generally regarded as more likely to produce conflict (Østby 2008b; Østby et al. 2009; Stewart 2000). Fearon and Laitin (2003) maintain that a low per capita income is a symptom of weak state capacity, which generates favourable conditions for insurgency and erodes popular support for the regime.

A rapidly changing climate will have the most serious short-term effects on economies dependent on renewable primary commodities. Many developing countries will experience reduced agricultural yields, depriving them of means to spend on adaptive buffers, such as resilient infrastructure, irrigation systems and desalinization plants (Homer-Dixon 1999, p.105). To the extent that environmental changes vary substantially within countries, they may also amplify existing inter-group inequalities.

9.8   SOCIAL FRAGMENTATION

The connection between ethnicity and armed conflict is disputed in the literature. Some claim that heterogeneity increases the baseline risk of civil war (Blimes 2006); others argue for the importance of particular configurations of heterogeneity, for example, dominance (Collier and Hoeffler 2004b); polarization (Esteban and Ray 2008; Reynal-Querol 2002); or exclusion (Buhaug et al. 2008a; Cederman and Girardin 2007). Some see ethnicity as irrelevant for the onset of conflict (Fearon et al. 2007).

Regardless of the origin of civil war, ethnicity is widely regarded as a facilitator for mobilization. Language, religion and nationality often serve as lines of demarcation between contending groups, eventually resulting in a reinforcing relationship between ethnic identity and hostilities. For example, Gurr (2000b) argues that the notion of a shared Eritrean nationality emerged slowly during the prolonged war of independence. Similarly, Suliman (1997) and Prunier (2007) emphasize that historically low ethnic barriers in Darfur have been heightened by prolonged conflict.

Climate change is unlikely to affect the ethnic composition of countries in the short run, with a possible exception for rapid, disaster-induced population displacement. In a slightly longer perspective, however, we may witness substantial intra- and inter-state migration as global warming makes environmentally vulnerable areas less sustainable.

9.9 MIGRATION

Migration enters the causal model in Figure 9.3 at two stages, as both a cause and effect of deteriorating environmental conditions. Climate-induced migration is argued to lead to violent conflict in receiving areas through four complementary processes (Reuveny 2007). First, the arrival of newcomers can lead to competition over diminishing natural and economic resources, especially where property rights are under-developed. Second, migrants of a different ethnic origin may give rise to ethnic tension and solidification of identities. Third, large flows of migrants may cause mistrust between the sending and receiving state. Finally, climate-induced migration may create or exacerbate traditional faultlines, for instance when migrant pastoralists and local sedentary farmers compete over the use of land. While there is some evidence for a link between transnational refugee flows and the outbreak of armed conflict (Buhaug and Gleditsch 2008; Salehyan 2007), it is not obvious that environment-induced population flows will have the same security implications as conflict migrants. Long-distance permanent mass displacement is seen as likely for slower moving environmental processes only (Piguet 2010). Due mainly to data limitations, no empirical study has been able explore the general consequences of 'environmental migration' across cases. Overall, this area remains critically understudied, and it is not clear whether we should expect climate-induced migration to blend with the ubiquitous urbanization or follow a radically different path.

9.10 INAPPROPRIATE RESPONSE

Inadvertent consequences of human reactions to climate change are rarely acknowledged as a potential catalyst of social friction. At a macro level, draconian measures to reduce CO_2 emissions may have large, unforeseen (or underestimated) effects on the global and regional economic system (Lomborg 2007). Stagnation or even reversal of economic growth could lead to political instability and civil unrest in some contexts. On a smaller scale, dam building and development of irrigation systems to counter projected changes in precipitation patterns may have direct adverse environmental effects on local communities (Baechler 1999, p. 91). The expansion of biofuel programmes could have serious implications for the regional, if not necessarily global, food situation. In fact, the last few years have seen a rise in food prices after decades of decline (Gleditsch and Theisen 2010). In Mexico, a reported 70,000 people took to the streets to protest against mounting tortilla prices caused by increasing US demands for Mexican corn for biofuel production (Watts 2007). So far, research on security implications of climate change has not paid much attention to these potential catalysts.

Climate change could also influence how armed conflicts are perceived and justified. In illiberal regimes, global warming may constitute a much-needed political escape. For instance, some claim that the origins of the Darfur conflict can be traced back to the decades-old Sahelian drought (see, for example, UNEP 2007a). While such claims may have some merit (though see de Waal 2007), they are nonetheless problematic as they may relieve the main actors of their own responsibility. In fact, the UN has been accused of using climate change as an excuse for its inability to halt the killings in Darfur (*The Times*, 23 June 2007). The high profile of the climate issue entails a significant risk that political actors with hidden agendas rally around the popular notion of global warming constituting the greatest security challenge of our time (Salehyan 2008).

9.11   CONTEXTUAL MEDIATORS

These mechanisms potentially linking climate change and variability to conflict are not likely to play out in all societies. In fact, many of the same factors that expose a society to deteriorating climatic conditions also influence the risk that the negative consequences will result in violence. Negative security impacts of future climatic change are likely to be observed primarily in regions that host armed conflicts today: that is, the East-Central parts of Africa, the Middle East, and Central and East Asia. This is where international peacebuilding and development efforts may be needed most urgently.

The physical consequences of climate change ignore state boundaries. Similarly, contemporary conflicts often cross porous borders, driven by proliferation of small arms and know-how, transnational ethnic linkages, refugee flows, and the need for safe havens (Buhaug and Gleditsch 2008). Accordingly, efforts to address harmful societal consequences of climate change need to apply a regional perspective. The Kurdish question in Iraq can hardly be resolved without acknowledging the role of neighbouring Turkey, Syria and Iran.

9.12   ASSESSING THE EMPIRICAL LITERATURE

Statistical comparative studies tend to model the scarcity–conflict relationship in rather simplistic ways. The first true multivariate assessment (Hauge and Ellingsen 1998) found that land degradation, freshwater scarcity, population density and deforestation had direct, positive effects on the incidence of civil conflict, while no indirect associations were uncovered. The contemporaneous Phase II of the State Failure Task Force (SFTF; now the Political Instability Task Force, PITF) project (Esty et al. 1998), by contrast, did not find any direct relationship between indicators of environmental scarcity and state failure. While differences in data and research designs provide some explanation for the lack of correspondence between these pioneering studies, Theisen (2008) shows that Hauge and Ellingsen's results cannot be reproduced. Later studies on water availability and civil war have not come closer to a robust conclusion. Miguel et al. (2004) find that negative deviation in annual precipitation – their instrument for economic shock – increases the risk of civil war in Sub-Saharan Africa. A similar result is reported by Hendrix and Glaser (2007), using the same data. Raleigh and Urdal (2007) also find water scarcity and soil degradation to increase the risk of armed conflict, but the effects are more pronounced in developing countries, contrary to theoretical arguments on the topic. In contrast, Buhaug and Theisen (2012) and Theisen et al. (2011/12), expanding the temporal and spatial scope of Miguel et al., find no robust association between rainfall and civil war and Ciccone (2011) finds that Miguel et al.'s results are not robust when looking at deviations from the long-term mean rather than interannual variations (see also Koubi et al. 2012). A widely publicized article claimed that warmer years have higher civil war risk (Burke et al. 2009), although this result is not robust to small alterations in model specification and estimation technique (Buhaug 2010). In a study of a much longer time period, Tol and Wagner (2010) find that lower temperatures are associated with lower food production and more wars in the pre-industrial era in Europe and China. The relationship is weaker for the more recent period, leading the authors to question whether temperature has much relevance to conflict in the present day.

Moreover, de Soysa (2002) finds that rural population density in combination with renewable resource wealth increases the conflict risk, while Binningsbø et al. (2007) report that higher levels of accumulated consumption of renewable resources (the so-called 'ecological footprint') is associated with a lower risk of civil conflict. Reflecting the current state of knowledge, Theisen (2008) finds environmental and demographic factors to be insignificant and demonstrates that several earlier findings are not replicable or do not hold with improved data. Research on natural disasters and conflict is less developed, but a few recent studies find statistical support for the general disaster–conflict hypothesis (Brancati 2007; Drury and Olson 1998; Nel and Righarts 2008), although little is known about the causal mechanisms. Above all, the results appear to be driven primarily by geological rather than climatic events. Slettebak (2012) finds that when the civil war model is better specified, the empirical results provide more support for a proposition from disaster sociology; that affected countries write in the face of adversity.

Despite a lack of convergence on any of the important proposed linkages, it would be premature to conclude that environmental factors generally and climate changes specifically are unrelated to conflict risk. Underdeveloped theoretical models, poor data quality, and inappropriate research designs cast doubt on possible inferences to be drawn from the reported (non-)findings. We identify five crucial limitations in the current literature that should be addressed in future work.

The first problem is that most large-N studies have failed to account adequately for proposed indirect and conditional effects of climate change. Of the mediating factors presented in Figure 9.3, at best only simple interaction terms have been used. However, there is no a priori reason why such intermediate effects should be linear and multiplicative; rather, they may be characterized by threshold effects and apply only under certain conditions. Furthermore, interactive effects might consist of a complex web of multiple factors, making it harder to test environmental security arguments with conventional statistical methods without a well-developed theoretical model. One possibility is to employ so-called 'fuzzy methods', which are more suitable for dealing with multiple interactive factors (Ragin 1987).

Second, large-N investigations of environmental scarcity and armed conflict suffer from overly aggregated research designs (Buhaug 2007; Buhaug and Lujala 2005; O'Lear and Diehl 2007). Unrest rarely engulfs entire states and many conflict-ridden countries today, such as India and Turkey, appear relatively unaffected by the local violence. Studies of the environment–conflict relationship at the country level may fall prey to an ecological fallacy – explaining local phenomena from aggregated data.

Recent advances in geographic information systems (GIS) and remote sensing make it feasible to adopt a disaggregated design for statistical analyses (Buhaug et al. 2008a; Buhaug and Rød 2006; Urdal 2008).

A third significant limitation is that almost all statistical assessments of environmental scarcity and conflict look only at the most severe forms of organized violence: civil and inter-state war. Yet, the cost of fighting a government army is considerable, so deprived groups may simply be too weak to engage in serious conflict with state forces (Klare 2001). This suggests that lower-level violence (without direct state involvement) is a more likely outcome of deteriorating climatic conditions than civil war or inter-state war. Indeed, much of the case literature that claims a causal link between scarcities of renewable resources and armed violence refers to local, small-scale inter-ethnic conflict (Kahl 2006; Martin 2005; Suliman 1999a, 1999b). The emerging quantitative literature on single countries thus far provides mixed results (Meier et al. 2007; Østby et al. 2011; Theisen 2012; Urdal 2008; Witsenburg and Adano 2009). Future research should also pay attention to the influence of the environment on conflict dynamics (duration, severity and diffusion), which until now has been almost completely overlooked.

Fourth, research in the field has long suffered from a dearth of reliable environmental data. In fact, SFTF's analyses (Esty et al. 1998) analyses were based on models that exclude nearly half of the world's states due to missing data. The temporal dimension – so crucial if we are to gauge the dynamics in resource availability – is another challenge as most environmental data are static or cover changes in the most recent years only. A third data limitation concerns the level of spatial resolution. Environmental data are often aggregated and released at the country level (Miguel et al. 2004) even when the underlying data have been collected at a higher resolution.

Finally, the case study literature tends to select cases on the dependent and main independent variables; that is, to study only countries where both conflict and scarcity are prevalent. Gleditsch's (1998) critique that much of this literature suffers from complex, untestable models, confusion of level of analysis, and inference based on speculations and anecdotal evidence remains valid. Other criticisms point to a possible spurious link between resource scarcity and armed conflict, a lack of focus on the agency of the actors involved (Peluso and Watts 2001b), and a refusal to attempt to rank the causal factors (for example, Homer-Dixon 1999, p. 7).

9.13 CONCLUSION

The physical effects of climate change have a variety of potential consequences for the livelihood of humans. The broad scope of these challenges
adds to the urgency of the climate change debate. Hardly a single important facet of our daily life is free from some hypothesized effect of climate
change. The good news is that support for policies of mitigation and adaptation can mobilize a broad section of the public because climate change is
relevant virtually to everyone. The bad news is that such broad debates are
in danger of being hijacked by actors with special agendas. We believe that
this has happened to some extent in the debate about climate change and
conflict, where NGOs and security establishments have vested interests in
presenting their own mission as one that is also particularly well suited to
the climate change agenda.

In stark contrast to popular perception – which has been boosted by
massive media attention, alarmist claims by high-profile actors, and the
2007 Nobel Peace Prize award – the empirical foundation for a general
relationship between resource scarcity and armed conflict is indicative at
best and numerous questions regarding the nature of the proposed causal
association between climate change and conflict remain to be answered
(Bernauer et al. 2012; Scheffran et al. 2012). Case-based research offers
several examples of conflicts where environmental degradation (anthropo-
genic as well as due to climate variability) plausibly has had some influence
on the initiation and continuation of violence. However, environmental
problems abound but armed conflict is a very rare phenomenon, so the
case for a general link between the two still appears to rest on a weak foundation. To the extent that policy advice from the academic community
should be founded on robust findings in peer-reviewed research, the literature on environmental conflict has surprisingly little to offer. Yet, we are
still only beginning to experience the physical changes imposed by global
warming, so a lack of systematic association between the environment
and armed conflict today need not imply that such a connection cannot
materialize tomorrow.

There is considerable room for improved case studies but in our view
the most important need is for better statistical research. Case studies can
provide advance warning of problems in selected areas, but global climate
change policy is crucially dependent upon the early warning of events in
areas that may have no such problems in the past. For this reason, we need
better generalizable knowledge. Data limitations, rigid research designs,
and overly bold assumptions have so far effectively prevented direct and
thorough evaluations of prevailing causal theories. These challenges are
not insurmountable. Recent and ongoing advances in data collection

and statistical software, notably within geographic information systems, coupled with refinement of theoretical models, facilitate more precise and localized analysis of environment–conflict linkages. Eventually, a multi-disciplinary research programme, combining the best of the two research traditions, would provide the best foundation for an assessment of the security implications of climate change.

10 Demography and armed conflict
Henrik Urdal

10.1 INTRODUCTION

Demographic and environmental pressures have featured prominently in
the debate over the new security challenges in the aftermath of the Cold
War. The attention has primarily been on two arguably distinctive sets of
population–conflict dynamics; the effect of population growth on dwin-
dling resources, and the importance of age structure transition, or 'youth
bulges'. In the resource scarcity literature, high population growth and
density are seen as major causes of scarcity of renewable resources such
as arable land, fresh water, forests and fisheries. Arguably, such scarcities
may trigger armed conflict over resource access (see, for example, Baechler
1999; Ehrlich 1968; Homer-Dixon and Blitt 1998; Kahl 2006; Kaplan
1994).

Population-induced resource scarcity has been considered to be a security threat primarily in developing countries with low capacity to prevent
and adapt to scarcities (see, for example, Homer-Dixon 1999). Generally,
one of the most robust findings in the quantitative conflict literature is that
impoverished and institutionally weak countries with low GDP per capita
have an exceptionally high risk of armed conflict and civil war (Collier and
Hoeffler 2004b; Fearon and Laitin 2003; Hegre and Sambanis 2006). Two
key trends arguably contribute to extend the relevance of population pressure and resource scarcity into the coming decades. First, despite declining
population growth rates globally, low-income countries, particularly in
parts of Asia and Sub-Saharan Africa will continue to experience very
significant population growth rates in the near future. Second, these areas
are also the ones expected to face the most severe consequences of global
climate change (Stern Review 2006).

The second demographic concern relates to whether countries and areas
undergoing age-structure transitions, resulting in very youthful populations or 'youth bulges', are increasingly susceptible to political violence.
Youth bulges have become a focus of current political upheavals in the
Arab world, including the most recent revolutions in Tunisia and Egypt,
as well as for recruitment to international terrorist networks. In a background article surveying the root causes of the September 11, 2001, terrorist attacks on the US, *Newsweek* editor Fareed Zakaria argues that youth

bulges combined with slow economic and social change has provided a foundation for an Islamic resurgence in the Arab world (Zakaria 2001, p. 24).

About the same time, Samuel Huntington qualified his 'Clash of Civilizations' thesis by adding the dimension of age structure:

> I don't think Islam is any more violent than any other religions . . . But the key factor is the demographic factor. Generally speaking, the people who go out and kill other people are males between the ages of 16 and 30. During the 1960s, 70s and 80s there were high birth rates in the Muslim world, and this has given rise to a huge youth bulge. But the bulge will fade. Muslim birth rates are going down; in fact, they have dropped dramatically in some countries. (Steinberger 2001)

The challenges pertaining to large youth bulges relate not to demography alone, but to a very considerable degree also the availability of opportunities of large youth cohorts for completing an education, for getting into the labour market and for participating in governance. While the failure of governments to deliver opportunities to youth can lead to increased conflict risks, young age structures alone do not make countries destined for violence. Where opportunities for participation in economic, social and political life exist, large youth bulges can even be a blessing rather than a curse. In the context of declining fertility and thus lower dependency ratios, large youth cohorts can be a vehicle for economic development, a so-called 'demographic dividend', rather than conflict (for example, Kelley and Schmidt 2001).

This chapter discusses the two major demographic security perspectives and presents results from recent quantitative studies of systematic empirical relationships between demographic change and armed conflict. Before doing so, however, it briefly presents the current demographic trends that form the basis for these security concerns.

10.2 GLOBAL POPULATION TRENDS

The total world population has increased from 2.5 billion in 1950 to reach 7 billion by late 2011 (United Nations 2009b, p. 4). Population growth accelerated after the Second World War, when many developing countries entered into the early phase of the demographic transition with decreasing mortality and continued high fertility. The rapid population growth in most developing countries spurred concerns in the 1960s and 1970s that food production would not keep up, and that burgeoning populations would seriously deplete natural resources (Ehrlich 1968, p. xi).

The gloomiest scenarios proved unfounded as food production has kept pace with population increases in most parts of the world, and fertility is now declining in all world regions. As shown in Figure 10.1, the latest medium projection of the United Nations Population Division suggests a total world population of around 9.1 billion by year 2050 (United Nations 2009b). The strongest growth will take place in South-Central Asia and Sub-Saharan Africa. In relative terms, the population of these regions has grown from 28 per cent of the total world population in 1950 to around 38 per cent in 2010, and it is projected to constitute 46 per cent of the world population by 2050 according to the United Nations medium projection.

Using the official UN youth definition (15–24 years), youth bulges are referred to here as the percentage of the population aged 15–24 in the adult population, defined as those aged 15 or above. While youth in OECD countries typically constitute 10–15 per cent of the adult population, Sub-Saharan Africa has by far the largest relative youth population at above 35 per cent in 2010. The Middle East and North Africa (MENA) have youth populations equalling 29 per cent of the adult population, while the similar number for both Asia and Latin America (LAC) is around 24 per cent. Youth bulges are expected to drop considerably over the next decades, to around 25.5 per cent in Sub-Saharan Africa in 2050, 16.5 per cent in the Middle East and North Africa, and around 14.5 per cent in Asia and Latin America and the Caribbean.

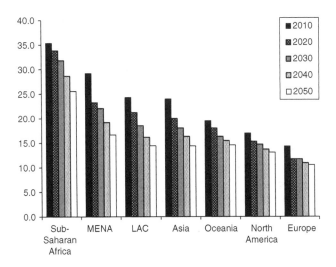

Figure 10.1   Youth bulges across world regions, 2010–2050

10.3   POPULATION GROWTH, NATURAL RESOURCE SCARCITY, AND CONFLICT

Resource scarcity is seen as a product of three different factors interacting – population growth, resource degradation, and the distribution of resources between individuals and groups. Homer-Dixon has called this 'demand-induced', 'supply-induced' and 'structural scarcity', respectively (Homer-Dixon 1999; Homer-Dixon and Blitt 1998). The distributional aspect is central in all the most influential frameworks of the resource scarcity tradition (Baechler 1999; Homer-Dixon 1999; Kahl 2006). The three sources of scarcity may exert different impacts from case to case, and frequently interact. Homer-Dixon (1999) argues that two types of interaction are particularly common. Resource capture occurs in a situation of resource degradation and population growth, providing incentives for powerful groups to take control over scarce resources on the expense of weaker and poorer groups. Ecological marginalization denotes a situation where great land inequality and population growth leads people to move into more ecologically fragile areas. While many countries have the ability to adapt to environmental change, some countries, particularly poor and institutionally weak states, are likely to be more vulnerable to environmentally related violence (Baechler 1999, p.xvi; Homer-Dixon 1999, p.181). Resource scarcity arguably also has the potential to aggravate social segmentation (Homer-Dixon 1999, p.96). While demographic and environmental pressures are seen as unlikely causes of international wars, it is claimed that such factors may spur local violent low-intensity disputes (Baechler 1999; Homer-Dixon 1999; Kahl 2006).

The resource scarcity framework has traditionally relied heavily on the state weakness hypothesis, positing that the impact of resource scarcity will weaken state institutions and provide opportunities for potential rebel groups to challenge state authority. Episodes of regime collapse and regime transitions may thus provide particularly great opportunities for violent conflict driven by demographic and environmental pressures. However, even when demographic and environmental factors are not the primary drivers of state failure, relatively weaker states are more likely to experience resource scarcity conflicts, first because they are less capable of mitigating the effects of resource scarcity, and second because they are generally more likely to be militarily challenged by opposition groups.

Challenging the conventional reliance on the state weakness approach, Kahl (2006) has identified two alternative 'state-centric' causal pathways from resource scarcity to internal violent conflict: the state failure and the state exploitation hypotheses. Both start from the premise that demographic and environmental stress factors may put severe pressure both on society at large and on state institutions. When the interaction between resource degradation, population growth and unequal resource distribution leads to lower per capita availability of land resources and the expansions into more marginal land, this is assumed to put a greater downward pressure on agricultural wages and contribute to economic marginalization which can further lead to migration and inter-ethnic tensions. According to Kahl, this represents an opportunity for weakened states to bolster their support base through mobilizing ethnic groups to capture scarce resources. When regimes experience increased grievances and opposition due to resource scarcity, they may be likely to instigate inter-ethnic violence as a means to divert attention from their inability to meet these demands at the same time as they consolidate support among groups that may capture resources at the expense of contending groups.

10.4 CRITIQUES OF THE RESOURCE SCARCITY PERSPECTIVE

The major challenges to the resource scarcity perspective come from the traditions of neoclassical economics and political ecology. Neoclassical economists, often also referred to as cornucopians or resource optimists, have posed three sets of challenges to the view that resource scarcities are likely to bolster conflict. First, they argue that most renewable resources are not scarce at the global level, and markets, technological developments and resource substitution are likely to help us adapt to situations of local scarcity (Lomborg 2001; Maddox 1972). Furthermore, in virtually all areas of the world, people are responding to lower mortality by reducing their fertility, albeit at different speeds. A second argument is that high population pressure and resource scarcity may be a vehicle for development. High population growth and increasing scarcity of resources provide incentives for finding ways to mitigate scarcity by means of technological development and resource substitution (for example, Boserup and Schultz 1990; Simon 1989). Hence, high population pressure will eventually lead to declining resource dependence and less scarcity. The third neoclassical argument is that it is resource abundance that causes conflict, not scarcity, either because rich resources may be captured for personal enrichment or for conflict financing, or because resource abundance works indirectly by paving the way for corruption and 'Dutch disease', hence weakening state institutions. While the scarcity and abundance perspectives are by no means theoretically exclusive, the first two neoclassical arguments directly challenge some of the assumptions of the resource scarcity perspective. The argument that renewable resources are not globally scarce and that markets, technological innovations and demographic adaptation may mute local scarcities is not entirely rejected by scholars associated with the resource scarcity perspective. In fact, Homer-Dixon (1999, p.108) acknowledges that what he terms 'technical and social ingenuity' is likely to help many societies overcome resource scarcities. However, in many developing countries, markets, property rights, government structures, infrastructure and human capital 'are imperfect, absent altogether, or distorted in ways that actually compound resource problems' (Kahl 2006, p.17). Similarly, population growth could be a source of conflict in the short run even if the long-term consequences may very well be greater adaptive capacity and peace.

The second tradition challenging the resource scarcity perspective, political ecology, sees resource distribution as the main mediating factor between the environment and conflict (for example, Peluso and Watts 2001a). While political ecologists argue that local cases of 'scarcity' may very well happen in the context of local abundance, they also argue that the resource scarcity perspective mostly ignores important sources of resource degradation caused by resource extraction in the forms of mining and logging, dam construction and other forms of industrial activity (ibid., p.26). Implicitly, political ecologists critique proponents of the resource scarcity perspective for blaming the poor for causing scarcity and violence (for example, Hartmann 2001, p.50). While it is true that Homer-Dixon's case studies mainly address local violent responses, resource distribution plays a major role in many of Homer-Dixon's cases, and for this reason he has been criticized for diluting the concept of resource scarcity (Gleditsch and Urdal 2002). Population growth and resource degradation may play an aggravating role, a fact often overlooked by political ecologists.

10.5   EMPIRICAL STUDIES OF POPULATION PRESSURE, ENVIRONMENT AND CONFLICT

Previous quantitative studies have found mixed evidence for the resource scarcity and conflict nexus. Two early and influential quantitative studies in the field, the State Failure Task Force Report (Esty et al. 1998) and Hauge and Ellingsen (1998), reported different results. Esty et al. found no effects of soil degradation, deforestation and freshwater supply on the risk of state failure. Hauge and Ellingsen, on the contrary, concluded that the same environmental problems as well as high population density were indeed positively associated with civil war, but that the magnitude of the effects was secondary to political and economic factors. However, these results have, for unknown reasons, proven not to be replicable even with

Table 10.1 Summary of quantitative studies on population pressure and
violent conflict

Variables	Cross-national studies	Subnational studies
Population density, growth, and their interaction	*Population density* Positive effect: Hauge and Ellingsen (1998); de Soysa (2002)	*Population density*
	No effect: Collier and Hoeffler (2004b); Esty et al. (1998); Hegre and Sambanis (2006); Theisen (2008); Urdal (2005)	No effect: Buhaug and Rød (2006) (Sub-Saharan Africa)
	Growth and density interaction Marginal effect: Urdal (2005) (positive for the 1970–79 period only)	*Growth and density interaction* Weak positive effect: Raleigh and Urdal (2007) (low-income countries only, global); Urdal (2008) (rural population density and growth, India)
High urban population growth	No effect: Urdal (2005) (negative for the post-Cold War period)	No effect: Urdal (2008) (India, negative for armed conflict)

the assistance of the authors, and are also not reproduced in an analysis of extended time-series resource scarcity data (Theisen 2008). Assessing the issue of land scarcity, de Soysa (2002) found a significant effect of population density on domestic armed conflict. These and other quantitative studies on population pressure and internal armed conflict are summarized in Table 10.1.

The cross-national correlations of population pressure and internal conflict were studied more thoroughly in Urdal (2005). The study included all sovereign states and politically dependent areas (colonies, occupied territories and dependencies) for the 1950–2000 period, and assessed the impact on the risk of low-intensity internal conflict (Gleditsch et al. 2002) of high population growth and great population density, measured as low per capita availability of potentially productive land.

The results of the study indicated that national-level aggregate demographic pressures are not strongly related to armed conflict. The interaction between population growth and density is not robustly associated with the onset of an armed conflict. In fact, in countries with negligible population growth, high population densities seem to lower risk of conflict somewhat. Nor are urban growth rates statistically associated with

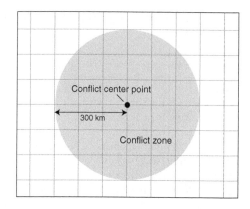

Figure 10.2   Conflict zones on grid squares

conflict onset. While running a subset of the models for different time periods, it appears that the interaction of population growth and density was clearly associated with an increased risk of conflict in the 1970s. However, the frequent claim that resource scarcity has become more pertinent as a driver of armed conflict in the post-Cold War era receives no support. In fact, urban growth is statistically associated with lower risk of conflict onset in this period.

Two subnational studies were later conducted to investigate whether the null-findings were simply a result of a too high level of aggregation, where local conflicts driven by population pressure-resource dynamics would not be captured. In a global study of small geographical squares of 100 × 100 km, Raleigh and Urdal (2007) investigated whether local level demographic and environmental factors determine the location of armed conflict. The study addressed three different demographic and environmental concerns, population pressure, land degradation and water scarcity, starting from the assumption that high population density, degradation and water scarcity should be more strongly associated with conflict in areas with increasing population pressure. The dataset comprised 13,199 polygon squares and covered civil conflicts observed from 1990 to 2004, using low intensity UCDP/PRIO conflict data with location information (Buhaug and Gates 2002). Figure 10.2 displays a hypothetical conflict zone set on grid squares.

For the full global sample, there was a robust effect on conflict of the interactions between population growth and density, as well as population growth and water scarcity. No empirical support was found for any mediating effects of the proxies used to measure state capacity or governance. When looking exclusively at the poorer half of the globe, which presumably should be more susceptible to conflict generated by demographic and environmental pressures, the only consistent and robust effect found was for the interaction between population growth and density.

All sample models for low-income countries showed very consistent results. Both population growth interacted with water availability as well as population growth interacted with population density were found to be consistently associated with an increasing risk of conflict, while the traditional national-level variables such as GDP, political institutions and the subnational population density account for a considerable amount of conflict across states. The inclusion of economic and political control variables did not alter the impact of any of the demographic and environmental variables. This ran counter to the expectation that state weakness variables would capture some of the variance explained by resource scarcity variables. In conclusion, models on the low-income subsample indicated limited effects of demographic and environmental pressures for conflict behaviour in those areas that should, according to the resource scarcity perspective, experience the most pronounced effects.

An alternative disaggregated approach is to study whether variations in demographic and environmental factors are associated with variations in levels of political violence within one state, implicitly controlling for type and strength of government. Urdal (2008) addressed the relationships between demography, environment and political violence in 27 states of India from 1956 to 2002. The advantage of such design is the availability of data comparable over time and space. The study used three different and independently collected measures of political violence including armed conflict, incidence counts of political violence, and a count measure of Hindu–Muslim riots.

The results generally provided more support for the resource scarcity and conflict nexus than the global studies. Scarcity of productive rural land was associated with higher risks of political violence, particularly when interacted with high rural population growth and low agricultural yield. Other central aspects of the resource scarcity scenario were not supported. Structural scarcity (measured by rural inequality) and high urbanization rates were not found to increase the risk of political violence. Hindu–Muslim riots, a predominantly urban phenomenon, did not seem to be related to population pressure, not even to rapid urbanization.

10.6 YOUTH BULGES AND POLITICAL VIOLENCE

It has been proposed that youth cohorts may develop a generational consciousness, and especially so out of awareness of belonging to a generation of an extraordinary size and strength, enabling them to act collectively (Braungart 1984; Feuer 1969; Goldstone 1991). However, violent conflict between groups only divided by age are rare. The generational approach has some serious shortcomings with regard to the explanatory power of the relationship between youth bulges and violence. In principle, the development of generational consciousness may explain the formation of youth movements that can function as identity groups, and some form of collective identity is necessary before collective violent action can take place. But it is clearly not necessary that identity groups are generation based for youth bulges to increase the likelihood of armed conflict. Furthermore, the generational approach does not offer explanations for the motives of youth rebellion nor does it provide a sufficient explanation for the opportunities of conflict. It is clear that if large youth bulges that hold a common generational consciousness would always produce conflict, we would have seen a lot more of violent youth revolts. Conditions that provide youth bulges with the necessary motives and opportunities for armed conflict are discussed below, starting from what we may call the opportunity and the motive perspectives.

The opportunity literature has its roots in economic theory and focuses on structural conditions that provide opportunities for a rebel group to wage war against a government (Collier 2000a; Collier and Hoeffler 2004b). These are conditions that provide the rebel group with the financial means to fight, or factors that reduce the cost of rebellion, such as unusually low recruitment costs for rebel soldiers. Paul Collier has suggested that relatively large youth cohorts may be a factor that reduces recruitment costs through the abundant supply of rebel labour with low opportunity cost, increasing the risk of armed conflict (Collier 2000a, p. 94). According to the opportunity perspective, rebellion is feasible only when the potential gain from joining is so high and the expected costs so low that rebel recruits will favour joining over alternative income-earning opportunities. The motive-oriented tradition has its origins in relative deprivation theory and tends to see the eruption of political violence as a rational means to redress economic or political grievances (Gurr 1970; Sambanis 2002, p. 223). Motives for committing political violence can be economic – such as poverty, economic recession or inequality – or political – such as lack of democracy, absence of minority representation or self-governance. Most of the literature on youth bulges and political violence arguably falls into this tradition. It focuses on how large youth cohorts facing institutional crowding in the labour market or educational system, lack of political openness, and crowding in urban centres may be aggrieved, paving the way for political violence (Braungart 1984; Choucri 1974; Goldstone 1991, 2001).

The distinction between the motive and opportunity perspectives should not be overstated. First, in its simplest form, the motive perspective over-predicts political violence; the existence of serious grievances is not sufficient for collective violent action to erupt (Kahl 1998). The likelihood that motives are redressed through political violence increases when opportunity arises from availability of financial means, low costs or a weak state. Second, while opportunity factors may better explain why civil wars break out, actors can also have strong motives (Sambanis 2002, p. 224). Third, many factors may equally well be described as representing both opportunity and motive. A young impoverished person may be considered both a potential low-cost recruit, and at the same time an aggrieved individual motivated by economic and political exclusion. Below, I discuss the most relevant contextual factors suggested to affect the relationship between large youth cohorts and conflict.

First, the mere existence of an extraordinary large pool of youth is a factor that lowers the cost of recruitment since the opportunity cost for a young person generally is low (Collier 2000a, p. 94). Additionally, research in economic demography suggests that the alternative cost of individuals belonging to larger youth cohorts is generally lower compared to members of smaller cohorts. This is called the 'cohort-size effect'. So not only do youth bulges provide an unusually high supply of individuals with low opportunity cost, but an individual belonging to a relatively large youth cohort generally also has a lower opportunity cost relative to a young person born into a smaller cohort. The influence of the size of youth cohorts on unemployment is also emphasized in the motive-oriented literature on civil violence (Braungart 1984; Choucri 1974; Cincotta et al. 2003; Goldstone 1991, 2001; Moller 1968). If the labour market cannot absorb a sudden surplus of young job-seekers, a large pool of unemployed youths will generate strong frustration.

Second, for large youth cohorts, the economic climate at the time they enter into the labour market is particularly crucial. Large youth cohorts are likely be rendered particularly susceptible to lower-income opportunities when economic conditions generally deteriorate, reducing the income they forgo by signing up as a rebel. Similarly, the motive-oriented literature posits that youth belonging to large cohorts will be especially vulnerable to unemployment if their entry into the labour force coincides with periods of serious economic decline. Such coincidences may generate despair among young people that moves them towards the use of violence (Choucri 1974, p. 73).

Third, according to the opportunity perspective, increasing education increases the income-earning opportunities of an individual, assuming a negative relationship between education and rebel recruitment. While this is not inconsistent with the motive-oriented literature, it has been suggested that when countries respond to large youth cohorts by expanding opportunities for higher education, this may produce a much larger group of highly educated youths than can be accommodated in the normal economy. Raising the expectations among large youth groups and failing to deliver employment opportunities could carry a risk for radicalizing and mobilizing an increasingly competent youth population.

Regarding the role of democracy, the opportunity and motive perspectives yield opposite predictions. The opportunity literature suggests that the opportunity for political violence is greater the less autocratic a state is, while the motive-oriented literature argues that the greater the political oppression, the greater the motive for political violence. Civil war studies have found an 'inverted U' relationship between democracy and conflict, suggesting that starkly autocratic regimes and highly democratic societies are the most peaceful (Hegre et al. 2001). This relationship is assumed to reflect a mix of both opportunities and motives in 'semi-democracies'. In particular, when large youth groups aspiring to political positions are excluded from participation in the political processes, they may engage in violent conflict behaviour in an attempt to force democratic reform (Goldstone 2001).

Finally, it has been suggested that if youth are abundant in relatively compact geographical locations, such as urban areas, this may increase the likelihood that grievances caused by crowding in the labour market or educational institutions arise (Goldstone 1991, 2001). Youth often constitute a disproportionately large part of rural-to-urban migrants, hence strong urbanization may be expected to lead to an extraordinary crowding of youth in urban centres, potentially increasing the risk of political violence.

Two highly influential civil war studies, Fearon and Laitin (2003) and Collier and Hoeffler (2004b) found no effect of youth bulges on the risk of civil war outbreak. However, both studies used a flawed measure of youth bulges, dividing those aged 15 to 24 years by the total population, including all cohorts under the age of 15 years in the denominator. Such a definition is highly problematic both theoretically and empirically. These studies also use a relatively high battle-deaths threshold and thus only include major civil wars.

In a cross-national time-series study of the 1950–2000 period using the low-intensity UCDP/PRIO conflict data (Gleditsch et al. 2002), Urdal found that the presence of youth bulges increased the risk of conflict outbreak significantly (Urdal 2006). Similar results were reported by Cincotta et al. (2003). The statistical relationship in Urdal (2006) held even when controlling for a number of other factors such as level of development, democracy and conflict history. For each percentage point increase in youth bulges, the risk of conflict increases by more than 4 per cent. When youth make up more than 35 per cent of the adult population, which they do in many developing countries, the risk of armed conflict is 150 per cent higher than in countries with an age structure similar to most developed countries. However, there does not appear to be threshold effects as suggested by Huntington (1996). Assessing possible interaction effects, the conflict risk associated with youth bulges does not seem to increase when youth bulges coincide with long-term per capita economic decline, expansions in higher education or strong urban growth. However, the results suggest that the effect of youth bulges is greater in the most autocratic regimes as well as in the most democratic states. It could indicate that youth bulges provide greater opportunities in autocracies and greater motives in democracies.

Finally, the study on India reported above (Urdal 2008) also included age structure measures. Generally, the results supported the findings from the global study. A young age structure was the only demographic factor in that study to be statistically associated with increased risks of all three forms of political violence. The impact of youth bulges on the risk of armed conflict was particularly pronounced in Indian states where men were in the majority. Hindu–Muslim riots were found to be more likely in states where youth bulges coincided with greater levels of urban inequality. High urban growth rates, on the other hand, appeared to be unrelated to the youth bulge–conflict nexus.

10.7 CONCLUSION

This chapter provided a review of recent research on the relationship between demographic factors and internal armed conflict that goes beyond the extensive case-study literature on the topic. The principal question was whether countries experiencing demographic pressures and age structure transitions are generally at a higher risk of experiencing armed conflict and other forms of political violence. Empirical results from a set of quantitative studies were discussed.

A main conclusion was that high levels of population growth and high ratios of population to productive land do not make countries more susceptible to armed conflict. Furthermore, there is no indication that the conflict proneness of poor countries results from greater population pressure on natural resources. These findings resonate well with previous cross-national studies that have found little support for the resource scarcity perspective. In addition, there seems to be little reason to fear that the rapid and massive urbanization that we currently witness in many developing countries is something that generally will lead to greater destabilization and more armed conflicts.

Geographically disaggregated studies provide somewhat greater support for the relationship between population pressure on natural resources and conflict, albeit with some important qualifications. The findings underscore that environmental scarcity and conflict relationships should also be studied systematically at the local level. The combined findings of cross-national and disaggregated studies indicate that while overall demographic pressures and resource scarcity do not seem to make states more conflict prone, the internal distribution and management of resources seem to contribute to explain the geographical distribution of political violence. Hence, relative regional differences in access to natural resources seem to impact the risk of conflict, even in the absence of any 'absolute' scarcity in the country as a whole. Furthermore, the relationship between regional resource scarcity and conflict could be seen as originating from the lack of ability or willingness by central governments to address relative resource scarcity, in the inability by regional and local governments to adopt measures to reduce resource scarcity, or in low adaptability and mobility of people from certain regions.

A young age structure can be both a blessing and a curse. From a more optimistic perspective, youth bulges can be regarded as an increased supply of labour that can boost an economy. This could further be expected to reduce conflict propensity, a 'peace dividend'. While such development is certainly possible, structural aspects of the economy will shape each country's ability to make use of favourable age structural transitions. While the youth bulge hypothesis in general is supported by empirical evidence, indicating that countries and areas with large youth cohorts are generally at a greater risk of low-intensity conflict, the causal pathways relating youth bulges to increased conflict propensity remain largely unexplored quantitatively. The studies presented here suggest that youth bulges, poor governance, failing economic growth and greater inequalities can be explosive. This represents a considerable security challenge to many developing countries, particularly in Sub-Saharan Africa, Asia and parts of the Arab world. While the challenge is real, states are not hostages to demographic developments beyond their influence. States are to some extent able to reduce the risk through the provision of opportunities for young people, primarily by providing education and employment opportunities, and offering political participation.

11 Rethinking durable solutions for refugees
Katy Long

11.1 INTRODUCTION

This chapter argues that there is a need for a paradigmatic shift in international approaches to durable solutions for refugees. Human mobility should be fully integrated into the durable solutions framework. Such a change would recognize the value human mobility can add to the economic, social, political and cultural life of both the individual and wider communities affected by displacement.

In particular, there is an urgent need to revise practices and understandings of repatriation, so that this durable solution is no longer understood to be incompatible with continued use of mobile and migratory livelihood strategies. Repatriation should be firmly conceptualized as a political act, involving the remaking of citizenship and consequent re-accessing of rights through reavailment of national protection in the country of action. It may often – but need not always – involve physical return. Especially in fragile post-conflict states with inadequate capacity to meet their citizens' basic social and economic needs, physical return may actually harm reconstruction efforts by exacerbating state fragility, even as refugees' political repatriation is a necessary condition for recovery and state-strengthening.

While it may at first appear counterintuitive to connect the idea of repatriation to refugees' continued movement, splitting citizenship from residency would open up new space within the durable solutions framework to build more flexible and more resilient solutions. Such a development within UNHCR's policies on repatriation would also help to combat the continued insistence of some states on the notion of repatriation as a return 'home': an aspiration which has been heavily and repeatedly critiqued by a number of forced migration researchers (Hammond 2004; Malkki 1995; Warner 1994).

This chapter is divided as follows. Section 11.2 (Repatriation deconstructed) considers the flaws in current practices and understandings of refugee repatriation and post-conflict reconstruction, as well as the value, scope and limits of the protection that incorporating mobility into repatriation can provide. Section 11.3 (Repatriation reconstructed) outlines a possible framework for integrating migratory strategies into understandings of repatriation and reconstruction. Section 11.4 concludes.

11.2   REPATRIATION DECONSTRUCTED

11.2.1   What Is Repatriation?

Refugee repatriation, at its most basic, has been traditionally equated with the physical return of refugees to their country of origin. This is the 'popular' understanding of repatriation – a 'return home' from exile. It is an interpretation that states have been keen to endorse: a refugee's return to a non-political 'home' represents a restoration of 'the national order of things' (Malkki 1995). Physical return removes the international dimension of the refugee crisis, reducing states' international obligations and increasing interregional stability, while also reducing the threat of xenophobic domestic political tensions in host states. In this sense, it is the physical movement of refugee populations that 'solves' the international community's geopolitical refugee 'problem', as well as any domestic refugee 'problem' in host communities.

Yet refugee repatriation cannot be equated with mere movement or simple return. Repatriation involves the re-linking of refugees to forms of national protection, symbolized through their physical return to their country of origin. Refugees are recognized to have need of international protection not because they are merely displaced, from their country of origin, but because of the inability – or active unwillingness – of their own national state to provide protection of their fundamental human rights. Repatriation – as a 'solution' to refugee status – must therefore involve the restoration of these fundamental rights. Given current forms of international political organization that provide for the distribution of universal human rights through national citizenship, the protection which needs to be restored should be understood to include a broad range of political, social and civil rights that collectively amount to a meaningful citizenship. In this sense, repatriation can be understood as the restoration of a refugee's 'right to have rights' through the restoration of citizenship (Arendt 1967, p. 267).

Repatriation, then, is not just return. It is a political process, involving the remaking of political community in order that refugees' rights – political, social, economic and cultural – are restored in an effective and meaningful manner. Understanding the key to repatriation to be a return to citizenship – rather than a return to physical territory – opens up the possibility of disassociating repatriation from return, by splitting the rights and resources attached to citizenship and those attached to residency. This in turn opens up the possibility of connecting mobility to understandings of 'repatriation'. Embracing a 'complementarity of solutions' allows for the restoration of national citizenship through repatriation and allows for an adequate response to socioeconomic needs that may in fact be best met through migration and mobility (Guterres 2008, p. 3).

11.2.2   Repatriation: An 'Ideal' Solution?

Refugee repatriation has traditionally been considered by the international community to represent the 'ideal' solution to displacement (Long 2012; United Nations 1997). In operational and policy terms, the early post-Cold War period between 1989 and 1997 saw the most emphatic endorsement of repatriation by UNHCR. Political confidence in the possibilities of a global shift towards liberal democratization helped to foster massive returns in Central America, Asia and Africa. Between 1991 and 1996, nine million refugees repatriated (Loescher 2001). Measured in terms of global numbers returned 'home', results during this period were indeed impressive.

In protection terms, however, the achievement of many such 'voluntary' repatriation programmes during the 1990s was considerably more questionable. Although throughout the 1990s UNHCR continued to insist publicly that repatriation must be voluntary, vigorous internal debate about the possibility of replacing 'voluntariness' with a more effective measuring of 'safety' took place. Some argued that the post-Cold War reality of fragile states, civil and regional conflicts, shrinking humanitarian space and massive ethno-national refugee flows made UNHCR engagement in 'imposed return' necessary (McNamara 1998). The 'voluntariness' requirement in repatriation was increasingly seen – particularly by states – as an obstacle to finding 'the right balance between protecting refugees and solving the refugee problem' (UNHCR 1993).

UNHCR's involvement in two repatriations that were judged by human rights organizations to be 'tantamount to forcible repatriation' (Amnesty International 1996) – the Rohingyan return from Bangladesh to Burma in 1994, and the Rwandan return from Tanzania at the end of 1996 – is now seen by senior staff within the organization as the point at which UNHCR turned away from the extremes of such practices[1]. After 1997, the language of voluntary repatriation turned away from that of 'ideal' solution to that of a 'preferred solution' to be used 'when appropriate' alongside 'conditions furthering reconciliation and long-term development in countries of return' (United Nations 1998). This formula – with its explicit connection of return to reconciliation and reconstruction processes – still broadly reflects the current UNHCR approach to repatriation. The organization has continued to be involved in massive

---

[1]   Author interviews with UNHCR staff, various dates.

repatriation operations in the past decade, most notably in Afghanistan and Southern Sudan.

However, repatriation remains a problematic concept on both the level of principle and that of practice. Despite the UNHCR's movements towards a more nuanced an integrated approach to the durable solutions framework, states frequently continue to insist on repatriation as the only possible permanent or long-term solution to mass refugee flows, and to operationalize such policies. Recent forcible returns of Burundians from Tanzania, and of Rwandans from Uganda and Tanzania are illustrative of the interests of host states in expediting gradual 'voluntary' return programmes Tactics used have included the burning of camps housing and the forcible round-up of refugees at gunpoint.

11.2.3 Returning 'Home'

A second problem with current international conceptions of repatriation is the persistent reinforcement that repatriation is a 'return home'. This continuing 'sedentary bias' (Bakewell 2008) in understanding durable solutions sees repatriation equated with the process of physical return to a status quo ante, or 'home'. Understanding repatriation in these terms helps to strengthen the idea that the political connections that exist between nation and state, or the cultural connections that associate people and place, are 'natural' rather than constructed. This assumption in turn helps to reinforce the structure of contemporary international political organization. Yet it is clear from the work of several anthropologists and sociologists that repatriation cannot be understood as a return home. Warner (1994), Malkki (1995) and Hammond (2004) are among those who have stressed the processes of home-making that stem from refugee repatriation, particularly after longer-term periods of exile. Refugees' life experiences – including the experiences of flight and exile themselves – make a return to a pre-flight 'home' both frequently undesirable and sociologically impossible.

Particularly following long-term exile, refugees may have little interest in a physical return home, even if they recognize the value that a restoration of citizenship and the reconstruction of their communities of origin may bring. Long-term refugees may be embedded in socioeconomic networks in their host communities even if they have no access to formal naturalization processes at state level. Importantly, extended exile is the norm for the majority of refugees. In 2004, 61 per cent of refugees remained in Protracted Refugee Situations (PRS). The result is that many refugees will not have ever seen the home to which they are supposedly eager to return. Geographically, return movements may also correspond to broader processes of industrialization and urbanization that mean socio-economic opportunities may also lie outside of the pre-flight home. In the 1990s for example, three-quarters of Guatemalan refugees repatriated to Guatemala did not return to their previous villages, but instead bought new land and formed new returnee communities (Worby 1999, p. 21).

11.2.4 Fragile States and Return

The questions surrounding voluntariness in repatriation can be seen as indicative of the tensions between practice and principles in return. Similarly, the continued insistence of some elements of the international community on representing repatriation as a return home is reflective of the continuing conceptual and political barriers impeding acceptance of refugee repatriation as a process involving positive political change and transformation. A third problem with contemporary practices of repatriation, however, is more practical. Recent conclusions from UNHCR's ExCom – including one passed at an extraordinary meeting held in December 2009 on PRS – explicitly state that 'voluntary repatriation should not necessarily be conditioned on the accomplishment of political solutions in the country of origin' (UNHCR 2009b). Most recent mass repatriation operations – such as those to Afghanistan, to South Sudan, to Liberia and Sierra Leone, to Burundi – have involved return to fragile post-conflict states and communities emerging from serious intra-state conflict, with weak public institutions and civil society and damaged socio-economic capacities. These conditions create serious obstacles to refugees' durable return.

The UNHCR ExCom paragraph's intended purpose is to ensure that political preconditions do not 'impede the exercise of the refugees' right to return'. Yet in reality, a refugee's right to return is not often threatened. In fact, refugee repatriation to fragile post-conflict states and communities is often likely to occur as soon as is possible, under significant pressure from host countries interested in 'solving' their refugee problem and in the interest of donor states keen to equate mass return with visible progress on post-conflict reconstruction. This form of premature return may 'plac[e] fragile institutions in the country of origin under significant strain . . . further undermining peacebuilding efforts' (Milner 2009, p. 26).

Similarly, for many refugees, the major obstacle to their repatriation – once their state of origin begins to emerge from conflict – is not a lack of desire to return, but a lack of confidence in the ability of the state and its authorities to guarantee basic security and dignity. Even following the agreement of a peacebuilding framework which includes an agreed pathway for refugee return – such as the 1995 Dayton Peace Accords for

Bosnia, the Bonn Agreement for Afghanistan in 2001 or the 2005 Sudanese Comprehensive Peace Agreement – violence and insecurity may persist locally on the ground. An absence of state capacity to absorb refugee flows may often result in serious obstacles to the securing of viable and dignified socioeconomic livelihoods. In Afghanistan, for example, the massive numbers who chose to repatriate were unexpected, and led to serious stress being placed on extremely limited Afghan resources. Given the fact that 'many returnees found themselves in a worse position after their return than before . . . the scale and speed of the return helped to divert yet more of the limited funds available for reconstruction into emergency assistance', Turton and Marsden argue that even the facilitation of this Afghan return by the UNHCR was misguided (2002, p. 3). Surveying Afghanistan today, it is difficult to dispute the recent conclusion of the International Crisis Group that 'as security deteriorates in and around Afghanistan, the successful repatriation of millions of refugees appears ever more elusive' (International Crisis Group 2009). Institutional incapacity – and the resulting corruption which frequently accompanies such weaknesses – has also frequently created obstacles for returnees interested in reclaiming or accessing land. This may not only prevent returnees' access to sustainable livelihoods, but may also reignite intra-community conflicts or create new divisions between returnees and 'stayees', as has occurred for example in Southern Sudan (Duffield et al. 2009; Pantuliano et al. 2008).

In addition to these threats posed by repatriation to fragile communities and states, the impact of fragile state repatriation on refugees themselves must also be acknowledged. Continuing insecurity and violence (whether targeted at returnees or a more general phenomenon), socioeconomic deprivation or even destitution and cultural shock (particularly in PRS and especially apparent if state fragility has resulted in a loss of gender-based freedoms) may all contribute to the non-sustainability of repatriation to fragile states. Furthermore, leaving a host community or state may result in measurable losses, particularly in terms of economic opportunities, cultural freedoms and access to education and training. This is especially true for women and youth. There is also a clear link between the success of return and subsequent internally displaced person (IDP) movements within fragile states of origin, as seen in both Afghanistan and Sudan (International Crisis Group 2009).

These concerns raise serious questions about how the success of refugee repatriation can best be measured. In a 2004 paper, Black and Gent argue that that the goal of the international community should be to secure refugees 'the right to sustainable return' (as per the definition used by the United Nations Mission in Kosovo) (Black and Gent 2004). This aim for sustainable return reflects their assessment that in reality, circular migration movements and transnational or mobile livelihoods play an important role in supporting refugee repatriation (Stepputat 2004). Sustainability in return clearly requires a significant institutional commitment to social and political capacity building at a state level, but – in Black and Gent's terms – it also can involve the fostering of transnational links: 'refugee return could be particularly valuable in terms of promoting sustainability by opening up economic, social or cultural linkages with former countries of asylum that could help the home country to withstand shocks' (p.16). Importantly, this approach to repatriation moves away not only from measuring success in repatriation by the absolute permanency of return, but also encourages a community-focused rather than an individual approach to measuring the impact of repatriation (ibid., p.15).

In summary, current practices of organized mass refugee repatriation frequently fail to respect recognized standards of voluntariness. This is largely because states have a continued political interest in expediting refugee populations' physical return to their country of origin. States also continue to insist on an understanding of repatriation as a sedentary return home, despite the considerable body of research showing that successful repatriation is a transformative and creative process building new understandings of home. This is again because of political interest in the 're-rooting' of populations. These pressures for early repatriation have led to several refugee repatriation operations not being able to sustain long-term reintegration, particularly in fragile post-conflict states with little internal capacity for political or socioeconomic resilience. Given this failure to foster sustainable form of repatriation and reconstruction, it is clear that a new approach is needed in order to create the conditions necessary to ensure refugees' sustainable and voluntary repatriation.

11.2.5 Repatriation and Reconstruction

In order for refugee repatriation to offer good prospects for sustainable reintegration in post-conflict states, it is clear that repatriation must be linked to reconstruction, in both political and socioeconomic terms. However, it is important to note that the concepts of 'state-building', 'state-strengthening' and 'capacity-building' that underpin contemporary approaches to post-conflict reconstruction are not unproblematic themselves. This is evident if the ways in which refugee repatriation has been linked to reconstruction are considered. Given the international communities' controversial recent involvement in 'rebuilding' Iraq and Afghanistan, it is now widely acknowledged that many state-building processes are frequently over-technocratic and often exacerbate rather than address deficits in state legitimacy and regime accountability (Bickerton 2007; Chandler 2006; see Ghani et al. 2005 for a good example of a technocratic account of state-building).

Understanding repatriation to be an integral component of nascent peacebuilding – rather than a response to a fundamental change of circumstances that would in time lead to the cessation of refugee status under the 1951 Convention – is not a new practice. The 1979–80 Zimbabwean repatriations were intended to ensure the return of Zimbabweans to the country in time to participate in the 1980 General Election that would signal the end of white rule in Southern Rhodesia (Jackson 1994). In 1993, refugee return to Cambodia after the signing of the Paris Peace Accords was similarly intended to ensure mass participation in the Cambodian elections. Yet these early examples show the dangers inherent in linking repatriation movements to symbolic moments of state reconstruction. In Zimbabwe, demographic manipulation of the repatriation process by Robert Mugabe's ZANU (Zimbabwe African National Union) ensured the scale of their victory in the elections. In Cambodia, although the actual movement of refugees across the Cambodian border was extraordinarily effective, reintegration itself was fragile.

Acute land shortages meant that by the end of 1993, 73 per cent of returnees were still classed as 'needy' or 'at risk' by the World Food Programme. Many were seen by neighbours and relatives as both community outsiders (for departing) and community burdens (for their failure to reach economic self-sufficiency) (Garcia-Rodicio 2001). Furthermore, in 1992 the Khmer Rouge had opted out of the peace process that precipitated repatriation efforts (Eastmond and Öjendal 1999, pp. 43–4). Long-term post-conflict reconstruction concepts such as security, development and restorative justice were therefore far more elusive to locate in Cambodian return (Garcia-Rodicio 2001, pp. 123–4).

The controversies surrounding the 2009 Afghan elections, although not directly linked to refugee repatriation, have also provided a very recent reminder of the folly of relying on the completion of technical exercises in democracy to demonstrate progress in building accountable and responsible political communities. Similarly, the difficulties that have plagued repatriation processes in Southern Sudan (Pantuliano et al. 2008) were directly connected to preparations for the 2010 secession referendum. These provide clear evidence that focus on what might be termed the 'demographics of democracy' – in the interests of reinforcing claims of national sovereignty – prioritizes the return of people rather than the content of their citizenship. Without basic security and socioeconomic sustenance to complement technical participation in elections, return is unlikely to provide a sustainable solution to exile.

Repatriation has, of course, long been linked to broader reconstruction and development aspirations. High Commissioner Ruud Lubbers' introduction of the concept of the '4Rs' – repatriation, reintegration, rehabilitation and reconstruction – in 2003 highlighted processes of linking repatriation to development that had begun as early as the ICARA II conferences in the mid-1980s (Lippmann and Malik 2004; Loescher et al. 2008). Such activities were in part prompted by the need to prevent recurrent cycles of flight due to continuing instability in areas of return. By connecting repatriation to the notion of development as a pathway to long-term state stability, some claims could be made to justify the act of repatriating refugees to fragile and insecure states such as Bosnia or Afghanistan. It was through UNHCR's 'efforts to consolidate the durable solution of repatriation and reintegration in countries of origin [that it is] . . . reducing the risk that violence, armed conflict and population displacements will recur' (Crisp 1999, p. 9).

Linking repatriation and reconstruction therefore serves a double purpose. On the one hand, it provides a means of addressing the 'root causes' of flight, and offers a welcome recognition that repatriation is not just return, but involves complex, long-term and gradual processes of reintegration and reconciliation. Yet less positively, it has also been argued by senior UNHCR staff members that such activities not only stretch UNHCR's mandate well beyond comfort, but also help to mask the real political causes of continued flight (ibid., pp. 19–20). Contemporary refugee crises in areas such as Congo, Somalia and Afghanistan lend weight to the argument, advanced by MacRae (1999) as early as 1999, that such displacements should be understood as symptomatic of chronic political failure and the absence of a sufficiently robust state to enforce the basic norms of social order. This has serious implications for development or capacity-building projects, because while the distribution of emergency relief may be imagined as purely humanitarian in certain circumstances, longer-term development is a necessarily political project requiring some form of relationship with state power and authority (ibid., p. 22).

A further problem with return-as-reconstruction is that return processes have frequently been used as a cipher for successful reconstruction: a visible 'safe' return provides donor countries with the opportunity to signal the 'success' of reconstruction efforts, providing a justification for political and financial disengagement. It also allows state of origin governments to point to returning populations as 'proof' of the legitimacy of their rule and the success of reconstruction. Furthermore, it is clear that linking the return of refugees to state-building and reconstruction discourses has been at least in part prompted by a decline in the political space made available for asylum-seekers in Western donor states. By presenting return as a necessary component for any successful state rebuilding process, donor governments are able to understand the uncertainty of qualities such as 'safety' in Afghanistan or Iraq in terms of 'obstacles to return' rather than 'justifications to stay' (Zimmerman 2009). These interests in promoting the 'success' of reconstruction and in closing off Western national space to refugee populations in response to domestic political agendas helps to explain why the UK government insisted in 2003 that Iraqi refugees had 'a moral obligation to return and assist in the rebuilding of the country' (Amnesty International 2003).

This overview suggests that 'good' practices of post-conflict reconstruction – gradual, informed by local practices and political cultures, focusing on building a political community and not completing technocratic exercises – do indeed benefit from refugee repatriation, understood as a form of political reconnection. Repatriation of refugees adds legitimacy to the process of state-strengthening and ensures that national inclusion is the basis for future political settlements. Exposure to new cultural values and better educational opportunities may in some cases mean that repatriates are able to act as 'promoters' of human rights, playing a strong role in constructing a new civil society. More practical skills accumulation and easier access to financial resources may also result in repatriates playing an important role in socioeconomic reconstruction. As Milner's work has recently emphasized, leaving refugees out of peace-building plans is likely to risk the long-term disruption of state reconstruction. In these terms, it is clear that repatriation should be connected to reconstruction (Milner 2009).

The problem, however, arises when repatriation is equated with immediate physical return. Early return may serve to create the appearance of a resolution of a refugee crisis before refugees' rights can be genuinely and meaningfully restored. This may respond to states' political interests in restoring populations to their 'natural' places and thus strengthen the security of nation states, but it is unlikely to lead to improvements to refugees' and other citizens' human security. To avoid the risks of early return being assumed to equate to full repatriation or a desirable component of post-conflict reconstruction, a new approach to reconstruction and repatriation processes is needed. One such approach may be integrate opportunities for mobility alongside those for physical return in formulating plans for refugee repatriation and post-conflict reconstruction.

11.2.6   The Value of Mobility

Current practices of repatriation and reconstruction are therefore problematic for a number of reasons. 'Voluntariness' in repatriation is often difficult to guarantee. The idealized notion of a 'return home' often reflects neither the wishes of refugees nor the possibilities afforded by repatriation, particularly in PRS. Fragile states are often ill-equipped to deal with the political, social and economic consequences of mass return influxes. Focusing on the demographics of return mean that 'proving' the success of reconstruction may become a technical exercise in which return marks the completion of the process, rather than the beginning of longer complex efforts to produce a responsible and responsive state. In all these cases, it is physical return, rather than 'repatriation' – understood as a political process of reconnection with the state – that creates many of the difficulties. Mobility in repatriation may, however, offer an opportunity to combine the best elements of repatriation and reconstruction and enhance the sustainability of both processes, to the benefit of both refugees and states.

Why does mobility matter? Is mobility a means to an end, or an end in itself? If we are to move towards the incorporation of mobility into durable solutions, it is important to answer these questions so that we can understand on what basis and under what conditions we should protect mobility.

Clearly, mobility has a role to play as a method of facilitating access to important rights and resources. Particularly in terms of socioeconomic strategies, it is clear that migration can play a crucial role in securing access to sustainable livelihoods. In terms of refugee repatriation and post-conflict reconstruction, as discussed above, mobility offers a possible means to offset many of the weaknesses of physical return programmes by providing access to alternative social, economic and cultural resources outside of the state of origin that may benefit refugees, their families and communities, and their home state.

This role that migration can play in development processes has been recognized for the past decade, particularly in terms of remittance contributions. Nyberg-Sorensen et al.'s seminal study of the migration–development nexus in 2002 noted that 'remittances are double the size of aid and at least as well targeted at the poor' (Nyberg-Sorensen et al. 2002, p. 5). These findings have developed into a general consensus among the international community that migration can be a positive force for development, with research findings suggesting that the economic power structures associated with remittance-led development may thus have a profound role in shaping the structures of states emerging from conflict (Fagen 2006; Ratha 2003). Migration offers opportunities to access sustainable livelihoods that may simply not exist in the community of origin, leading Nyberg-Sorensen et al. to argue that 'the most important resource for the development of LDCs is people connected by transnational networks' (p. 24). The World Bank estimates that even despite the current global recession, remittances to developing countries will total some $290 billion (World Bank 2009b). The UK Department for International Development is not alone in promoting donor development programmes that acknowledge that 'migration can make a positive contribution to poverty reduction and development' (DFID 2007, p. 24). Migration also not only makes economic contributions to development. Migrants may 'contribute new skills and life views, whether they return or not' (Nyberg-Sorensen et al. 2002, p. 10). Although it is important to guard against overly simplistic views of the impact of migration upon communities of origin (some of the potential pitfalls – such as remittance dependency, increased intra-community inequality and tensions, and reduced political accountability – will be discussed below), this brief overview confirms that mobility in repatriation and reconstruction could play a functional role, facilitating broader development processes and access to greater economic and social opportunities.

Yet mobility is more than just migration, a means to the end of socio-economic remittances. Mobility is in fact an end in itself, a good worth protecting for its own sake. In a recent report from the UNDP on the general relationship between mobility and human development, de Haas argued that mobility should be understood as 'a fundamental capabilities-enhancing freedom itself', not least because such movements allow the expression of individual agency (de Haas et al. 2009, pp. 1–2). The UNHCR recognizes freedom of movement to be 'a principle enshrined in international human rights law'. Article 13 of the Universal Declaration of Human Rights similarly states that 'everyone has the right to freedom of movement and residence within the borders of each state . . . Everyone has the right to leave any country, including his own, and to return to his country'. While the wording of Article 13 underlines the difficulties in balancing the right to human movement against the expression of state sovereignty through the control of entry to state territory, it is nonetheless obvious that freedom of movement – even if limited by states' political interests – should be considered a fundamental human freedom essential to the protection of 'inherent human dignity'. Protecting and enhancing refugees' mobility (within the limits of the law) is therefore an essential task for the UNHCR to undertake in itself. This need for mobility is further compounded in the case of repatriation. Recognizing freedom of movement as a human right underlines the importance that any return home be a refugee's choice rather than a product of expectations or obligations imposed by the international community.

Far from being a simple adjunct to durable solutions, allowing a neat circumvention of the problems caused by the shrinkage of resettlement options or the return of refugees to still-fragile states, the protection of mobility should therefore be seen as a central goal of the international refugee regime. This is not as radical as might at first be assumed: Nansen passports – the pre-UNHCR refugee identity document created under the League of Nations in the 1920s and 1930s – were after all initially intended to facilitate refugees' freedom of movement across international borders in search of viable employment (Skran 1995). In developing a discourse which links refugee protection with mobility, migration and the securing of socioeconomic livelihoods, contemporary discussions may in fact be returning full circle to a central principle of earlier protection regimes.

Mobility in repatriation might involve the integration or combination of repatriation processes with opportunities for access to regularized labour migration channels, or continued temporary or permanent residency in a host community. It is conceivable that mobile repatriation might be a precursor to eventual physical return pending reconstruction, or it might represent a durable solution in itself in which a state's political community broadens to include transnational and diasporic members. The possible forms mobility in repatriation might take will be discussed in more detail in Section 11.3, but what is clear is that access to mobility needs to be understood as a central component of any approach to refugee protection, a facilitator of refugees' access to rights and an important freedom in itself. In the last three years, UNHCR policy has begun to reflect just such considerations.

11.2.7   Mobility, Solutions and the UNHCR

Recognizing the value that mobility could bring to practices of repatriation reflects a wider shift within the UNHCR since 2006 towards the embrace of mobility and its integration into the durable solutions framework. Policy documents issued in the past three years have repeatedly stressed the potential value mobility could add in rethinking durable solutions to take account of new complexities and challenges, particularly in dealing with PRS populations and in cases where political causes of flight may also be connected to economic needs for continued migration, such as might result from endemic state fragility (for example, in Zimbabwe or Afghanistan).

To date, mobility has largely been presented by the UNHCR in terms of refugees' potential access to labour migration channels. The UNHCR's January 2007 10-Point Action Plan on Mixed Migration and Refugee Protection suggested that 'beyond the classic durable solutions, legal migration opportunities may open up a complementary avenue for some refugees' (UNHCR 2007b, para. 7). In a discussion paper prepared for the High Commissioner's Dialogue on Protection Challenges held in December 2007, this idea was expanded upon. The UNHCR pointed to the potential benefits which could accrue to both host state and the state of origin if refugees are able to remain in the state of asylum even after the original cause of flight has disappeared:

> [B]y living and working abroad, such people effectively reduce the competi-
> tion for jobs and other scarce resources in their country of origin, and thereby
> contribute to the peacebuilding process. As far as countries of asylum are
> concerned, the continued presence of refugees . . . may make a valuable contri-
> bution to the growth and productivity of both local and national economies.
> (UNHCR 2007a, para. 51)

In June 2009, the Department of International Protection Services released a further commentary on refugee protection and mixed migration, which explicitly highlighted the role international migration could play in meeting the socioeconomic needs of refugees from or being hosted in fragile states:

> In the context of globalization, and at a time when many host countries and
> countries of origin in a post-conflict phase cannot yet offer adequate jobs and
> livelihoods . . . legal migration to a third country could offer an alternative,
> either short term or permanently. (UNHCR 2009a)

Other policy documents have also reinforced this emphasis on freedom of movement and refugee mobility as important and positive contribu-tors to refugee protection, particularly when connected to durable solu-tions. As already noted, the 2008 Policy on Return and Reintegration activities makes clear that post-repatriation freedom of movement should be protected, and no attempt made to contain returnee popula-tions within communities of origin. The September 2009 Urban Refugee Policy also stresses freedom of movement within these terms, emphasiz-ing the need for solutions to be based around the provision of 'effective protection':

> A refugee who is unable to live in decent and dignified conditions and who has
> no real prospect of finding a durable solution in or from their country of asylum
> within a reasonable timeframe cannot be considered to have found effective
> protection. When a refugee moves to seek reunification with immediate family
> members who are not in a position to reunite in that person's country of first
> asylum, and when a refugee moves as a result of other strong linkages with the
> country of destination, the onward movement may also be justified. (UNHCR
> 2009c, para.15)

UNHCR's interest in mobility as a part of a durable solutions framework is undoubtedly linked to its work on the Afghan Comprehensive Solutions

Framework from 2003 onwards, and by its recent experiences in using the ECOWAS (Economic Community of West African States) Protocol on Free Movement to deal with residual Liberian and Sierra Leonean populations in hosting West African states (Adepoju et al. 2007). Yet in reality, beyond these cases there has been little attempt to move beyond a growing recognition of the potential value of mobility to refugee protection in general policy statements towards an understanding of how mobility as a component of repatriation and return processes could work in practice. Section 11.3 now offers some suggestions about possible frameworks for such an implementation.

11.3　REPATRIATION RECONSTRUCTED

11.3.1　The Value of Mobility in Repatriating to Fragile States

It is clear that the success of mass repatriation is inextricably connected to the complex processes underpinning post-conflict reconstruction and vice versa. The survey of contemporary repatriation and reconstruction practices, however, demonstrates that it is extremely difficult to negotiate between the demand for swift refugee return and the reality of slow, tentative peacebuilding. In 2006, speaking about the prospect of a durable refugee return to Southern Sudan, UNHCR High Commissioner Antonio Guterres underlined the difficult symbiotic relationship between repatriation processes and broader post-conflict reconstruction:

> Large-scale population returns are difficult to sustain if development stalls and instability grows. Without adequate resources for development, institution-building and reconciliation, societies can unravel again, dormant conflicts can reignite, and civilians can be forcibly displaced once more ... [Yet] over and over, we see that their [refugees] participation is necessary for the consolidation of both peace and post-conflict economic recovery. Sustainable peace and recovery are necessary to allow refugee returns. Yes. But refugee returns are every bit as essential to sustained peace and recovery. (Guterres 2006)

It is highly questionable whether in terms of early post-conflict reconstruction it is the physical return of refugees which is crucial to success. However, what is necessary is a political reconnection between the refugee diaspora and the state, in order to reinforce the legitimacy of the post-conflict state's claim to exercise sovereignty on behalf of and distribute rights to the national population, and provide refugees with access to those political rights. This political 'repatriation' – a process of national incorporation – is clearly essential to ensure sustainable peacebuilding.

The fragility of most post-conflict states means that encouraging repatriates to seek mobile livelihoods may reduce pressure on fragile state infrastructure, help finance reconstruction and on an individual level offer greater autonomy and opportunities to such 'repatriates', pending their eventual physical return at a later and more stable stage of the peace consolidation process.

11.3.2   De Facto Mobile Repatriation

These observations are borne out by considering refugee-returnees' own practices. Evidence shows that the model of return as a mono-directional process from a host state to a home community does not reflect the reality of refugees' search for solutions. Turton and Marsden (2002), for example, suggest that at least 200,000 of the refugees who repatriated to Afghanistan in 2002 had left the country by the end of the year. This was not simply a response to the difficulties encountered in returning to a fragile state (although these did play an important role), but also reflected refugee returnees following patterns of seasonal migration or returning to better employment prospects in Iran and Pakistan (having picked up repatriation assistance packages). In these cases, their decision to leave Afghanistan should not be classed as ricochet flight or displacement, but understood as a rational socioeconomic decision. Furthermore, the fact that their physical return was not permanent should not be taken to suggest that they were not participating in repatriation and reconstruction processes through circular migration and remittance sending.

In her study of Somaliland return migration, Nyberg-Sorensen confirms these observations, classifying returns – particularly from the wider and more educated diaspora – as often involving 'staggered' or 'revolving' repatriation (Nyberg-Sorensen 2004, p. 15). Staggered repatriation involves the splitting of family units, as one member (usually a male head of household) returns, leaving the rest of the family in a host community until safety and security in the state of origin can be assured. This has also been reflected in Afghan return patterns, as returnees work in Afghanistan for the reconstruction effort (commanding higher equivalent salaries than are available in Pakistan), while their family remains resident in Pakistan (International Crisis Group 2009). The reverse form of rational economic leverage has also been observed in Afghanistan among less-skilled migrants. Monsutti (2008) reports that such Afghan labourers may return their families to their community of origin, accessing the support of kin networks, before joining seasonal or circular transnational migration flows outside the state's borders.

Revolving returnees are described by Nyberg-Sorensen in terms of failure, as:

> [Those who] after an intended 'permanent' return go back to Europe or North America, either because they have been unable to renew their contract within the 'development industry', have failed in their business efforts, or have been unable to convince their families in the wider diaspora to join them. (Nyberg-Sorensen 2004, p. 15)

Currently practices of refugee repatriation do not often allow for such revolving return under regular processes. There is often little opportunity for a regularized return to a host community if physical return fails to provide adequate livelihood opportunities. However, some recent innovations have tried to better reflect the fact that repatriation may not always offer a successful outcome for refugees, particularly in post-conflict and fragile societies, in their return programmes. One example is the Danish Repatriation Act, passed in 2000, which gives those recognized refugees who have repatriated an opportunity to change their minds and return to Denmark within a year of their repatriation. Since 2000, 306 Iraqis have elected to repatriate, with 73 ultimately choosing not to remain in Iraq and to return to Denmark (Nielsen et al. 2010, p. 1).

Another response to this revolving return of educated diaspora is particularly intended to harness the potential contributions to reconstruction of refugees who have already found a 'durable solution' through naturalization or dual citizenship. There has been a marked growth in the number of formal programmes designed to encourage short-term returns to societies undergoing post-conflict reconstruction: these visits allow educated and skilled members of the diaspora to contribute to reconstruction, despite the fact that they are extremely unlikely to return permanently. This kind of repatriation seeks to benefit both refugee and the community of origin by connecting 'old' and 'new' identities. Recent examples of such programmes specifically targeted at diaspora populations displaced through conflict include have included the World Bank Afghanistan Directory of Expertise and the IOM's (International Organization for Migration) Return of Qualified Afghans programmes.

Other forms of flexible repatriation that belie a simple association between return and durable solutions can also be identified. Some members of the Iraqi refugee diaspora, for example, can be characterized as transborder 'commuter' repatriates, remaining in Jordan, Lebanon or Syria but making regular visits back to Iraq to collect rents, check on land and visit family (Crisp et al. 2009). Similar behaviour has been observed among IDPs in Darfur, where camps are used as secure 'dormitories' for IDPs who continue to participate in rural life.

The sum of these analyses is a clear indication that the relationship between reconstruction and return is extremely complex and difficult to define. There are clearly many forms of return which can contribute to reconstruction, and for many refugees continued mobility appears to be a crucial aspect of any sustainable post-conflict repatriation strategy. It is thus difficult to disagree with Nyberg-Sorensen's conclusion that 'so-called durable solutions are not bound to be either integration or repatriation but could well combine the two in durable transnational, transregional or translocal strategies' (2004, p. 21). This echoes Stepputat's assertion that '"sustainable return" may involve continued mobility within and between borders' (Stepputat 2004, p. 3).

But how does increased refugee mobility enhance prospects for post-conflict reconstruction and sustainable return? And what – if any – is an appropriate role for international involvement in protecting such mobility? Four basic assumptions appear to lie behind both researchers' interest and refugees' uses of mobility. First, that increased mobility offers opportunities for increased remittance flows. Second, that increased freedom of movement also offers opportunities to preserve professional skills in states where educated refugees professionals can access the infrastructure necessary to undertake training and to work, and then through return at a later point transfer these skills to their communities of origin as a form of 'brain gain'. Third, that building up an economic diaspora offers opportunities to use transnational political pressures to build new political forms of accountable governance. Fourth, that the incorporation of mobility increases refugees' autonomy in choosing how to respond to their political, social, economic and cultural needs. Mobile repatriates may physically return at a later date having contributed to reconstruction in absentia, or some may find an eventual solution in naturalization or dual citizenship. Above all, a conceptual movement towards embracing mobility allows the international community to distance itself from the all-or-nothing approach that has traditionally governed its approach to refugee return, and move instead towards a more nuanced and holistic approach to durable solutions.

It is important, however, to investigate in more detail the assumptions on which such claims rest. In particular, what is the role played by refugee remittances in supporting post-conflict reconstruction? How does this role link to prospects for sustainable return? What are the social and political roles that such mobile repatriates play in reconstruction and are these conducive to sustainable reconstruction? Perhaps most importantly of all, what impact might these new forms of migration-centred return have on the lives of such mobile repatriates themselves?

11.3.3 Remittances

In recent years, the value of remittances in supporting development has been recognized by the international community. In 2009, the World Bank estimated a total remittance flow of $290 billion to developing countries, and highlighted the resilience of remittance flows despite the global economic recession. The potential for remittances to contribute to development agendas has been greeted enthusiastically by donor states (DFID 2007), although researchers have repeatedly warned that states should not assume that remittance-led development may eventually reduce outmigration (Nyberg-Sorensen et al. 2002, p. 5). Nevertheless, remittances are now assessed as being a key component of development programmes: 'considerably larger than the size of development aid and at least as well targeted at the poor in both conflict ridden and stable developing countries' (Nyberg-Sorensen 2004, p. 11).

The vast majority of research into remittance flows has not considered the particular dynamics that are likely to influence refugee remittances, far less the impact of refugee remittance practices on the likelihood of return. Clearly, there are some important distinctions between migrant and refugee remittance sending: most obviously, while refugees may become remittance senders, this is not their motive for leaving their community of origin. Furthermore, the vast majority of refugees do not send remittances: there is evidence from Kenya and Ghana that a substantial number particularly in PRS actually depend on receiving remittances (Lindley 2007). Yet there is a growing body of work that focuses on the role of remittances in conflict and crisis (for example, Fagen 2006; Lindley 2009) and which does have some important ramifications for connecting mobility, repatriation and reconstruction.

One general finding about repatriation which is particularly relevant to our concern with the role that mobility can play in encouraging sustainable repatriation and reconstruction is the finding that remittance-led development may in fact increase intra-community financial inequality. As Van Hear's work has shown, the range of a migrant or refugee's mobility is to a great extent correlated with their economic and social status in their community of origin (Van Hear 2004). Mobility is dependent upon class: 'long distance mobility is increasingly the preserve of those who can afford to pay migration agents' inflated fees' (Koser and Van Hear 2003, p. 7).

Inequalities may also widen between different sectors of a fragile-state population because remittances are largely directed towards private recipients and family groups. Although remittance flows may therefore help to secure the livelihoods of those who have access to personal remittances, and in times of conflict prevent some further displacement, the inequality of access to remittance funds mean that such benefits will not be evenly distributed. This is particularly true given the evidence that in conflict-torn societies, remittances tend to be used to meet daily subsistence needs and provide access to services such as healthcare and education rather than to invest in infrastructure or development projects which are more likely to benefit wider groups (ibid., p. 7). This reluctance or inability to invest in more long-term projects clearly becomes less of an obstacle once reconstruction begins. Community-based projects and 'Hometown Associations' provide an example of how remittances can be used to encourage more productive development projects, such as the case of Tamil youth in France who set up funds for Sri Lankan secondary education (Sriskandarajah 2002, p. 305). However, the fact remains that remittances tend to operate as a private good, hence the World Bank's recommendation that governments should treat remittances like any other source of private income.

Remittances nevertheless represent a significant and even vital contribution to families, communities and states emerging from conflict and crisis. Lindley's work mapping the contributions of the Somali diaspora, for example, suggests that on average $3,110 a year were remitted by the Somali diaspora to family networks: community and investment transfers brought the total remitted to an average of $4,440 (Lindley 2009). This is likely to often represent a vital lifeline during the disruptions of conflict, and can provide a significant boost to early reconstruction. It is not, however, evident that such contributions to reconstruction will immediately lead to better prospects for such refugee remitters' physical returns. Lindley's work also reports that 'many refugees with family connections in the more stable parts of the Somali regions would like to return permanently; however, relatively few do so, for a variety of reasons, often including the fact that people back home depend on their remittances' (ibid., p. 1328). States may also actively encourage continued migration even as they simultaneously promote continued financial and social repatriation. For example, since independence the Eritrean diaspora has been asked to contribute 2 per cent of income to the state as a 'healing tax' (Koser and Van Hear 2003, p. 15).

Greater refugee mobility may result in increased access to remittances and better prospects for sustainable reconstruction (at least at substate levels). Yet this evidence suggests that such developments may not increase the prospects for physical return. However, as Koser and Van Hear (p. 17) note, 'physical return is not the only way to integrate refugees in post-conflict reconstruction'. Connecting repatriation to mobility while simultaneously reducing the insistence on prioritizing return as a solution may help to empower refugees and provide economic security to a wider community. Yet it is also necessary to recognize that if remittance dependency obstructs the prospects for refugee return, this may not be a positive development, but reflect the abdication of wider international responsibilities to contribute to post-conflict recovery. As Lindley remarks: 'a diaspora perspective makes it clear that someone – somewhere – pays, a fact too often lost in the overwhelming focus of the literature in migrants' countries of origin' (2009, p. 1330).

11.4   CONCLUSIONS

Durable solutions for refugees – local integration, resettlement and repatriation – all provide for a return to citizenship. It is this return to citizenship that provides a political remedy to the political deprivation of refugees' rights as a result of either the incapacity or the active hostility of their state of origin. This means that it is a political reconnection with the state, rather than the physical movement involved in return, which is central to providing access to durable solutions for refugees in exile. Sustainable repatriation is thus closely connected to the prospects for success in broader post-conflict reconstruction and peacebuilding efforts.

Post-conflict reconstruction efforts themselves demand the early inclusion of refugee populations, both to legitimate the emerging state and to contribute in economic terms to reconstruction. However it is clear that inclusion through physical return, particularly at an early state of recovery, can be detrimental to the sustainability of reconstruction and return. Weak and fragile states do not have the practical capacity to support large return populations (especially in socioeconomic terms), even if they are eager to do so in theory. In practice, considerable numbers of refugees who return to fragile states of origin emerging from conflict develop livelihood strategies that involve continued mobility rather than return. Such mobility may involve entry into established seasonal or transnational labour markets, the 'staggering' of family return to spread risk between two economies or even long-term migration alongside a more abstract repatriation which is marked by the regaining or retention of formal citizenship and the sending of remittances to families and communities. These strategies contribute to reconstruction prospects. In doing so they increase the prospects for an eventual physical return to represent both a voluntary choice and a sustainable outcome.

Mobility could therefore play a vital role in facilitating sustainable repatriation and reconstruction. Recognizing this, UNHCR has begun to move towards the integration of mobility into its policies on return and reintegration. Notably, facilitation of mobility has played an important role in dealing with residual refugee populations in the ECOWAS region and confronting the considerable challenges posed by the continuing Afghan refugee crisis. These cases also illustrate the difficulties which are likely to be faced in encouraging the international community to embrace pro-mobility strategies, especially in terms of state responses to continued or increased population movements.

Nevertheless, there is a growing consensus that sustainable reconstruction and refugee repatriation/returns will involve a growing use of mobile livelihood strategies. These offer an important coping strategy in states with weak infrastructure, allowing families and communities greater resilience in withstanding the shocks that fragile states themselves may struggle to overcome. In the longer term, repatriates' continued or increased mobility may also represent a positive outcome of reconstruction: there is considerable evidence to suggest that an increase in a population's mobility is in fact associated with successful economic development and increased equity of access to a globalized modern economy.

It is important to recognize that practices of mobility may bring their own challenges. In particular, remittance-led reconstruction may exacerbate inequality within communities and between families based upon residents' access to such funds which are overwhelmingly remitted to individuals. In political terms, the involvement of wealthy diaspora in repatriation efforts may exacerbate class tensions: there is also a need to avoid the 'capturing' of the state by returning diaspora elites, as has occurred in Rwanda and Afghanistan.

However, the likelihood that repatriate mobility will strengthen community and individual power over and above state institutions should not be seen as a limitation on the usefulness of mobility-led strategies. This finding should instead be cause for the international community to reconsider both its approach to and its aims in financing state-building operations. Community-based local structures of power may prove to be more legitimate, more resilient and better reflect historical and cultural realities than relatively abstract concepts of a single national state. Strengthening community structures able to effectively protect repatriates and provide other citizens with meaningful human security may in fact be easier and more successful than attempting to build states.

Proposing such a paradigm shift in approaches to reconstruction and repatriation is likely to be controversial, especially among states concerned with their own border securitization. Yet it is impossible to ignore the deep crises in state sovereignty that have led to a considerable number of states in the global south suffering from endemic fragility and a chronic deficit of legitimacy. It is the fragility of such states which is the 'root cause' of many PRS, particularly in terms of continuing obstacles to effective return. Mobility may provide a remedy to some of the constraints experienced by the populations of fragile states. However, it is important that in incorporating mobility into a durable solutions framework, the UNHCR does not lose sight of the deeper and more problematic structural failures of the international states system.

Integrating mobility into repatriation programmes may take several forms and is likely to depend on the particular local setting and the refugee population's particular protection needs. All such strategies reflect the need for the international community to move away from the idea of one-way movements and solutions. Return is not synonymous with repatriation: movement is not the cause of displacement but a symptom, and may in fact provide an important remedy to some refugees' needs. Similarly, repatriation should be understood as an opportunity for positive political transformation, rather than as an elusive search to 're-anchor' refugees at 'home'.

Ultimately, incorporating mobility within repatriation recognizes that durable solutions must be framed to protect choice. It is the absence of choice in their movement – the absence of effective rights or autonomy – which marks the refugee out as needing international protection. Protecting and encouraging mobility restores this choice, and reminds us that the UNHCR was not set up to contain movement, but to protect those in need from political persecution. Embracing mobility – which in itself is a significant decision – is therefore also part of a broader and arguabley still more significant paradigm-shift towards understanding the UNHCR's protection work within a rights-based framework. Refugees are in essence citizens who have been deprived of their fundamental rights: the aim of the international community must be to restore such rights. Linking repatriation, reconstruction and mobility therefore represents one small – but significant – step towards the development of this broader rights-based approach to protection.

12 Rebel recruitment
Yvan Guichaoua

12.1 INTRODUCTION

Recruitment within irregular armed groups is commonly understood as
the process through which non-combatants abandon – at least partially,
and for some time – their civilian life to pledge loyalty to social groupings whose direct or indirect aim is to carry out violent actions against
their perceived enemies, whether governmental or not. By definition
then, recruitment involves two sides, a person breaking some pre-existing
social routines and a violent, not necessarily formal, organization accepting her – and most probably, him – in its ranks. Rebel recruitment is the
encounter of at least two agencies. Being willing to enlist is an important
step towards individual inclusion in an armed group but may not suffice
to become a combatant. Likewise, hiring new fighters is a trickier operation than just tapping into a reserve army of serviceable and obeying
soldiers.

Rebel recruitment intersects with two logics, ordinarily studied separately by theories of participation and organizations, respectively. A
useful way to reconcile these subfields of research conceptually consists
in portraying recruitment as a matching process whereby the strategic
needs of the combat organization are met with the aspirations of would-be
fighters. What further complicates this process though is that it generally
happens in highly volatile contexts, in which the decisions of protagonists
are subjected to myopia, stress, fear or physical threats. Under such circumstances, people adapt and transform constantly, hence pushing analysts of participation in collective political violence to do away with static
one-dimensional approaches and produce modest explanations with only
temporary and local validity.

The following review owes a lot to the recent shift of academic attention
towards micro-level social processes in civil wars. The studies on social
movements and revolutions in the 1970s were holistic and emphasized
class interests as major drivers of violent uprisings (Skocpol 1982). They
were replaced in the post-Cold War context by rational choice-oriented
approaches highlighting the role played by 'greed' in provoking state
collapse (Collier and Hoeffler 1998). These streams of research lacked
sound micro foundations: collective violence was either produced by the

deterministic interplay of overarching social forces or by the calculations of groups behaving like unitary entities. Besides, past approaches have tended to equate conflict with violence, hence obscuring what arguably constitutes the ontology of political violence: specific contingent processes in which macro and micro cleavages intimately enmesh (Kalyvas 2003). As aptly put by Brubaker and Laitin (1998, p. 426), political violence is not 'something that occurs automatically when the conflict reaches a certain intensity, a certain temperature'. Political violence has a life of its own whose dynamics amply help shape rebel recruitment.

The chapter proceeds as follows. Section 12.2 reviews the alternative drivers of personal violent enlistment. Section 12.3 discusses the recruitment strategies designed by armed organizations and their influence on combatants' profiles. Section 12.4 concludes.

12.2 MAPPING OUT NON-RIVAL EXPLANATIONS OF INDIVIDUAL PARTICIPATION IN POLITICAL COLLECTIVE VIOLENCE

No single pattern of drivers of personal violent enlistment prevails empirically to which a general theory of participation in violence could be anchored. In fact the real intellectual challenge resides not so much in the identification of the drivers of enlistment than in the understanding of their dominance in particular contexts. One should then take the wide plurality of findings in the literature as non-rival explanatory frameworks (Humphreys and Weinstein 2008).

We propose a simple way of representing the mounting evidence available on personal enlistment in collective violence (Figure 12.1). Models could be arranged according to the relative choice availability agents are confronted with, reflecting the objective circumstances they face. Agents may join irregular armed groups voluntarily or be coerced to do so. Models also differ according to the kind of subjective calculations they assume agents implement. One could situate at one end of the spectrum rudimentary types of decision-making processes, for example in the form of maximization of strictly material benefits. At the other end of the spectrum one may consider more complex behavioural logics where individual calculations endogenize social objects (such as norms or preferences); are dependent on decisions made by others; or include learning processes. We can then map out most of the recent alternative models of violent enlistment by using a two-dimensional diagram in which choice availability is represented on the horizontal axis while the complexity of behavioural logics hypothesized is represented on the vertical axis.

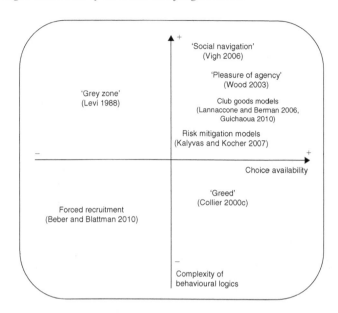

Figure 12.1 Alternative models of individual enlistment in violent groups

Unsurprisingly, the northeast quadrant of our diagram is the most replete with models. It may encompass the representations most likely to reflect real-life situations where agents have some degree of decisional room for manoeuvre and pursue complex strategies. Other quadrants might have narrower, yet non-trivial, empirical validity.

The left-hand side of Figure 12.1 corresponds to situations of extreme coercion, where members of an armed organization are actually recruited by force. Such practices have been observed in the past decades, in Sri Lanka, Sierra Leone, Uganda or Mozambique. They often target young-sters. An obvious reason for this is that young recruits offer a relatively cheap labour force to which non-combatant roles may be assigned. Underage recruits resist camp discipline and exploitation less than adults. A wide range of low cost but often extremely cruel techniques are employed to extract obedience from them and create exclusive bonds of allegiance to the group (Beber and Blattman 2010; Geffray 1990).

Child soldiering or some instances of enrolment of women in armed groups constitute possible illustrations of the realm of phenomena covered by the southwest side of Figure 12.1. However, many authors have chal-lenged pure coercion models and argued that persons submitted to intense oppressive orders may still mobilize agentive capacities to alleviate the abuses they suffer or simply survive (Hart 2011; Utas 2005). Therefore, social spaces ruled by such oppressive groups may more realistically be portrayed as 'grey zones', as described by Levi (1988), where avoidance tactics are elaborated and reciprocal brutalization emerges as a valid survival strategy. While Levi's grey zones were fashioned to describe life in Nazis labour camps, their behavioural principles may apply more broadly to situations where agents' cooperation is obtained by force.

'Choiceless choices' abound in civil wars, yet one may consider that the decision to join an armed group can, in most cases, be weighed against alternative options. When the rationale of such decision is exclusively driven by economic calculations, then rebellion can analytically be equated to criminal activity (see the southeast quadrant in Figure 12.1). According to the economics of crime rationale, the bigger the prize, the smaller the opportunity cost of crime and the chance of getting caught, the higher the incentive to perpetrate crime (Becker 1968). This approach sees poverty and joblessness as major predictors of violent enlistment as they lower the opportunity cost of joining insurgency. The perception of rebellion as a criminal activity gained currency following the post-Cold War's so-called 'New Wars' in the late 1990s (for a critical review of the New Wars discourse, see Kalyvas 2001).

Do economic incentives actually trigger violent mobilization? This hypothesis has received substantial anecdotal support emanating from non-governmental organizations (NGOs) (Human Rights Watch 2005), as well as from journalistic accounts portraying the protagonists of New Wars as disenfranchised, egoistic 'loose molecules' (Kaplan 2000). In the academic field this hypothesis was further developed and popularized by Collier and Hoeffler (Collier 2000a; Collier and Hoeffler 1998). Its 'easy to understand' nature and its pretty straightforward convertibility into policy recommendations are arguably two reasons for its success in the development community. In the two authors' view, top of the rebels' agenda is their desire to appropriate the 'national cake', a rationale seemingly congruent with their econometric finding that poor countries, economically dependent on primary commodities, are relatively more prone to civil conflicts. However, recent studies have shown that the relationship between the onset of conflict and economic dependence on primary commodities operates through institutional channels unacknowledged by Collier and Hoeffler's original model. The 'greed' component of the natural resource curse literature is consequently largely dismissed (Fearon 2005; Humphreys 2005; Le Billon 2007).

In addition, even though the relationship between conflict onset and the poverty of nations remains econometrically robust, a significant cross-country correlation is not equivalent to a causal mechanism on the individual level. No behavioural conclusions can thus be inferred from its significance. Also, should it be empirically proven, the observation that the poor have a greater propensity to join armed groups does not tell much about their actual motives: is it because they expect material benefits, out of grievance, or out of some other confounding factor?

Several studies are now available which investigate the nexus between poverty and violence on the individual level. Their findings are equivocal. Krueger and Maleckova (2003, p. 119) research the profiles of suicide bombers in the Middle East and come to the conclusion that terrorism 'is more accurately viewed as a response to political conditions and long-standing feelings of indignity and frustration that have little to do with economics'. Suicide bombing might be perpetrated by overly dedicated combatants though, and the above findings might not apply to more ordinary irregular combatants facing less lethal prospects. Indeed, Humphreys and Weinstein (2008) find a significant relationship between poverty and enlistment in Sierra Leone's Revolutionary United Front (RUF) in the 1990s. But their econometric analysis yields much richer results: lack of access to education, material incentives to join, pre-existing social connections within the armed factions, or the search for safety under the auspices of armed groups, are all significant predictors of enlistment. The authors therefore stress the coexistence of multiple 'logics of participation . . . in a single civil war' (p. 437).

Some of these non-economic logics may still be framed within a rational choice framework, notably when they relate to risk (see the northeast quadrant in Figure 12.1). Kalyvas and Kocher (2007) challenge the conventional wisdom stating that members of a combat organization incur relatively higher risks of victimization than non-members. When civilians feel at risk of indiscriminate repression by armed opposition, then armed groups may constitute safe refuges. In instances of low-intensity conflicts where the risk is more diffuse and includes arbitrary violence but also morbidity or theft, group membership can be desired as it secures access to club goods, that is, exclusive forms of group solidarity involving risk-sharing arrangements. Hamas in Palestine or Hizbullah in Lebanon have been characterized as typical club goods providers (Iannaccone and Berman 2006). Some Nigerian ethnic militias also function as 'moral economies' whose members enjoy relative physical but also psychological security (Guichaoua 2010).

The above models insist on individual calculations aiming at maximizing personal utilities, disregarding others' utilities. But rebelling is a collective business comprising a wide range of interpersonal connections. One obvious one is that would-be fighters may embrace a cause that reaches beyond their immediate interests. Marxist rhetoric may not be part of the fighters' ideological toolkit anymore, but insurgents continue to think and act according to beliefs or shared worldviews; and these need careful analysis. 'Moral outrage', which we borrow from Wood's illuminating study of the civil war in El Salvador (Wood 2003), may best encapsulate the mechanism of participation which appeals to individuals' sense of collective justice and fairness. The expression refers to the sentiments advanced by participants in insurgencies to justify their engagement. These views might be instigated by leaders through ideological training, yet numerous case studies convincingly show their practical mode of operation.

Wood's account of the conflict in El Salvador demonstrates how feelings of oppression by large landowners and liberation theology worked to entrench a deep-seated resentment among the campesinos who, as a result, experienced a genuine 'pleasure of agency' when they eventually joined the armed insurgency. Similarly, Marshall-Fratani (2006) and Fofana (2009) show how central the issue of citizenship was in Côte d'Ivoire's civil war. The authorities' rejection of the northern leader Alassane Ouattara's candidacy in the presidential elections on the basis of his 'dubious' nationality generated massive discontent among his co-ethnics who felt downgraded to 'second-class citizens' by their own government. Grievances may take a generational tone, as shown by Lecocq (2004) in Niger and Mali, and Chauveau and Richards (2008) in Sierra Leone. In these cases, the authors argue, violent mobilization was primarily directed against a gerontocratic order which impeded youths' upward social mobility.

Collective loyalties do not need to be essentialized and made objective causes of blind enlistment. They may be assessed critically by the participants themselves and are reversible. Guichaoua (2009) shows that Tuareg low-level combatants during the 2007 Niger rebellion vocally expressed 'moral outrage' as members of a marginalized ethnic group but offered simultaneously very conditional support to their leaders whose decisions were subjected to scrutiny and discussed in small affinity-based groups of combatants. Defection could result from critical thinking. Adaptive and revisable loyalty may explain why violent engagement can become intermittent, as observed in Niger (ibid.) or Chad (Debos 2008).

A last series of models (top of the northeast quadrant of Figure 12.1) pays greater attention to behavioural rather than attitudinal aspects of participation in armed violence. Attitudinal approaches raise serious epistemological and methodological issues pertaining to the heuristic value of subjective accounts, the biases of *ex post* testimonies or the distortions of remote and traumatized memories (Browning 2010; Mariot 2003). Behavioural approaches get around these obstacles by assigning a great importance to situational factors as drivers of violent enlistment. Therefore they prolong some of the models reviewed above centring on individual responses to risks (Kalyvas and Kocher 2007). Situational factors correspond to mundane concerns attached to the idiosyncratic course of events lived by individuals during wartime. Many environmental features need on-the-spot assessment and demand quick responses: who controls the territory (Kalyvas 2006); how physically dangerous are the circumstances; which social connections can be activated to get assistance; how intense is the peer pressure; and so on. Answers to these questions define the set of feasible options available to agents and combine with plausible opportunities they discern in a blurred landscape: ways to escape or make money but also, quite trivially . . . have fun.

Not only are concrete obstacles to individual agency overwhelming during wartime, but they are also constantly changing. They inform and reshape the ways decisions are taken, sometimes irreversibly. Individuals' decision-making processes in unstable environments are permanently subjected to myopia and under constant revision. 'Social navigation' (Vigh 2006) best captures this improvised behavioural logic. Decisions should then be integrated within an 'eventful temporality' (Sewell 2005). From this perspective, violent enlistment may lose its dramatic character and becomes the outcome of instant decisions temporarily perceived as appropriate. Joining an armed group is one event concatenated to the many others that war produces at an accelerated pace. The banal character of such a move may prove particularly true in societies where brutality is pervasive and 'peacetime' experiences are no less traumatizing than wartime experiences.

As mentioned in the introduction, models of individual participation in collective political violence just tell one half of the rebel recruitment story. The other half relates to the choices elaborated inside the recruiting agency. Rebellions or militias are wrongly portrayed as welcoming anyone and everyone into their ranks. In practice, they have specific qualitative and quantitative human resource needs, which lead them to figure out adequate recruitment strategies (Gutierrez Sanin 2011). Irregular armed organizations' intentions may not concretize according to plans yet they help shape the profiles of combatants eventually admitted into their ranks.

12.3   GATHERING TROOPS: ORGANIZATIONAL PUZZLES AND THE DIVERSITY OF OUTCOMES

'Activating, connecting, coordinating, and representing' are the four activities generally undertaken by entrepreneurs of violence, as identified by Charles Tilly (2003). These tasks form the general puzzle every irregular armed organization seeking efficiency has to solve. In practice, the diversity of outcomes is great. Broad-based rebel initiatives firmly entrenched within local communities might be pursued, making entry within the group as easy as possible. Conversely, sectarian radicalization may also happen, entailing horrendous practices such as forced recruitment and slave labour. We briefly expose below some general questions that recruitment policies of irregular armed groups have to address and review potential explanations for the diversity of the empirical answers provided.

The public rhetoric stance adopted by the group is one fundamental element of its recruiting strategy. Entrepreneurs of violence typically tailor 'master cleavages' breeding readiness to violence among followers by providing emotional narratives and cognitive categories simplifying complex social phenomena (Petersen 2002). Their discourses help shape the boundaries between 'them' and 'us', which in turn fosters enmity and fear. These discourses carry huge 'performative' potential (Brass 2006) as the example of Radio 1000 Collines in pre-genocide Rwanda notoriously shows: hateful messages were endlessly broadcast by extremist Hutu leaders, presenting Tutsis as poisonous 'cockroaches' to be eliminated (Mamdani 2001; Straus 2006).

Importantly, for mobilizing discourses to be effective, hatred does not need to be their most salient feature. Promises of economic or political emancipation have historically served longer-term revolutionary and anti-imperial projects typical of the Cold War era. As highlighted by Wood (2003) among others, liberation theology played a central role in Latin American agrarian revolts. Marxist rhetoric is still a major feature of the Revolutionary Armed Forces of Colombia's ideological combatant training programme (Gutierrez Sanin 2004).

Problematically, by definition, irregular armed groups have to operate underground. Therefore, as put by Gutierrez Sanin (2011), they may not be able to implement an open entry recruitment policy consistent with their universal discourse (phrased, for instance, in terms of proletarian or peasant emancipation), due to risk of informational leaks and betrayal from inside. The recruitment puzzle is a tricky one, for any misjudgement may have lethal consequence. Open entry policies are also a menace to groups' viability as inflows of recruits change the logistical constraints they bear. Potential newcomers need to be contacted in the first place then selected, tested, geographically deployed, accommodated, fed, trained, possibly armed, while, at the same time, combats may take place. Furthermore, as any organization seeking sustainability over time, irregular armed groups need competent personnel fitting their specific demands in such heterogeneous fields as intelligence, knowledge of terrain, fundraising abilities, managerial and commanding skills, and, of course, military capacity. Whether women should be enlisted is an additional dilemma. Among other prejudices, women might be perceived as physically and morally unfit for combat or factors of division. But many irregular armed groups have actually held opposite views. Recruiting females actually involves some strategic and practical advantages. Dietrich Ortega (2011) mentions four of them. First, liberation movements enhance their public image as promoters of deep societal change and equality when they accept women in their ranks. Second, women may profitably be used to accomplish certain logistical tasks, such as smuggling arms or spying. Third, women assigned conventional caregiving roles may facilitate the relations between armed groups and civilians. Finally, they may stimulate male recruitment as their mere presence in the group challenges men's aspiration to masculinity: if women can fight why shouldn't men fight, too? Africanist scholars have also insisted on the magical assistance women may offer through the privileged connexions with the spiritual world they enjoy in certain belief systems (Nolte 2008).

Mobilizing discourses do not suffice. To meet their recruitment needs and minimize the risks evoked above – and notably information asymmetries – rebel leaders have to concretely act as brokers. In the field of conflict analysis, unlike the study of criminal gangs (see Morselli 2009), little is known about the structures of networks most conducive to large-scale violent mobilization. The form of social relations most often suggested in recent literature is political patronage: violent entrepreneurs simply hire thugs to spread chaos by offering them material rewards (in the form of money or tacit authorization to loot). The widespread recruitment of 'area boys' or, more broadly, ethnic militias in Nigeria each time elections have been held since the 'democratic' transition in 1999, illustrate this process (Human Rights Watch 2008). Brass (2006) describes similarly politically manipulated riots in India as part of what he calls an 'institutionalized riot system', aimed at polarizing communal affiliations and reaping the inherent electoral benefits. But this top-down organization of collective violence may be only one of the many ways in which social connections operate in violent episodes.

Other situations seem to involve more horizontal networks, composed of friends, immediate relatives or neighbours. Comparing the profiles of Nigerian rioters and non-rioters in Kaduna and Jos, Scacco (2010) suggests that strong social connectedness at ward level (the smallest urban unit in Nigeria) is a significant predictor of participation in riots. She suggests that the social ties relevant to violent mobilization are not hierarchical but highly local and horizontal: proximity networks carry information; help spread rumours and worldviews; sustain economic solidarity; and engender bonds of affection. They may also produce bandwagon effects, especially among youths. Longer-term associations may require oath-taking ceremonies, as a way to secure permanent allegiance (Wlodarczyk 2009). These practices typically belong to parochial/ethnic movements while broad-based groups might adopt more 'industrial' approaches to recruitment compatible with the numerous constraints exposed above.

What actually explains the empirical diversity of recruitment strategies is still debated among academics. The origins of differences between armed groups' features and trajectories are likely to be found in some determining factors 'outside' the groups. Weinstein (2006) equates this 'outside' with the 'initial conditions' prevailing when rebellious projects are designed. His laudably parsimonious approach contends that access to finance is the key 'initial condition' that shapes recruitment strategies. Weinstein suggests that two types of rebellion exist – 'activist' and 'opportunist' – and argues that the ratio of politicized activists to opportunists within a rebel group stems directly from the financial constraints faced by the rebel leaders. Well-funded rebellions tend to attract opportunists, that is, recruits driven by the immediate prospects of profit; while financially constrained rebellions have to resort to activists, that is, recruits who can be primarily mobilized through social bonds and ideological training. In short, armed groups build up on two sorts of endowments, alternatively economic or social. Weinstein then explores the implications of these choices on violence and durability of armed groups.

The strong appeal of Weinstein's perspective is that it articulates various levels of analysis into a coherent framework, ranging from the macro (the economic constraints faced by rebel leaders) to the micro (the profiles of individual recruits and the types of violence perpetrated). Yet a fundamental problem with Weinstein's typology of armed groups is that it ultimately relies on a static dichotomy. It is hard in practice to disentangle between the types of resources mobilized by armed organizations: not only are economic and social resources likely to be mobilized simultaneously, but they might also be symbiotically and dynamically intertwined, hence reshaping constantly armed groups' capacity to recruit, in quantity and in quality. Moreover, whether the group is military challenged or not dramatically alters its personnel needs. Repression and, more broadly, strategic interaction with governmental opponents as well as rivalry from other groups (Metelits 2009) are largely contingent factors of changes in recruitment policy independent of resource endowments that are not yet fully understood.

12.4   CONCLUSION: BECOMING A FIGHTER AND BEYOND

Rebel recruitment can be conceived of as the matching process of two agencies, each moved by idiosyncratic expectations and dealing with a constrained set of alternative choices shaped by war. As detailed above, myopic decisions may result, based on a highly diverse range of circumstantial considerations. A great intellectual challenge ahead consists in the improved understanding of the great diversity of empirical forms of matching dynamics.

In some pervasively brutalized contexts, the particular encounter that admission within an armed group represents may not have deep life-changing impact as the break with pre-existing routines may not be so dramatic. In many other cases, for those who survive the experience, violent enlistment has implications that last long after the group has dissolved and critically hamper their life prospects in the post-conflict. Socialization in violent environments has more harmful consequences than recruitment within armed collective *per se*. However, as a crucial transitory phase towards violent socialization, recruitment demands critical attention.

13 Violent conflict and human capital accumulation

Patricia Justino

13.1 INTRODUCTION

Violent conflict is one of the most important development challenges facing the world today.* Although the incidence of civil wars has decreased in recent years (Harbom and Wallensteen 2009), the legacy of violence persists across many countries around the world, especially in Africa, Caucasia, the Balkans, and the Middle East. The economic, political and social consequences of civil wars are immense. War displaces people, destroys capital and infrastructure, disrupts schooling, damages the social fabric, endangers civil liberties, and creates health and famine crises. Almost 750,000 people die as a result of armed conflict each year (Geneva Declaration Secretariat 2008), and more than 20 million people were internally displaced by civil wars at the end of 2007. Any of these effects will have considerable consequences for long-term development outcomes. Yet while there is a growing consensus that development interventions and the promotion of democracy worldwide cannot be disassociated from the restrictions caused by violent conflict, we have limited rigorous evidence on how violent conflict affects development outcomes, the economy or the lives of people exposed to violence.

One fundamental mechanism by which violent conflict may affect long-term development outcomes is through the accumulation of human capital, a central mechanism in economic growth and development processes (Galor and Weil 2000; Lucas 1988, 2002; Schultz 1961). The objective of this chapter is to review the available evidence on one important micro-level mechanism linking civil wars and long-term development outcomes, namely the level and access to education of civilian and combatant populations affected by violence. The chapter is

* An earlier version of this paper entitled 'How does violent conflict impact on individual educational outcomes? The evidence so far' has appeared as a background paper for the Education For All Global Monitoring Report 2011 produced by UNESCO. The author is very grateful for discussions and comments from Pauline Rose, Anna Haas and Patrick Montjourides. Alexander Cornelius has provided excellent research assistance.

particularly concerned with the long-term human capital consequences of lost education.

13.2   VIOLENT CONFLICT AND HUMAN CAPITAL ACCUMULATION: THEORETICAL CONSIDERATIONS

From a theoretical point of view, the long-term developmental effects of violent conflict are unclear. Neoclassical models predict rapid catch-up growth in the post-conflict period as the economy converges to its steady state growth rate. In particular, the temporary destruction of capital can be overcome in the long term by higher investments in affected areas that will bring the overall economy to its steady growth path (see discussion in Blattman and Annan 2009). Davis and Weinstein (2002), employing a unique dataset on Japanese regional populations, look at the effects of the Allied bombing of Japanese cities during the Second World War. Their findings reveal that cities that suffered the largest population declines due to the bombing tended to have the fastest post-war growth rates. The typical city in Japan affected by the bombings recovered its former relative size fully within 15 years following the end of the Second World War. Brakman et al. (2004) arrive at similar conclusions in their analysis of the impact of the bombing of German cities during the Second World War on post-war German city growth. Miguel and Roland (2006) present similar findings using the extensive variation in US bombing intensity across 584 districts in Vietnam. Their results show that the bombing had no long-term impact on economic growth across regions in Vietnam affected by the war. Justino and Verwimp (2006) find evidence for this form of convergence across provinces in Rwanda following the 1994 genocide. Chen et al. (2008) find, across a sample of 41 countries that experienced civil war between 1960 and 2003, that once civil war ends, recovery in economic performance, health, education and political development increases significantly. Other cross-country studies reiterate these findings of rapid economic recovery in post-war economies (Cerra and Saxena 2008; Organski and Kugler 1977, 1980; Przeworski et al. 2000). Civil wars may also promote state formation and nation-building as was the case in Europe (Tilly 1978, 1990), and may induce social progress via greater popular participation in civic and political institutions (Blattman and Annan 2007; Wood 2003).

Other studies point to the long-term destructive effects of civil wars that may remain entrenched in certain regions even if economic growth converges at the aggregate level. Civil wars break social cohesion, destroy infrastructure and create political instability and insecurity in property rights (European Report on Development 2009; OECD 2009). The destruction entailed by warfare, combined with the erosion of institutions and organizations, leads to a deterioration of the economic environment. This in turn leads to a reduction in the desired levels of factors of production. Some factors (such as physical and human capital) are more able to leave the country than others (such as arable land), giving rise to a gradual exodus of these more mobile factors (Collier 1999). Violent conflict may also affect severely the quality and functioning of institutions, the expansion of technology and social outcomes (Acemoglu and Robinson 2006). In particular, recent research on the micro-level effects of violent conflict has shown that negative impacts of civil wars on education, labour and health of individuals and households can be observed decades after the conflict (Alderman et al. 2006; Bundervoet et al. 2007; Shemyakina 2007). Although these effects may average out at the macroeconomic level, they may contribute to the emergence of poverty traps among specific population groups affected by violence (Justino 2009, 2010).

The impact of war on the accumulation of human capital among civilian populations affected by violence can be substantial and persistent. Not only do people living in war zones suffer injuries, death and have their property destroyed, they may also be displaced from their homes and lose their means of survival. Children are especially adversely affected by the destruction of physical capital and the deterioration of economic conditions given the age-specific aspects of many human capital investments. Civil wars and associated physical destruction can interrupt the education of children through the damage to schools, absence of teachers, fears of insecurity and changes in family structures and household income. Children can also be negatively affected by the worsening of their health due to the association of violent conflict with famines, widespread malnutrition, outbreaks of infectious diseases, post-war trauma, and the destruction of health facilities. The destruction of human capital during childhood is a well-documented mechanism leading to poverty traps, given the severe long-run effects it can have on individual and household welfare via the future labour market outcomes and economic performance of affected children (Becker 1962; Mincer 1974; Schultz 1961).

These micro-level effects of civil wars remain largely underresearched. This is unsurprising given that large-scale, high-quality micro-level data for developing countries affected by civil war is generally not available. When it is available it is difficult to identify whether and under which circumstances household coping behaviour is induced by civil war events or by other economic conditions that may have taken place simultaneously. Detailed measures of conflict and associated destruction are often not available, and such information is difficult to collect from countries that have just emerged or are emerging from armed conflict. In the next section, we discuss in more detail the available empirical evidence on the impact of violent conflict on education. Section 13.4 explores the different mechanisms that may link the outbreak of violent conflict with educational outcomes, an area that has remained unexplored in the literatures on conflict and on education.

13.3   VIOLENT CONFLICT AND HUMAN CAPITAL ACCUMULATION: THE EVIDENCE SO FAR

Violent conflict results in deaths, injuries, disability and psychological trauma to men, women and children. These outcomes of violence may often be enough to push previously vulnerable households below critical thresholds. These may become impossible to overcome if the household is unable to replace labour or capital, and may last across generations if the impact on children's education and health is significant (Case and Paxson 2006; Maccini and Young 2009). Below we review emerging empirical literature on the impact of violent conflict on educational outcomes among children and young men and women affected by violence.

Research on the consequences of violent conflict has long focused on estimating the aggregate costs that civil wars impose on countries (Collier 1999; Knight et al. 1996; Stewart, Fitzgerald and Associates 2001). Programmes of conflict resolution have also been typically driven by concerns with state security and state capacity (see United Nations 2004a, 2005). This country-level perspective has come under criticism in recent years due to insufficient attention paid to the impact of armed conflicts on the lives of individuals and households affected by violence (see Justino 2009; Verwimp et al. 2009). Better data and improvements in microeconomic research in developing countries have led in recent years to an increased focus of research and policy on the consequences of violent conflict on the long-term human capital of people affected by violence (see review in Justino 2010).

Although still in its infancy, emerging empirical evidence on the micro-level effects of violent conflict has found that in general civil wars have a negative impact on educational attainments. Alderman et al. (2006) find that Zimbabwean children affected by the civil war in the 1970s completed fewer grades of schooling and/or started school later than those not affected by the shocks. Similar results are found by Akresh and de Walque (2008) for Rwanda, Angrist and Kugler (2008) and Rodriguez and Sanchez (2009) for Colombia, Chamarbagwala and Morán (2008) for Guatemala, de Walque (2006) for Cambodia, Shemyakina (2007) for Tajikistan and Swee (2009) for Bosnia.

As with any new area of research, results are still ambiguous and generally not yet comparable. For example, Shemyakina (2007) finds from her empirical work in Tajikistan, that it is girls who suffer the greatest loss in education due to concerns over safety and low returns to girls' education. In contrast, Akresh and de Walque (2008) find that, in Rwanda, it is among the male children in non-poor households that these negative shocks are strongest, potentially due to a levelling-off of educational achievements to a low level for everyone. Some consistent patterns have, however, started to emerge.

The first is that relatively minor shocks to educational access can lead to significant and long-lasting detrimental effects on individual human capital formation in terms of educational attainment, health outcomes and labour market opportunities. Akbulut-Yuksel (2009) provides causal evidence on the long-term consequences of large-scale physical destruction caused by the Second World War on the educational attainment, health status and labour market outcomes of German children. This study combines a unique dataset on city-level destruction in Germany caused by Allied Air Forces bombing during the war, with individual survey data from the German Socio-Economic Panel (GSOEP). She finds significant, long-lasting detrimental effects of bombing on human capital, health and labour market outcomes of individuals who were of school age during the war. Sixty years after the end of the war, these individuals had 0.4 fewer years of schooling on average in adulthood compared with those not affected by the bombing. Those in the most hard-hit cities completed 1.2 fewer years of schooling in relation to those not affected by the bombing. They were also about one centimetre shorter and had lower self-reported health satisfaction in adulthood. Despite the seemingly small educational impact of war exposure (between 0.4 and 1.2 years on average), individuals who as children lived in areas of high intense bombing experienced on average a very significant reduction of 6 per cent in labour market earnings in relation to those not affected by the bombing. Another piece of research which resonates with these findings is that of Ichino and Winter-Ebner (2004). This paper shows that in two European countries involved in the Second World War – Austria and Germany – children who were 10 years old during the conflict were significantly less likely to proceed into higher education and lost around 20 per cent of a year of schooling on average. No effect is found for individuals in the same cohorts living in countries not involved in the war. Their results show that the negative educational effects of the war, and consequent reduction in earnings, led to GDP in Germany being at least 0.36 per cent lower in 1986 than it should have been without the war. The loss for Austrian GDP in 1983 is larger, around 0.67 per cent. Merrouche (2006) adds to these findings with an interesting piece of research on the long-run effects of landmine contamination on human capital in Cambodia after 30 years of war during the Khmer Rouge regime. Cambodia is one of the most heavily landmine-contaminated countries in the world, with about one mine planted for each inhabitant. The study finds that landmine contamination has caused significant educational losses in Cambodia. A conservative estimate at the mean level of landmine exposure suggests a loss of about 0.4 years of education. This again represents a very large education setback given a sample average number of years of education of about 4.5 years in 1997.

The second pattern emerging from this area of research is that the destruction of infrastructure, the absence of teachers and reduction in schooling capacity during violent conflicts across the world seem to have affected secondary schooling disproportionately. Chen et al. (2008) find that the average recovery rate for primary-school enrolment in the period between 1960 and 2003 was larger than that of secondary enrolment in post-conflict countries. Stewart et al. (2001) find that primary-school enrolments decreased in only three out of 18 countries in their sample of countries affected by civil wars. These effects recur also in micro-level studies. Akresh and De Walque (2008) examined the impact of Rwanda's 1994 genocide on children's schooling. They find that school-age children exposed to the genocide experienced a drop in educational achievement of almost half a year of completed schooling, and are 15 per cent less likely to complete 3rd or 4th grade. The most likely mechanism linking the genocide to educational attainment is through lack of progression to higher secondary schooling grades. Swee (2009) provides evidence on the effects of the civil war in Bosnia (1992–95) on schooling attainment of the cohorts who were in the process of completing their primary and secondary schooling during the war. He finds that individuals in cohorts affected by the civil war are less likely to complete secondary schooling if they resided in municipalities that experienced higher levels of war intensity. He finds no noticeable effects on primary schooling, which might indicate successful organization of war schools at the primary level. Swee argues that youth soldiering may be the key mechanism explaining these effects.

The third pattern is that the exposure of households to violence results in significant gender differentials in individual educational outcomes. Shemyakina (2007) examines the effects of the armed conflict (1992–98) in Tajikistan. Her results indicate that exposure to the conflict had a large, significant and negative effect on the enrolment of girls. She observes little or no effect on the enrolment of boys. Girls who were of school age during the conflict, and lived in conflict-affected regions, were 12.3 per cent less likely to complete mandatory schooling as compared to girls who completed their schooling before the conflict started. They are also 7 per cent less likely to complete school than girls of the same age who lived in regions relatively unaffected by the civil war. Furthermore, Shemyakina finds that the probability of completing the mandatory nine grades is 4 and 7 per cent lower for boys and girls, respectively. The probability decreases by another 5 per cent for girls born between 1978 and 1986 who lived in regions affected by the conflict during their schooling years. These results suggest that households affected by conflict invested more in the schooling of boys, for whom there is less perceived risk of violence, harassment or abduction. Due to the destruction of industries and infrastructure, job opportunities for skilled labour may become scarce, in which case it may make more economic sense to educate boys as they may be more likely than girls to take up higher-paid jobs. In a similar paper, Chamarbagwala and Morán (2008) examine how the worst period of the civil war in Guatemala (1979–84) affected human capital accumulation among affected children. This study examines the effects of war on years of schooling and grade completion among different social groups. Like Shemyakina's, this empirical analysis exploits variation in war intensity across departments and across cohorts of school age during the war. The results show a strong negative impact of the civil war on female education. Girls exposed to the 1979–84 war during their school-age years completed 0.44 years of school (or 12 per cent) less than girls living in departments not affected by the fighting. Older female cohorts exposed to the war completed 0.64 years (17 per cent) less schooling than those not affected by warfare. The effect for males is smaller. Female education continued to lag behind male education throughout the country, but especially so in areas of high war intensity between 1979 and 1984, almost two decades after the worst conflict outbreak (in 2002). The study suggests that loss of property and massive displacement led households to reallocate limited resources towards providing young boys and, to a lesser extent, young girls, with at least some primary education. While both boys and girls received less secondary and high school education as a result of the civil war, the effects were more pronounced for girls. As in the Tajikistan study, considerations regarding higher education returns for boys and fear of abduction and rape of girls may explain these results. Like Akresh and de Walque (2008), Chamarbagwala and Morán find that a lower probability of progressing from one grade to another rather than not attaining any education appears to drive the results.

13.4   CAUSAL MECHANISMS LINKING VIOLENT CONFLICT AND EDUCATIONAL OUTCOMES

The literature reviewed above shows a clear negative legacy of violent conflict on the human capital of individuals (and consequently of families) exposed to violence. Among the results discussed, a debate has emerged as to what causal mechanisms explain the negative link between violent conflict and educational outcomes. While it is clear that civil wars affect household education attainment and schooling decisions, it is much less apparent through which channels and for how long these effects will impact on the long-term ability of individuals and households to survive economically, access sustainable forms of livelihood, and make long-term production, consumption or labour decisions. More research therefore needs to be done in terms of uncovering the precise mechanisms through which the relationship operates. Detailed knowledge of the mechanisms that support this negative relationship between conflict and educational outcomes are crucial towards creating and implementing effective policy to ensure that these negative consequences are dampened.

Civil wars affect educational outcomes negatively because, during violent conflict, children are removed from school, are prevented from attending school or the conditions under which they attend school do not provide them with education of sufficient quality. Below we discuss several types of mechanisms that explain the absence or reduction in schooling of children affected by fighting. We discuss below six possible mechanisms: soldiering, household labour allocation decisions, fear, changes in returns to education, targeting of schools, teachers and students and displacement.

13.4.1   Child Soldiering

The recruitment of child soldiers is a tactic used widely by armies and rebel groups alike to increase the number of fighters, improve logistical support, spread fear and reduce resistance among local populations. Children in armies are used as fighters, porters, messengers, cooks and are often forced to provide sexual services (USAID 2007). It is believed that violent conflicts around the world have involved around 300,000 children, both boys and girls, under the age of 18 (Blattman and Annan 2007; World Bank 2005b). Most of the (few) available empirical studies of child soldiers focus on boys, although there is wide recognition of the involvement of girls in armed forces, as combatants and as non-combatants (used as cooks, cleaners, nurses and so forth), and as victims of sexual slavery, forced 'marriages', rape and other forms of sexual violence (Annan et al. 2009;

UNHCR/OSCE 2002). Estimates from 2005 suggest that of the approximately 300,000 child soldiers involved in combat worldwide, 40 per cent of them are girls (Save the Children UK 2005). The military recruitment of children, either by armed non-state groups or by national armies, is however still widely underreported, taking place in a variety of forms in over 86 countries and territories worldwide (USAID 2007).

The recruitment of children into armed groups and armies has considerable impacts on their educational attainment, with consequences on their level of human capital. In particular, participation in armed groups affects negatively the long-term economic performance of child soldiers in terms of skills, productivity and earnings because military activities are not good substitutes for the benefits that individuals will acquire through education and work experience (Blattman and Annan 2007). Boys and girls exposed to conflict may also experience severe psychological effects that may continue long after the war is over and affect their educational outcomes. Weak economic opportunities in turn may serve to exacerbate the conflict if individuals have more to gain from soldiering when peacetime economic opportunities are limited (Grossmann 2002; Walter 2004).

13.4.2 Household Labour Allocation Decisions

Households in conflict-affected countries tend to replace dead, injured or physically and mentally disabled adult workers with children, if these have not become fighters themselves, in order to compensate for the unexpected reduction in the financial resources available to households during wartime. The use of children as a form of economic security mechanism is widely reported in the development economics literature (see Dasgupta 1993; Nugent and Gillaspy 1983), as is the resort to child labour as a form of compensating for low incomes (Basu and Van 1998; Duryea et al. 2007). In India, for example, agricultural households use seasonal school non-attendance by children and child labour as a form of self-insurance in the lean times (Jacoby and Skoufias 1997). Similarly, in Indonesia, many households were forced to decrease their spending on education after the 1998 financial crisis (Thomas et al. 2004). These studies assume that households in general favour investing in the education of their children. However, when facing unexpected income shocks, households tend to trade off future consumption with maintaining current consumption (often food) levels. Income uncertainty may therefore adversely affect the quality and quantity of children's education, and have severe negative consequences on the long-term welfare of households.

Children that are needed to replace labour may be removed from school, which may in turn deplete the household of their stock of human capital for future generations. Akresh and de Walque (2008), Merrouche (2006), Shemyakina (2007) and Swee (2009) point to this mechanism as an explanation for the reduction in educational attainment and enrolment observed in contexts of civil war. In a recent paper, Rodriguez and Sanchez (2009) test directly the effect of war on child labour and find that violent attacks in Colombian municipalities by armed groups have increased significantly the probability of school drop-out, and have increased the inclusion of children in the labour market. They show that increased mortality risks, negative economic shocks and reduction in school quality due to violence are the main channels through which armed conflict reduces human capital investments at the household level and increases child labour.

The social legacy of the conflict becomes even more profound when we remember that data allow us to observe information only on those individuals who survive the conflict. In addition, poor individual health and the loss of family members may create serious restraints on access to schooling. In one such study, Evans and Miguel (2004) find that young children in rural Kenya are more likely to drop out of school after a parent's death and that the effect is particularly strong for children who lost their mothers.

13.4.3   Changes in Returns to Education

Violent conflict may affect considerably the level and distribution of returns to education across social groups and gender. Returns to education in turn play a large role in households' decisions. Due to destruction of industries and infrastructure, job opportunities for skilled labour in conflict-affected countries generally become scarce. Households may respond to job scarcity by redistributing their resources away from investments with lower returns. In wartime contexts, this may mean investing more in the education of boys rather than girls as boys may have a higher probability of finding better-paid jobs. This effect is found in Shemyakina (2007) and Chamarbagwala and Morán (2008), as discussed above. Evidence on how this mechanism operates in different conflicts and across different population groups is, however, still scarce.

13.4.4   Fear

Fear plays an important part in explaining the removal of children from schools during violent events. A recently reported fighting strategy in Afghanistan has been the direct targeting of schoolchildren on their way to or from school. More than 100 children were killed in this way between 2006 and 2008, according to UNICEF. This tactic for spreading fear has resulted in the closure of around 670 schools in early 2009, depriving around 170,000 children of access to education (IRIN 2009). Rape and other sexual violence are common behaviour among fighting groups (IRIN 2004). Fear of physical attacks and sexual violence is likely to hinder the ability of children, particularly although not exclusively girls, to enrol in schools. In such contexts of fear and terror, households may attempt to protect vulnerable members by keeping them at home or sending away to relatives and friends in more secure locations.

13.4.5 Targeting of Schools, Teachers, Students and Staff

In several conflict-affected countries, access to good-quality education is seriously imperilled, not only due to the direct effects of fighting, but also because schools, teachers, students and staff are often targeted by violent attacks. The types of attack include the burning, shelling and bombing of schools, the occupation of schools by armed forces, the murder, torture, abduction and rape of teachers, students, education aid workers and school staff by armed groups or military forces, and the forced recruitment of child soldiers (O'Malley 2007). These attacks lead to the death of teachers and students, the destruction of infrastructure, and result also in severe psychological trauma to those exposed to them. In the face of repeated incidents and threats of attack, children are afraid to go to school, parents will be scared to send them to school and teachers will be afraid to go to work. Schools will be closed to prevent attacks (UNESCO 2010), and governments may be reluctant to reopen schools because threats of attack may still be present (Mulkeen 2007). They will also find it difficult to replace teachers in the areas targeted (ibid.). Motives for these attacks on schools, students and staff vary according to circumstances. In some cases, schools are the only visible symbol of government rule, making them easy targets for rebel groups (O'Malley 2007). Attacks are also used as a form of control of the population to impose religious, linguistic or cultural identities, and to recruit personnel, or provide shelter for troops. Teachers are also perceived as leaders of communities. Threats and attacks to teachers tend to take place due to their opposition to the forced recruitment of children by armed groups, their positions of leadership in the community, and accusations they face by armed groups of collaborating with opposing groups (Amnesty International 2007; Novelli 2008). All these effects will have long-term consequences for the type and quality of schooling available to children in areas of violence.

13.4.6   Displacement and Forced Migration

More than 27 million children are estimated to be out of education as a result of emergency situations. A large proportion of these are internally displaced (Mooney and French 2005). Displaced children are deprived of education but also of the support provided by educational structures in difficult, often persistently violent, environments. Access to education is an important element to the successful integration of internally displaced populations into their communities, as the disruption to normal life and insecurity inherent in refugee and displacement camps can harm children's physical, intellectual, psychological, cultural and social development with long-term consequences to their welfare and that of their children (UNHCR 1994, pp. 38–9).

Education is increasingly viewed as the 'fourth pillar' of humanitarian response, alongside nourishment, shelter and health services (ICWAC 2000; Norwegian Refugee Council 1999). Education can help to reduce children's exposure to threats including sexual exploitation, physical attack and recruitment into armed groups. Classrooms can also be effective means to disseminate information on how to avoid landmines, reducing the risk of HIV/AIDS and other preventive measures. Access to education may also facilitate the integration of displaced populations into local communities as schools may provide a means to promote community cohesion.

Very often education is viewed as a long-term post-conflict development aim and does not constitute a central element in emergency interventions among displaced populations. However, violent conflict and resulting displacement can last decades, leaving whole generations without access to education and the social structures provided by schools and teachers. The availability of education in IDP (internally displaced person) camps is typically disorganized, when it exists at all. Where schools do exist they tend to be temporary, underresourced, overcrowded and limited to primary education. Accessing schools outside the camps may not be an option due to issues of safety. The loss or confiscation of personal documents also makes enrolment difficult for displaced populations (Aguilar and Retamal 1998). School fees, the cost of school supplies and travel costs may also pose constraints to the access of education by displaced children (UNHCR/OSCE 2002). While some governments have implemented fee waivers for displaced children, these policies are rarely observed.

In addition, displaced children do not attend school when their labour is needed to contribute to household income. Boys are employed in farming and other activities, while girls are needed to help with domestic work, childcare and agricultural tasks. For those who do manage to get schooling while still working, there are losses in the quality of their education due to chronic fatigue and stress (Brookings Institution-SAIS 2003). In Colombia, where in 1999 only an estimated 15 per cent of IDP children received some form of education, the academic performance was found to be significantly constrained by high rates of malnutrition, trauma and cognitive disorders (Mooney and French 2005).

13.5   CONCLUSION

This chapter provided a review of available empirical evidence on the impact of violent conflict, largely civil wars, on education outcomes among civilian and combatant populations affected by violence. The literature reviewed shows a clear negative legacy of violent conflict on the educational outcomes of individuals and households exposed to violence. Three main themes emerge from existing empirical literature. The first is that even relatively minor shocks to a population's level of education can cause significant and long-lasting detrimental effects on human capital formation. These effects persist well after the conflict has ended, with long-term intergenerational consequences in terms of school achievement, health outcomes and future earnings. Second, violent conflict seems to affect secondary schooling more critically than primary schooling. This might indicate successful organization of war schools at the primary level, and an indication that families and organizations try to give their children at the very least some primary education even in circumstances of persistent violence. Third, education effects are not gender neutral. Conflict can change social, economic and political relations in such a way that makes returns to schooling for some social groups (usually girls) less attractive. Due to the destruction of industries and infrastructure, job opportunities for skilled labour, particularly women, may become scarce, leading households to value the education of boys higher than that of girls. The vulnerability of girls to sexual attacks and abduction may also explain the lower educational attainment of girls observed during violent conflict.

Evidence on the specific casual mechanisms that mediate these effects is scarce. The analysis of empirical studies and policy reports allowed us to review some important channels reported in the relevant literature, with important policy implications. These include the recruitment of child and youth soldiers, the need of children to contribute to household income, changes in returns to education during conflict, fear and attacks and displacement. Evidence on these channels, as well as the patterns emerging from recent empirical research, point to the importance of human capital accumulation for the well-being and economic outcomes among households and individuals affected by armed conflict and violence. We expect more to emerge as this area of research matures and we come to a better understanding of what specific factors are likely to affect education, who is likely to be affected and the causal pathways through which these changes occur in order to help policy makers to deal more effectively with the loss of education that violent conflict inflicts.

14 Education and violent conflict
Birgitte Refslund Sørensen

14.1 INTRODUCTION

Education has assumed an increasingly prominent position in interventions and analyses of violent conflicts and their aftermath over the past 20 years. The empirical connections between education and violent conflicts are many and complex, but I propose that efforts to understand and analyse these can be divided into three separate, but interrelated analytical approaches: the humanitarian perspective, the conflict perspective, and the citizenship perspective, which I outline and discuss in this chapter. Briefly, the humanitarian perspective considers education as a social good that is disrupted and destroyed by violent conflicts, and focuses on how to ensure that children continue to have access to education in times of crises. The conflict perspective instead argues that education may in fact contribute to the eruption of violent conflicts by producing and disseminating opinionated images and attitudes of 'self' and 'other' and creating structural inequalities, and focuses on how to foster peace and social cohesion through educational reforms. The citizenship perspective shares this view of education as an active force in the formation of subjects and societies, and suggests that attention is paid to the political socialization of children, not only in conflict societies, but everywhere. The citizenship perspective accentuates the strategic importance of education in establishing contemporary citizenship, and sheds light on education as a highly politicized and contested arena that many different actors have an interest in shaping and controlling.

14.2 THE HUMANITARIAN PERSPECTIVE

'Internal conflicts', 'ethnic wars', 'complex political emergencies' or simply 'the new wars' are some of the common labels attached to the violent conflicts that erupted in the post-colonial and post-socialist world in the 1970s and 1980s, and which have remained high on the global agenda due to the lack of sustainable solutions. What distinguishes them in particular from the inter-state wars of the past is that civilian populations are directly involved, as targets and victims and often also as collaborators and combatants. This makes 'women, children and other vulnerable groups' a new major category in the international aid vocabulary and a new target group of humanitarian and post-conflict interventions.

For children, the disruption of education is one of the most severe impacts of violent hostilities, which affects their everyday lives here and now, but also has ramifications for their future (see for instance Boyden and de Berry 2004; Crisp et al. 2001; Davies 2004a, 2006; Sommers 2002; World Bank 2005). Education is disturbed by conflict in innumerable ways, and the literature written from the humanitarian perspective provides ample descriptive accounts of these with the objective of improving programming and policy making. The literature, for instance, documents how the escalation of violence and military activities may force teachers as well as children and their families to flee their community for shorter or longer periods, often repeatedly. Parents may also keep their children at home, as they risk being attacked by armed groups, abducted or maimed by a landmine as they travel between home and school. The combination of mobility and insecurity makes it impossible to continue regular schooling, and children are left either with no education at all or with only basic education, for instance in refugee camps or at home. Another major threat to children's education occurs when school buildings cease to be available or usable for education. Buildings may be demolished by armed forces in order to disturb social life and install fear, looted by civilians in search of saleable goods, or as often happens, turned into temporary shelters for refugees or occupied by the armed forces to make local military presence possible. Militarization of schools also occurs because many militant groups consider them apposite locations for the dissemination of their political propaganda, and recruitment and training of their cadres. In some situations, schools and teachers are also directly targeted by militant groups for their alleged political and social roles. A different kind of challenge lies in the lack of food and medicine during crisis, which leads to a deterioration in children's health and hence their ability to concentrate in schools, just as difficulties to secure a reasonable household income may force them to drop out of school and work instead. Finally, the maintenance of an education system is obstructed when governments redirect financial allocations from schools and education to military purposes, which negatively affects recruitment of qualified teachers, maintenance of schools and availability of teaching materials.

Initially, emergency relief and reconstruction initiatives largely built on experiences from natural disasters. Interventions relied on a linear model with a clearly demarcated before, during and after conflict, and a medical understanding of basic needs that included shelter, water, sanitation, food and healthcare, but not education. According to this view, education is not perceived as a life-saving activity, which is illustrated by the fact that it is not included in the humanitarian charter of the Sphere Handbook that was first published in 1998.[1] Rather, education is commonly postponed until the reconstruction and development phases, for which governments and international development actors, not the humanitarian agencies, are responsible. Suggestions to support education during emergencies are often met with reservations by governments, in part because it is feared that the provision of education to refugees and other war-affected people would serve as a pull factor and contribute to making refugee settlements permanent, and in part because the government may itself be taking part in the conflict with the group deprived of education. However, at the World Education Forum in Dakar 2000, special emphasis was put on how to secure free primary education for 'children in difficult circumstances and those belonging to ethnic minorities' and on how to 'meet the needs of education systems affected by conflict'.[2] Discussions at the Forum resulted in the establishment of the open global Inter-Agency Network for Education in Emergencies (INEE), representing non-governmental organizations (NGOs), UN agencies, donor agencies, governments, academics and concerned individuals. The network's objective is to mainstream education as a priority humanitarian response. Almost 10 years later, in 2009, a companionship agreement was signed between the Sphere Project and the INEE in order to further integrate education into emergency responses and improve the quality of interventions by the development of key indicators and standards (The Sphere Project and INEE 2009; see also Davies 2004a and Sommers 2002).

Education interventions in times of conflict are typically based on an understanding of children as vulnerable and dependent victims of war, and of education as a life-sustaining, life-saving, protective activity. Education is regarded as a means to restore routines and normalcy in children's everyday lives, which help children cope with their suffering and heal their wounds, while simultaneously providing them with a safe environment. Education is also employed as a way to resocialize and reintegrate children who have been enmeshed in a sociality defined by the rules and values of war, as, for example, sex slaves or child soldiers, while providing them with useful knowledge and skills. Interventions are always based on somebody's definition of something as a problem and the concomitant identification of somebody as a target or beneficiary

---

[1]   The Sphere project is a global consultative process that aims to improve quality and accountability in humanitarian assistance, available at: http://www.sphereproject.org/.

[2]   The Dakar Framework for Action (2000), available at: http://unesdoc.unesco.org/images/0012/001211/121147e.pdf (last accessed 7 July 2011).

group. Interventions in the field of education pose no exception, and categories such as 'refugee children', 'child ex-soldiers', 'orphans', 'disabled children' and 'girls', who each in their own way are, or are at risk of being, marginalized and excluded from education, have emerged as particularly worthy of attention. It is beyond doubt that these children are in need of some assistance, but there is a lack of reflection of the fact that these categories are social constructions of reality, not neutral mirror images, that conceal as much as they reveal. It is important to examine who is excluded and who is included when adopting a particular categorization and with what consequences. It is also critical to understand that when children are identified according to certain principles of marginality or vulnerability, these aspects are accentuated and other dimensions of their lives are overlooked. Children's particular competencies, aspirations and agency and the constructive role they play as, for example, caretakers and protectors of siblings and friends, contributors to a household economy, are easily unnoticed and unacknowledged, either due to an agency's inclination to see war-affected individuals primarily as victims, a common perception of children as helpless and dependent, or because the skills, knowledge and values that they have developed during a conflict are not deemed relevant for post-conflict reconstruction and peacebuilding (Boyden 2007).

Apart from identifying relevant target groups and making education accessible to them even under very difficult circumstances, humanitarian agencies have also encouraged and supported the development of training that addresses the particular dangers and challenges that children face during a violent conflict or emergency (Crisp et al. 2001). Knowledge about how to spot landmines and what to do if you find one, knowledge about good hygiene and how to avoid contagious and sexually transmitted diseases, information about children's rights, and training in how to cope with loss and grief are all important and useful issues that are usually not covered by the ordinary curriculum.

In addition to education and training that addresses emergency-related problems, a variety of educational programmes that concentrate on the aftermath of conflicts are being offered by international and local organizations and sometimes incorporated into the curriculum of formal education. The gist of these programmes is that through vocational training and education on issues such as human rights, democracy and peace, development can be supported and sustained, democracy can be established and violent conflicts prevented. While the intentions of such initiatives are laudable, there are many traps. One recurrent issue is the fact that in most cases, these programmes build on historical experiences, theoretical concepts, cultural values, and ideological and political convictions that emanate from countries in 'the West'. Ideals and ideas derived from a Western experience may not be well understood or regarded as relevant and appropriate elsewhere. The historical development of state and nation, the nature of political culture, the degree of socioeconomic (in)equality, and religious and cultural worldviews are all matters that shape official and popular understandings and expectations of 'peace', 'stability', 'democracy' and 'justice'. Moreover, post-conflict reconstruction and peacebuilding activities are by nature political activities, and post-conflict societies, many of which are also post-colonial, are cautious that foreign assistance does not threaten their hard-won sovereignty. From a political perspective, education in human rights and peace may be resisted by governments, because it imposes a new political culture that is largely defined and controlled by the international community and bypasses the government as it builds alliances with civil society. There are many good reasons for wanting to involve children and youth in peace programmes, but it may add to their vulnerability *vis-à-vis* strong political actors.

To summarize, the humanitarian literature on education in emergencies has made a momentous contribution by documenting how violent conflict affects education and children's livelihoods, and inserting education on the agenda of humanitarian agencies. Important work is also being carried out in order to re-establish educational infrastructure, and to make interventions more effective, sustainable and appropriate. For the most part, however, the literature is descriptive and generalizing, and predominantly framed by the mandates, objectives, categories and reasoning of the humanitarian agencies. There is a dearth of rigid analysis based on in-depth ethnographic field research and too many anecdotal examples removed from their political, economic, social and cultural context, but also growing awareness that this is the case, and that policy and programmes can gain from research. Likewise, there is little critical scrutiny of the field's own assumptions, especially as regards the normative constructions of the category of the child and of education, but also of policy and programming as a social activity that involves many actors and is far more complex and untidy than a project cycle makes us believe.

As humanitarian actors and scholars expanded their empirical knowledge about education in emergencies, it became ever clearer that the question that had guided the humanitarian perspective, 'how does violent conflict affect education?' only revealed part of the picture, and the next generation of literature was guided by the much broader question, 'how does education relate to (violent) conflicts?'.

14.3   THE CONFLICT PERSPECTIVE

A growing number of scholars who conduct empirical research in schools or within the broader field of education, are writing against the common trust in education as inherently beneficial and a solution to social problems that characterizes the humanitarian perspective. Increasingly, education is also seen as a factor contributing to conflict (see Bush and Saltarelli 2000; Davies 2004a; Matthews 1995; Sørensen 2008). They argue that despite the global rhetoric of 'Education for All', education is in fact far from being inclusive and leaves many children behind, and although the discourse on merits and achievements suggests certain fairness, education systems are hardly ever equitable. The widespread belief that education results in social mobility and progress also appears elusive for many, and high hopes are replaced by growing despair (Chopra and Jeffery 2005; Jeffrey et al. 2008; Meinert 2009; Valentin 2005). Finally, schools do not always provide the safe environment they are claimed to, but are home to many forms of violence. Indeed, in her comprehensive discussion of education and conflict Lynn Davies reaches the sinister verdict that education generally contributes more to conflict than to peace (Davies 2004). In the following I delineate some of the processes and issues that have contributed to this conclusion.

Conflict-oriented studies of education have paid particular attention to the curriculum, which directly affects what knowledge, skills and values children are supposed to learn (Bush and Saltarelli 2000; Davies 2004a; Tawil and Harley 2004). The curriculum plays an important role in children's formation of identity and sense of belonging, and their understanding of and attitudes towards diversity. The subject of history, for instance, never transmits an objective account of what happened, but gives selective and positioned representations of prominent persons and significant events according to which some groups are classified as victors and heroes, and others as intruders, traitors and enemies or are written out of history altogether. Historical 'evidence' is used to add authenticity and moral value to contemporary claims for power and may feed into processes of negative ethnic stereotyping that can escalate into violent conflict. Subjects such as archaeology and geography likewise serve to legitimize certain power constellations. The presence of ancient ruins and relics and the use of particular placenames both serve to demonstrate a strong link between group and territory that may legitimize the denial of other groups' equal status and equal rights. And social studies offer children an understanding of how their society is organized and what constitutes social order, and provide them with ways to think about gender, race, ethnicity or diversity more generally. A common feature that may generate conflict is the moral categorization of some groups as civilized and modern on the basis of their language, cultural values and social practices, and the concurrent labelling of others as backwards, primitive or simply strange. When children are exposed to such moral and normative label-ling, it shapes their understanding of 'self' and 'other' and may legitimize that they treat others as inferior, or even dehumanize and demonize them (Bush and Saltarelli 2000; Bekerman 2003).

A link between education and violent conflict is not only made pos-sible by the design of a curriculum, its subjects and contents. An equally important factor is the choice of language(s) of instruction (Chopra and Jeffery 2005; Jeffrey et al. 2008; Lauder et al. 2006). At first, this may appear a relatively neutral and practical decision, but language is integral to cultural identity, and language proficiency determines future possibilities, hence making the choice of language of instruction in schools a highly political matter. In situations where policy makers aim at increasing enrolment rates, the vernacular languages may be favoured as they are argued to facilitate learning, especially during the early years. Parents may object, however, arguing that vernacular education does not promote social mobility and furthermore, if vernacular schools receive fewer resources than more internationally oriented schools, this is likely to evoke feelings of discrimination. Moreover, as language is deeply embedded in whom we are, the language chosen for instruction supports particular kinds of identity formation and shapes the power relationship between different groups. While receiving education in their own language may help children to develop their cultural identity, this contributes to the essentialization of identities and may result in cultural stigmatiza-tion. In contrast, instruction in a foreign language may result in cultural alienation, but may also facilitate social mobility. Decisions about which languages to accept as media of instruction not only have implications for the individual child's sense of self and future prospects, they also affect the economic and social construction of the nation-state. Thus the choice to upgrade English-medium instruction is often motivated by a desire to compete on global markets, and may be resisted by some and even result in violent riots. More importantly, perhaps, the political decision regard-ing what language(s) can be used in teaching is a strong indication of how a country deals with cultural diversity in general. The decision to social-ize and assimilate all children into a common national identity regardless of their background may lead to discrimination and violence if carried out through coercion, but may also ease inter-ethnic relations. A multi-linguistic educational policy may be respectful of children's cultural back-ground, but can also contribute to national fragmentation. As shown, the language issue is extremely complex and what constitutes a wise decision is context dependent.

The growing realization that education is in many cases complicit in the escalation of violence has generated widespread international calls for educational reforms as part of post-conflict reconstruction processes (Bekerman 2005; Coulby et al. 2000; Tawil and Harley 2004). In accordance with the above presentation of what is perceived as key problems, these reforms typically entail a revision of existing subjects and textbooks to remove discriminatory content, and the introduction of new subjects and teaching material on subjects envisaged to generate social cohesion. Such initiatives are important, but they tend to overlook the importance of what is commonly termed the 'hidden curriculum' and which refers to the implicit knowledge, opinions and values embedded in school culture (Jackson 1990). Children not only learn what is written in their books or directly communicated by their teachers. The physical layout of a school, the style of teaching and testing, the performances at morning assemblies, activities during breaks, teachers' attendance, inspection of students' clothes and hygiene, the distribution of rewards and sanctions all carry important messages about hierarchy, authority, justice and acceptable social behaviour. One aspect of the hidden curriculum that has received considerable attention is violence in schools. Schools are expected to be safe environments for children, but often they are not. Schools are part of the social environment, and if this practises and accepts violence that often reflects in school culture. In some places schoolchildren bring weapons to school and organize in gangs in order to protect themselves. Violence, however, is also embedded in the ordinary practices of schools, as when teachers employ corporal punishment or use more subtle psychological violence through lack of recognition, exclusion, harassment and humiliation in order to discipline children. Violence is not only present in the hierarchical relations between teachers and students. Ragging and bullying are common practices among students who establish hierarchical social relationships among students and form social peer groups. While there is wide agreement that schools should be violence free, empirical research shows that certain forms of violence may be perceived as helpful and necessary.

Another area that is receiving growing attention in studies of education in conflict settings is governance structures and management, which can be considered a particular aspect of the hidden curriculum (Chopra and Jeffery 2005; Tawil and Harley 2004). Governance structures influence how and by whom decisions about education are made. Due to the central economic, social and cultural role of education, the state often plays a key role in the education sector and guards it carefully. In the context of violent identity conflicts the state often adopts a centralized, top-down approach as it operates the education system to serve its own interests and reduce the influence of others. In some situations politicians take control over education and other essential social services and use these to gain and maintain political power, by making generous promises of services in exchange for votes or other expressions of loyalty (Sørensen 2011). The result is an education system that develops unevenly, as access, resources and results are distributed among political followers. The politicization of education thus undermines trust in education as a common social good, and instead turns it into a privilege of particular groups. Politically motivated distribution of resources generates different material conditions for teachers and children, but more than that, it also serves as a forceful symbolic language about recognition and derecognition of identity, about inclusion and exclusion from the nation-state (Sørensen 2008). One overlooked result of the uneven distribution of quality education is that the privileged may be the ones who mobilize in protest, if their educational achievements do not translate into jobs and social mobility as expected.

Recently, studies of governance in the field of education have singled out corruption as a rising problem. Rather than being a characteristic of particular societies and cultures, corruption within the field of education is often caused by an intensified competition for good education as a means to achieve social mobility and prosperity. As quality education is not available for all, educational officers and principals may accept bribes to produce necessary documents and enrol a child in a good school, or demand 'voluntary fees' from parents despite an official policy of free education. And once enrolled, teachers may accept bribes to let children pass important exams that will allow them to continue their education. When corruption is accepted, it undermines the values of merits and achievements and instead demonstrates and legitimizes the power of the resourceful and well connected. The long-term consequences include a deterioration of the school system as principals and teachers may be employed without having the required qualifications, and moreover, children are socialized to accept bribery and corruption as effective ways to get things done.

The conflict perspective constitutes an important addition to the humanitarian view, as it demonstrates that education systems are not external to conflicts, but may in fact be deeply entangled in these, providing multiple causes for conflict as well as an empirical scene for their enactment. Moreover, the conflict perspective has exposed the limitations of the humanitarian perspective's generalized narratives and showed that the exact link between education and violent conflict is dependent on such factors as the particular constitution of the educational system; the attitudes and performance of politicians, the public, teachers and students; and prevailing socioeconomic conditions and governance structures. In my view, one of the analytical limitations of the conflict perspective is that it tends to operate with a very narrow delineation of the empirical field, often the education system or a school in a conflict setting. This prevents us from fully understanding how the field of education is linked to the wider national and global world, and how the school may indeed be complicit in 'small wars, peacetime crimes and invisible genocides' not only in the zones of violent conflicts, but in all societies, as Nancy Scheper-Hughes (2007, p. 181) suggests. The citizenship literature, to which I now turn, attempts to understand the connections between education and conflicts from this wider perspective.

14.4   THE CITIZENSHIP PERSPECTIVE

The citizenship perspective is concerned with many of the issues taken up under the conflict perspective, but also offers some new and interesting ones. A main difference between the two perspectives stems from the fact that while the conflict perspective concentrates on situations where conflict has erupted or is on the verge of doing so, the citizenship perspective is used in both non-conflict and conflict settings and thus allows for a broader comparative analysis. Sometimes, the citizenship perspective also advocates for an education that is more critical and that aims at a more fundamental transformation of societies.

In the conventional understanding of the term, citizenship connotes a political, legal relationship between a state and its subjects, and part of the citizenship literature takes its point of departure in a rights perspective. According to the Convention of the Rights of the Child, all children enjoy a legitimate right to primary education, and the nation-state carries the main responsibility to provide this. When a state denies children access to education or fails to deliver the necessary resources to establish and maintain a reasonable education system, this constitutes a violation of these rights. In conflict situations, states often grant access and distribute resources on the basis of ethnic identity or political allegiance, which in practice means that it practises gradual citizenship, so that certain groups only have status as second-rank citizens (Sørensen 2008). Children of ethnic or religious minorities, refugee children and undocumented children are particularly at risk of being derecognized as proper citizens.

More commonly, the citizenship perspective in educational research is based on the fact that schools and mass education were historically developed as part of the formation of nation-states, and hence schooling has always also been about the creation of (national) citizens (Bénéï 2005; Davies 2004a; Fuller 1991; Lauder et al. 2006; Lee et al. 2004; Sørensen 2008). From this angle, analyses similar to those of the conflict perspective, of how different groups are either assimilated within the dominant national culture or marginalized as of lesser status, have emerged. A recurrent question that occupies scholars is whether the notion of citizenship can possibly be detached from its national heritage and offer people a post-national type of identity, global citizenship, based on equal rights (Davies 2004a, 2004b). Another trajectory is to investigate more generally how schools practise political socialization of children and what kind of political agency children learn in school (ibid., Lazar 2010; Stevick and Levinson 2007). Contrary to theories of social reproduction (Bourdieu and Passeron 1990 [1997]), which see children as the product of prevailing structures, this approach usually assumes that teachers and children have agency and contribute both to the system's reproduction and its alteration, and to the formation of themselves as citizens (Ong 1996). This approach thus emphasizes people's own imaginaries of citizenship and their strategies and actions to develop their citizenship as it takes place in particular social and cultural contexts (Davies 2004; Lazar 2010; Smith and Vaux 2003; Stevick and Levinson 2007).

Writings on the transformation of children into citizens tend to be normative and focus on what kind of citizens one would like the schooling process to produce. From a national government point of view this would usually be the loyal national citizen, from the international donor perspective it would be a democratic and mobile citizen, while many academics and activists have as their ideal the critical citizen who are able to understand the causes and consequences of social issues as they affect different groups, and who employ political agency not only to participate, but to make claims for a more just and equitable world.

A final contribution of the citizenship perspective that deserves mention here is its global orientation, which opens up the topic for comparative analysis. As has been evident from the previous discussion, the analysis of education has commonly been framed by the nation-state, but the field of education is thoroughly affected by globalization (see for example, Anderson-Levitt 2003; Chopra and Jeffery 2005; Colby et al. 2000; Daun 2002; Tikly 2001, 2009). First, teachers, parents and schoolchildren live not only in local worlds, but also in a global world that add to their imaginations of and aspirations for possible futures. Second, globalization is introducing a plethora of new actors and agendas in the field of education that needs to be taken into account. In situations of emergency, the most notable example of this is the presence of humanitarian organizations, which may be accountable to international organizations, national donors, religious denominations or civic groups and which target different groups with alternative offers of education. These actors produce competing environments and some citizens may turn to them instead with their political claims for resources and recognition, and in the process be defined and define themselves according to their criteria (Ong 1996). If the nation-state does not feel its sovereignty threatened it may acquiescently accept this, otherwise it may increase surveillance and control. Global actors not only enter the field of education in emergencies. Education itself is increasingly globalized, as providers of education market their degrees and courses globally, and schoolchildren and youth seek to qualify for a job on the global market. In the field of education, we are witnessing a more and more desperate struggle to get access to quality education and degrees from recognized institutions of learning. The outcome is not necessarily positive, and may include an increase in psychological stress among children and youth who try to cope with the growing demands and who are afraid of not succeeding. And even among those who succeed in completing their education there is growing frustration, as they join the ranks of the unemployed and see their dreams shattered. At the same time, politicians worldwide continue to advocate for education for all and learning for life.

If the conflict perspective makes us understand how educational practices may contribute to the escalation of conflict in a particular place mainly through various forms of discrimination, the citizenship perspective accentuates the political and moral formation of subjects in general. The approach does not focus on violent conflicts exclusively, but it effectively shows that struggles to succeed and become recognized as citizen are intense, and that education plays a significant role in this process. If this holds true, we should not be surprised to find different kinds of violence present in the field of education, also outside the zones of violent conflict. Citizenship education or civic education is entering the curriculum in many places as a way to counteract violence and injustice in its different shapes and to establish a culture based on equal rights and democratic principles, but at the same time the economic and social inequalities that generate conflicts seem to be growing, thus suggesting that the introduction of a single new subject will hardly be sufficient to remove violence from the field of education.

14.5 CONCLUSION

In this chapter, I have sought to demonstrate that education is more central to violent conflicts than is often assumed, and that indeed, violence may also be a more fundamental aspect of education than commonly believed. I have summarized three different ways in which practitioners and academics see a link between education and violent conflict. In reality, they coexist, overlap and appear less coherent, but they have been treated as distinct here in order to emphasize dominant assumptions and viewpoints in the field. As the existing literature shows, education is linked to violent conflicts in many and complex ways that are context specific. However, in-depth, rigid empirical research is still scarce and needs to be strengthened in order to enhance our understanding of how global, national and local actors, political, economic, social and cultural dimensions, and institutional and individual agendas affect each other and shape the dynamics of particular educational fields. So far, research on education and violent conflicts has tended to focus on cases where conflict has erupted, but it has become clear from recent research that education is everywhere becoming increasingly central to the production of inequality, vulnerability, marginality and derecognition, which generate frustrations, despair, tensions and conflict, and this deserves more attention. In addition, there is a need for better analytical concepts and tools that can grasp and explain such complexities. Practitioners working in emergencies are greatly helped by initiatives such as the INEE–Sphere project, but some kind of conflict assessment might also be useful to incorporate in policy making and implementation outside the zones of conflict.

15 International dimensions of internal conflict

Nils W. Metternich, Kristian Skrede Gleditsch, Han Dorussen and Andrea Ruggeri

15.1 INTRODUCTION

Civil wars are by definition violent conflicts between a state and some form of non-state actors (Sambanis 2004b). Perhaps not surprisingly, most scholars have looked for features within countries to account for why such conflicts break out and how they evolve (Blattman and Miguel 2010). However, it is misleading to simply equate civil wars with domestic conflict and look exclusively within countries to understand civil war.

Transnational factors can play an important role for the initial outbreak of civil wars and the escalation and dynamics of conflict once underway. But transnational factors also can contribute to the resolution and mitigation of such conflicts. Indeed, since civil conflicts are not necessarily limited to an individual state and often involve participation by other states in various forms, a strict dichotomy between civil and inter-state wars is often untenable and inappropriate. Failing to theoretically and empirically account for the transnational dimension of civil wars is likely to lead to biased conclusions about the onset, duration and intensity of such conflicts. Moreover, many policy prescriptions based exclusively on a domestic understanding of civil war can be highly misleading and potentially counterproductive.

15.2 THE TRANSNATIONAL CONTEXT OF STATES AND CIVIL WAR

Most research implicitly or explicitly adopts a 'closed polity' approach to civil war, where civil war is driven exclusively by features and events within individual countries. The conventional wisdom on civil war tends to portray civil wars as problems of poor and weak states (Fearon 2005), largely driven by the greater opportunities for conflict when states are unable to enforce control or deter protest (Herbst 2000a). In addition, poor and weak states are thought to provide greater incentives for

Note: Location of intra-state conflicts (circles) and internationalized intra-state conflicts (squares).

Source: Based on the Conflict Site Dataset (Hallberg 2012).

Figure 15.1 Location of armed conflicts, 1946–2005

participation in conflict when the formal economy affords few rewards for normal economic activities (Collier and Hoeffler 2004b). It is often inferred that civil wars are best prevented through shoring up the capacity of the central government, achieving sustainable economic growth, and more controversially, establishing more representative political institutions or power-sharing institutions (Hartzell and Hoddie 2003b).

The transnational dimension can make many of these inferences problematic. Political processes do not stop at the water's edge, and countries are not isolated units, impervious to events and actors outside their boundaries (Franzese and Hays 2008; Gleditsch and Ward 2006). This insight is neatly summarized in Tobler's (1970, p. 236) First Law of Geography: 'Everything is related to everything else, but near things are more related than distant things'. Indeed, when looking at Figure 15.1, displaying a map of the geographical centre points of intra-state conflicts between 1946 and 2005, we observe a strong tendency for civil conflicts to cluster geographically. Certain regions, such as the Caucasus and Western Africa, have an especially large number of conflicts over this period, while Northern Europe and Eastern Asia experience only a few armed conflicts. This in turn suggests that individual conflicts may not be independent of one another, and that the risk of conflict is dependent on actors and events outside its borders (Buhaug and Gleditsch 2008). While political interdependencies are likely to extend beyond the geographical dimension (Beck et al. 2006), there is much reason to believe that in the context of civil wars the geographical dimension is especially important.

15.2.1 An Example of the Transnational Dimension

The Albanian insurgency in Macedonia in 2001 provides a helpful example highlighting many transnational dimensions of civil war. Any new state will be less well consolidated than older states, and Albanians clearly were marginalized in the new and explicitly ethnic Macedonian nation-state. However, violent conflict erupted 10 years after independence in 1991, and at a point where the state was much better established. Moreover, the insurgency actually emerged in the aftermath of notable concessions to Albanian parties by the Macedonian government. Hence, the outbreak of the conflict clearly contradicts what one would expect from purely domestic conceptions of civil war.

In this example, the transnational context provides a helpful frame to understand the timing of the civil war as well as the specific conduct. While the Albanian population in Macedonia by itself is small and lacks significant resources, it is clearly part of a larger Albanian community in neighbouring Albania and Kosovo. Moreover, the Albanian community in Kosovo had a long history of mobilization, and had recently seen violent conflict following the emergence of the Kosovo Liberation Army (KLA), which challenged the Yugoslav government by violent means (as opposed to older organizations such as the Democratic League of Kosovo party, which favoured non-violent strategies). In the aftermath of the Kosovo war, an Albanian organization similar to the KLA called the National Liberation Army emerged in Macedonia, drawing on individuals that had previously participated in the Kosovo conflict, as well as arms and resources from the previous war in neighbouring Kosovo. The fact that the fighting overwhelmingly took place in border areas attests to the close links between the insurgency and the Kosovo war.

The 2001 Albanian insurgency in Macedonia provides a compelling example where transnational features were important for the outbreak, and it seems unlikely that conflict would have come about without the linkages to the external prior conflict in Kosovo. However, sceptics may wonder whether this is an isolated case, and how representative the example may be. Although there can be many important transnational linkages, we shall here focus on a set of common transnational mechanisms that often affect the risk of conflict, which we shall discuss under the labels 'transnational actors', 'transborder conflicts', and 'transnational conflict externalities and spillovers'.

15.3 TRANSNATIONAL ACTORS

The actors in civil wars are not necessarily confined within individual countries. For example, ethnic groups often span international boundaries, and transnational kin frequently participate in or provide important support for insurgencies in other states (Cederman et al. 2009). Resources mobilized transnationally can often be more difficult for governments to control or target. As such, the domestic political status and resources of an ethnic group can be a poor guide to the motivation for violence and the events that influence mobilization and changes in political strategies. Cederman et al. (2009) provide systematic evidence suggesting that transnational groups are much more likely to engage in conflict than would be expected on purely domestic characteristics. They extend a purely domestic model of conflict among excluded ethnic groups and a central government, where the risk of conflict is proportional to the relative size of the ethnic group, to consider the difference between groups with and without transnational segments. Figure 15.2 illustrates the core empirical findings, with the solid line representing the predicted risk of conflict over the period from 1946 to 2003 for a group with transnational segments and the dashed line the predictions for a purely domestically confined group. Figure 15.2 demonstrates that conflict is dramatically more likely for groups with transnational kin. As an illustrative example, in the case of the Kurds in Turkey we have a relative group size of 0.14, or about seven Turks for every Kurd. If this were an isolated ethnic group, the

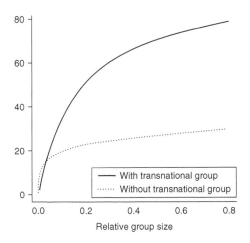

Figure 15.2   Risk of ethnic conflict by relative ethnic group size and transnational ethnic kin

model would imply a predicted probability of conflict of less than 20 per cent. However, given the presence of Kurds in neighbouring states (that is, Iran, Iraq and Syria), there is a much higher predicted risk of conflict, that is, 43 per cent. The opportunities for the Kurdish Workers Party (PKK) to operate out of Syria and more recently Iraq have been important for the organizations ability to engage the Turkish government in conflict over the repeated outbreaks of the violent conflict. From the perspective of accommodation, Dorussen (2005, 2009) finds that groups with transnational kin also are more likely to receive concessions from governments, reflecting their stronger bargaining power. More generally, Salehyan (2009) demonstrates that rebel organizations frequently find sanctuaries in bordering countries, which makes it difficult for the government to successfully defeat insurgents. In addition, Salehyan (2007) argues that transnational rebels complicate the bargaining environment. First, the government has less verifiable information about transnational rebels as they operate and hide beyond its borders. This increases informational problems and leads to a higher probability of bargaining failure. Second, any agreement between the government and the rebels will involve the demobilization of military forces. In addition, there are incentives for the rebel organization to keep forces beyond the borders of a state, which gives rise to commitment problems that can prevent peaceful settlements.

15.4 TRANSBORDER CONFLICTS: EXTERNAL SUPPORT AND ESCALATION

The examples reviewed illustrate how fighting and mobilization in civil wars often takes place in border areas. Although borders in a technical sense are just lines in the sand and often not difficult to cross from a purely military perspective, the status of international borders generates different constraints and opportunities for governments and rebels. The fact that borders formally delineate state sovereignty makes it more difficult for governments to violate the sovereignty of other countries, while such constraints are less relevant for rebels. Governments risk retaliation from neighbouring countries from territorial incursions, and face difficulties in targeting transnational support. This in turn means that rebels can have a logistical advantage in operating out of extra-territorial bases, and transnational rebel movements can be more difficult for governments to deter or defeat (Salehyan 2009).

Buhaug and Gates (2002) demonstrate more systematically that a large share of civil wars tend to be fought in border areas. This prevalence of fighting in border locations in civil wars in turn raises the question about whether rebels operate in neighbouring countries with the explicit consent of other states. Although there are situations where inter-state conflicts have emerged out of direct support for insurgent groups (such as the 1978–79 Tanzanian Ugandan war that toppled Idi Amin), direct intervention on the side of insurgents is a very costly action for states. Support is more likely to come in the form of indirect military support, and such support is often officially denied by the supporting state. Salehyan et al. (2011) estimate that about 45 per cent of all the civil wars in the post-1945 era saw rebel organizations receiving support from a foreign state. External support requires both some degree of demand by insurgents and supply by a potential supporting state. It can be shown that support seems more likely in instances when groups have transnational segments, states have a history of antagonisms, and rebel groups are moderately strong relative to the government. One interpretation of the last aspect is that rebels must be sufficiently weak for foreign support to be attractive, given the problems that this may entail with respect to potentially competing goals of the patron state and the potential loss of legitimacy arising from external backing. At the same time, a rebel organization must also be sufficiently strong to be considered a plausible candidate by potential supporters.

15.5 TRANSNATIONAL CONFLICT EXTERNALITIES AND SPILLOVERS

The general notion in the literature is that conflicts that include transnational actors and are closely located to international borders are more difficult to resolve and more likely to escalate. In the last section we highlight another important aspect of the transnational dimension of civil wars: the risk of contagion through conflict externalities and spillovers. Recalling Tobler's (1970) First Law of Geography: 'Everything is related to everything else, but near things are more related than distant things' (p. 236) alludes to the risk of conflict diffusion and clustering. Indeed, Gleditsch (2007) finds that countries with neighbours experiencing civil war are at a greater risk of conflict than would be expected by their purely domestic characteristics. Although this in part may be due to transnational actors, fighting can also create externalities and spillover mechanisms that by themselves increase the risk of conflict. The presence of conflict in another state can help facilitate violent mobilization even in the absence of direct linkages between actors, through either emulation of successful rebellions, or the direct import of arms and combatants.

Put differently, spatial dependency goes beyond the assumption that near things simply experience similar structural conditions and are therefore related to each other. From our perspective, transnational dependencies arise from interactions between the relevant conflict actors and their strategic dependencies.

In the context of economic policies Simmons et al. (2006) discuss four mechanisms that can easily be related to the transnational dimension of civil wars. The first mechanism is coercion, which may be direct or indirect and hard or soft. Coercion is frequently exercised by external actors that try to influence the dynamics of civil wars. Interventions by international organizations or neighbouring countries are commonly observed in civil conflicts (Gleditsch and Beardsley 2004). These direct interventions may include military, economic and diplomatic aspects to change the course of an armed confrontation. More indirect measures might be the toleration of transnational rebels on its territory (Salehyan 2009).

The second mechanism highlights that civil war actors can learn across borders (Horowitz 1985, p. 6). This extends the idea that learning and informational updating only occurs between the belligerents (Slantchev 2003; Smith and Stam 2004). For example, rebel organizations might learn from insurgents in neighbouring countries which strategies and logistical networks are successful in an armed struggle. Similarly, governments are able to observe successful policies to prevent and mitigate armed conflicts.

Governments can also observe the behaviour of the international community and form expectations about potential international interventions on their or the rebels' behalf. Therefore, learning is a powerful mechanism that leads to transnational dependencies.

The third mechanism, competition, refers to pressures that actions within one country place on surrounding ones. Armed conflicts within one country are likely to have externalities that affect proximate countries (Murdoch and Sandler 2004). For example, negative externalities arise when countries have important economic ties and dependencies with a country that experiences civil war. But in some cases armed conflict can have short-term positive externalities for surrounding countries. The civil conflict in Iraq, for example, hampers oil production in one of the largest exporters, thus decreasing the global supply of oil and benefiting other oil-exporting states in the Gulf region.

The potential impact of externalities should also have an effect on whether surrounding countries consider coercive transnational interventions. Competition might also refer to more indirect consequences of, for example, economic development. If proximate countries experience strong economic competition, this should lead to regional economic development in the long run. However, we know that economic development is negatively related to civil war and thus transnational economic activities can potentially lead to a lower risk of armed conflict.

Civil wars can also decrease the government's military competitiveness *vis-à-vis* neighbouring countries (Gleditsch et al. 2008). While the government has to allocate its forces against an internal threat, this may increase the risk of inter-state violence by lowering the neighbours' expected costs or increasing the expected benefits of using military force. Civil wars and insurgencies expose and exacerbate weaknesses in the state's military capabilities and divert resources away from defence against foreign enemies. This position of weakness may invite opportunistic attacks against the state, which would not have taken place in the absence of the internal conflict. In such cases, the attacker is not concerned with the outcome of the civil war and does not necessarily sympathize with rebel aims, but is primarily motivated by capturing territory or resources. In some cases, conflicts arise over the externalities generated by conflicts, including refugees and collateral damage.

Many disputes arise out of border violations, where government forces pursue rebels into the territory of neighbouring states. Conflict may also arise out of alleged support for rebels. In some cases, states may respond to alleged support for insurgents by neighbouring countries, by either direct military retaliation or support for insurgent groups in the neighbouring states. Western Africa in the 1990s provides many examples of governments supporting insurgencies in neighbouring countries. Finally, many studies document large negative social and economic effects of civil wars for neighbouring countries, which in turn could undermine political stability. This attests to how civil war cannot be considered exclusively domestic problems, but in many cases will constitute transnational security issues and challenges for other states.

The fourth mechanism is emulation, which refers to behaviour that is not coerced or responsive to competition and learning. In the context of civil wars, emulation has gained little attention. However, ideological movements frequently seem to follow this mechanism by attaching themselves to a momentarily in-vogue ideology. Leftist movements in South America or Islamist movements in Southeast Asia represent spatially clustered organizations which do not obviously result from the success of similar movements (learning) or identical external support (coercion).

Finally, Franzese and Hays (2008) add a fifth category to the diffusion mechanisms proposed by Simmons et al. (2006): migration. The relationship between migration and conflict diffusion has received some notable attention. Salehyan and Gleditsch (2006) point out that migration is an important aspect of conflict diffusion. First, refugee flows from war-torn countries can imply the direct influx of combatants, arms and ideologies from neighbouring states that facilitate the spread of conflict. Second, rather than fighting openly with the host government, refugee populations can provide resources and support to domestic opposition groups of a similar ethnicity or political faction. Third, as a negative externality, refugee flows can change the ethnic balance in a country, sparking discontent among local populations towards the refugees as well as the government that allows access. Finally, refugees may pose actual or perceived negative economic externalities because they compete with locals over scarce resources such as employment, housing, land and water, constituting an economic 'threat'.

16 Theories of ethnic mobilization: overview and recent trends
Peter Vermeersch

16.1 INTRODUCTION

Even though violent ethnic conflicts often look like highly unorganized and spontaneous outbursts of popular anger, in reality they always involve a certain degree of planning, organizational effort and strategic deliberation. An ethnic conflict occurs only when a critical number of people have made the calculated decision to pursue their goals with violent means (Wolff 2007, p. 6). Such a decision is part of a longer history of political organizing along ethnic lines. This longer process can be called 'ethnic mobilization'; leaders decide to speak for 'their' ethnic group, thereby making the abstract idea of ethnic belonging a somewhat more tangible reality, and engage the members of this group into political action. This does not mean that such mobilization inevitably leads to violence; as Brubaker and Laitin (1998, p. 88) have argued, 'measured against the universe of possible instances, actual instances of ethnic and nationalist violence remain rare'. In many cases ethnic mobilization remains firmly within the limits of peaceful democratic political competition (Habyarimana et al. 2008). Nor does it mean that the grievances invoked by such political action are not deeply felt by the population *prior* to the process of mobilization, or that the population is not genuinely or spontaneously angered by 'the ethnic other'. But the step from grievances to ethnic strife should never simply be regarded as an automatic linear chain from cause to consequence; ethnic mobilization is a complex, multidirectional and not necessarily convergent or coherent process. Therefore, it needs careful examination.

It is the purpose of this chapter to present a brief and non-exhaustive overview of recent thinking and research on ethnic mobilization in the social sciences. I shall do this as follows. Section 16.2 will define the term 'mobilization' and situate the literature on ethnic mobilization within the larger body of scholarly inquiry on political mobilization and social movements. Section 16.3 will consider the main theoretical strands in the study of ethnic mobilization. Here I shall distinguish between culturalist, reactive, competition and institutionalist perspectives. And finally, in the brief Section 16.4, which also functions as a conclusion to the chapter, I shall explore the question of differentiated outcomes: what factors account for the radicalization of ethnic claims and the turn from ethnic mobilization to ethnic violence?

16.2   WHAT IS 'ETHNIC MOBILIZATION'?

Political mobilization can be defined as the process whereby political actors encourage people to participate in some form of political action. In its concrete manifestation this process can take on many different shapes. Political mobilizers typically persuade people to vote, petition, protest, rally, or join a political party, trade union or a politically active civic organization (for more on the definition of political mobilization, see Johnston 2007; Vermeersch 2010).

All political mobilization has in common that it is initiated by mobilizing agencies looking for adherents to a collective cause. These agencies try to persuade potential adherents to take part in public actions in order to defend that cause. Therefore, political mobilization usually has a distinctly collective dimension to it. There is strength in numbers, mobilizers know, and so they seek to influence the behaviour of large groups of citizens in order to achieve well-defined political aims. These aims, however, may vary. There are myriad types of public action that are considered to best serve these causes, and there are many strategies used to persuade people to participate.

In order to situate the phenomenon of ethnic mobilization adequately in a wider sociopolitical context, one needs a broad conceptualization of the term 'political mobilization', one that goes beyond merely the field of electoral politics. Traditionally, political mobilization is often understood as closely tied to elections (for example, Rosenstone and Hansen 1993); studies of political mobilization, for example, focus on the effects of electoral campaigning (for example, Shanto and Simon 2000) or seek to explain fluctuations in voter turnout (for example, Franklin 2004). Mobilization in this sense is seen as consisting of those actions that elites undertake in order to garner a growing group of supporters and persuade them to express their affinity through the ballot box. Among the questions that researchers have traditionally asked are: what determines voters' decisions, and to what extent is the success of electoral mobilization dependent on existing affiliations, organizational capacities, or persuasive ideas? More specifically, the study of *ethnic electoral* mobilization weighs the relative importance of different potential sources of ethnic voting: cultural affiliation, political manipulation by elites, and existing socio-economic divisions that coincide with ethnic boundaries (for example, Leighley 2001).

Political scientists, however, would have only a narrow understanding of the process of ethnic mobilization if they were to exclude from their scope those forms of political action that take place outside the electoral process, ranging from peaceful protest to violent revolutions. So, there is a need to adopt a broader definition of political mobilization in order to study the complexity of ethnic mobilization. The notion has to be extended to include the field of unconventional political action, or as it is sometimes referred to, 'contentious politics'. Many now view extra-electoral action as an inherent aspect of political mobilization. Such non-electoral initiatives – including protest marches and civil disobedience, but also lobbying, strategic litigation and press conferences – may have profound consequences on policy making, even though researchers still disagree on how effective their influence is (Amenta et al. 2010; Baumgartner and Mahoney 2005; Skocpol 2003). Despite that disagreement, political scientists generally agree on the idea that such unconventional expressions are ever more becoming a part of regular politics. It is a form of politics that does not diminish with the advent of modernization. In fact, especially in advanced democracies they are increasingly viewed as a 'normal' characteristic of politics. Political mobilization thus covers a broad spectrum of public action, from the covert to the disruptive, and from the institutionalized to the unconventional.

The study of political mobilization outside electoral politics has deep roots in political sociology and, in particular, in the study of mass protest and social movements (Amenta et al. 2010; della Porta and Diani 1999; Edelman 2001). This sociological view on political mobilization has allowed analysts to look for factors beyond electoral campaigns. These studies have examined the way in which protest waves and social movements have emerged, how they have developed, and what impact they have had on policy outcomes or social change. They have brought several new dimensions of mobilization to the attention of political scientists: the social grievances underlying collective action, the importance of resources, the role of meaning manipulation and ideas, and the political context (the opportunities and constraints) shaping such action. For example, contemporary researchers do not simply view the American black civil rights movement as a spontaneous mass response to social grievances (for example, McAdam 1982). They have examined the political opportunity structures that have shaped this movement, the resources that have supported it, and the global spread of human rights norms that has given the movement's ideas, claims and demands a universal validity (Jackson 2006).

Social movement research has thus considerably altered political scientists' understanding of what is 'political' in mobilization. Political scientists are now increasingly inclined to question the neat division social scientists once made between the political significance of political parties and interest representation in state institutions, on the one hand, and the social and cultural (but supposedly less political) weight of social movements, on the other. Of course, social movements have important cultural and social implications; but they are also inherently political, even when they, as they sometimes do, propagate methods that are disruptive to political and social stability and peace such as rioting or ethnic cleansing. Sometimes the mobilization of people into non-electoral and non-institutionalized types of public action may lead to new and stable political interest cleavages. These interest cleavages, in turn, may serve as a new basis of electoral mobilization.

Ethnic mobilization is thus far more than electoral campaigning on the basis of ethnicity. It occurs not only at the time of elections but also during other points in time, most likely at the time of particular events that can form a basis for mass action, be it in the form of collective street protests or less visible forms of petitioning.

16.3   THEORIES OF ETHNIC MOBILIZATION

It is perhaps surprising that theorizing on ethnic mobilization in political science literature cannot look back upon a long history. Traditionally, political scientists did not attach much importance to the ethnic aspects of political mobilization. Not that ethnic politics was entirely discounted; but scholars often assumed that the politics of ethnic solidarity would disappear with the ongoing development of modernization and the spread of liberal–democratic values (Kymlicka 2000, p. 184). For others, mainly before the 1960s, ethnicity was a transitional phenomenon or a factor that did not, and would not, have any influence on the formal political system (Taylor 1996, p. 886). In some cases this argument was inspired by the Marxist reasoning that class identity would prevail over other types of identity through the struggle against capitalism. Still others, especially in the 1980s, dismissed the subject, and even predicted the decline of ethnic attachments because of the advancement of liberal democracy. Glazer and Moynihan dubbed this the 'liberal expectancy' (Glazer and Moynihan 1974, p. 33); ethnic identities were seen as merely transitory and were assumed to vanish into the inevitably growing cosmopolitan ethnic melting pot (Moynihan 1993, pp. 27–8).

The resurgence of political mobilization of territorially based linguistic groups in Western Europe in the 1970s – think of the mobilizations of the Bretons and Corsicans in France, the Celtic-speaking populations in Great Britain, or the Flemish–Walloon cleavage in Belgium – clearly contradicted the expectations of classical social theory (Ragin 1987, p. 133). Ethnic differences within one country did not seem to erode over time, a phenomenon that made the need felt for additional theorizing. However, it was the surge in ethnic conflict in the last decade of the twentieth century that changed views on ethnic mobilization most profoundly. This historical development called for a refocusing of attention on the need to think about the relationship between ethnicity and politics. Indeed since the 1990s, political scientists have written a considerable amount of literature on the phenomenon.

In this broad literature, which has its roots in the 1960s but grew considerably in the 1990s, one can now discern roughly four different theoretical perspectives on ethnic mobilization:

1. the 'culturalist' perspective, which emphasizes the significance of strong subjective bonding and values within ethnic groups for shaping the lines of ethnic mobilization;
2. the 'reactive ethnicity' perspective, which uses an economic perspective to argue that the primary cause of ethnic mobilization lies in the coincidence of ethnic bonding and relative deprivation;
3. the 'competition' perspective, which focuses on ethnic leaders making rational calculations about their identity and invoking ethnicity in their struggle for resources and power; and
4. the 'political process' perspective, which emphasizes the role of the macropolitical context, consisting of (i) the institutional environment and (ii) the dominant political discursive context.

Each perspective takes a different set of factors to be primarily responsible for causing and shaping ethnic mobilization. This four-pronged distinction is of course a rough analytical device, but it offers an opportunity to structure the literature and gain insight into the pattern of explanatory variables that theorists have considered to be pivotal in driving ethnic mobilization. I shall consider these perspectives in turn.

16.3.1 Culturalist Approaches to Ethnic Mobilization

Culturalist perspectives distinguish themselves from other approaches by their view on the role of culture in the process of ethnic mobilization. Culturalists regard the cultural socialization process as the most fundamental factor explaining ethnic mobilization. In other words, the fact that members of an ethnic group share a common culture is seen as determinant for the group's pattern of mobilization. The view is close to that of primordialism. According to Fearon (2004, p. 6), primordialists claim that

> [Ethnic groups] are naturally political, either because they have biological roots or because they are so deeply set in history and culture as to be unchangeable,

'givens' of social and political life. In other words, primordialists assume that
certain ethnic categories are always socially relevant, and that political relevance follows automatically from social relevance.

Most authors denounce the idea that there is a biological basis to ethnic
solidarity, but the view that ethnic identities are based on cultural affini-
ties that have an overpowering emotional and non-rational quality is
more widely accepted (Allahar 1996; Oberschall 2000, p. 982). One school
of thought in international relations literature, for example, argues that
culture should be seen as the crucial independent variable explaining
economic and political developments (Harrison and Huntington 2000).
Throughout long periods of history, it is argued, cultural attributes such
as religion or community traditions have influenced population groups so
profoundly that it becomes relatively easy to engage them in a process of
collective action or even conflict on the basis of these attributes.

The basic assumption that governs this literature is that ethnic mobilization is the natural reflection of cultural structure. The obvious conclusion,
then, is that people from the same ethnic group will have some sort of a
fundamental connection because of their shared culture and will therefore
organize in similar ways. Their political or economic position may to a
certain extent facilitate or suppress that mobilization, but it is ultimately
the cultural content that forms the backbone of the mobilization process.
On the basis of the assumption that action is expressive of culture, the
argument is made that each ethnic group should exhibit a unique mobilization pattern (Ireland 1994, p. 8). The same ethnic group in different
societies is expected to adopt roughly similar forms of mobilization.

Several criticisms have been made against culturalist perspectives. The
first criticism is that culturalists have too readily taken for granted that an
ethnic group is characterized by a shared culture. Yet, so critics contend,
it is difficult to define the cultural essence of an ethnic group, and therefore culture is too diffuse to be a useful explanatory variable. As Nathan
Glazer has argued: 'What does Italy in the large tell us about the typical
Italian immigrant, poor, from the south, uneducated? Are we to take him
as an example of the culture and civilization of Catholic Europe, of the
Mediterranean, of peasant life, all of which and more may be considered
to mark him?' (Glazer 2000, p. 223).

Second, some authors contend that culturalist explanations of ethnic
mobilization tend to be tautological. The culturalist perspective considers ethnic identity to be determined by culture, but suggests at the same
time that the individuals of a group have a common culture *because* of
their common ethnic identity. Obviously, such reasoning leads to circular
explanations of ethnic mobilization.

Another criticism argues that culturalist descriptions fail to appreciate the role of agency. By excluding the role of agency, these theories manifestly fail to account for the fact that individuals and groups can change both their culture and their ethnic identity, consciously or unconsciously, or that their ethnic identity can assume a different meaning over time, dependent on the political circumstances. This criticism points, for example, to cases where there is empirical evidence that clearly shows that leadership and strategy have exerted a great deal of influence on ethnic bonding and ethnic movement patterns (Ireland 2000, p. 270).

16.3.2   Reactive Ethnicity

The 'reactive ethnicity' approach considers the rise of ethnic mobilization as a process prompted by the unequal division of resources along ethnic lines. The term itself is strongly associated with the work of Michael Hechter on politics in the Celtic fringe of the British Isles in the early 1970s (Hechter 1975). In Hechter's, formulation, reactive ethnicity means that ethno-regional loyalties and conflict within a state may be strengthened as a result of increasing levels of economic inequalities between the core and the ethnically distinct periphery. Although Hechter applied this approach specifically to offer an explanation for territorially based ethnic identities in a particular region, similar theoretical perspectives were applied to explain other instances of ethnic mobilization that have clearly been less connected to the core–periphery distinction. A prominent example of this line of reasoning was Bonacich's 'split labor market theory' (Bonacich 1972), which holds that ethnic antagonism is generated by the competition arising from a differential price of labour for the same occupation. Ethnic mobilization in this version is dependent on the economic competition between ethnically differentiated segments of the working class. Theories that could be considered as similar to the 'reactive ethnicity' approach have also been applied to explain revolts in American ghettos (Blauner 1969) and more recently to explain ethnic mobilization patterns among immigrant minorities in Western Europe (Drury 1994, p. 16).

This theoretical approach, too, has met with a number of criticisms. First of all, economic disadvantage is clearly not a *sufficient* condition for the occurrence of ethnic mobilization. It is not that difficult to find examples of economically disadvantaged ethnic groups that do not engage in politics or protest. The level of mobilization does not seem to be dependent on the level of disadvantage. Conversely, if ethnic mobilization occurs, it is not necessarily accompanied by economic disadvantage. Some scholars, for example, have pointed to the resurgence of ethnic solidarities in regions that are economically advantaged relative to other areas in the state (Coughlan and Samarasinghe 1991, p. 4). Furthermore, social movement scholars have argued that there is little or no relationship between variations of relative deprivation and the pace and timing of collective protest (Piven and Cloward 1995).

In response, a number of social movement scholars have instead focused on the resources that movement organizations and movement entrepreneurs need in order to be able to engage in political action, including ethnic action; their approach has become known as 'resource mobilization theory'. Resources such as money, expertise, access to networks and people permit social actors to take strategic decisions with the purpose of mobilizing for social and political change. Taking social movement actors as rational actors has provided an important inspiration for theorists on ethnic mobilization focusing on the role of leaders. This is what I call the 'ethnic competition' perspective.

16.3.3   Ethnic Competition

According to the competition model, society revolves around a struggle for scarce resources. It argues that it is not economic deprivation itself, or at least not alone, that gets people to mobilize. On the contrary, economic advancement of previously disadvantaged groups can result in an escalation of inter-group conflict. According to this view, the mere fact that groups can compete for the same resources as a result of their economic advancement may contribute to conflict. This competition will be greater when the inequalities increase both on the elite and the mass level (see, for example, Langer 2005). In addition, some proponents of the competition perspective emphasize 'the entrepreneurial role in ethnic politics: how the mobilization of ethnic groups in collective action is effected by leaders who pursue a political enterprise' (Barth 1994, p. 12). Within this perspective, emphasis is placed on the ability of elite political entrepreneurs to respond to economic and political circumstances. This perspective usually does not pay much attention to mass beliefs in common origin or mass culture, but instead it claims that the idea of an ethnic group refers sociologically to an overlap between patterns of (positive or negative) recognition of ethnicity and of resource allocation (in the broadest sense, of which economic resources are simply one important instance) along those officially recognized ethnic lines (Crowley 2001, p. 102).

In contrast to most culturalist and reactive ethnicity approaches, the competition perspective usually regards ethnic group identity not so much as a pre-existing fact as a phenomenon that arises, or at least gains new meaning, during the process of ethnic competition. In order to defend material interests, self-proclaimed group leaders invoke an ethnic group identity or apply new meaning and interest-based connotations to existing ethnic terms. In this way identity and interests are mutually reinforced.

In this perspective the existence of an ethnic group is thus not a given. It is the result of the act of making one label more prominent and more relevant as a frame for identification and affiliation. The making of an ethnic group is something that is actively pursued (through discrimination or through emancipation) not by the abstract collective of a pre-existing group itself, but by particular actors, including organizations and individual ethno-political activists. Somewhat more provocatively formulated, one could say that this perspective argues that ethnic activists or ethno-political entrepreneurs 'produce' ethnic groups, not the other way around.

According to Daniel Bell, ethnicity in the competition perspective 'is best understood not as a primordial phenomenon in which deeply held identities have to re-emerge, but as a strategic choice by individuals who, in other circumstances, would choose other group memberships as a means of gaining some power and privilege' (Bell 1975, p. 171). The assumption here is that politics is not an automatic reflection of ethnic divisions; on the contrary, ethnic divisions are invoked through a political struggle against situations of marginalization and inequality. For example, certain leaders may find it useful to organize a group around a common ethnic identity when they sense that this group has been placed in a specific position in the workplace, experiences a common form of discrimination, or suffers from income inequality. Other authors approaching ethnicity from this perspective have emphasized that it is not only the economic position that contributes to the construction of certain patterns of ethnic minority mobilization, but also the differential distribution of *political* power (Oberschall 2000, p. 983).

The competition perspective has been inspired by what has been called an 'instrumentalist critique of primordialism'. Instrumentalists disagree with the assumption held in primordialist (and culturalist) accounts that ethnicity is strongly determined by common ancestry and traditions. Instrumentalism has directed attention towards ethnicity as a calculation of social, economic and political profits carried out by political elites. Joane Nagel, for example, has argued that the occurrence of ethnic minority mobilization is the result of individuals engaging 'in continuous assessment of situation and audience, emphasizing or deemphasizing particular dimensions of ethnicity according to some measure of utility or feasibility' (Nagel 1996, p. 23). Some theorists have contended that ethnic identity directly evolves out of elite competition (Brass 1991).

One of the important points of reference in this literature is the work by social anthropologist Fredrik Barth. Although the element of political competition was only implicit in his most influential work – written in

1969 – on ethnic groups and boundaries, by 1994 Barth was contending that political factors deserve more attention. He suggested that the creation of ethnicity should not be seen as taking place only on the interpersonal level but that it is also dependent on collective action (Barth calls this the 'median level'). The importance of Barth's view for students of political relations was primarily that it cleared a way for studying the role of elites and their strategic action in the construction of ethnic boundaries. In other words, the interactional element introduced by Barth's 1969 article was taken a step further and brought into the scope of theories of political competition. The competition model is discernible in the writings of a number of political scientists, including Paul Brass (1991), Abner Cohen (1996) and Michael Hechter (1975). In different ways they have all adopted a more or less explicit instrumentalist view of ethnic identity formation, offering a great deal of attention to the role of elites who engage in struggle for political power, maximization of preferences and rational choice. A number of these authors have also devoted attention to the circumstances that constrain the making of strategic decisions. Also Barth himself had become increasingly aware of this; in 1994 he argued that the state should be taken into consideration as an important factor determining mobilization patterns (Barth 1994, p. 19). Consequently, several other researchers have begun to draw attention specifically to the fact that ethnic identities appear to be dependent on ethnic classifications promoted by political elites and the state.

16.3.4 Political Process Approaches to Ethnic Mobilization: Opportunity Structures and Framing

The 'political process' perspective seeks to fuse attention to competition with attention to a socially structured context. Like the competition perspective, the political process perspective regards a number of organizational aspects as key: the activities of those who present themselves as leaders of ethnic minorities, their resources, their ability to make public claims in the name of the minority, and their attempts to garner mass support. But the political process perspective directs attention to two additional elements: 'political opportunity structure' and 'framing'. The inspiration has been drawn from the literature on social movements, which argues that collective action is more than just the result of strategic and instrumental rationality (Cohen and Arato 1995, p. 510). It is important to recognize, this literature argues, that social movements evolve around the articulation of identity and the awareness of the influence of power relations on the creation of identity.

Divisions in society are not simply reflected in politics, nor are they merely the result of strategic action. Divisions are constructed through politics within the context of dominant perceptions in society. In contrast to the culturalist and the competition perspectives, the political process perspective on ethnic mobilization argues that there is a two-way relationship between political action and interests. Interests are not just 'out there', waiting for ethnic leaders to organize around, but are shaped by the institutional environment and the dominant discursive context.

While the competition perspective focuses on resource competition as the most important factor influencing patterns of ethnic mobilization, the political process perspective attaches crucial importance to the institutional environment (the political opportunity structure) and the symbolic and discursive dimensions of mobilization (framing processes) – both fields of influence that have been taken into account in the comparative analysis of social movements (McAdam et al. 1996). This approach sets ethnic identity against the broader picture of social movements utilizing identity as a basis for mobilization in search of access to political power, material resources, and the control of representation. Let me, in turn, discuss the concepts of 'political opportunity structure' and 'framing'.

The 'political opportunity structure' (often abbreviated as POS) is the complex compound of formal and informal political conditions into which a movement, including an ethnic one, must enter when it becomes active (ibid.; Tarrow 1994). It includes what can be regarded as the stable properties of the institutional environment, such as the state's propensity to repression or the openness of the institutionalized system (in the case of ethnic movements, the official recognition of ethnic groups or the existence of special channels for ethnic representation). It also includes less stable factors such as the presence or absence of elite allies, or the shifts in political alliances (in the case of ethnic movements, for example, the political position of other identity groups).

According to a brief definition offered by Sidney Tarrow, the POS comprises 'consistent – but not necessarily formal or permanent – dimensions of the political environment that provide incentives for people to undertake collective action by affecting their expectations for success or failure' (Tarrow 1994, p. 18). A frequently used way of conceptualizing the POS is offered by Hanspeter Kriesi and Marco Giugni (1995, pp. xiii–xvi). These authors have argued that the POS is made up of four components:

- national cleavage structures (the established political conflicts in a country, which arguably impose important constraints on newly emerging movements);
- formal institutional structures (institutional make-up of the stable

elements of the political system, such as parliament, public administration, or other more direct democratic procedures);
- prevailing informal strategies in dealing with social movements
(strategies members of the political system typically employ to deal
with social movements); and
- alliance structure (cyclical elements of change in the political system
such as the availability of influential allies or the shifts in ruling
alignments).

POS perspectives have mainly been developed in the context of the study
of social movements. In the structural–functionalist approaches from the
1950s and 1960s (think of the work of Arthur William Kornhauser 1959, or
Neil Smelser 1963) any social action was regarded as an uncalculated and
irrational by product of a large-scale social transformation (della Porta
and Diani 1999, p. 7). Resource mobilization criticized this perspective
(Oberschall 1973; Zald and Ash 1966), as it did other collective behaviour
perspectives that conceived social movements as collective responses to
a changing environment. The resource mobilization approach construed
collective movements as forms of political behaviour driven by actors who
calculate the costs and benefits of their collective action in relation to the
limited material or non-material resources available. Social movements
were thus no longer seen as simply reactive or grievance-based collective
phenomena, but as conscious efforts by professionally organized actors,
making rational choices within the political system (della Porta and Diani
1999, p. 9). Resource mobilization approaches in turn were criticized for
ignoring the structural context of contentious politics. The political and
institutional environment, and particularly the relation between institutional political actors and social protest, was the main concern of those
who became known as the 'political process' theorists (ibid., p. 9). Key to
their line of argumentation was that particular characteristics of the external environment, especially the openness or closure of the political system,
were relevant to the development of social movements (Eisinger 1973).

For authors such as Doug McAdam (1982) and Sidney Tarrow (1983),
POS referred to both the general receptivity of a given political system to
the collective contention by social challengers and the formal access points
they have to the institutions of the political system (McAdam 1996). In
the 'new social movements' tradition researchers applied the POS concept
mostly in comparative research designs, trying to account for the cross-
national differences in the appearance and organizational form of comparable movements on the basis of the properties of the national political
systems in which they are embedded.

The POS perspective provides an important point of support for studying the formation of ethnic mobilization. Scholars writing about ethnic minority mobilization within this perspective have been attentive to the properties of the political context that facilitate or constrain the formation of a certain movement identity. Moreover, the theory is compelling because it responds to an intuitive feeling that social movements will act in accord with the institutional opportunities and constraints with which they are confronted in a given political system. Such an idea is also related to what James March and Johan Olsen have labelled 'the logic of appropriateness' (March and Olsen 1989). This is the logic according to which the strategies and preferences of actors are determined and created by institutions. 'Institutions create or socially construct the actors' identities, belongings, definitions of reality and shared meanings' (Rothstein 2000, p. 147).

Interestingly, the POS perspective has served as a primary source of inspiration for an emerging research tradition among scholars who have attempted to understand the political mobilization of immigrant minorities in established Western European democracies (Martiniello and Statham 1999). The argument held in common by these researchers is that the shape of the institutional political context is a key variable influencing and fostering the ethnic mobilization of minorities.

However, we should be aware that the current studies that have applied POS theory as a point of departure for empirical research have not remained entirely without problems. Hassan Bousetta has shown that formal and informal organizational processes that take place *inside* an ethnic movement and give rise to certain strategic choices (a field which he calls 'infra-politics') are often left out of sight when exclusive use of the POS perspective is employed (Boussetta 2001, pp. 19–20). In other words, the internal organizational processes should be considered an integral part of the political mobilization of ethnic minorities, but remain hidden when importance is attached only to the 'institutionalized' processes. Struggles surrounding strategic choices or questions of representation and group boundaries may take place between actors within the organizational realm of an ethnic movement. These may have a certain impact on how a movement will develop and will need to be conceptualized as an area of research.

Furthermore, POS studies have also been criticized for overemphasizing the institutional political context as a causal variable and de-emphasizing other factors that may have contributed to the formation of opportunities. It must be realized that opportunities and constraints are not simply given. They have to be perceived as opportunities first before they will be able to function as such (Jenson 1998).

Many authors on social movements agree that these problems can to some extent be avoided when the POS perspective is integrated with insights that have been developed in the 'framing' literature (McAdam et al. 1996). In various types of research the term 'frame' has been used to denote, in its most general sense, a schema of interpretation. The verb 'to frame' refers then to a process through which meaning is reproduced in society. Most studies in social science that use the concept of framing offer a definition derived from the writings of Erving Goffman, in particular his book *Frame Analysis* (Goffman 1975). Goffman used the designation 'primary framework' to refer to what he called a 'conceptual structure' that organizes interpretation. The concept became an important source of inspiration for scholars interested in the development of social movements (McAdam et al. 1996). These scholars shifted the focus away from frames as pure cognition and started to concentrate on the power of deliberate framing within the organizational and collective processes that are part of mobilization (Johnston 1995, p. 217). For them, frames not only perform an interpretative function, as suggested by Goffman. They are also 'made' by movement leaders with the specific intention 'to mobilize potential adherents and constituents, to garner bystander support, and to demobilize antagonists' (Snow and Benford 1998, p. 198).

Social movement scholars in general have been interested in framing when understood as the way in which movement actors disseminate their understanding of social reality in order to appeal to a constituency. Different authors have often highlighted different aspects of the framing process, some emphasizing the individual control over framing processes. On this view, research has to focus on the ability of activists to actively assign meaning to social reality, promote a certain understanding of reality, and intentionally choose a frame for mobilization. They define framing as 'the conscious strategic efforts by groups of people to fashion a shared understanding of the world and of themselves that legitimate and motivate collective action' (McAdam 1996, p. 6). Others, however, have emphasized that the process of framing does not take place in a vacuum (Benford and Snow 2000, p. 628). For them, research should not discard the fact that framing is always negotiated and is to a certain degree shaped by the complex, multi-organizational, multi-institutional arenas in which it takes place. These authors have stressed that frame diffusion (how frames spread) and frame resonance (how frames become effective) is affected by the cultural and political environment. In this way, Robert D. Benford and David A. Snow have defined framing as the generation and diffusion by movement actors of mobilizing and countermobilizing ideas and meanings, a process which is facilitated or constrained by the cultural and political context, including the framing/counterframings of the elites in power (Benford and Snow 2000). Defined as such, the concept of 'framing' creates an opportunity to examine both the element of *choice* in the construction of ethnic identity (the use of intentional frames) and the element of *designation* (the presence of countermobilizing frames or the (in)ability of a frame to resonate in a given context).

The concept of framing has offered a useful contribution to the study of ethnic mobilization. With regard to movement identity, it can be said that such an identity is created through framing. Constituencies do not exist until they are defined through an identity frame (Jenson 1998, p. 5). Identity frames are central to the process of ethnic minority mobilization, but it is likely that also other related frames will be employed during this process. Indeed, it is the contention of social movement scholars such as Benford and Snow that different types of framing processes help to shape a social movement and its outcome. In their view, any movement has a number of core framing tasks: 'diagnostic framing' (problem identification and attribution), 'prognostic framing' (perspectives on how to remedy a certain problem), and 'motivational framing' (providing a rationale for action) (Benford and Snow 2000).

16.4   DIFFERENT OUTCOMES: WHAT EXPLAINS THE RADICALIZATION OF ETHNIC CLAIMS?

Why do some forms of ethnic mobilization lead to radicalization and conflict, while others remain moderate and stay within the confines of the existing states system? Different theories have been formulated to explain the widely different outcomes of ethnic mobilization. One theoretical approach argues that the democratic state has an overwhelming responsibility in the creation of ethnic conflict. Michael Mann, for example, argues that murderous 'ethnic cleansing is a hazard of the age of democracy since amid multiethnicity the ideal of rule by the people began to entwine the *demos* with the dominant *ethnos*, generating organic conceptions of the nation and the state that encourage the cleansing of minorities' (Mann 2005, p. 3) His theory is based on a historical survey of democratizing states throughout the twentieth century. The work of Paul Collier (2009) seems to offer contemporary evidence for that same idea. On the basis of an analysis of contemporary civil wars, Collier argues that the spread of elections and peace settlements in the world's most dangerous countries may not lead to lasting peace but rather to more conflict, *if* the wrong features of democracy are promoted. More in particular, democracy introduces the concepts of 'minority' and 'majority', and without the proper checks and balances and methods of representation such division may soon instil resentment among majorities as well as minorities. When these majorities and minorities are defined on the basis of ethnic characteristics, an ethnic war may easily ensue. In his research on ethnic rioting in India, Ashutosh Varshney (2003) finds that democratic attitudes – more in particular, engagement in civic life – are an effective prevention mechanism against ethnic conflict. Thus, while democracy as an institutional system may create ethnic violence, fostering democratic attitudes may be an adequate way to avoid such violence. In his work, Varshney shows that networks of civic engagement (in the form of integrated business organizations, trade unions, political parties and professional associations) that function across community boundaries – in his case they bring Hindu and Muslim urban communities together – are a key factor in controlling outbreaks of ethnic conflict.

While the sudden introduction of a democratic system in countries where there is no tradition of democratic values might be one element stimulating ethnic conflict, the expanding literature on the topic brings a broad range of other factors into view. Most authors currently start from the assumption that there is no single factor responsible for tipping the balance towards violence. They look for interactions between various sets of factors such as the institutional context, the political climate and the specific traits and interests of the political players involved. Karl Cordell and Stefan Wolff, for example, have developed an analytical framework that attaches key importance to the interplay between three sets of factors, which they call 'motives', 'means' and 'opportunities' (Cordell and Wolff 2010, p. 44). If these three sets of factors, of which two are actor related (means and motives) and one is rather more a matter of context, are present then the chances for ethnic conflict rise.

Theoretical writing about ethnic conflict can indeed fruitfully be analysed with the help of this framework. Yet through such an analysis it will become clear that some researchers tend to emphasize actor-related factors while others tend to stick to their belief in the key impact of environment-related factors. Of those who continue to emphasize context, for example, there are some who have argued that ethnic claims are more likely to radicalize when a power vacuum exists or when an ethnically defined population fears that it will be exploited. Others have put more responsibility in the hands of elites. Elite competition theories, for example, look at the motives of powerholders and ethnic leaders who build on existing ethnic loyalties to mobilize political support for violence. These theories argue that variation is caused by shifting motives among the mobilizing elites. Rational choice approaches build on such analysis. Erin Jenne (2007), for example, who researched the matter in the European context (she investigated and compared different episodes of ethnic mobilization across a range of cases in Central and Southeastern Europe), argues that we need a theory that explains variation in ethnic mobilization outcomes by considering these outcomes as results of bargaining processes between actors. Her 'ethnic bargaining model' attaches crucial importance to the bargaining between putative minority representatives, state institutions and external lobbies (that is, any other state, organization, or private interest that lobbies directly on behalf of the minority). By examining how these actors are linked to each other in a bargaining game, one should be able to predict more precisely when and why ethnic minority mobilizers will radicalize their claims.

One may conclude that while there is growing consensus about the hypothesis that not one but *various* interacting factors are responsible for turning ethnic mobilization into violent ethnic conflict, there is no consensus yet on which elements to include in a definite list of factors. More empirical research will no doubt be needed before social scientists will come to such a list. On the other hand, a critical note with regard to the attempt of making such a list might be in order. When attempting to analyse the emergence of ethnic conflict it is important to keep in mind that 'ethnic conflict' is a diverse phenomenon. As Rogers Brubaker and David Laitin have argued already in 1998: instances of ethnic violence are 'composite and causally heterogeneous, consisting not of an assemblage of causally identical unit instances of ethnic violence but of a number of different types of actions, processes, occurrences, and events' (Brubaker and Laitin 1998, p. 446). Therefore, so Brubaker and Laitin argue, we need to see the existing variety within what we all too often casually call 'ethnic conflict'. Such a plea for disaggregation has lost nothing of its validity in current times. Before we engage in a further debate about the factors that might explain ethnic conflict, it is important that we gain a better and more nuanced understanding of what it is exactly that we seek to explain.

17 Transitions from war to peace
Caroline A. Hartzell

17.1 INTRODUCTION

El Salvador, the site of a civil war from 1979 to 1992, has not experienced any recurrence of fighting since the end of that conflict. The country has become more democratic in the ensuing years, recently electing a member of the Farabundo Martí National Liberation Front, the former mass-based guerrilla group's political party, to the presidency, and its economy has registered steady economic growth following a period of post-war recovery. El Salvador's transition from war to peace can be contrasted with that of Chad. Six civil wars have been fought in Chad since that country's independence in 1960. Although opposition parties were legalized following the end of one of Chad's armed conflicts, the last set of presidential elections was boycotted by the opposition. The country, which is plagued by corruption, has consistently been ranked as one of the poorest in the world.

How much do we know about why some countries, such as El Salvador, have been able to make the transition from war to peace while others, like Chad, struggle with serial civil wars? An overview of the growing literature on civil war termination indicates that although scholars have identified some factors that can facilitate the shift from war to peace – for example, the presence of peacekeeping forces – there is much we still must learn in order to be able to provide useful advice to countries emerging from civil war. In particular there is a need to revisit what has been the central argument of theories regarding the ability of countries successfully to move from war to peace – that is, that the means by which a country ends its civil war plays a central role in determining whether the peace will prove stable or war will recur. If, as evidence now suggests, these outcomes do not have the type of impact on the peace they traditionally have been thought to exercise, researchers will need to develop new models to help us understand why some countries are more readily able to build peace after civil war than are others.

This chapter assesses the state of current knowledge regarding transitions from war to peace following intra-state conflicts. I begin by discussing what we thought we knew, evaluating long-held claims regarding the relationship between civil war outcomes and the stability of the peace (Section 17.2). I next review what we know about the factors that facilitate or impede the transition from civil war to a civil peace (Section 17.3). I conclude with some thoughts on what we need to learn (Section 17.4) focusing on two themes: what we mean by the peace, the ability of the international community to promote different versions of the peace, and the content of the peace or the types of civil war settlements adversaries construct to end civil wars.

17.2 WHAT WE THOUGHT WE KNEW: CIVIL WAR OUTCOMES AND THE STABILITY OF THE PEACE

One of the longest-held tenets in research on transitions from civil war to peace is that the outcomes of intra-state conflicts play a central role in determining whether or not countries will experience a durable peace. I review this claim below, taking note of changing trends in civil war outcomes and the inconclusive results that have been produced by efforts to test this claim.

17.2.1 Trends in Civil War Outcomes

Civil wars have ended in a number of different ways during the post-Second World War period. The most common means by which these conflicts have been terminated is military victory. Fifty-five (51 per cent) of the 108 civil wars that were fought and ended, at least for some period of time, between 1945 and 1999 were concluded with one party claiming victory and the other(s) admitting defeat. Negotiated agreements ended 38 civil wars (35 per cent) after the representatives of opposing factions met to discuss and agree to the terms on which they would terminate the fighting. Eleven civil wars (10 per cent) were concluded following negotiated truces, an outcome which saw adversaries focus on the modalities of stopping the fighting in the short term while delaying an ultimate resolution of war-related issues. Four civil wars (4 per cent) ended with the imposition of a peace by third parties acting either on their own or in conjunction with one of the sets of combatants (Hartzell and Hoddie 2007). Finally, some civil wars peter out for a while, with the number of deaths in the conflict falling below civil war thresholds, only to flare back up at a later point in time.

Table 17.1 highlights trends in the means by which civil wars were ended during the 1945–99 period. During the Cold War period the majority of intra-state conflicts (69 per cent) were terminated via military victory. The first post-Cold War decade saw a major change in the way civil wars

Table 17.1   Trends in civil war termination, 1945–1999

Termination type	1940s	1950s	1960s	1970s	1980s	1990s
Military victory	5	11	8	13	8	10
	(62.5%)	(79%)	(80%)	(65%)	(62%)	(23%)
Negotiated agreement	2	3	1	6	3	23
	(25%)	(21%)	(10%)	(30%)	(23%)	(54%)
Negotiated truces	0	0	0	0	1	10
					(8%)	(23%)
Peace negotiated with or imposed by third parties	1	0	1	1	1	
	(12.5%)		(10%)	(5%)	(8%)	

Source: Data from Hartzell and Hoddie (2007).

were ended, with 54 per cent of the conflicts concluded through negotiated agreements and another 23 per cent through negotiated truces. Employing somewhat different datasets, both Fortna (2009) and Toft (2010) identify the same trends in civil war termination for the Cold War and post-Cold War eras. This trend in civil war outcomes has become even more pronounced during the first decade of the twenty-first century with negotiated agreements stopping the fighting in 12 of the 16 civil wars ending between 2000 and 2007.[1]

17.2.2   Claims Regarding the Effects Civil War Outcomes Have on the Peace

The means by which civil wars end has been the focus of an ongoing debate among scholars who believe that these outcomes play an important role in the process of securing a durable peace.[2] At the heart of this debate is the argument that war, once initiated, will only end when adversaries arrive at a bargain they prefer to continuing to fight and that peace will last only as long as the groups remain committed to the new bargain (Fearon 1995, 1998; Reiter 2003). Parties will stick to their bargains, and the peace will endure, as long as rival groups have convergent expectations regarding the outcome of a future hypothetical war. As a number of scholars have

---

[1]   Identification of trend based on author's data. Although he uses a lower battle-death threshold to identify civil wars, Mack (2008) also finds that a growing percentage of intrastate conflicts have been ended via negotiated agreements.

[2]   This section draws on Hartzell (2009b).

pointed out, however, agreements are not likely to be adhered to, and war will become more likely, if these expectations change (Wagner 1993; Werner and Yuen 2005). Based on this explanation of civil war recurrence, the challenge for those who seek to foster an enduring peace is to find the best means to reduce uncertainty and to stabilize expectations among the parties to the conflict.

What is the best method for accomplishing this? According to one group of scholars, it is to end civil wars via military victory (Licklider 1995; Luttwak 1999; Wagner 1993; Walter 1997). The claim in this case is that the victors of civil wars use their superior strength to destroy or dismantle the organizations of their adversaries, thereby checking future armed challenges to their power. By leaving the defeated parties with little doubt regarding the outcome of future military encounters, military victories increase the likelihood that the losers will stick to the bargain they agreed to at the war's end. According to this school of thought, in the absence of the information that the defeat and destruction of rival factions' organizations is thought to produce, groups' expectations regarding the possibility of winning a future war and thus securing a better deal for themselves may change, thereby encouraging a return to war. It is for this reason that the post-Cold War trend of ending civil wars via negotiated agreements is of concern to scholars who believe that it may be followed by a wave of renewed intra-state conflicts initiated by factions seeking new and better bargains for themselves.

Other scholars have argued that, if properly constructed, negotiated agreements can serve to secure the peace. This school of thought posits that negotiated agreements can also be used to secure the peace, not that they are the *only* means of doing so. Agreements that provide rival groups with a means of checking one another's actions and that include provisions that raise the costs to the groups of returning to war can serve to stabilize expectations and reduce uncertainty (Hartzell and Hoddie 2007; Mattes and Savun 2000). Particularly useful in this respect is the inclusion in agreements of power-sharing measures, provisions that call for the distribution of political, military, territorial, and/or economic power among contending groups. Agreements by adversaries to share power can prolong the peace, according to this school of thought, by providing rivals with a stake in the future in the form of access to state power. Power-sharing bargains can also alter rivals' preferences in a manner that makes for a stable peace. Finally, because power-sharing provisions such as those that mandate the integration of rivals' troops into the state's military make it more difficult for adversaries to return to armed conflict, opposing factions that implement these measures should be more likely to abide by the terms of the bargain they agree to at the war's end.

Which of these sets of arguments does the evidence best support? Tests of the effects military victories and negotiated agreements have on the stability of the peace following civil war have produced a variety of different results. Licklider (1995) finds support for the argument that military victories yield long periods of peace while negotiated settlements are more apt to be followed by recurring war. Doyle and Sambanis (2006) find that ending wars via treaties or negotiated agreements makes for a more durable peace while ending wars via military victory has no significant effect on the peace. Walter (2004) fails to identify either type of war outcome as having a significant effect on the duration of the peace. Toft (2010) finds that military victories by rebel groups (but not by the government) produce more durable settlements of civil war while negotiated agreements are more apt to be followed by renewed civil war. Quinn et al. (2007) conclude that both rebel victories and negotiated agreements supported by peacekeeping forces serve to stabilize the peace. Finally, Fortna (2008a) and Hartzell (2009b) find that both military victories and negotiated settlements can produce a durable peace.

What can one conclude about the relationship between civil war outcomes and the duration of the peace given these results? None of these results can be considered conclusive because none of the studies directly tests the effects that the two different types of civil war outcomes are hypothesized to have on the stability of the peace. Scholars have assumed, for example, that military victories result in the destruction of the losers' organizational structures while negotiated agreements preserve them. In the absence of data on the fate of factions at the end of civil wars it has been difficult to know whether this is a reasonable assumption. Scholars have also assumed that power-sharing measures are associated only with negotiated settlements of civil wars. Lacking data on whether offers to share power have been made following military victories it has been difficult to assess the stabilizing effects of these measures. In short, even in those instances in which an association was found between military victories and/or negotiated agreements and the duration of the peace, we cannot be certain why the type of outcome had the effect it did on the peace.

A new dataset on power-sharing measures and the fate of factions following all civil wars fought and ended at some point between 1945 and 1999 sheds some light on these issues. Among other things, the data indicate that military victories do not consistently give rise to the destruction of rival groups' organizational structures at the end of civil wars. In fact, nearly 42 per cent of all wars that end via military victory see the preservation of the organizational structures of factions other than that of the victor. In addition, fully one-fifth of the wars that end in negotiated agreements see the destruction of the organizational structures of all but the winning faction. Interesting details regarding power-sharing measures also emerge from the data. These indicate that provisions for power sharing have been agreed to following some military victories and negotiated agreements sometimes include very limited or no measures for sharing power (Hartzell 2009b).

Tests of the impact civil war outcomes have on the stability of the peace when one controls for the fate of factions and power-sharing measures yield some interesting results. First, the destruction of rival factions' organizational structures is found not to have any significant effect on the duration of the peace. Second, the inclusion of power-sharing measures in a war-ending agreement is associated with a longer-lived peace. Finally, both military victories and negotiated settlements are found to lower the likelihood that peace will fail (ibid.).

The foregoing results suggest two avenues for further research regarding the relationship between the means by which wars are ended and the ability of countries to establish a stable peace. One is to think theoretically about other features of war outcomes that have a stabilizing influence on the peace. Since both military victories and negotiated agreements have a positive impact on the duration of the peace, it may be that they share some common, as yet undiscovered, characteristics that produce this effect. An alternative path scholars should consider focusing on is to look not at war outcomes but on the effect civil war settlements have on the peace. I return to this issue later in this chapter. First, however, I review what we have learned about the impact a number of factors have on the transition from war to peace.

17.3   WHAT WE KNOW: FACTORS THAT IMPACT ON THE TRANSITION FROM WAR TO PEACE

Studies indicate that a handful of factors appear to have an effect – in some cases positive and in other cases negative – on the likelihood that countries will successfully make the transition from war to peace. Given differences in the datasets and methodologies researchers employ, the fact that these factors have been found to exercise an effect on the peace across a number of studies speaks to their significance. For the sake of convenience, I divide these factors into three categories:

'inherited risk factors' (Bigombe et al. 2000), characteristics of previous conflicts, and the presence of peacekeepers. I address each of these below.

17.3.1   Inherited Risk Factors[3]

Countries with low levels of economic development have been found to be particularly vulnerable to lapsing back into armed conflict (Collier et al. 2003; Doyle and Sambanis 2006; Hartzell 2009b; Quinn et al. 2007; Walter 2004). One explanation that has been offered for this relationship is that the cost of recruiting people to fight is very low in poverty-stricken societies. Finding themselves with few economic options, individuals are believed to be more willing to join rebel forces. In light of the negative economic effects that civil war has on a country's economy, individuals may be faced with even more stark choices regarding strategies for survival in the aftermath of such a conflict. Low levels of economic development have also been hypothesized to be a proxy for state weakness (Fearon and Laitin 2003). In this instance, states, weakened by civil war, are thought to be at a higher risk for renewed conflict because of their inability to exercise control effectively over their territory, including contending with any remaining pockets of armed resistance.

Rates of post-conflict economic growth have also been found to have an impact on countries' ability to make a successful transition to peace (Collier et al. 2003). Countries with higher rates of post-conflict economic growth should see a lower risk of conflict to the extent that that growth provides economic opportunities for the population. Economic growth that is achieved through policies that seek to promote social inclusion – for example, government spending on education and healthcare – has been found to play a particularly important role in stabilizing the peace after war (Collier and Hoeffler 2004a). By prioritizing inclusive social policies following a civil war, governments are thought to signal their commitment to the peace. In addition to proving reassuring to former rebel groups, such a move may encourage foreign investors to invest domestically with positive effects on the economic growth rate and thus on the peace.

---

[3]   Although a number of additional risk factors, such as the extent of natural resource rents and factors related to ethnicity have been identified in the literature, I do not discuss them here because of the contradictory results produced by studies that have employed these measures. See Section 17.2 for extensive discussion of these various factors.

17.3.2 Characteristics of Previous Conflicts[4]

Attributes of civil wars have been found to have an impact on the likelihood that a country will make a successful transition to an enduring peace. One such feature is the duration of a civil war. Numerous studies have found that lengthy civil wars lower the likelihood that armed conflict will recur (Doyle and Sambanis 2000; Fortna 2008a; Quinn et al. 2007; Walter 2004). Long civil wars are thought to have this effect by providing parties to the conflict with an extended opportunity to gather information concerning their chances for victory (Mason et al. 1999). Wars that drag on for many years are believed to produce a sense of pessimism among belligerents regarding their potential for winning a future conflict. This has the effect of encouraging them to stick to the peace once a war ends.

The intensity of a civil war, or the number of deaths produced by the violence, also has been found to have an impact on the duration of the peace (Fortna 2008a; Hartzell 2009b; Mukherjee 2006; Quinn et al. 2007). In this instance, more intense civil wars make it more likely that countries will slip back into armed civil conflict. Wars characterized by high casualty rates are thought to foster low levels of trust among actors and a desire for retribution once the conflict ends. These factors make it less likely that former opponents will be able to cooperate to manage conflict in the post-war state. High levels of war deaths also lower a society's stock of human and social capital, making it more difficult to recover economically from the war (Doyle and Sambanis 2000). Together, these factors erode antagonists' commitment to the newly established peace.

17.3.3 Presence of Peacekeepers

The deployment of peacekeeping forces in the aftermath of civil wars has been found to be helpful in facilitating countries' transition from civil war to peace. Peacekeeping missions, which have been led by the United Nations, regional organizations, and ad hoc groups of states, have been found significantly to reduce the risk that civil war will resume. Peacekeepers are thought to have this effect by altering parties' incentives to engage in conflict, by providing adversaries with reliable information regarding each other's intentions, and by helping to prevent and/or cope

---

[4] A number of scholars have focused on the effects whether or not a previous conflict was fought over identity issues – that is, issues pertaining to ethnicity, race, religion and/or language – have on the stability of the peace. I do not focus on this characteristic here because a clear consensus has yet to emerge on the significance of this factor to the transition from war to peace.

with accidental violations of the peace (Fortna 2008a). Although peace-keeping forces at times fail to keep the peace following civil war, this may well reflect the fact that these missions tend to be deployed to some of the most challenging cases of civil war (Bigombe et al. 2000; Fortna 2008a).

17.4   WHAT WE NEED TO LEARN

There is, of course, a great deal we still need to learn about transitions from war to peace. Rather than construct an exhaustive list of all of these topics, I concentrate here on two factors that I believe should be at the top of any agenda for future research and action on this issue.

17.4.1   What We Mean by 'Peace' and the International Community's Capacity to Promote Different Versions of the Peace

Thus far I have focused on the current state of knowledge regarding transitions from civil war to a durable peace. Although the stability of the peace is clearly important, it is not the only component of the peace that post-conflict societies and other actors care about. Other relevant issues include personal security and a respect for human rights, democracy, and economic development and the provision of public goods.

Can all of these elements of a post-civil war peace be advanced at the same time with some real degree of success? Should they be sequenced in some particular fashion (Lake 2010)? What if there are trade-offs involved among some of these peace-related goals? If that is found to be the case, which definition of the peace should be given prevalence – one that emphasizes stability, democracy, or development? What version of the peace do the leaders and populations of post-conflict countries support? Despite a lack of answers to such questions, international actors have sought to promote a variety of these goals as part of a model of post-conflict reconstruction. How well has the international community fared in its efforts to implement a multi-faceted version of the peace? Not well, according to one analyst who notes that this 'is due both to the enormous difficulty of the undertaking and to the fact that in most countries the international community lacks the political will to really try' (Ottaway 2003, p. 315)

This dilemma highlights the need for the international community to come to some agreement regarding what it means by peace. This decision should be based, in no small measure, on an evaluation of the ability of international actors to help promote transitions to different versions of the peace. Although, as I noted above, we know something about the factors that have an impact on the stability of the peace, we know much less about what is involved in establishing a wider-ranging 'participatory peace' (Doyle and Sambanis 2006). Topics in need of study include, for example, an assessment of the impact democracy assistance programmes have on democratic outcomes and the stability of the peace; an appraisal of the effects security sector reform (SSR) and demobilization, demilitarization, and reintegration (DDR) programmes have on peace duration and domestic security; and an evaluation of the effects IMF and World Bank programmes to liberalize post-conflict economies have on development, human rights and the stability of the peace. Although they do not focus specifically on post-conflict countries, Abouharb and Cingranelli (2007) find evidence that IMF and World Bank structural adjustment programmes, used to promote economic liberalization, have adverse effects on a range of human rights practices and increase the probability of rebellion. Hartzell et al. (2010) find that IMF structural adjustment programmes increase the risk of civil war onset. If we find that efforts to promote some of these goals negatively affect other objectives, difficult choices will need to be made. Doing so in an informed fashion is critical, however, since failed efforts to promote more complex versions of the peace could have a variety of negative effects. These include undermining a stable peace, eroding domestic actors' commitment to the peace, and weakening the international community's willingness to participate in future efforts to help countries make the transition from war to peace.

17.4.2   The Effects Civil War Settlements have on the Peace

We should seek to learn more about how countries can successfully make the transition from civil war to peace via means that rely less intensively on the actions of the international community. I do not make this point in order to absolve the international community from any responsibility it has to play a role in helping to end civil wars. Rather, I seek to take into account three limitations associated with depending too heavily on the international community to play the central role in this process. First, as actively as international actors have been involved in helping to end civil wars in the past two decades, not all post-conflict cases see the level and types of international resources directed to them that have been associated with successful efforts to secure the peace (Ottaway 2003). Fortna (2004b) finds, for example, that international peacekeepers were deployed in only 36 per cent of the civil wars that were ended between 1947 and 1999. Second, recent developments such as the costly wars the United States is fighting in Afghanistan and Iraq, in conjunction with the current global economic crisis, raise questions about external actors' ability and willingness to dedicate attention and resources to helping countries make the transition from civil war to peace. Finally, and perhaps most importantly, a durable peace requires that post-conflict governments be seen as legitimate by their societies. This is an objective that regimes that are perceived to be overly dependent on the international community for their survival may be particularly hard-pressed to achieve.

Focusing on the settlements constructed at the end of civil wars holds promise as a means of learning more about what actors in civil war states have done to construct a lasting peace in some instances and one that has failed to hold in others. Virtually all civil wars, whatever their outcome – military victory, negotiated agreement, or truce – see adversaries agree to terms of some kind at the war's end (Iklé 1991; Kecskemeti 1958; Reiter 2003; Wagner 1993). These terms, or civil war settlements, consist of decisions regarding 'who gets what and when' in the post-conflict state (Werner and Yuen 2005, p. 262). One can distinguish among civil war settlements on the basis of the rules they construct regarding these issues. Broadly speaking, settlements whose terms eliminate some of the factions that participated in civil wars or that seek to limit their ability to participate in efforts to determine the benefits of the peace may be deemed *exclusionary* in nature. Settlements whose terms call for allocating state power and resources among adversaries can be conceived of as being of a *distributive* type (Hartzell 2009a).

Why focus on the role settlements play in the transition from war to peace? One important reason is because the terms of settlements are subject to human intervention. If we find that particular types of terms increase the likelihood that the peace will prove durable or serve better to protect human rights or to promote development in the post-war environment, civil war adversaries can be encouraged to construct settlements of that nature while also tailoring them to their country's particular circumstances. Second, as the evidence cited earlier noting that power-sharing measures have been adopted in the wake of military victories and rival factions' organizational structures have sometimes been eliminated following negotiated agreements suggests, settlement terms are not necessarily determined by war outcomes. This is important since it means that no matter what the trend is by which civil wars are being ended, agency matters: actors have the latitude to design settlements, including, hopefully, those whose terms can help facilitate the transition from war to peace. Finally, once we know more about the effects different types of settlements have on the peace, members of the international community can be encouraged to support the design and implementation of settlements that are most appropriate for helping countries make the transition from war to peace.

17.5   CONCLUSION

The fact that most intra-state conflicts now end via negotiated agreements and that these are followed by a more durable peace than was associated with this type of civil war outcome in the past suggests that something has changed in such a manner as to help facilitate the transition from war to peace (Mack 2008). Just what the nature of this change is we do not know. Part of the explanation is likely to be found in the international community's increased support for post-conflict peacebuilding, although not all of these efforts have been equally fruitful. This chapter has suggested that we also take a closer look at the choices conflict actors have been making as they craft civil war settlements. One thing is clear. Some countries have been able to make the transition from war to peace more successfully than others. Learning more about why and how some countries succeed in securing the peace could prove useful to other countries as they seek to end civil wars.

18 Fragile states and civil wars: is mediation the answer?

Carmela Lutmar and Jacob Bercovitch

18.1 INTRODUCTION

Since the end of the Cold War and the changes it induced in the social, economic and political environments, a lot of scholarly attention has been given to the nature of conflict in the new post-Cold War environment. The traditional bipolar international system changed into a different system; East–West relations have been altered, and alignment tensions decreased, and with it came the expectation that a prolonged period of stability would characterize the new system. The great powers, acting through, and on behalf of, the international community, would effectively prevent any conflict from breaking out. The end of the Cold War, so we were led to believe, marked the end of conflict, or as some scholars said even the 'end of history' (Fukuyama 1989). An era of long peace was what we all expected at the dawn of the 1990s.

What we have seen since 1991 is not a decrease, but rather an increase in the number and intensity of conflicts. The post-Cold War period has been characterized by an outbreak of nationalism, the accentuation of national and religious identity, and the eruption of violent conflicts in diverse places all over the globe such as Angola, Myanmar (formerly Burma), Sudan, Iraq, Russia, Turkey, Lebanon, Rwanda, Sudan, India, Ethiopia, Bosnia and so on. These conflicts, largely generated within state boundaries, have become known as civil wars. By one account only seven out of 111 militarized conflicts in the 12 years after 1989 were of the traditional conflicts between two sovereign states, and even these may have had a strong internal or communal dimension (Sollenberg and Wallensteen 2001). Clearly, as the study of these conflicts began to take the central stage of scholarly attention it became essential to begin to understand them and to develop policies designed to deal with them, ameliorate their destructive manifestations, and examine how we can reach agreements at the end of the conflicts and to make sure they are fully implemented.

Civil wars are among the most dangerous types of conflict in the international system. Not only do they bring death and destruction to the belligerent parties, they also inflict considerable harm upon the civilian populations in the countries in which they occur through geno-cide, population displacements, and long-term negative consequences for public health (Ghobarah et al. 2003; Harff 2003; Krain 1997; Moore and Shellman 2004; Schmeidl 1997). Because they have a propensity to internationalize themselves, and to spill over into neighbouring countries, and sometimes to a whole region, civil wars also represent a broader threat to the international community. UN Security Council resolutions have repeatedly underscored the belief that civil wars pose a 'threat to international peace and security'. For these reasons, under-standing the ways in which civil conflicts can be managed, and solved, has become increasingly important for both scholars and practitioners. In this chapter, we argue that one of the main features of fragile states is the prevalence of civil wars, and that one of the main characteristics, but less studied, of civil wars is that they tend to become intractable and produce deadlocks. These prevent any quick and satisfactory termina-tion, whether through negotiation between the warring parties or other means. We hope to contribute to the existing literature by examining how deadlocks affect civil wars and how best to break through them. First, we shall offer some conceptual definitions and identify typologies that can help us discuss deadlocks in civil wars in a more systematic manner. Then we shall go on to investigate how deadlocks may affect outcomes in civil wars.

We argue here that one important mechanism that can be used to termi-nate deadlocks in civil wars is mediation, and we distinguish between civil wars that are best suited to mediation from those where mediation may not be the best option to pursue.

A sizeable body of literature has focused on examining the causes of civil war (see Dixon 2009), the conditions under which settlements occur, and the conditions that promote the durability of these settlements (see, for example, Collier and Hoeffler 2004b; Doyle and Sambanis 2000; Elbadawi and Sambanis 2002; Fearon and Laitin 2003; Hartzell and Hoddie 2003a; Hartzell et al. 2001; Hegre et al. 2001; Hegre and Sambanis 2006; Licklider 1995; Mason and Fett 1996; Sambanis 2004a; Walter 1997, 2004). In general, however, the existing literature has suf-fered from two key weaknesses. First, although the literature has placed considerable emphasis on the outcomes of civil wars and civil war con-flict management efforts, it has placed less emphasis on the question of when and why most forms of conflict management in civil wars produce deadlocks, and at what stage of the conflict is it wise to initiate manage-ment efforts? This omission is especially important to studies of civil war termination, and successful implementation of peace agreements, due to the problem of selection bias. Identifying the conditions under which deadlocks in negotiation attempts occur during civil wars is as important as understanding when and how such deadlocks can be overcome. Without controlling for selection bias, empirical analyses of the conditions associated with civil war termination and getting out of impasses in negotiations may yield faulty inferences. In addition, understanding when third-party interventions in mediating the conflict occur, and when those attempts might yield positive outcomes, can shed light on the prospects of solving civil wars, and the ways practitioners can, and should, approach such conflicts.

The second weakness is one that applies to the conflict management literature in general, and to studies on mediation in particular, and not just to the subset of the civil war literature. In those studies that do focus upon the conditions under which conflict management takes place (for example, Gilligan and Stedman 2003; Greig 2005; Mullenbach 2005), the literature tends to examine different types of conflict management largely in isolation from one another, focusing upon when mediation or peacekeeping individually occur, without referring to the occurrence of other types of conflict management. Although this type of work provides valuable insights into specific types of conflict management efforts, it fails to take into account the fact that policy makers have a choice not only regarding whether or not to attempt to manage a conflict, but also in terms of the type of conflict management to be applied. Moreover, it is imperative to examine when those conflict management efforts reach a deadlock, and most importantly, how various tools of breaking those deadlocks operate separately and in conjunction with one another.

From a practical standpoint, third parties, be they a state or an international organization, upon deciding to manage a civil war, can choose between a reliance upon wholly diplomatic strategies or move towards approaches such as peacekeeping and peace enforcement that involve military force. In this way, different conflict management tools can be substitutable for one another, with each approach carrying different benefits and drawbacks. In this study, we take one step forward by addressing the concept of deadlock in the context of negotiation in civil wars, and by focusing on two possible ways of breaking those – mediation and leadership change. It is just a first step as there are other techniques for breaking deadlocks in negotiations such as UN involvement, issuing UN Security Council resolutions ('naming and shaming'), applying economic sanctions, arbitration, or even one-sided military intervention. Most and Starr (1984, 1989) developed the concept of foreign policy substitutability, but it has also been applied to domestic political contexts (for example, Moore 1998). Fundamental to this concept is the idea that decision makers choose from a range of policy options, all of which may lead to the same desired outcome. Decision makers choose from the available options according to their preferences and their estimates of the probability of success for each option (Moore 2000; Palmer and Bhandari 2000). Key to this conceptualization is the principle that it is difficult to empirically find a strong impact for explanatory variables if only one of the available policy options is included in a model while other options are excluded.

In this chapter, we seek to discuss first the notion of fragile states and their characteristics. Then we shall discuss the concept of deadlock, and to better understand the response of the international community to its occurrence in civil conflicts by focusing upon four key questions. First, what are deadlocks, and how can we conceptualize them? Second, under what conditions do deadlocks occur in negotiations in civil wars? Third, when international efforts are made to break a deadlock in a civil conflict, what conditions influence the choice between various tools such as mediation or leadership change in one of the warring states or both? We argue here that the main mechanism that can be used to terminate deadlocks in civil wars is mediation. However, not all civil conflicts are equally suited to this mechanism. Therefore, we shall distinguish between civil wars that are best suited to mediation from those where mediation is unlikely to produce a favourable outcome. We argue that whether or not a deadlock is tackled by the mechanism mentioned earlier depends upon the degree to which mediation is deemed to be necessary, the extent to which interests important to third parties are at stake in the conflict, the costs inherent to not intervening, and the regime type in both warring states. We think that the more democratic a state is, the more open it will be to accept mediation offers, and the higher the probability of success of these efforts. When mediation takes place, the form of mediation that is chosen is tied to the urgency the civil conflict demonstrates for external intervention coupled with the risks the conflict would pose for the mediators. Thus, the political decision to engage in mediation or to wait for a later time is in fact a two-level decision-making process. At the first stage, third parties identify whether the negotiation reached a deadlock, and if so whether to intervene at all or remain silent; at the second stage they choose between mediation now and (maybe) mediation at a later stage.

Following a discussion on the characteristics of fragile states, and where they are more likely to emerge, we offer a definition of deadlocks in negotiations, and the potential danger they pose, then we discuss in detail the possible means used to terminate the deadlocks – mediation. We explain the merits and shortcomings of the option and conclude by offering additional paths for future research.

18.2 CONFLICT IN THE POST-COLD WAR ERA

For more than four decades the Cold War shaped every facet of the international environment. It created an incompatibility of goals and interests between two superpowers and their spheres of influence, and led to tensions and conflicts at both the international and intranational levels. While there was an exceptional level of stability at the superpower level, the Third World became the de facto location of the majority of conflict, with the after-effects of colonialism – namely internal division and economic decline – leaving many Third World countries ripe for external interference and suppressed internal conflict. The United States and the Soviet Union were not directly engaged in a conflict, but rather indirectly, allowing or encouraging their respective client states (mostly in Asia and Africa) to go to war against each other.

Conflict management during that period was characterized mostly by deterrence, suppression and diversion (proxy conflicts) rather than resolution. The United States and the Soviet Union intervened unilaterally in a number of conflicts, but their interventions served limited interests, mostly those of leaders or groups supported by either superpower. Conflict suppression as a strategy, under the big umbrella of deterrence and the spheres of superpower influence, served paradoxically to intensify latent demands for political identity of various groups.

18.3 FRAGILE STATES

Countries vary in their population size, wealth, ambitions, state capacity, capabilities and the level of rights constituents enjoy. If we adopt the definition that 'nation-states exist to provide a decentralized method of delivering political (public) goods to persons living within designated parameters (borders)' (Rotberg 2003, p. 2), and that 'they organize and channel the interests of their people . . . they buffer or manipulate external forces and influences, champion the local or particular of their adherents, and mediate between the constraints and challenges of the international arena and the dynamism of their own internal economic, political, and social realities' (ibid., p. 2), then we can also say that fragile states are those states that do not perform well, or even fail, on any of those dimensions. The ability to deliver the political public goods, and the effectiveness by which they are delivered, distinguishes between strong and weak states, and between weak states and fragile states (which may eventually collapse or fail).

The variation in states' performance, and in their performance when it comes to the delivery of political public goods to their constituents can be explained by the strength of their institutions. The stronger they are, the better they can provide these goods to their citizens. Weak states are characterized by unstable institutions, often as a result of domestic unrest, civil wars, or a prolonged inter-state war. Strong states exhibit full control within their borders on the use of force, they perform well on a range of indicators such as GDP, level of democracy, civil rights, low level of corruption and high levels of economic development. Weak states on the other hand, are characterized by higher levels of corruption, the rule of law is not fully (or at all) enforced, low level of political, religious and civil liberties, and in many cases internal violence that originates in tensions among ethnic, religious, or other groups in the society, and the weakness of the institutions and the government's inability to take full control of the use of force.

In fact, we can locate the above-mentioned categories on one continuum where, at one end we find strong states, and at the other, failed (or failing) states. Fragile states are closer to this end, in that they do not fully perform on one (or more) dimension(s), and as time goes on, they might totally collapse (or fail) – Somalia being the classic example.

Fragile states are characterized by rivalries between various groups within the society, and those often lead to violent clashes between government forces and armed groups. As Rotberg (ibid., p. 5) comments:

> [I]t is not the absolute intensity of violence that identifies a failed state . . . rather, it is the enduring character of that violence (as in Angola, Burundi and the Sudan), the fact that much of the violence is directed against the existing government or regime, and the inflamed character of the political or geographical demands for shared power or autonomy that rationalize or justify that violence in the minds of the main insurgents.

Although we do distinguish between fragile and failed states in that they are proximate categories on the same continuum, they are both quite similar when it comes to the prevalence of civil wars. And it is to the analysis of civil wars that we now turn.

18.4   CIVIL WARS

The term 'civil war' is broadly used to describe a wide range of internal conflicts. The scholarly literature refers to all of them as civil wars, though some would argue that ethnic conflicts are a subsct, one of many, of civil wars. However, our focus in this chapter will be on the broader category known as civil wars.

A civil war is thus a conflict that involves two or more groups within a state. Although civil wars are not unlike other forms of internal violence (for example, coups, genocide), we usually reserve the term 'civil wars' to those conflicts where the government is one of the parties in conflict. The other group or conflict party may have territorial, political, or economic ambitions which the government is desperately trying not to concede. Traditionally we think of a conflict situation as a civil war if it resulted in 1,000 or more fatalities on both sides. Even with such a high threshold it is worth noting that some 37 per cent of all countries have experienced civil wars in the 1990s (Fearon and Laitin 2003).

Civil wars arise when non-state groups with a separate sense of identity perceive their governing structure to be incapable of addressing their basic needs and grievances. When such needs are denied, or are not met, various grievances are formed, and demands that the situation be redressed become more and more voluble. Perceived need deprivation, or the desire to gain control of scarce resources (usually coal, diamonds and petroleum) are the basic condition of civil wars. The desire to remove a perceived deprivation or greed for resources is characteristic of the development and conduct of many such conflicts.

If we see civil wars as a new wave sweeping across different regions of the world, engulfing them in convulsive fits of violence in the wake of the collapse of the Soviet Union, then explanations of their causes and proposals for their management, and eventual resolution, are likely to be quite different than if we view them over a much longer term. Scholars have relied too much on end of the Cold War elements in their analyses of civil wars. Ethnic groups and civil wars that originate in grievances between two or more ethnic groups have been around for centuries, hence we cannot explain either their occurrence, or their duration, management and resolution, merely in terms of some structural readjustment that took place 20 years ago (Lake and Rothchild 1996). Ethnicity is not a new phenomenon; it may play a salient role in many conflicts, but that does not mean it plays a sufficient one. It takes a substantial effort to have issues of ethnicity and identity transformed into violent conflicts (not all or even most conflicts of identity become violent). We should be mindful of this.

Civil wars are associated with high costs, major disruption, refugee flows, persistent violence, economic dislocation and breakdown in civil society. It has been estimated that civil wars have accounted for 16 million fatalities in the last 45 years (Fearon and Laitin 2003). There can be no doubt that civil wars are the main source of disruption and volatility to the international environment. Another feature of civil wars that makes them so difficult to deal with is their tendency to expand geographically and bring in new actors and expand the scope of the original conflict. This makes an original civil war an internationalized phenomenon.

There are a number of processes which may transform a civil war into an international one (Ganguly and Taras 1998; Gurr 2000b). Civil wars can become internationalized through the spread of refugees across borders, or where one ethnic group is spread across several states, or when ethnic leaders in one state seek sanctuary in another. They can become internationalized through terrorist activities, or partisan interventions on behalf of one of the groups. Finally, there are a number of conflicts with significant ethnic components that become internationalized through international diplomatic activities (such as UN intervention, diplomatic efforts of various statespeople). Bearing in mind the nexus between internal and international conflicts, Bercovitch (2003) suggests that it might be useful to think of different categories of conflict and to examine how each manifests itself and how each can be managed, controlled or prevented. Broadly speaking we can talk about two kinds of conflicts; (a) internationalized civil wars (civil wars which become internationalized through refugees or spread of conflict, and conflicts where external demands for territory, resource, or regime change are superimposed on ethnic identity), and (b) inter-state conflicts (where an international conflict affects and exacerbates ethnic identities within a state). They are different conflicts in structure and nature and may require different forms of intervention and termination.

Many of the conflicts that have occupied a prominent place on the international agenda in the last decade or so, such as Sri Lanka, Iraq (*vis-à-vis* the Kurds), Israel, or Afghanistan, began as civil wars, but quickly spilled over to involve more than one state. In a globalized age, state boundaries become increasingly more porous; thus conflicts that started within a state's borders will have consequences that affect the international system, or the international community may take measures that affect domestic conflicts. Either way, such conflicts rarely remain an internal phenomenon only.

One of the features we wish to examine in this chapter is the way in which each of these conflicts leads to its resolution, and the various mechanisms used to do so. In an empirical examination of 309 international conflicts between 1945 and 1995, Bercovitch and Jackson (1997) find that 131 of the conflicts had a significant ethnic component, and later developed into internationalized conflicts.

18.4.1   Characteristics of Internationalized Civil Wars

Clearly a substantial number of conflicts since 1945 can be described as internationalized conflicts with ethnicity as their salient focus. What are the main features and characteristics of such conflicts, and to what extent do these affect their management and eventual resolution? Internationalized civil wars are both very violent and protracted in nature. Carment's (1993) examination of international conflicts from 1945 to 1981 found that civil wars with an ethnic component were characterized by a high level of violence in 40 per cent of conflicts compared with 30 per cent of non-ethnic conflicts. Miall's (1992) findings from the 1945–85 period reinforce this, with internal conflicts being four times more likely to be categorized as 'major violent' than international conflicts during the same period. The year 1994 saw the highest number of conflict-related deaths since 1971, with a total of over one million for the year, many of them civilian (Sivard 1996). Today, more than 90 per cent of all casualties are non-combatants, with violence directed against civilian populations evident in conflicts such as Chechnya, Rwanda, Kosovo and Afghanistan (ibid.).

An analysis of 131 conflicts with a significant ethnic component reveals that most of them (106) involved the highest hostility level in conflict (with hostility examined on a three-point scale from display of force to war), and a very substantial number of these (59) had gone on for three years or more.

Internationalized civil wars are characterized by a high level of perceived cultural differences. In civil wars with an ethnic component, cultural, linguistic, or religious distinctions play a vital role in shaping the disputants' ways of thinking and influencing their perceptions of themselves and others. The first fact of ethnicity is the application of systematic distinction between insiders and outsiders in a process of inclusion and exclusion that defines the 'group'. The ability of a protest group to develop and sustain a dispute with the government depends on the group perceiving both a distributional and an identification element. Without distributional deprivation, identification remains a positive factor and not a motivation for conflict; without an identification element, distributional inequalities remain unfocused and non-mobilizing. Ethnicity provides a focus around which individuals can unite and a basis upon which to construct and maintain a community based on certain features that are perceived and shared within the group. Internal unity and cohesiveness is dependent on a group's ability to clearly define itself as an entity, an in-group, and to distinguish itself from the out-group(s).

Another feature of internationalized civil wars is that they rarely remain dyadic. Civil wars usually spawn a multiplicity of groups, alliances and subgroups. These groups sometimes spill over into other countries, and cause the conflict to involve even more countries. It is also very difficult to establish proper leadership or control channels in such conflicts where so many diffuse and ill-defined groups coexist. This clearly compounds the problems faced by policy makers or conflict practitioners.

Internationalized civil wars are also characterized by specific issues over which the conflict is typically fought. These are predicated upon value-related issues and fundamental beliefs such as identification, loyalties, individual beliefs, group identities, ethnic relations, and perceptions of separateness and discrimination. Ethnic issues are, like other value-related issues, intangible, intractable, and do not lend themselves easily to political compromise or a negotiated settlement.

Unlike traditional inter-state conflicts, which usually end with negotiation and a settlement of sorts, internationalized civil wars often end in expulsion, surrender, or extermination. Most internationalized civil wars either continue for a long time or re-emerge again within 24 months. Zartman (1995) found that less than a third of civil wars in the twentieth century led to negotiations. In a much discussed paper, Kaufman (1996) argued that there was only one possible outcome to violent civil wars with an ethnic component, and that is permanent separation of the parties. Paul Pillar's (1983) study shows that about two-thirds of inter-state wars terminated through negotiation, compared to about one-third of internal conflicts. Stedman, after eliminating colonial wars and other 'special' cases, found that the incidence of civil wars terminating by negotiation declined to approximately 15 per cent (Stedman 1991; Walter 1997).

18.4.2   Parties and Issues in Internationalized Civil Wars

Gurr's Minorities at Risk project (1993, 2000b) provides a useful classification of political actors in internationalized civil wars. The actors in question are defined as ethno-political actors. Two criteria must be met for an actor to be defined as such: (a) collectively suffer, or benefit from, discriminatory policies, (b) collective action, mobilization and defence of own interest are undertaken by such actors. Many shared attributes, of which ethnicity is one, might however lead to collective actions.

Gurr makes a basic distinction between two broad categories of ethno-political groups: national peoples and minority peoples. National peoples include ethno-nationalists (regionally concentrated people who pursue autonomy), national minorities and indigenous peoples. Minority peoples include ethno-classes (ethnically distinct people, occupying a distinct social status), communal contenders (culturally distinct people who seek a share in state power) and religious sects. On the basis of these criteria Gurr identifies 275 ethno-political groups, the majority of which are communal contenders (68) or indigenous peoples (66). In another study, Bercovitch (2011) found that ethno-nationalist groups and communal contenders have been involved in more than 78 per cent of the 131 conflicts. Clearly, any approach to conflict management has to be predicated on the nature and identity of the parties in conflict.

One further dimension that needs to be investigated pertains to the issues that mobilize ethno-political groups to engage in conflict. Issues in internationalized civil wars represent the political articulation of some grievance, demands, or strategies. Bercovitch identifies a tenfold categorization of issues in internationalized civil wars that distinguishes between several types of civil wars:

1. *Secessionist conflicts*   These concern the attempt by an ethnic group claiming a homeland withdrawing with its territory from the state.
2. *Irredentist conflicts*   Such conflicts are characterized by the movement by members of an ethnic group party to retrieve territory that had once been (or is considered to have been) part of their territory.
3. *Autonomy conflicts*   These reflect an ethnic group's desire for the right of self-government of their ethnic group.
4. *De-colonization conflicts*   These are predicated on the desire of an ethnic group to gain independence from a colonial power.
5. *Religious conflicts*   These are founded on concerned ethnic parties that are organized in defence or promotion of their religious beliefs.
6. *Political voice*   Conflicts defined as political voice concern the distribution of political influence between relative ethnic groups.
7. *Ideology conflicts*   Such conflicts involve ethnic groups mobilizing to contest the dominant political or economic ideology.
8. *Resource conflicts*   These are characterized by different ethnic groups contesting the distribution and control of resources.
9. *Political control conflicts*   These concern conflict between parties over total regime and control of authority changes.
10. *Genocide*   These are conflicts in which there is a policy of deliberately killing members of a specific ethnic group.

Based on the empirical evidence, Bercovitch also finds that most internationalized civil wars are fought over issues of secession, autonomy and ideology. All are intangible issues that do not easily lend themselves to a resolution. In other words, they often produce a deadlock in the negotiations between the warring parties.

18.4.3   Terminating Internationalized Civil Wars

Managing and terminating internationalized civil wars is a difficult and complex process, but it is not much different from managing any other kinds of conflict. Like other intractable conflicts, civil wars are not unmanageable. Rather than devise a variety of constitutional accommodative arrangements (ranging from autonomy to federalism), we need to think

Table 18.1   Mediation outcomes in internationalized civil wars

	Frequency	Percent
Mediation offered only	141	8.1
Unsuccessful	934	53.6
Ceasefire	207	11.9
Partial agreement	406	23.3
Full settlement	53	3.0
Total	1,741	100.0*

Note: *Rounded.

of how to deal with them in terms of the three basic methods of conflict management that apply to all conflicts. Parties in any conflict may resort to different levels of coercion (physical and psychological) to manage their conflict. They may settle the conflict through peaceful forms such as bargaining and negotiation on their own initiative, or the conflict may be managed through the intervention (binding or otherwise) of some third party. Although there is a common perception that most civil wars are terminated through victory by one side, an analysis of all conflict management activities in our 131 cases of conflict reveals that the practice of external, non-coercive intervention by third-party mediation was the most common method of dealing with internationalized civil wars.

Non-coercive interventions can be defined according to the degree of involvement by a third party in the conflict management process (see Touval 1982) (Table 18.1). Fisher and Keashly (1991) provide a framework for describing such efforts. Using their terminology, it can be said that conciliation involves a trusted intermediary who provides an informal communication link between the parties with the purposes of identifying the issues, reducing tensions and encouraging the parties to shift their negotiating positions. Arbitration and adjudication involve a legitimate and authoritative third party that renders a binding judgement to the parties. Consultation, or problem solving, involves a third party facilitating analysis of the conflict and the development of alternatives through communication and diagnosis based on an analysis and understanding of conflict processes. The fourth form of intervention is peacekeeping, which involves the provision of military personnel by a third party, or parties, to supervise and monitor a ceasefire, to undertake humanitarian activities, or attempt to prevent open hostilities between the parties. The final form of third-party intervention is mediation and involves the intervention of an intermediary who attempts to facilitate a negotiated settlement of the substantive issues in the conflict.

Deadlocks in the termination of civil wars

Conflict management efforts can – and often do – grind to a halt, where progress towards any form of settlement or resolution stalls. This phenomenon may be defined as a 'deadlock' or 'stalemate'. A deadlock stops progress in conflict management. It represents a protracted situation of no agreement between the warring sides, where parties simply cannot move forward whatever they do. This is particularly the case with internationalized civil wars. A deadlock can be best perceived as a situation where there is no agreement coupled with an obvious halt in the cycle of negotiations. This is thus a situation where there is no progress, no concessions, continued violence, and where a perception of immobility and inactivity takes hold. It is in short a situation of little or no progress or cooperation. As such, a deadlock may trigger escalation and renewed violence between the belligerent parties, and create a feeling that a compromise is no longer possible. Or a deadlock can help negotiators to reverse their course of action and work harder towards a compromise. Deadlocks and stalemates are very typical of civil wars. This is why deadlocks are so important for us to conceptualize and understand, and also why we need to know their causes in order to find out the best way of getting out of a deadlock.

We may think of deadlocks in civil wars structurally and suggest that they can be of two kinds; strategic (where a deadlock relates to real and genuine basic incompatibilities between the parties) or it can be tactical (where it results because of failures to coordinate the process of negotiation). Or we may analyse deadlocks in process terms and suggest three types of deadlocks; a genuine stalemate in the process of negotiations, an extended delay in the process, and a complete breakdown in the process. Each of these types of deadlock may require different coping strategies if the parties in conflict are to transform their situation.

While a military victory is a decisive event that may terminate a civil war, a deadlock occurs in the context of non-violent conflict management efforts. A deadlock is not limited to situations where parties exhibit a low motivation to reduce or resolve the conflict (Bloomfield et al., 1998, p. 99). A deadlock may occur, *inter alia*, because of inflexible positions, lack of commitment or desire to resolve a conflict, or political leaders' commitment to their official position. On the international stage, the conflicts surrounding the break-up of Yugoslavia in the 1990s represent an excellent example of the difficult realities faced by negotiators. The issues and complications involved in these conflicts were diverse and included ethnic, religious and economic factors. In the early stages of the conflict, a combined negotiation effort involving the foreign ministers of Luxembourg, Italy and the Netherlands was initiated, yet despite their continued efforts, substantive progress towards some form of ceasefire was never achieved (Weller 1992, p. 571).

Deadlocks may represent a major barrier to the dynamics and possible success of any conflict management effort. They are characterized by a high degree of uncertainty and a low degree of progress. Underdaal (1983), in an early study, presents four primary causes for negotiation deadlock. First, there is the issue of uncertainty. This occurs when disputants are uncertain about aspects of the negotiation process such as the preferences, perceptions and beliefs of their opposition, or there is uncertainty about the actual effects of certain proposals. When uncertainty is high, parties will fail to realize possible shared interests and gains, and thus increase the likelihood of a deadlock. Second, and related to the issue of uncertainty, is the idea of imperfect (and often inaccurate) information as a possible cause of deadlocks. Both imperfect information and uncertainty will make disputants cautious about moving away from the status quo and particularly sceptical about making any commitments. A third factor which may produce a deadlock in negotiation is the tendency for the process to reinforce certain 'stakes'. When negotiations begin in this fashion, the likelihood of deadlock is pretty high. For example, the very act of entering negotiations may have serious repercussions for some parties in terms of reputation, standing and position (for example, for the US to enter into direct negotiations with Iran may in itself send a series of messages that could affect the US position and reputation in other cases). Finally, some negotiations are destined simply to reach a deadlock or fail, simply due to the absence of a politically acceptable solution model (for example, any negotiations between Israel and the Palestinian faction of Hamas will reach a deadlock in the very first session of negotiations). Deadlocks can thus occur because of any one (or more) of these factors cited above.

To these initial factors we may add further elements that may produce deadlocks. Here we can mention factors such as the number of negotiating parties (for example, when many parties are involved, a deadlock is more likely to occur), openness and publicity of negotiations (the more secret the negotiations, the higher the chances of a successful outcome), the nature of the issues in conflict (for example, the more substantive the issues the higher the likelihood of a deadlock), and the rank of negotiators (negotiations conducted by heads of states or prime ministers are less likely to result in a deadlock). Each and every one of these can produce a serious disruption to any negotiation process.

The causes of deadlocks fall into two main groups – process and structural. Process factors relate to the way the negotiation process unfolds (for example, when parties engage in too much bluffing, posturing and lying, or when they feel they have no incentive to make concessions). Structural factors relate to such causes as asymmetry of power between the parties (which may result in the stronger party simply stonewalling), or because of certain institutional constraints on negotiations (for example, a lack of clear guidelines on such issues as chairmanship, prominence of issues, level of representation, and so on which stymied the Madrid Peace Negotiations in 1992). The last, though by no means the most important factor, is the one we propose to examine here. This argues that deadlocks occur because of certain domestic political structures and interests (for example, some political leaders may feel that their interests would be better served by creating deadlocks and inducing a sense of crisis than by achieving an agreement). We believe that this is an important cause of deadlocks and will spend some time below developing and examining this idea.

Lewicki and Litterer (1985, p. 281) suggest that once a deadlock emerges there are six main factors that characterize it, and make the whole conflict management effort that much more complicated. These factors are both of a strategic and psychological nature. First, a deadlocked environment is charged with anger and frustration and these sentiments are directed at the opposing negotiator. Second, as a result of this anger and frustration, disputants' positions become increasingly entrenched and rather than searching for ways to make concessions, parties become firmer in their initial demands and resort to threats and deceptions in an effort to force their opposite to back down. Third, channels of communication which had been active are no longer viable except for the purpose of criticism and apportion of blame. Fourth, the original issues at stake in the conflict have become distorted and ill-defined. Fifth, the parties perceive extreme differences between their respective positions and areas of commonality are perceived as either minimal or non-existent. Finally, the in-group dynamics of the disputants will change. Disputants will tend to view those on the same side more favourably and minimize any differences that exist. In an effort to present a united front to opponents, leaders will demand more uniformity within their team and increasingly autocratic and militant leadership styles will emerge (Blake and Mouton, 1961). Whichever way we look at it, deadlocks are very difficult social situations with serious consequences negotiation at any level.

Breaking or overcoming deadlocks in civil wars

As mentioned earlier, deadlocks present major obstacles preventing progress towards a reduction in conflict. In fact, we can say that deadlocks may actually intensify conflict as disputants become increasingly entrenched in their positions. And yet, on some levels it may be posited that deadlocks actually create opportunities for conflict management, for if nothing else, they at least provide us with signposts as to the real state of the negotiation. Is it possible to see deadlocks as opportunities? There are very few studies that attempt to address this issue. Yet, we must clearly see deadlocks as a warning sign as well as an opportunity. Our task is to ensure that the opportunities are grasped and the deadlock broken. This is not an easy task when the causes of a deadlock are structural.

Some scholars believe that all it takes to break a deadlock is to educate the parties and refocus their efforts. William Ury (1991) provides a good example of such an approach. Ury states that certain negotiation situations are particularly susceptible to deadlock and that these situations call for more than just ordinary negotiation skills. These situations are generally characterized by the presence of particularly difficult issues, and clearly hostile disputants. The combination of these two factors creates a deadlock of some sort. To overcome such deadlocks, Ury provides negotiators with a five-step process, which he refers to as 'breakthrough negotiation'. The first step emphasizes the importance of avoiding an adverse reaction to initial positions. This can be achieved by stepping back from the conflict and attempting to distance actions from impulses and reactions. Second, disputants must diffuse their anger, fears and suspicions. Third, Ury emphasizes the importance of reframing an opponent's position rather than rejecting it, as this generally only strengthens and reinforces it. Fourth, mediators should be enlisted to help disputants to save face and provide them with an easy way out of the conflict. Finally, if one party is still committed to unilateral methods (that is, violence) in the hope of achieving all its objectives, that party must be educated by third parties and others, as to the folly of this course of action (ibid.). Ury's conception of negotiations as a process that can just keep on moving forward irrespective of circumstances is as touching as it is erroneous.

In a similar vein, Bloomfield et al. (1998, p.99) outline a number of 'tried and tested techniques' which may be useful for overcoming situations of deadlock. The first of these is the idea of building a 'coalition of commitment' between members of both the parties who still value the negotiation process. A strong pro-negotiation coalition can increase pressure on those causing the deadlock by the implicit threat that they will take the blame if the talks stall or collapse. A second technique is the use of unofficial channels of communication, which can supplement the official negotiation process. Where a specific issue is causing deadlock, the use of subgroups or subcommittees may be convened to address that specific issue. The use of subgroups can divide the agenda into more manageable segments. A further technique for dealing with specific issues, particularly when emotions are running high, is the use of 'proximity talks'. This technique eases the pressure on the disputants by separating them into different locations (but in relatively close proximity, for example, different rooms of the same building). Disputants will then communicate entirely through a nominated chairperson.

Lewicki and Litterer (1985, p. 280) also discuss the problem of how to break a negotiation deadlock. They make an important point by noting that negotiation techniques are particularly difficult to implement 'in the heat of the battle'. Under conditions of mistrust and suspicion, disputants will often view indications of cooperation or concession as tricks or ploys aimed at luring their own party into a position of vulnerability. Lewicki and Litterer introduce a range of methods to help move disputants away from deadlock. These can be summarized as techniques to reduce or release tension; improvement of the accuracy of communication; controlling the issues that are under negotiation; establishing commonalities; and techniques regarding how to make preferred options more desirable to the opponent (ibid., pp. 282–99).

A common theme regarding the causes of deadlock is that the fear of one or both disputants losing face will prevent them from moving towards agreement (Deutsch 1973; Rubin and Brown 1975; Tjosvold 1974). Examples of situations where maintaining face has hindered negotiations include the 1951 Korean ceasefire negotiations, the 1972 Vietnam talks in Paris, and the continuing negotiations in the Middle East (see Brown 1977, pp. 275–6). In response to this, a deadlock may be broken, by allowing disputants time to present options to their constituents, and seek approval for their actions (see Bloomfield et al. 1998, pp. 99–102). Additionally, negotiators may shift responsibility for any concessions on to a mediator, so that they at least can be seen as sticking to their original position.

While acknowledging the importance of saving face in negotiations, Hawkins and Hudson (1990) argue negotiation deadlock primarily occurs when either one or both of the disputants are not having their important needs met. As such, the first step to resolving deadlock is to re-evaluate the disputants' needs to ensure that they are accurately identified. Once disputant needs are accurately identified, the content of discussion, and negotiation style and behaviour should be changed accordingly. Processes such as redefining issues in a new and different manner; finding a bridging issue; recapping areas of agreement; recollection of previous good association; and discussion of the failure to negotiate are all put forward as additional techniques to help disputants move beyond deadlock (ibid., pp. 109–10).

Rubin et al. (1994) suggest a further explanation for negotiation deadlock, arguing that stalemate is commonly caused by entrapment. Once disputants invest a certain amount in a conflict, they become increasingly reluctant to sacrifice that investment, regardless of how fruitless the conflict has become. On a large scale, the American involvement in the

Vietnam War, or the Soviet invasion of Afghanistan provide us with good examples of how costly entrapment can become (ibid., p. 209). A range of strategies are recommended to overcome problems of entrapment such as setting limits; ensuring disputants stick to these limits; and reminding disputants of the costs involved (ibid., pp. 215–16).

What has been considered so far could be described as the 'conventional' approaches to negotiation deadlock. Most of these approaches simply see deadlock as a result of problems in the way in which negotiation is applied. As such, the techniques prescribed to deal with deadlock essentially amount to an extension of the negotiation process, for example clarification of positions, or allowing disputants' time to cool their heels. Some research considering negotiation deadlock discusses approaches to the problem which are distinct from the basic negotiation process. Lewicki and Litterer (1985) suggest that when negotiations become deadlocked, it may be necessary to introduce a new form of conflict management. Arbitration, mediation and process consultation are put forward as potential alternative forms of conflict management. The benefits of moving to a completely new form of conflict management, such as mediation, have been identified by a number of scholars (Bloomfield et al. 1998, pp. 108–9; Pruitt and Carnevale 1993).

18.4.4   Mediation in Civil Wars

Mediation is an important method of dealing with conflict, and it is the first one we discuss as a way to break deadlocks in negotiations in civil wars. For many reasons it is a favoured form of peaceful third-party involvement. Unlike conciliation, mediation allows a mediator to take a more active formal role in the process. Mediation may also include more informal forms of third-party intervention such as the provision of good offices, inquiry, or fact-finding. At its best, mediation can help the parties address the substantive issues in a conflict. A mediator is able to steer the parties towards agreement through communication and diagnosis, and may press and reward the parties so as to have a degree of control over the context of the conflict and its process.

Mediation, in comparison to other methods of peaceful intervention such as arbitration and adjudication, is a voluntary process in which a third party offers non-binding assistance (in various forms) to the disputants to help them move towards a mutually acceptable agreement. Given the voluntary, non-coercive nature of mediation, and the polarized and entrenched nature of internationalized ethnic conflict, mediation provides, on the face of it, a non-threatening way of transforming, de-escalating, or settling such conflicts.

Mediation is best viewed as a process that is used worldwide in numerous kinds of conflicts, inter-state as well as intra-state, and can be systematically studied within the broader context of negotiation and conflict management. Definitions of mediation may focus on mediation behaviour, mediator identity, or mediator resources (Fisher 1995). Some definitions are broad; others are quite specific. Given the immense scope of mediation, Bercovitch et al. (1991, p. 8) offer the following broad definition. Mediation is:

> A process of conflict management where disputants seek the assistance of, or accept an offer of help from, an individual, group, state or organization to settle their conflict or resolve their differences without resorting to physical violence or invoking the authority of the law.

Parties in conflict, whether domestic or international, have alternatives other than mediation. They choose it voluntarily because mediation embodies some international norms they wish to uphold, or because they expect greater payoffs from mediation than from other conflict management methods. Either way mediation is an adaptive form of conflict management – the context of each conflict situation is highly variable in terms of the nature of the parties, the issues, the dispute and the mediator. Mediation must develop and respond to the context of a conflict if it is to be effective. It is well suited to the reality of civil wars, as parties in such conflicts rarely have the desire or inclination to talk to each other, and their high level of hostility and violence means that talking and communicating with the other is precisely what is required. Outsiders can have a positive influence on the process and evolution of a civil war through discouraging violence or providing facilities to determine resource distribution. Under some well-established conditions mediation may prove to be a decisive factor in the termination of civil wars.

Mediation success in civil wars

A number of approaches to the study of mediation have dominated the literature (see Bercovitch and Houston 1996). Broadly speaking these approaches represent the single case study tradition (see Ott 1972), experimental studies, interviews and observations (see Kolb 1983), and the systematic, empirical tradition (see Bercovitch 1986). This tradition examines a large number of mediation cases, and tries to relate mediation outcomes to a wide array of independent variables describing the context and process of any conflict situation. Wall et al. (2001) refer to this aspect of the literature as 'aggregate outcome determinants'.

Which are the most important independent variables in affecting, or determining mediation outcomes? The literature on mediation is consistent in identifying four factors as likely to have the most effect on mediation outcomes (Henderson 1996). These are (a) issues in conflict, (b) conflict level or intensity, (c) mediator rank, and (d) timing of mediation. Let us review each of these in turn.

Issues in conflict are invariably seen as affecting mediation outcomes. Issues define the underlying causes of a conflict. They may not always be clear, but the parties' perception of issues in conflict defines the parameters of any conflict. When dealing with inter-state conflicts, we study issues of territory, sovereignty, security and ideology. Here, we are interested in the relationship between mediation and our tenfold classification of issues that characterize internationalized civil wars.

Conflict level or intensity refers to the level of costs incurred by both actors in conflict. Conflict costs can be computed to include material costs, human costs, or any other kind of costs (for example, reputation and so on). The idea here is that there is some relationship between conflict costs and mediation outcomes. Two contradictory strands characterize the literature: some argue that this relationship is direct, others that it is inverse. Which way does this relationship hold in the case of internationalized civil wars?

The literature on mediation often alludes to the importance of the personal factor (see Young 1968). Just how important is mediator identity in this equation? While we can hardly evaluate the impact of mediators' personal traits and attributes, we can perhaps analyse the extent to which different mediators, representing different bodies and organizations can bring their organizational attributes and resources to bear. Do impartial mediators or high-rank mediators achieve greater success in internationalized civil wars? Is rank related to outcome? These are all fascinating questions, but beyond the scope of this chapter.

Finally, the notion of mediation timing seems to be used by many as a predictor of a successful outcome (for example, Edmead 1971; Pruitt 1981). To be effective, mediation must take place at a propitious moment in the life cycle of a conflict. But how exactly can we recognize a propitious moment? Some argue that it occurs early in a conflict, others suggest that this moment occurs much later (see Northedge and Donelan 1971). Timing certainly affects mediation effectiveness, but in which way? Bercovitch and Lutmar (2010) find that mediation is more likely to occur in international conflicts when there is a leadership change in one (or both) states involved. This brings us to discuss the second way we think can break a deadlock in negotiations in civil wars – leadership change.

18.5 CONCLUSIONS

Fragile (or failed) states have been plagued by civil wars for many years now. They are among the most difficult of all forms of conflict. Civil war causes fatalities, most of them non-combatants, they are nasty and brutish, they are very hard to terminate or resolve, and they cause regional and international instability. What is more, they also tend to recur, often with more violence and destruction. Deaths from social dislocation, economic and social collapse which are typical of intense civil wars run into the millions. Whichever way we look at it, it is clear that civil wars merit a very serious analysis indeed.

In this chapter we tried to address the issues of fragile states and civil wars by defining the concepts, distinguishing their various forms, suggesting patterns in the occurrence of civil wars, and highlighting the tendency of most civil wars to internationalize. We have argued that this last feature makes civil war termination even more difficult to achieve. When it comes to termination, most studies address the issue in terms of a military victory (which produces a decisive outcome) and negotiation efforts (which produces at best a murky and uncertain outcome). Our aim has been to try to explore this issue from a different perspective.

We argue above that any form of conflict management in civil wars is likely to produce a stalemate or a deadlock, given the intractable realities of entrenched parties, difficult issues, and a sense of identity and grievance that parties bring with them to a civil war. Conflict management is hardly likely to be a linear process in civil wars. Given that we are likely to face a deadlock in our negotiation efforts, how best to break it? How best to overcome it and move to another phase of conflict management? In this chapter we advance two propositions. We argue that non-coercive intervention by an outsider, or outsiders is the best process to break out of a deadlock.

Outsiders, acting as mediators, can help parties in a civil war establish some lines of communication, think about goals and means, and work to develop some credible commitments to a peaceful outcome. Given the complex nature of civil wars where parties do not even countenance talking to each other, it seems that outside intervention is one of the best means of helping to terminate a civil war.

We have presented some initial and tentative data that support our ideas. This is an exploratory chapter and we believe that more research is needed on these two social processes and their contribution to the termination of civil wars. More research is warranted in this area. We need to be able to evaluate the success (whatever that may mean) of these processes. In addition, we need to examine whether they lead to longer periods of peace and reduced chances of recurrence. Many of these questions are still open to debate, and we hope to revisit a few of these questions in our future efforts.

19 Disarmament, demobilization and reintegration
Robert Muggah

19.1 INTRODUCTION

More than 60 disarmament, demobilization and reintegration (DDR) initiatives have taken place around the world since the early 1990s. Most of these were launched in the wake of violent international and civil conflicts and conceived following the defeat of one of the parties or as part of a peace-support operation. Whether mandated by a peace agreement, a UN Security Council resolution, or unilaterally by a government, each DDR operation has featured unique characteristics and particularities. Notwithstanding their distinctive origins and bureaucratic manifestations, the shape and direction of DDR evolved in parallel with wider shifts in peacekeeping doctrine and the discourse on security and development. Specifically, peace-support operations expanded from a comparatively limited (minimalist) focus on peacekeeping designed to maintain stability between demarcated parties and on the basis of a negotiated ceasefire to include more multidimensional (maximalist) mandates and integrated approaches, with explicit military, policing, rule of law and social welfare objectives.

Since the early 1990s, DDR interventions have shifted from a relatively narrow preoccupation with ex-combatants ('spoilers') and reductions in national military expenditure ('peace dividend') to a concerted emphasis on consolidating peace and promoting reconstruction and development. Geographically, the vast majority of these have taken place in Africa, though many have also been administered in Latin America and the Caribbean, Southeastern Europe, Central and South Asia and the South Pacific. Temporally and institutionally, DDR programmes are getting longer, drawing on an ever larger caseload of combatants and (vulnerable) dependants and becoming more expensive. Because of the way DDR is designed to reinforce and extend the reach and legitimacy of state authority, it has increasingly been singled out by political scientists and specific practitioners for careful investigation. It is precisely because it has the intended consequences of allowing states to reassert their monopoly of violence that DDR is recognized as an inherently political and politicizing process and of special concern to social scientists.

The following review offers a range of critical reflections on policy and theoretical innovations in DDR since the early 1990s to the present day. Drawing on a wide-ranging (and non-exhaustive) review of the policy and scholarly literature, it highlights key trends in the character and shape of DDR activities. While noting the distinct features and dynamics of DDR processes around the world, it observes a progressive shift from minimalist (security-first) to maximalist (development-oriented) programming. This shift mirrors the expanding engagement of multilateral and bilateral security and development sectors in the DDR debate. Although tensions persist over a host of issues – including the merits of cash/ non-cash benefits, individual versus collective targeting, and sequencing of interventions – the review nevertheless detects a progressive professionalization and standardization of DDR practice within key expert constituencies. Likewise, in examining particularly recent theoretical debates, it detects a shifting of priorities and areas of focus from first- to second-generation scholars. Interest has evolved from a consideration of DDR as a bounded cluster of discourses and practices to a more complex social process connected to actor agency, peace negotiations, justice and security sector reform, state-building and ultimately war recurrence. This shift mirrors a widening array of disciplinary perspectives as well as methodological advances. It also highlights evidence of a longstanding practitioner–academic praxis.

19.2   MAPPING DDR TRENDS

The scale and distribution of peace support operations is unprecedented in the twenty-first century. There are more than twice as many peacekeepers deployed in post-conflict settings today than a decade ago. Global preoccupation with stabilizing fragile states is at an all-time high, as reflected in overseas development flows to such contexts. Policy makers and practitioners are investing considerable resources in enhancing their coordination and coherence and integrating efforts where possible. A host of security promotion activities have emerged over the past few decades to guarantee security and, ultimately, development. DDR activities are among a host of interventions designed to, *inter alia*, stem war recurrence, reduce military expenditure, stimulate spending on social welfare, prevent spoilers from disrupting peace processes, enhance opportunities for their livelihoods, disrupt the command and control of armed groups, and prevent resort to the weapons of war.

With more than 60 DDR operations launched since the 1990s, most of them in the past five years, DDR can be described as something of a 'growth industry'. There are a host of recurring patterns that unify what are otherwise disparate DDR experiences. Approximately two-thirds of these DDR interventions were launched in Africa, with the remainder in Latin America and the Caribbean, Southeastern Europe, Central and South Asia and the South Pacific. Well over a million 'combatants' have participated in some aspect of DDR, with annual aggregate expenditure now surpassing US$630 million. Moreover, national DDR interventions have gradually adopted more 'regional' or multi-country approaches as recognition of the 'spillover' and 'contagion' effects of armed conflicts widened. Likewise, the caseload of prospective beneficiaries for DDR has also expanded from ex-combatants alone, to 'vulnerable groups' (children, women, disabled), dependants, and others of concern (refugees and internally displaced persons) (Harpviken 2008). Now widely considered a pillar of the international peace-support and peacebuilding architecture, more than 20 UN agencies and dozens of non-governmental organizations (NGOs) are engaged in supporting DDR activities. While unable to directly fund disarmament activities, the World Bank is a lead agency in many DDR activities.

DDR programmes also appear to have converged around a set of conventional orthodoxies. First, is the critical role attached by policy makers and practitioners to (national) ownership of DDR and the signal importance of predictable and adequate external assistance. In virtually every country where DDR has been pursued, UN and World Bank representatives have sought (sometimes unsuccessfully) to ensure that national authorities assumed a key role in various aspects of its preparation and implementation. Engagement has ranged from deciding on the scope and timing of the exercise through to negotiating eligibility criteria and implementation modalities, management and monitoring. In most cases, an institutional entity – usually a national commission or focal point – was established to articulate strategic direction and filter policy priorities.

Second, DDR has gradually been recast as not a 'technical' programme but rather a process of stabilization and state-building, even if not explicitly recognized as such. This process has often come after repeated failures, as in Afghanistan (Giustozzi 2009), Eritrea, or Timor-Leste (Peake 2008). Depending on the context, including the duration and severity of the war preceding DDR, practitioners have come to recognize the tremendous political, economic, infrastructural, institutional and social reconciliation challenges entailed in DDR. Although still often erroneously conceived as a kind of magic bullet that automatically and simultaneously cares for a wide range of development and security challenges (Kingma 2000, p. 241; Muggah 2005), approaches to DDR are being tailored to account for the political economy of (in)security. Indeed, a host of complementary processes such as security sector reform and transitional justice are now being consciously examined in relation to DDR programming (Bryden 2007; Grodsky 2009). Needless to say, it was not always this way.

More positively, over the past two decades, those associated with the DDR enterprise have realized that DDR is a process of social engineering. It is not just a 'technical' programme and cannot be treated in isolation of other activities and dynamics underway. Rather most, if not all, aspects of DDR are negotiated and decided in the context of wider political and economic expediencies (Torjesen 2006). An intensely complex process of bargaining invariably defines the parameters of a DDR – including the establishment of what may ultimately represent an appropriate, effective and adequately flexible institutional framework. While some of this nego-tiation takes places in the 'formal' domain – between donors, among state representatives and between agencies (defined as 'turf battles') – much of it occurs informally out of sight of international actors. But it is 'informal' negotiations – between former commanders, erstwhile combatants, elites and community leaders, and families and dependants – that are often key to DDR success or failure. Yet formal conditions are routinely imposed on DDR activities, even if they may not be appropriate or required, while in other instances not all the standard components of DDR are necessary. For example, while it may appeal to some military actors, cantonment may not be appropriate. Ultimately, a common mantra today is that DDR must never be based on a fixed blueprint. Rather, innovation and creativ-ity and a sensitivity to 'context' always remain important for efficient and effective interventions.

As noted above, the literature indicates that the international peace-support, peacebuilding and development architecture has expanded in tandem with international preoccupation over state fragility, stabilization and reconstruction. Often under the auspices of 'integrated' or 'joined-up' peace-support missions, a vast array of multilateral and bilateral agencies have invested in short- and medium-term security promotion efforts, especially DDR and security sector reform (SSR), but also interim stabilization and second-generation efforts (Colleta and Muggah 2009). Regardless of the specific 'social technology', a defining characteristic of this emergent stabilization and reconstruction agenda is the explicit merging of security and development agendas, institutions and actors. In practice, this has been achieved through 'whole-of-government' and 'whole-of-system' approaches, the practical expression of which is most obviously 'integrated missions' (Bryden 2007; Muggah 2009b, 2009c). As such, DDR can and should be regarded as just one of many instru-mental means of preventing states and societies from slipping back into 'instability' and ultimately war.

In the twenty-first century, DDR is firmly wedded to the logic of stabilization, reconstruction and ultimately reconstituting effective states and state–civil society bargaining (Vines and Oruitemeka 2008; Zyck 2009). While reflecting wider trends in the privatization of security more generally, the implementation of DDR is paradoxically also being delegated to private security companies. These trends are hardly surprising since DDR mirrors the strategic and bureaucratic priorities of the security and development sectors and thus the discourse and policy priorities of international donors and power-holding elites. Irrespective of the (apparently now diminished) Western appetite for a liberal peace-support agenda, the effectiveness of the broad spectrum treatment for contemporary post-war landscapes remains critically untested (Egnell and Haldén 2009; Muggah and Krause 2009). And notwithstanding an apparent consensus on the imperative for DDR from Colombia and Haiti to Afghanistan, Iraq and Sudan, there are also still fundamental tensions concerning how it is expected to be achieved, its indicators of success (or effectiveness), the parameters of targeting, or how to reconcile 'security' and 'justice' imperatives (Ucko 2008). Not surprisingly, some critical scholars have examined how the labels and terms of DDR are also freighted with political connotations. For example, in some countries, the concept of DDR is fundamentally rejected in favour of less 'securitized' terminology. Maoist fighters in Nepal and Moros combatants in Mindanao fundamentally rejected the 'discourse' of DDR (Colleta and Muggah 2009).

19.3   POLICY INNOVATIONS

Over the past five years an array of policy initiatives have sought to distil core lessons emerging from DDR policy and practice. Many of these processes yielded prescriptive international guidelines and standards. For example, in 2006 – after a process of several years of analysis and internal and external consultations – the UN generated a set of Integrated Disarmament, Demobilization and Reintegration Standards (UN-IDDRS). The IDDRS represent the agreed guidelines and procedures of the UN for preparing and executing DDR programmes in peacekeeping operations (United Nations 2006a). These guidelines acknowledge the inherent complexity of DDR and its essentially political dynamics. The IDDRS also demonstrated the inherent tension between UN policy guidance on DDR and the need for national ownership of DDR processes. As many hardened UN veterans know too well, during peacekeeping operations it is difficult to live up to the demands of 'national ownership'. Although the IDDRS is the most comprehensive set of good practices in

DDR and offers a loose doctrine for decision makers and practitioners alike, it also risks fuelling 'template thinking'. This could unintentionally inhibit flexibility in responding to the specific needs as they occur or result in the disempowering of national institutions.

Meanwhile, new IDDRS modules are being added and old ones revised. For example, the latest module to be established aims to clarify the nexus between DDR and SSR (Bendix and Stanley 2008; Bryden 2007; Knight 2008). The expectation is that these and other inputs can assist host governments and associated agencies in converting former combatants into legitimate security providers. A variety of important entry-points relate to the design and sharing of management information systems (MIS) between DDR, SSR, transitional justice and related planners and managers. At a programmatic level, it is assumed that these same actors can usefully establish clear and transparent criteria for the integration of former combatants into the security sector (that reflect national priorities and stipulate appropriate skills and backgrounds). In addition to clarifying roles and re-training requirements of different security bodies, DDR, SSR and transitional justice planners can purportedly better ensure transparent (and equitable) chains of payment to existing and newly integrated security sector and justice personnel (Ozerdem 2003).

Two other relevant documents that currently guide DDR processes focus primarily on children (below the age of 18). Endorsed at a ministerial meeting held in 2007, these include the Paris Commitments to Protect Children Unlawfully Recruited or Used by Armed Forces or Armed Groups and the Paris Principles and Guidelines on Children Associated with Armed Forces or Armed Groups. These documents build on the Cape Town Principles adopted in 1997 and the ongoing experience of UNICEF and other national and international agencies. They underscore the humanitarian imperative for unconditional release of children from armed forces and armed groups at all times, even in the midst of violent conflict. It is also important to note that several years of activism and research has led to the adoption of UN Resolution 1325, which urges the international community to enhance the role of women at all levels in peace processes. It includes indications of how women's roles should be strengthened in relation to DDR design and implementation (BICC 2001; Hauge 2009).

Despite the emergence of prescriptions and guidelines, many decision makers operating in the security and development sectors continue to wrestle with the conceptual dimensions of DDR (Kilroy 2008). While norm-setting exercises offer important signposts, they only take planners so far. As was indicated above, each DDR exercise needs to be designed and negotiated according to the specific circumstances on the ground even if most operations are guided by supply-side matrices and check-list thinking. At the international level, a lingering concern among some UN agencies and governments, for example, relates to the institutional and bureaucratic 'integration' of disparate multilateral and bilateral agencies mandated to deal with DDR and the best ways of ensuring the 'reinsertion' and 'reintegration' of former fighters and associated groups. In the context of wider UN reforms, there is a vibrant debate over how best to coordinate the international DDR architecture among disparate security and development agencies, and whether they can practicably 'deliver the goods'. Nevertheless, the choice of which international agency(ies) would play a role in a specific DDR operation remains dependent on their specific comparative advantages and the preference of local actors, in particular the relevant government.

Although peacekeepers and civilian personnel working in the face of simmering violence are struggling to generate results, the priority is naturally more towards delivery than regular monitoring and evaluation. Even so, in a donor climate increasingly dominated by results-based management, many operational agencies are also conscious of the critical importance of moving away from prescriptive approaches towards evidence-based interventions that promote genuine safety and security but have few examples of how to move the agenda forward. Appropriate metrics of success, the indicators, impacts and outcomes of DDR – together with analysis of what and why it does or does not work – are all urgently required.

19.4   PROGRAMMING INNOVATIONS

A recurring dilemma for DDR planners and practitioners relates to the issue of 'targeting' of disarmament, demobilization, reinsertion and reintegration support. It is widely accepted that in most DDR operations the ex-combatants receive an initial assistance package, usually entailing a monetary component. Whether reintegration support within the DDR programme should be provided specifically to the ex-combatant and her/his family unit has long been a point of debate. Related to this is the difficulty of discerning between combatants and non-combatants – a problem certainly not limited to DDR programming and one aggravated by the so-called 'new wars' of the post-Cold War era. As research has amply shown, targeted direct support to the ex-combatants and their immediate family is likely to contribute more effectively to immediate stabilization, but it can and does routinely engender disquiet among the wider population. Most reintegration support efforts have sought to achieve a balance.

An alternative (non-monetary) mechanism includes the provision of specific information, counselling and referral services to ex-combatants. Such assistance can potentially assist ex-combatants consider their needs and preferences and be guided towards appropriate reintegration opportunities – whether through some specific legal advice, participation in a rural development programme, the opportunity to return to school, or an economic opportunity in the market. Although conventional individual approaches to targeting reinsertion and reintegration assistance persist, alternative approaches have emerged over the past two decades. These build on the 'collective' approaches and also include 'community-centred' and 'area-based' interventions including in Haiti, Mozambique, the Philippines, the Democratic Republic of Congo and Sudan (Muggah 2009c; Specker 2008). The core innovation of these approaches is not necessarily in their specific institutional or even programmatic design, but rather the pragmatic acknowledgement that they flow from a diagnosis of the context in which they operate. Very generally, they recognize that individuated incentives can not only fuel resentment and communal tension, but they are often inadequate, wasted and contribute to moral hazard. Collective targeting – from weapons lotteries and inter-community competitions to quick impact projects and scaled-up sector assistance – seemed to circumvent many of these challenges.

Although the number and intensity of armed conflicts has declined since the mid-1990s, post-war violence simmers on. Certain lessons associated with preventing and reducing armed violence in multiple contexts are being learned. Over the past decade, security promotion activities are adjusting to the dynamic landscapes of post-war armed violence (Muggah and Krause 2009). Both 'second-generation peacekeeping' in the wake of operations in the former Yugoslavia and Somalia and more recent 'stabilization' missions following interventions from Afghanistan and Iraq to Timor-Leste and Haiti have emphasized the value of joining up military and civilian activities. Such evolution and adaptation is suggestive of an element of experimentation and pragmatism. Together with mainstream post-war activities, such as mine clearance, truth and reconciliation interventions and international criminal courts, interventions seeking to promote safety and security are flourishing (Knight 2008). In some cases, security promotion activities once confined to war zones are now being applied in ostensibly non-war environments. And while evidence of 'success' of these newer practices remains comparatively thin, these interventions potentially complement and reinforce conventional strategies.

As indicated above, at least two clusters of emerging practices – interim stabilization and second-generation activities – are suggestive of a new horizon of experimentation. Interim stabilization measures feature clear and immediate objectives. These are to dramatically reduce armed violence; consolidate peace and real and perceived security; build confidence and trust; and buy time and space for the macro conditions to ripen for more conventional security promotion activities such as DDR and SSR to take hold, including second-generation initiatives. Meanwhile, second-generation security promotion approaches are fast emerging as alternatives and complements to DDR and SSR, particularly in Latin America and the Caribbean. They tend to be evidence-led, focusing at the outset on identifying and mitigating demonstrated risk factors, enhancing resilience and protective factors at the metropolitan and community levels, and constructing interventions on the basis of identified needs.

19.5 THEORETICAL INNOVATIONS

While not necessarily a discipline or field of enquiry in its own right, the study of DDR has expanded considerably over the past two decades. Beginning with a relatively modest number of specialists with expertise in international relations and political science (Berdal 1996; Colleta 1995; Colleta et al. 1996; Collier 1994), the landscape has widened to include experts in development studies, security, policing and military studies, econometrics, anthropology, sociology, criminology, law, psychology and behavioural studies, human geography, public health and others. Much of this expansion was inspired by policy and programming interest expressed in multilateral and bilateral policy arenas. Action-oriented researchers frequently imparted 'lessons from the field' in the academic environment, including international conferences. Likewise, practitioners have also in some cases been encouraged to invest in evidence-based policy and programming, thus advancing the exchange. DDR research could therefore be characterized as a classic case of research-practice praxis – a fully iterative and dynamic exchange.

Research and practice on DDR has been motivated predominantly by programmatic and operational concerns rather than more esoteric scholarly interests such as war recurrence (Glassmyer and Sambanis 2008). Academic investigation has focused on practical aspects of the project cycle – from designing robust DDR interventions to monitoring and evaluating outputs and outcomes. In what amounts to the first generation of DDR research from the mid-1990s to the mid-2000s, researchers from predominantly US, UK and Western European institutions (both university and research institute based) focused on more qualitative and case-specific phenomena in Africa. This first wave began with general assessments of DDR and its relationship with wider peacebuilding and state-building processes (Berdal 1996). Researchers were mobilized to examine specific aspects of combatant and ex-combatant motivations and skill-sets, access to and availability of weapons and munitions, the relative trade-offs between cash and non-cash incentives for participation, absorptive potential in areas of return and repatriation, long-term dividends of reintegration assistance, the trade-offs between individual and collective renumeration and recidivism of DDR participants. In some cases, findings have featured in both scholarly and practitioner-oriented journals.

A major focus of first-wave scholars was with the specific institutional features of DDR itself – namely disarmament, demobilization and reintegration. As such, research focused on the dynamic outcomes of each phase, the logic of sequencing, and the dilemmas associated with each activity rather than the wider array of processes occurring before, after or in parallel with DDR. Theoretical approaches tended to assume rational agency models and focused, if at all, on primarily economic criteria of demobilization and reintegration effectiveness. First-generation scholars were especially preoccupied with defining the target groups (Jensen and Stepputat 2001), the security dilemmas associated with asymmetrical disarmament (Stedman et al. 2002), the perils of partial demobilization (Colleta et al. 1996; Kingma and Sayers 1994), the adequacy of reintegration assistance inputs (Kingma 2000), and the consistency of funding (Ball and Hendrickson 2005). As such, DDR was conceived as a bounded activity, spatially, temporally and socially remote from other activities. While drawing important conceptual parameters around the debate on DDR, these early studies did not address fundamental questions of causality or correlation, actor agency, or intervention outcomes.

More recently, scholarly attention to DDR has evolved to begin testing assumptions, undertaking comparative assessments and breaking new disciplinary ground. In what could be described as the second generation of DDR research (from the mid-2000s to the present), a growing number of academics are investing in statistical assessments drawing on large-n sample studies and more experimental design to test counterfactual arguments with examples from Latin America and the Caribbean, Sub-Saharan Africa, the Balkans, South Asia and the South Pacific. Specifically, researchers have begun to examine large numbers of DDR interventions (from 1989–present) to examine the determinants of DDR and the strength of their statistical contribution to war (non-)recurrence or homicide reduction (Blake 2009; ECP 2007; Restrepo and Muggah 2009). This expansion in research mirrors, in part, a widening of engagement in DDR from multilateral and bilateral development agencies, foreign policy establishments and policy think-tanks.

The sheer diversity of theoretical and practical innovation is bewildering. The list of topics of interest has expanded to include not just core aspects of DDR, but also wider intersectoral relationships between DDR and transitional justice (Morgenstein 2008), SSR (Berdal and Ucko 2009; Bryden 2007; Egnell and Haldén 2009), and state-building processes. More focused investigations include microeconomic assessments of demobilized combatant behaviour/outcomes in comparison with non-participant cohorts (Christensen and Utas 2008; Humphreys and Weinstein 2007, 2008). Others might include randomized survey-based assessments of the incentives shaping child involvement in armed groups and the likely determinants of their successful exit (Blattman and Annan 2009). Meanwhile, some DDR specialists began focusing on assisting programmers on influencing the 'design' and 'implementation' of interventions so as to better measure programme effectiveness. In Aceh (Barron 2009), Burundi (Douma 2008), Liberia (Pugel 2009), Sierra Leone (Humphreys and Weinstein 2007; Mitton 2008), and elsewhere, researchers sought to encourage the randomization of DDR entitlements to identify the actual probability of effective political and economic reintegration outcomes. Even as it may have stirred up controversy, their work has also served to refine the metrics of reintegration success and failure.

In the course of these two waves of academic enquiry, a professional field of experts has emerged to help guide DDR design, management, outputs and outcomes. Many of these specialists work directly for the Department of Peacekeeping Operations (DPKO), the United Nations Development Programme (UNDP), the World Bank, the International Organisation for Migration (IOM) and various bilateral partners (Douglas et al. 2004; European Union 2006; USAID 2005a). Composed of a military and police, development practitioners, social science researchers and many others, this nascent epistemic community is fast producing lessons that reveal some common trends and patterns across time and space. For example, there is an emerging consensus that DDR should be considered early on in a given peace process (preferably in negotiations and in the peace agreement itself) (Buchanan and Widmer 2006), that it be meaningfully owned and managed by legitimate national institutions (with attention to political economies), that it combine a combination of cash and non-monetized incentives targeting individuals and collectives (Ozerdem and Podder 2011; Willibald 2006), and that the division of labour for its various components be based on a coherent vision and according to the comparative advantages of the actors involved (in a so-called 'integrated' approach or otherwise) (Greene et al. 2008; Muggah 2009a). Another important lesson relates to humility and effective communication, especially concerning what can be realistically achieved by DDR in usually complex environments (Berdal and Ucko 2009).

20 Obstacles to peace settlements
Roy Licklider

20.1 INTRODUCTION

We know more about how wars begin than how they end. Intellectually, the problem of negotiating an end to a civil war is daunting; how do you make peace and agree to live in the same state with people who have killed your friends and family? How do you live with these people for the rest of your life? How do you trust them enough to work with them economically and socially to create a functioning political system?

The problem is made much more difficult by the likely conditions under which this trust must be created. Typically, war or civil violence has not solved the problems that caused it. If two groups of people have been antagonistic towards each other, large-scale killing is unlikely to have improved relations. If maldistribution of economic resources has been a problem, the destruction of the economy will not help. The list can be extended.

Peace, after all, is not the primary goal of the parties. On the contrary, the violence arose precisely because both sides felt there were other issues more important, things that were worth dying and killing for. Nor is this inappropriate. An unjust peace, whatever that means, is not necessarily a good bargain. This analysis does not assume that peace should be the primary goal; it only assumes that peace sometimes is and that, at such times, it is useful to have some idea about the conditions under which peace may be obtained.

An 'ideal type' of post-war society might look like this: economically the infrastructure has been destroyed; the currency has been undermined; commerce is at a standstill; agriculture has been devastated; unemployment is high, which means there are no jobs for former soldiers; and there is no basis for exports. The country's society has been undercut by the mutual dislike between warring groups, which is not any weaker than before the war; the wide distribution of weapons within the population; the people's habit of non-obedience to government and authority generally; the undermining of traditional sources of authority; the need to demobilize and disarm at least two armies quickly; and the prevalence of young soldiers with no skills other than killing. The old political process has been discredited (you do not want to re-create the political system that resulted in civil war), there is no single legitimate government, there is a low tolerance for legitimate oppositions, there is often little democratic tradition, and the police and judicial systems are seen (usually correctly) as part of the problem rather than as part of the solution because they have no legitimacy for much of the population.

Civil war looks more likely to start than to end under these conditions. It is thus not surprising that a number of analysts have found that civil wars are less likely to end in negotiated settlements than are inter-state wars (Licklider 1995; Pillar 1983; Stedman 1991; Walter 1997). Nor is it incredible that most settlements of civil wars do not last (Walter 1997, 2001); it is perhaps surprising that any do. But we also know that historically every major state has gone through at least one such transition (the French Revolution, the Chinese Revolution, the English Civil War, the Russian Revolution, the American Civil War, and the American Revolution), so we know that it does happen. We also know that, since 1945, settlements of civil wars that have lasted about five years have seldom later collapsed into future violence. But we do not know much about the dynamics of these processes or the conditions under which they are more or less likely to succeed.

20.2 WHY HAVE COMBATANTS INCREASINGLY SOUGHT SETTLEMENT THROUGH POLITICAL RATHER THAN MILITARY MEANS?

Conventionally, civil wars were expected to end by a military victory for one side or the other, on the model of the American Civil War or the French and Russian Revolutions. The theory was straightforward: in inter-state wars foreign conquerors might leave at some point, but in civil wars where the stakes were permanent control of the government, losing such control would be fatal to the interests of either side, and therefore compromise was impossible (Iklé 1991). Analyses of civil wars during the Cold War period confirmed that negotiated settlements were rare, although not unknown (Licklider 1995; Pillar 1983; Stedman 1991; Walter 1997).

More recently, however, combatants seem more willing to work out negotiated settlements involving compromises, some of which seem to work (El Salvador, South Africa and Nicaragua) and some of which do not (Angola and Sudan). Both internal and external factors seem to be contributing to this trend.

Internally, military victories seem harder to come by these days.

Increasingly, the issues in civil wars tend to be about identity rather than ideology, a trend that began several decades ago (Gurr 2000a, p. 53; Licklider 1995, pp. 685–6). Identity conflicts may be harder to resolve; settlements do not seem to hold as well (Licklider 1995). We can imagine why this may be true. In an ideological conflict (for example, Cambodia), it is possible to imagine converting the enemy to your own position by re-education. It is striking that in China, for example, the communists asked thousands of Kuomintang officials to remain in office after the revolution once organized resistance had ceased (Teiwes 1987, p. 74).

In an identity conflict, on the other hand, conversion is practically impossible. The victor has only a few alternatives: removal of the other group by genocide or ethnic cleansing (which explains why these policies have become more common); repression, which presumably makes a future outbreak of violence more likely in the long run; and conciliation, which can never be fully effective because the victor cannot risk losing control of the state, which is the most important stake. A fourth alternative is integration, which would produce new alliances that cross former divisions and make the identity conflict irrelevant. Integration, however, is attractive in concept but extremely difficult to bring about, especially in the short run.

This stalemate is increasingly likely to be the result of civil war. But stalemate by itself does not produce negotiated settlements. As I. William Zartman has pointed out (Zartman 1989, 1993), stalemate is not necessarily a bad outcome for the parties; one may control the state apparatus and be able to gain some resources from its international connections, while the other may control a substantial part of the state's population and territory and run a shadow state, again benefiting those in control. Thus the elites of both sides may find stalemate a comfortable outcome, although it may be less attractive to those in whose name they govern.

At the same time, external resources for long-term civil wars are generally declining. Because the Cold War has ended, the superpowers are much less interested in financing such activities; thus there was an outbreak of peace in the early 1990s (Ayres 2000; Gurr 2000a). Regional powers often remain willing and able to intervene (Syria in Lebanon is a conspicuous example) but the increased stress on economic performance rather than on conventional security issues seems to have reduced this tendency somewhat as well. Both sides in such wars thus increasingly feel under pressure to end the violence as the situation moved to what Zartman (1989) has called a 'hurting stalemate', in which each side expects things to get worse in the future unless some change occurs. It is interesting that explanations for the continuation of some current conflicts often stress access to portable economic resources that can be looted, such as diamonds and oil in

Zaire and Angola; these ideas in turn are part of a recent, serious interest in the economic basis for civil war.

20.3   WHY IS IT SO DIFFICULT FOR THESE PEACE SETTLEMENTS TO HOLD?

Negotiated settlements seem an attractive way to end large-scale violence. Presumably, each side gets enough concessions to encourage it to participate in a common government that will alleviate societal problems, build ties with former adversaries, and make future conflict less likely. Negotiated settlements also hold the promise of not enforcing a vindictive peace that may lead to resentment and renewed violence. Indeed, negotiated settlements have become the gold standard for ending civil wars after the Cold War, part of the good practice by which Ted Gurr (2000a) explains their recent increase.

However, some theorists and practitioners believe that negotiated settlements will not generally hold as well as military victories will. A plausible general argument is that different factors cause groups to (i) initiate negotiations, (ii) reach agreement, and (iii) implement those agreements and that considerable slippage between these different stages is thus predictable (Walter 2001). Negotiated settlements create a series of veto groups in internal politics, making it difficult for the new government to act decisively. Moreover, the groups remain in existence, so political crises may be followed by renewed resort to violence. Military victory, on the other hand, destroys the internal organization of one side, allowing the winners to take strong actions, although obviously not guaranteeing success, and making it very difficult for the losers to successfully resort to violence (Wagner 1993). Some analysis suggests that this theory may be correct; of the approximately 80 civil wars between 1945 and 1993, 15 per cent of the military victories were followed by renewed wars, while 50 per cent of the negotiated settlements were (Carment and Harvey 2000; Licklider 1995).

Why do negotiated settlements often not work well? Such agreements have a number of serious potential problems, and it is important to remember that the collapse of an agreement need not signal bad faith or irreconcilable differences. Negotiated settlements by definition involve compromises; both sides have to abandon some of their goals to reach agreement. Negotiated settlements are thus always second-best solutions. As a result, no party is totally committed to the terms of the settlement itself. It may be the best outcome they can get, but it is unlikely to inspire passionate loyalty from either side, at least at the beginning. This lack of automatic support puts it constantly at risk, particularly if circumstances change (Werner 1999).

Often the two sides have effectively developed separate states, areas and peoples under the control of a working government. The settlement will usually require both sides to abandon these separate structures to create a new structure that those who have been deadly enemies share. It is not surprising that the prospect may be greeted with real concern, even if goodwill is present.

Within each side, a settlement will threaten the interests of individuals and organizations who have the ability to undercut it, those Stephen Stedman (1997, 1998) has called 'spoilers'. Peace may make obsolete the expertise of specialists in violence and diminish their political dominance. They and others often are benefiting economically from the war as well; large amounts of money are being used, and there are a variety of ways, more and less legitimate, to profit from it (Collier and Hoeffler 2000). The settlement is often driven by a new coalition of moderates from both camps. But it may be opposed by a similarly cross-cutting coalition of extremists in both camps tacitly allied in opposition to the agreement. Outsiders often assume that the moderates have a natural advantage since they are advocating peace, but the spoilers may have access to important resources and be aided by the inherent difficulties of negotiating an end to a civil war.

20.4   ROLES FOR OUTSIDERS

Many of the factors that explain the rise of negotiated settlements are the result of external actions or lack of them: the end of the Cold War with the corresponding decline in support for violence, an international intellectual climate less sympathetic to violence, non-governmental organizations (NGOs) dedicated to ending violence, and so on. In many cases international pressure has pushed the parties to negotiate when they otherwise might not have done so. Once the process has begun, outsiders have transmitted information, acted as mediators, and offered incentives to reach settlements. Several studies have found that these activities are more common in cases in which settlements are reached (Miall 1992; Richardson and Wang 1993). On the other hand, at least one study found that UN intervention seemed to make inter-state disputes more intense (Diehl et al. 1996).

External pressure does not always promote peace, of course. Ostensibly, internal violence is often promoted or made possible by outside assistance of various sorts, such as that provided by the United States in Afghanistan under Soviet occupation and by South Africa in Mozambique. Borrowing from, among other cases, the settlement for Zimbabwe, outsiders attempting to end wars have frequently tried to resolve the problems with external powers first, in order to have a better chance of success when moving on to the internal disputes that are usually at the heart of the matter.

But external pressure seems increasingly to be oriented towards bringing about peace, which in practice means some sort of negotiated settlement, even if some players want the settlements skewed in favour of one side or another. External diplomatic involvement is not necessary to reach a settlement; in Colombia in 1957 and North Yemen in 1970 the local protagonists negotiated and enforced agreements (Walter 1997). However, external involvement is often helpful in facilitating this process, albeit only when the local parties prove ready to take advantage.

Interestingly, we do not have much systematic research on what qualities of a peace settlement make it more likely to endure. In the absence of parsimonious, empirically supported theory, practitioners and analysts have developed a number of plausible suggestions to guide policy choices of outsiders trying to encourage such behaviour.

20.4.1 Inclusiveness

A workable settlement usually has to involve all the major parties (Hampson 1996, p. 217). This is easy to say but hard to accomplish. Civil wars often involve loose alliances of moderates and extremists on both sides. It is tempting to negotiate with the moderates and try to leave the extremists out; the moderates are much more willing to make agreements, and more likely to keep them, may have more supporters, and are often much more attractive individuals.

But this is often a mistake. Negotiated settlements to civil wars are delicate affairs; persuading enemies to disarm and leave themselves vulnerable is not a simple task, and even after the agreement is reached, implementation remains extremely fragile (Walter 2001). The process can often be derailed by relatively small acts of violence or even symbolic gestures, particularly early in the process, before personal trust has developed among the former antagonists. Civil war settlement is not a democratic process: even a small but dedicated group can commit a series of violent acts that can bring about the collapse of the peace process, as when Ulster Catholic and Protestant militants have undercut popular Ulster peace agreements. It is important, then, to make every effort to include all the major groups involved in the conflict, particularly at first. At the same time, such inclusion need not imply granting the extremists a permanent veto. Over time an effective coalition may develop between the moderates of both sides. If this coalition is strong enough, it may be able to survive the violent defection of extremists. Cambodia is an interesting example; the Khmer Rouge defected from the settlement and caused considerable trouble, but over time the settlement gained momentum and the Khmer Rouge subsided into irrelevance.

Outsiders have promoted inclusiveness by encouraging the different sides to meet, selecting the meeting places, empowering the weaker groups, and funding the process. In the process they may effectively select the parties who will meet. They should exert every effort to bring all of the important players in the conflict into the process as soon as possible. Experience suggests that they need to resist the temptation to settle for an easy agreement with moderates, even if it means that the killing will go on longer, because such settlements are very likely to fail, reinforcing distrust and making future negotiations more difficult.

20.4.2   Elite Integration

In practice, a coalition of moderates is critical for negotiated settlement. Effectively, this means that the more moderate members of the elites from both sides of the war must be integrated and given a stake in the settlement. Recently, two important theories have been developed to explain this process.

Elisabeth Wood's impressive work (2000) focuses particularly on El Salvador and South Africa. Her theory applies to states where elite power depends on control of the labour of the masses in ways that go beyond the conventional employer–employee relationship. The resulting civil war is likely to have a large dose of class conflict, although ethnic issues may also be involved, creating what Gurr (1993, p. 21) has called an ethno-class struggle, as in South Africa. If the war continues, this elite control will be weakened, and profits in this sector will decline. Members of the elite will shift their investments to other activities that do not require such control. As these activities become dominant within the elite, its interests change; the elites now have an economic interest in peace, and as a result a new coalition of moderates on both sides becomes possible.

Marie-Joëlle Zahar (1999) proposes an alternative theory in her analysis of militia leaders, who, although usually seen as the most difficult people to work with, have in fact sometimes been amenable to peace settlements in places as highly charged as Lebanon and Bosnia. She argues that militias develop social and political institutions in order to fight their wars successfully, but that these institutions in turn open new opportunities that change the costs and benefits of various strategies. In particular, militias become more vulnerable to military losses and develop economic interests that can be traded off against their original political goals, sometimes making them more amenable to negotiated settlements.

Because of the importance of ethnicity in current violence, it is particularly important that both theories seem to explain settlement in places such as South Africa, Bosnia and Lebanon. If they work in these very unpromising conflicts, this suggests that ethnic conflicts may not be all that different from others in some significant qualities.

The general point of both Wood and Zahar is that interests of the parties may change as the conflict goes on, sometimes making compromise possible. Zartman (1989) has argued that conflicts may become 'ripe for resolution' when a mutual, hurting stalemate occurs, that is, when each side believes that things will get worse if the status quo continues and that another alternative (settlement) is available that will be better than continued war. This concept has been difficult to apply because we have no way to measure the degree of ripeness separate from the success or failure of settlements, but the underlying idea remains important – namely, that there may be times when the interests of elites change, making peace possible.

However, integration does not mean that everyone participates in and benefits from a peace settlement; despite the conflict resolution rhetoric, settlements are not a win–win outcome for all the participants. Every peace settlement has losers and winners (Stedman 1993, pp. 159–60); effective settlements include those who have the power to disrupt, often leaving out others who may seem more deserving but are less threatening. Zimbabwe is a good example. The Lancaster House settlement resulted in an election that established a black government led by Robert Mugabe. Mugabe then decided to allow the white settlers to remain and to keep their land and money in return for their allegiance to him and their withdrawal from politics; indeed, he even kept the white heads of the army and intelligence until they became involved in an anti-government plot. This meant that he could not keep his promises of land reform to his own soldiers; they gained political rights (no small thing, of course), but their economic situation did not change much. The settlement was not necessarily a bad thing; it allowed Zimbabwe to retain the export sector of its economy during the transition and eased the concerns of European powers and the United States. But it is a useful reminder that, despite the conflict resolution rhetoric, negotiated settlements are not simply win–win solutions but political 'deals' (Waterman 1993) in which some people win a great deal more than others.

Civil wars go on for a long time because at least some people and institutions find it useful that the wars do so. In order to change this incentive system, outsiders need to find ways to make peace pay more than war for the competing elites. Apparently it does not have to pay equally for everyone; Hugh Miall (1992, p. 186) found that, as long as one side did not clearly lose outright, agreement was possible with different levels of benefits.

Once the fighting itself has stopped, elites need to be encouraged to work together. This can be done in a variety of ways: aid is often tied to agreements among them or targeted to institutions in which they work together, for example. The key is to develop and strengthen a coalition of moderates from both sides (although they need not have been moderates during the war) because it is practically inevitable that some people will find themselves less well off in peace and form an alternative, if often implicit, coalition of extremists resisting the settlement. Outsiders may be too quick to assume that the moderate coalition, which often has control of the governmental institutions and receives external support, will automatically win such a conflict. This is a bad assumption to make if it encourages outsiders to reduce support for post-settlement governments that face enormous challenges.

20.4.3   Resolve the Security Dilemma

Several studies show that since 1940 civil wars have been much less likely than inter-state wars to end in negotiated settlements. Figures vary somewhat with the time and definitions: 15 to 68 per cent (ibid., p. 124); 32 to 68 per cent (Pillar 1983, p. 25); 15 to 68 per cent (Stedman 1991 refines Pillar's civil war data and does not dispute the inter-state war figure); and 20 to 55 per cent (Walter 1997, p. 335). Some analysts have attributed this to the different stakes involved in civil wars (Iklé 1991; Licklider 1995). Barbara Walter (1997, pp. 336–41; 2001) argues persuasively, however, that the difference is that a negotiated end to an inter-state war may leave each side with enough military power to defend itself, while a comparable settlement in a civil war requires that both sides disarm themselves, leaving each vulnerable to destruction.

Analysts have borrowed the term 'security dilemma' from international politics to describe the situation (Fearon 1998; Posen 1993; Walter and Snyder 1999). Disarmament is necessary for internal security, but for each side it is enormously risky; what if the other side takes advantage of its weakness to destroy it? But if one side does not disarm, the other assumes that it is planning an attack and rearms. More seriously, each side has a strong incentive to rearm even when it has ambiguous information that the other side is doing the same, and of course each side knows this about the other. Thus even people who want to disarm may find it too risky and wind up undercutting the settlement they support. Naturally, those who oppose the settlement on both sides will use these issues as arguments against it.

The importance of the security dilemma can be exaggerated. Many civil war settlements collapse, not because of real fear of attack, but because one or more of the antagonists were unhappy with the outcomes and felt that violence was a preferred alternative. Security dilemma theorists sometimes make it sound as though every civil war could be settled if we could just resolve this particular issue, which is obviously untrue. But the security dilemma remains a major problem, both in the short term during the transition from war to building shared institutions, and later, as the new government tries to cope with its very substantial problems.

Much attention has focused on the transition period. It usually is very unstable politically. The alliances of the preceding war are coming apart as the rule and rewards change. People with guns are uneasy about their future, which is always a recipe for trouble. The country is often close to anarchy. Some new political structure is being created, but no one is certain what it is or what its effects will be. The existing political institutions cannot be trusted.

It seems reasonable that third parties could play an essential role in bridging the transition, reassuring each side that the other is complying long enough for mutual trust to build and infant institutions to develop, perhaps formally guaranteeing the process. Outsiders may also offer alliances in case the settlement fails, thus reducing the security dilemma (Stedman 1996; Walter 1997; Walter 1999, 2001). In fact, the effects of such guarantees are unclear. Walter (1997, pp. 349–51) identified 16 successful civil war settlements between 1940 and 1990; 14 of them included third-party guarantees and every case in which such a guarantee was given was a success (see also Hartzell et al. 2001). Aside from the raw figures, when nine cases of failed settlements are analysed, negotiations often foundered on the issue of security during the transition. When peacekeeping troops were in place but withdrawn after settlement – Laos in 1973 and Vietnam in 1975 – fighting resumed. Similarly, when peacekeepers failed to arrive – Uganda in 1985, Chad in 1979 – the settlements collapsed. In a later version of the analysis, Walter (2001, chs 4–5) identified 59 civil wars ending between 1940 and 1995, 12 by successful settlement; she found that third-party security guarantees were one of the strongest predictors of successful implementation of civil war negotiated settlements. At the same time, Caroline Hartzell (1999) looked at settlements from 1945 to 1997 and Suzanne Werner (1999) examined settlements from 1815 to 1992; both found that third-party guarantees did not matter much.

Outside intervention comes in different forms. Classical conflict resolution theory calls for neutral peacekeepers, but in several of these cases the outsiders were not neutral (the United States in the Dominican Republic and Britain in Zimbabwe are examples). This is probably a good thing; even though outside states with an interest in a civil war are likely to be biased, states without such an interest may not be willing to make the commitment that is useful in ending the violence.

Walter (1997) also argues that foreign troops can help resolve the security dilemma by enforcing the terms of the agreement and providing reliable information to the parties about compliance of the other parties. We now have examples in the former Yugoslavia in which foreign soldiers actually enforced such agreements among locals – a radical change from conventional peacekeeping (which is sometimes called 'peacemaking'). Western governments seem to have decided that they can carry out such activities only as long as casualties are low; the ominous example of Somalia hangs over them, despite research that suggests that the US public in fact did not demand withdrawal after the débâcle (Kull and Ramsay 2000). As a result they are inclined to use air power and artillery instead of ground forces when resistance is likely. If one side decides to reopen the civil war, strategies such as these that often produce civilian casualties do not seem the best way to end the violence, as suggested by the vigorous debate over the ethics of the Kosovo intervention.

20.4.4   Establish a Working Government

Post-violence states have major social problems: '[p]ractically all war-torn societies require comprehensive reforms in their political, economic, social, and security sectors' (Kumar 1997, p.3). In particular these problems require a strong state, at a minimum able to provide security for its citizens, make decisions in a politically acceptable way, and create organizations that will implement these decisions and extract resources from the population to pay for the whole process. Each set of problems is formidable, and outsiders have attempted to assist with all of them at various times.

Security
Perhaps the most fundamental task of the state is providing security for its population. This is often very difficult for the post-conflict state. Civil war armies are often not well disciplined under the best of circumstances, one explanation for the seemingly pointless brutality that often accompanies such conflicts. When the fighting ends, they often disintegrate, releasing thousands of armed young men with no civilian skills at all. At the same time, the public security forces of the old regime were deeply implicated in its bad actions and cannot continue their repressive behaviour because of

the political settlement. All this happens precisely when people who have often been terribly injured by the war desperately need reassurances in order to resume their normal lives:

> In communities tormented by repeated violence . . . safety is the most compelling motive for action. Unstable conditions tend to be exacerbated by the return of community members who fled during earlier bouts of fighting; land disputes, threats, retribution, and intimidation are common. Individuals may be frightened by other individuals or gangs, identity groups as a whole may be afraid of large-scale retribution or attacks based on association, and the community at large may be threatened by other regions, the military, or government persecution. Healing under these conditions can be extremely difficult. Therefore, freedom of movement within the community, absence of personal or group threats or attacks, property security, and access to community resources are necessary first steps on the path to recovery. The principle of safety must apply to all members of the community, regardless of status. (Maynard 1999, p. 132)

The problem of establishing security for citizens confronts every society after civil war. At one level it seems to be fairly simple: a police force has to be created. But in fact this is extraordinarily difficult. If it seems inappropriate to use personnel from the earlier security forces, where are trained and competent personnel, fluent in the local language and versed in the local customs and geography, to be found in short order? Anarchy in the streets will not wait for the establishment of a new policy academy, determination of a curriculum, recruitment of new officers, completion of coursework, and initiation into the complexities of police work. Given the time constraints, veterans from the earlier security forces have to be used. Outsiders can encourage purging those guilty of the worst excesses and providing some sort of training to the rest, even if it is only on the job.

In fact, however, a police force is only part of the solution. A police force needs a set of laws to enforce, and the previous set dates from the old regime and is now widely seen as illegitimate. It also needs a judicial system with judges and lawyers, who are likely to be in short supply after a civil war in which they were likely targets. After trials, a prison system is needed, and again this will likely have to be built from the ground up. In other words, it needs a government. But who should control such a government? That is precisely what the civil war was all about (for a useful collection on this whole process, see Oakley et al. 1998).

At another level, the security system attempts to limit individual violence within the society. The usual upsurge in such violence is the result of fighters who find that crime is the easiest way to prosper economically. Clearly it is more efficient to demobilize and integrate these individuals into the national economy than to try to deal with them as an internal security problem. Obviously this will reduce the security dilemma as well.

Demobilization usually involves assembling the fighters to disarm them and give them some preparation for re-entering civilian life, perhaps including some skills and basic education, and providing them with some basic resources for some time. It is a complex and expensive process, and delays often seem inevitable. However, such delays raise the threat that the civil war armies may reform, undermining confidence in the settlement, and they should be avoided if possible (Ball 1996).

Outsiders have often played a central part in such activities, by providing intellectual leadership, resources and personnel to supervise the process. Demobilization succeeded in Namibia, where 7,500 people from the United Nations were present; it failed in Angola, where there were only 425. On the other hand, numbers are sometimes not enough: the Khmer Rouge refused to be disarmed despite the presence of over 15,000 military personnel associated with the United Nations. This raised the delicate question of whether the United Nations should have been prepared to use force to enforce demobilization; the combat records of the Khmer Rouge and the United Nations suggest this may have been a bad idea (Hampson 1996). Nonetheless, the general point remains that demobilization and disarmament are critical and that third parties often play a central role in making it happen.

An interesting alternative is community-based security, in which arms are retained under the authority of local councils. This approach seems to have worked in Somaliland and produced significant disarmament without foreign assistance (von Hippel 2000a).

Outsiders have often been reluctant to become involved in these activities. Outsiders do not like to spend money on police and prisons; it is much more satisfying to feed starving children than to establish a justice system that may reduce corruption so they can get food on their own. In addition, some organizations, including the US military, are forbidden to aid police (Kumar 1997). This reluctance may explain why the same sorts of problems seem to confront us repeatedly and why international learning on this subject seems to have been rather slow.

Any outside troops on the scene will be pressed into service as police, but they will not like it. Soldiers and police are not trained to do the same things, even if they both are armed. Moreover, the soldiers as outsiders have no legitimacy. So the military will pressure the civilians to get some sort of police force, almost any kind, on the streets so that they can get back to their job. In Panama, for example, the Americans created a special group of reservists who had been police in the United States, some of whom also spoke Spanish, to go on patrol with the new Panamanian police officers. However, this did not last long because the US military is forbidden to train foreign police (Donnelly et al. 1991). In Somalia, a police force was created in Mogadishu from former police after the initial intervention by the US-directed UNITAF (United Nations Task Force), but when the United Nations took over, its personnel felt that there should be a government before there was a police force and allowed the rather vestigial force to decay (Hirsch and Oakley 1995). In Haiti an interim police force was formed from diaspora Haitians and members of the armed forces who had been non-political and given a few days of training. Simultaneously a separate, permanent police force was recruited and given more extensive training by both the United States and the United Nations; over time it replaced the interim force (von Hippel 2000a).

Similar problems arose in Panama, El Salvador and Haiti, despite the different roles for the United States and the United Nations. The new security forces had insufficient physical equipment and fiscal support, first from the external sponsors and later from the local government. They found it extremely difficult to recruit high-level officials who had not been involved in the previous government's security systems and suffered public scandals as a result. They were handicapped by the lack of an effective judicial system, including courts, lawyers, prisons and so on. They clearly had a much better human rights record than their predecessors (which would not have been difficult), and the local populations generally viewed them fairly favourably initially, but local support declined as crime rose after the settlement and the police seemed unwilling or unable to cope with it (Licklider 1999; Stanley and Call 1997; University of Illinois Office of International Criminal Justice 1990; von Hippel 2000a).

Some organizations have stepped forward to fill the gap with training, notably the International Criminal Investigative Training Assistance Program, sponsored by the US Department of Justice, and the United Nations CIVPOL; the Stanley Foundation (2000) recently suggested developing an International Legal Assistance Consortium. Nonetheless, the lack of capability within the international community is a major problem, as shown most clearly in Bosnia (von Hippel 2000a).

Power sharing

The most important issue in any civil war settlement is the distribution of political power in the successor state(s). That is, ultimately, what the war has been about. People are willing to fight and die over it because they know it will determine their future and that of their children.

Western governments, particularly the United States, seem to believe that democracy is the form of government most likely to allow people to live together peacefully, and indeed it seems reasonable that people are more likely to be content if they have some say in their government. Several authors have tried to develop empirical theories about how democracy may emerge from civil war. Wood (2000) concludes that changing elite interests in oligarchies make continuation of civil war too expensive and makes democracy an attractive alternative. Leonard Wantchekon and Zvika Neeman (2002) suggest that elites in conflict prefer basic decisions to be made by the population at large rather than by their opponents, since the interests of the population are more divided and therefore more likely to be neutral.

However, simple majoritarian democracy is unlikely to be acceptable to groups who see themselves as permanent minorities. This means that the conventional parliamentary system, which most European states exported to their colonies, will not work well. The US system of divided powers specified by a written constitution, perhaps reinforced by a federal system, may seem more attractive, but it is not clear how the legal checks on executive authority can be enforced. The more common strategy is a parliamentary system with some sort of proportional representation (Hartzell 1999); this guarantees access to the government but risks producing weak governments.

There are two different types of power sharing: assuring all groups a voice in political decisions at the centre of the state and dispersing central power to regional or local centres. They may be used together, of course. Timothy Sisk (1996, p. 46) has argued that dispersal of power is an appropriate response to situations in which groups are regionally concentrated (often these are ethnic groups), while central distribution is more helpful in other cases. Regional autonomy settlements have often been effective in resolving ethnic and communal conflicts, although they are not a panacea (Gurr 1993, pp. 298–305; Lapidoth 1996).

Power sharing is not necessarily democratic; in fact, it is often designed precisely to prevent simple majorities from ruling. More significantly, it can take place among elites with very little role for other segments of the society (Rothchild 1997; Rothchild and Foley 1988). We do not have good evidence about whether democratic post-settlement governments make renewed civil war less likely, in part because in the post-Second World War era there have not been many such governments or renewed civil wars. However, some tentative work suggests that there may not be much of a connection. Democracy was not significantly associated with decreased likelihood of renewed civil war in an analysis of 83 cases from 1945 to 1993. Further analysis specified a number of causal processes, including intermediate variables, by which democracy would be expected to have this impact; some of the specified intermediate variables were not uniquely linked to democracy, and others seemed to have little impact on renewed civil war (Licklider 2000). Democracy may be a superior form of government for a variety of reasons, but it is not clear that it prevents renewed civil war.

Third-party forces may be useful during the transition, but they cannot remain forever. We are usually talking about a period of a few years. Aside from stopping the killing, the most important function of the transition is to establish a set of political institutions through which societal conflicts may be pursued without large-scale violence. Boutros Boutros-Ghali (1992) has called this 'post-conflict peacebuilding'.

Hartzell (1999) has shown that successful settlements are overwhelmingly characterized by agreements that specify in some detail (a) rules about the use of coercive force, particularly during the transitional period, when the security dilemma is most acute, (b) rules concerning the distribution of political power after the transition, and (c) rules concerning the distribution of economic resources after the transition. This research suggests that (i) power sharing is likely to be essential in a settlement and (ii) the time to get the agreement is when the initial settlement is being negotiated, not in a later conference when the urgency to end the violence has passed and compromise has become more difficult (Hampson 1996; Stedman 1996).

Can outsiders significantly increase the chances of stable democratic post-settlement governments? The evidence is thin at this point because there are very few cases; the whole idea of using democracy after civil wars is fairly new. One interesting analysis argues that democracy, like settlement, is a second choice for elites at war, who not surprisingly prefer victory and domination. Democracy, then, is much more likely when a single elite does not feel able to control the situation, as in a negotiated settlement. Democracy is not an automatic result of settlement, but it is more likely here than after a military victory. Outsiders in such a situation may find that incentives to retain democracy are more useful than sanctions against non-democratic behaviour (Krain 2000). At the same time, two large-N statistical analyses find that whether a war ended in military victory or not is unrelated to subsequent democratization (Doyle and Sambanis 2000; Wantchekon and Nickerson 1999), while it does seem to be linked to pre-war democratization (Sambanis 2000).

Although often overlooked, the German and Japanese occupations after the Second World War demonstrated that outsiders could in fact create working democracies that would receive local support for over 50 years. Germany and Japan, of course, were different from our current concerns; they were literate and industrialized and were totally controlled by foreign governments that believed they had a vital national interest in instituting democracy (von Hippel 2000a, pp. 12–13, 185–6). At the same time, the outsiders had just killed several million of their citizens, had no clear idea how to create democracy, and expended relatively limited resources over only a few years (Licklider 1999, pp. 85–90). Certainly the failure of contemporaneous Soviet efforts in Eastern Europe is striking. The failure of the United States in Vietnam suggests the difficulties in establishing democracy even when substantial resources are deployed. Karin von Hippel (2000a, pp. 18–22) attributes the US failure to a lack of coordination and more concern with fighting communism than building democracy.

Building democracy has been a new activity for the United Nations since 1989. Some of its missions have achieved impressive results in unpromising situations, such as El Salvador, Mozambique and Namibia. Others, such as Somalia, Angola and Rwanda, have been resounding failures. In these missions, the United Nations works under several handicaps: member concern about the precedent of undermining sovereignty; a neutrality tradition that contradicts peacebuilding, which is inherently political; and the potential conflict between the goals of establishing security and creating a democratic political system (Bertram 1995). The record of individual states is similarly mixed. The United States has found itself engaged in similar state-building exercises in Panama, Somalia, Haiti, Bosnia and Kosovo. In general, the military aspects of these interventions have gone well, but it is not at all clear that the US government knows how to create a working state in a country where none exists, much less how to make it self-sufficient and democratic (Licklider 1999; von Hippel 2000a, 2000b).

Part of the problem is simple ignorance:

> The international community has accumulated a vast body of technical knowledge in designing and implementing economic and, to some extent, social assistance programs during the past three decades. Although the knowledge is not highly satisfactory, it is nonetheless adequate for all practical purposes. However, no such claims can be made for assistance in the political arena ... Consequently, those charged with designing and implementing political rehabilitation interventions lack appropriate conceptual frameworks, intervention models, concepts, policy instruments, and methodologies for assistance programs to rebuild civil society, establish and nurture democratic institutions, promote a culture favourable to the protection of human rights, reconstruct law enforcement systems, or facilitate ethnic reconciliation in a highly unstable political and social environment. (Kumar 1997, pp. 33–4)

We know that some efforts to build democracy have backfired (Adamson 2000). Moreover, almost all work in this area has been guided by the assumption that democracy is necessary to prevent renewed civil war (much as it was earlier seen as a barrier to communism). As suggested earlier, we do not have much empirical support for this proposition, but its widespread acceptance has meant that a working government is defined as democratic.

This in turn has sometimes allowed outsiders to justify focusing almost exclusively on free elections as the most appropriate strategy to create and legitimize a new, democratic political system. A careful analysis of post-conflict elections, however, including those which failed, led Krishna Kumar and Marina Ottaway (1998) to suggest that several preconditions are necessary: a working state, a societal consensus on boundaries and how the government should function, a democratic commitment among all parties strong enough so that they are prepared to accept losing, and progress towards demobilization. They suggest that in the absence of these preconditions it may be better to delay elections for some time, using a coalition government or one largely controlled by outsiders, in order to establish the conditions that make elections appropriate.

Intellectually, it is plausible that democracy may be more trouble than it is worth and that elite power sharing may be a better political strategy in some cases. However, it would be very difficult for Western governments and organizations to support a government that is avowedly not democratic. Under the circumstances, we seem to have no alternative other than to support democracy, although of course the locals may choose to do something else altogether. Given this, a major contribution by outsiders is the development and reinforcement of the norms that are central to democracy, such as tolerance, rule of law and respect for human rights (Hampson 1996).

Can we say anything more that is useful about what works and what does not? A recent analysis of 1815–1990 (an unusually long period) finds that multilateral interventions are much more likely to result in a more democratic regime than previously (Wantchekon and Nickerson 1999). A sophisticated analysis of 124 post-Second World War civil wars concludes that UN mediation by itself is not sufficient to establish basic democratization but that UN operations that involve a variety of activities (traditional peacekeeping, economic development and building political institutions) have a major positive impact (Doyle and Sambanis 2000). A separate analysis of unilateral interventions concludes that mixed strategies work better than purely military strategies in establishing peace (Regan 2000, pp. 82–99), results that seem similar to those for multilateral interventions, although Regan looks for peace rather than democratization.

20.4.5 Creating a Responsive, Effective and Reasonably Honest State Apparatus

Outsiders often focus on the political leadership of the post-settlement government, and this is clearly important. It is difficult to imagine South Africa's peaceful transition without Nelson Mandela, for example. But in order for settlements to hold, governments must be able to deliver services and collect revenues to pay for them in a manner that the population finds acceptable. This is done by state employees, civil servants, bureaucrats and so on, not elected politicians. For example, the government of Panama after the US invasion essentially consisted of three men: a president and two vice presidents. They had been fairly elected, although the election had been nullified by Manuel Noriega. When the United States invaded, most members of the government, who had naturally been linked to Noriega, decamped, often taking with them whatever resources were available. The three men were powerless; the US military had to step in until locals could be brought in to take over, which took months.

Internal security is so immediate and important that it has been discussed in an earlier section, but many of the same problems appear in other areas of government. Skilled personnel are in short supply. Loyalty to political leaders or groups often is more important than competence in getting jobs. Supporters expect to be rewarded, and this is especially complex when there are several sides to be satisfied at the same time. The prior government has often not offered a useful model of governance, even for those with good intentions.

Taxation policy is particularly critical. In many cases an unjust taxation system was one of the spurs to civil war in the first place; this tradition, combined with a general culture of resistance, makes it very difficult to establish a taxation system based on income and sales taxes across the population, which most economists now see as the best way to encourage economic growth. It is often tempting instead to rely on taxation of export industries and resource producers, since this can be done fairly easily. As Charles Tilly (1990) pointed out, however, this is a dangerous strategy because it allows the state to avoid reaching an agreement with the productive sectors of society, which is the basis for long-term government. The more recent notion of the 'resource curse' suggests that states with resources that can easily be seized (drugs, oil, some kinds of diamonds) will find it very difficult to end civil violence because the rebels can use these resources to finance their wars; Angola and Congo are examples (Collier and Hoeffler 2000).

The good news is that the new government does not have to produce Weber's ideal-type bureaucrats in large numbers. Standards of governance have usually been abysmal, so fairly low levels of competence can actually look pretty good, and a certain amount of corruption may be acceptable, depending on the society. The important thing is that the new government is perceived to be acting fairly and reasonably competently.

Outsiders can be very helpful by training personnel and sending experienced people to help get the various organizations of modern government established. However, none of this will work unless the locals fairly quickly acquire both access to local resources and a sense of ownership.

20.4.6 Create a Working Economy

A recent sophisticated econometric study links two economic factors to civil war renewal: a high percentage of GDP acquired from natural resources and the lack of economic opportunities, particularly for young men (Collier 2000b; Collier and Hoeffler 2000). This analysis presents the policy maker with a dilemma, since one way to increase opportunities is to focus on resource extraction. These findings suggest the importance of creating a working economy, both to reduce dependence on easily looted resources, and to increase economic opportunities. This opinion is widely supported by anecdotal evidence in various cases. But this is easier to say than to do when the country has been devastated by civil war; the infrastructure is often in ruins; equipment and factories have been destroyed; workers and managers have been dispersed; the banking and financial systems have been destroyed; and the government is weak and without planning expertise or resources.

Economically, outsiders can bring important resources to the table and add incentives to make peace more attractive for everyone (Cortright 1997). Kumar (1997) notes that we have had a lot of experience with economic development assistance, so we do not have a good excuse if it does not work. Moreover, it is commonplace that economic development is critical to the stability of post-settlement governments. Thus most settlements now include economic assistance from states, intergovernmental organizations and NGOs.

However, there is no consensus on how such economic assistance should be given. In particular there is disagreement about whether the new governments should be encouraged to establish fiscal responsibility by limiting expenditures quickly or be allowed to respond to the massive social needs for several years, even at the risk of discouraging foreign investment that may be essential for their long-term futures. The International Monetary Fund has become the lightning rod for this issue, and we have not made much progress in resolving it.

The problem would be simplified, although not eliminated, by the provision of economic resources from outsiders, and such commitments are often part of the settlement. Unfortunately, donors often do not deliver on their promises, in part because a successful negotiation ends the violence, which in turn makes the issue seem less pressing to outsiders, whose attention may then shift to another instance of violence. Even when promises are kept, the inability of the international community to coordinate its activities means that the real impact of such aid may be less than expected (Forman and Stewart 2000).

All of this assumes that foreign assistance leads to economic development, which in turn makes renewed civil war less likely. Aside from a good deal of anecdotal argument, a recent study shows that higher levels of net current economic transfers (which include aid of all sorts) and local economic capabilities are indeed associated with a substantially higher probability of achieving a basic level of democracy; they even seem to compensate somewhat for higher levels of hostility that reduce this probability (Doyle and Sambanis 2000). At the same time, some analysts argue that economic aid may actually increase conflict on the ground (Anderson 1991).

20.4.7   Transitional Justice/Retribution

Civil war fighters often do terrible things to their enemies and to more or less innocent bystanders: needless killing, torture, rape, robbery, expulsion and so on. After the war, the people who did these things are still in the country, in many cases living close to their victims. This presents two separate questions: what, if anything, should be done about them, and what in fact can be done about them?

What should be done?
One school of thought holds that individuals who have done such things, or have ordered them done, should be punished in courts of law, either in the country where the atrocities occurred or elsewhere, or at least publicly confess and repent. The legal argument rests on the assumption that international norms and conventions increasingly adopt this position; the agreement on the International Criminal Court is perhaps the most striking recent example. There are two political arguments: (a) punishment of such crimes deters future crimes and (b) borrowing from psychology, neither victims nor perpetrators will be able to live with the other until the crimes are acknowledged and some punishment, compensation, or sign of remorse is given. This position dominates the current literature on peacebuilding and has resulted in the creation of a variety of institutions to discover the truth and, in some cases, to administer justice, from international war crimes courts to truth commissions with varying charters (Kritz 1995). An interesting variation of this is communalization, in which victims and perpetrators share memories of what happened in small communities such as villages (Maynard 1999).

The opposing argument is that the only way that people live together, whether in families or states, is to forget the things that divide them, that truth is elusive and in the mind of the beholder, and that justice cannot and will not be administered fairly. Tony Judt's comments about the Second World War apply in recent civil wars as well:

> [H]ow do you punish tens of thousands, perhaps millions of people for activities that were approved, legalized, and even encouraged by those in power . . .? But how do you justify leaving unpunished actions that were manifestly criminal even before they fell under the aegis of 'victor's justice'? How do you choose whom to punish and for what actions? Who does the choosing? At what precise moment is a purge sufficient to meet elementary demands for justice and revenge, and not yet so divisive as to damage still further a rent social fabric? (Judt 2000, pp. 300–301)

In a civil war, everyone has been guilty of collaborating with one side or the other (usually both) at different times; who is to draw the line? Those condemned as criminals by some will be seen as martyrs by others, and the net result may well deepen and harden existing divisions, undermining the settlement, weakening the already fragile post-settlement state, and making future violence more rather than less likely. This position is often held by people in the group in post-settlement situations, although it is not politically popular.

We simply do not know whether transitional justice makes future violence more or less likely. Reconciliation, after all, is likely to take generations. It is, however, interesting to compare two cases from the last century: Germany and the Jews and Turkey and the Armenians. Germany has since become the poster child of transition justice, after the Nuremberg trials embarking on an extensive programme of apologies and compensations to both individual Jews and the state of Israel (Gardner Feldman 1984; Lavy 1996; Olick and Levy 1997; Wolffsohn 1993). Turkey has never even acknowledged any responsibility for the death of the Armenians, much less done anything to show remorse (Chorbajian and Shirinian 1999; Dadrian 1997; Hovannisian 1999; Tölöyan 1987). Clearly relations between Germany and the Jews are better than relations between Turkey and the Armenians, suggesting that something like transitional justice may facilitate reconciliation. However, neither government had to live with large numbers of the victims in its own state afterward, so their experiences are not really comparable to modern cases such as Cambodia or Rwanda.

Practical limits
In practice, each situation has different limitations on what can actually be done. There is a fundamental contradiction between negotiating a settlement with someone and subjecting that person to trial for war crimes. If

the settlement was negotiated, presumably the leaders of both sides have built in amnesty for themselves and their followers; otherwise they would not have agreed in the first place. More generally, there is always the risk that rigorous transitional justice programmes will trigger new violence. The American Civil War, for example, is usually seen as a military victory, but it is hard to imagine that Southerners would have laid down their arms and gone home if the government had announced that every soldier in the rebel army would be tried for treason and executed, as it clearly could have done legally. Often the leaders who signed the peace agreement are among the most complicit, but arresting them may cause a renewed outbreak of civil war; peace and justice may thus be directly opposed.

There are also enormous practical problems. Major human rights violations may involve thousands of people. Post-settlement states do not have the resources to give fair trials to so many people, so decisions about who will be punished are necessarily arbitrary and unfair. The international tribunals have found it difficult to function effectively, both because of the intrinsic difficulty of the task and because of lack of resources. Truth commissions find their reports disregarded or attacked. In the storm of problems confronted by a new government, how important is transitional justice?

Recently, there has been a tendency to accept mutual amnesty in order to reach a settlement and then change the terms later, when one side is weaker politically and presumably less able to resist; the Pinochet case in Chile has elements of this. Aside from the details of the particular case, this policy has broader and riskier implications for conflict management. Disowning such amnesty guarantees may make political leaders more reluctant to accept future negotiated settlements to civil wars.

Third parties have been extremely important in encouraging transitional justice institutions of various sorts. In many places the whole idea of transitional justice, as opposed to the traditional strategies of direct reprisal or amnesty, has been imported; even when the impulse has been local, information about alternatives and fiscal and political support have come from the outside. When outsiders have this much impact, they take on a correspondingly high level of responsibility for the outcomes. It is particularly troubling that much of this work is being done with no clear evidence of its impact on the prospects for reconciliation within the target society.

20.4.8 Renegotiation of the Settlement

Carrying out the terms of the peace settlement is often seen as one measure of its success. Indeed, its success often depends on the assumption by all concerned that this will happen; this is particularly true for the political and security provisions, as we have seen, and without such assurances the violence may well resume.

However, the settlement itself often is not the best framework for the post-war government. The American Civil War formally ended in 1865 with the Confederacy surrendering and Reconstruction governments established in Southern states. But in fact resistance was so intense (possibly constituting an extension of the war by our current coding schemes) that a second settlement was reached in 1877, under which white Southerners agreed to abandon slavery and not to secede but were allowed to eliminate all political rights for black Southerners. A civil war ended in Colombia with a model power-sharing agreement that actually worked for decades, but the rise of a new civil war was due in part to the settlement that kept new groups out of power (Hartlyn 1993). The Cambodia war ended with a power-sharing settlement that was replaced by a dictatorship but did not develop into a new war. The French, Chinese and Russian Revolutions all ended in governments that were replaced by more extreme elements within a few years.

Theoretically, this is not hard to understand. Settlements focus on current issues, primarily those of the civil war. But once those issues have been handled, at least for a short time, the political coalitions on both sides break up, and new issues become more important; indeed in several recent cases the first violence after the settlement was between former allies, not former adversaries (Atlas and Licklider 1999). The US constitutional convention almost foundered on the issue of large versus small states, but once the issue was settled by having two houses of Congress, no issue has ever separated the large from the small states. A successful settlement is precisely one that makes its own issues less relevant and thus makes itself obsolete.

Thus there is a paradox: a civil war settlement must seem permanent but in fact should probably be temporary. But the short-term need is stability, expectations that the terms of the settlement will endure. On balance, it is probably not a good idea to try to formally build the possibility of change into the system; the renegotiation process may well trigger new violence (Werner 1999). However, we need to remember that change is inevitable in politics and that civil war settlements must not be immune from such processes. In the short run, ambiguous provisions in the settlement will have to be negotiated. As time goes on, changes will have to be made to make the settlement work, and eventually the intractable issues that were omitted from the settlement will have to be tackled. Presumably the process culminates in a permanent political process within the country itself, but third parties can be critical in encouraging the negotiating process and supporting those who are willing to be involved in it.

20.4.9   Coordination within the International Community

Much of our discussion has assumed that the international community is effectively a single actor, with common goals and strategies, and that the key question is to decide how it should act. Of course this is not true. There is some general agreement on goals (peace is better than war, democracy is better than authoritarianism, economic development is important for peace, and so forth) among most of those involved in interventions in civil war. But once we move beyond this very general consensus, major divisions are quickly revealed.

Karin von Hippel (2000a, p. 205) identifies five international communities that need to be coordinated: donor governments, militaries, multilateral organizations, the private sector and NGOs. Governments bring the most resources to bear (when they choose to do so) but are not usually well organized to deliver the goods and services that will be helpful in making a civil war settlement work. Militaries are often very good at violence and organization but, especially in the United States, have problems working with civilian organizations on development and political projects. Multilateral organizations (United Nations agencies and regional organizations) have great potential, but they are necessarily responsive to the often conflicting imperatives of the governments that control them. The private sector has generally been neglected, but it clearly can bring major resources and often has considerable influence with both governments and rebel groups; on the other hand it often has no obvious reason to become involved.

The recent explosion in activities of humanitarian NGOs has changed the face of international response to civil wars. Such organizations tend to be highly specialized in function and/or targets (medical care, food, negotiation, civil society, children, refugees, former combatants, AIDS, democracy, legal systems) and independently financed and controlled. They can respond quickly, bringing appropriate and vital resources to the task at hand, including experienced personnel, and they are often accepted when governmental organizations are not. On the other hand, their limited missions may encourage rigid standard operating procedures, regardless of the local situation, sometimes disregarding the wishes of the local population. They are also very concerned both to remain independent and to appear to be independent from others. Many of them are particularly concerned not to be associated with military forces and missions, which causes difficulty in those peacemaking activities that require security and humanitarian missions to be carried out in concert.

These divisions are convenient for analysis, but it is important to realize that there is no reason to expect that any two organizations in the same category will agree on policy decisions. Each organization has its own mission and set of goals, organizational culture, sources of support, and dominant constituency. The incentives for cooperation are generally low; indeed, in many cases organizations fear that they will suffer if they are associated with others. Advanced planning is an important part of the cultures of the military and, to a lesser extent, the private sector; NGOs have great difficulty in getting the necessary resources to indulge in it. Moreover, all of these organizations share a division between those in the field and those at headquarters (Maynard 1999).

At the same time, there is a general realization that coordination is a problem, and some progress is being made in this area. Reforms in the United Nations seem to have improved things considerably. Groups of representatives from different organizations – such as the Burundi Forum, the Afghanistan Programming Board, the Monitoring and Steering Group in Liberia, and the Somalia Aid Coordination Body – have coalesced around particular countries or problems. Military, governmental, and NGOs now participate in common training exercises and planning.

Coordination between the military and political organization is both particularly critical and particularly difficult; it thus serves as a useful proxy for the more general problem. Clearly all concerned have learned a good deal about how to work together (von Hippel 2000a; Weiss 1999; Williams 1998). Given the world we live in, we are likely to see soon whether they have learned enough.

21 Pitfalls and prospects in the peacekeeping literature

Virginia Page Fortna and Lise Morjé Howard

21.1 INTRODUCTION

Following closely the practice of peacekeeping, the literature on the subject has come in three waves – one small and two larger. Peacekeeping was invented during the Cold War, but its use exploded only after the rivalry between the superpowers ended. More missions were deployed from 1988 through 1993 than had been in the previous four decades. At the same time, peacekeeping evolved from a practice used primarily between warring states to a tool used to maintain peace after civil wars as well. A perceived crisis in peacekeeping, beginning in June 1993, was the result of well-publicized dysfunction, failure and paralysis, first in Somalia, and then in Rwanda, Angola and Bosnia, despite many successful missions elsewhere. A lull followed, with very few new, important missions launched until 1999. After attempts to reform the practice of peacekeeping (epitomized by the Brahimi Report, described below), peacekeeping rebounded; a number of major missions were initiated from 1999 to 2004. There are more peacekeepers deployed around the world currently than at any time in the past.

The literature has followed these ups and downs. A few classic works on peacekeeping were written during the Cold War, but one could hardly call the body of work a 'literature' until the explosion of interest in the 1990s. Within this new wave of literature, brief optimism about the practice of peacekeeping in the first years of the post-Cold War era was followed by a period of soul-searching and pessimism about its limitations and faults. A third wave of peacekeeping studies emerged in the mid-2000s. Although the literature as a whole remains largely descriptive and prescriptive, the latest wave of works on peacekeeping has matured considerably, becoming more theoretical and, perhaps most significant, much more methodologically rigorous.

Until this most recent wave, the literature was unable to answer the most basic question about the impact of peacekeeping: does it keep peace? The early literature consists largely of descriptions of the general practice and principles of peacekeeping, or of detailed case histories. Although many of these case studies discuss the role of peacekeepers in keeping peace, or failing to do so, they necessarily rely on (often implicit) counterfactuals. Only in the past few years has the literature concerned itself with any variation between success and failure, or, more fundamentally, between peacekeeping and non-peacekeeping cases, that could give more systematic analytical leverage over basic empirical questions about the effectiveness of peacekeeping or the causes of peacekeeping outcomes. The emerging consensus within these new, more systematic studies is much more optimistic than the tenor of the preceding wave, indicating that peacekeeping does indeed help keep peace.

In short, the intellectual history of the literature with respect to the issue of peacekeeping's effectiveness could be described as follows: first, a long period including the sporadic studies during the Cold War; second, the newfound interest in peacekeeping in the 1990s, which turned quickly to a focus on failure, dysfunction and unintended consequences; and third, the advent of systematic qualitative and quantitative studies that have tested peacekeeping's impact empirically, showing that despite its limitations, peacekeeping is an extremely effective policy tool. The more theoretically and methodologically mature studies of the most recent wave have allowed more serious debate and analysis of related questions on peacekeeping effectiveness: whether peacekeeping is best conducted by the United Nations or by other organizations or regional actors; the effectiveness of the use of force; whether and when more intrusive and longer-term transitional administrations are effective; and the impact of peacekeeping not only on stable peace but also on other goals, such as democratization. The newer studies have also included more nuanced analysis of effects on local political actors and local populations. These issues have not yet been addressed definitively but represent active research agendas and fruitful avenues for future research as the literature continues to mature.

This chapter provides a roughly chronological intellectual history of the study of peacekeeping. It is by no means comprehensive, as the literature is too vast to cover exhaustively. Instead we focus here primarily on the major trends in the literature, and what it tells us about the effectiveness and effects of this policy tool.

21.2 WHAT IS PEACEKEEPING?

The term 'peacekeeping' generally refers to the deployment of international personnel to help maintain peace and security. Some studies of peacekeeping include efforts to contain or terminate hostilities (for example, Gilligan and Sergenti 2007; Greig and Diehl 2005; Walter and

Snyder 1999), or even to prevent hostilities (for example, Rikhye 1984, pp. 1–2), whereas others restrict the definition to efforts to prevent the recurrence of war once a ceasefire is in place (for example, Fortna 2008a; Hillen 1998; Howard 2008). The definition of peacekeeping has also changed over time, as has the practice. The definition in the 1990 edition of *The Blue Helmets* (United Nations 1990, p. 4), the UN's review of operations, notes that peacekeeping personnel deploy 'without enforcement powers' and refers specifically to '*international* peace and security' (our emphasis). Interestingly, the preface of the 1996 edition, written by Boutros Boutros-Ghali, drops the definition altogether (United Nations 1996). By this time, peacekeeping was firmly established as a technique for maintaining peace in internal as well as inter-state conflicts, and the line separating peacekeeping and peace enforcement missions had blurred considerably. However, some studies continue to restrict the definition of peacekeeping to consent-based missions that are authorized to use force solely for self-defensive purposes, as opposed to peace enforcement missions. Findlay (2002), for example, makes this distinction, using the term 'peace operations' to cover both types of mission. In UN lingo, this distinction separates Chapter VI and Chapter VII missions, in reference to the relevant parts of the UN Charter. Technically, however, these labels are misnomers, as nowhere does the UN Charter refer to the practice of peacekeeping. Even though peacekeeping has now become a central activity of the UN, it was a practice improvised after the Charter was written, and in many ways fell between the activities discussed in Chapter VI and Chapter VII. Former UN Secretary-General Dag Hammarskjöld famously described peacekeeping as 'chapter six and a half'.

As peacekeeping was adapted for use in civil conflict zones, it evolved far beyond monitoring ceasefire lines and troop withdrawals or interposing personnel between opposing national armies to include many more civilian tasks: human rights monitoring, monitoring and running elections, monitoring and training police forces, providing humanitarian assistance, and assisting with the rebuilding of judicial institutions. In terms of military-related tasks, peacekeepers moved from merely observing troop movements after inter-state wars to actively assisting with troop demobilization, reintegration, retraining, and the construction of national military forces after civil wars. Many studies thus distinguish between 'traditional' peacekeeping and 'multidimensional' missions (for example, Doyle and Sambanis 2000, 2006; Findlay 2002; Fortna 2008a; Howard 2008). Most recently, the UN has begun to call the more complex peacekeeping operations 'integrated missions'. These missions are designed in conjunction with the UN development and humanitarian agencies, and seek to go beyond shorter-term peacekeeping to include elements of longer-term post-conflict economic, social and political development or 'peacebuilding'.

Most studies restrict their analysis to peacekeeping operations undertaken by the UN, but others (for example, Bellamy and Williams 2005; Dobbins et al. 2003; Fortna 2008a; Rikhye 1984) include peacekeeping missions mounted by regional organizations or other coalitions of states. Such missions are often authorized and legitimized by a UN resolution, as, for example, in Bosnia, Liberia and Afghanistan.

21.3 THE CLASSICS: PEACEKEEPING STUDIES DURING THE COLD WAR

Among the early studies of peacekeeping, some focused on the prospects for improving or developing peacekeeping as an effective tool of conflict resolution (for example, Bloomfield 1964; Cox 1967; Fabian 1971; International Peace Academy 1984; Wiseman 1983). However, most of these classics consist primarily of detailed case histories. The Wainhouse compendiums (1966, 1973), for example, provide detailed accounts of all the international peace observation missions and peacekeeping missions, respectively, undertaken before those books were published. Burns and Heathcote (1963) survey the early missions in the Middle East and then thoroughly dissect the searing experience of the UN in the Congo. Higgins (1969–81) provides a four-volume set of cases, including relevant documents, from the first four decades of peacekeeping. Pelcovits (1984) and Mackinlay (1989) focus on peacekeeping in Middle East cases.

Rikhye (1984) similarly provides rich descriptions of the various missions mounted by the UN and by regional organizations. His book is organized around the functions of peacekeeping (for example, peace observation, separation of forces and maintaining peace), and although he does not set out to assess the effectiveness of peacekeeping as such, his case studies provide implicitly counterfactual arguments about how peacekeeping helped to keep peace (see, for example, pp. 94, 99–100).

Despite their titles, Rikhye's *Theory and Practice of Peacekeeping* (1984) focuses much more on the politics, particularly between the superpowers, involved in launching (or not) peacekeeping missions and their management, whereas James' *The Politics of PeaceKeeping* (1969) presents something much closer to a causal theory of how peacekeeping might work. James discusses the practical political limits of peacekeeping, given the propensity of either the parties to the conflict or the superpowers to thwart peacekeepers' efforts. James focuses much more explicitly than most of the literature, either during this era or subsequent ones, on what would now be called the causal mechanisms of peacekeeping. He describes, often in colorful metaphors, the myriad ways that peacekeepers can serve to 'patch-up' conflicts or provide 'prophylaxis' against things getting worse or violence recurring, as well as some methods for 'proselytism' of changing regimes or state policies. (See also James 1990.) Although these studies include some cases of peacekeeping in internal conflicts (in the Congo and Cyprus, for example), their focus on inter-state peacekeeping reflects the fact that for its first 40 years, peacekeeping was used primarily to keep peace between states, not within them.

Early attempts to test empirically the effect of peacekeeping (among other efforts by the UN) on conflict management also focus on inter-state conflict. These studies present contradictory findings, most likely because of methodological limitations. Studies by Haas and his colleagues (Haas 1986; Haas et al. 1972) and by Wilkenfeld and Brecher (1984) examine both conflicts in which the UN was involved and those with no UN involvement, avoiding the problem of the vast majority of the literature, not just in this era but until quite recently, which examines only peacekeeping cases. Haas reports UN military operations to be generally successful, but the measure of success is coded only for disputes referred to the UN, making a direct comparison or assessment of the UN's effects impossible. Wilkenfeld and Brecher make a direct comparison and find that UN involvement makes agreement more likely than when the UN is not involved, but that the UN has no effect on the recurrence of crises. In other words, the UN is good at making peace but not at keeping it. However, despite the fact that they explicitly study selection effects, noting that the UN tends to get involved in the most serious cases, Wilkenfeld and Brecher do not adjust for this when concluding that the UN has little effect in preventing the recurrence of crises. It would be 15–20 years before studies directly compared peacekeeping and non-peacekeeping cases, taking the non-random selection of peacekeeping into account.

21.4 BOOM AND BUST IN THE 1990s

With the end of the Cold War, peacekeeping came into its own as an important international instrument for ending wars and maintaining peace primarily within, rather than between, states. With the end of the superpower rivalry, the deadlock in the UN Security Council eased, producing agreement in a number of areas, and very often in peacekeeping. For almost a decade, from the second half of 1978 through 1987, the UN fielded not a single new peacekeeping mission (and only 13 in the 1948–78 period) – but from 1988 to 1993, the UN launched a staggering 20 new missions. Secretary-General Boutros Boutros-Ghali's *An Agenda for Peace* was the central policy document, outlining a series of activities for which the UN should be responsible, from peacekeeping to peace enforcement to peacebuilding (United Nations 1992). This text directly reflected the optimism and confidence of the UN Secretariat at the time. There was a pervasive sense that finally, after decades of disagreement, the UN would be instrumental in resolving disputes across the globe.

But the optimism faded quickly in the face of several débâcles. First, in Somalia, in June 1993, 24 Pakistani troops under the UN flag were killed, followed by 18 US rangers (deployed under the US flag), one of whom was brutally dragged through the streets in front of live TV cameras, as depicted in the movie *Black Hawk Down*. This pivotal event was followed by devastating failures in Rwanda, Angola and Srebrenica (in Bosnia), where genocide, mass killing and ethnic cleansing raged while UN peacekeepers looked on helplessly. Most of the scholarly literature reflecting on the 1990s, as well as most newspaper and policy analyzes, focuses on these crushing cases of failure despite many significant cases of peacekeeping success: for example, in Namibia, El Salvador, Cambodia, Mozambique and Eastern Slavonia (a region of Croatia). Books with such hyperbolic titles as *Why Peacekeeping Fails* (Jett 1999), *Peacekeeping Fiascoes of the 1990s* (Fleitz 2002), and *Peacekeeping in the Abyss* (Cassidy 2004), and a seminal article in *Foreign Affairs* called 'Give war a chance' (Luttwak 1999), epitomize the pervasive sense of pessimism. But even the less tendentious literature about this time period focuses primarily on the cases of failure (see, for example, Biermann and Vadset 1999; Boulden 2001; Clarke and Herbst 1997; Crocker et al. 2005; Cousens et al. 2001; Daniel et al. 1999; Hawk 2002; Hillen 1998; Mayall 1996; Moxon-Browne 1998; Thakur and Thayer 1995; Walter and Snyder 1999; Weiss 1995). Of the numerous works, only two texts are concerned primarily with comparing successful cases (Doyle et al. 1997; Krasno et al. 2003).

In addition to the focus on failure, this wave of the peacekeeping literature is characterized by its lack of attention to systematic causal arguments (similar to the early works in peacekeeping). In general, this wave of the literature is not particularly concerned with explanation or positive social science analysis, nor are the debates particularly cumulative. Instead, the literature of this period tends to explore different themes associated with peacekeeping. Most are edited volumes with excellent, detailed case studies (Brown 1996b; Crocker et al. 1999a; Durch 1993, 1996; Otunnu and Doyle 1998; Weiss 1995). The practitioners of peacekeeping also began to move into the business of analysis, with major works by peacekeeping architects Brian Urquhart (1972, 1987) and Marrack Goulding (2002); Secretaries-General Javier Pérez de Cuéllar (1997) and Boutros Boutros-Ghali (1999);

and articles by top-level UN diplomats such as Alvaro de Soto (de Soto and del Castillo 1994) and Shashi Tharoor (1995–96). Some studies seek to apply an international law framework (Bailey 1994; Caron 1993; Harper 1994; Ratner 1995; White 1990). Analysts also began to explore the merits of post-conflict peacebuilding as an integral and necessary part of keeping peace in the longer term (Chopra 1999; Ginifer 1997; Kumar 1998; Lederach 1997).

Many studies also seek to describe the evolution of one case, one issue in peacekeeping, or the relationship between a single state and UN peacekeeping. Examples of single case studies include Doyle (1995) on Cambodia, Clarke and Herbst (1997) on Somalia, Johnstone (1995) on El Salvador, Howard (2002) on Namibia, and Barnett (2002) on Rwanda. Issue-specific studies of various aspects of multidimensional peacekeeping operations include the work of Lehmann (1999) on UN information offices; Berdal (1996) and the UN Institute for Disarmament Research series on disarmament (UNIDIR 1995–98); and specialized works on elections monitoring (Kumar 1998), civilian policing (Call and Barnett 1999; Oakley et al. 1998), human rights protection (Katayanagi 2002), humanitarian intervention (Hoffmann 1996; Murphy 1996), and the effects of the media (Minear et al. 1996). Stedman et al. (2002) include both a section organized by 'implementation tasks' and a section devoted to individual case studies. Yet other authors seek to explore single-state involvement in multilateral peacekeeping, usually focusing on US, Japanese, or Canadian roles. Books and articles analysing the role of the United States include those by Ruggie (1994), Daalder (1994), Coate (1994) and MacKinnon (2000). Harrison and Nishihara (1995) and Morrison and Kiras (1996) examine Japan, and Jockel (1994) and Coulon (1998) explore the role of Canada in peacekeeping.

All of the works mentioned above develop either implicit or explicit arguments about why peacekeeping fails (or in the rare analysis, succeeds). They tend to be extremely rich in description, and in making suggestions for policy changes, but the use of social science tools for comparing cases is scarce (with the notable exception of Diehl 1993).

Reflecting the pessimistic mood in the policy-oriented literature has been the tenor of the works in 'critical theory', which also focus primarily on the historical period of peacekeeping in the 1990s. The critical turn emerged in opposition to 'problem-solving theory' (Bellamy 2004, p. 18) and was critical in the sense of being interested in exploring the negative side-effects and consequences (both intended and unintended) of peacekeeping. See, for example, analyzes by Debrix (1999), Whitworth (2004) and Mendelson (2005); and a special edition of the journal *International Peacekeeping* edited by Pugh (2004).

Meanwhile, the UN had all but turned away from peacekeeping after the débâcles in Somalia, Angola, Rwanda and Srebrenica. From late 1993 to 1998, the organization fielded only one new large mission, in Eastern Slavonia. There were several smaller missions, but none with the breadth or mandate of those of the previous era. The pessimism of the mid- to late 1990s affected both the practice and the study of peacekeeping.

21.5 THE POSITIVE TURN IN PRACTICE AND IN THEORY

With the close of the decade, however, the political tide shifted back in favor of peacekeeping. After scathing, self-critical UN reports on the genocides in Rwanda (Carlsson et al. 1999) and Srebrenica (Annan 1999), a more positive mood began to envelop the UN. Secretary-General Kofi Annan, who had previously served as the head of the Department of Peacekeeping Operations and thus was intimately familiar with and interested in the issues, had won a second term. His stature as a trusted hand at peacekeeping was matched by that of the new US Ambassador to the UN, Richard Holbrooke, who had played a pivotal role in securing the Dayton Agreement in Bosnia (Holbrooke 1999). While the top-level leadership expressed general support for UN peacekeeping, of the many peace processes under way across the globe, four in particular lurched toward agreements, with opposing sides expressing an interest in having the UN play a central peacekeeping role. In 1999 alone, four large missions with robust mandates were launched in Kosovo, Sierra Leone, the Democratic Republic of Congo and East Timor. These were followed by another wave of missions of substantial size and mandate in Liberia, Côte d'Ivoire, Burundi and Haiti in 2003–04. As of the end of 2007, an unprecedented number of UN peacekeepers (more than 83,000) were deployed around the world.

The new operations came in tandem with discussions, and institutionalization, of the 'Brahimi Report' (UN 2000b). This report and subsequent reforms were named for the Algerian diplomat Lakhdar Brahimi, who was the chair of a panel in 2000 to draft a comprehensive review of all aspects of UN peacekeeping. The report articulated a strategic perspective on peacekeeping (one matching means to ends and resources to challenges). It ushered in a doubling of the staff of the UN's Department of Peacekeeping Operations in New York; streamlined processes of procurement and logistics; and created a renewed sense at UN headquarters that the UN could 'say no' to operations it deemed underfunded or given an inadequate mandate (as in Iraq).

The positive mood around UN headquarters coincided with a positive (in the social science sense of the word) turn in peacekeeping research. This work has attempted to address, in a more explicit and social scientifically rigorous way than past scholarship on the subject, basic empirical questions such as whether peacekeeping makes peace more durable, and why some missions are more successful than others. These questions have been addressed using both quantitative and qualitative methods. As noted above, much of the second-wave literature on peacekeeping examines cases where peacekeepers were deployed, not cases in which no such intervention occurred, making it impossible to assess empirically the 'value added' of peacekeeping. Statistical surveys of all wars have solved this problem.

A few of these quantitative studies have examined peacekeeping in its 'traditional' inter-state setting. Diehl et al. (1996) argue that UN intervention has no effect on the recurrence of inter-state conflict. Fortna (2004a), however, finds that 'peace lasts substantially longer when international personnel deploy than when states are left to maintain peace on their own' (p. 517). (For studies of the durability of peace after inter-state war more generally, see Werner 1999; Fortna 2004c; Werner and Yuen 2005.) Even fewer studies examine peacekeeping in both inter-state and civil wars or explicitly compare the two settings. Many assume that peacekeeping is more difficult and therefore will be less successful in civil wars (for example, Diehl 1993; Weiss 1995), but the few studies that examine peacekeeping in both inter-state and civil wars (Fortna 2003; Heldt 2001/2002) show that peacekeeping is at least as effective in civil conflicts as in inter-state ones.

The bulk of the quantitative work on peacekeeping's effects focuses on civil wars (perhaps not surprisingly, as most of the current need for peacekeeping is in internal conflicts). It is now possible to say that these studies have reached a consensus, and it is an optimistic one. One or two studies cast doubt on the effectiveness of peacekeeping in general (for example, Dubey 2002), and several distinguish between the effects of peacekeepers on making peace in the first place and on keeping it once it is established, finding that peacekeepers are not so good at the former (Gilligan and Sergenti 2007; Greig and Diehl 2005). (Note the contrast to Wilkenfeld and Brecher's (1984) findings, discussed above.) However, the finding that peacekeeping makes civil war much less likely to resume once a ceasefire is in place has emerged as a strongly robust result in the quantitative literature. Using different datasets and statistical models, and covering slightly different time periods, a number of studies (Doyle and Sambanis 2000, 2006; Fortna 2004b, 2008a; Gilligan and Sergenti 2007; Hartzell et al. 2001; United Nations 2004c; Walter 2002) find that peacekeeping has a large and statistically significant effect on the duration of peace after civil wars. In other words, despite its limitations and the dysfunction highlighted in the previous wave of studies, peacekeeping keeps peace surprisingly well. Although in some cases peacekeepers have trouble leaving (for example, Cyprus or more recently Kosovo) for fear that war will reerupt as soon as they leave, peacekeepers have generally been quite good at establishing self-sustaining peace that lasts after the mission departs. Examples are found in Namibia, Mozambique, El Salvador, Croatia and the West African peacekeeping mission in Guinea-Bissau. (For a discussion of the implications of this distinction for testing peacekeeping's effects, see Fortna 2008a, ch. 5.) In short, peace is substantially more likely to last, all else equal, when peacekeepers deploy – and even after they go home – than when belligerents are left to their own devices.

Many of these studies of peacekeeping's effects on the recurrence of war have explicitly addressed, albeit in different ways, the fact that all is not equal. Peacekeeping is not employed at random; it is endogenous to other factors that affect whether peace lasts. Instrumental variables to deal with this endogeneity are hard to come by. Gilligan and Sergenti (2007) use matching techniques to handle endogeneity, and Fortna (2008a, especially ch. 2) engages in extensive analysis of where peacekeepers go so as to control for possible spuriousness.

This question, where peacekeepers go, is interesting in its own right (for example, Gilligan and Stedman 2003). It has been examined quantitatively and qualitatively, on its own and within larger studies of the effects of peacekeeping. Much of this literature has focused, understandably, on the interests of the permanent five members of the UN Security Council (the 'P5' in UN jargon) as determining where peacekeepers go (Beardsley 2004; de Jonge Oudraat 1996; Gibbs 1997; Jakobsen 1996; Mullenbach 2005; see also Diehl 1993, p. 86; Durch 1993, pp. 22–3). Others emphasize the interests of the international community in remaking war-torn societies as liberal democratic states (Andersson 2000; Marten 2004; Paris 2004), or in responding to a humanitarian impulse (Beardsley 2004; Gilligan and Stedman 2003; Jakobsen 1996). Few of these studies examine the selection process from the standpoint of the belligerents themselves, even though consent-based peacekeeping, by definition, requires the acceptance of the parties to the conflict (the perspectives of the 'peacekept' are discussed below). Fortna (2008a) is one exception, arguing that the demand for peacekeeping from local actors is just as important as the supply from the international community.

Of particular interest to the question of peacekeeping's effectiveness is whether peacekeepers tend to undertake easier cases or harder ones. If the former, then the putative effects of peacekeeping may be spurious – peacekeepers cannot make much of a difference if they go only where peace is likely to last in any case. However, if peacekeepers tend to go to more difficult situations, then successful cases of peacekeeping are all the more noteworthy (Howard 2008). Carter (2007) argues the former, that the UN strategically selects cases where the probability of success is high, and some of the findings of Gilligan and Stedman (2003) would suggest that peacekeeping is more likely in easier cases. De Jonge Oudraat (1996) argues the opposite, however, and Fortna (2004a,b, 2008a) finds empirically that peacekeepers select into the most difficult cases.

The turn towards rigorous research design has not been limited to quantitative studies; it has affected qualitative research on peacekeeping as well, and more and more the two types of analysis are conducted together. For example, Doyle and Sambanis (2006) combine statistical findings with case studies of peacekeeping success and failure. Noting that peacekeeping generally has a positive effect on civil war outcomes, Howard (2008) asks why some missions fail while many others succeed. She employs qualitative methods to compare systematically the set of most similar, completed UN peacekeeping missions, defining success in terms of both mandate implementation and the ability of domestic institutions to function after the departure of the peacekeeping mission. The central finding is that 'organizational learning' – that is, increasing ability to gather and disseminate information, engage with the local population, coordinate among units, and provide strong leadership – while a peacekeeping mission is deployed in the field, is one of three necessary sources of success. Fortna (2008a) uses quantitative analysis to test whether peacekeeping has an effect and qualitative analysis (fieldwork and interviews) of both peacekeeping and non-peacekeeping cases to examine how it has an effect, that is, the causal mechanisms of peacekeeping.

21.6   OPEN QUESTIONS AND DIRECTIONS FOR FUTURE RESEARCH

Having established that peacekeeping works in general, the literature is turning to secondary questions. These include the relative effectiveness of different types of peacekeepers, the tools of peace enforcement and transitional administrations, links between peacekeeping and democratization, and perspectives of the 'peacekept'. Each is explored below.

21.6.1   Peacekeeping by Whom?

Although the UN has deployed more peacekeeping operations than any other organization or single state, it has never had a monopoly on peacekeeping. Debates over who should undertake peace operations are as old as peacekeeping itself (the issue arose, for example, over the Arab League's involvement in Palestine in 1948 and the Organization of American States mission in the Dominican Republic in 1965). However, with the launching of a number of non-UN missions in the late 1990s and early 2000s, especially those of NATO in Kosovo and ECOWAS (Economic Community of West African States) in several conflicts in West Africa, the issues of who does and who should keep peace have re-emerged. There has been a lively policy debate on this topic (reviewed by Bellamy and Williams 2005), but the empirical study of the question remains embryonic. Durch and Berkman (2006) assess the strengths and weaknesses (in terms of legitimacy, military effectiveness and so on) of various providers of peacekeeping, including the UN, NATO, various regional and subregional organizations, states, coalitions of states, and even private firms. Bellamy and Williams (2005) evaluate a number of recent non-UN missions along similar lines. Quantitative comparisons include those of Heldt (2004), who finds no difference in the success rate of UN and non-UN missions, and of Sambanis and Schulhofer-Wohl (2007), who find UN operations to be much more effective than non-UN missions. Clearly, more research is needed on this topic, particularly research that disaggregates non-UN missions.

21.6.2 Peace Enforcement

Related to the question of who keeps peace is who enforces peace, and how peace enforcement might be done most effectively. Whereas peacekeeping is primarily a task of implementing long-negotiated peace agreements, peace enforcement generally concerns the use of limited force until the non-cooperative party is defeated or agrees to a peace agreement – as occurred, for example, in Bosnia, Kosovo, East Timor, Sierra Leone, Liberia, the Democratic Republic of Congo and Côte d'Ivoire. In all of these cases, single states (for example, Australia, the United Kingdom) or regional organizations (for example, NATO, ECOWAS) used force, often with the endorsement of the UN, in order to stop the fighting and pave the way for less coercive, multidimensional UN peacekeeping operations. Howard (2008) argues that, contrary to those who advocate for the development of a force capacity within the UN, the emerging division of labor – with regional organizations and single states enforcing peace, and the UN conducting the follow-on peacekeeping – is both effective and legitimate. A number of US-led interventions have been conducted in the name of post-conflict stability or nation-building, which are often included in the category of peace enforcement. The current, troubled, and much discussed efforts in Iraq and Afghanistan have cast a shadow over examinations of the effectiveness of the use of force to secure peace. In general, in this literature, policy considerations tend to overshadow social scientific explorations. Marten (2004), in comparing several recent peace enforcement operations with colonial efforts of the past, provides a forceful and provocative argument for why attempts by the West to remake foreign polities in their own image falter, despite good intentions. However, this work focuses only on descriptions of the cases of failure, and thus misses the cases of success (for example, in Sierra Leone) and possible sources of that success. Similarly, von Hippel (2000a), Dobbins et al. (2003) and O'Hanlon (2003) provide masterful descriptions of US attempts to enforce peace, while Findlay (2002) traces the history of the use of force by the UN and the development of norms about the use of force by the organization. These works are concerned less with causal explanation than with policy recommendations. Finnemore (2003) provides a constructivist theoretical understanding of why military intervention in the name of peace (humanitarian intervention) has become the norm in international relations. Mirroring Finnemore's theoretical argument concerning the changing purposes of military intervention, in 2006, the UN Security Council ratified the 'establishment of the foundations for a new normative and operational consensus on the role of military intervention for humanitarian purposes' (Thakur 2002, p.323) by passing a resolution on 'the responsibility to protect populations from genocide, war crimes, ethnic cleansing and crimes against humanity' (United Nations 2006b). The resolution was cited in the UN's decision in August 2007 to send a peace enforcement mission to Darfur. The current conventional wisdom (emerging in part from the Brahimi process) holds that more robust peacekeeping missions mandated under Chapter VII are more effective at keeping peace than are Chapter VI missions. However, Fortna (2008a) finds no strong difference between the effects of Chapter VI and Chapter VII missions. She argues that this is because most of the causal mechanisms through which peacekeeping influences the parties to a conflict are non-military, having instead to do with political and economic leverage, signaling intentions, and preventing accidental escalation, *inter alia*. While clearly there is a lot of movement in both the practice and theory of peace enforcement, the literature remains inconclusive about the conditions under which force may be most effective in the context of keeping peace.

21.6.3   Transitional Administrations

Another important issue in peacekeeping relates to the most intrusive of the multidimensional or integrated missions: UN transitional administrations (also called 'transitional authorities'). Transitional administration mandates generally resemble those of typical multidimensional peacekeeping operations, but with the added requirement that the UN hold executive authority over the state administration. Sometimes this means the UN mission merely has veto power over the decisions of a transitional government (as in Namibia). At the other end of the spectrum, the UN is asked to take over the very governing of the state (as in East Timor), putting members of the international civil service in executive, legislative and judicial positions that would usually be held by the citizens of the state in question. Although transitional administration has become a major topic of discussion in the literature and in policy circles (see Chopra 2000; Marten 2004; Paris 2004; Pouligny et al. 2007), it has only been attempted (in its modern form) in five places – Namibia, Cambodia, Eastern Slavonia (Croatia), Kosovo and East Timor – rendering social scientific generalizations somewhat difficult. In all these cases, the UN sought to play the role of 'benevolent autocrat' (Chesterman 2004), violating the norms of sovereignty and democracy with the goals of establishing sovereignty and democracy. The central debate in the transitional administration literature is over the extent to which third-party actors may be able to build states for others. Some authors argue that longer, more concerted efforts at delaying the disruptive effects of democratization and marketization are more conducive to long-term peacebuilding (Paris 2004), whereas others argue that such attempts mirror the negative aspects of colonial occupations of the past (Edelstein 2008; Marten 2004; von Hippel 2000). Questions center on both moral concerns (for example, which actors may hold legitimate authority in a state?) and practical considerations (for example, is the UN, or any third party, physically capable of governing another country?). Both practical and moral questions are related to effectiveness, and we do not yet have definitive answers. The real-world trend appears to be that the UN is moving away from attempting to launch new transitional administrative missions. (Tiny and dysfunctional Haiti would have been an obvious recent candidate, but as per the Brahimi reforms, the UN 'said no'.) However, outside the domain of the UN, the US efforts in Afghanistan and Iraq mirror quite closely those of transitional administrations, with the same moral and practical considerations under debate.

21.6.4 Peacekeeping and Democratization

A closely related debate concerns the effects of peacekeeping on democratization. Second only to stable peace, democratization is a core goal of the international community when it undertakes peacekeeping missions, whether transitional administrations or less intrusive forms of peacekeeping (Andersson 2000; Ottaway 2002; Paris 2004). However, the effectiveness of peacekeeping in fostering democracy is contested in the existing literature. Wantchekon (2004) argues that impartial peacekeepers provide one of the conditions for democracy to emerge from civil war. Doyle and Sambanis (2006) contend that peacekeeping helps to foster at least a minimal level of democracy as a condition of a negotiated settlement in which factions agree to disarm in return for political participation. Both Heldt (2007) and Pickering and Peceny (2006) find empirical support for the notion that UN intervention fosters a transition to democracy. Others, however, argue that peacekeeping has negligible or even detrimental effects on democracy. Gurses and Mason (2006) find no significant effect of UN peacekeeping on democratization. Marten (2004) proposes that peacekeepers should limit their goals to providing stability and not try to transform societies: 'The notion of imposing liberal democracy abroad is a pipedream' (p. 155). Weinstein (2005) holds that outsiders' attempts at state- and democracy-building can impede the development of strong and democratic political and economic institutions, and that in some cases at least, post-war societies would be better off left to their own devices in a process of 'autonomous recovery' (see also Wantchekon and Neeman 2002). Bueno de Mesquita and Downs (2006) argue that intervention, including that by the UN, is unlikely to lead to democracy and may even lead to its erosion. Fortna (2008b) finds that peacekeeping has no clear effect on post-war democratization because positive and negative effects cancel each other out. Although peacekeeping promotes stable peace, which in turn enables democracy to take root, it also thwarts democratization by crowding out indigenous processes of political development and by removing war itself as an incentive to democratize. Some of the differences in findings result from differences in research design – whether the study examines change in democracy scores or a country crossing a threshold to democracy, whether the study includes only civil wars or also inter-state conflicts, whether the study examines only peacekeeping or intervention more broadly and so on. The empirical debate over the effects of peacekeeping on democracy in war-torn states remains to be resolved.

21.6.5   Perspectives of the 'Peacekept'

The vast majority of the literature on peacekeeping focuses on the peacekeepers rather than the 'peacekept'. This term, coined (to our knowledge) by Clapham (1998), refers to the parties to the conflict – government and rebel decision makers, as well as the greater population – among whom peacekeepers are attempting to keep peace. That the success of peacekeeping depends on the political will of the parties to the conflict is acknowledged; indeed it has become something of a cliché in the peace-keeping literature. But there the attention to these parties usually ends. A few studies have started to rectify this problem. Clapham argues that peacekeepers and the peacekept often have very different perspectives. For example, whereas peacekeepers prioritize a non-violent conflict resolution process, the peacekept care more about the substance of who wins what. Peacekeepers see themselves as providing solutions to conflicts, while the peacekept see them as bringing resources, including resources that can be manipulated by the peacekept. Peacekeepers think in the short term; the peacekept think about the long term. Fortna (2008a) interviews govern-ment and rebel decision makers to obtain their perspective on whether and how peacekeeping affects the incentives of the peacekept and the information on which they base decisions. Pouligny (2006) focuses less on decision-making elites, providing instead an account of the percep-tions local populations have of peacekeepers intervening in their countries (see also Talentino 2007). Other studies have begun to assess the effects of peacekeeping at the micro level, for example by surveying both ex-combatants who were exposed to UN peacekeepers and those who were not (Humphreys and Weinstein 2007; Mvukiyehe et al. 2007). However, in general, analyzes from the vantage point of those on the receiving end of peacekeeping operations have only just begun to develop.

21.7   CONCLUSION

The peacekeeping literature has emerged in three waves: one smaller and two larger. Studies in the first wave focus on the traditional operations during the Cold War, when peacekeeping was primarily used as an instru-ment to monitor ceasefires between formerly warring states. These studies come to contradictory findings about the effectiveness of peacekeeping. After the end of the Cold War, and the explosion of peacekeeping practice in civil wars, came the second wave of literature, which focuses largely on peacekeeping failures and negative effects. Works in these first two waves do not generally draw on systematic quantitative or qualitative methods to compare and evaluate cases, focusing instead on somewhat arbitrarily selected case-study descriptions and analyzes. By the turn of the millennium, a third wave began to crest. This literature has been much more careful in its use of systematic research methods and has come to much more robust findings about the positive effects of peacekeeping, and the sources of success and failure. Since this third wave emerged, the peacekeeping literature has also branched out into related debates about who does, and ought to do, peacekeeping; the pros and cons of peace enforcement; the contradictions of transitional administrations; the links between peacekeeping and democratization; and the perspectives of the peacekept. In contrast to the consensus on the effectiveness of peace-keeping for maintaining peace after civil war, these new directions in the literature are, to date, far less conclusive. However, they should make for important and lively future developments in the peacekeeping literature, extending our knowledge of this important policy tool.

22 Transitional justice in post-conflict societies
Phil Clark

22.1 INTRODUCTION

In the last 20 years, transitional justice has become a ubiquitous response to conflict or repressive rule. It encompasses both practical and lofty dimensions, seeking to rebuild the physical, political and judicial infrastructure of recovering societies, as well as reconciling fractured communities, reshaping contested memories, and healing emotional and psychological wounds. This combination of pragmatic and profound objectives reflects the enormous ambitions – and tensions – of transitional justice.

This chapter explores two main themes. First, it defines and delineates six key concepts in transitional justice. This theoretical section clarifies key terms in this field which are frequently ill-defined and conflated. It also underscores important theoretical tensions that arise wherever transitional societies wrestle with the most appropriate means to move from a conflicted past to a more stable, harmonious future.

Second, this chapter addresses some of the key practical and policy debates in transitional justice, which in some cases are linked to the theoretical concerns addressed in Section 22.2. Together, these sections highlight that the enormous aspirations of this field – not least aiming for societal transformation – in the face of horrific conflict and repressive government have led to unclear concepts, untested assumptions and recurring challenges for scholars and practitioners alike.

22.2 KEY CONCEPTS AND THEORETICAL TENSIONS IN TRANSITIONAL JUSTICE

This section defines and distinguishes six key transitional justice concepts – reconciliation, peace, justice, healing, forgiveness and truth – which constitute important objectives following conflict or repressive rule. This theoretical framework is not intended to be exhaustive but simply to clarify some common terms employed in most transitional settings.

At the heart of discussions of transitional justice are questions of what reconstructive objectives post-conflict societies should pursue and how they should pursue them. Different transitional societies choose different objectives and different methods for achieving them, usually because of political, social, economic and legal constraints after conflict. The truth commissions of Central and South America in the 1980s and 1990s sought to establish the truth about crimes committed by political and social elites and, in most instances, offered these individuals amnesty in exchange for the truth (Hayner 1994). The South African Truth and Reconciliation Commission (TRC) similarly offered amnesty to apartheid leaders in exchange for disclosure about their crimes against the black majority. However, the TRC differed from previous truth commissions by enshrining reconciliation as a key objective. This policy represented a turning-point in the ideas and practices of post-conflict institutions globally. The TRC in South Africa has since served as a touchstone for other transitional institutions, inspiring in many cases (usually implicitly) the expressed pursuit of reconciliation, for example in Sierra Leone, the Democratic Republic of Congo, the Solomon Islands and Timor-Leste. Even the Statute of the United Nations International Criminal Tribunal for Rwanda (ICTR) – an institution designed primarily to prosecute and punish the main orchestrators of the Rwandan genocide – states that 'prosecution . . . would . . . contribute to the process of national reconciliation and to the restoration and maintenance of peace'.

Out of the central question of transitional justice – what reconstructive objectives should post-conflict societies pursue? – two recurring questions emerge. First, is it necessary and feasible to punish the perpetrators of mass crimes? Second, if punishment is necessary and feasible, what is it designed to achieve: to fulfil a moral obligation to bring the guilty to account, to deter future perpetrators, or to contribute to wider social objectives such as reconciliation?

The creators of the Central and South American truth commissions argued that it was not feasible to punish perpetrators if they were to persuade them to tell the truth about their crimes (Hayner 1994). The South African TRC held that punishing apartheid leaders was likely to foment civil conflict, and that therefore a political compromise – trading amnesty for the truth about crimes and for national reconciliation – was more appropriate (Sarkin 1996). The ICTR holds that it is necessary to punish perpetrators, in order to fulfil a moral obligation to bring them to account, but also contribute to national peace and reconciliation. In the South African case, punishment and reconciliation were deemed to be contradictory objectives. The ICTR, however, holds that punishment is a prerequisite of peace and reconciliation. What these examples show is that, not only do different post-conflict institutions explicitly aim for different political, social or legal outcomes, but even in cases where they claim to pursue the same objectives – as in the South African TRC's and the ICTR's claimed pursuit of reconciliation – they often define the same objectives, or the methods for achieving these objectives, in very different ways. Given the malleability and inconsistent use of key terms such as 'justice' and 'reconciliation', a high degree of conceptual precision is required.

22.2.1   Justice

Justice, the first of the six transitional concepts considered here, is perhaps the most commonly discussed by scholars and practitioners. However, this regular usage has not always ensured clear articulations of *models* and *processes* of justice. First, models of justice in transitional societies can be divided into three broad categories: retributive, deterrent and restorative. Retributive justice holds that perpetrators must be punished, to bring them to account and to give them what they supposedly 'deserve'. Some authors argue that retributive justice is also necessary for states to adhere to international legal conventions (Orentlicher 1991). The deterrent view of justice meanwhile holds that punishment is necessary, but not simply because perpetrators deserve it. Rather, punishment should help discourage a convicted perpetrator from committing another crime, for fear of receiving punishment, as he or she has in the past, and also to discourage current or potential criminals from continuing or initiating offences, lest they also be punished. Finally, a restorative conception of justice differs from the retributive or deterrent models, by holding that punishment alone is insufficient; it is necessary but should be facilitated in ways that allow perpetrators and victims to rebuild relationships, for example by requiring perpetrators to compensate victims or provide reparations, which may contribute to restoring fractured relations.

Second, methods of justice can be divided into two broad categories: formal and negotiated. In the formal interpretation, transitional institutions arrive at justice via predetermined (usually legal) statutes and procedures. Due process during criminal hearings constitutes a key component of most formal models. In the negotiated interpretation, institutions achieve justice predominantly through communal discussions of evidence related to mass crimes. Negotiated justice emphasizes the role of the community in discussing and debating different versions of the truth about the past, and the responses that truth requires, for example, whether perpetrators should be punished and what form of punishment they should receive. These two broad methods of justice – formal and negotiated – are not mutually exclusive. An institution could, theoretically, rely on very broad legal statutes that permit a large degree of communal negotiation within those formal boundaries.

At the theoretical level, formal and negotiated methods may lead to some combination of retributive, deterrent or restorative outcomes. For example, retributive or deterrent justice may be achieved via both formal or negotiated means: in the first instance, independent judges operating in the controlled environment of a conventional courtroom, adhering strictly to predetermined legal statutes governing the running and the range of judicial outcomes of hearings, may punish perpetrators in a fashion consistent with the requirements of retributive or deterrent justice. These requirements could also be fulfilled via a negotiated process that affords the community a central role in debating and judging cases, but that still punishes perpetrators. Similarly, restorative justice could theoretically be achieved by either formal or negotiated means. For example, the formal requirements of a judicial process could dictate that punishment be systematically directed towards rebuilding relationships between parties, or in the case of negotiated processes, if the very nature of the participatory methods employed were viewed as a means towards restorative ends.

22.2.2   Reconciliation

In the broadest sense, reconciliation involves the rebuilding of fractured individual and communal relationships after conflict, with a view towards encouraging meaningful interaction and cooperation between former antagonists. Reconciliation entails much more than peaceful coexistence, which requires only that parties no longer act violently towards one another. Non-violence may mean that the parties concerned simply avoid each other, seeking separation rather than mended relationships. Reconciliation requires the reshaping of parties' relationships, to lay the foundation for future engagement between them.

Reconciliation is both a process and an endpoint, requiring individuals and groups to interact and cooperate in often difficult circumstances, to discover solutions to their problems and thus to build stronger future relationships. Reconciliation is both backward and forward looking, seeking to address the causes of past conflict in order to produce a more positive dynamic in the future. Reconciliation must honestly and directly address the root causes of conflict, and the overwhelming feelings of grievance and anger that may have compounded over generations and led to violence, if the parties concerned are to overcome serious divisions in the future.

In defining reconciliation, it is also necessary to differentiate it from two terms with which it is often confused: peace and healing (both discussed separately below). First, reconciliation differs from peace or any of its related processes such as peacekeeping or peacebuilding. The Report of the Panel on United Nations Peace Operations defines peacebuilding as 'activities undertaken on the far side of conflict to reassemble the foundations of peace and provide the tools for building on those foundations something that is more than just the absence of war', including, 'promoting conflict resolution and reconciliation techniques' (United Nations 2000b). Peace should be viewed as a prerequisite of reconciliation. If violence continues, it is nearly impossible for individuals and groups to consider rebuilding their relationships. The broader, systemic, society-wide peacebuilding aims of ending violence and safeguarding against future conflict therefore pave the way for reconciliation's deeper, interpersonal, relationship-focused processes.

Second, reconciliation differs from healing, which refers primarily to the ability of individuals and groups to overcome trauma. Authors such as Johan Galtung often conflate reconciliation and healing: for Galtung (2001, p. 3), reconciliation entails 'the process of healing the traumas of both victims and perpetrators after violence, providing a closure of the bad relation'. Reconciliation, however, with its focus on rebuilding broken relationships, constitutes much more than overcoming trauma, although this – like peacebuilding – is often an important prerequisite of reconciliation.

22.2.3 Peace

Transitional institutions that pursue justice in some form are usually connected to the objective of peace through the idea of deterrence. If we punish the orchestrators and perpetrators of mass violence, the argument goes, then we will send a clear message that future criminals will also be punished, thus dissuading them from committing atrocities. Often on the basis deterrence, transitional institutions are regularly viewed as tools of peacebuilding, which the UN defines as 'in the aftermath of conflict . . . identifying and supporting measures and structures which will solidify peace and build trust and interaction among former enemies, in order to avoid a relapse into conflict'[1] this definition of peacebuilding contains two aspects of 'peace': a negative component, in which peace (usually defined as the absence of conflict) has already been achieved, but must now be solidified in the immediate aftermath of violence; and a positive component, in which peace is a long-term condition that must be facilitated for

---

[1] United Nations, 'Glossary of UN Peacekeeping Terms.' Available at: http://www. un.org/.

the future, through building trust and encouraging greater interaction between previously antagonistic parties.

Each of these components comprises an interpretation of the timeframe and the necessary measures to bring about peace. In the negative version, peace involves short-term maintenance that shores up a recently achieved situation of non-violence. In the positive component, peace constitutes a long-term process that requires building deeper mechanisms in a community to ensure that combatants do not return to conflict. Positive peace seeks to overcome what David Crocker describes as the 'temptation in post-conflict or post-authoritarian societies . . . to permit euphoria (which comes from the cessation of hostilities . . .) to pre-empt the hard work needed to remove the fundamental causes of injustice and guard against their repetition' (Crocker 2000, p. 107). Negative peace requires simply that the parties involved maintain security and stability, and no longer act violently towards one another. Such processes constitute forms of peacekeeping or peace enforcement. Positive peace, meanwhile, entails deeper engagement between previous protagonists, requiring new conflict resolution methods to safeguard against violence in the long term. Negative peace is generally interpreted as a prerequisite of positive peace, as security and stability are necessary for the parties involved to begin constructing safeguards against future conflict. Both components of peace should be viewed as prerequisites of reconciliation, as negative peace helps facilitate positive peace, which in turn may help parties to resolve their conflicts more effectively in the future and therefore build stronger, longer-lasting relationships.

22.2.4   Healing

The concept of healing has only recently become associated with the field of transitional justice. In recent years, greater attention has been paid to issues of psycho-social healing after conflict, largely as a result of the South African TRC, where Archbishop Desmond Tutu emphasized the importance of truth, forgiveness and communal healing in the daily running of the TRC (Tutu 1999). Where post-conflict reconstruction was once solely the domain of politicians and legal experts, trauma counsellors and other psychological experts now play a greater role in helping individuals come to terms with their personal experiences of conflict.

Underlying this shift towards a greater consideration of psycho-social issues is a recognition that conflict not only damages entire nations or cultural groups, as emphasized in the use of the term 'genocide', but also the individuals within those groups. Post-conflict healing holds that societies require rebuilding from the level of the individual upward, in concert with nationwide pursuits. Rebuilding from the level of the individual is a complicated undertaking because individuals' needs are both highly varied and difficult to assess without evaluating the specific case of every person in the transitional society. As Mahmood Mamdani argues, however, overcoming individuals' feelings of trauma, resentment and victimhood after conflict is vital because these perceptions have long-lasting effects, producing subsequent feelings of victimhood in future generations that plant the seeds of further violence. Mamdani argues that, in the Rwandan case, a Hutu self-view of victimhood, particularly in the twentieth century, provided an emotional and psychological foundation for Hutu violence against Tutsi, as Hutu attempted to overcome their victim status and to gain a greater sense of empowerment (Mamdani 2001). The intergenerational effects of trauma remind us of the need to facilitate healing not only to help individuals rebuild their lives, but also to protect entire societies from descending into further conflict. Healing therefore is integral to achieving positive peace and ultimately reconciliation.

Healing relates to crucial questions of individual identity. Processes of healing comprise important internal and external elements, as healing entails what Malvern Lumsden (1997, p. 381) describes as 'rebuilding a coherent sense of self and sense of community'. Post-conflict healing relates to individuals' regaining a sense of inner wholeness; that is, healing of their own identity, as captured in the phrase 'to find oneself again'. Re-establishing individuals' sense of inner coherence often requires rebuilding a sense of how they as individuals relate to their communities, from which they gain much of their sense of self-worth and the meaning of their lives as a whole. Lisa Schirch (2001, p. 152) argues that it is often necessary to 'rehumanize' survivors and perpetrators after violence. These individuals have forfeited much of their personal sense of humanity through either perpetrating, or being the victims of, mass crimes. Perpetrators often dehumanize their victims in order to justify their violent actions and in turn may suffer forms of dehumanization themselves by committing crimes, when they forfeit feelings of common humanity and empathy towards their victims. Thus, healing requires rehumanizing survivors and perpetrators to overcome the negative identities that they assumed during conflict.

22.2.5   Forgiveness

Similar to questions related to healing, the debates over the concept of forgiveness are a recent development in the study of transitional societies. Forgiveness is an even more controversial and more rarely discussed issue in this context because it is so readily connected with religious perspectives to which many people do not subscribe. Some commentators argue that any discussion of forgiveness will inevitably require forfeiting retributive or deterrent justice; that is, perpetrators will not receive the punishment they deserve or that may be necessary to discourage future criminality. Some critics also argue that forgiveness will entail the enforced forgetting of crimes and an unjust demand for survivors to 'move on' from their pain and loss. For all these reasons, it is often considered too emotionally costly or coercive to advocate forgiveness after mass violence.

Most political thought on post-conflict forgiveness has occurred within the last decade. However, Hannah Arendt explored the appropriateness of forgiveness in the aftermath of the Second World War and provided an important analysis of the relevance of this term after mass conflict. Arendt argues that 'forgiveness is the exact opposite of vengeance, which acts in the form of re-acting against an original trespassing, whereby far from putting an end to the consequences of the first misdeed, everybody remains bound to the process' (Arendt 1958, p. 241). Direct retribution, Arendt argues, fuels the cycle of violence. Therefore, forgiveness, which entails forgoing feelings of resentment and a desire for personal, direct retribution, is necessary to start afresh and to allow people to deal with memories of the past in a more constructive manner. 'Forgiveness does not imply forgetting' 'giving up', 'turning the other cheek' or 'letting the other off the hook', argues Wendy Lambourne (1999, p. 4). Rather, forgiveness should be seen as a 'complex act of consciousness' that overcomes injury in order to restore lost relationships. Forgiveness therefore requires active, sometimes public acknowledgement of crimes committed, and leaves open the possibility that victims will seek redress from perpetrators and perhaps insist on punishing them.

On this basis, forgiveness is not inherently opposed to all forms of punishment, provided that punishment does not involve personal, direct retribution or ongoing calls for retribution even after perpetrators have been punished. Because forgiveness suggests some form of renewed relationship between perpetrator and victim, it is often confused with reconciliation. The two concepts, however, are distinct. While forgiveness may, in practice, lead to parties' resolving their differences to the extent that a renewed form of relationship is possible, nothing in the concept of forgiveness requires parties to reconcile. A victim may justifiably forgive his or her transgressor and still refuse to engage with him or her again, perhaps for fear of repeat offences. Forgiveness requires only that a victim forgo feelings of resentment and a desire for direct revenge against the perpetrator.

22.2.6   Truth

The theme of truth, its discovery, propagation and the extent to which it should be pursued along with other objectives is a perennial consideration in transitional societies. Victims of violence often seek the truth of who organized, perpetrated and covered up crimes, and how they were able to do so. From the perspective of policy makers, a key reason why questions over truth arise so regularly is that the debate in many transitional settings is framed as a stark choice between pursuing justice or truth (Gutmann and Thompson 2000). Specifically, policy makers are often faced with deciding between establishing some sort of judicial mechanism, whether domestic, international or some combination, which may try an individual without establishing a full account of the past, or creating some type of truth commission, which often incorporates a promise of amnesty in exchange for full disclosure of the truth.

What does 'truth' entail in the context of post-conflict societies? Generally speaking, truth after conflict relates to people's understandings of what occurred during periods of mass violence. As Robert Rotberg (2000, p. 3) argues, 'if societies are to prevent recurrence of past atrocities and to cleanse themselves of the corrosive enduring effects of massive injuries to individuals and whole groups, societies must understand – at the deepest possible levels – what occurred and why'. Truth can be achieved through various processes, for example, a legal process, if it involves the provision and weighing of evidence related to crimes, or an emotional process, when it concerns testimony related to personal experiences of conflict. A controversial feature of the truth commissions established in South and Central America was their attempts to construct an 'official' version of the truth by producing reports that synthesized evidence gathered from thousands of citizens who had experienced, or witnessed, alleged atrocities (Bronkhorst 1995). Individuals' and groups' recollections of the past regularly clash, and may be expressed for a variety of well-intentioned or cynically instrumentalist reasons. Therefore, attempts to produce an account of the past that will adequately represent, and be acceptable to, all individuals and groups who engage in the post-conflict truth process are inherently limited and likely to prove acrimonious.

Three processes related to uncovering truth after conflict can be distinguished: what I term 'truth-telling', 'truth-hearing' and 'truth-shaping'. First, truth-telling relates to parties' public articulation of the truth, for example with the aim of providing legal evidence at a war crimes tribunal, or in pursuit of some form of catharsis through emotional expression in front of a truth commission. In these instances, legal evidence that leads to the conviction and sentencing of alleged perpetrators exemplifies how truth can constitute a means towards certain forms of justice; in the case of emotional discourse, truth may help facilitate healing.

Second, truth-hearing entails the reception of truth-telling, focusing on the ways in which different audiences respond to evidence or emotional expressions. Truth-telling and truth-hearing constitute the halves of a post-conflict dialogue; in the case of legal settings, this dialogue is less pronounced, as truth-hearers are usually judges who engage in dialogue only in so far as they ask questions of those providing evidence. In more negotiated settings, such as truth and reconciliation commissions or the *gacaca* community courts in Rwanda, there is a greater sense of dialogue, as perpetrators and victims are encouraged to speak face to face.

Third, truth-shaping relates to the ways in which parties external to the initial truth-telling and truth-hearing receive and re-mould evidence to serve purposes for which the original participants may not have intended their discourse. For example, historians and political leaders engage in truth-shaping when they use evidence gleaned from transitional institutions to serve wider social or political purposes, such as to reinterpret historical events or to teach the population moral lessons. This phenomenon can be abused, for example when elites manipulate evidence to serve self-interested, even corrupt purposes, such as purging history of their own crimes.

One source of complexity and controversy in the TRC in South Africa was that all three truth processes – truth-telling, truth-hearing and truth-shaping – occurred within the same institution. Individual perpetrators and victims engaged in face-to-face dialogue, and their discourse was recorded, debated and interpreted by a range of external parties, not least by the commissioners of the TRC tasked with producing the Commission's Final Report, which was supposed to provide a basis for post-apartheid nation-building (Cronin 1999). That the truth related to past crimes emanates from many different sources and is expressed, and subsequently deployed, for many different reasons ensures that the three processes of truth often intersect and overlap and are invariably controversial.

22.3   KEY ISSUES AND DEBATES IN TRANSITIONAL JUSTICE

This section highlights three key conceptual and practical problems in the field of transitional justice that affect a wide range of conflict and post-conflict societies. Some of the issues raised in this section derive from the problem of lack of conceptual clarity, as discussed in the previous section, and others from specific policy challenges that arise in multiple transitional settings.

22.3.1 Peace versus Justice: The Problem of Binaries

First, a symptom of unclear transitional justice concepts, as discussed above, is a tendency towards binary debates in this field: peace versus justice, justice versus forgiveness, punishment versus reconciliation, retributive versus restorative justice, law versus politics, local versus international, individual versus collective. As suggested in the previous section, in most cases these terms are not mutually exclusive and conceiving them as such prevents the possibility of combining different objectives and approaches. It narrows the options and generates unnecessarily polarized discussions and policy formulations.

Exemplifying this trend, the Juba peace talks between the Ugandan government and the Lord's Resistance Army (LRA) in 2006–08 were hampered by the binary framing of much of the negotiations – by the parties themselves and their numerous donor and civil society interlocutors (Waddell and Clark 2009). Advocates of 'retributive justice' through the International Criminal Court (ICC) claimed that law should supersede politics and that any attempts to defer or remove the ICC indictments of the LRA leadership would contravene international law. On the other side, supporters of 'restorative justice' and 'peace' advocated the use of community cleansing and reintegration rituals and claimed that support for the ICC elevated abstract legal norms over the practical necessity of achieving peace in northern Uganda. Confined by the narrow conceptual architecture of the 'peace versus justice' debate, the parties continually talked past each other, undermining the potential for creative and consensual solutions to the serious problems on the table in Juba.

22.3.2 Tensions between Advocacy and Analysis

The field of transitional justice balances uneasily between analysis and advocacy, which is further complicated by the fact that many academics and practitioners engage in both processes. Human rights actors have been powerful in transitional justice from the outset, providing many of its intellectual, institutional and financial resources. Advocacy organizations such as Amnesty International (AI) and Human Rights Watch (HRW) play a central role in many transitional justice debates. The influence of such advocates, however, has not been universally positive. Human rights ideology – a firm belief, for example, in the need for international judicial responses to human rights violations – has often trumped finer-grained theoretical and empirical analysis, leading to 'faith-based' rather than 'fact-based' prescriptions (Thoms et al. 2008, p. 3).

These ideologically based influences undermine the ability the scholars and practitioners in transitional justice to objectively question their assumptions. In particular, what if the advocated responses to massive violations diverge from particular conditions and context-specific needs within transitional societies? The fervent certainty of much human rights advocacy has often hampered the tasks of impartial research and informed policy making. It is important therefore to challenge the central assumptions that human rights advocates and others make about transitional justice and to subject them to conceptual and field-based interrogation – to begin with analysis and debate before considering practical and policy implications.

22.3.3 Institutions before Objectives

Finally, closely linked to the concern over advocacy and ideology is a trend in transitional justice towards emphasizing technical institutional responses to past violations, often without sufficient clarity regarding the objectives of those institutions. In a field replete with 'toolkits', 'toolboxes', 'menus' and 'templates' (Franke 2006; Hamber 2009), the rush to implement certain ready-made models has precluded careful consideration of the *needs* of particular transitional settings, the *aims* they engender and *which processes* are most appropriate to pursue particular objectives. The toolkit approach to transitional justice begins with institutions and appears to work backwards through questions of needs and objectives.

The supposed success of the South African TRC sparked the proliferation of similar truth commission models in Timor-Leste, the Solomon Islands, Sierra Leone, the Democratic Republic of Congo and elsewhere – models transplanted from the particular circumstances of post-apartheid transition in South Africa into very different contexts. Meanwhile human rights advocates' attachment to a narrow range of (mainly legal) institutional responses was one catalyst of the unhelpful 'peace versus justice' debate surrounding the Ugandan peace talks in 2006–08. A constant stream of advocacy reports and press releases from AI, HRW and others throughout the negotiations proclaimed the ICC as the only justifiable response to crimes committed during the northern Ugandan conflict and rejected outright other potential approaches, including local reintegration rituals, reform of the national civilian and military courts and national reparations programmes (see, for example, Amnesty International 2008a, 2008b). Here, we see again the uneasy relationship between ideological positions and contextual factors.

The narrow institutional approach to transitional justice elicits several discrete but connected problems. At the level of agents, the emphasis on global models affords immense power to international donors and consultants in shaping the transitional justice agenda, often to the detriment of domestic actors. Foreign generalists, who often lack a deep knowledge of particular transitional societies, wield significant influence because of their mastery of supposedly universal templates. Their models gain an international currency through a plethora of workshops and training courses and the funding of like-minded research and policy projects in transitional societies. The danger is that dissenting domestic voices – and a great deal of local insight, legitimacy and accountability to affected communities – are ignored.

In methodological terms, the technical institutional approach views in-depth, society-specific knowledge as a luxury. If domestic political, social and cultural dimensions are considered important it is as elements to be grafted on in the final stages of implementation. This impulse largely explains why domestic outreach programmes – designed to inform affected communities about international judicial developments – have been among the last components enacted by international criminal tribunals (Peskin 2005). Engagement and consultation with local populations are often afterthoughts. A more justifiable (and effective) starting point involves determining the impact of conflict on the domestic population, its needs and which of those needs should be addressed by certain mechanisms. Particular histories, social norms and cultural practices of affected communities must shape how transitional justice is conceived and will inevitably determine its impact.

Closely connected to these methodological concerns are questions over the legitimacy of transitional justice processes. Given that the template approach to transitional mechanisms preferences predetermined, universalist models and the agency of foreign actors, it often struggles to produce processes that are considered legitimate by affected societies. A surfeit of legitimacy in turn dulls the effectiveness of transitional justice processes because they invariably rely on the participation and cooperation of local communities, for example as witnesses in criminal trials or truth commissions. The toolkit approach to transitional justice also appears to ignore the fact that international actors and institutions *per se* lack legitimacy in many transitional societies because of long histories of colonialism and fraught engagement with multilateral financial institutions, foreign donors, peacekeeping missions and corporations. These historical dimensions hamper international interventions from the outset, necessitating sustained consultation and cooperation with local communities to build trust and confidence.

Regarding the justifications for global models, the short-term objectives of these templates are often overly ambitious and their ultimate objectives are rarely explicit. In the short term, there is still major disagreement among transitional justice scholars and practitioners over what particular 'toolkit' institutions can feasibly achieve: echoing the theoretical questions raised in Section 22.2, should international courts and tribunals aim only to prosecute suspects of serious crimes or pursue more ambitious ends such as reconciliation? Can truth commissions feasibly aim to recover the truth about the past as well as facilitate healing, reconciliation and some form of catharsis? Connected to the earlier concern regarding conceptual clarity in transitional justice, the field still struggles to elucidate the precise *purposes* of common transitional processes. Expectations of such processes are often too high, necessitating clearer understandings of what particular approaches to transitional justice can realistically achieve.

Frequently, the broader aim of transitional justice is assumed to be democratization, facilitating the transition of societies towards governance and institutional structures that reflect liberal democratic concerns for individual freedoms, the protection of human rights and the rule of law. This tendency no doubt derives from prevailing modernization and democratization theories in the early years of transitional justice. The close linkage between transitional justice and democratization, however, makes a teleological assumption that all societies should be encouraged towards similar forms of democracy. Such a view proves problematic when translated to the diverse political, social, cultural and historical settings in which transitional justice takes place. Furthermore, it emphasizes forward- over backward-looking concerns, holding that redress for past wrongs always contributes to future democratic entrenchment. The implied objective of democratization also privileges – with insufficient justification – society-wide concerns over the harm done to discrete individuals and groups.

In policy-making terms, this trend constrains the choices that transitional societies can make. It suggests that they must select from a preexisting list of options, without considering whether revised versions of extant domestic institutions or completely new processes are necessary. One reason why the *gacaca* jurisdictions in Rwanda were initially greeted with such hostility from the international human rights community (see, for example, Amnesty International 2002; Des Forges and Roth 2002) was because the hybrid nature of the community-based process – part courtroom, part truth commission, with the local population playing a central role in all aspects of the genocide trials – did not fit easily into accepted templates of transitional justice (Clark 2007). The decision to employ *gacaca* reflected Rwanda's recognition that – despite donor pressure to conform to international norms (OHCHR 1996) – the existing models were not up to the task of handling hundreds of thousands of genocide cases. Most of the orthodox options presupposed small numbers of perpetrators, victims and survivors and were ill-equipped to address atrocity on this scale. Therefore, new approaches, fusing international and local influences, were required.

22.4   CONCLUSION

Transitional justice is an immensely diverse and ambitious field of scholarship and practice. The scale of that diversity and ambition is a key reason why it has encountered the conceptual and policy challenges discussed above. Aiming to address individual, interpersonal, communal and national concerns after conflict or repressive rule, the field arguably aims to do too much, without sufficiently clear concepts, objectives and processes. The ability of transitional justice to respond effectively to conflict in the future will hinge on more sober aspirations, greater consultation with affected communities, and the tailoring of reconstructive aims and methods to the specific contexts of transitional societies.

23 Collective conflict management

Chester A. Crocker, Fen Osler Hampson and Pamela Aall

23.1 INTRODUCTION

We have entered an era in which the risks of discord, fragmentation and competition are manifest, and in which leading countries are buffeted by economic pressures and distracted by political divisions. There is a risk that among 'established' powers, short-term agendas and internal pressures will crowd out visionary, cooperative initiatives to increase global security. While 'emerging' powers increasingly have global interests and embody changes in preferences and priorities, they are not themselves necessarily prepared to assume responsibility for international order. Meanwhile, the current world governance structure suffers from trade-offs between effectiveness and legitimacy. In these circumstances, the obstacles to productive international governance and reform are daunting.

Today's security challenges are also increasingly diverse, differentiated and fragmented. Nowhere is this more evident than in the evolving problems of combating terrorism and the growing dispersion of global terrorist networks. However, the increasing dispersion and regionalization of threats are not confined to terrorism. Many of today's security challenges are generated within individual societies, spread across borders to their surrounding environment, and exacerbated by unhealthy regional dynamics. Still others, such as the western hemisphere narcotics syndicates, originate on one side of the world but target and exploit vulnerable societies on the other side. To complicate the picture further, today's security threats encompass challenges to human security and a whole series of social and environmental ills, such as pandemic disease, piracy, illicit trafficking and environmental degradation along with traditional military security challenges. And they occur in a time of bewildering connectivity and advancing political complexity as the world becomes increasingly and simultaneously interlinked and multicentric. How is the world responding to these complex security challenges? As we argue here, new patterns of international cooperation are emerging which are largely ad hoc, informal, improvised and opportunistic. We refer to this new form of security cooperation as 'collective conflict management' (CCM). The term itself is hardly new. Writing in 1993, Ernst B. Haas (1993, p. 84) argued that the 'remarkable record of the UN since 1985 is a case of adapting to new challenges and opportunities without rethinking the basic rules of international life or considering the very foundations of international order'. He recognized the obstacles, but advocated that the US and other leading states support a UN-centred multilateral security system. The term CCM was broadened and developed in the late 1990s by the late Joseph Lepgold, Thomas G. Weiss and Paul F. Diehl to describe an emerging type of inter-state and intergovernmental collaboration between NATO and the United Nations on peacekeeping operations (Diehl and Lepgold 2003; Lepgold and Weiss 1998). By late 2010 the wheel of conflict management had turned again, as global institutions appear to have their hands full. We are building on this earlier work to refocus and amplify the concept to take account of increasingly evident patterns of ad hoc coalition-building. The broadened concept covers a wider range of multilateral collective endeavours that includes the participation of civil society groups such as non-governmental organizations (NGOs), professional bodies and task-specific international agencies, as well as regional organizations, individual states and international organizations working in dedicated coalitions to deal with non-traditional as well as traditional security threats.

The observations in this chapter grow out of a multi-year, multi-author study on regional security and regional conflict management (see Crocker et al. 2011a). Experts from Europe, the Middle East, Africa, Asia and the Americas were asked to identify the major security threats to their respective regions and assess their region's capacity to address these threats. While the project was not looking for patterns of collective action outside the regional institutional context, the regional authors identified a number of examples of collaboration among various state-based, regional, global and occasionally non-governmental institutions in response to regional challenges. This result led the book's editors to seek out other examples of collective conflict management. We see some common features emerging across these collaborative arrangements, and explore examples here that shed light on criteria for success or failure and raise interesting questions for policy makers.

Unlike traditional approaches to security management, such as collective defence or collective security which involve formal obligations to undertake joint action in response to the actions of an aggressive state (for the classic discussion of these concepts, see Claude 2006), today's cooperative ventures seem to involve improvised strategies of collective action, often in response to one or more of a wide array of diverse security challenges ranging from 'traditional' security threats such as the outbreak of civil war or regional conflict to 'non-traditional' threats such as organized crime, piracy, kidnapping, arms trading, narcotics trafficking and conflict-related commodity rents, as well as protecting individuals from gross human rights abuses (Haacke and Williams 2009; Maybee 2009). Faced with such challenges, states and sometimes regional groupings seek remedies where they are available – from international agencies, regional organizations, bilateral official or non-official partners, or joint 'neighbourhood watch' initiatives. This chapter explores why these new collective conflict management ventures have emerged, what effect they have had, and whether some principles can be identified that may lead to more effective action.

23.2   THE CHANGING GLOBAL CONTEXT OF SECURITY MANAGEMENT

Before examining these collective arrangements, it will be useful to examine the interrelationship between security and conflict management over the past 40 years, during which there have been significant changes in official and popular perceptions of security threats and conflict management responsibilities. When he wrote *Politics among Nations*, Hans Morgenthau (1985) defined security in national terms: as the expectation that, through its 'monopoly of organized violence', the state would protect the citizen and the institutions of the state. In the succeeding years, expert circles generally framed security challenges as arising from the competitive power struggles between states, epitomized by the Cold War military and political confrontation between the Soviet Union and the United States.

During the Cold War there was little official interest in conflict management – that is, the use of non-military means such as mediation, 'good offices' or pre-emptive diplomatic engagement to promote negotiated alternatives to violence and political upheaval. Although nuclear deterrence was underpinned by diplomacy and the credible threat to use force, conflict management was generally viewed in unidimensional terms. The dominant powers in a bipolar international system sought to 'manage' their conflicts in order to avoid a loss of face or strategic setbacks and to prevent their conflicts from escalating 'out of control' (Waltz 2000; Wohlforth 1998). However, they had little interest in using the tools of negotiation, mediation and preventive statecraft more broadly to promote durable settlements, institution-building, good governance, development and the promotion of the rule of law.

The East–West conflict found expression in proxy wars – initially in Greece, then in Korea, Vietnam, southern Africa, central America, Afghanistan and other places – but, with the exception of those in Korea and Vietnam, these wars were generally limited in scale and scope (Gaddis 1986). While lip service was paid to the role of collective security instruments, such as the United Nations, in resolving conflicts, it was clear that the ability to freeze or manage conflicts lay with the powerful states, not with international or regional organizations. The UN's conflict management potential was confined to those cases where there was some measure of East–West tolerance or consensus, and its actions consisted mainly of good offices, electoral support in decolonization processes, and 'traditional' peacekeeping operations in consensual settings such as Cyprus, Israel/Egypt (the Sinai Desert), or Israel/Syria (the Golan Heights).

During these Cold War years, more interest in conflict management was shown by scholars, religious and secular activists, and others outside government who sought to popularize a very different discourse about national security (Kreisberg 2007). This discourse focused on the threat of nuclear annihilation as a consequence either of direct attack or of a 'nuclear winter'. Proponents believed that 'conflict management' (more usually expressed in terms of 'peace movements' at the time) consisted of pushing their own governments towards arms control and then eventually nuclear disarmament, thereby reducing stockpiles and removing the weapons from national armouries (see, for example, Meyer 1995; Miller 1994). Such activity by civil society actors gained some traction in a few Western countries; however, it was virtually absent within the Soviet bloc.

In the years immediately after the end of the Cold War, the world's attention shifted from tracking superpower rivalry to witnessing the outbreak on nearly every continent of civil wars: wars that habitually spilled over state boundaries to contaminate entire neighbourhoods. Global security was redefined in local and regional terms, and the tasks undertaken to provide security widened to protecting civilians from massacre by their own governments as well as shoring up weak states threatened by struggles among factional militias (see, for example, Hampson 2008).

No longer was international security 'indivisible' as it had been during the Cold War. Instead, it became fragmented as governments, institutions and individuals attempted to address a wide range of security challenges and threats (see United Nations 2004a). Powerful actors assumed a 'third party' conflict management role – often successful – in other people's conflicts, and the UN undertook peacemaking efforts in Africa, Asia, Central America and Europe. A number of studies noted a decline in the outbreak and lethality of conflict. At least one report attributed this trend to UN engagement; others pointed to the embrace of notions of human security and a growing acceptance of the normative 'responsibility to protect' (see Human Security Centre 2005; International Commission on Intervention and State Sovereignty 2001).

Conflict management became the business of large and small states alike. However, with the terrorist attacks in the United States and Europe in the 2000s, this global consensus broke down. The US and its coalition partners went to war in Afghanistan and Iraq, big power politics came back to the fore, and the UN and other conflict management organizations were pushed aside. At the same time, according to data published by the University of Maryland, the steady decline in the number of active conflicts levelled off, and the current trend seems to be an upturn in armed conflict and violence in many countries (Hewitt et al. 2010). Many of the peace agreements that were concluded in the 1980s and 1990s to end sectarian strife have either failed, as in the Democratic Republic of Congo, Somalia and the Philippines–Mindanao, or are barely holding together, as in the cases of Nepal, Sudan and Colombia.

Many countries continue to suffer problems of chronic instability because of persistent social, political and economic problems. This produces conflict patterns that are multidimensional, featuring a range of traditional and emerging features – sectarian and factional strife, criminal networks, state-building crises and regional rivalries. The annual 'failed state index', developed by the Fund For Peace and Foreign Policy magazine, identifies some 60 countries as being at risk of political and economic collapse. At the top of the list are Somalia, Zimbabwe, Sudan, Chad, the Democratic Republic of Congo, Iraq, Afghanistan, the Central African Republic, Guinea and Pakistan – large parts of Africa and the greater Middle East.

The fact that so many countries are susceptible to internal conflict and social disintegration suggests that there is enormous potential for instability in the international system. While these conflicts and global threats may have made the link between national security and conflict management more apparent to policy makers around the world, the countries and institutions that provided conflict management in the 1990s are either marginalized by current wars or overburdened by the number and gravity of ongoing crises. In this environment, major powers and international security bodies have scrambled for politically sustainable and doctrinally coherent strategies. The policy catchphrases aimed at generating the political will for action – such as 'failed states', 'loose nukes', 'post-conflict stabilization and reconstruction', genocide prevention' and 'the war on terrorism' have failed to capture public imagination or to mobilize consistent international action. As discussed below, the impetus behind collective action in response to security challenges is widely shared. The evidence clearly suggests that no one wants unilateral ownership of today's security agenda. The motives behind this lurch towards collective action need to be unpacked.

23.3 THE GLOBAL RESPONSE: COLLECTIVE CONFLICT MANAGEMENT

Moments of geopolitical change often produce new institutions as a response to that change (on the historical evolution of contemporary multilateral institutions, see, for example, Heinbecker and Goff 2005; Kennedy 2006; Talbott 2008). The end of the First World War brought the League of Nations, which attempted but failed to create a global order through international cooperation on security matters. The end of the Second World War produced a host of institutions, most of which still function today – the United Nations, the North Atlantic Treaty Organization (NATO), the International Monetary Fund, the World Bank, and the European Coal and Steel Community which has transformed over time into the European Union. However, the end of the Cold War did not result in much new global institution-building. Instead, the past two decades have seen existing institutions adapt their missions and doctrines, expand their membership, and engage in a series of agonizing reappraisals of their identity and purpose. The G7, founded in the mid-1970s as a group of the wealthiest, most developed countries with an initial focus on financial and economic issues gradually moved into terrain of a more political and security-oriented character. Over 20 years later, in 1997, Russia was invited to join the group (a possible consolation prize for having to stand aside and watch NATO and EU expansion). By 2005 leading European members were pressing for the inclusion of emerging and developing nations, and the so-called 'Outreach Five' (Brazil, China, India, Mexico and South Africa) joined some of the proceedings. By this point the meetings were addressing everything from finance to terrorism, African development, climate change and the scourge of paedophilia. Meanwhile, since 1999 the G20 meetings of finance ministers and central bank governors have developed into the premier body for consultation on governance of the international financial system: G20 summits began in 2008.

Advances in financial sector governance have not been matched in the field of international security. At first, the late 1980s and the 1990s seemed to mark a new era of the United Nations as the global mechanism through which conflicts could be monitored, managed and resolved. The institution had some notable successes in all corners of the world – Namibia, Mozambique, Cambodia, El Salvador and, more recently, East Timor. The success rate, however, was matched by a 'failure rate', as the UN fell short of effective action in Bosnia, Somalia, Rwanda and Haiti, and was marginalized in the face of the terrorist attacks on the United States of 11 September 2001 and the consequent American decisions to attack

Afghanistan and Iraq. At the same time, scandals and inefficiencies plagued the institution, and calls for its reform were joined by calls for its dissolution. Serious and well-intentioned reform efforts made modest headway, but were deflected by political disputes and a lack of underlying consensus among leading states and groups of states (Stedman 2007). NATO, the most effective of Cold War institutions, has often seemed caught in a bramble of self-doubt, as questions about its mission in the post-Cold War environment are heard both inside and outside the organization. Every 10 years its guiding 'strategic concept' becomes subject to review and examination (Betts 2009; De Jonge Oudraat 2011). The 2009–10 review cycle, which culminated in Lisbon in November, embraced a broad array of goals and missions, but has probably not resolved the organization's Afghanistan dilemma or the internal contradictions among members.

Instead of building strengthened global security institutions, the general international pattern has been to cast doubts on the relevance of established ones. The UN and NATO were not dismantled in the post-Cold War period, but they were weakened as much by a thousand cuts as by any direct challenge to their mission. Instead of innovation, we have witnessed expansion, dilution and confusion. This history raises the question, however, whether the world needs another institutional approach to conflict management and security. Would a new institution be capable of responding to the complex challenges of present-day conflict? Do we understand the nature of the challenge well enough to design a capable institution? While there may be growing recognition that local, regional and global security are linked and that national security is connected to preventing or managing conflicts, the exact nature of these links remains obscure. Also obscure is the road ahead as far as reform and innovation in global institutions are concerned. There are three reasons for this: first, there are huge political hurdles to real reform, as the example of the UN Security Council makes clear; second, security has become divisible, making the quest for consensus and coherence elusive; and third, many actors prefer that the current institutional endowment remains weak and imperfect.

Instead of looking to a new institution or a new set of responsibilities for an existing institution, we need to recognize that new collaborative patterns of behaviour are becoming apparent in the conflict management field. In these new patterns, approaches which depend on only one country or institution have been replaced by a growing network of formal and informal institutional arrangements that operate across national, subregional and regional boundaries. These arrangements occur for a variety of reasons – some encouraging, others less so – and the results appear to vary widely. It is important to understand these informal patterns of CCM in order to analyse why they may succeed or fail and what potential they may have to reshape conflict management strategy.

23.3.1 Collective Conflict Management in Action

The cases presented here – in Africa, Afghanistan/Pakistan, Southeast Asia, Latin America and Europe – are quite different from one another in nature, dynamics and composition. Some are responses to specific crises; others are organized around ongoing attempts to foster peace in long-standing conflicts. Some are set up by third parties, determined to take action to provide security; others have been established at the request of the conflict parties themselves. Several cases illustrate the informal, ad hoc qualities of improvised response that first attracted our attention. Others involve formal institutions, but point to a high level of inter-institutional collaboration. None of them, arguably, would have developed during earlier historical periods.

Horn of Africa piracy
In 2009, in response to escalating attacks by pirates on ships and merchant vessels crossing the Gulf of Aden and the Indian Ocean off the Horn of Africa, a combination of intergovernmental, regional, state and private actors mounted a collaborative effort to address this threat. Combined efforts to deal with piracy have involved joint, ad hoc naval coordination among key NATO, EU and coalition maritime forces; a major parallel role for the private sector, especially among those companies whose ships use these waters; the critical cooperation of Kenya in handling captured pirates; and more effective efforts by certain Somali non-state entities. Although there is no unified command structure among the three naval contingents, there has been extensive coordination at the tactical level, in dealing with Somali pirates.

In a parallel development, merchant shipping lines have made improved efforts to protect their own vessels. Up to 70 per cent of pirate attacks are now being defeated by merchant ships' crews themselves. As a consequence, pirates face significant risks and less likelihood of reward if they attack merchant ships. While Kenya has agreed to prosecute pirates who are apprehended, other regional states have lacked the necessary legislation or political will to cooperate with international efforts to provide legal support for direct naval action against pirates.

Interestingly, the UN Security Council in its Resolution 1851 (2008) authorized and endorsed – in everything but name – the voluntaristic, 'neighbourhood watch' characteristics of the ongoing response to the Somali piracy challenge. Specifically, it called upon 'States, regional and international organizations that have the capacity to do so, to take part actively in the fight against piracy and armed robbery off the coast of Somalia'. It also invited 'all States and regional organizations' engaged in the fight to conclude special arrangements with countries surrounding Somalia to allow for the embarking of 'shipriders' to facilitate the detention and prosecution of detainees. In addition, it urged the creation of an 'international cooperation mechanism to act as a common point of contact between and among states, regional and international organizations on all aspects of combating piracy . . . at sea off Somalia's coast'. Finally, it encouraged UN member states to 'enhance the capacity of relevant states in the region to combat piracy, including judicial capacity'.

In a sweeping illustration of the new normative environment, the resolution went on to urge member states to collaborate with the shipping and insurance industries and the International Maritime Organization in developing 'avoidance, evasion, and defensive best practices and advisories to take when under attack or when sailing in waters off the coast of Somalia'. The ad hoc, case-specific nature of this pattern of collective action is also spelled out in categorical terms aimed at limiting the impact of the Somalia decisions on the existing, rules-based international maritime order, while also maintaining at least a figleaf for Somali sovereignty.

Naval operations are ultimately no substitute for greater efforts to tackle the sociopolitical and economic challenges within Somalia. However, even here there has been some modest progress as a result of encouraging political developments in the autonomous regions of Somaliland and Puntland. It is also now recognized that security sector reform is necessary, particularly in terms of building regional 'brown-water' naval and coastguard capacities. This does not mean that the threat itself has diminished. However, there is something of an evolving network of global, regional, and state and non-state actors cooperating to address the piracy problem.

The Afghanistan–Pakistan border dispute
The Dubai Process – a cross-border CCM venture facilitated by Canada – offers another illustration of the kinds of networks that are being spawned to deal with today's complex security challenges. Major, long-standing disagreements between Afghanistan and Pakistan over the issue of the Durand Line (which constitutes the de facto border between them) have for many years thwarted any kind of dialogue or security cooperation between the two countries on a wide range of border problems that include the cross-border movement of insurgents; the absence of proper infrastructure and customs management at key legal border crossing points (Waish-Chamam, Ghulam Khan and Torkham); the smuggling of

duty-free goods between Afghanistan and Pakistan; the illicit cross-border flow of narcotics; and illegal migration.

This initiative developed when Pakistan's then President, Pervez Musharraf, threatened to mine the border in response to pressure from the international community to assume greater responsibility for controlling the country's frontiers. Canada, a longstanding champion of the treaty banning anti-personnel landmines, stepped in to suggest an alternative approach to dealing with the myriad problems in the disputed border region. Since 2007, in keeping with the Potsdam Statement by G8 foreign ministers and the foreign ministers of Afghanistan and Pakistan (and the Pakistan–Afghanistan Joint Peace Jirga), the two countries have met on a regular basis under Canadian auspices in a series of technical, working-level workshops to discuss cooperating on managing their border. The five working areas of what is now referred to as the Dubai Process (named after the Persian Gulf emirate where the first meeting took place) are customs, counter-narcotics, managing the movement of people, law enforcement in border areas, and connecting government to people through social and economic development. The meetings are now part of an internationally recognized process which not only promotes dialogue between Afghan and Pakistani officials but also advances cooperation in each of these areas. Importantly, the process has engaged and mobilized a wide range of partners and stakeholders not only in the two countries, but also at the international level, including the US Border Management Task Force in Kabul and Islamabad, the United Nations Office on Drugs and Crime, the International Security Assistance Force (ISAF) Regional Command (South), the World Bank, the United Nations Assistance Mission in Afghanistan, the United Nations High Commissioner for Refugees, the International Organization for Migration, other organizations working on border management, and key donors such as Germany and Denmark.

The Liberia peace process
The 2003 Liberian peace talks offer another illustration of a CCM undertaking in a peacemaking context. Many international, regional/subregional and local actors and institutions supported negotiations to end a bloody and protracted civil war between President Charles Taylor's National Patriotic Party (NPP) and two rebel groups, the Liberians United for Reconciliation and Democracy (LURD) and the Movement for Democracy in Liberia (MODEL). The negotiations, which took place in Ghana, were mediated by former Nigerian President General Abdulsalami Abubakar under the auspices of a subregional entity, the Economic Community of West African States (ECOWAS). ECOWAS had a strong interest in ending the conflict, both because it had sent

peacekeeping troops into the country during the civil war in the 1990s and because the Liberian conflict threatened neighbouring ECOWAS members, notably Sierra Leone, Guinea and Côte d'Ivoire.

Other international and regional actors participating in the negotiations were the US, the EU, the International Contact Group on Liberia, the African Union (AU) and the United Nations. In addition, the key parties attending the talks included Liberian civil society organizations which maintained constant pressure on the negotiating parties in both Ghana and Liberia to reach an agreement. These groups represented inter-religious interests, human rights, women's rights and legal interests. Many had even risked their lives by travelling through an unstable Côte d'Ivoire to reach the talks in Ghana. Among the most forceful was the team of 150–200 members from the Women of Liberia Mass Action for Peace group, which at one point even barred delegates from leaving the room during the course of negotiations until they had reached an agreement (Hayner 2007).

Philippines–Mindanao talks
The Philippines International Contact Group (ICG), established to support the peace talks between the Government of the Republic of the Philippines (GRP) and the Moro Islamic Liberation Front (MILF), provides an interesting example of collective conflict management in Southeast Asia. The ICG's assignment is to assist a Malaysian-led mediation process, building trust between parties, helping to monitor compliance with agreements, and providing expertise in and conducting research on matters of interest to the peace talks. Unlike the anti-piracy example, however, this group is not the result of third parties initiating CCM, but of an agreement between the parties to the conflict – the GRP and the MILF – to mobilize additional external support and participation in the talks that reopened in December 2009. The state members of the ICG include the UK, Japan and Turkey. The Organization of Islamic Conference (OIC), while not a member of the ICG, has ties to this group through Turkey. In addition, OIC member Malaysia leads the mediation, while fellow OIC members Brunei and Libya are participating in the international monitoring team which monitors the ceasefire between the GRP and MILF.

Interestingly enough, the GRP and MILF also asked two NGOs, the Asia Foundation and the Centre for Humanitarian Dialogue (HDC), to join the contact group, and requested that the Centre act as its secretariat. The Asia Foundation has a long history of engagement in the Philippines and in Mindanao, the governance of which is critical to the peace talks. HDC's involvement in the Philippines is of more recent date and has focused on the conflicts between the government and the communist rebel group the New People's Army. Its contribution lies in the fact that it specializes in mediation and facilitation, and can draw on its experience from other conflicts. Presumably, the addition of the ICG to the existing Malaysian-led mediation process will also add to the transparency of the process. While it is too early to assess the effectiveness of this elaborate structure, the fact that the parties sought assistance from this diverse set of countries and institutions shows recognition that a variety of talents and perspectives may be required to manage a complex situation.

Western hemisphere mechanisms
The OAS (Organization of American States) is a very robust organization for dealing with security problems in the western hemisphere. Its work, however, is also complemented by a wide variety of subregional and ad hoc groupings and entities, such as the Rio Group, the Guarantors of the Peru–Ecuador Treaty, and the summit meetings of hemispheric presidents and defence ministers – all of which have contributed significantly to building an environment in which conflict management is the norm. CCM norms are also reinforced by two bodies that deal with nuclear matters – the Agency for the Prohibition of Nuclear Weapons in Latin America and the Caribbean, and the Brazilian–Argentine Nuclear Accounting Agency. Regional economic cooperative endeavours such as Mercosul, UNASUR (Union of South American Nations) and the Andean Community also help foster a common security agenda. These arrangements underscore the importance of formal institutional mechanisms and confidence-building instruments in the CCM equation because they contribute to legality, transparency and widespread political 'buy-in' from members through direct institution-to-institution partnerships (Herz 2011).

ASEAN-based CCMs
Formal regional organizations can also serve as the launchpad or pivot for a wide variety of CCM ventures of the more informal variety that extend beyond the direct membership of the organization. ASEAN (the Association of South-East Asian Nations) has established several forums for the promotion of regional security within the wider Asia–Pacific region, including dealing with ongoing or potential disputes. Among these are the ASEAN summit of member states to discuss and resolve regional issues and tensions; security-building dialogues with countries outside ASEAN, for example with China, Japan and South Korea in ASEAN+3, and with Australia and New Zealand; and the ASEAN Regional Forum (ARF) which comprises 26 countries including all the major powers plus the EU. The ARF's activities reflect its strong focus on confidence-building and the creation of a sense of strategic community, as well as encouraging

preventive diplomacy and conflict management. The explosion of bilateral and multilateral free trade and economic partnership agreements in the Asia–Pacific region also underpins the CCM enterprise by deepening the bonds of cooperation through rapidly growing levels of economic interdependence (Bitzinger and Desker 2011). At the same time, ASEAN and its outreach adjunct bodies have some potential to serve as a forum for airing and debating divisive issues and for bringing balancing pressure to bear against a powerful state, as Chinese officials have experienced.

Transnational law enforcement cooperation in Southeastern Europe
The OSCE's Strategic Police Matters Unit (SPMU) has worked to expand adherence to the United Nations Convention against Transnational Organized Crime, and to this end has entered into partnerships with subregional police and prosecutors' organizations. One subregional body – the Southeast European Cooperative Initiative Regional Centre for Combating Transborder Crime (SECI Centre) – has been in existence since 1995. Teaming up with these and other subregional organizations, the SPMU promotes adherence to the Police Cooperation Convention for Southeast Europe, which fosters cross-border coordination to facilitate seizures and arrests of narcotics traffickers. Such cooperative activity has obvious potential for addressing other security challenges such as human trafficking, other forms of criminal business enterprise and terrorism. Given the evident linkages between criminal mafias, conflict prevention and conflict management, such law enforcement initiatives represent a real contribution to security. This cooperative model has potential for development in other challenged regions such as Central Asia.

23.4   A CLOSER LOOK AT CCM

As seen from these examples, CCM describes an emerging phenomenon in international relations in which countries, international and regional/ subregional organizations, and, importantly, non-official institutions or private actors address potential or actual security threats by taking concerted action in order (i) to control, diminish or end the violence associated with the conflict through combined peace operations and/or mediation, conflict prevention and avoidance; (ii) to assist, where appropriate, with a negotiated settlement through peacebuilding, cross-border management and other cooperative efforts and measures; (iii) to help address the political, economic and/or social issues that underlie the conflict; and/or (iv) to provide political, diplomatic and economic guarantees or other long-term measures to improve local security conditions.

What are the characteristics of these new, cooperative forms of conflict management? First, there are no universal rules of the road or consistent principles behind CCM. Consequently, this pattern of cooperation in international affairs varies according to the severity of the security challenges being addressed, who participates in responding, and who takes the lead in these ventures. A distinguishing feature, however, is that they tend to span global, regional and local levels in terms of their institutional and individual membership or composition. Many CCM ventures also typically involve a combination of public (intergovernmental) and private (non-state) partners.

In one sense CCM follows on in the traditions of collective defence and collective security (see Table 23.1). However, unlike collective defence and collective security, which involve formal obligations to undertake joint action in response to the actions of an aggressive state, CCM is a voluntary and improvised form of collective action in response to any of a number of diverse security challenges, ranging from traditional security threats, such as the outbreak of civil war or regional conflict, to non-traditional threats such as organized crime, piracy, kidnapping, arms trading, narcotics trafficking, illegal migration and conflict-related commodity trade. Faced with such problems, states or regions seek remedies where they are available – from international agencies, regional organizations, bilateral official or non-official partners, or joint 'neighbourhood watch' initiatives.

Second, CCM ranges across a large spectrum of activities, as the examples above have shown. It tends to be informal (rather than treaty based), improvised, ad hoc and opportunistic. Pragmatism reigns, sometimes (but not always) at the expense of the norms embodied in formal charters or alliances. CCM choices are also shaped by the national preferences of lead actors and reflect prevailing regional security cultures or norms. Stated in less theoretical terms, many CCM undertakings are make-do arrangements to deal with specific security challenges and immediate conflict management needs.

Third, CCM action is effective when one or more key actors at the official or unofficial level are prepared to take the lead and mobilize partners who are willing to support a shared undertaking. For example, NATO took the initial lead in mobilizing a regional and international constituency to address the growing problem of piracy in the Gulf of Aden and the Arabian Sea. Canada was instrumental in serving as a catalyst to promote a more cooperative regional approach to festering border problems between Afghanistan and Pakistan. The Philippines International Contact Group emerged from the bottom up as a means of engaging a wide range of local and international, official and non-governmental partners to support the protracted peace process in Mindanao. Although there is an

Table 23.1 Differing approaches to conflict and security management

	Actors	Security threats	Forms of cooperation	Degree of institutionalization	Patterns of leadership
Collective defence	State signatories to a treaty, which is rooted in a multi-party alliance	Military threats from the outside	Formal and rules based	High	Centralized, hegemonic
Collective security	State signatories to a treaty, which is collective and supported by an organization, and does not draw lines to keep anybody out	Any military threat to one or more of the members of the organization	Formal and rules based	High	Centralized, oligopolistic
Collective conflict management	Informal coalitions or networks of state, intergovernmental and non-state actors	External or internal, traditional and non-traditional threats	Ad hoc, on a case-by-case basis, evolutionary, open structure	Low	Diffuse, shared, pragmatic, and ad hoc (and opportunistic)

Source: Crocker et al. (2011b).

element of spontaneity to the way CCM ventures arise, these loose coalitions, if they are to be successful, require guidance and leadership from their key members as well as buy-in from the different partners. Beyond this, success would also appear to depend on other factors such as the level of effective consensus within the CCM team and the degree to which its members have the right skills and resources for the task at hand.

These observations lead us to focus more closely on the question of motivations and other 'drivers' that may account for the increasing recourse to CCM by decision makers. A range of factors and a variety of motivations may bring CCM into play. Today's security challenges are often multidimensional and require tools, insights, experience, resources and specialized capabilities that often lie outside the grasp of single-actor conflict managers. Individual states, coalitions, alliances, and international as well as regional organizations band together in collective activity in part because – as suggested earlier – they recognize the limits of their resources. Decision makers also appear to recognize the need to share the 'ownership' of conflict responses with others and gain legitimacy from others; the political benefits of acting (and being seen to act) on a broad basis of support; and the importance of including actors with specific skills and assets relevant to the security problem being addressed. Ever fewer national and organizational decision makers choose to act unilaterally and to assume sole responsibility for any of today's security problems.

Of course, there is a negative side to some of these positive drivers. The urge for collective responses may disguise a lack of firm commitment to see things through on one's own. The readiness to borrow leverage from others could descend into mere 'buck-passing', in order to be seen doing something but avoid any real responsibility. Joining a collective enterprise may be motivated by a desire to show domestic audiences that the country is important and relevant without intending to do any serious heavy lifting.

In some instances, CCM ventures may be derailed by the conflicting motivations of regional/global partners that for various reasons are reluctant to see any variation from the status quo. This appears to be the fate of the Minsk group (comprising representatives from a dozen countries and co-chaired by France, Russia and the United States), which was set up to mediate a resolution to the conflict over Nagorno-Karabakh between Azerbaijan and Armenia. As Thomas de Waal (2010, p. 160), a close observer of this conflict, writes: 'Although the Minsk Process has appeared poised to deliver success on several occasions, it seems stuck in a perpetual cycle of frustration and disappointment'. Part of the reason for this is the presence of powerful Armenian diaspora communities in France, Russia and the US which are keen to see Armenia maintain its control over the Nagorno-Karabakh region and do not want to jeopardize relations with Yerevan. Some believe that Russia is also using the continuing dispute to exert pressure on Baku, which has been trying to reduce Russian influence over its energy sector and export markets. The EU, which could potentially play an important role in resolving the conflict, has been kept at bay by France and Russia, the latter having objected to the deployment of a full-scale EU mission.

Another 'frozen' conflict is the situation in Moldova, which has also defied any sort of successful CCM ventures via the Organization for Security and Cooperation in Europe (OSCE) or EU, because of the presence of large-scale criminal networks in the unrecognized separatist region of Transdniestria which are tied to Ukraine and Russia. Transdniestrian elites have shown little appetite for engagement in any kind of peace process bolstered by the presence of Russian troops, Russian economic aid and Russian sanctions against Moldovan exports (International Crisis Group 2006; OSCE 2010). As both of these examples illustrate, in the worst-case CCM translates into no CM at all (See the balance sheet on the pros and cons of multi-party mediation efforts in Crocker et al. 1999b).

But CCM may occur not only because of the perceived benefits of collective action; it may also be the result of enablers that facilitate such action. Internet-enabled open architecture is one such enabler, as defence thinkers in the US, the UK, NATO, Australia, Sweden and Singapore (members of the International Transformation Chairs Network founded in 2004) have argued. While the ideas germinating in the US Navy remain at a formative stage and are meeting predictable resistance, its 2007 'Cooperative Strategy for twenty-first Century Seapower' outlined what may become seminal ideas that go beyond traditional naval roles to include cooperative maritime security, humanitarian assistance and disaster response based on interoperability and engagement with a broad spectrum of US and international partners (official and non-official). Two years earlier, Admiral Mike Mullen, then US Chief of Naval Operations, proposed a Global Maritime Partnership centred on the vision of a 1,000-ship navy consisting of over 300 US ships and 700 vessels from partner nations that wished to be part of the initiative. Henrik Friman, a scholar at the Swedish National Research Agency, sees the 1,000-ship navy proposal as an early example of 'WikiForce', a new way of organizing and sharing information and security tasks on a collective basis, based on transformational technologies and new modes of multilateral organization. Meanwhile, humanitarian and disaster response initiatives in which technology-enabled networks link a wide spectrum of official and non-official agencies are already a reality in some settings (Friman 2009; see also Wells and Christman 2009). Such ideas are not alliance based and are not confined to joint training; in the maritime security sphere they represent operational collaboration on humanitarian issues that are increasingly viewed as part of the security agenda of major powers.

23.5   SOME KEY CAVEATS

When the political environment is supportive, networks of conflict managers can help to develop effective engagement strategies of negotiation and mediation that reinforce each other. They also have a key role to play in supporting peacebuilding and conflict transformation processes from their inception to their conclusion, including the implementation of formal peace settlements. These ad hoc 'coalitions', rather than any new institution, may be the best tailor-made conflict management instruments available for the job. However, there are some important questions to consider before applauding the emergence of these arrangements unequivocally.

First, many NGOs are uneasy at being coopted by governments and military authorities in conflict zones such as Iraq and Afghanistan. While some NGOs specializing in conflict management, such as the Crisis Management Initiative run by former President Martti Ahtisaari of Finland, have gone so far as to design communication systems for specific conflict locations so that military and civilian/NGO partners can work more effectively together, others have been reluctant to engage with governments, especially their military units. To make CCM initiatives combining official and non-official actors effective, the two sectors will have to agree on some general 'rules of engagement' that respect the status and special nature (and limitations) of NGOs. The NGOs, in turn, will need to decide whether or not to accept the constraints of operating in insecure locales and relying on others for security and physical survival. Improvised networks among conflict management actors will feature a flattening of vertical hierarchy and a reduction in status disparity, especially (as previously discussed) when networks are linked to the resources of information technology. This aspect of modern CCM places a premium on the presence of key people who know their counterparts in different participating entities, who understand the arts of informal, lateral communication, and who are culturally sensitive. Research on the possibilities of cooperation and coordination among different types of third-party intermediaries points to the importance of improved relations and communication while also identifying limitations and barriers to operational coordination (Fisher 2006; Strimling 2006).

Second, we also need to understand more about the durability of the CCM phenomenon. It is an open question whether CCM is a transitional practice – a halfway house to more formal, binding forms of cooperative action – or a step backwards because of the failure of existing institutions of conflict management to address collective security challenges. This is a significant issue. If CCM turns out to be an ephemeral or half-hearted response to security challenges; if participants engage only in order to be seen 'doing something' about a problem; if they dabble at the problem and fail to 'finish the job', losing interest once immediate threats are removed – then CCM will have only a minor role in global security.

An interesting test case will be the longevity of the Proliferation Security Initiative (PSI), founded in March 2003 and now 'endorsed' by some 95 countries whose act of adherence consists of officially subscribing to a set of principles. The PSI aims to detect and intercept WMD (weapons of mass destruction) materials and related finance, and is described in official US statements as 'a flexible, voluntary initiative geared toward enhancing individual and collective partner nations' capabilities to take appropriate and timely actions to meet the fast-moving situations involving proliferation threats'. Emphasis is placed on 'voluntary actions by states that are consistent with their national legal authorities and relevant international law and frameworks'.[1] The PSI has principles in lieu of a formal charter, and it conducts operational and training activities rather than regularized meetings or summits. It has no headquarters or dedicated facilities and no intergovernmental budget. Interestingly, President Barack Obama has called for the PSI to become 'a durable international institution'.[2]

Third, there is great diversity in CCM practices and choices: national preferences and different regional 'security cultures' are two variables that seem to influence both. But it also matters a great deal whether powerful regional actors assert themselves in order to shape their environment. In today's divisible security environment, it still matters whether extra-regional states are available to help out as conflict management partners, as Canada has done in the Dubai Process. Clearly, we need a sharper understanding of the motives and incentives that drive states, international and regional actors, and NGOs to develop further their cooperative arrangements and doctrines. One driver may be the absence or uneven presence of global assistance and support to fill the 'security gap' (Call and Schmitt 2009). The suggestion here is that regional or private ownership of conflict management roles evolves to fill a vacuum. A related driver may be the perception by local and regional actors that they have specific and

[1]   US State Department website, http://www.state.gov/t/isn/c10390.htm.
[2]   See http://www.whitehouse.gov/the_press_office/Remarks-By-President-Barack-Obama-In-Prague-As-Delivered/.

unique attributes, skills and cultural insights that more distant, external bodies or states lack.

Further, each region has its own peculiarities and distinctive normative framework for cooperation. European norms shape much of the regional security agenda of the members and would-be members of Europe's institutions, but not beyond this geographical zone. Cooperation in the OAS rests on a culture of regional self-help that is tied to subregional forums and networks of cooperation in Latin America. We also have to recognize that many evolving 'global' norms, such as the 'responsibility to protect', rest uneasily on the most fragile consensus and are not universally shared across different regions.

Fourth, in some regions there may be evidence of another driver: a sense of a developing incompatibility between the doctrines and normative priorities of global actors and those of regional states. For example, it is unlikely that the Shanghai Cooperation Organization (or the Collective Security Treaty Organization) and the OSCE would place the same degree of emphasis on governance norms in approaching the challenges of combating terrorism and maintaining border security in Central Asia. African peacekeeping missions could be encountering a parallel dilemma: UN and Western agencies and NGOs may have one set of conditions for achieving a legitimate 'exit' from military operations, and African leaders may have quite a different one reflecting the realities of patronage and 'wealth-sharing' in many societies (de Waal 2010).

Additional drivers of regional innovation and capacity-building are to be found in reactions to perceived global 'interventionism' (under whatever guise) and the assertion by external parties (official or non-official) of the need to act on behalf of 'universal' values that may not, in fact, be so universally admired or respected. To some degree, then, collective conflict management – as it unfolds in individual regions – may be partly a regional response and a reaction to the perceived shortcomings of external policy and doctrine. When major powers seek to project their priorities into distant places, privileging a single issue such as non-proliferation or counterterrorism or anti-corruption, there will be pushback and a possible 'opening' for regionally defined CCM initiatives.

A final consideration is the prospect that some CCM ventures may develop without a legal basis or any agreed source of official authorization. While there are few, if any, examples of this happening, it is possible to imagine that improvisation could run amok leaving a potential minefield of unanswered questions: who is responsible when a CCM initiative results in (or aggravates) a humanitarian disaster, what laws apply to which participants, and who is financially liable for the direct or collateral effects of an apparently worthy undertaking? Identifying the questions is easier than finding answers. Placing existing international bodies 'in charge' of CCM activity would seem to contradict the basic dynamic behind the emergence of CCM and to devalue the source of its attraction to participants.

23.6   THE CCM BALANCE SHEET

The world is very uneven in terms of regional capacities for self-determination in the conflict management and security spheres; and the nature of post-9/11 geopolitics makes CCM a strong reflection of the age. Many of the threats facing groups, countries and regions today are beyond the capability of any one actor to resolve, and no one really wants to own them. Hence CCM occurs within regions, between regions and global actors, and between neighbouring regions. Its operation in any specific instance depends on (i) the readiness of global actors to engage in regional conflict management, (ii) the availability and power of non-official entities to make contributions across the spectrum of conflict prevention, management and peacebuilding, (iii) the presence or absence of 'lead nations' to drive a response forward and (iv) the readiness of regional bodies and key regional states to seek external help when needed.

Any balance sheet on CCM should reflect the rapidly changing threat landscapes of different regions. If criminal business enterprises or al-Qaeda are moving towards regional franchises or branches with local/regional roots as noted above, the CM response will need to be similarly agile. The balance sheet should, however, also reflect the element of impermanence – that is, today's arrangements in response to today's challenge (for example, piracy or WMD proliferation) may not be suitable for coping with other challenges that could arise tomorrow. Having said this, however, it is possible that CCM will become a seed of future institutional development. It has happened before: the European Coal and Steel Community was the germ of the EU; ECOWAS was the germ and incubator for ECOMOG (Economic Community of West African States Monitoring Group); the Helsinki Accords were the seedbed for the OSCE.

In this fragmented era there is no common 'cookie cutter' approach to conflict management. Moreover, the main powerful actors are all – in one way or another – troubled by economic pressures and facing short-term political imperatives over issues of identity, employment, health, ageing, trade and jobs. In such a world, the degree of interest in working for a new global order is very unevenly spread. The international arena is witnessing something quite different from a new global order – CCM may not be pretty, but it is the best we are going to get.

24 The political economy of fragile states
Tony Addison

24.1 INTRODUCTION

Fragile states have very mixed characteristics. Some are experiencing violent conflict, some are 'post-conflict', some have avoided large-scale violence – so far. Many are resource poor, but some are resource rich. Many are landlocked, but certainly not all. What they do have in common is that aid donors find it tough to work with them. Weak governance and weak implementation capacity dominate donor discussion of fragile states.

Running alongside the focus of aid donors on fragility is increasing attention to growth in recipient countries, in an attempt to reduce aid dependence. Another reason is the perceived link between low growth and conflict. But there is more to the economics of fragility than simply growth, and inequality matters as well. This chapter explores the political economy of fragility, using examples from countries that have, at one time or another, been on most donors' lists of fragile states (definitions of fragile states do of course vary).

The chapter is divided as follows. The next section reviews the evidence on the relationship between growth, fragility and civil war (Section 24.2). It emphasizes the need to look at the *quality* of growth not just the *quantity*. The chapter then turns to growth's relationship to livelihoods and poverty in fragile states (Section 24.3). We assess two engines of growth. The first is *internal*, namely ways to build growth around the needs and capacities of poor people. The second is *external*, entailing better engagement with the global economy, changing the incentives of elites, and mobilizing the diaspora.

Section 24.4 discusses public finance, which is central to building states, distributing growth's benefits, the politics of fragility, and post-conflict recovery. Without any underlying change in the distributional politics, growth that delivers more revenue to the state will simply accentuate unequal fiscal incidence and associated grievances. The chapter concludes, in Section 24.5, that closer engagement in the global economy is a way forward for fragile states. But this strategy has risks, not least in the present global economic turbulence, and governments would be wise to invest in their internal engine of growth as well, especially if they build growth around the capacities of poor people.

24.2   GROWTH AND CIVIL WAR

Fragile states have a high risk of violent conflict. So even in fragile states without histories of large-scale conflict, we are right to be worried. This goes alongside a frustration over their politics that keeps them on trajectories of instability and violence. Donors want to cut through the Gordian Knot of politics with a simple and effective tool. Economic growth seems to offer that tool.

Cross-country statistical studies, notably foundational research by Paul Collier and Anke Hoeffler, conclude that a higher per capita income is associated with a lower probability of civil war (Collier and Hoeffler 1998, 2004b). In that sense, economic growth reduces the chances of civil war. Quite how this works is still debated, and almost certainly varies across types of economy and society.

The growth-to-peace linkage has great appeal for aid donors. If aid can raise growth then it might help prevent civil war and secure peace after conflict. The cost–benefit ratio looks promising given that the typical civil war does about US$64 billion of damage (this is almost certainly an underestimate, see Addison 2004; estimate from Collier and Hoeffler 2004a), including the monetary value of the lost human life (to use the 'bloodless' terminology of economic science). Therefore the use of aid to raise growth, and thereby possibly avert conflict, seems to be good value. However, it is not that easy. There are several stings in the growth tail, to which we now turn.

24.2.1   Exceptions to the Rule

There are many examples of political instability and violent conflict occurring after periods of strong growth or while growth is ongoing. Without being exhaustive, or going into detail on each case, they include the following. Kenya's conflict in 2008 followed five years of strong economic growth, which was running at over 6 per cent immediately before the 2008 crisis (IMF 2007, p. 4). Pakistan has achieved 6.5 per cent growth since 2003, and significant poverty reduction, but otherwise looks like a failing state. Madagascar's political instability over 2009 followed 5 per cent annual economic growth from 2002 (World Bank 2009a). Northern Uganda's conflict continued despite the national economy's strong recovery from the turmoil of the Amin and Obote years. Naxalite conflicts have risen despite India's emerging-economy success story. And Gujarat has the highest growth of all Indian states (12 per cent in 2007) but some of the nation's worst communal violence (Justino 2009). Turmoil in Egypt and Tunisia in 2011, as well as Libya's civil war, followed a decade of higher growth.

These conflicts could have occurred earlier, or have been worse (in duration and depth), without economic growth. We do not know. However, these examples certainly do illustrate the point – emphasized by the cross-section studies – that while growth might lower the likelihood of conflict, it certainly does not eliminate the possibility. In some countries the nature of the growth process might be conflict inducing, in which case a high growth rate will translate into an *increased* probability of conflict. Growth's unequal distributional impact has been an important part of the conflict story in each of these 'successful' growth cases. So it is to distribution that we now turn.

24.2.2 Unpacking Growth

Growth needs unpacking to understand its link to conflict through the distribution of its benefits. The first generation of cross-country statistical studies found that grievance measures, including inequality, but also ethnic polarization, and religious fractionalization, had only weak effects on the likelihood of conflict (Collier and Hoeffler 1998, 2004b). Subsequent studies using larger datasets, notably Nafziger and Auvinen (2002), find that inequality measures have greater importance in explaining conflict's occurrence. So do case studies and systematic comparisons across case-study countries (see, for example, Cramer 2003; Cramer 2006; Nafziger et al. 2000; Tadjoeddin and Chowdhury 2009; Ylönen 2005).

This is bad news: it is far harder to reduce inequality than it is to raise economic growth. It is very difficult when inequality is strongly horizontal or group in nature (Stewart 2008b). Land reform across ethnic groups is especially hard. If GDP is static, then redistribution becomes win–lose for the groups involved. The trick is to achieve *redistribution alongside growth*, so that the *absolute* well-being of all groups improves, but the well-being of the previously excluded improves faster – so that their *share* of the social pie rises over time. This has been recognized since 'Redistribution with Growth' in the early 1970s, but is no less true today (Chenery et al. 1974). Economic diversification further reduces the political problem. It creates economic opportunities for the excluded, thereby helping them escape spatial poverty traps and 'adverse incorporation' as landless and indebted labourers in rural areas – a mobility that is enhanced by investing in their education (CPRC 2008).

Inequality has been reduced alongside growth, and in the aftermath of conflict. Taiwan and South Korea reconstructed from the Chinese civil war and the Korean War, respectively, and then grew strongly with inequality falling as labour rapidly shifted out of agriculture and into labour-intensive manufacturing. But a strong ethnic or religious dimension did not characterize their social inequality as it does today's fragile states. Horizontal inequality was reduced alongside economic growth in Malaysia, but this is one of the few success stories (Stewart et al. 2008).

To take the discussion further, the distribution of growth's benefits can be split into two areas of concern. The first is the creation of more and better livelihoods and, related to that, the question of what constitutes the *engines of growth*. The second is public finance, and how to gather the revenue generated by the growth process and use it well. We now turn to these issues, starting with livelihoods.

24.3   LIVELIHOODS AND THE ENGINES OF GROWTH

24.3.1   Post-war Growth 'Bounces'

Poverty remains deep in the absence of productive livelihoods, making it easier for warlords and other organized criminals to recruit followers. High unemployment alongside high inequality is a combustible mixture and a warning that conflict is likely; examples include Nepal and Sierra Leone (Keen 2005; Murshed and Gates 2005).

Growth will 'bounce' after war, provided that peace is maintained. Refugees move back to their farms, factories reopen and hire again, and private capital and aid donors return to rebuild infrastructure – thereby absorbing unemployed labour (often reinforced through labour-intensive public works). The growth bounce is desirable – it underpins the political settlement and supports the reintegration of ex-fighters – but it can create false optimism, and the immediate post-war gains need to be followed by sustained and broad (inequality-reducing) growth.

Informalization also characterizes fragile states. Under weak governance, businesses avoid registering (thereby limiting tax revenue, which exacerbates the state's revenue problem). There are very few small and medium-sized enterprises (SMEs) of the type that drive innovation and employment generation in growth's success stories. Informalization rises dramatically under conflict. Consequently, there is a 'missing middle' in their private sectors.

Fragile economies are characterized by underinvestment in production (outside of the extractive industries) and overinvestment in trade – for the latter has rapid returns and needs little of the fixed capital investment that makes production vulnerable to predation (Addison and Murshed 2005). Smallholders retreat into subsistence and away from higher-earning, but more vulnerable, cash crops – thereby exacerbating rural poverty (Brück 2004). If the economy remains specialized in point resources, then lack of diversification also keeps it vulnerable to conflict (Welsch 2008). And undiversified economies are more vulnerable to shocks, and growth shocks are associated with increased conflict (Miguel et al. 2004).

The *quality* of growth must therefore be improved. Establishing credibility, both in economic policy and towards peace, is vital to securing long-term investment outside of mining and hydrocarbons. The Central African Republic, Chad, Guinea-Bissau and the Democratic Republic of Congo (DRC) illustrate how difficult it is to recover credibility once lost.

24.3.2   Success and New Challenges

Examples of success include Ethiopia, Mozambique and Uganda, three countries that have, over the last two decades, been in recovery from war. Since the end of the war in 1992, Mozambique has been one of Africa's fastest-growing economies and poverty has fallen significantly with recovery in rural areas, which bore the brunt of the fighting (Virtanen and Ehrenpreis 2007). In Uganda, national poverty fell from 55.7 to 35.2 per cent over 1992–99 (Lawson et al. 2003). This was at a time when the economy was shifting from its earlier post-conflict recovery phase into sustained growth. In Ethiopia, national poverty fell, but more so in rural than urban areas, jumped during the 1998–2000 war with Eritrea, and then continued its decline (Dercon 2006).

Despite growth, poverty can remain resilient in areas with poor infrastructure that are weakly connected to national and international markets, or in areas where conflict remains. If they continue to be left behind, then *spatial inequality* widens with growth. Grievance is not just driven by low levels of income and human development. People worry about their group's standard of living relative to others. Grievance intensifies when spatial inequality is rising – even if people are absolutely better off. Secession becomes attractive when the lagging region is resource rich and the fiscal mechanism fails to redistribute the rents. Examples include Nigeria's Delta region and southern Sudan.

Spatial inequality is one reason why poverty can remain chronic despite growth – lasting throughout a person's (short) lifetime and being 'transmitted' to their children (and their children). Thus despite Uganda's impressive record in growth and poverty reduction – that lifted nearly 30 per cent of households out of poverty by 1999 – about 19 per cent of households who were poor in 1992 were still poor in 1999 (Lawson et al. 2003).

24.3.3   Building Growth around the Poor

'New' poverty can emerge with economic success. Growth raises the returns on land and other natural capital and therefore their value. When property rights are insecure, land-grabbing drives people into poverty. Land values rise as cities prosper, putting pressure on poor urban communities – evident in Bangladesh with its impressive growth, but also in Addis Ababa and other African cities.

In Uganda, 10 per cent of non-poor households fell into poverty despite the decline in national poverty as the economy recovered (ibid.). Spatial inequality, land-grabbing and the conflict in northern Uganda are the main reasons. This complexity in the growth-poverty picture is why it is crucial to understand poverty over time ('poverty dynamics') through a multidimensional and multidisciplinary approach (Addison et al. 2009). Governments need to invest in regular data collection, not least to help generate a better-informed political debate over priorities and trade-offs.

Lagging regions and the continued risk of falling into poverty despite growth can make the public sceptical about growth itself. Governments and donors need to recognize this for they oversell the growth story, neglecting the downside. Social protection could increase growth by reducing the fear of rapid economic change – especially openness to international trade (Rodrik 2007). Growth in turn generates the revenue to finance social protection, but only if tax institutions are strengthened.

Social protection offers a way to move from short-run imperatives to sustained and cost-effective poverty reduction (CPRC 2008). For fragile states, conditional cash transfers (CCTs) linked to schooling, especially for girls, should be effective. Educational reform and investment to raise schooling quality will be necessary as well. In building female human capital, and therefore women's livelihoods, education for girls can offset some of the gender bias inherent in public works that are typically aimed at absorbing young male fighters after conflict. Educating girls and women (for many women lose educational opportunities during wartime) is a powerful means to improve the quality of growth by improving the quality of women's livelihoods.

We do not yet know how strong the national growth effects of social protection are. But we do know that social protection can have significant effects on local economies. Much of the additional cash is spent on locally produced goods and services, acting as a demand multiplier. With a bigger local market, private investment is encouraged, and the returns to micro-finance increase. CTTs for education can reduce spatial inequality, offsetting growth's tendency to widen the gap between regions with locational and resource advantages and those without. In resource-rich countries, social protection can distribute resource rents more widely and, through its productive effects, help diversify growth away from dependence on extractive industries.

Social protection offers a way for the state to demonstrate commitment to redressing distributive injustice (Addison 2009). Post-conflict Guatemala and El Salvador are contrasting examples. The indigenous majority predominates among Guatemala's poor (de Ferranti et al. 2004). These grievances fed 36 years of civil war, but peace has seen little progress. El Salvador, which also went through a brutal civil war, reduced poverty from 65 per cent in the early 1990s to 41 per cent by 2004 (IDB 2005; World Bank 2000). A conditional cash transfer programme, *Red Solidaria*, is contributing to this success (Soares and Britto 2007).

In summary, building growth around poor people – their needs and capacities – strengthens the *internal* engine of growth, and improves growth's quality (more diversification, less volatility, more social inclusion). Yet, an internal growth engine is insufficient. Fragile states must make their way in the global economy, through the *external* growth engine as well.

24.3.4   Engagement with the Global Economy

Fragile economies are mostly small, the result of small populations and low per capita incomes. Of the 35 countries on DFID's list of 35 fragile states, more than half (19) have populations around 10 million or less (DFID 2005). Conflict reduces the size of the internal market further. The post-war growth bounce stimulates internal demand. But even if Sierra Leone (to take one example) doubled its per capita income (which is half that of Tanzania) its economy would still only be 16 per cent the size of Tanzania's – and Tanzania is a very small economy (less than 20 per cent the size of Nigeria's).

The internal engine will be prominent in countries with large populations (for example, Indonesia and Nigeria, countries which have appeared on some lists of fragile states). Market size provides local producers with economies of scale in these countries. But most fragile states are otherwise reliant on the external growth engine; the small size of their economies limits their internal growth engine until per capita incomes rise to levels that offset the disadvantage of small populations.

However, we must recognize that the present engagement of fragile states with the global economy is highly problematic. To help, we need to understand the difficulties facing each country. Is it simply that the costs of engaging are high – so that they export too few goods and services, and too much labour, to the world? Is regional conflict the main issue? Is it limited policy capacity – they find international (World Trade Organization: WTO) trade rules difficult to navigate? Is limited business knowledge the problem – their entrepreneurs cannot connect to the supply chains that underpin globalization? Are they facing the destruction of key sectors by climate change, thereby making it more risky to invest? Or are these countries worst-case scenarios? That is, do they engage in the global economy in entirely the wrong ways; through blood diamonds and other minerals, narcotics, illegally cut timber, money laundering and human trafficking.

Much depends on what is happening within the state itself. So we need to understand that. Are honest politicians hamstrung by states with weak implementation capacities? Are politicians driven more by personal wealth-building than state-building? Do they run predatory states? Does the state's remit no longer hold within the nation's frontiers? In summary, the economic diagnosis must be simultaneously a political diagnosis. This amounts to growth diagnostics within a conflict perspective (for an application to north Africa, see Addison and Baliamoune-Lutz 2006).

24.3.5 Firing-up the External Engine

Economists argue among themselves over how to produce external-led growth. Should the state or the market drive exports forward? What is the role for import substitution? The jury is still out. Nevertheless, it is difficult to envisage many of the present fragile states deploying the kind of state-led growth strategies that moved Taiwan and South Korea from post-conflict recovery and into fast and sustained growth. That is not to rule out 'industrial policy' ('industrial' in the sense of creating new sectors with high value added). Ethiopia's leaders say they draw valuable lessons from East Asia. But fragile states are defined by their weak implementation capacity. Spending that capacity on trying to pick too many 'winners' risks diverting policy makers from fundamental but demanding reforms, particularly in public finance. Therefore while an industrial policy might be helpful, it needs to be well crafted, and not just consist of a list of unrealistic projects.

So what can be done to fire up the external growth engine? One way into the problem is to start by recognizing that elites have many *exit options* – their fortunes are only partially linked to economic and social progress in their own countries. They can move wealth abroad, whereas most citizens' prosperity is tied to domestic, largely immobile, assets (a community's access to a forest, for example). The elite's wealth accordingly grows as the global economy grows, independently of their own country's fortunes. Therefore reducing the gap between the returns that elites derive at home and abroad, bringing their own prosperity into closer alignment with that of their country, gives them an incentive to encourage private investment and growth. Mancur Olson called this 'an encompassing interest' (McGuire and Olson 1996).

This amounts to discouraging the export of capital, and encouraging its return. Capital controls cannot prevent capital export – fragile states are too weak to apply them. And the governing elite will not tolerate measures that run counter to its own interest. Capital that has flown is free to move across the world – it can only be forced back with difficulty (Sani Abacha's millions are still somewhere in the world financial system, little as yet has been driven back to Nigeria). So drastic steps are necessary. With limited credibility, policy has to be restrained to reduce the risks of hyperinflation and currency runs, thereby raising investor confidence – including that of the elite. This implies dollarization or the adoption of a currency board (as in Bosnia and Herzegovina). Potential investors also watch sovereign-debt ratings closely. Official debt relief, most recently the Enhanced HIPC (heavily indebted poor countries) Initiative and the MDRI (multilateral debt relief initiative), have helped to improve credit ratings, thereby sending a positive signal to potential investors. Missing, however, are more substantial efforts at the international level to provide, for example, more compensatory finance to assist countries vulnerable to external shocks (such as those emanating from the global financial crisis of the last few years).

For *predatory elites*, the world has started to tighten their access to opportunities elsewhere in the global economy. In 2009, the attempt by a senior member of Zimbabwe's government to sell large amounts of gold (originally mined in the DRC) was blocked under EU sanctions (against 200 of Zimbabwe's elite who stand accused of human rights abuses). Action against international organized crime disrupts the (growing) linkages between Latin American drugs cartels and elites in West Africa, including Guinea-Bissau where the cartels helped to assassinate President João Bernardo Vieira in 2009. The recent moves to reduce bank secrecy in rich countries, the product of a crackdown on tax havens and money laundering by organized crime and terrorists, assist as well. So does the prosecution of those in the rich world who facilitate corruption in the South, and the UK has recently strengthened its anti-bribery legislation (although critics argue that this needs to go further).

Predatory-elite capital forced back home may then be reinvested in the domestic economy to deliver some growth, providing the elite with at least a partial interest in property rights – although mainly as they affect their own interests. This has a chance in countries that have not slid too far. But we may be clutching at straws as far as the very worst cases go. Charles Taylor's election as Liberia's president in 1997 offered him the opportunity to develop Liberia alongside his own wealth. But instead his greed drove the economy into the ground, and Liberia back to civil war. Ultimately, predatory elites must be brought to justice when they commit gross human rights abuses and impoverish their people – the latter is as much a crime as political murder, and potentially easier to prove (Addison 2009).

24.3.6 Growth as a Stabilizing and Destabilizing Process

There is another way of going at the problem, which can be pursued simultaneously. This is to accelerate the creation of a middle class. Historically, the expansion of the middle class alongside growth eventually contained the power of traditional ruling elites. The middle class, together with the class of skilled labour created by growth, built institutions through which to exercise *countervailing powers*. Democratization followed. It was supported by a greater diffusion in economic power, including the co-option of traditional elites into the new sources of wealth generated by diversifying and growing economies.

An improvement in the quality of growth is simultaneously *destabilizing* – it undermines old orders – and *stabilizing*; it moves societies towards a new set of rules that have wider popular support. The process is therefore far from smooth, with political crises (and sometimes bloodshed) along the way.

This process has a trade dimension. Today, countries with the right external growth engine converge much faster towards rich-world living standards – including a large middle class – than was possible in past industrial revolutions. South Korea and Taiwan took only 10 years from the mid-1960s to reach their middle-income level, while the United Kingdom took 54 years from the late eighteenth century onwards (Parente and Prescott 2000). Today's global economy provides more markets and more economies of scale in production, more 'off-the-shelf' technologies for late developers, and more capital.

But here we come to the stalemate in which fragile states find themselves. Their middle classes are thin – the result of limited private sector development – leaving most people poor, and a very few wealthy. It is another 'missing middle', and one related to the other missing middle: the lack of SMEs in the private sector, discussed earlier.

What can be done? There are no easy answers, but one route forward might be to try and 'import' a middle class. That is, turn to a group containing people with capital who know their country and its risks best; the *diaspora*. Diasporas are large. Sub-Saharan Africa's diaspora consists of at least 16 million people (Ratha and Shaw 2007). Stable countries, with unstable pasts, have used their diasporas in reconstruction; Ethiopia,

Ghana and Uganda are examples. Diasporas have resources, entrepreneurial talent, experience of global value chains, a greater ability to assess risk than other foreign investors (they are willing to invest during conflict if it is profitable), and some loyalty to their countries (unless persecuted, but even then they may be persuaded to return as Uganda's Asians did). Their return soon after conflict sends a confidence signal to other investors with less information and ability to 'price risk' into their decisions. This externality might be worth a public subsidy, and financial assistance from governments and donors.

Diaspora capital also contributes to filling the private sector's 'missing middle' of SMEs. Post-conflict financial systems are damaged, undercapitalized, and reluctant to lend to all but the safest borrowers (Addison et al. 2005). SMEs are low on their priorities – unless connected to the local elite. Moreover, banks are not good at judging loan applications from potential export businesses; hence their preference for 'safe' assets such as urban construction. Rebuilding and reforming the financial system provides deposit, lending and insurance services to domestic entrepreneurs and the returning diaspora, and reduces the costs of remittances (and reliance on informal money-transfer systems that sometimes transmit terrorist funds). To take one example, fees for remittances from the UK to Rwanda average 15 per cent of the amount sent[1] In the meantime, the capital of the diaspora – and their ability to borrow abroad – can initiate investment while financial reconstruction is still to begin. As banks recapitalize – which usually requires foreign funds – states must allocate scarce implementation capacity into effective financial regulation and supervision. As they do so, they should assess how the financial system can assist the external growth engine and help find ways to tap diaspora capital and expertise (including that necessary to rebuild the financial system itself). It is in this area that states can construct a useful industrial policy.

If the diaspora returns home and invests then countries stand a chance of moving themselves onto a trajectory of quality growth. Diaspora investment is valuable to the internal growth engine – including one kick-started by social protection – but essential to the external engine, given the global entrepreneurial networks in which diasporas embed. Together with measures to encourage domestic capital to stay home, this may start a growth process that has buy-in from at least part of the ruling elite.

None of these positive outcomes is predetermined. Growth is both destabilizing and stabilizing as emphasized earlier. It also requires an opportune political moment to begin the process. Some ruling elites will

[1]   Source: http://remittanceprices.worldbank.org/RemittanceCosts.

resist – it is unlikely that Colonel Gaddafi or Kim Jong-il would have signed up. When the ruling elite enjoys generous resource rents that also provide the means to defend itself – or generous external patrons – then it has less interest in economic diversification (Mobutu's Zaire, for example). Countries can, and do, exist in this condition for many years. One example is Myanmar (Burma). Then the thinness of the middle class, and the absence of a skilled-labour class, implies weak countervailing powers; few business associations that are not co-opted by the ruling elite, small trade unions without much (if any) independence from the state, and little in the way of an independent media.

Finally, to end this section, another word of caution: in nudging countries out of their fragile state we expose them to a new set of risks. In integrating more closely with the global economy, countries open themselves to different kinds of external shock. This is the potential risk in seeking global opportunities for quality growth. So again the state needs to conserve but also build its policy-making and implementation capacity to meet the new risks and help the private sector find the new opportunities. Policy makers require a thorough understanding of how the global economy works. Supporting international finance is also required.

24.4　GROWTH AND PUBLIC FINANCE

We now discuss another vital part of the fragility equation, that of public finance. This is central to building states, the distribution of growth's benefits, the politics of fragility, and to post-conflict recovery (Addison and Roe 2004; Boyce and O'Donnell 2007; Brautigam et al. 2008). All other reforms are secondary compared to the primacy of public finance. This is not to say that they are unimportant. But reforms in the areas of regulation, finance, trade, and agriculture require effective execution by the state, and effective states rest upon a system of effective public finance.

Growth is *potentially* state-building. Growth creates the revenues with which to reform and construct state institutions. The value of market transactions increases with growth; as more transactions take place through the formal sector (including via SMEs) and as indirect taxes become easier to collect (provided that policy, including tax policy, is pro-business). The introduction of VAT (the most efficient form of indirect tax) further raises revenue (and minimizes economic distortions compared to other types of sales taxes).

The value of imports grows alongside economic growth, delivering more revenue to the state if the customs and excise service is reformed. Import quotas must be converted into tariffs to deliver revenue to the state not rents to import-licence holders. And tariff schedules need to be simplified as overcomplex schedules create economic distortions and are more easily manipulated by corrupt officials. The average tariff rate must then come down, to reduce the cost of the intermediate and capital goods needed by businesses as they invest and expand.

Post-conflict countries experience a surge in imports of raw materials and capital equipment to rebuild shattered infrastructure and to get business restarted. Reforms facilitating that surge should be placed at the top of the revenue reform agenda. And the reforms must be innovative when state capacity is initially weak. The post-war government of Mozambique subcontracted the management of the customs service to crown agents to revitalize the organization and reduce corruption, for example (McCoy and van Dunem 2009). This generated additional revenue and a more efficient and fast service that reduced transactions costs for business.

In summary, strengthening tax institutions (or constructing them from scratch as in newly independent Eritrea and Timor-Leste) must be the first fiscal action point. There is a lot of technical work to be done, as there is in the planning and budgeting of public expenditures to use the additional revenue effectively.

24.4.1   The Distributional Politics of Public Finance

We turn now to the politics of how public finance distributes growth's benefits. Public spending often favours one or two ethnic groups over others, thereby reinforcing their wealth and political power. Combined with taxation systems that grant non-transparent exemptions to privileged groups, the net incidence of public finance is often grossly unequal across ethnic groups (or by other characteristics, sometimes overlapping, such as region and religion).

When ethnic groups are concentrated geographically, the spatial distribution of public spending (as well as its trend) indicates whether the state is reinforcing horizontal inequality or reducing it (this is also a potential warning sign of conflict to come). Given the budgetary data, it is straightforward to construct 'privilege indices' showing the spatial distribution of public spending (and actual services and investments). One such exercise for Burundi, found that almost all public investment went to areas of the minority Tutsi elite (Ngaruko and Nkurunziza 2000, p. 382).

Without any underlying change in this distributional politics, growth that delivers more revenue will simply accentuate the unequal fiscal incidence and associated grievances. Collecting revenue from the rising tax base is also harder; those who are neglected by public spending will rightly regard the taxation as unjust.

The politics of public finance is crucial in mineral-rich countries for it is the *quality* of their growth that is the problem not, at present, the *quantity* of growth. Mineral-rich but fragile economies are found among some of the fastest growers. Of the eight countries whose real GDP per capita rose by more than 50 per cent over 1997–2007, five were resource rich (and fragile): Chad, Myanmar, Nigeria, Sierra Leone and Tajikistan (Ahmed 2008, p. 10). The employment link that distributes growth's benefits is weaker when the growth pole is an extractive industry using capital-intensive, high-skill labour (West Africa's offshore oil for example). And the 'Dutch disease' effect of the resource windfall often limits growth outside the enclave. So GDP expands rapidly but along a very narrow path.

These problems can be managed. Linkages to the rest of the economy can be built, thereby raising labour demand. And Dutch disease can be offset by investing in infrastructure and services in the non-resource sectors. Most resource-rich countries can afford social protection from their ample revenues, thereby adding to the internal growth engine. All these interventions raise growth's quality. The impact is greatest when the growth potential outside of extractive industries is high (the case for Angola and Nigeria with their agricultural potential, for example). When the country's growth potential is limited by endowments or location (Chad and Niger in the Sahel, for instance) quality can still be raised, by using resource rents to create human capital.

All these interventions require effective public finance systems to allocate the resource rents and raise additional (tax) revenues to enlarge the required budget envelope. Creating these institutions is far from easy, but they should be a priority, especially in the early years of post-conflict reconstruction.

The windfall from 'point resources' (hydrocarbons and metals) differs from that of 'diffuse resources' (soils whose productivity is enhanced by a new agricultural technology, for example). The gains from the latter are widely spread unless access to the requisite natural capital (land, in particular) is very unequal. The rents from point resources are easier to channel into a few hands. If sated, predatory elites then have no personal or political need to build tax institutions – and certainly no desire to swap *real* representation for taxation (multi-party elections are often mere formalities). Resource-rich states therefore tend to limit their tax effort. Tax revenues fall by 2 per cent for every 10 per cent rise in hydrocarbon revenue, on average (Bornhorst et al. 2009).

Consequently, the growth-to-poverty link is weakest in mineral-rich countries when it is mediated through systems of public finance that are manipulated by elites for their own gain. Poverty-reducing expenditure in Guinea, which has the world's largest bauxite reserves, averages only 25 per cent of government revenue, and has shown no improvement since 1999 – during a global commodity boom (IDA and IMF 2006, p. 30).

In stark contrast stand Ethiopia, Mozambique and Uganda, three countries with far fewer point resources. Poverty reduction in these three is supported by increased budgetary allocations to education, basic health-care and other pro-poor expenditure; tax reform and growth provided resources as did the enhanced HIPC Initiative. Poverty-reducing expenditure as a share of public revenue rose over 1999–2006 from 61 to 89 per cent in Ethiopia; from 52 to 122 per cent in Mozambique; and from 40 to 85 per cent in Uganda (ibid.).

Aid provided substantial budget support to all three. The results also demonstrate the importance of debt relief in a post-conflict setting. Yet, the decision to grant official debt relief is still largely determined by *economic* performance criteria, rather than *political* progress – which should be given at least equal weight when politicians and civil society are making peace work (Addison and Murshed 2003a). At present, the reward (debt relief) for progress comes too long after the start of peacebuilding (when the resources from debt relief could be used earlier to support the peace process).

The success of Ethiopia, Mozambique and Uganda in comparison to the resource-rich countries such as Guinea supports the view that resource revenues are less transformational than aid (see, for example, Collier 2006). Indeed, destruction rather than transformation best describes many resource booms when they are used to fund more military capability, both equipment and mercenaries, to use against internal dissent. 'National security' is often cited to justify keeping resource revenues off-budget and, indeed, to classify them as a state secret. Conflict in Darfur continued despite Sudan's 7 per cent annual growth after 2000. Growth raised the revenue base; up to 60 per cent of Sudan's oil revenue went to the military, doubling over 1999–2001, according to one estimate (Rone 2003, p. 464). Khartoum's ability to pursue predatory military action was thereby strengthened. The use of oil revenue in this way is another reason why we should be wary of inflated claims regarding growth's potential to reduce conflict.

The politics of public finance is sometimes gloomy, but not irredeemable. Change is possible. To take one final example, Angola still spends far too little on human capital formation, especially among the poor. And it could afford comprehensive social protection. Nevertheless, Angola is showing progress in diversifying the economy. The quality of growth has risen. The Angolan elite is exporting less of its capital, and investing more at home. The diaspora is reinvesting. The private sector is therefore expanding beyond the *Empresários de confiança* ('the few trusted enterprises'), diluting their influence (Aguilar 2003). The resulting political dynamics could eventually nudge Angola towards a more socially inclusive pattern of development and a fuller democratization. Time will tell.

24.5   CONCLUSIONS

This chapter has emphasized the importance of unpacking the growth process. The quality of growth matters as much as the quantity in fragile states. A 'growth bounce' occurs once countries come out of conflict, but this can be too narrow in its benefits for poverty reduction. Countries that have not yet fallen into conflict need to spread livelihood generation as widely as possible, especially by reducing spatial inequality.

This chapter urges increased action on social protection as a way to strengthen growth's ability to reduce poverty. This can then provide an important *internal* source of demand for growth, stimulating the private sector. The chapter also argues, however, that this growth engine will be insufficient given the small size of most fragile economies. An *external* engine of growth is required, through international trade and the related investment, including that by the large diasporas associated with fragile states.

Export-led growth, especially by investing in diversifying the traditional export base, can be the fastest means to generate quality growth, and with growth comes revenue to build the state and to construct a better relationship with its people. Trade builds states, and potentially a social contract that underpins peace. But this strategy has risks, not least in the present global economic turbulence. Rich countries as well as emerging economies need to recognize that self-interested responses to the management of the global economy could easily derail progress in fragile states. Therefore, governments in fragile states would be wise to invest in their internal engines of growth as well, especially in ways that build growth around poor people and their capacities.

25 Conflict resolution versus democratic governance: can elections bridge the divide?

Pauline H. Baker

25.1 INTRODUCTION

A widely held assumption in the international community is that in post-conflict situations peace-building and democratization are virtually synonymous; creating the conditions for the one does so for both, and the two processes will be reciprocal and mutually supportive. This suggests the policy issues will be simple. But the reality could be very different. Choices have to be addressed between requisites for peace and conditions for democracy; and over the kind of 'democracy' and its relation to other essential developments like state-building.

(Burnell 2006, p. 1)

While considerable progress has been made since the end of the Cold War in ending internal wars, and it is clear that pro-democracy forces worldwide are growing, these dual processes do not always reinforce each other, as might be expected. Two distinct schools of thought exist on the best route to democratic peacebuilding in societies undergoing profound political transformation. 'Conflict resolution managers' emphasize the necessity for promoting peace; they seek to end or avoid bloodshed as soon as possible, even if that means including parties with unsavory histories, overlooking human rights abuses, and compromising on democratic principles. 'Democratizers', by contrast, while urging an end to violence, stress the critical importance of ensuring that democratic and human rights principles are upheld to have a durable peace, even if that means a longer and bloodier road to stability. A historical example of the diplomatic approach of the 'conflict resolution managers' is the Dayton Accords on Bosnia (Holbrooke 1998). An example of the 'democratizers' approach is the transition to majority rule in South Africa (see, for example, Waldmeir 1997). The debate over which of these approaches should be applied to societies in transition is sharpest when international policy makers and local parties face key questions on how and when to convene elections.

All countries, including authoritarian regimes, pay lip service to the need to hold elections, irrespective of whether they are free, fair or frequent. Elections are the linchpin of legitimate authority. And, with some exceptions, such as China, Russia and smaller authoritarian states, most governments, regional organizations and international institutions endorse the use of elections as the principal vehicle for promoting genuine democratic change. While there is a consensus that holding elections is essential to reaching democratic governance, how to accomplish that goal is more problematic. Conflict managers tend to see elections as a cure-all. It is not only as an instrument to legitimize authority but it is a way to end ongoing conflicts. 'The best guarantor of stability is democracy', concluded *The Economist* (5 February 2011, p. 15) in an editorial during the 2011 Egyptian uprising. The journal endorsed the view that elections should be held quickly, even if the country lacked the institutions and leadership that would ensure a smooth transition and there was a risk of a rise in the influence of undemocratic Islamist parties.

But elections, like revolutions, can be hijacked by well-organized undemocratic forces if there is too rapid a change in power and the processes and conditions leading up to the polls do not allow truly free and fair voting to take place. Many observers, including representatives of the US government, warned of the need to move slowly in Egypt, for example, when pressure was mounting on President Hosni Mubarak to step down. For example, Hossam Bahgat and Soha Abdelaty (2011), the executive director and deputy director of the Egypt Initiative for Personal Rights who were committed to 'an immediate end to the Mubarak era', warned that quick change could undermine the goals of the popular revolution that had electrified the world and inspired similar revolts in the region. Ensuring that democratic principles were first established before elections are held was 'the only way out of our nation's crisis', they maintained. Egyptian protesters themselves expressed this view after Mubarak was pushed out of office. Some felt that the military should be given a chance to fulfill its promises of amending the constitution before holding elections within six months, as had been promised, while others wanted to remain in Tahrir Square, the center of the revolution, to keep up the pressure until an entirely new political system under civilian rule was established. The latter view called for all the Mubarak-appointed civilian ministers and high-level appointees to resign immediately.

The Egyptian crisis is not the first in which the debate over the role of elections has arisen, but it shows how notions of electoral democracy have changed over time. In established democracies, elections have not only been regarded as central to freedom, but also as vital to stability, even if, as several commentators have argued, election campaigns have become too influenced by special interests, too prone to rhetorical excess, too dependent upon private funds, and prone to lapsing too often into unhealthy partisanship. Mature democracies may regret the quality of such campaigns, but they rarely fear that contentious contests will present existential threats to the state. Democracy, after all, is messy. However, in mature democracies, there are state institutions that mitigate the potential for conflict, such as judicial appeals, alternative routes to office (Marschall et al. 2011), term limits, checks and balances that limit power, and constitutionally protected human and civil rights that permit peaceful protest. In fragile or strongman states that are on the brink of, or emerging from, civil conflict or autocratic rule, such safeguards are often non-existent or dysfunctional. Typically, one political party, dynastic elite, ethnic group or economic oligarchy is dominant; judicial institutions are weak or controlled by the ruling regime; and a winner-takes-all mentality prevails, with no term limits, few alternative routes to power, and no checks and balances. The violation of human and civil rights – including the rights to free expression and assembly that are essential to holding free and fair elections – are not well protected. In fact, with the exception of 'liberation elections', election controversies in a series of countries, ranging from Burma to Kenya, Iraq and Haiti, show that elections can, and often do, trigger conflict. Even in cases where change takes place at the top, elections will neither bring peace nor democracy if the outcome is generally deemed illegitimate (Côte d'Ivoire), competition for office is restricted (Iran), sectarian splits are deepened (Lebanon), and state-sponsored crackdowns on the opposition take place (Zimbabwe).

Despite such risks, elections remain the main mechanism for managing political transitions. They are seen as the best way to facilitate legitimate regime change and fundamental changes in the structure of the state, as well as ensuring the consent of the governed. But many questions remain. When should elections be held, and under what conditions, to ensure that they are free and fair? Who should conduct the elections in shattered societies where the government is either not capable or regarded as likely to rig the elections? Should elections be held even if basic human rights and democratic principles are not guaranteed? What are the minimum institutional requirements that should exist if the foundation of a democracy is to be built? Should peace (holding elections to achieve change) be pursued at the expense of justice (insisting on political inclusion of all parties in the elections and granting amnesty for those who committed atrocities)? Or should elections be delayed, despite public pressure to move forward, in order to construct a more solid democratic foundation that respects human rights and ensures institutional checks on power? These issues are what divide the two approaches (for additional discussion on the two schools, see Baker 2001; for other insightful discussions of this issue, see Jarstad and Sisk 2008).

There are no universally accepted answers to these questions – nor a consensus on the goals, sequencing, scope, conditions or resources that

Table 25.1   Peacemaker profiles

Conflict managers	Democratizers
Inclusive approach	Exclusive approach
Goal is reconciliation	Goal is justice
Pragmatic focus	Principled focus
Emphasis is on the process	Emphasis is on the outcome
Stress the particular norms and cultures of the societies in conflict	Stress universal norms endorsed by the international community
Assume moral equivalence	Insist on moral accountability
Conflict resolution is negotiable	Justice is not negotiable
Outside actors should be politically neutral	Outside actors cannot be morally neutral

Source: Derived from Baker (2001).

should be invested in elections in states undergoing rapid political transitions. Yet, the controversy over elections is bound to continue as a technologically savvy younger generation of democracy advocates challenge autocratic rule, quicken the pace of transformation, demand a greater voice in government, protest inequality and injustice, and express outrage over elite corruption. With this agenda, the tension between conflict resolution and democratic governance is bound to be a larger debate as policy makers pursue sustainable security in the twenty-first century.

25.2   DIVERGENT PATHS TO PEACE

Peace and democracy should go together. But while the ideals generate agreement, the means of achieving them do not. Conflict managers engage in a range of peacebuilding activities, from preventive diplomacy and mediation to dispute resolution, in order to identify common ground among all hostile parties to prevent or stop violence. While also pursuing peace, democratizers advocate human rights, democratic institutions, the rule of law, and the prosecution of those who commit war crimes and atrocities, ranking the need for accountability above the desire for political inclusion. Indeed, democratizers usually oppose the political inclusion of leaders and parties believed to have committed mass atrocities.

It is important to state that there are no pure forms of either school. And the goals and activities of each camp may overlap or be complementary. Yet, despite some gray areas in which collaboration may be possible, the two approaches start from different premises, have different definitions of success, and employ different strategies, as can be seen in Table 25.1. As the table shows, conflict managers seek an inclusive approach and strive for reconciliation among all rival parties. They stress the importance of dialogue to build trust and confidence in the peace process, and emphasize the uniqueness of the history, norms and cultures of the societies in question. Eschewing any moral position on the superiority or rightness of any party, conflict managers are politically and ethically neutral; they urge negotiations until agreement is reached by the contesting factions. They point out that the primary human right is the right to life, even if the means for achieving it is not necessarily in compliance with universal human rights norms. If peace can be attained at the cost of not bringing human rights abusers to justice or, indeed, even includes them in a power-sharing agreement, then so be it. The main objective is to stop the fighting and save lives, not to hold people accountable – a goal which the local government or international tribunals can pursue later, if at all. Conflict resolution managers also are acutely aware of the cultural foundations for peace, such as bringing in traditional rulers (for example, elders, tribal or clan heads) or religious authorities, even though they are not democratically elected. Such leaders can often claim people's loyalties over secular or elected politicians.

Although there are occasionally shared attitudes about certain players, democratizers take the opposite position. Richard Holbrooke, for example, was a conflict manager but he was unequivocal in his dislike of the Serbian leaders with which he was negotiating. In this sense, he shared a characteristic with the democratizers. But pragmatism made him conclude that he had to treat Serbian leaders with respect as they were vital to reach agreement (Holbrooke 1998). Democratizers urge the exclusion from power of those who are known human rights abusers, particularly the leaders who must be held accountable for their crimes. Democratizers seek justice and the maintenance of basic democratic principles as ways to build a foundation of public trust in the outcome of negotiations or elections. They stress universal norms endorsed by the international community, not the unique circumstances of the conflict or the culture. Insisting on moral accountability and arguing that justice is not negotiable, democratizers maintain that their position is not only morally right, but more pragmatic because it is more likely to achieve long-term stability. Peace without justice might be achieved, they argue, but it will not last long and could ignite deeper grievances down the road. Ending impunity is necessary to stop the cycle of violence. Moral neutrality, for many human rights advocates, is equivalent to moral complicity in the atrocities committed.

In sum, conflict managers see peace as a precondition for democracy, whereas democratizers see democracy and human rights as preconditions for peace. Both positions have some validity. It is certainly true that each conflict must be viewed on its own terms, and the solutions adopted in one case do not necessarily apply to others. Conflict resolution techniques may be better suited to some instances, while democracy principles are dominant in others.

Still, experience suggests that, in general, political settlements in societies emerging from conflict that are built on solid democratic foundations have a better chance of achieving sustainable security, compared to crises that are resolved by accepting the lowest-common-denominator arrangements in shaky power-sharing agreements forced by the international community or local vested interests. Power-sharing agreements may succeed in ending civil unrest in the short term, but they do not usually offer a long-term solution, especially if they institutionalize sectarian and ethnic rivalries. Hidden tensions could erupt during subsequent elections or in the wake of post-war peace agreements where unfinished business, such as disarmament of military forces or revenue-sharing agreements, is also unsettled. Moreover, such agreements can give a false sense of security or finality, leading the international community to abandon the peace process too early. Power-sharing agreements and liberation elections are often viewed as the 'end-game' rather than the beginning of a long process of democratic state-building.

The friction between democracy and conflict resolution, however, is neither inevitable nor insurmountable. Given sufficient planning and resources, decision makers can make progress toward meeting the goals of both approaches, especially where elections are concerned. One major step in that process would be to better understand the role of elections in societies in conflict.

25.3   A TYPOLOGY OF ELECTIONS

Elections can be beneficial or detrimental to both the peace process and to democratization. If not conducted properly or run under the right conditions, they can promote factionalism, intensify ethnic rivalries, and encourage the use of hate speech or ethnic slurs to denigrate opponents. Elections foster elite competition that, in the extreme, can drive a simmering conflict into civil war, authoritarian oppression, ethnic cleansing and even genocide. Thus, one must distinguish between different types of elections, not by the type of electoral system that exists or the mechanics of voting, but rather by outcomes – the impact elections have on conflict and democratic governance in societies undergoing rapid political change.

Five different types of elections in transition societies are outlined here. They are not mutually exclusive. An authoritarian election can also entrench sectarian differences and be illegitimate, for example. Rather, this typology is meant to be suggestive, and is used here as a way of illustrating the range of possible electoral outcomes that can impact democratic peacebuilding.

25.3.1   Liberation Elections

The most dramatic and inspiring of all elections, liberation contests held at politically defining moments in history tend to have the greatest potential to blend the concerns of both conflict resolution managers and democratizers. In such circumstances, elections are an ideal instrument of non-violent change, crowning a wave of political activity in which there is a widely agreed political settlement, a constitutional framework, and a forward-looking plan on how to transfer power from one set of elites to another. In these circumstances, elections facilitate conflict resolution among rival factions, as well as institutionalize democratic governance. To fully achieve these goals, steps must be taken before elections to ensure political inclusion (a chance for all major groups to contest office), electoral transparency, and an institutional or constitutional framework based on representative government. Liberation elections are held at pivotal times, for example, when there is a pending shift in power from colonial rule to independence, a managed secession or political partition (South Sudan), or the downfall of a regime not considered legitimate by the majority population (South Africa). Typically, such elections (and referenda) generate high voter turn-out, extensive international media coverage, and generous international electoral and training assistance, all of which enhance the chances for a successful ballot. Although elections are merely one event in a long process, they are nonetheless heralded as the culmination of the transition, rather than what they really are: the beginning of a new era of democratic politics.

Examples of liberation elections include Poland's 1989 free elections that led to the first non-Communist government just six months before the Berlin Wall crumbled. Another historic turning point was South Africa's 1994 election, the first non-racial contest in the country that was based on universal suffrage. The 1989 elections in Namibia, contests accompanying the 'colour revolutions', such as those in Georgia and Ukraine, and the 2011 referendum for independence in South Sudan all also qualify as liberation elections.

While of epic significance at the time, liberation elections also can contain the seeds of democratic backsliding and future conflict. 'Normal' politics often sets in quickly, with constituent groups demanding more economic benefits and more political power for their own interests. Heroes of the liberation fade away and new leaders and factions emerge. In post-war conflicts, the danger exists that extremists may be brought to power, autocratic rule re-emerges under new strongmen, and criminal connections arise, as former militants or unemployed youths turn to violence to survive. To ensure that liberation elections do not reignite conflict and are not oversold, the enthusiasm surrounding them should be channeled as soon as possible into building the institutional foundations of democratic governance that can withstand future political storms and contain new rivalries.

But even that may not be enough. The euphoria of the Orange Revolution dissipated in Ukraine, as deep divisions within the country eventually brought back the *ancien régime*. In Georgia, the Rose Revolution faded as Mikhail Saakashvili employed authoritarian tactics against his opponents, confronted scandals, failed to resolve the separatist movements in Abkhazia and South Ossetia, and plunged the country into a disastrous war with Russia. In Poland, after serving one term as President, Lech Walesa lost his bid for a second term. A decade after leading Solidarity's successful trade union rebellion against communist rule, Walesa garnered less than 1 per cent of the vote when he tried to recapture the presidency once again in 2000. Similarly, in South Africa, the post-apartheid transformation has maintained strong democratic institutions, but the country's leadership has not applied the same human rights standards in other states that it demanded for itself (for example, in Zimbabwe); demonstrated the same tolerance for criticism and opposition as its first iconic president, Nelson Mandela; or made sufficient headway in eliminating poverty, which has spawned protests against extremely high 30 per cent unemployment and inadequate public services. Problems will arise in other recent liberation elections, including South Sudan, a desperately poor but potentially oil-rich state, where 99 per cent of the electorate voted for secession, and in post-revolutionary Middle East, where a technology-savvy generation of unemployed youths, middle-class professionals and the rise of Islamacists are driving dramatic changes in a new thrust for freedom that will have a ripple effect globally that is yet to be fully understood.

25.3.2   Authoritarian Elections

Although an instrument of democracy, elections have often served despotic rule. From the post-independence kleptocracy of Mobutu Sese Seko in the Democratic Republic of the Congo that lasted for decades to the resurrection of a Soviet-style regime of Aleksandr Lukashenko in Belarus, authoritarian elections have been used to thwart democratic change and suppress dissent. Commenting on the 2010 authoritarian elections in Belarus, in which the state launched the most brutal crackdown on the opposition in Europe since martial law was declared in Poland in 1981, US Senators John Kerry and Joe Lieberman (*Washington Post*, 30 January 2011) described the voting as 'patently unfair and undemocratic', though they were applauded by Venezuela's Hugo Chavez, who ceded to himself new powers to bypass Parliament, control the media, limit communications, and weed out non-governmental organizations. Authoritarian elections erode the public's faith in the democratic process and cultivate a widespread cynicism, if not docility, that is hard to overcome, if and when conditions improve. They undermine the goals of democracy: creating legitimate authority, encouraging citizen participation, and fostering social peace. Indeed, the opposite usually occurs – illegitimate authority is installed, citizen participation is restricted and stability is enforced through police tactics.

There are numerous other examples of authoritarian elections. Ukraine, once hailed as a country with new freedoms during the Orange Revolution, reversed course when internal divisions persisted. In 2010, the electorate returned to power Viktor Yanukovich, the former communist ruler who was pushed out in the 2004 revolution. He campaigned as a 'changed man' who promised to respect media and political freedoms and have good relations with both East and West. Yet his old impulses returned after he came to power. He suppressed opponents by mirroring the prosecutorial tactics used by Vladimir Putin in Russia to delegitimize and imprison challengers.

Zimbabwe is another example of a country using authoritarian methods, including elections, to maintain decades of strongman rule. Besides manipulating electoral results, Robert Mugabe has not hesitated to use violence to beat the opposition into submission. Pressured by the international community, he accepted a power-sharing agreement after the 2008 post-election violence. The agreement, however, has not challenged his authoritarian control and Mugabe has not honored all its provisions, leaving the country vulnerable to future conflict.

Another example of authoritarian elections is Iran. There is some limited competition, but clerics rule with the backing of the military because elections are controlled, from the beginning, by a nomination process in which reformist candidates are weeded out before the voting takes place.

Authoritarian elections worsen conflict and undermine democracy, not only within the country but also among policy makers and peacebuilders outside the country who are divided in how to react. Moreover, the use of authoritarian elections to remain in power undermines the state itself, not just the regime. Mugabe's power base, like Mubarak's, is weak because the state itself is so fragile. 'Strongman states' are inherently weak, regardless of the size of their security apparatus, because they lack the institutional capacity to manage crises and turn to repression or bribery when challenged. Once the leadership is removed, however, things fall apart. Although there were different circumstances surrounding each of them, Yugoslavia, the Soviet Union, Iraq, Somalia, Libya and Tunisia all quickly unraveled once the top leaders were overthrown or irreparably weakened by circumstances they could no longer control. If it were not for the military and the unity of the people, the same thing could have occurred in Egypt during the revolutionary upheaval that led to Mubarak's downfall; even then, the country entered a period of instability with an uncertain outcome. Iraq is another example of a strongman state that was very weak. After the US invasion, the state collapsed, followed by insurgency and civil war. Authoritarian elections may buy time, but they do not buy acceptance by the people.

25.3.3 Sectarian Elections

In socially divided societies, where strong group identities exist, elections are riskier than most – particularly if they are conducted during or immediately after conflict. Relatively homogeneous authoritarian states are rarely threatened with territorial disintegration. The 2011 Egyptian revolution was driven by a strong current of nationalism and patriotism. Egyptian civilization goes back seven centuries, its people are largely secular, and national solidarity from a broad cross-section of the population was evident as protestors waved flags and demanded a 'new Egypt'. Other countries in the Middle East, such as Yemen, are not as fortunate. Tribal identities are stronger than national ones and the unrest there threatens to break up the state.

Heterogeneous societies far outnumber homogeneous ones in Asia, Africa, Latin America and the Middle East where conflict resolution frequently clashes with democratization. Sectarian differences were evident during elections in Iraq, for example, and continued to plague that country as foreign combat troops were drawn down. The Shiite–Sunni–Kurdish balance remains tenuous (with Sunnis feeling marginalized), and tribal and clan affiliations claim a strong influence on people's loyalties. Deep sectarian divisions operate in Lebanon as well, where sectarian quotas are embedded in the system. The Lebanese government fell in early 2010 due to the withdrawal of Hezbollah and its allies from the ruling coalition, though it had been paralyzed for months. Hezbollah's action was a response to the crisis over a UN tribunal investigating the assassination of former Prime Minister Rafiq al-Harari, whose son led the collapsed government. Although Hezbollah's core constituency is based among the Shiite minority, it has grown to become the most important political player in the country, with the strongest army. 'The country, always teetering on the brink of a flare-up, could easily fall into a sectarian war, with the potential to spill over into a larger regional conflict', commented the *Washington Post* (14 January 2011).

Sectarian electoral contests that are held during, or soon after a civil war, often produce controversial results, with no clear winner, multiple accusations of fraud, and waves of violent protests. In such circumstances, conflict managers try to push hostile forces into some kind of coalition government. Some involve complex proportional representation systems that divide government into inefficient, rival ministries that entrench ethnic differences. In 2011, after months of wrangling, Iraq decided to use a controversial point formula to form a government in which the relative prestige of each cabinet portfolio was given points and linked to a party's electoral performance. In such systems, parties bid for cabinet posts based on matching their seats in Parliament to the value assigned to each portfolio. Finance, Foreign Affairs and Oil ministries were rated at three points each; Health and Electricity two points each, and Human Rights and Displaced Persons one-and-a-half points each (revealing the low value placed on human rights). Ministries were seen as personal or party fiefdoms to balance rival sectarian interests. The process was described as 'a bazaar where wild Iraqi desires for enrichment and influence meet clashing regional and international agendas' (*Wall Street Journal*, 9 December 2010). Indeed, the conflict in Syria spilled over the border and created violent clashes among Lebanon's own sectarian population.

Similarly, the elections held in 2011 in Afghanistan created insecurity, disaffection and accusations of fraud, when the results showed a reduction in the representation of the country's largest ethnic group, the Pashtuns. Instead of promoting peace and democracy, Afghan elections shifted power toward northern ethnic minorities and embittered Pashtuns. Some tribes and Pashtun provinces won no seats in Parliament at all, due to the fact that the election commissioner banned them in order to avoid accusations of fraud that had surrounded the previous elections in 2009. As a result, many areas where the insurgency was most active were disenfranchised. This stoked fears of worsening sectarian divisions, intensified the insurgency, and raised fears of a creeping ethnic civil war.

25.3.4   Illegitimate Elections

Besides being illegitimate in authoritarian states, elections can also lose credibility in semi-democratic or partly free states, where there are limited civic and political freedoms. Semi-democratic societies are positioned somewhere between non-democratic states that are willing to suppress dissent and use force, and functioning democracies that recognize minority rights, protect civil liberties, and tolerate political opposition. In semi-democratic states, elections lose legitimacy in the eyes of the electorate usually because of repeated irregularities. Recent research suggests that early stages of democratization are the most dangerous; statistically, they have the highest incidence of intra-state armed conflict compared to stable autocracies and mature democracies. The Index of Electoral Malpractice, produced at the University of Essex, calculated that there were 15 different forms of electoral malpractice in 136 elections held between 1995 and 2006 in 57 new and semi-democracies in Latin America, Eastern Europe, the Former Soviet Union and Sub-Saharan Africa. It is not only the prospect of a shift in power that induces armed conflict in semi-democracies. 'Consolidated semi-democracies, where no significant political change has occurred for some time, are still more conflict prone', noted Soderberg and Ohlson (2003, p. 6).

Haiti, the poorest country in the Western Hemisphere, is an example of a country with a history of unstable governments, corrupt leaders and flawed elections which the public tends to see as illegitimate. The 28 November 2010 elections attracted considerable attention, coming on the heels of the devastating January 2010 earthquake that had killed hundreds of thousands of people. The electoral council had originally declared Mirlande Manigat, a former first lady, the winner; Jude Celestin, the protégé of outgoing President Rene Preval, was announced as the second-largest vote-getter, over Michel Martelly, a popular musician. This would have allowed Celestin in the run-off with Manigat. Haitians took to the streets and, in demonstrations that turned violent, demanded that their right to a legitimate vote be respected. After a two-and-a-half month standoff, the electoral council, under pressure from international experts from the Organization of American States (OAS), the UN and the US, removed Celestin from the second round of voting, allowing Manigat and Martelly to compete in the 20 March run-off. The OAS found widespread fraud, missing votes and altered ballots, and condemned all three leading candidates for trying to steal votes. Complicating matters was the planned return of two former presidents, 'Baby Doc' Jean-Claude Duvalier, who had to face corruption and human rights charges from his rule, and Jean-Bertrand Aristide, a populist priest and former president installed and then removed from power. Both former presidents said they were committed to reconciliation, but both have caused major upheavals in their country, adding to the deep cynicism of the public in national elections. In the first round of the November 2010 voting, only 28 per cent of the electorate had voted, underscoring the public's scorn for the fraud, incompetence and contentiousness of the process which revolves around personalities, not issues. 'Even among the usually engaged, disgust has become conventional wisdom', reported *The New York Times* (7 February 2011). Unless the electorate concludes that elections are legitimate, the country could plunge into turmoil once again. Despite slow recovery from the earthquake, a cholera outbreak and flooding, the Haitian electorate rose up and mobilized as a serious force that will not accept illegitimate elections.

Nigeria is another example of a semi-democracy in which elections are sources of armed conflict. Elections have always been controversial in Nigeria, but those held since 1999, when the country transitioned from military to civilian rule, have been judged to not be credible by international observers and, more importantly, the electorate.[1] However, the results were said to be 'good enough' both by the electorate and the international community. In 1999, they were a way to get the soldiers back in the barracks, even though the victor, Olushegun Obasanjo, was a former military general. In 2003, elections retained civilian rule. In 2007, elections were 'good enough' to transfer power from one civilian regime to another, Olushegun Obasanjo to Umaru Musa Yar'Adua, Obasanjo's hand-picked successor. When Yar'Adua died from natural causes while still in office, Vice President Goodluck Jonathan, a native of the Niger Delta, succeeded him, shifting power from the politically dominant North to the South. The 2011 elections, though applauded by international observers as one of the country's best-held elections, was held by the North as fraudulent, and there was considerable post-election violence in that regard. Nigeria is coping with ethno-religious riots, a simmering insurgency and a spate of kidnapping in the oil-producing region of the Niger Delta, terrorist incidents, an active radical Islamic sect, and rising crime.

The violence in Nigeria is more symptomatic of a weak or failing state than a rising tide of unified national opposition to illegitimate governance, as in Haiti or Egypt. Human rights are abused not because of a heavy-handed dictator, but because of the weak rule of law, corrupted institutions, the politics of patronage, and weak leadership. Still, illegitimate elections contribute to the problems in this country. It has an abundance of wealth from oil and other commodities, but the majority of the population still lives in poverty. If these trends continue, the fear is

---

[1] This author served on delegations sponsored by the National Democratic Institute to monitor the Nigerian elections of 1999, 2003 and 2007. Each election was more fraudulent than its predecessor. Under the leadership of President Goodluck Jonathan, preparations for the 2011 election got off to a better start with a new Independent Election Commission appointed under the leadership of a respected academic, a new voters' roll prepared, and an ample, independent budget authorized that was not subject to presidential manipulation as previous funding had been.

not that Nigeria would have a popular revolution though that is possible, but would likely fragment and, possibly, disintegrate. Well-run elections, however, could just as well reverse this negative trend, and with improved leadership, launch the country in a new direction. Thus, while the conflict drivers in Nigeria are complex, elections could be a positive turning point or a negative last stop.

25.3.5   Stalemated or Stillborn Elections

Finally, there are elections that cannot be held for a variety of reasons: continued fighting (Somalia), the electorate cannot be determined (Western Sahara), or the results are not honored by the sitting government (Côte d'Ivoire). Stalemated or stillborn elections are manifestations of the failure of peacebuilding efforts, the absence of democracy and human rights standards, and the lack of the institutional foundations for credible elections to take place.

Somalia has been anarchic since 1991. There have been at least 14 attempts at a negotiated resolution, all of which have failed. In 2009, a Transitional Federal Government (TFG) was elected by a 550 member Somali Parliament, which meets infrequently, mostly outside the country. The TFG has very little capacity, no civil service, and holds only Mogadishu, the capital, with the assistance of 8,000 African Union (AU) peacekeepers, known as AMISON. The Somali Parliament is composed of clan heads, warlords, businessmen, Islamic representatives and civil society heads. In 2009, the Parliament elected Sheikh Sharif Sheikh Ahmed as president. He is sustaining the fight against al-Shebaab, an al-Qaeda-backed insurgency, with assistance from Uganda and Burundi, who are backed by the US, Europe, the AU and the UN. There are no elections involving the larger society. Besides the insurgency, Somalia has two autonomous regions, Somaliland and Puntland, and a shoreline that is dominated by increasingly brazen pirates. Somalia has consistently taken first place in The Fund for Peace's Failed States Index and is likely to retain that distinction for some time. Elections for peacebuilding are a long way off.

Western Sahara is a different model: that of a frozen conflict since 1975, when Morocco forcibly took over the territory. Rabat has since poured considerable economic resources into the area, but has refused to hold an election or a self-determination referendum, arguing that the territory belongs to Morocco alone. The King of Morocco has offered to negotiate with the Sahawi nationalists based on his internal decentralization program which would give more autonomy to the territory. The most difficult problem through the years, however, even if the parties came to an agreement, would be determining who is qualified to vote.

Polisario, the representative of the Sahrawi people, wants a referendum that allows refugees living in Algeria and the Diaspora, as well as local Sahrawis, to participate. Morocco wants Moroccan immigrants who are not of Sahrawi descent be allowed to vote and questions the authenticity of the residents in the refugee camps, suggesting that Algerians have infiltrated them and are not all of native origin. No residency or nationality standards have been agreed upon, and no census has been conducted, to determine those who might be eligible, even if agreement were reached on the terms of a referendum.

Côte d'Ivoire, which held an election in November 2010 to heal the wounds of a five-year war that had literally split the country in half, had been in turmoil since the 1999 *coup d'état*. The provisions of a 2007 peace agreement called for elections in 2009, which were delayed until 2010. The presidential run-off election between President Laurent Gbagbo, who controls the south, and Alassane Ouattara, whose Forces Nouvelle (FN) control the north, resulted in confusion and defiance. The electoral commission had first announced that Ouattara had won, but the constitutional council composed of Gbagbo supporters overturned the results and declared Gbagbo the winner. The international community, including the UN, the AU, most African and European states, and international monitors supported the election commission's findings, but Gbagbo refused to concede. For months, fighting resumed and the country was split in two, with a threat of a revival of civil war. There were two claimants to the presidency, two prime ministers, two cabinets and two armies. In this case, it was not the rigging of elections *per se* that caused the conflict, as the results were widely known and, at least, initially correctly announced. What caused the crisis was the nullification of the results by a leader who refused to step down. Finally, UN and French forces took military action along with local forces, Gbagbo was arrested and sent to the International Criminal Court (ICC) in the Hague.

In all three examples, neither peace nor democracy was advanced by elections. Moreover, all three had international peacekeeping missions. Troop presence did not avert, nor resolve, the crises. In Côte d'Ivoire and Somalia, international peacekeepers were simply protecting one side in the conflict; in the case of Côte d'Ivoire, the internationally recognized electoral winner and, in the case of Somalia, the internationally recognized Transitional Federal Government.

The prospect of election stalemate is not limited to these examples. In Iraq, it took nine months after the 2010 election for Prime Minister Nuri al-Malaki to form a government. That was accomplished only after considerable international pressure from the US and Iran, plus Malaki's agreement to form a new National Strategic Council headed by Ayad

Allawi, whose party marginally surpassed Malaki's in the election. But Allawi could not form a winning coalition. The new council, a kind of power-sharing mechanism that would recognize Allawi's status, was an invention. It is not mentioned in the constitution, and its name, capacity and powers were not spelled out, leaving open the question of just how much power would be shared.

Nepal offers another example of a recently stalemated election. A parliamentary stalemate was broken when the legislature – after violent protests, seven months of debate and 17 ballots – elected a prime minister in early 2011. The Maoist faction, which held the majority of seats in Parliament, had declared a general strike and demanded that the former prime minister resign because of his lack of progress on integrating guerrilla fighters into the army. Although the crisis was eventually resolved, it set back progress on writing a new constitution and on the peace process that had ended a decade-long insurgency.

In the Middle East, building a democratic peace in the wake of revolutionary uprisings could also lead to stalemates and flawed or stillborn elections, particularly in countries where existing state institutions had been hollowed out by decades of dictatorial rule and where there is no clear successor to the fallen strongmen. Elections will be critical to progress, but they may not quickly yield legitimate and stable governments and the outcome may include disproportionate influence of the military. In countries where repressive rule was previously overthrown, such as South Korea, Indonesia, the Philippines and Chile, the military played a constructive role toward a democratic transition. In Turkey, the military has also regarded itself as the guarantor of a secular state, though its influence has been somewhat contained of late. In Egypt, the military refused to fire on its own people and that was key to pushing Hosni Mubarak out without the violence that accompanied the uprising in Libya, Bahrain, Syria or Yemen. However, the military throughout the Middle East is an institution that has its own, often considerable, economic interests to protect. It reflects divisions within their own societies, and it is not that the generals will keep faith with the people. At best, the military can maintain order and be the steward of democratic change; at worst, it could take the opportunity to install a junta or leave a power vacuum that will be filled by extremist forces or new strongmen. But, even if it plays a constructive role, the military cannot fulfill the necessity for legitimacy that only free and fair elections can convey. That means writing or revising the constitutions, holding credible polls, and returning to the barracks as soon as possible in all the Middle East countries. Should that not happen, then alternative outcomes are possible, from stalemated situations to Somali-like anarchy, a Western Sahara-like frozen conflict, or a

Côte d'Ivoire-like split in the country. The outcome in each country will depend upon the history, institutional foundations, political party organization, civil society organizations and military leadership displayed.

25.4   NEXT STEPS IN DEMOCRATIC PEACEBUILDING

As indicated earlier, the gap between the two approaches to democratic peacebuilding need not be permanent or inevitable. It is likely to be sharpened as crises continue to mount, but a more coordinated approach is possible, because both schools have legitimate points that should be integrated into future strategies. There are basically three areas in which fresh approaches can be explored by the international community to promote democratic peacebuilding: (i) improving the logistics of elections; (ii) agreeing upon the preconditions needed for credible elections to take place; and (iii) creating more incentives and penalties for electoral behavior that conforms to, or deviates, from universal norms.

25.4.1   Improving Election Logistics

One way to improve logistical support is to give more influence to election monitors. In many cases, independent local and external monitors can assist, just by their presence, as election rigging may be minimized when eyes are on the perpetrators. But not always. Monitors often witness blatant rigging but are cautioned against intervening. Instead, they merely report what they saw. But if those reports are ignored, then their presence runs the risk of lending legitimacy to an illegitimate process; the host government disregards their recommendations, announces outcomes which are flagrantly incorrect, and often allows the same methods during the next elections, with no reforms whatsoever. The international community needs to develop rewards and punishments as incentives and disincentives for electoral behavior. This may include tying aid to electoral integrity, similar to the way the EU requires minimum human rights and democratic principles to be upheld before new members are approved for membership.

To a limited extent, this is already being done, notably in the standards used by the US Millennium Challenge Corporation, an independent development agency geared to rewarding good performers. Country eligibility for economic support is dependent upon how committed it is to just and democratic governance, how much it invests in its people, and the extent of economic freedom, all of which are measured by 17 different indicators, one of which includes free and fair elections (Voice and Accountability).

However, the emphasis upon electoral credibility has not been sufficiently featured in foreign aid strategies. Instead, the emphasis has been on a range of other goals, such as poverty reduction, strengthening civil society, building a free market and entrepreneurial business, and security concerns. All these goals, at some level, are related to democracy and peace. To give priority to democratic peacebuilding means more targeted aid to change agents within repressed societies (students, trade unions, religious organizations, human rights and democracy advocates, and so on) and state-building – building institutional capacity and professionalism in the civil service, the judiciary, police, the legislative and executive branches of government and even the military to ensure that state institutions remain consistent with democratic principles. One must be careful not to make scapegoats of such aid recipients, as oppressive regimes have often accused them of being Western agents. Nonetheless, since the US government began funneling aid to anti-apartheid forces in South Africa in the first outwardly 'political' aid program in the US, a number of other programs have bypassed host governments and supported the building of democratic institutions within nascent or semi-democracies, such as a free press, judicial integrity, legislative independence and human rights advocacy (Carothers 2009).

Other ways to improve elections and ensure their conformity to universal standards are to emphasize transparency, inclusion and limitations on power. For transparency, it is important, for example, for electoral authorities to publish the voting breakdowns for every polling station, local government, state and federal level when the results are released. This prevents rigging through secret enumeration, which is where a lot of rigging takes place. The publication of all votes down to the lowest level would allow monitors to be able to check their own figures at polling stations against final tallies.

Inclusion means ensuring that every voter is given the opportunity to register and cast his or her vote, so outreach to women, rural residents, and citizens living overseas must be made. Limitations on power means term limits, with strict constitutional prohibitions that prevent leaders from serving in office for decades, using patronage to lure or intimidate voters to 'stay on the gravy train'. Two terms are the universal standard for serving in executive office.

Other devices for ensuring good elections are creating special election courts to hear appeals after the results are announced, so that disputes can be settled rapidly and not allowed to linger months or years after the polling, with verdicts handed down shortly before the term of office is over. Electoral justice delayed is electoral democracy denied.

Finally, the international community should explore the possibility of creating an authoritative Index of Electoral Malpractices, based on reports of the dozens of independent local and international monitoring teams and verifiable reports from embassies around the world. Currently, such reports are not collected into one place, with a single rating system and analysis, issued annually to guide assistance and strategies. Such an annual report could serve a purpose similar to that of the annual US State Department Human Rights Report, which often exposes activities, influences policies, and impacts local actors who know that their activities are being monitored.

25.4.2 Election Preconditions

There is no one formula that will fit every country or situation, but historical experience has shown that some unnecessary conflicts were created due to untimely decisions. One issue is scheduling elections. The precise timetable for holding elections has to be determined on a case-by-case basis, but elections held too soon, during conflict or soon afterwards, without a cooling-off period may be doomed to fail. Success is enhanced if the rule of law is first established, showing that political violence is declining, the police are protecting the people, a constitution is being written, and normal life is coming back. The protection of basic rights, such as freedom of speech and assembly, must also be present. And the 'rules of the game' must be agreed upon in consultation with civil society by an independent and well-funded electoral commission led by trusted and respected officials. Without such conditions, there will be a shortage of public trust, voting will likely occur based on fear (with warlords being cast as the saviors), and contesting parties may be tempted to conduct their war by other means, such as election fraud. Instead of telling the public that elections are being delayed to establish the right conditions, they should be informed that these election preparations are as vital to the integrity of the vote as the casting of ballots, and invite them to participate. Civic society consultations in developing electoral preconditions would go a long way toward building the trust, patience and popular buy-in necessary for the peace process to succeed, in contrast to closed-door elite bargaining and decision making.

Although it may not be possible in all cases, another lesson learned from previous experience is that demobilization, disarmament and reintegration (DDR) of armed militias should precede voting. Otherwise, the losing side, which has access to arms and fighters, can return to fighting if it does not like the electoral outcome. To accomplish this, many weak states need outside assistance from the US or bilateral donors. It is a worthy investment but not likely to take place peacefully unless and until there is a political settlement that is widely agreed upon. DDR then becomes part of the process of confidence-building. Whether amnesty should be granted to those from government and rebel forces who committed abuses is a matter to be decided by the parties themselves. Sometimes, coming to terms with the past is dealt with by Truth and Reconciliation Commissions or by normal judicial processes after a transition takes place.

Transitional justice is one of the critical issues that divide the two peace-building camps, with conflict resolution advocates calling for leniency in the name of achieving peace, and democratizers calling for toughness to end the cycle of violence and impunity. Some societies, such as Rwanda, created their own justice system, using traditional communal-based methods to clear the jails of suspected killers in the 1994 genocide. Others, such as Cambodia, tended to avoid the issue as much as possible, until the alleged leaders who committed atrocities died or were judged according to a hybrid system that was not entirely objective. Thus, this is one area where local parties, country experts and constitutional specialists need to hammer out a strategy best for the country concerned, instead of applying the same template across the board. Some countries could be driven back into civil war if a sense of 'victor justice' appears to take hold while others may be better able to meet the challenge of promoting peace with justice. International players, such as the International Criminal Court (ICC), the Inter-American Human Rights Commission, or country or region-specific special tribunals could take up the task of indicting war criminals, relieving local leaders from the responsibility that could take on a partisan hue.

A dual strategy of intense diplomatic activity followed some time later by external judicial prosecution can also be useful, albeit highly controversial. This was what happened in Kenya, when former UN Secretary-General Kofi Annan played a key role in ending the election violence in 2007 that claimed over 1,000 lives. In the midst of a tenuous political calm, the ICC prosecutor, Louis Moremo-Ocampo announced three years after the disputed election that he intended to charge six Kenyans, including sitting members of the cabinet, with crimes against humanity, including murder, rape and deportation which they incited or failed to prevent. Democracy advocates applauded the move, arguing that it was the only way to end impunity, as prior acts of mob violence in Kenya had never been prosecuted before and the threat of ethnic conflict loomed again in the 2012 elections. Conflict managers, and many local Kenyans, argued that the selection of the six suspects was arbitrary; and others who may have committed worse crimes had not been identified. Moreover, justice, they maintain, must be meted out by Kenyans themselves, not imposed from the outside, even though there had been plenty of time for the government to do so and had not acted.

Democracy advocates say that this is a systemic problem. When governments do not act to investigate and prosecute abuses, only an outside tribunal can do it. Coming to grips with justice issues has had major implications in Kenyan politics and ethnic relations, all the more so because of the ethnic dangers in future elections. Holding former perpetrators to account has been regarded by some people as a necessary precondition to holding future democratic elections, and by others as an impediment to peace that will incite more violence at the polls.

25.4.3 Incentives and Penalties

There is broad consensus on the necessity of imposing sanctions on extreme human rights abuses. This was shown in the unprecedented act of the UN Security Council imposing a wide variety of penalties, including an arms embargo, freezing of assets, denial of travel visas, and referral to the ICC, for Libyan leader Muammar Gaddafi and some of his supporters for the violence they inflicted on their people in the 2011 uprising. Libya triggered an unprecedented unanimous Security Council vote to censure a leader, Gaddafi, based on his human rights violations. Similar actions, except for military interference taken against Bastior al-Assad for human rights violations in Syria

Various international sanctions have also been enacted against regimes for other reasons: defying UN resolutions on weapons of mass production programs (Iran, North Korea), violating World Trade Organization (WTO) trade obligations (China), harboring or supporting terrorists (Sudan, Syria), ideological opposition (Cuba), and military *coups d'état* or dictatorships (Honduras, Madagascar, Mauritania, Burma). While some of these reasons relate to the suspension of democracy, none was imposed directly to protest election malpractices as such. Sanctions were imposed on Zimbabwe for failure to honor the results of an election, but only after human rights abuses were committed. Moreover, there have been strong forces in the US arguing that these sanctions should be lifted, even though Robert Mugabe remains in power, the opposition continues to be harassed, and political and civil rights are still abused.

Sanctions do not always work. Smart measures need to be adopted that are proportional to the offense and do not do more harm than good. And, again, there are no rigid rules of application. However, if the international community is serious about promoting democracy, then there should be substantial support for enacting sanctions against regimes that deliberately hi-jack elections by rigging, suspending or nullifying elections. In addition, there ought to be incentives or rewards for semi-democracies that are headed in the right direction, even though they may not have reached the highest universal standards for electoral integrity.

The list of sanctions could range widely, from public listing in an Index of Election Malpractices to harsher measures for ruthless dictators or negligent regimes that inflict harm on electorates. Such a list would necessarily include influential countries, such as China and Russia, and allies, such as Saudi Arabia and the Gulf States which are absolute monarchies. Would this not harm bilateral relations? Perhaps. However, listing them as poor human rights performers in the annual State Department reports has not seriously affected bilateral relations. It is doubtful that similar listing on the grounds of election abuses would have any different effect. To the contrary, it would likely add pressure that could help internal democratic activists in repressive countries, elevate the importance of electoral integrity in foreign policy, and contribute to building common norms and coordinated actions in promoting good behavior.

The reward structure for exemplary electoral behavior would be equally, if not more important, as sanctions. The EU has successfully changed behavior in a number of countries seeking membership in the union, though this instrument is not available elsewhere. However, regional organizations could be encouraged to adopt similar measures, such as the AU's decision to suspend the membership of any African country in which government is changed through military force. The Organization of African States is geared to protect the democratic progress achieved in that region, chiefly through diplomacy. And the Arab League had for the first time sanctioned one of its own members, Libya, for the violence in that country. While such measures may not stop violence once it has begun, it can serve to influence aides who might defect, act as a prevention measure, and provide an incentive to bring a country back into the fold once it has adopted reforms. Rewards can be tangible, such as loans, economic assistance, WTO membership, high-level diplomatic trips, promotion of foreign private investment, or indirect, such as cultural and educational exchanges and military to military cooperation.

These suggestions are meant to offer some ideas that need to be widely discussed by the two communities of peacebuilders: conflict resolution managers and democracy and human rights advocates. They are not exhaustive, but contain the seeds of commonality that could enable the builders of peace to speak more forcefully with one voice, rather than engage in needless and unproductive rivalry. The truth is that peace and justice are both important for peacebuilding and, while there may be exceptions in specific cases, the world is changing too rapidly and the demand for effective actions is too important for the divisions to continue. Elections are the one area in which the divisions can be reduced, if not entirely eliminated, allowing peace to emerge among peacebuilders themselves.

26 Federations and managing nations
John McGarry and Brendan O'Leary

26.1 INTRODUCTION

Federalism is a normative political philosophy that recommends the use of federal principles, that is, combining joint action and self-government (King 1982). 'Federal political systems' is a descriptive catch-all term for all political organizations that combine what Daniel Elazar called 'shared rule and self-rule'. Federal political systems, thus broadly construed, include federations, confederations, unions, federacies, associated states, condominiums, leagues and cross-border functional authorities (Elazar 1987). Federations are very distinct federal political systems (Watts 1987, 1998). In a genuinely democratic federation there is a compound sovereign state, in which at least two governmental units, the federal and the regional, enjoy constitutionally separate competencies – although they may also have concurrent powers. Both the federal and the regional governments are empowered to deal directly with their citizens, and the relevant citizens directly elect (at least some components of) the federal and regional governments. In a federation the federal government usually cannot unilaterally alter the horizontal division of powers: constitutional change affecting competencies requires the consent of both levels of government. Therefore federation automatically implies a codified and written constitution, and normally is accompanied at the federal level by a supreme court, charged with umpiring differences between the governmental tiers, and by a bicameral legislature – in which the federal as opposed to the popular chamber may disproportionately represent the smallest regions. Elazar emphasized the 'covenantal' character of federations, that is, the authority of each government is derived from a constitution and convention rather than from another government.

Federations vary in the extent to which they are majoritarian in character, but most constrain the power of federation-wide majorities. They constrain the federal demos, though there is extensive variation in this respect (Stepan 2001, pp. 304–57). The United States, Australia and Brazil allow equal representation to each of their regions in the federal chamber, which means massive overrepresentation for the smaller ones. Other federations also overrepresent less populous units, but not to this extent. Federations differ additionally in the competences granted the federal chamber. Some, such as the US Senate are extremely powerful. The latter is arguably more powerful than the House of Representatives because of its special powers over nominations to public office and in treaty-making. Others, including those in Canada, India and Belgium are weak (Watts 1998). Constitutional change can be blocked by individual regions in some instances, although normally a veto requires a coalition of regions. A federation is majoritarian to the extent that it lacks consociational practices of executive power sharing, proportionality principles of representation and allocation, cultural autonomy and veto rights; and it is majoritarian to the extent that it lacks consensual institutions or practices – such as the separation of powers, bills of rights, and courts and monetary institutions insulated from immediate governing majorities. A majoritarian federation concentrates power resources at the federal level and facilitates executive and legislative dominance either by a popularly endorsed executive president or by a single-party premier and cabinet.

The federal principle of separate competencies says nothing about how much power each level enjoys. Regions in some federations may enjoy less de facto power than those in decentralized unitary states. The constitutional division of powers (even as interpreted by the courts) is not always an accurate guide to policy-making autonomy and discretion enjoyed by different tiers. Some powers may have fallen into abeyance, or the superior financial and political resources of one level (usually the federal) may allow it to interfere in the other's jurisdiction. A better indicator of the degree of autonomy enjoyed by regions may be the proportion of public spending that is under the control of the respective levels (Lijphart 1979, p.504; for such measures, see Watts 2001, p.29).

A key distinction for our purposes is that federations can be multi-national/multi-ethnic or mono-national in character (Table 26.1). In the former, the boundaries of the internal units are usually drawn in such a way that at least some of them are controlled by national or ethnic minorities. In addition, more than one nationality may be explicitly recognized as co-founders and co-owners of the federation. They have been developed on all continents. Canada was the first such federation, established in 1867. Switzerland, re-established in its current form in 1848, was conceived of as a national federation, but was always multi-lingual; most of its cantons, however, were dominated by either Protestants or Catholics, so we have coded it as a mixed case, a national federation with multi-ethnic characteristics. Ethiopia is officially a multi-national federation, and Nigeria was certainly one in its immediate post-colonial years,

Table 26.1   *Examples of national and multi-national or multi-ethnic*
federations

National federations	Duration	Multi-national or multi-ethnic federations	Duration
Argentina	1853–	Belgium	1993–
Australia	1901–	Bosnia and Herzegovina	1995–
Austria	1920–	Burma	1948–
Brazil	1891–	Cameroon	1961–72
Germany	1949–	Canada	1867–
Mexico	1917–	Czechoslovakia	1968–92
Switzerland	1848–)	Ethiopia	1992–
	with multi-	India****	1947–
	lingual	Iraq	2005
	character-	Malaya	1957–63
	istics	Malaysia	1963–
United Arab Emirates	1971–	Mali	1960–60
United States	1789–	Nigeria	1960–
Venezuela	1960–*	Pakistan**	1947–71
		Pakistan	1971–
		Russia	1993–
		Soviet Union	1918–91
		St. Kitts-Nevis	1983–
		West Indies Federation	1958–62
		Federal Republic of Yugoslavia	1992–
		(Serbia and Montenegro)	2003***
		Yugoslavia (Communist)	1953–92

Notes:
*   Venezuela abolished its Senate in 1999;
**   Pakistan (before the secession of Bangladesh);
***   The Federal Republic of Yugoslavia (Serbia and Montenegro) was transformed into the confederal union of Serbia and Montenegro in February 2003, and dissolved into the two separate states of Serbia and Montenegro in June 2006.
**** India is a union-state but since 1955 has organised most of its non-Hindi major language communities in their own states, giving it a multi-lingual form, and it is now a member of the Forum of Federation.

1960-66. Pakistan which emerged from British India was an Islamic but multi-ethnic federation; India, dominated by Hindus emerged as a multi-ethnic multi-religious but secular union-state, which soon took on the characteristics of a linguistic federation in all but name. The communist Soviet Union, Yugoslavia and Czechoslovakia were organized as multi-national federations, and the Russian Republic (RSFSR), one of the constituent units of the Soviet Union, was itself organized along federal lines.

These communist federations did not bestow genuine democratic self-government on their minorities, and fell apart in the early 1990s, although Yugoslavia continued as a dyadic federation incorporating Serbia and Montenegro until 2003, when it was transformed into a confederation renamed Serbia and Montenegro that dissolved into two independent states. Bosnia became a multi-national federation under the internationally enforced Dayton Agreement of 1995, with one of its units comprising another bi-national federation of Bosnians and Croats. Belgium has recently evolved into a federation, and both Euro-optimists and pessimists think that the European Union (EU) is moving in the same direction. Iraq became a multi-national federation in 2005, as did Sudan, although South Sudan seceded in 2011. Multi-national federations have been proposed for a significant number of other divided phases, including Afghanistan, Burma, China, Cyprus, Georgia and Indonesia.

National federations may be nationally or ethnically homogeneous (or predominantly so), or they are organized, often consciously, so as not to recognize more than one official nationality – often this happens in such a way that the state's national and ethnic minorities are also minorities in each of the constituent units. The intention behind national federalism is nation-building, the elimination of internal national (and perhaps also ethnic) differences. The founding and paradigmatic example of a national federation is the United States. Its model was adopted by the Latin American federations of Mexico, Argentina, Brazil and Venezuela. Germany, Austria, Australia, and the United Arab Emirates are also national federations. American and American-educated intellectuals often propose national federations as a way to deal with ethnic heterogeneity in post-colonial and post-communist societies.

Federations can also be distinguished according to their level of democracy. Some, such as Canada, the United States and Belgium should be seen as maturely democratic; others, such as Malaysia and Nigeria, as partially democratic; and still others, such as the communist federations of the Soviet Union, Yugoslavia and Czechoslovakia as not democratic. There is an increasingly popular view in the academic literature on federalism that this distinction is unimportant. A number of prominent American academics thus interpret the failings of the communist federations as an indictment of (multinational) federalism *per se* (Brubaker 1996; Bunce 1999; Leff 1998; Roeder 1991). This chapter is, however, about democratic federations; and one of our arguments is that democracy matters, crucially, as does the type of democratic system. Indeed, there is not yet an example of an established democratic multi-national federation failing.

This chapter is primarily concerned with multi-national and multi-ethnic federations because we regard national federations largely as devices associated with integrationist or assimilationist politics. We shall first discuss the debate on the value and feasibility of federations as management devices for ethnic and national differences, then the track-record of multi-national federations in mitigating conflict, and conclude with an analysis of the factors that contribute to their success and failure.

26.2 THE DEBATE: NATIONALISM AND FEDERALISM IN PRACTICAL POLITICAL DESIGN AND ARGUMENT

There are four important positions on the value of federalism and federation as a method of accommodating national and ethnic minorities, all of which have been articulated by intellectuals, constitutional lawyers and political scientists, and have had an effect on the design of particular states.

26.2.1 Jacobin Unitarism: Federalism as State Destroying

In the French revolutionary tradition, associated with the Jacobins, federalism was part of the counter-revolution, hostile to the necessity of linguistic homogenization, a road-block in the path of authentic, indivisible, monistic popular sovereignty. Rather than accommodating minorities through self-government, the Jacobins sought cultural assimilation; they were determined to make peasants into Frenchmen; and therefore they were deeply hostile to all forms of accommodation that inhibited this goal, including federalism. The Jacobin response to diversity was a strong unitary state and one French nation. This tradition survives in contemporary France, where it is central to the myth of the French Republic. Federalism, with its multiple governments, is seen by those in the Jacobin tradition as incompatible with equal citizenship and a sovereign people. This is not just a concern about regional governments creating uneven ('patchwork quilt') public policy provisions. Latter-day Jacobins cannot accept the federal principle that allows citizens in regions with small populations to be overrepresented at the expense of those in more populous regions, and they have difficulty with the federal idea of a judicial umpire who can overrule the people's elected representatives. Both facts explain the reported French astonishment at George W. Bush being elected US president in 2000 with fewer popular votes than his opponent (a result of the disproportionality inherent in the Electoral College, and a partial byproduct of the US's federal system), and the incumbency being effectively decided by the federal Supreme Court (Ferenczi 2004).

Modern Jacobins think that the accommodation of minorities and ethnocentrism go together. If minorities do not want to promote ethnocentrism, the argument goes, why do they seek self-government? They think that political recognition of multiple nations or ethnic communities leads to regressive government and discrimination against minorities dominated by local regional majorities, and institutionalizes and reinforces divisions, endangering national/state unity. These views are shared on the left and right. Communists claim that Paris's proposals to give self-government to Corsica will undermine 'solidarity between Corsican and French workers, who can only defend their interests by working together', and will lead to discriminatory measures against those on the island who are not of Corsican descent. The then French interior minister, Pierre Chevènement, resigned over the proposals, protesting that they would lead to an 'island ruled by an underworld that spends three-quarters of its energy settling accounts and internal battles'. While the proposals for Corsica fall short of federation, both Chevènement and the French President, Jacques Chirac, attacked them as leading in that direction: Brittany, Alsace, Savoy, as well as French Basques and Catalonians, would allegedly follow Corsica's lead (ibid.). Ultimately, in this view, federation promotes state break-up, with the attendant risks of ethnic cleansing and Matrioschka-doll secessions emerging as ethnic nationalism takes hold.

The Jacobin view that unitarism is needed for unity, if not always its support for civic equality and popular sovereignty, is replicated throughout the world. It was the dominant view in Great Britain until recently, particularly among Conservatives. Most ex-colonies in Africa, Asia and the Caribbean have shunned federalism as an obstacle to economic development, political stability and state unity. Post-colonial statebuilders' antipathy to federalism is now matched among the intellectuals and governing elites of Eastern Europe, who regard it as a recipe for disaster, given the Czechoslovakian, Yugoslavian and Soviet experiences. Federalism is their 'f' word. The recent emergent principle of international law, stemming from the report of the Badinter Commission on the former Yugoslavia, that permits the disintegration of federations along the lines of their existing regional units, may strengthen the belief that federations should not be considered a desirable form of multi-national or multi-ethnic accommodation (Horowitz 1998; Weller 1992). Several Eastern European states have moved in the opposite direction in recent years. They seceded from multi-national federations and replaced them with what Brubaker calls 'nationalizing' states, that is, homogenizing states that are tightly centralized and controlled by their dominant national community.

Ironically, the Jacobin argument that federalism is incompatible with nation-building is shared by 'hard-line' nationalists trapped inside states controlled by other nations. They concur that nation and state should be congruent, although they disagree on the appropriate boundaries. This has been the position of Quebec's Parti Quebecois, particularly the faction around the ex-Premier, Jacques Parizeau, and of Basque Nationalists in Batasuna. It was also the view of the Turkish Cypriot leadership under Rauf Denktash, the Chechens, and, until the early 2000s, the now defeated Liberation Tigers of Tamil Eelam. Such hard-liners seek independence as unitary, sovereign and indivisible nation-states, although some are prepared to consider confederation.

26.2.2 Federalism as Nation-building

Unlike the Jacobins, who see (state) nationalism and federalism as inconsistent, some exponents of federalism think that (state) nationalism and federalism go together. The earliest federalists in the German-speaking Swiss lands, and in what became the Netherlands, the USA, and the second German Reich were 'national federalists', that is, they saw the prime function of federalism as being 'to unite people living in different political units, who nevertheless shared a common language and culture' (Forsyth 1989, p. 4). They maintained that only an autonomous federal government could perform certain necessary functions that confederations or alliances found difficult to perform, especially a unified defence and external relations policy (Riker 1964). They advocated federation as a tool for nation-building and sometimes saw it as a stepping stone towards a more centralized unitary state.

The USA is the paradigm case of national federalism. Americans have little difficulty with what Jacobins consider the 'demos-constraining' features of federalism: radical autonomy for regions or states (noncentralization); the overrepresentation of small states in upper chambers, electoral colleges and constitutional amending formulas. In fact, Stepan has argued that the United States competes with Brazil for the title of the world's most demos-constraining federation (Stepan 2001, p. 334). The attractiveness of demos-constraining institutions reflect the historic stress of some Americans on liberty rather than equality. The American founding myth is of colonies that won independence from empire. Many Americans reject the strong state favoured by French republicans and praise federalism precisely because it diffuses power to multiple points. American exponents of federalism, such as Riker, have argued that the demos-constraining features of American federalism are liberal because they protect individuals from populist majorities (Riker 1964). Americans insisted on a federation for post-war Germany, because they were convinced it would make a resurgence of fascism less likely. The view that federalism is essential to liberty is central to American discourse, in spite of the chequered history of federalism in all of the Latin American federations, as well as in Pakistan, Nigeria and the USSR.

But America's makers and their celebrants have taken the position that federalism is antithetical to nation-building if it is multi-national, multi-ethnic or 'ethnofederal'. As the United States expanded southwestward from its original largely homogeneous (except for African slaves) 13 colonies, it was decided that no territory would receive statehood unless minorities were outnumbered by White Anglo-Saxon Protestants (WASPs) (Glazer 1983). Sometimes, the technique employed was to gerrymander state boundaries to ensure that Indians or Hispanics were outnumbered, as in Florida. At other times, as in Hawaii and the southwest, statehood was delayed until the region's longstanding residents could be swamped with enough WASP settlers. American authorities were even sceptical of immigrant groups concentrating in particular locations lest this lead to ethnically based demands for self-government, and grants of public land were denied to ethnic groups in order to promote their dispersal; William Penn dissuaded Welsh immigrants from setting up their own self-governing barony in Pennsylvania (Gordon 1964, p. 133). In consequence, the US federation shows 'little coincidence between ethnic groups and state boundaries' (Glazer 1983, p. 276). National federalism was part and parcel of American nation-building, aiding the homogenization of white settlers and immigrants in the famous melting pot of Anglo conformity (Gordon 1964). Celebration of the homogeneity of the founding people is evident in The Federalist Papers (see, especially, John Jay's assumptions in Madison et al. 1788[1987], paper II).

America's experience with federalism has informed an interesting argument on how federalism can be used to manage divisions in contemporary ethnically heterogeneous societies. Donald Horowitz (1985) and Daniel Elazar (1994), building on earlier work by S.M. Lipset (1960), and indeed, on an important American tradition that goes back to James Madison, suggest that federations can be partly designed to prevent ethnic minorities from becoming local provincial majorities. The strategic thinking here is to weaken potentially competing ethno-nationalisms: federalism's territorial merits are said to lie in the fact that it can be used as an instrument to prevent local majoritarianism with its attendant risks of tyrannies of the local majority, or of secessionist incentives. The provincial borders of the federated units on this argument, should be designed on 'balance of power' principles – proliferating, where possible, the points of power away from one focal centre, encouraging intra-ethnic conflict, and creating incentives for inter-ethnic cooperation (by designing provinces without majorities), and for alignments based on non-ethnic interests. This logic is interesting, but empirical support for it seems so far confined to the rather uninspiring case of post-bellum Nigeria (Suberu 2001, pp. 4–6). In most existing federations to re-draw regional borders deliberately to achieve these results would probably require the services of military dictators or one-party states. Historically mobilized ethno-national groups do not take kindly to efforts to disorganize them through the re-drawing of internal political boundaries. Belgium may, however, become an interesting exception to this scepticism: the Brussels region, created in the new federation, is neither Flemish nor Wallonian, and perhaps its heterogeneity will stabilize 'inter-national' relations in Belgium, because Flanders will not secede without Brussels and there is presently little prospect of Brussels obliging Flanders.

American republicans, with a small 'r', have shared with Jacobins the view that minority nationalists are backward, a 'revolt against modernity' (Lipset 1985) or people who 'tend to subordinate all free government to [their] uncompromising position' (Elazar 1994, pp. 128–9 and 163–4). They think that it is both counterproductive and unnecessary to accommodate minority nationalists. This view may have been strengthened by America's own experience, in the Deep South, of southern whites using their control of state governments to oppress blacks. America's experience with a disastrous civil war over secession attuned its intellectuals to the centrifugal potential of federalism, particularly when regions are controlled by distinct cultural communities. Eric Nordlinger, one of the first contemporary American political scientists to take an interest in ethnic conflict regulation, rejected the use of federalism as an instrument for accommodating minorities as he feared it would lead to state break-up and the abuse of power by ethnocentric minorities (Nordlinger 1972, pp. 32–3).

Reflecting these sentiments, a number of American academics have argued that the break-up of the former communist federations and the accompanying chaos, can be traced squarely to 'ethnofederal' structures (Brubaker 1996; Bunce 1999; Leff 1998; Roeder 1991). Rogers Brubaker (1996, p. 9) maintains that the Soviet regime went to 'remarkable lengths, long before glasnost and perestroika, to institutionalise both territorial nationhood and ethnocultural nationality as basic cognitive and social categories'. Once political space began to expand under Gorbachev, these categories quickly came to structure political perception, inform political rhetoric, and organize political action'. The implication is that (at least some of) these divisive identities did not exist before the Soviet Union federated and would not have come into play had it not federated. In Jack Snyder's view, 'ethnically based federalisms . . . *create* political organisations and media markets that are centred on ethnic differences' (our italics). According to him, 'the decision to establish ethnofedera- tions in the Soviet Union, Czechoslovakia, and Yugoslavia was *unneces- sary* (Snyder 2000, p. 327, our italics): 'Arguably, ethnofederalism was a strategy of rule actively chosen by its Communist founders not a necessity forced upon them by the irresistible demands of ethnic groups'. The results of ethnofederalism in his view were straightforward: only the communist federations broke up and 'nationalist violence happened *only* where . . . ethnofederal institutions channelled political activity along ethnic lines (USSR and Yugoslavia)' (ibid. p. 252, our italics)

26.2.3   Cosmopolitans, Federalism as a Stage in Nation-transcendence

A third perspective holds that federalism is capable of dissolving all national allegiances, including minority and majority nationalisms. It comes in two different variants. The first is represented by several nineteenth-century anarchist and liberal federalists, notably Joseph Proudhon and Carlo Cattaneo, who were resolutely hostile to nation- state nationalism (Majocchi 1991, p. 162), and by many twentieth-century liberal federalists, notably within the European movement (see, for example, Bosco 1992, Part III). Such federalists have been, and are, reso- lutely anti-nationalist, associating both state and minority nationalisms with ethnic exclusiveness, chauvinism, racism and parochially particularis- tic sentiments. For them federalism belongs to an entirely different cooper- ative philosophy, one that offers a non-nationalist logic of legitimacy, and an antidote to nationalism rather than a close relative. This viewpoint was most clearly articulated by Pierre Trudeau – educated by Elie Kedourie at the LSE (London School of Economics and Political Science) – before he became Canadian Prime Minister. Thinkers like Trudeau regard federal- ism as the denial of and the solution to nationalism, though occasionally they adopt the view that federalism must be built upon the success of nationalism which it then transcends in Hegelian fashion (Majocchi 1991, p. 161). In effect they echo Albert Einstein's reported remark that nation- alism is the measles of mankind.

A different perspective was articulated by the Austro-Marxists, Karl Renner and Otto Bauer, who proposed it in the last days of the Habsburg empire (see, for example, Bauer 2000; Hanf 1991; Pfabigan 1991). For them nationalism had to be accommodated en route to a global socialist and communist order. They thought it was feasible to combine national autonomy in federal and consociational formats. Lenin and Stalin pressed their arguments, in an adapted format, into service in the Soviet Union. Federalism was to be used to offer a limited accommodation to minority nationalism, but solely towards the end of building a socialist society. Minorities were to be offered the fiction, but not the fact, of national self-government. While this policy was superficially similar to that of multi-national federalists, Marxist–Leninists were, of course, formal cosmopolitans, committed to a post-nationalist global political order. However, pending the world revolution, they maintained that federal arrangements, 'national in form, socialist in content', were the optimal institutional path to global communism.

26.2.4   Multi-national Federalists: Multi-national Maintenance Engineers

Multi-national or multi-ethnic federalists, by contrast, advocate federation 'to unite people who seek the advantages of membership of a common political unit, but differ markedly in descent, language and culture' (Forsyth 1989, p. 4). They seek to express, institutionalize and protect at least two national or ethnic cultures, on a durable and often on a permanent basis. Any greater union or homogenization, if envisaged at all, is postponed for the future. They explicitly reject the strongly integrationist and/or assimilationist objectives of national and or post-national federalists, and see these as nation destroying rather than nation-building. They believe that dual or multiple national loyalties are possible, and indeed desirable. Multi-national federalists represent a third branch of liberalism, distinct from the Jacobin (federalism breeches civic equality), and American varieties (national federalism promotes individual liberty). For multi-national liberals, a proper understanding of liberal individual rights requires respect for the culture of individuals, and this means allowing minorities the power to protect and promote their culture (Kymlicka 1995; Stepan 1999, pp. 31–2). Unlike unitarists and national federalists, multi-national federalists reject the a priori view that minority-controlled governments are more backward or illiberal in their treatment of their own minorities than majority-controlled central or federal governments. Minority nationalisms are as likely to be of the civic variety as dominant nationalisms according to these liberals; indeed, Keating argues that contemporary minority nationalisms are strongly modernist, responding to the shift in power from the state to the global marketplace (Keating 2001; Kymlicka 1995).

Multi-national federalism has considerable, albeit critical support, among contemporary academics (Hechter 2000; Keating 2001; Kymlicka 1995; Linz 1999; McGarry and O'Leary 1993; Moore 2001; Stepan 1999; Watts 1998). Some supporters make quite remarkable claims for federalism. Von Beyme (1985, p. 121), referring to Western democracies, argued in 1985 that 'Canada is the only country in which federalism did not prove capable of solving . . . ethnic conflict'. Others are more modest: Kymlicka supports multi-national federalism normatively, while acknowledging that it faces considerable difficulties in practice (Kymlicka 2001). Multi-national federalists have been influential in the development of federations in the former British Empire, notably in Canada, the Caribbean, Nigeria, South Africa, India, Pakistan and Malaysia. Austro-Marxists and even some Marxist–Leninists were multi-national federalists, albeit of the transitional kind and have had an enduring impact in the post-communist development of the Russian Federation, Ethiopia and the rump Yugoslavia. While unitarists have presently been in the ascendancy in Eastern Europe, multi-national federalism has become more popular in Western Europe, both among proponents of the federalization of the European Union, and among power-holders in established states – as the decision to create a federation in Belgium attests. We should also note the novel and more decentralized devolutionary, regional and potentially federal institutions of Spain, the United Kingdom, France and Italy. Multi-national federalists are often soft minority nationalists, but they also include state elites who believe that accommodating national minorities holds the key to overall stability and unity. They include the Quebec Liberal Party, the Basque Nationalist Party (PNV), and the Catalan Convergencia I Unio. Contemporary Euro-federalists might be thought to be the most ambitious multi-national federalists of our age, but their sympathies in fact lie more in the direction of national federalism.

Plainly the multi-nationalists' defence of federation as a way of managing nations – to each nation let a province be given – is not able to accommodate those minorities that are so small in number or dispersed that they cannot control federal units or provinces. This includes francophones who live outside Quebec, Flemish-speakers in Wallonia, francophones in Flanders; and small and scattered indigenous peoples in Australia, India and the Americas. Multi-national federalists reject the view that every minority must inevitably seek its nation-state, and maintain that even among those that do they may settle for their own region instead. They argue that if the provincial borders of the component units of the federation match the boundaries of the relevant national, ethnic, religious or linguistic communities, that is, if there is a 'federal society' congruent with the federating institutions, then federation may be an effective harmonizing device. That is precisely because it makes an ethnically heterogeneous political society less heterogeneous through the creation of more homogeneous subunits. Multi-national federalism thus involves an explicit rejection of the unitarist and national federalist argument that self-rule for minorities necessarily conflicts with the territorial integrity of existing states. It is also a prima facie challenge to the tacit Gellnerian notion that in modern times the equilibrium condition is one sovereign state, one culture (or nation) (Gellner 1983). If we treat broadly the 'political unit' in Gellner's definition, to encompass regional or provincial units in a federation, then his theory can accommodate such arrangements, but at the significant concession of recognizing that federal systems are compatible with dual and possibly multiple nationalities.

National minorities within a multi-national federation often argue that they should have powers beyond those enjoyed by the federal units dominated by the national majority: they support asymmetrical federalism, insisting that their distinct status be officially recognized and institutionalized. They may seek to share in powers that are normally the prerogative of the centre or federal government: some minorities seek a role in federal foreign policy, or to be directly represented in international organizations. This may not mean the same as supporting confederation, because the minorities may be content for most purposes to remain part of a federation, but they are clearly stretching the limits of traditional federations, and moving in the direction of confederation.

Multi-national or multi-ethnic federations may originate from the union of previously self-governing ethnic communities, as happened in the case of Switzerland. However, in other cases, multi-national federalists may engage in deliberate democratic engineering to match certain ascriptive criteria with internal political borders. This occurred at Canada's founding, when the province of Canada was divided largely along linguistic lines into Ontario and Quebec. It also happened in post-independence India, but not until Jawaharlal ('Pandit') Nehru was forced to concede reorganization of internal state borders along linguistic boundaries (Arora and Verney 1995; Brass 1990). Nigeria has re-organized its internal boundaries on several occasions, to the advantage of certain minorities. Whereas its original tripartite federation was dominated by the Ibo, Hausa and Yoruba groups, its current 36 state structure includes 14 states that are dominated by other groups (Suberu 2001, p. 5). Switzerland carved a new canton of Jura (largely French and Catholic) out of the mostly German-speaking canton of Berne in 1979.

26.3   WEIGHING THE EVIDENCE

On first glance, it would seem that there is considerable evidence for the French and American republican argument that multi-national federalism has, as Snyder (2000, p. 327) puts it, 'a terrible track record'. However, multi-national or multi-ethnic federations which have either broken down, or failed to remain democratic, have been largely in the communist world or the post-colonial world. The federations of the Soviet Union, Yugoslavia and Czechoslovakia disintegrated during or soon after their respective democratizations. Indeed, of all the states in the former communist bloc of Eastern Europe, it was only federations that irretrievably broke apart, and all of them did. Of all these states, the federations experienced the most violent transitions. In the post-colonial world multinational or multi-ethnic federations failed, or failed to be successfully established, in the Caribbean, notably in the West Indies Federation. Even the miniature federation of St. Kitts-Nevis recently faced the prospect of break-up (Premdas 1998). Multi-national or multi-ethnic federations have failed in Sub-Saharan Africa, in Francophone West and Equatorial Africa, in British East Africa (Kenya, Uganda and Tanganikya), and in British Central Africa (Northern and Southern Rhodesia and Nyasaland), or have failed to remain durably democratic (Nigeria and Tanzania). The break-up of the Nigerian federation between 1966 and 1969 was prevented only after a secessionist conflict that caused approximately one million deaths. In the Arab world, only the United Arab Emirates has survived, but it is a national federation and hardly democratic. In independent Africa, federations have broken up in Ethiopia, Mali and Sudan, while Cameroon experienced forced unitarism after a federal beginning. In Asia there have been federative failures in Indochina, in Burma, in Pakistan (the secession of Bangladesh), and in the union of Malaya (the secession of Singapore). In short, new multi-national federations appear not to work as conflict-regulating devices – even where they allow a degree of minority self-government. They have broken down, or failed to be durably democratic, throughout Asia, Africa and the Caribbean. India stands out as the major exception in Asia, but it has important constitutional characteristics that are more typical of a unitary state than a federation. These cases, however may also suggest an indispensable link between authentic federalism, stability and extensive experience of liberal democracy.

It is obviously true that the territorial definition of regions within multinational federations facilitates secession. Federalism provides the minority with political and bureaucratic resources that it can use to launch a bid for independence. Giving a minority its own unit makes it possible for it to hold referendums on secession, which can be useful for gaining recognition. Multi-national federations implicitly suggest the principle that the accommodated minorities represent 'peoples' who might then be entitled to rights of self-determination under international law. It is far more likely that, as the Badinter Commission on the former Yugoslavia confirmed, the international community will recognize a bid for independence from a federal unit than from a group that lacks such a unit. This is why all of the full constituent units of the Soviet Union, Yugoslavia and Czechoslovakia that broke away are now seen as independent states, whereas breakaway regions that were not constituent units, such as Abkhazia, Trans-Dniestria, the Turkish Republic of Northern Cyprus, and Kosovo, have not been fully recognised, although Kosovo is much more recognised than the others. To this extent, unitarists and national federalists have a point – although it is a point that multi-national federalists have little difficulty conceding.

This bleak assessment of the track record of multi-national federations has to be qualified in five important ways. First, the major federal failures, including the Soviet Union, Yugoslavia, Czechoslovakia, Sudan and Nigeria were or have been, to a significant extent, sham or pseudo-federations. In several cases, they were forced together. The constitutional division of powers and the rule of law were often ignored in practice and they were not authentically representative (that is, democratic). There was, therefore, no possibility of genuine dialogue, never mind cooperation, among the different national communities involved. In sum, these states had weak or no overarching identities to begin with, and no democratic mechanism for developing them. While the United States can be seen as the paradigmatic example of national federalism, the Soviet Union is the most prominent case of pseudo-federalism. Territorially it consisted of those remnants of the Tsarist Empire that the Red Army was able to subjugate after the October Revolution, plus those countries (Estonia, Latvia, Lithuania and Moldova) it conquered as a result of the Ribbentrop–Molotov pact (1939) and its victory in the Second World War. While its state structure was federated from the beginning, real power lay in the tightly centralized Communist Party (the CPSU), which operated according to the principle of 'democratic centralism' (Lieven and McGarry 1993). The Union Republics were therefore not autonomous in any meaningful sense. Moreover, their legislatures (the Soviets), although in theory elected by local populations, were in fact rubber-stamp bodies nominated by the CPSU. Key institutions, including the army and police, were controlled by Moscow. No effective judicial review existed to decide on the division of rights and functional spheres between the centre and the republics. And while it is true that Yugoslavia was more decentralized than both the Soviet Union and Czechoslovakia, at least after reforms in the late 1960s, it was no less undemocratic, and was held together by the League of Communists.

The colonial federations arose out of colonies that had been arbitrarily consolidated by white imperialists. Even the very decision to federate at independence was made in some cases by the departing metropolitan rather than the colony's indigenous elites. Nigeria's original three-unit federation, which collapsed in the mid-1960s, was 'bequeathed' by the vacating British (Suberu 2001, p. 4). The Cameroon federation was a construct of British and French colonialists (particularly the latter), who wanted to preserve the dual personality they thought they had created (Elazar 1987, p. 240). It was converted into a unitary state by military strongmen soon after independence, while Nigeria has been ruled by centralizing military dictators for more than two-thirds of its post-independence history – and its presidential contenders in recent times have all been ex-generals. Even under democratic conditions, Nigeria is so centralized that it has been described as a 'hollow federation' and 'a unitary state in federal guise' (Suberu and Diamond 2000, p. 8). Corruption and abuse of power are so pervasive that the rule of law can hardly be said to exist (Suberu 2001).

These communist and post-colonial federations were additionally burdened by economic systems that were incapable of providing a reasonable or growing standard of living for their citizens. In each case, this caused resentment, not least among minorities in relatively enterprising regions of the state who saw their inclusion in the federation as a drag on their prospects. It was therefore not surprising that when the communist planning system became discredited and collapsed in the late 1980s it produced a legitimacy crisis.

Second, the case against multi-national federalism would be stronger if it could be shown, as critics claim, that it was unnecessary to accommodate national minorities, and that there were democratic civic nationalist (unitarist or national federalist) alternatives that would have worked better if not much better. Once this test is probed the critics' position looks less credible. The decision to create both the Soviet and Yugoslav federations was taken in the midst of bitter civil wars and external invasions, when parts of both states had seceded (Connor 1984, p. 198; Woodward 1995, p. 30). The decision was regarded as essential for restoring unity and luring breakaway regions back into the state, and was taken in both cases by socialist internationalists, neither of whom was ideologically committed to multi-national federalism. Before he assumed power, Lenin had expressed his vehement opposition to federalism and his clear preference for unitary structures. Tito, before taking power, appeared to be a conventional Leninist. If federalism was unnecessary, we must conclude that both Lenin and Tito were extraordinarily incompetent from their own perspectives. The thesis that communist multi-national federalism 'created' divisions cannot adequately explain why strong ethnic identities exist among groups that were not accommodated through federal institutions, such as the Chechens or Crimean Tatars. Similarly, while some have argued that Nigeria's divisions at the time of independence reflected British divide and rule strategies, few think that the state could have been (or could be) held together without some form of decentralized or federal structure. When an Ibo leader, General Ironsi, tried to convert Nigeria into a centralist state in 1966 it led to his downfall. Even though the Nigerian federation witnessed a failed and bloody bid for secession in Biafra (1967–70), the victors were careful to retain ethnofederal structures, albeit reformed, with new internal boundaries.

One reason to doubt the feasibility of civic nationalism, French or American, as an alternative to multi-national federation is that it has not been particularly successful when it has been applied, under more propitious circumstances, in multi-national states. Turkey still faces a large dissident Kurdish minority despite eight decades of 'Kemalist' civic nationalism. British civic nationalism within a tightly centralized union at the centre of a global empire could not prevent the break-away of Ireland in 1921 (McGarry 2001). Irish nationalists mobilized successfully without the advantages of their own self-governing institutions. They were able to establish democratic legitimacy without the need of a referendum, by winning the overwhelming majority of Ireland's seats in every election between 1885 and 1918. Britain's civic and unitary state proved incapable of preventing a nationalist rebellion in Northern Ireland from the late 1960s, or of preventing the resurgence of Scottish and Welsh nationalism. Even the home of Jacobinism that was able to turn peasants into Frenchmen in the nineteenth century has been unable to erode Corsican nationalism in the late twentieth century. The failure of unitarist or national federalist forms of civic nationalism may explain why all Western multi-national democracies, including the United Kingdom, Spain, Belgium, France and Denmark are now more disposed towards decentralized autonomy regimes if not full-blown multi-national federalism.

Third, if one accepts that federalism was necessary in the failed federations, the focus of blame for the violence accompanying their break-up can be shifted from multi-national federation *per se*. To some extent one can argue that secession – and violence – followed from attempts by certain groups to centralize these federations, that is, to move away from the spirit of multi-national federalism. Yugoslavia's break-up, including the de facto breakaway of Kosovo, followed successive Serbian-dominated moves against the autonomy of Yugoslavia's republics. The Soviet Union broke up after an abortive right-wing coup aimed at repudiating Mikhail Gorbachev's decentralizing initiatives. Violence was also caused by the centre's unwillingness to permit secession, that is, one can argue that federal constitutions with procedural and negotiable secession rules might have avoided violence better. In the former USSR, the most intense violence has been over Chechnya's right to secede; Yeltsin and

Putin did not accept that Chechnya had obtained recognition equivalent to that of a Soviet republic in the last days of Gorbachev's rule. Had it done so, it would likely have seceded with the other republics, and with as little violence as most of them. In many cases, one might argue that post-communist violence resulted from the absence of ethnofederalism, that is, from the lack of congruency between constituent unit and ethnic boundaries. In the case of Yugoslavia, Slovenia's secession was relatively peaceful because it was homogeneous. The 'velvet divorce' in Czechoslovakia was facilitated because there were few Czechs in Slovakia and few Slovaks in the Czech lands. War started in Croatia in 1991 largely because Croatia had a significant Serb population that wanted to stay united with Yugoslavia, and spread to Bosnia because it had Croats and Serbs who also wanted to stay linked to their respective ethnic kin. These groups were aided and abetted by Serbia and Croatia, respectively. Bosnia, the most multi-ethnic republic, was perhaps destined to be the most violent. In 2001, violent conflict broke out in Macedonia, whose significant Albanian minority resented the dominance of Slavs. War between Armenia and Azerbaijan was largely fought over the inclusion of an Armenian ethnic enclave (Nagorno-Karabakh) in the latter. In Georgia, two conflicts broke out between Georgians and South Ossetians cut off by Georgia's secession from their kin in North Ossetia (within Russia), and between Georgians and Abkhazians – who baulked at being included in what they saw as a Georgian state. The only other violence was in the Trans-Dniestrian region of Moldova, where Ukrainians and Russians resented their inclusion in Moldova. Just as communist federal break-up was fuelled by centralizing measures, the same could be said of the violence that arose in the newly independent, still heterogeneous, but unitary, republics. The wars in Croatia, Macedonia, the South Ossetian and Abkhazian regions of Georgia and Trans-Dniestria were all influenced by the majoritarian policies of the states' dominant groups. In Croatia, a minority rebellion broke out after the newly independent Croatian regime adopted a flag that resembled that of the wartime Croatian Ustashe regime that had committed genocide against the Serbs, and after it moved to disarm its Serbian policemen (Hayden 1992). Seen in this way, these conflicts were similar to those in the Kurdish region of Turkey or Iraq, or the Basque region of Spain under Franco, that is, they were reactions to centralization. It seems unreasonable simply to attribute them to multi-national federation *per se*.

Fourth, while it is true that only federations broke apart in communist Eastern Europe, this glosses over the more basic fact that the states that broke apart were also the most ethnonationally diverse states – which explains why they were federations. In the case of the Soviet Union,

Table 26.2   *The largest community's proportion of the population in the*
            communist states of Eastern Europe

Communist federations	Largest community	Percentage of population
Yugoslavia	Serbs	38.9
Soviet Union	Russians	51.0
Czechoslovakia	Czechs	63.0
Communist unitary states		
Bulgaria	Bulgarians	83.0
Albania	Albanians	95.0
Romania	Romanians	89.5
Hungary	Hungarians	89.9
Poland	Poles	97.6

Sources: CIA World Factbook 2001; Library of Congress Country Studies.

Russians had a bare majority of the total population (51 per cent), while in Czechoslovakia and Yugoslavia, the largest groups had 63 and 39 per cent, respectively. In none of the communist unitary states, did the total minority population constitute more than 17 per cent. The Turks of Bulgaria comprised the largest single minority group, with roughly 8 per cent of the population. It makes at least as much sense to argue that the instability of the communist federations resulted from their ethno-national diversity as their ethnofederal structures. In other research O'Leary has shown that national federations that are durably democratic and majoritarian have a Staatsvolk, a dominant people (O'Leary 2001). While lacking a Staatsvolk does not guarantee political instability in a federation, he claims that it makes it more likely. The United States, built around a historically dominant nationality of WASPs, proved more stable than Nigeria – which clearly lacks a numerically dominant people. The same comparison helps suggest why the Russian Federation is more stable and secession-proof, thus far, than the Soviet Union. Russians have a majority of 81.5 per cent in the Russian Federation; they had only 51 per cent in the USSR. The unitary states of Eastern Europe may have held together, in other words, not because they were not federations, but because each of them has a dominant community able to hold their state together if they had wanted to (see Table 26.2). Conversely, it is not at all certain that if, counterfactually, Yugoslavia had been a unitary state when it democratized, it would have stayed together. Ireland was able to secede from the much less diverse but unitary United Kingdom after the first universal male suffrage elections held in 1918.

Lastly, it is simply wrong to claim, as Snyder and others do, that 'ethnofederalism' is unworkable. One of the world's oldest and most stable regimes, the Canadian federation, is bi-national. It has endured since 1867, and has generally demonstrated that the accommodation of its French minority in an evolving bi-national arrangement is consistent with the advancement of propserity and the protection of human rights. India, the world's largest democracy and most successful post-colonial democracy, also has important ethnofederal characteristics in its practices. Belgium, while of more recent vintage, has adopted successful ethnofederalist structures, and so has Russia, if Chechnya is left aside. Within each of these states, there is plenty of evidence, including polling data and the positions of their political parties, that minorities are content with less than a sovereign state (Keating 2001, pp. 7–9). Together, these qualifications question the assumption that multi-national federalism is bound to fail. Our next task is to inquire into the conditions that make success more or less likely.

26.4   EXPLAINING SUCCESS AND FAILURE

The five conditions that facilitate, but do not guarantee successful multi-national federations are implicit in the preceding discussion. Here we spell them out.

26.4.1   The presence of a Staatsvolk

Table 26.1 would seem to demonstrate that national federations are more stable than multi-national federations. The latter appear more likely to fail or break up. The reason often proffered is straightforward: national federations are generally nationally homogeneous, or virtually so. However, O'Leary's data emphasizes the relative stability of multi-national federations and shows that it is related to the demographic preponderance of their largest national communities, to whether or not these constitute Staatsvolk. A Staatsvolk can feel secure – and live with the concessions attached to multi-national federations, and *ceteris paribus*, has the demographic strength and resources to resist secessionism by minority nationalities. Multi-national federations without a Staatsvolk are more likely to be unstable, face secessionism or break up, because minorities are more likely to think they can prevail (O'Leary 2001). Russia's future cannot be extrapolated from the experience of the Soviet Union, because Russians are far more dominant within the former than they were within the latter. The same argument implies that Nigeria and a future European federation will, *ceteris paribus*, be relatively unstable, as neither possesses a Staatsvolk. What must be considered in our '*ceteris paribus*' clause? We hypothesize as follows:

1. Multi-national federations without a Staatsvolk, if they are to survive as democratic entities, must develop consociational practices that protect the interests of all the encompassed national and ethnic communities with the capacity to break away.
2. The existence of a Staatsvolk, or the existence of consociational practices, will not by themselves assure the stabilization of a multi-national democratic federation, though they will separately or conjointly increase its survival prospects.
3. Other conducive external and internal political, economic and social relationships may decide the fate of a multi-national federation. The character of multi-national power sharing, whether a national minority has backing from a powerful neighbouring state and whether its region is on the border of the federation will assuredly matter, as will the democratic and legal character of the federation, its mode of formation, and its prosperity.

26.4.2   Consociationalism at the Centre

In a multi-national federation, consociational government at the centre may be required to give significant national communities pivotality in decision-making. When federalism is defended as a method of conflict regulation, the emphasis, as we have seen, is usually on how it can provide minorities with guaranteed powers of territorial self-government. Sometimes it is also argued that a virtue of federalism is that it avoids the 'winner-takes-all' outcome associated with Westminster-type regimes: a group that is excluded at the centre may be able to console itself with regional power. However, federalism is about 'shared rule' as well as 'self-rule', and national minorities are likely to want a federal government that represents them, that is inclusive, and indeed, we would say, consociational. National and ethnic minorities excluded from the federal government will have a reduced stake in the federation and the federal government will be less inclined to promote their interests. It is not surprising, then, that all of the durably democratic multi-national federations have practised consociational forms of democracy within the federal government. Such arrangements involve four features: cross-community executive power sharing, proportional representation of groups throughout the state sector (including the police and judiciary), ethnic autonomy in culture (especially in religion or language), and formal or informal minority-veto rights (Lijphart 1977). Consociational practices within the federal government are relatively undisputed in the case of Canada, Switzerland and Belgium (Hooghe 2003; Noel 1993; Steiner 1989), and Lijphart has recently claimed that India had effective consociational traits during its most stable period under Nehru (Adeney 2002; Lijphart 1996). Since Congress's decline, India has been governed by a broad multi-party coalition representing its diversity. Even if one does not count India as consociational in respect of having cross-community executive power sharing in New Delhi, it has usually had descriptively diverse representation of religious, ethnic and linguistic groups in the cabinet and civil service.

We can see the salience of consociational organization in the federal government in the case of many of the failed federations, where centrifugal pressures were often exacerbated by unrepresentative federal governments. In Pakistan, before the secession of Bangladesh, a crucial federal agency, the Army, was dominated by the West (Nasr 2001). This was also a serious problem in Yugoslavia, where the army, one of the most important federal institutions (absorbing two-thirds of the federal budget), was dominated by Serb officers, many of them from Serbian minorities who shared Slobodan Milošević's vision of a re-centralized state. The Yugoslav Federal Council, the most important political institution, and one based on (non-democratic) consociational principles, was subject from the late 1980s to an undisguised take-over by Serbian politicians. After having suspended the autonomy of Kosovo and Vojvodina, the Serbia–Montenegrin alliance gained control of four of the Federal Council's seven seats, plunging the federation into crisis. The Soviet Union broke up after an abortive take-over of the central government by conservatives opposed to decentralization. The episode undermined Gorbachev's attempt to re-organize the federation in ways that would have given the republics more self-government and better representation in Moscow. The breakdown of the Nigerian federation in 1966–67, which included anti-Ibo violence in the northern Hausa region and the bloody Biafran war of secession, arose after a coup which led to the centre being dominated by Ibo officers and a counter-coup in which these officers were overthrown (Suberu 2001). Much of Nigeria's post-1970 conflict, including sectarian warfare between Muslims and Christians and the rise of violent separatism in the oil-rich Delta area, has also been traced to the lack of inclusiveness at the level of the centre (Suberu and Diamond 2000, pp. 6–13). The breakdown of the West Indies federation was linked to Jamaicans' lack of representation and influence at the centre, and in the case of the federation of Nyasaland, Northern and Southern Rhodesia, it was black Africans who were underrepresented.

This suggests that it will not be sufficient for the Nigerian, Ethiopian and Pakistani federations or any prospective Iraqi federation to practise democracy. Past evidence suggests that they will need to adopt and maintain consociational governance at the federal centre. It also suggests that calls to have a fully fledged European federation, with the classic bicameral arrangements of the USA, to address the so-called 'democratic deficit' in the European Union will fail unless such calls are accompanied by strong commitments to consociational devices. Consociational governance would imply strong mechanisms to ensure the inclusive and effective representation of all the nationalities of the European Union in its core executive institutions, proportionate representation of its nationalities in its public bureaucracies and legal institutions, national autonomy in all cultural matters deemed of profound cultural significance (for example, language, religion, education), and last, but not least, national vetoes to protect national communities from being out-voted through majoritarian rules. In short, many of the current consociational and confederal features of the EU which some federalists want to weaken or temper in their pursuit of formal federation are in fact required to ensure the EU's prospects as a multi-national democratic federation. The EU's greatest current danger stems from its ardent majoritarian federalists.

This argument about the importance of accommodation through consociational devices is different from that put forward by Linz and Stepan (1992). They put their faith in the ability of federation-wide political parties to win support from all groups, to balance majority and minority concerns, and to build what Linz calls '*bundestreue*', an overarching loyalty to the state (Linz 1999). In their view, the key reason for the disintegration of the Yugoslav and Soviet federations was that the first democratic elections were held in the republics rather than the state (whereas in post-Franco Spain it was the other way around). In Yugoslavia this sequencing gave divisive republican elites the resources and space to promote break-up, and obstructed the organization of federation-wide parties with an interest in holding the state together. Had federal elections been held first, federation-wide parties would have been able to act as unifying forces.

This reasoning is, however, questionable. State-wide parties may well be likely to do better in state-wide elections than in regional elections, but there is no guarantee, or even likelihood, that they will do well at any level in societies with noticeable national divisions. In the United Kingdom's first democratic elections, in the mid-1880s, the overwhelming majority of Irish seats were won by Irish nationalist parties. The fact that they were elected in state-wide elections, as opposed to regional elections, does not

Table 26.3   *Relative demographic size and electoral support for minority groups in Bulgaria, Romania and Poland, 1990–1991*

State/year of election	Minority group/proportion (% of population)	Support for minority party (% of votes cast)
Bulgaria 1990	Turks, 8.5%	6.0%[a]
Romania 1990	Magyars, 7.8%	7.2%
Poland 1991[b]	Germans, 1%	1.2%

Notes:
[a]   The 1990 election was to elect a constitutional assembly. The first parliamentary elections took place in 1991. The Turkish minority party, the Movement for Human Rights and Freedoms, won 7.5 per cent on this occasion.
[b]   These were the first parliamentary elections. Presidential elections were held in 1990.

Sources: Centre for the Study of Public Policy: Mass Behaviour in New Democracies, at: http://www.cspp.strath.ac.uk/index.html?bulgelec.html; the University of Essex's Project on Political Transformation and the Electoral Process in Post-Communist Europe, at; http://www.essex.ac.uk/elections/; Elections in Central and Eastern Europe at: http://www2.essex.ac.uk/elect/electer/pl_er_nl.htm#pl91.

appear to have coloured their view of the UK, or their ability to secede from it, and they won despite the presence of competitors from state-wide parties. Czechoslovakia's first democratic elections, which involved concurrent state-wide and regional elections, produced no state-wide parties at the state-wide (federal) elections other than the discredited communists, who won 23 of the country's 150 seats – but even they subsequently divided into Czech and Slovak factions. All of the other parties that won seats were based on the Czech, the Slovak, or the Hungarian populations (Leff 1998, p. 98). Perhaps this political party fragmentation into ethnonational blocs was due, as Leff claims, to the simultaneity of elections at both levels, that is, to the fact that the federal election was not held in advance.

But how, then, are we to explain the first democratic election returns in the unitary states of Eastern Europe, where there were no regional elections? In these cases, party support still broke down almost exactly along ethnonational lines (see Table 26.3), with little evidence of integrative vote-pooling activities by either party elites or voters. These results are difficult to square with Linz and Stepan's assumption that Yugoslav state-wide elections would have produced strong Yugoslav state-wide parties, unless one is to assume that Yugoslavia was a good deal less divided than its neighbours. Given that it was the only state in Eastern Europe whose major communities had persons who had butchered each other within living memory (1941–45), this assumption is implausible. This comparative evidence suggests that state-wide elections in

Yugoslavia would have resulted in elections that reflected its national divisions. Hoping for state-wide parties to hold Yugoslavia together was probably wishful thinking. Stability would have required successful bargaining among the different minority nationalist parties on a new consociational and confederal constitution. Such bargaining as there was on this agenda did not succeed.

26.4.3 Authentic (Democratic) Multi-national Federations Are More Likely to be Successful than Pseudo-(undemocratic) Federations

An authentic multi-national federation is democratic. It allows the representatives of its respective national communities to engage in dialogue and open bargaining about their interests, grievances and aspirations. Such democratic dialogue is a prerequisite for the development of cooperative practices. Democratic multi-national federalism may help to preclude the systematic transgression of individual and group rights. It can prevent minority (secessionist) elites from exaggerating support for their preferences (Linz 1999). An authentic multi-national federation is also based on the rule of law, law that recognizes national, ethnic, or communal rights, a constitutional division of powers, and legal powers that approach those of impartial umpires. There is not yet an example of an established democratic multi-national federation failing (though the number of cases is small), although there are, as we have seen, numerous examples of democratizing federations that have not worked. The evidence, limited as it is, suggests that we should not automatically assume that Canada, Switzerland, Spain, India or Belgium will go the way of the flawed communist or post-colonial federations.

26.4.4 'Voluntary' or 'Holding Together' Multi-national Federations Are More Likely to Endure Under Democratic Conditions than Those that Are Coercively Constructed After Modern Social Mobilizations

Stepan distinguishes between three types of multi-national federation (Stepan 1999, pp. 19–34):

1. those that voluntarily come together from distinct polities/colonies, like the Swiss and Canadian federations;
2. those that are created from unitary states in an attempt to 'hold' the polity together, such as Belgium, and, one might argue, India; and
3. those that are forced together (or 'put' together) by a dominant group, such as the Soviet Union.

Federations that are consensually established as a result of elite bargaining, whether of the holding or voluntary variety, are more likely to be considered as legitimate by their citizens, and are more likely to survive than those that result from coercion. A foundational act of cooperation is also more likely than one of coercion to promote traditions of accommodation. Canada's success is owed in part to the fact that it originated in 1867 from a compact between Anglophone and Francophone elites led by John A. MacDonald and George Etienne Cartier. The Swiss federation was also the result of different groups agreeing to 'con-federate'. While the Spanish and Belgian federations emerged from unitary states, they too were based on agreement between representative elites. India, which stands out as one of the few post-colonial federal success stories, is also one of the few where indigenous elites took the decision to federate by themselves – albeit reluctantly, and albeit after prior British tutelage (Adeney 2002). Most of the failed federations, on the other hand, were put together without the consent of minority leaders. This does not augur well for Bosnia and Herzegovina, which exists as a federation because of the internationally imposed Dayton Accords.

26.4.5   Prosperous Multi-national Federations (or States) Are More Likely to Endure than Those that Are Not

Walker Connor has correctly counselled us against exaggerating the importance of materialism when questions of national identity are at stake. Prosperity should not be considered a sufficient or even a necessary condition (as the example of India shows) for holding a multi-national federation together (Connor 1984, pp. 145–64). Nonetheless, *ceteris paribus*, prosperity – and distributive fairness – may matter. The plight of the communist federations and post-colonial federations was plainly exacerbated by their inability to provide materially for their citizens and by the discrediting of communist central planning. In the Ukraine and the Baltic republics, even Russians voted for the break-up of the USSR. In both Yugoslavia and the Soviet Union, the catalyst for break-up was necessary economic reforms, and the charge was led in both cases by those republics (Slovenia and Croatia in the case of Yugoslavia, the Baltic republics in the case of the Soviet Union) which had the most to gain materially from going it alone. And we need not labour the obvious point that distributive fiscal and expenditure issues are the meat and drink of political controversy in those federations which do not use equitable formulae for fiscal equalization.

26.5   CONCLUSION

We have attempted to offer a more balanced and nuanced assessment of the value and durability of multi-national federations than that put forward by critics of 'ethnofederalism'. Democratic federalism did not cause the break-up of the communist states, as these were not authentic democratic (or economically efficient) federations. Clearly, this chapter demonstrates that not all multi-national federations have failed. There are a small number of remarkable success stories. We have tried to identify conditions that are conducive to the success of multi-national federations. It is imperative that they be democratic and that they respect the rule of law. It helps if they are prosperous. It helps if they came together voluntarily. If federations develop from a unitary state, our arguments suggest that early and generous responses to expressed demands for minority self-government will work better than delayed and grudging responses. The demographic composition of the federation matters: a federation with a dominant ethnonational community is likely to be more stable than one that does not. Lastly federalism is usually not enough: consociational practices, particularly at the level of the federal government, are very important to the success of multi-national federalism if there is no Staatsvolk.

27 Post-conflict recovery
John Ohiorhenuan

27.1 INTRODUCTION: THE CHALLENGE OF POST-CONFLICT RECOVERY

Countries emerging from violent conflict face extraordinary constraints mobilizing the human and financial resources that are urgently needed, first for humanitarian relief and subsequently for reconstruction and economic recovery. They are typically critically short of almost all types of expertise and yet have to deal simultaneously with several major challenges. They have to preserve the peace and safeguard security, reintegrate ex-combatants, resettle internally displaced persons (IDPs) and returning refugees, rehabilitate essential infrastructure and key public institutions, and restore private investors' confidence. They must also revive the public finance regime and reassert control over key national assets. Finally, they must promote conditions that make the resumption of conflict less likely, including by generating employment opportunities, tackling horizontal inequalities and by re-establishing the rule of law.

The post-conflict economy is not simply a 'normal' economy that happens to be in great distress. The massive destruction of assets, the disruption of social networks and the distortion of signals and incentives that generally constitute the legacy of violent conflict indicate a long transition to normalcy. This transition or recovery process consists of a series of overlapping processes – like colours in a rainbow – requiring that the sequencing of economic and social policies be particularly creative. This chapter discusses the approaches, policies and partnerships that are required to consolidate peace and restart economic development in the aftermath of violent conflict. It highlights what actions national authorities should take and how the international community can be most helpful.

The next section outlines the parameters of recovery. Section 27.3 describes briefly the impact of violent conflict on people, livelihoods and on the economy. Section 27.4 outlines the approach that is increasingly emerging as the most promising for sustained recovery. Section 27.5 examines the issue of appropriate economic policy for revitalizing the economy. Section 27.6 looks at the issue of partnerships for post-conflict recovery, focusing on the potential for private sector involvement and the role of external assistance. Section 27.7 provides some concluding remarks.

27.2   DEFINING POST-CONFLICT RECOVERY

Terms such as 'recovery', 'reconstruction' and 'rebuilding' tend to suggest a return to the status quo before the conflict. Typically, however, developmental pathologies such as extreme inequality, poverty, corruption, exclusion, institutional decay and poor economic management would have contributed to armed conflicts in the first instance and would have been further exacerbated during conflict. In the aftermath of war, recovery could mean a return to pre-conflict economic growth and employment rates. Indeed, one perspective views recovery as a return to the highest level of gross domestic product (GDP) per capita attained during the five years preceding the conflict (Flores and Nooruddin 2009). In many cases, however, growth rates in the period immediately before the outbreak of violence have been very low, or even negative. Returning to the pre-war GDP growth trajectory is clearly not good enough in such situations. A narrow emphasis on growth alone may also understate the sheer complexity of managing the economic consequences of conflict. For instance, if growth favours only a small segment of the population, it risks perpetuating or exacerbating grievances that may have contributed to conflict in the first place (Addison and Murshed 2003a).

A broader perspective that sees recovery as achieving broad socioeconomic well-being is also possible. This would include restoring citizen and societal security, ensuring food security, restoring shelter, public health and educational systems, as well as reconstructing the physical infrastructure, generating employment, opening markets, re-establishing prudential systems for banking and financial institutions (Mendelson-Forman 2002). There is a risk, however, that such a maximalist definition could conflate recovery from conflict with attaining economic development more broadly. The international peacebuilding and development community works with several notions of recovery. For instance, the World Bank advances the notion of post-conflict reconstruction, which it defines as 'the rebuilding of the socio-economic framework of society' and 'the reconstruction of the enabling conditions for a functioning peacetime society, explicitly including governance and rule of law as essential components' (World Bank 1998). The United Nations Development Programme (UNDP) sees recovery as the process of return to a 'normal' development trajectory, where a country has 'reacquired the capability to make and implement economic policy as part of a largely self-sustaining process of economic governance' (UNDP 2005).

While eschewing a maximalist approach, successful economic recovery cannot simply be a return to pre-war income levels and growth rates. Rather, it must involve growth rates that permit a structural break with the past. This means that growth must be sustained at significantly higher than historical rates, and should be accompanied by significant employment creation and by action to reduce severe horizontal inequalities. In essence, post-conflict recovery does not mean simply restoring pre-war economic or institutional arrangements. It involves a socioeconomic transformation and it requires a combination of far-reaching economic, institutional, legal and policy reforms that allow war-torn countries to re-establish the foundations for self-sustaining development. Recovery means creating a new political economy dispensation. It means building back differently and better.

A critical dimension of post-conflict recovery is that despite their many similarities, post-conflict economies do vary in many ways from country to country. The actual situation depends on the length, scope and intensity of the armed conflict, the terms of the peace and the level of development prior to conflict. Some countries emerge from war with a reserve of economic assets, human capital, functioning institutions and a formal economy that still works. Others are not so lucky and face large hurdles both to sustainable peace and to economic recovery.

Recent civil conflicts have increasingly been concentrated in poor countries with large rural populations. Combat often provides an attractive occupational option for young rural males, reducing the supply of labour as much as demand. This makes employment and livelihood creation particularly crucial at the end of conflict to rehabilitate ex-combatants as well as those displaced from jobs and communities by war. Moreover, as many of these economies were not performing well before lapsing into conflict, creating large numbers of decent jobs is particularly urgent (McLeod and Dávalos 2007).

27.3   THE IMPACT OF VIOLENT CONFLICT ON PEOPLE, ASSETS AND INSTITUTIONS

Conflict diverts resources from production to destruction. The economic legacy of conflict includes the widespread destruction and degradation of human and physical capital; the collapse of growth and flight of capital; loss of employment and livelihoods; and weakened governance institutions and social networks. The distorted system of asset acquisition, resource use and incentives that conflict leaves behind represents a disabling environment for legitimate private sector investment. Capital flight and investor confidence can be particularly difficult to reverse when hostilities end. Markets will have been severely compromised at all levels from village produce exchanges to national commodity and financial exchanges.

Table 27.1   Battle deaths and total deaths in selected African countries

Country	Years	Estimated total war deaths	Battle deaths	Battle deaths as % of total war deaths
Sudan (Anya Nya rebellion)	1963–73	250,000–750,000	20,000	3–8
Nigeria (Biafra rebellion)	1967–70	500,000–2 million	75,000	4–15
Angola	1975–2002	1.5 million	160,475	11
Ethiopia (not including Eritrean insurgency)	1976–91	1–2 million	16,000	<2
Mozambique	1976–92	500,000–1 million	145,400	15–29
Somalia	1981–96	250,000–350,000	66,750	19–27
Sudan	1983–2002	2 million	55,000	3
Liberia	1989–96	150,000–200,000	23,500	12–16
Democratic Republic of Congo	1998–2001	2.5 million	145,000	6

Source: Lacina and Gleditsch (2005); cited in Human Security Centre (2005, p. 128).

As legitimate economic activity is devastated, illicit activities economies often flourish that may fuel the conflict further.

27.3.1   The Human Costs

Armed conflicts generally result in the reduction of a country's stock of human capital. While the most direct human capital costs are deaths as a result of war-related violence, battle deaths usually constitute a small proportion of the total number of casualties. Non-battle deaths, due to war-exacerbated disease and malnutrition, are substantially larger than battle deaths. As shown in Table 27.1, for a sample of conflicts in Africa, actual battle deaths have ranged from under 2 per cent to at most 30 per cent of total war deaths.

The large numbers of indirect deaths are due to famine and disease. War reduces the availability of food and it changes entitlements as food prices rise and people lose their jobs or livelihoods. Famine, resulting from this combination, often accounts for a large number of deaths. Mortality rates also tend to rise due to the spread of killer diseases such as HIV/ AIDS, malaria, tuberculosis and other infectious diseases in situations where healthcare systems have collapsed. World Health Organization (WHO) data on 23 major diseases indicate that armed conflicts substantially increase the incidence of contagious diseases (Ghobarah et al. 2003). Although the interplay between violence and infectious diseases is complex and variable, evidence suggests that the greater the wartime violence and the poorer and more vulnerable the country, the greater the number of people who get seriously ill or die from these diseases (Human Security Centre 2005).

The educational system is often another major casualty of civil conflict. Conflict reduces the stock of people with high levels of education and productive skills due to death, injury death or migration. It may also induce some deskilling among combatants, as they lose some of their previously acquired professional skills during years spent fighting. The destruction of a country's educational infrastructure can be very widespread and often has serious long-term effects on a post-conflict country's economic recovery and development. For instance, during Liberia's 15-year civil war, at least 50 per cent of all schools were destroyed (Li 2007), depriving 800,000 children of education (Dukuly 2004). In Timor-Leste, the percentage was even higher with an estimated 95 per cent of classrooms destroyed or severely damaged in the violent aftermath of the 1999 referendum on independence. In Kosovo, Bosnia and Herzegovina, and Mozambique, respectively, 65, 50 and 45 per cent of schools required repair or reconstruction after war (World Bank 2005b). The loss of providers of education can also be very substantial during conflict. In Rwanda, for instance, more than two-thirds of the primary and secondary school teachers either fled or were murdered, while the educational system in Cambodia was almost completely bereft of any trained or experienced teachers at the end of the Khmer Rouge terror regime (ibid.).

Population displacement is another major human capital cost. The 2005 Human Security Report noted that while wars in the 1950s, 1960s and 1970s were associated with high death rates, they did not generate very large flows of displaced people (Human Security Centre 2005). In contrast, contemporary armed conflicts usually result in large numbers of internally displaced persons and refugees. Human capital is also lost as a result of the emigration of skilled talent and labour. Entrepreneurs, professionals and intellectuals often leave conflict countries for better personal security and opportunities abroad.

27.3.2   Physical Capital

The destruction of infrastructure is often the most visible consequence of armed conflict. The warring parties often directly target bridges and roads in order to gain a strategic advantage. Government spending on infra-structural maintenance also typically declines during conflict, due to the insecurity, a general decline in government revenues, and an increase in military spending. The loss of physical capital may be very substantial and can severely restrict the capacity for economic recovery in the post-conflict period. For instance, during the civil war in Mozambique some 40 per cent of immobile capital in the agriculture, communications and administrative sectors was destroyed (Brück 2001). The damage to physical capital has a significant impact on a country's productive capabilities. It also imposes serious hardships on civilian populations through the loss of safe drinking water, sanitation and power systems. Three years after the end of Liberia's civil war, for example, pipe-borne water and sanitation services were still mostly not available. Before the war, 45 per cent of the urban population and 23 per cent of those in rural areas had such access (UNDP Liberia 2006).

In post-conflict countries large land areas are frequently rendered inac-cessible by landmines and other unexploded ordnance. In 2001, 25 years after the end of war, Cambodia still had more landmines and unexploded ordnance than any other country in the world. There were 6,422 villages (46 per cent of the total) contaminated (Collier et al. 2003). Clearly, the prospects of economic recovery are severely hampered in such situations, by the risk to life and discouragement of agricultural production. The assets of the poor are often lost or abandoned following forced migration or expropriation by combatants. In Uganda, a survey among households who fled the violence in the centre of the country during the civil war in the mid-1980s, found that two-thirds of respondents had lost all their assets as a result of the violence as well as the extensive looting by both sides (Matovu and Stewart 2001).

27.3.3 Economic Performance

Conflict almost always affects the rate of growth of a country's economy as a result of the negative impacts on physical and human capital as well as disrupted markets and reduced trust. The growth impact of conflict differs significantly from country to country, depending in part on the proportion of the population actually fighting, the duration and geographical spread of the conflict, and the extent to which the central government has col-lapsed. For instance, where armed conflicts are concentrated in peripheral areas, such as with Uganda's northern insurgency, the economic engine of the country may be largely unaffected. However, where armed conflicts spread throughout a country's territory, as in Afghanistan, Cambodia and Mozambique, they usually cause immense economic damage.

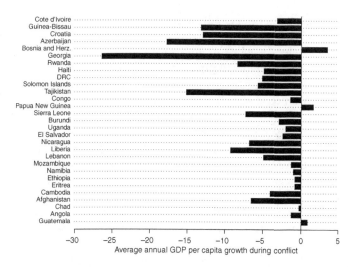

Note: Countries are ranked from left to right with the countries with the shortest conflicts on the left and the ones with the longest on the right. The conflict periods considered are those during which economic activity is likely to have been most affected on a continuous basis.

Sources: World Development Indicators, and Heston et al. (2002).

Figure 27.1   Change in GDP per capita in selected conflict-affected countries

Figure 27.1 shows the impact of conflict on GDP in selected post-conflict countries. While there are significant differences in the reduction in GDP per capita among conflict-affected countries, the effect of war is typically largely negative. The overall effect of a conflict on a country's GDP per capita depends on the average growth rate it is able to maintain during conflict and on the duration of its conflict. GDP per capita growth during conflict was strongly negative in Afghanistan, Azerbaijan, Croatia, Georgia, Guinea-Bissau, Liberia, Nicaragua, Rwanda, Sierra Leone, Solomon Islands and Tajikistan. In Angola, Chad, Mozambique and Uganda, the average annual decline in GDP per capita was more modest at below 2 per cent. In exceptional cases, a few countries have experienced positive growth over their conflict periods, with Bosnia and Herzegovina, Guatemala and Papua New Guinea having higher levels of GDP per capita at the end of conflict than at the beginning. Several factors may account for these differences in growth trajectories, including the characteristics of the country's economy, the reaction of the international community and the geographical scope, intensity and duration of the conflict.

27.4 OBJECTIVES AND APPROACH TO POST-CONFLICT RECOVERY

Post-conflict recovery is not a return to the status quo ante bellum. Indeed the country's existential conditions may have contributed to the onset of conflict. Recovery involves a number of competing urgent actions, including the restoration of basic safety and security, the rehabilitation of ex-combatants, IDPs and returning refugees, and the restoration of core government functions at the national local and community levels. It also means restoring basic social services, particularly water and sanitation, primary education and health services, restoring political processes and promoting reconciliation, and rehabilitating the economy, including through employment generation and livelihoods restoration, as well as the rehabilitation of basic infrastructure (United Nations 2009a).

Appropriate timing and sequencing among priorities often require trade-offs within a recovery strategy. Promoting conditions that make the resumption of conflict less likely is clearly a primordial requirement. The insecurity and sporadic violence that often persist, even after the ostensible end of conflict, require early emphasis on security. Similarly, generating livelihood opportunities and addressing land and property issues may also require early emphasis because they engender confidence in people of a return to normalcy. On the other hand, while electoral processes can help restore political legitimacy, rushing into them could be a major source of tension and renewed conflict. Historical evidence seems to indicate that the most important challenge of the first two years after conflict is to ensure that actions or decisions do not prejudice the long-term sustainability of peace (United Nations 2009a).

27.4.1 Indigenous Drivers of Recovery

As indicated in the introduction, it is useful to view economic recovery as a series of overlapping policy actions. The sets of action may be clustered into four categories: strengthening indigenous drivers of recovery, rebuilding state capacity, promoting inclusive economic policy and cultivating appropriate partnerships (see Figure 27.2). The obvious starting point is to promote indigenous drivers. In even the most war-damaged environments, economic activities have been continuing and populations have retained some ability to rebuild, based on their own resources, ingenuity and energies. There is always some spontaneous initiation of recovery as soon as conflict ends. People return to their homes and livelihoods, or adapt to new conditions and begin to engage in various types of income-generating

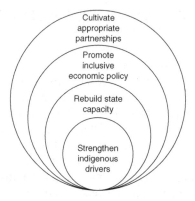

Figure 27.2   Main phases of post-conflict economic recovery

activity. The natural foundation for economic recovery lies in mobilizing this energy and nurturing the 'indigenous drivers' of economic recovery.

This means promoting the efforts and initiatives of local communities, individuals, households and enterprises that stimulate and impel economic activities. Local actors have the strongest incentives to rehabilitate their own livelihoods after war. Post-conflict recovery policies that harness and build on local capacities and on social processes and interactions on the ground are more likely to be successful and self-sustaining in the long run, because they respect local conditions and people's actual circumstances.

The indigenous drivers' emphasis suggests that 'national ownership' should be non-negotiable. It insists that people and communities, as well as national institutions, should lead in establishing the specific priorities for reshaping or reforming institutions and restarting the economy. It also goes beyond the familiar notion of capacity-building. Nurturing indigenous drivers requires explicitly identifying the capacities, capabilities and tensions inherent in systems and processes and in organizational, community and even national dynamics as observed in the immediate aftermath of conflict. Recovery policies should respect these dynamics even as they determine where they may need to be modified or strengthened.

The following are among the key requirements for nurturing indigenous drivers:

- National actors must take the lead in the recovery process. The best support for post-conflict countries is to work with them to build the leadership capability in the shortest possible time.
- It is essential to build on what is left after the conflict. For instance, to help the quick restart of the next crop cycle, partially damaged

crops could be salvaged, and seeds and tools (such as farm implements, fishing nets and canoes) provided.

- Where pre-war structures and practices were not a source of tension, it is important to draw on them to re-establish local consultative mechanisms and local capacity for economic and social development.

This approach places local actors, institutions and resources at the centre of economic recovery, but it extends, just as crucially to the national level. At the national level, considerable resources are required after war for rehabilitation and reconstruction. A key factor in determining whether the early impetus for economic revival translates into sustainable recovery and longer-term development is the leadership and capacity of the post-conflict state. Dynamic leadership is needed to ensure that the productive energies and assets of households, communities and enterprises can be channelled towards the recovery effort.

27.4.2 Rebuilding State Capacity

The leadership of the state is needed to foster and protect an enabling environment for economic activity that can promote both security and growth. The efforts of communities will be hindered unless state institutions quickly become effective and are able to provide essential public goods. Since conflict invariably undermines the legitimacy of the state, one of the most important priorities for the post-conflict leadership is, perhaps, to re-establish legitimacy and rebuild its authority. The notion of indigenous drivers applies with equal force at this level also. The broad peacebuilding community now generally recognizes the indispensability of local leadership in re-establishing a functioning state after conflict ends (OECD 2007). This is why it has now placed a high premium on assisting war-torn states to rebuild the institutions, rules and capacities for accountable and effective governance and, in some cases, to redress the legitimacy and capacity deficits that may have contributed to armed conflict in the first place.

The ultimate measure of an authoritative, legitimate and effective state is one that has established a 'social contract' entailing the reciprocity between the state's provision of essential services and citizen acceptance of its authority. Restoring state legitimacy requires the restoration or installation of institutions that foster an inclusive political process. Promoting an inclusive political system is really critical where exclusion is severe. It mitigates the risks of conflict recurrence that may be posed by an absence of voice for some groups in dealing with extant socioeconomic and inter-group inequalities.

The post-conflict government should quickly install the core capacities it needs to provide basic services and essential public safety, strengthen the rule of law, and protect citizens' rights. Visible peace dividends that are attributable to the national authorities, such as employment generation or returnee rehabilitation, are critical to building the confidence in the post-conflict government. To regain the confidence of the population and rebuild trust after years of uncertainty and violence requires the provision of jobs and basic social services for individuals and households. For communities and local government that means revenue sharing, institutional strengthening and relative fiscal autonomy. For business, it means political stability, clearly articulated economic policies and a commitment to rebuilding investment-enabling institutions. Restoring public services is an excellent start to restoring the social contract.

Training or retraining civil servants and public sector managers is essential as soon as hostilities end. Incentives should be developed to attract displaced nationals and those in diaspora to return to the service. Among the most critical institutional requirements is the establishment of mechanisms for oversight, accountability and financial controls. Sustainable economic recovery requires that the post-conflict government has the institutional, administrative and fiscal means to underwrite the provision of these services. This depends, in turn, on its ability to mobilize, allocate and spend domestic revenues. The payment of taxes by the citizenry is an essential aspect of the social contract that needs to be rewritten. Restoring fiscal capacity means strengthening capacities at the local and community levels also for revenue mobilization. It is also essential to control corruption and rent seeking, especially in states with abundant natural resources.

Recovery efforts must work with and from the political, institutional and resource endowments actually available on the ground. These may include informal institutions and forms of governance that lie outside the generally accepted model of the developed countries.

27.5   POST-CONFLICT ECONOMIC POLICY

Conflict typically leaves countries with severe macroeconomic problems. A shrunken economic base, moderate to high inflation, chronic fiscal deficits, high levels of external and domestic government debt and low domestic government revenues are among the more prominent features of these economies.

The first few post-conflict years are crucial to long-term economic recovery. While quick action is often required, this is not necessarily a time for radical action. Rather it is a period for establishing policies that are most appropriate to creating the conditions for recovery. Good post-conflict macroeconomic performance requires a sequential approach to reforms. It strives to bring down inflation as soon as possible to single digits. It actively promotes job creation and the expansion of livelihoods and it solicits the return of private investment.

A return to steady and respectable growth is essential for sustainable economic recovery, but growth alone does not define recovery. It is particularly important in post-conflict settings that growth be inclusive, broad based and conflict sensitive. Recovery is likely to be more sustainable when it benefits the vast majority of the population, rather than a small group. Restoring jobs and livelihoods helps consolidate peace by giving young people alternative opportunities and incomes. Macroeconomic policy must also give priority to minimizing conflict risk, even as it promotes growth. Conflict-sensitive economic policy may mean, for instance, tolerating some macroeconomic heterodoxy. For instance, most post-conflict countries are beset by hyperinflation, which needs to be brought down as soon as possible. It may be necessary, however, to tolerate in the short term, higher inflation and budget deficit levels than would be considered 'normal'. While there is no unique path to recovery, experience shows that post-conflict countries that have emphasized social inclusion and equity enjoy a stronger recovery and are less likely to fall back into conflict. The promotion of growth must be self-consciously broadbased and inclusive.

The sequencing of policy actions is particularly important in post-conflict settings. The imperative of reducing conflict risk indicates pragmatic macroeconomic policy. Done properly, sequencing of reforms strengthens the reformers in government and builds the political will and institutional capacity to design and implement more difficult reforms later on. Such a gradual approach also allows post-conflict authorities to build the self-confidence and general goodwill that can then be deployed for more complex reforms. More complex reforms, particularly in the domains of financial liberalization and privatization, risk backfiring if the appropriate regulatory regime is not in place. Reforms should be introduced in a way that is compatible with the realities of the domestic political economy in each country. Specifically, successful recovery requires the leadership of governments and domestic political elites that are serious about economic reform and consolidating peace.

Employment creation and the recovery of livelihoods are particularly urgent because they help reduce the probability of conflict resuming and ultimately save on outlays for security and crime prevention. Employment programmes are especially important for ex-combatants, as regular work

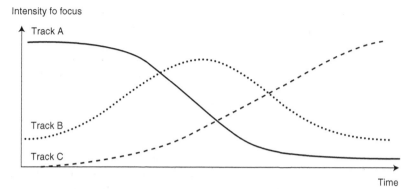

Intensity fo focus

Track A: Direct employment/income generation schemes. *Focus on targeting groups*
Track B: Local economic recovery/area-based development programmes. *Focus on communities*
Track C: Long-term employment/decent work interventions. *Focus on national level*

Note: 'Intensity of focus' is both qualitative and quantitative, denoting the extent of policy and programme commitment to each avenue for employment creation. It captures the idea that over time emphasis shifts from one track to another as the economy returns to 'normalcy'.

Source: Based on United Nations (2008a, p. 17).

Figure 27.3 The three tracks of a post-conflict employment strategy

in civilian jobs helps create a sense of normalcy and routine, which contributes to social stability. Public employment schemes also serve as transitory mechanisms: private sector employment begins to kick in only after recovery has gained some momentum. Moreover, civilian employment helps ex-combatants recover more 'normal' social and emotional networks, which were lost while they were in a military unit (McLeod and Dávalos 2007).

A useful approach to post-conflict employment creation is the three-track approach proposed recently by the United Nations (United Nations 2008a). Developed to guide the work of UN entities at country level, the policy proposes three distinct but mutually reinforcing tracks of employment policies and programmes (see Figure 27.3). The first track aims to consolidate security and stability with high-visibility, labour-intensive public work programmes that provide temporary jobs, strengthen local skills and rebuild economic and social infrastructures. It contains short-term responses such as emergency employment schemes and basic start-up grants, and it targets primarily (but not exclusively) conflict-affected individuals, such as youths and ex-combatants, who are at a high risk of relapsing into violence. Ideally, public work programmes should support indigenous drivers by, for instance, awarding contracts to local organizations and firms to help build skills and foster local enterprise capacities.

The second track focuses on the larger community and is aimed at building local labour demand by stimulating local economic recovery. This entails investments to restore the local economic infrastructure and local institutions, rebuild local government capacity and stimulate private sector development, for instance, by offering employers wage supplements. The third track is national in scope and aims at long-term employment creation and stimulation of decent work opportunities via macroeconomic policy. The goals include changing industrial structures, nurturing the domestic private sector, stimulating labour-intensive industries and inducing foreign investment. It begins, ideally, immediately after conflict ends and is intensified as stability is restored. A major aim of the whole process is to encourage a transition from aid-supported employment creation that predominates in Track A to self-sustaining private and public sector job creation.

Three considerations are important regarding post-conflict employment creation. First, the three tracks should be activated as soon as conflict ends. Sometimes, it is possible for some efforts to be initiated even before hostilities have subsided totally. At the very least, a substantial part of the planning should take place before the end of conflict. Second, as the private sector is the only effective guarantee of jobs in the long run, it should be involved in activities from the beginning. Third, the private sector is quite small in many post-conflict situations. It is important in these situations to nurture the creation of small enterprises by removing administrative and other barriers and providing incentives such as low taxes and wage subsidies.

27.6 CULTIVATING ESSENTIAL PARTNERSHIPS

Recovery is anchored at the community level and it requires not only state support, but also active partnership with the private sector. Community efforts to rebuild and strengthen their livelihoods will be constrained unless private investment recreates markets and generates employment (Addison and Murshed 2003a). Moreover, while the indigenous driver approach to recovery places community and national level actors, institutions and resources at its centre, it also recognizes that the considerable resources required after war are usually beyond the means of governments. External assistance is needed to support and complement the activities and actions of the national drivers.

27.6.1   Attracting Private Investment

Recovering economies need to be particularly creative in soliciting the return of private investment. Attracting the private sector requires the assurance, as soon as possible, of physical security, property rights pro- tection and transparency in the justice system. These requirements are particularly central to improving the business climate in the high-risk environments of post-conflict economies. Laying the basis for these in the immediate aftermath of the conflict may raise the confidence of domestic and foreign investors alike in the future of the economy. It is important to empower local entrepreneurs in the first instance. The revitalization of local enterprise is not only essential to economic recovery, but it also signals the beginning of a return to 'normalcy'. Important steps for engag- ing the local business community include providing access to finance and, even more importantly, cultivating its continuing participation in policy dialogue with the government and policy makers.

Promoting foreign investment is equally urgent. The risk perception of private enterprise delays its entry into post-conflict environments. For instance, even in resource-rich economies, investors may be quick to pursue exploration contracts, but may delay long-term investments in production until they are better assured of a country's stability. Incentives such as tax allowances and political risk insurance may encourage foreign investors to enter the post-conflict market earlier. Extending political risk coverage to domestic and regional investors may encourage them to invest earlier than they were previously considering.

It is important, however, to be realistic about investment opportunities. The active participation of large foreign corporate enterprises and transna- tional corporations in the post-conflict situation would represent a strong vote of confidence in local stability. However, investment from these enti- ties is unlikely to materialize in the short term. Policy makers may want to focus, therefore, on smaller investors from within or from countries in the immediate region. These actors would have greater familiarity with local conditions and may well have a stake in local economic recovery beyond simple economic calculus. The reasons for such additional interest from regional enterprises may well include strong cultural linkages.

Perhaps the most important incentive would be a mechanism that enables risk sharing. A robust risk-sharing facility would help bridge the gap between private and social returns that is a typical feature of post- conflict situations. While private returns to the investor may be low, the social returns are usually considerable. These include the signalling that peace has returned that may attract in additional investment, and the employment generated that may reduce conflict risk. This divergence between private and social returns suggests that a publicly funded financial facility may be an especially important market failure correction mechanism. Such a facility could, for instance, bear much of the cost of doing project design and financial structuring in a fully consultative and conflict-sensitive manner. It could also share in the cost of borrowing as an incentive for early entry into high-priority sectors such as energy, construction or export industries (UNDP 2008).

27.6.2 Mobilizing External Assistance

It is now overwhelmingly accepted that the overriding principle behind all external assistance must be to 'do no harm'. This means, in the first instance, that any action that could stir up social tensions or otherwise increase the likelihood of a relapse into conflict must be avoided. External assistance strategies must thus take full account of the political, ethnic and religious dynamics that have emerged from or may have contributed to conflict in the first place.

Specifically, external assistance must aim to support and complement ongoing indigenous efforts. The obvious starting point would be to go beyond the usual post-conflict needs assessments that the international community undertake in the immediate aftermath of conflict. These should be complemented with a capabilities assessment to determine what exists. Additionally, a 'quick and dirty' analysis of the broader political economy issues would help ensure that aid is properly grounded on what and how people are already contributing to the recovery process.

Substantively, external assistance should aim to provide a stronger platform for further locally grown initiatives, paying particular attention to the obstacles and unmet needs that may be constraining the efforts of community- and national-level actors. Partners should invest in local resources, procure supplies locally as much as possible and enhance the capacity of the private sector. External partners need to avoid excessive reliance on parallel mechanisms to deliver development assistance. Instead, they should carefully weigh the additional costs of routing assistance through relatively weak state systems against the benefits of building the state's capacity to manage and deliver services to its citizens.

External assistance can provide much-needed breathing space to governments to build political consensus and goodwill, engage in broad internal consultations and plan better for the medium term. This requires from external partners early and more predictable disbursements of aid, as well as faster and deeper debt relief, in a manner that gives additional discretion to the beneficiaries. For governments of countries in recovery, it means using the early dividends and space provided by external assistance to restore and reform institutional capacities and the policy-making process.

External assistance should be provided under limited conditionality as much as possible. This would give post-conflict national leaderships the discretion to make context-appropriate decisions on the utilization of aid. Post-conflict countries may wish to use aid to cover some of their budget deficits, which are often quite large. By providing financing to cover part of the gap between domestic revenues and expenditures, aid complements domestic revenues and enables the implementation of additional priority expenditures. External resources, including aid, can also be 'saved', to build up reserves, lower debt and help stabilize their exchange and inflation rates. Questions regarding what proportion should be spent, what amount should be absorbed and for what purpose, must be based on a sound analysis of the needs and constraints facing the economy. Typically, a strong case can be made for spending most of the official development aid received so as to help finance larger fiscal deficits in the face of massive recovery needs. But it may also make sense to save some of it, depending on such considerations as the level of debt and the characteristics of the export sector.

A substantial amount of external assistance in post-conflict settings is typically provided in the form of technical assistance. In these situations, also, the theme should be to build up local capacities. It is now mostly accepted that relying too heavily on imported capacity can undermine local capacities and the rebuilding of skilled domestic competencies by putting off investment in domestic human resources. Drawing on its accumulated experience from supporting dozens of countries emerging from conflict, the United Nations recommends using and supporting national capacity as the first preference for international assistance. Where there is need for international expertise, regional experts would be most effective, given their knowledge of local languages and conditions. The substitution of international capacity to perform critical recovery tasks should not undermine or replace existing national capacities and should be accompanied by efforts to develop the necessary capacity. In particular, external partners should provide 'early and sustained support' to the civil service and local institutions to provide adequate compensation and conditions for professionals who remain within domestic structures, where their contribution to recovery may have the greatest impact, rather than move to work with international organizations (United Nations 2009a).

National actors should take the lead in reviving the economy and restoring institutional capacities. Again, the United Nations recommends that when the international community is requested to provide technical capacity to support line functions in national governments, a capacity development programme must be part of such support. Allowing for local personnel to work and train alongside foreign experts may temporarily raise the cost of recovery programme. But, in the longer term it strengthens the recovery process by reconstituting domestic capacity on a more sustainable basis.

27.7 CONCLUSION

This chapter examined the notion of post-conflict recovery and discussed the actors, policies and partnerships that are required to restart economic development in the aftermath of violent conflict. It highlights what actions national authorities should take and how the international community can be most helpful.

Successful post-conflict recovery requires growth rates that permit a structural break with the past. It also requires a pattern of growth that helps to reduce the risk of conflict recurring. As such, growth must be accompanied by employment expansion and action to reduce horizontal inequalities.

Conflict diverts resources from production to destruction. The economic legacy of conflict includes the widespread destruction and degradation of human and physical capital; the collapse of growth and flight of capital; loss of employment and livelihoods; and weakened governance institutions and social networks.

Because post-conflict countries differ from one another in important respects, a fundamental requirement is for recovery programmes to be context appropriate and based on an assessment of the particular circumstances of the country. In even the most war-damaged environments, economic activities have been continuing and populations have retained some ability to rebuild, based on their own resources, ingenuity and energies. When conflicts end, people return to their homes and livelihoods, or adapt to new conditions as necessary. The natural foundation for economic recovery lies in mobilizing this energy and nurturing the 'indigenous drivers' of economic recovery.

The leadership of the state is needed to foster and protect an enabling environment for economic activity that can promote both security and growth. The efforts of communities and the private sector will be constrained unless state institutions are able to provide essential public goods. The post-conflict government needs to quickly install the core capacities to provide basic services and essential public safety, strengthen the rule of law, and protect citizen rights. Visible peace dividends are critical to regaining the confidence of the population and rebuilding trust after years of uncertainty and violence.

Conflict typically leaves countries with severe macroeconomic problems, including a shrunken economic base, moderate to high inflation, chronic fiscal deficits, high levels of external and domestic government debt and low domestic government revenues. Macroeconomic policies must give priority to minimizing conflict risk, even as they promote growth. This may mean accepting some heterodoxy, such as tolerating moderate inflation and budget deficits for a time.

Reforms should be introduced in a way that is compatible with the realities of the domestic political economy in each country. Specifically, successful recovery requires the leadership of governments and domestic political elites that are serious about economic reform and consolidating peace.

Employment programmes are especially important in post-conflict situations, especially to reintegrate ex-combatants and other displaced people. Employment creation requires a three-track approach, beginning with an initial focus on restoring stability with public work programmes that provide temporary jobs and rebuild war-damaged economic and social infrastructures. The second and third tracks focus, respectively, on community-level programmes and national and macro-level initiatives.

Community efforts to rebuild and strengthen their livelihoods will be constrained unless private investment recreates markets and generates employment. Attracting the private sector requires the assurance, as soon as possible, of physical security, property rights protection and transparency in the justice system. It is important to empower local entrepreneurs in the first instance. The revitalization of local enterprise is not only essential to economic recovery, but it also signals the beginning of a return to 'normalcy'.

It is important, however, to be realistic about investment opportunities. While the active participation of large foreign corporate enterprises would represent a strong vote of confidence in local stability, this is unlikely to materialize in the short term. Policy makers should focus, therefore, on smaller investors from within or from countries in the immediate region.

The considerable resources required after war are usually beyond the means of post-conflict governments. External assistance is needed to support and complement the activities of the national drivers. Specifically, external assistance must aim to support and complement ongoing indigenous efforts. The international community should complement the usual needs assessment with a capabilities assessment to determine what exists on the ground. A 'quick and dirty' analysis of the broader political economy issues would also help ensure that aid is properly grounded.

Substantively, external assistance should aim to provide a stronger platform for further locally grown initiatives, paying particular attention to the obstacles and unmet needs that may be constraining the efforts of community- and national-level actors. External assistance can be very important for recovery, especially in the early stages. But the management of aid must be subject to the logic on promoting and using indigenous drivers and should never be a vehicle to promote parallel systems.

28 Gendering violent conflicts
Birgitte Refslund Sørensen

28.1 INTRODUCTION

Violent conflicts and wars cannot be accounted for without consideration of gender. The statement is simple and often made, but how to incorporate a gender perspective continues to be the object of discussion and contestation. The history of armed conflicts in the Western world is dominated by inter-state wars, the analysis of which has focused on such issues as political objectives and military strategies, the relationship between the technical development of military equipment and war efficiency, economic costs and the deployment of soldiers. The analytical focus has thus predominantly been on male perspectives, interests and activities, which have been cast as gender neutral, leaving aside a discussion of the multiple roles that women played in these wars. The escalation of a new kind of wars, the intra-state or internal wars, that occurred in the wake of decolonization and the post-Cold War period, as nation-states failed to satisfactorily settle issues of identity, resources and power, profoundly challenged our habitual understanding of war as a political and social phenomenon. In these wars, the frontline moved to the villages and neighborhoods where people live, and war became embedded in civilians' everyday lives in numerous and multifarious ways.

Media images of infinite crowds of refugee women fleeing violence with their dependent children and elderly relatives in search of security, food and health, and of women who have been tortured, maimed and sexually abused, made the relevance of a gender perspective apparent to everyone. Over the past 15 years, many academics and activists have contributed significantly to enhancing our understanding of the entanglement of gender and violent conflicts, with detailed documentation, and critical analysis and reflection (see, for example, Enloe 2000; Moser and Clarke 2001; Youngs 2009). These studies confirm the relevance and urgency of gender, but more importantly, they challenge stereotype and simplified images, and suggest new and more apposite analytical frameworks and policy objectives.

Three cross-cutting issues run through the literature and are important to be aware of as they shape underlying assumptions as well as conclusions. First, recent studies of gender in the context of violent conflict raise the question of *representation* (for example, De Mel 2007; Thiruchandran 1999). Divergences in this regard reflect not only different disciplinary traditions, but also diverse ideological positions and cultural traditions. It has been pointed out that even when gender identities, roles and relations are to some extent premised on the biological sex, they are always socially constructed and not naturally given. This has important implications for discussions of the reproduction and transformation of gender identities. Related to this, discussions of gender typically focus on women. Another recurrent critique of mainstream representations concerns the tendency to depict women (and men) as autonomous individuals in accordance with Western liberal ideology, and disregarding that in other traditions, individuals are recognized only as parts of larger social relations, and their agency is embedded in these relationships. The question of how to address gender and represent women and men, and the politics of this question, is reflected in different choices of categories. A given female individual living in a context of armed conflict might be described as a 'woman', 'mother', 'war-widow', 'refugee', 'victim', 'survivor', 'actor', 'citizen' or with reference to her occupation, religion, ethnicity or age (Kaufman and Williams 2007; Moser and Clark 2001; Turshen and Twagiramariya 1998). Any of these categories will capture who she is, but only partly so, as other dimensions are left out. Whatever categorization is selected will have consequences for what we expect from her and how we assess her actions.

Second, studies of gender and violence conflicts propose different *framings* of the analysis, and the framing impacts on what is excluded or included as relevant for understanding gender identities, roles and relationships. One kind of framing is temporal. The typical temporal framework is linear with a distinguishable and sequential 'before', 'during' and 'after' conflict. In conflict theory this model has been challenged and more dynamic alternatives developed, but studies of gender largely continue to describe, compare and assess women's and men's changing status, roles and activities according to this model. Another form of framing is spatial. Here, scholars are emphasizing that even though incidents of violence and conflicts are lived and experienced locally, they are always linked to wider national, transnational and global processes. International actors shape the dynamics of conflict and hence the condition of local lives through political intervention and their supply of emergency assistance and weapons, and local actors access transnational social networks and establish contacts to international organizations in their attempt to improve access to protection, resources and a better future.

The third issue that permeates studies of gender in conflict settings has to do with a study's ultimate *purpose*. Anthropological studies generally aim to provide in-depth ethnographic accounts of how people live violent conflicts, but usually do not engage in normative discussions of how to improve people's lives (Coulter 2006; Ring 2006). This, however, is the driving force in policy-oriented studies that aim to provide humanitarian organizations with information they can use to develop better policies and programs (for example, Bouta et al. 2005). This literature is largely confined by the mandates, categories and assumptions of the organizations, and a common critique is that organizations tend to operate with stereotype understandings of gender identities and roles. A third kind of literature that is also oriented towards change, although of a more radical nature, is the feminist or post-structuralist literature. It is argued that real peace depends on a fundamental transformation of gender identities, roles and relationships (see Lorentzen and Turpin 1998; Mikell 1997). Situations where societal conflicts have escalated are seen as potent windows of opportunities, but transformation is not restricted to such circumstances. Instead, an attempt is made to reveal the occurrence of gendered violence in different contexts and to demonstrate the profound linkages that exist between violence at different levels.

In the remaining sections of this chapter, I present a number of central themes and debates in the field, based on a policy-oriented studies, ethnographic accounts and theoretical deliberations.

28.2   VICTIM AND ACTOR

As mentioned above, it was the replacement of wounded male soldiers with civilian women as the main casualties of violent conflict that made gender an item on the agenda of humanitarian organizations and conflict researchers alike. In the mid-1990s there was a boom in literature documenting how armed conflicts around the world impact on women's lives, resulting in a growing realization that women and men experience conflict and its aftermath differently. One area where gender is observed to make a difference is mobility. Case studies show that men more often than women leave their families and homes behind to join the armed forces or to escape forced recruitment, which adds to the tasks, burdens and responsibilities of their wives. Men are also more likely to be encouraged and supported to go abroad to seek asylum than women, whereas women often outnumber men among internally displaced people. Women can sometimes travel more freely locally, as they are perceived as less threatening, but in some conflicts their mobility is severely restricted to protect the honor and integrity of the family. Another issue that is dealt with extensively in the literature is violence. Women are raped by enemy soldiers, often as a symbolic act of power to humiliate her male relatives, and subjected to trafficking, sex slavery and forced prostitution with serious health consequences (see, for example, Farr et al. 2009; Lentin 1997). At the same time, many women experience an increase in violence in the domestic sphere. The third kind of negative impacts that receives considerable attention is related to women's economic and social livelihoods. Destruction of infrastructure, diminishing security, decreasing availability of goods and rising prices together with a reduction of a household's (male) labor force adds to a woman's hardships, as she assumes main responsibility for providing for the family. Violent conflicts typically result in deteriorating standards of nutrition and hygiene, and an increase in communicable diseases, which affects women in particular. As these examples illustrate, the literature that comes out from the mid-1990s is occupied with documenting how the new wars directly affect women's lives, and soon women are turned into 'vulnerable victims' which legitimizes humanitarian interventions.

Troubled by the passive role of women that the above categorization entails, an effort is now made to demonstrate that women are also capable, resourceful and creative actors. Women engage in trade, business and agriculture in new ways and become the new breadwinners; they establish and run health and education facilities; organize and engage in local informal peacebuilding activities; and generally play a key role in the social reproduction of family and community. Women's responses and activities are often presented as examples of coping mechanisms and self-help strategies, which accentuates their traditional roles as wives and mothers, and a close affiliation with the (female) domestic sphere. Experiences show, however, that women are transgressing gender boundaries and take up what is traditionally conceived of as typical male activities, including combat and torture, and become increasingly visible in public space and interact more frequently with the authorities (Ali-Ali 2007; Moser and Clark 2001). While such accounts demonstrate that women's roles change during violent conflicts and that they are actors with multiple responsibilities, they do not really challenge the essentialized understanding of gender identities and the prevailing association of female with the domestic, and male with the public sphere. Nor do they necessarily demonstrate how gender is constructed socially or how other markers of identity and status such as class, ethnicity, race or age contribute to the creating of huge and important differences within the categories of 'men' and 'women'. The discussion of whether women are victims or actors, and efforts to conceptually get beyond this dichotomy is central to much of the literature on gender and violent conflict.

28.3   PUBLIC AND PRIVATE DOMAINS

The discussion of gender identities and roles has partly been taken forward as a critique of the common distinction between the public and the private spheres, considering male and female domains, respectively, which influence both popular understandings and policies (Youngs 2009). In relation to violence, the distinction sometimes implies that violence against women that takes place in the domestic sphere or perpetrated by close relatives is not fully recognized by the authorities, just as certain aspects of reproductive health may be considered a private matter. However, state and other actors in a conflict may also seek to control women's bodies as they are important symbols of the nation and necessary for procreation. Such interventions illustrate the blurred boundaries between public and private. The gendered definitions of the public and private spheres have also been contested from an economic point of view. In many conflicts women make a significant contribution in the health and education sectors. Others often see this as a natural extension of a woman's reproductive and nurturing domestic roles and capacities. This typically means that she receives no or less remuneration, and that she is excluded from capacity-building initiatives. It is also documented that women are more often occupied in the informal economy, where there is less security, regulation and where the pay is lower. Although women can earn an income, it also adds to their vulnerability. A similar pattern of marginalization in society is found when it comes to peace negotiations and peacebuilding, as women are generally not invited to participate in formal processes. Their association with the domestic sphere separates them from the political arena. However, women living in conflicts have repeatedly shown their political interests and capacities, as they have established civil society organizations that have lobbied for public recognition of so-called 'private matters'; organized relief in support of marginalized and needy groups; and challenged state authorities to be more accountable and respectful of human rights. Research shows that while it does make sense to distinguish between a public and a private sphere, they should not be seen as hierarchical and the linkages between them are important to acknowledge in order to challenge gender inequalities.

28.4   MILITARIZATION OF SOCIAL LIFE

The interest in militarization is relatively recent and an attempt to understand the social processes that support violent conflicts (see, for example, Ali-Ali and Pratt 2009; Enloe 2000). By implication, it is also an attempt to enhance our understanding of how women are involved in violent conflicts, not only as victims or actors who assist people and communities to cope and recover, but also as direct and indirect supporters of violent conflict. Militarization is commonly viewed as the process through which the military take ascendancy over civilian institutions and as a particular ideology that influences our thoughts. Militarization is highly gendered and builds on ideas of femininity and masculinity, which are learned and disseminated in the family, school and wider society. The most explicit example of militarization is the introduction of checkpoints, surveillance and strict regulations of mobility, which in the name of security subject men and women to different kinds of control and install the anticipation of violence. Women may be complicit in the militarization of society and its normalization in many and subtler ways than joining the army as soldiers. Mothers' socialization of their sons and daughters may include playing wargames, playing with toy guns, watching films and staging role plays with warriors and heroes, but also conveying certain gendered attitudes of being tough, enduring hardships and respecting authorities, which are all important aspects of militarization. In schools, too, many social practices bear a strong resemblance to military practices such as marching, uniforms and hoisting the national flag. In times of violent conflict the two institutions come even closer, as schoolchildren may be expected to perform ceremonies in support of their soldiers and in honor of dead heroes, or even be trained in handling weapons. It is often pointed out that the moral support that soldiers' wives and mothers extend to their husbands and sons, by keeping the home in order and keeping up appearances, is crucial. It not only sustains the individual soldier, however, but also gives legitimacy to his actions and the cause he is fighting for. The military acknowledges this when they give their support to voluntary networks of close relatives. Women, just like men, also lend some kind of support to militarization as employees in the weapons industry, and in the economic and social sectors that service the military in different ways. Through a focus on militarization, scholars have shown how violent conflicts and wars seep into ordinary everyday life, become normalized and constitute a particular sociality. From this perspective, the men and women who are spectators of public commemorative ceremonies, consume daily news reports from the front, and watch their children play wargames, are as important for our understanding of gender and violent conflicts as are the male and female soldiers and refugees. Interestingly, this perspective also brings to the foreground the similarities that exist among different violent conflicts and wars, which the focus on ethnicity, religion has tended to conceal in its radical othering.

28.5   GENDER, STATE AND POLITICAL PARTICIPATION

The modern nation-state plays a central role in many internal violent conflicts, and derecognition of certain social or ethnic groups, discriminatory policies, the lack of capacity or will to protect people and abuse of power constitute important contributory factors. Feminist scholars point out that the state is gendered, and it generally favors masculinity and the male population (Lister 1997 [2003]; Thiruchandran 1999). Laws regulating mobility, marriage, ownership and inheritance, employment, criminality and justice, and political representation and participation, policies regulating the distribution of resources, and the nation-state's reliance on war and security as founding principle, are all gendered and tend to marginalize women in so far as they take a male perspective. Women in conflict situations daily experience the consequences, and engage in activities that either supplement or challenge and oppose the state. When women organize community-based health facilities and education activities, they in fact take over some of the state's responsibilities, and many states rely on the voluntary social work of its citizens. Labor migration is another state-supporting activity, and remittances constitute a significant economic resource. One way in which women contest the state is through women's organizations that use the women's moral authority as mothers and demand that the state is held accountable for the killings, displacements and disappearances that have affected their families.

A different kind of contestation lies in women's participation in formal peace initiatives. There is considerable debate about whether women are more peace-loving than men due to their reproductive roles, but it is more relevant to explore exactly what resources and potentials women in different conflict situations have for supporting peace and reconciliation (see, for example, Mazurana and Kay 1999). In some contexts they creatively build on traditional social or religious practices and roles and their inherent authority, while in others they adopt new strategies and establish non-governmental organizations (NGOs) that have power from being part of an international network with access to a powerful discourse and external resources. The critical question is to what extent such informal initiatives are linked to or able to inform more the formal processes that are the basis of political agreements and policy decisions. Contrary to the perception of women as belonging to the domestic, non-political sphere, women generally become increasingly involved in politics during violent conflicts. That is because they have to take on new responsibilities and have more contacts with authorities, and because their life is severely affected by conflict. Research suggests that while women may initially focus on matters that are close to their personal life, they gradually develop a broader agenda and often one that focuses on social justice. While women do play an active role in what is commonly referred to as 'civil society', they are underrepresented in formal political parties and governments, and many efforts are made to increase their numbers, assuming that not only will these bodies become more representative, but they will also take up women's issues more systematically. However, this perspective reproduces an essentialized understanding of gender and neglects that women are a highly heterogeneous group, and assumes that women will automatically take up women's concerns. Many recent studies suggest a slightly different approach by focusing more on the state-building process itself and on the relationship between state and citizens. Such a perspective escapes the rigid opposition between women and men and the homogenization of each group, and directs its focus toward the legal and moral obligations of the nation-state. Although critical, this approach also makes it possible to reframe women's demands for accountability and claims for recognition as a constructive effort to strengthen the capacities of the state to be more inclusive and just. And significantly, it takes a transformative approach to the future, asking what kind of states and societies we want to develop.

28.6   CONCLUSION

The documentation of women's and men's experiences of violent conflicts has helped to generate a better understanding of how deeply a conflict reaches into people's everyday lives and into the fundamental structures and values of a society. And the documentation of women's and men's activities during and after conflict is a testimony of the resilience and creativity that exist, but also witnesses that people are greatly concerned about and willing to engage in the reconfiguration of the modern nation-state despite the risks it entails. For women this work implies getting recognized as citizens and political actors, who have a right and a duty to contribute equally to the development of their society and state.

The literature on gender and violent conflict has continued to grow over the past 15 years and it is an impossible task to do justice to this in such a short chapter as the present. It is also impossible to develop a general conclusion regarding the status of gender in violent conflicts, as the experiences are many and diverse. So let me conclude, instead, by suggesting some aspects that need further scholarly attention.

First, we know that violent conflicts empower some and disempower others, and that the post-conflict period may alter the situation fundamentally. While gender and power does have a significant impact on these processes, it is also clear that factors such as generation, class, religion and ethnicity are equally important and sometimes even more so. Anthropological studies of particular social communities demonstrate the dynamics of identity and status in everyday life and thus challenge stereotypical categories and give emphasis to lived experiences and the heterogeneity and complexity of life.

Second, studies of violent conflicts have obviously tended to focus on the war zones themselves and the categories of people they generate. There is a need for more studies of the interaction between different actors and how they mutually constitute each other. In relation to gender, there is now an abundance of studies on women, while men who do not belong to the groups of combatants, child soldiers or demobilized soldiers are often overlooked as are the non-military aspects of their lives. There is also a need to expand the field geographically. Important research is already being carried out in relation to migration and remittances and to some extent also on humanitarian assistance and NGOs. More difficult, but no less important would be issues such as trafficking, private businesses, and the weapons industry, which also influence the dynamics of local conflicts and the potentials people have for coping with these.

Third, researchers have focused on the eruption and escalation of conflicts that so severely disrupt the livelihoods of people, but perhaps it is the post-conflict situation that is the most critical. It is at this moment when important choices about future social structures and decisions about governance are made, that a transformation of gender identities and roles must be addressed, in the context of establishing social justice, human rights and equality for all groups.

29 Complex power sharing
Stefan Wolff

29.1 INTRODUCTION

The democratic governance of divided societies can pose particular challenges. This well-rehearsed mantra among students of ethnic conflict and conflict settlement has its origins in John Stuart Mill's scepticism of even the possibility of democracy 'in a country made up of different nationalities' (Mill 1861 [1962], p. 230), as well as in empirically observable violent ethnic conflict around the globe. Yet, while ethnic diversity is the predominant demographic rule in most countries today, violent ethnic conflict remains the exception. Thus, diversity need not inevitably result in either prolonged violent ethnic conflict or the break-up of existing states. Rather, existing literature on the subject offers both normative accounts of the desirability, and empirical evidence of the feasibility, of designing institutional frameworks within which disputes between different conflict parties can be accommodated to such an extent that political compromise becomes preferable to violent struggle, at least for the majority of parties involved in the conflict in question. The flipside of this argument is that 'it is . . . in divided societies that institutional arrangements have the greatest impact [and that] institutional design can systematically favour or disadvantage ethnic, national, and religious groups' (Belmont et al. 2002, p. 3). Consequently, while there is agreement that institutions matter because they can provide the context in which differences can be accommodated and managed in a non-violent, political way, the existing literature on conflict settlement *qua* institutional design offers no consensus view about which are the most suitable institutions to achieve this. This debate about how to design institutions to achieve sustainable peace in divided societies has engulfed the theory and practice of ethnic conflict resolution for more than four decades, and has mainly been fought between advocates of consociationalism and their opponents. The disagreements between them have not subsided over the years and remain as divisive as ever.

In the context of this contribution, three main schools of thought are of particular relevance: centripetalism, consociationalism and power dividing. They offer a range of distinct prescriptions on how to ensure that differences of identity do not translate into violence. In this sense, they are both realistic about the fact that differences of identity exist and can create politically relevant and salient cleavages (that is, divided societies) and optimistic about the possibility that such cleavages can be managed by accommodating distinct identities and the demands they give rise to (see Horowitz 2002; McGarry and O'Leary 2004a). In so doing, they often go beyond 'politics at the centre' and hold views on territorial dimensions of ethnic conflict settlement as well. While the latter are not central to the following exploration, the three main schools of thought that will be discussed cannot be completely understood without reference to their territorial preferences, and these will thus form part of the discussion below as necessary. Using very broad conceptualizations of the three main schools' approaches, and in fact the determination that there are in fact three such schools, cannot but be a convenient shorthand for analytical purposes that glosses over the diversity of approaches within each school. Limitations of length further necessitate that I shall concentrate on what I believe are the main proponents of particular approaches, rather than offer a full-length intellectual history of each school of thought. Following a brief section outlining the main challenges to institutional design in divided societies, I shall treat centripetalism, power sharing and power dividing in separate sections, summarizing the main tenets of each and paying particular attention to their prescriptions for divided societies. As the three schools are critical of each other, and as critics of one are normally proponents of another, I shall not devote much space to a critique of each individual approach. Rather, I shall use a concluding section comparing the three schools to one another and showing their limitations as theories of conflict settlement against a new practice of conflict settlement that is best described as complex power sharing, and eclipses the much narrower approaches taken by each school of thought individually.

29.2   INSTITUTIONAL DESIGN IN DIVIDED SOCIETIES

Advocating the settlement of self-determination conflicts through institutional design assumes that such conflicts can be addressed through an institutional bargain that establishes macro-level structures through which micro-level incentives are provided to elites (and their supporters). This is a rational choice approach to institutions that presumes that institutions are chosen and will be stable when the actors involved in them have – and will continue to have – an incentive to adhere to them and, thus, 'reproduce' them. In other words, one needs to distinguish between incentive structures, that is, the macro-level frameworks that allow for incentives to be enjoyed by elites and their supporters in a predictable and repetitive way, and the incentives themselves. From this perspective, centripetalism, consociationalism, power dividing and other conflict resolution mechanisms prescribe the macro-level structures which provide incentives such as power, status, security, economic gain, and so on. The stability of these macro-level structures, from a rational choice perspective, depends on both the general desirability of the incentives they provide and whether these incentives can be gained through alternative arrangements. If the incentives provided are desirable and cannot be gained otherwise, existing arrangements would appear to be acceptable and their maintenance desirable, and they would thus be likely to be stable.

As far as conflict settlement in divided societies is concerned, institutional design of macro-level structures needs to address three broad sets of issues.

First, the question of the state's overall construction needs to be decided, and here the most important institutional design challenge has to do with the territorial organization of the state. While the principal choice is generally between unitary and federal systems, there is a great deal of variation within these two main categories, and there are a number of hybrid forms as well. Further choices in this area relate to the number of (federal) units and the degree to which these should be ethnically homogeneous or heterogeneous.

Second, several questions in the relationship between the different branches of government need to be addressed, including the nature of the government system, that is, whether it is a parliamentary, presidential or semi-presidential system. A second dimension is the issue of whether executive power sharing is mandatory, and if so, what is the extent of prescribed inclusiveness. Inclusiveness, at the same time, is also an important feature of legislative design and is primarily realized through the choice of an electoral system. A final issue in this regard is the overall relationship between the three institutions of government, that is, the degree of separation of powers between them. While this partially relates to the choice of government system (see above), it is also about the degree of independence of the judicial branch and its powers of legislative and executive oversight.

A third set of issues concerns the relationship between individual citizens, identity groups and the state. Institutional design in this area is about the recognition and protection of different identities by the state. This relates to human and minority rights legislation, that is, the degree to which every citizen's individual human rights are protected, including civil and political rights, as well as the extent to which the rights of different identity groups are recognized and protected. While there may be a certain degree of tension between them, such as between a human rights prerogative of equality and non-discrimination and a minority rights approach emphasizing differential treatment and affirmative action, the two are not contradictory but need to complement each other in ways that reflect the diversity of divided societies and contribute to its peaceful accommodation.

While it is important analytically to treat these three areas separately, it is equally important to bear in mind that institutions in practice work as a package; that is, they 'interact in complex ways' (Belmont et al. 2002, p. 4). Thus, while it may be possible to make a theoretically valid argument about the utility of using the single transferable vote (STV) as an electoral system to induce moderation among politicians, district magnitude and local ethnic demography can easily 'conspire' against such an outcome (see Wolff 2005). What matters, therefore, is that different dimensions of institutional design fit each other to enable overall outcomes that are conducive to lasting peace in divided societies.

29.3 INSTITUTIONAL DESIGN IN EXISTING THEORIES OF CONFLICT RESOLUTION

Existing theories of conflict resolution generally acknowledge the importance and usefulness of institutional design in conflict resolution, but offer rather different prescriptions as to the most appropriate models to achieve stable conflict settlements. Three such theories are of particular significance as they speak directly to the three areas of institutional design identified above: power sharing in the form of its liberal consociational variant, centripetalism, and power dividing. Discussing the main tenets of these three sets of theories now in turn, I focus on their recommendations in each of the three areas of institutional design outlined above, but cannot, for reasons of space, claim either to offer a comprehensive examination of these theories or to assess how practically feasible or morally justifiable they are.

29.3.1 Liberal Consociationalism

The term 'consociational democracy' has been most closely associated with the work of Arend Lijphart, as well as more recently with that of John McGarry and Brendan O'Leary. Lijphart began to examine this particular type of democratic system in greater detail for the first time in the late 1960s, when making reference to the political systems of Scandinavian countries and of the Netherlands and Belgium (Lijphart 1968). He followed up with further studies of political stability in cases of severely socially fragmented societies, eventually leading to his groundbreaking work *Democracy in*

Plural Societies (Lijphart 1977). The phenomenon Lijphart was describing, however, was not new. As a pattern of social structure, characterizing a society fragmented by religious, linguistic, ideological or other cultural segmentation, it had existed and been studied (albeit not as extensively) long before the 1960s. These structural aspects, studied among others by Lorwin (1971), were not the primary concern of Lijphart, who was more interested in why, despite their fragmentation, such societies maintained a stable political process, and identified the behaviour of political elites as the main, but not the only, reason for stability. Furthermore, Lijphart (1977, pp. 25–52) identified four features shared by consociational systems – a grand coalition government (between parties from different segments of society), segmental autonomy (in the cultural sector), proportionality (in the voting system and in public sector employment) and minority veto. These characteristics, more or less prominently, were exhibited by all the classic examples of consociationalism: Lebanon, Cyprus, Switzerland, Austria, the Netherlands, Belgium, Fiji and Malaysia. With some of these consociations having succeeded, such as in Switzerland, Austria, the Netherlands and Belgium, and others having failed, such as Lebanon, Cyprus, Fiji and Malaysia, Lijphart also established conditions conducive to consociational democracy. These included overarching, that is, territorial, loyalties, a small number of political parties in each segment, about equal size of the different segments, and the existence of some cross-cutting cleavages with otherwise segmental isolation. The small size of the territory to which a consociational structure is applied and the direct and indirect internal and external consequences of this, as well as a tradition of compromise among political elites are also emphasized by Lijphart as conditions enhancing the stability of the consociational settlement (ibid., pp. 53–103).

Of course, Lijphart's assumptions and prescriptions did not go unchallenged. He and other advocates of consociational approaches to ethnic conflict settlement responded in two ways – by offering a robust defence of their views and by gradually developing consociational theory further. Lijphart himself engaged his critics most comprehensively in his book *Power Sharing in South Africa* (Lijphart 1985, pp. 83–117) and in his contribution to Andrew Reynolds's *The Architecture of Democracy* (Lijphart 2002, pp. 39–45). In the latter, he also offers a substantive revision of his original approach, now describing power sharing and autonomy (that is, grand coalition government and segmental autonomy) as 'primary characteristics', while proportionality and minority veto are relegated to 'secondary characteristics' (ibid., p. 39). Yet, in relation to his grand coalition requirement, Lijphart maintains his earlier position that such executive power sharing means 'participation of representatives of all significant groups in political decision making' (ibid., p. 41).

Subsequent developments of consociational theory, especially by John McGarry and Brendan O'Leary (McGarry 2006; McGarry and O'Leary 2004a, 2004b, 2006a, 2006b) have made one important modification in particular in this respect. O'Leary contends that 'grand coalition' (in the sense of an executive encompassing all leaders of all significant parties of all significant communities) is not a necessary criterion; rather, he demonstrates that what matters for a democratic consociation 'is meaningful cross-community executive power sharing in which each significant segment is represented in the government with at least plurality levels of support within its segment' (O'Leary 2005a, p. 13).

In order to appreciate fully the current state of consociational theory, it is useful to examine McGarry and O'Leary's (2004b) *The Northern Ireland Conflict: Consociational Engagements* (a collection of their joint and individual writings on this conflict from 1987 to 2002), in particular its co-authored introduction on the lessons that Northern Ireland holds for consociational theory more broadly. Northern Ireland and its 1998 Agreement, McGarry and O'Leary maintain, 'highlights six important weaknesses in traditional consociational theory' (McGarry and O'Leary 2004a, p. 5). These are the neglect of external actors; the trans-state nature of some self-determination disputes and the necessary institutional arrangements to address them; the increasing complexity of conflict settlements in which consociational arrangements form an important element but require complementary mechanisms to deal with 'the design of the police, demilitarization, the return of exiles to their homes, the management of prisoners, education reform, economic policy, and the promotion of language and other group rights' (ibid., p. 13); terminological and conceptual inaccuracies, primarily associated with Lijphart's grand coalition requirement; the merits of preferential proportional electoral systems, that is, STV; and the allocation of cabinet positions by means of sequential proportionality rules, that is, the d'Hondt mechanism. In dealing with these weaknesses, McGarry and O'Leary offer both refinements of, and advancements to, traditional consociational theory. The refinements relate, first, to the technical side of consociational institutions, where the authors recommend STV instead of List-PR (proportional representation) as an electoral system as it militates against the proliferation of micro parties. Second, McGarry and O'Leary elaborate the usefulness of sequential proportionality rules, such as the d'Hondt mechanism or the Sainte-Laguë method, in the allocation of cabinet positions in order to avoid protracted bargaining between parties and increase parties' incentives to remain part of cross-communal coalitions.

The advancements to traditional consociational theory offered here, as well as elsewhere in their recent writings (for example, McGarry 2006;

O'Leary 2005a), are a significant step forward in that they address both longstanding criticisms of consociationalism and a gap between consociational theory and conflict resolution practice. McGarry's and O'Leary's observations on external actors bring consociational theory in line with an established debate in international relations on the role of third parties in conflict resolution (see, for example, contributions in Carment and Schnabel 2003; Diehl and Lepgold 2003; Otunnu and Doyle 1998; Pugh and Singh Sidhu 2003; Thakur and Schnabel 2001; van Houten and Wolff 2007; Walter and Snyder 1999; Wolff and Weller 2008). Equally importantly, their discussion of the provisions in the 1998 Agreement that go beyond domestic institutions and address the specific 'Irish dimension' of the Northern Ireland conflict reflect a growing awareness among scholars and practitioners of conflict resolution that many ethnic conflicts have causes and consequences beyond the boundaries of the states in which they occur and that for settlements to be durable and stable, these dimensions need addressing as well. In the case of the 1998 Agreement for Northern Ireland, McGarry and O'Leary highlight three dimensions: cross-border institutions which formalize cooperation between the Northern Ireland Executive and the Irish government (the so-called North–South Ministerial Council) and renew British-Irish inter-governmental cooperation (the British-Irish Inter-governmental Conference); the explicit recognition of the two governments of the right to self-determination of the people in Northern Ireland and the Republic, that is, the possibility for them to bring about, in separate referenda, a united Ireland if that is the wish of respective majorities; and new institutions of regional cooperation, incorporating the UK and Irish governments, and the executive organs of the other two devolved regions in the UK and its three dependent island territories in the Channel and the Irish Sea.

These arrangements have earlier precedents in the history of conflict settlement in Northern Ireland, but they are not unique to this case alone. Institutions of cross-border cooperation have been utilized as part of comprehensive peace settlements elsewhere as well – for example, in South Tyrol, and Bosnia and Herzegovina – and exist, of course, in less conflict-prone situations as part of arrangements between sovereign states and/or substate entities – for example, in the EU's Euro regions. The EU itself, at the same time, is one of the most successful cases of regional integration (albeit among 'equal' partners at the state or substate level), while the Nordic Council offers arrangements similar to the British–Irish Council in bringing together sovereign states and self-governing territories within them (see Danspeckgruber 2005).

As far as the possibility of future status changes is concerned, this, too, is not unique to Northern Ireland or indeed the 1998 Agreement.

In recent Northern Ireland history, a so-called border poll took place in 1973 but was near-completely boycotted by Nationalists and Republicans. There had also been an initial British commitment to hold such polls in 10-year intervals, but this was unceremoniously and quietly abandoned. Farther afield, the people of the Autonomous Republic of Gagauzia in Moldova have a one-time opportunity to exercise their right to (external) self-determination if Moldova were to join Romania. The Comprehensive Peace Agreement for Sudan offers the people in the South a referendum on independence after six years, while the Bougainville Peace Agreement includes a clause that envisages a referendum on independence to be held in Bougainville after 10–15 years. Crucially, in all these situations and including Northern Ireland, the signatory parties have committed to respecting the outcome of these referenda.

A final, and perhaps the most significant, advancement of consociational theory is McGarry and O'Leary's contention that Lijphart's grand coalition requirement is overstated, as 'what makes consociations feasible and work is joint consent across the significant communities, with the emphasis on jointness' (McGarry and O'Leary 2004a, p. 15). On that basis, they distinguish 'unanimous consociations (grand coalitions), concurrent consociations (in which the executive has majority support in each significant segment) and weak consociations (where the executive may have only a plurality level of support amongst one or more segments)'. Jointness, more generally, implies equality and cooperation across blocs and some genuine consent among the relevant mass publics for a democratic consociation and thus excludes just any coalition, as well as cooptation of unrepresentative minority 'leaders'.

The more recent writings by Lijphart, McGarry and O'Leary also indicate a clear move from corporate towards liberal consociational power sharing. The main difference between the two is that a 'corporate consociation accommodates groups according to ascriptive criteria, and rests on the assumption that group identities are fixed, and that groups are both internally homogeneous and externally bounded', while 'liberal . . . consociation . . . rewards whatever salient political identities emerge in democratic elections, whether these are based on ethnic groups, or on sub-group or trans-group identities' (McGarry 2006, p. 3; see also Lijphart 1995; O'Leary 2005a). This is another important modification of consociational theory that addresses one of its more profound, and empirically more valid, criticisms, namely that (corporate) consociations further entrench and institutionalize pre-existing, and often conflict-hardened, ethnic identities, thus decreasing the incentives for elites to moderate (see, for example, Horowitz 1985, pp. 566–76; 1991, pp. 167f.f; 2003, p. 119).

Territorial self-governance is an accepted feature within the liberal consociational approach emphasizing that the self-governing territory should define itself from the bottom up, rather than be prescribed top down. Liberal consociationalists also support the principle of asymmetric devolution of powers, that is, the possibility for some self-governing entities to enjoy more (or fewer) competences than others, depending on the preferences of their populations (see McGarry 2007). However, self-governance needs to be complemented with what liberal consociationalists term 'shared rule', that is, the exercise of power at and by the centre and across the state as a whole. While grand coalitions, proportionality and minority veto rights continue to be favoured by liberal consociationalists, the emphasis is on cooperation and consensus among democratically legitimized elites, regardless of whether they emerge on the basis of group identities, ideology or other common interest. They thus favour parliamentary systems, proportional (List-PR) or proportional preferential (STV) electoral systems, decision-making procedures that require qualified and/or concurrent majorities, and have also advocated, at times, the application of the d'Hondt rule for the formation of executives (see Lijphart 2004; O'Leary 2005a; see also Wolff 2003).

This means that liberal consociationalists prefer what O'Leary refers to as 'pluralist federations' in which co-sovereign substate and central governments have clearly defined exclusive competences (albeit with the possibility of some concurrent competences) whose assignment to either level of authority is constitutionally and, ideally, internationally, protected, in which decision making at the centre is consensual (between self-governing entities and the centre, and among elites representing different interest groups), and which recognize, and protect the presence of different self-determined identities (O'Leary 2005b). This preference for pluralist federations, however, remains context dependent, and is not *per se* part of liberal consociational thinking. In some circumstances, for example, where ethnic communities are not ethnonational (that is, demanding their own governance institutions), it is quite possible that a unitary state with power sharing at the centre will suffice as a mechanism to settle conflicts.

In order to protect individuals against the abuse of powers by majorities at the state level or the level of self-governing entities, liberal consociationalism offers two remedies – the replication of its core institutional prescriptions within the self-governing entity, and the establishment and enforcement of strong human and minority rights regimes both at the state and substate levels. In addition, the rights of communities – minorities and majorities alike – are best protected in a liberal consociational system if its key provisions are enshrined in the constitution and if the interpretation and upholding of the constitution is left to an independent and representative constitutional court whose decisions are binding on executive and legislature (ibid., pp. 55–8).

Key to liberal consociational prescriptions of institutional design in divided societies is, therefore, the emphasis on the protection of self-determined (rather than predetermined) identity groups through ensuring both their representation and effective participation in decision making, especially in the legislature and executive. The underlying assumption here is that representation and participation together will ensure that different identity groups recognize that their aims can be achieved, and interests protected, by political means and do not require recourse to violence.

29.3.2   Centripetalism

Centripetalism emphasizes that rather than designing rigid institutions in which elected representatives have to work together after elections, 'intergroup political accommodation' is achieved by 'electoral systems that provide incentives for parties to form coalitions across group lines or in other ways moderate their ethnocentric political behaviour' Horowitz (2004, pp. 507–8). This school of thought is most prominently associated with the work of Donald Horowitz (1985, 1990, 1991, 2002), as well as with that of Timothy D. Sisk (1996), Matthijs Bogaards (1998, 2000, 2003), Benjamin Reilly (1997, 2001, 2006) and Andreas Wimmer (2003).

Horowitz remains the standard-setting centripetalist scholar, and his work will be analysed in more detail below. However, it is worth noting significant contributions by other authors as well. Reilly has developed an explicit theory of centripetalism, emphasizing that, in practice, centripetalism tries to encourage, among others,

> (i) *electoral incentives* for campaigning politicians to reach out to and attract votes from a range of ethnic groups other than their own . . . (ii) *arenas of bargaining*, under which political actors from different groups have an incentive to come together to negotiate and bargain in the search for cross-partisan and cross-ethnic vote-pooling deals . . . and (iii) *centrist, aggregative political parties* or coalitions which seek multi-ethnic support . . . (Reilly 2001, p. 11, emphasis in original)

The empirical evidence offered in support of the utility of centripetal mechanisms in his 2001 volume was focused primarily on Papua New Guinea, while a much broader study published in 2006 was based on a wider variety of cases across Asia–Pacific. On this basis, Reilly (2006, p. 171) concluded:

The limited use to date of explicit power sharing requirements, the troubled experiments with grand coalition cabinets in Indonesia and Fiji, and the strong association of such practices with political instability, all underscore aversion towards consociational measures. By contrast, informal power sharing approaches, in which political inclusion is a result of deal-making rather than law, appears to have become successfully institutionalised in a number of cases.

An attempt to apply in practice centripetalist conclusions about which institutional designs can provide lasting peace and stability in divided societies is Wimmer's proposals for the post-war constitution of Iraq. He recommends introducing 'an electoral system that fosters moderation and accommodation across the ethnic divides', including a requirement for the 'most powerful elected official . . . to be the choice not only of a majority of the population, but of states or provinces of the country, too', the use of the alternative vote (AV) procedure, and a political party law demanding that 'all parties contesting elections . . . be organised in a minimum number of provinces' (Wimmer 2003, p. 122). In addition, Wimmer advocates non-ethnic federation, at least in the sense that there should be more federal entities than ethnic groups, even if a majority of those entities would be more or less ethnically homogeneous or be dominated by one ethnic group. Furthermore, 'a strong minority rights regime at the central level, a powerful independent judiciary system and effective enforcement mechanisms are needed', according to Wimmer (ibid., p. 125).

In what remains a classic work in the field of ethnic conflict and conflict resolution theories, Donald L. Horowitz (1985) discusses a range of structural techniques and preferential policies to reduce ethnic conflict. Among them, he emphasizes that 'the most potent way to assure that federalism or autonomy will not become just a step to secession is to reinforce those specific interests that groups have in the undivided state' (ibid., p. 628). Horowitz also makes an explicit case for federation in his proposals for constitutional design in post-apartheid South Africa (Horowitz 1991, pp. 214–26) and argues, not dissimilar to power-dividing advocates, for federation based on ethnically heterogeneous entities. In a later study, more explicitly focused on federation as a mechanism for conflict reduction, Horowitz (2007) accepts that homogeneous provinces, too, can prove useful for this purpose, but argues that rather than the aim being to facilitate group autonomy (the consociational rationale), homogeneous provinces offer the possibility to foster intra-group competition (ibid., pp. 960–61; see also Horowitz 2008, p. 1218). In an earlier contribution to the debate, Horowitz had recognized the need for federal or autonomy provisions, but cautioned that they could only contribute to mitigating secessionist demands if '[c]ombined with policies that give regionally concentrated groups a strong stake in the centre' (Horowitz 1993, p. 36).

Similar to Wimmer, Horowitz, citing the Nigerian experience, sees utility in splitting large ethnic groups into several provinces as this potentially encourages the proliferation of political parties within one ethnic group resulting in intra-group competition and a lessened impact of relative numerical superiority of one group over others.

While centripetalism is thus open to engaging with, among others, territorial approaches to conflict settlement, 'its principal tool is . . . the provision of incentives, usually *electoral incentives*, that accord an advantage to ethnically based parties that are willing to appeal, at the margin and usually through coalition partners of other ethnic groups, to voters other than their own' (Horowitz 2008, p. 1217, my emphasis). In particular, Horowitz emphasizes the utility of electoral systems that are most likely to produce a Condorcet winner, that is, a candidate who would have been victorious in a two-way contest with every other candidate in a given constituency. The most prominent such electoral system is the AV, a preferential majoritarian electoral system, that is said to induce moderation among parties and their candidates as they require electoral support from beyond their own ethnic group in heterogeneous, single-seat constituencies (Horowitz 2003, pp. 122–5). However, the intended benefits are not always forthcoming, nor are the consequences of the introduction of electoral systems that aim to encourage moderation through inter-ethnic vote pooling always and only the benign ones sought. Horowitz admits that 'there has sometimes been deterioration of interethnic harmony, or the durability of accommodative institutions, or the quality of democracy' (Horowitz 2008, p. 1223), but as the debate between him and Fraenkel and Grofman on the case of Fiji and the use of the AV more generally indicates (Fraenkel and Grofman 2004, 2006; Horowitz 2004, 2006), there is little if any common ground between those who advocate centrepetalist strategies in conflict resolution and those who doubt their utility. The only modest consensus that does seem to exist between the different schools of thought is that preferential electoral systems, majoritarian or proportional, offer benefits in the context of conflict resolution that non-preferential systems cannot provide, that is, they offer at least the theoretical possibility, under context-specific circumstances, that moderation and a degree of inter-ethnic cooperation can be induced.

The debate on electoral systems is also apparent in arguments about whether divided societies are served better by a presidential or a parliamentarian system. The debate here is primarily about whether presidential systems heighten divisiveness. Among consociationalists, Lijphart is an exemplary defender of the parliamentary system, while McGarry and O'Leary accept that especially collective, or multi-member, presidencies can be useful in mitigating divisions, thereby extending consociational principles to presidential systems. For Horowitz, on the other hand, it is the electoral system that is crucial in determining whether the president's is a uniting or dividing election and office, and he argues for an electoral system 'that ensures broadly distributed support for the president' (Horowitz 1990, p. 76). Citing Nigeria and Sri Lanka as examples, Horowitz offers two different ways of achieving the election of a president with such broadly distributed support: a combination of total votes cast and votes cast in individual states (Nigerian federation) or a version of AV in which the two top candidates (those with the highest number of first preference votes) would be put into an instant run-off second round in which lower-order preferences cast for eliminated candidates would be redistributed until one of the two top candidates had an overall majority.

In summary of the centripetalist approach, then, it is clear that conflict reduction is to be achieved through inducing inter-ethnic cooperation before and at the polls rather than after elections. This idea permeates centripetalist institutional choices throughout: in relation to the structure and organization of the state as a whole (for example, federal versus unitary designs); with regard to the composition and powers of the executive, legislative and judicial branches of government and the relationship between them (for example, parliamentary versus presidential systems); and when it comes to the relationship between individual citizens, identity groups and the state (for example, the degree to which specific groups are to enjoy particular privileges).

29.3.3 Power Dividing

Power dividing, as put forward by Philip Roeder and the late Donald Rothchild in their co-edited volume *Sustainable Peace: Power and Democracy after Civil Wars* (Roeder and Rothchild 2005b), is the latest contribution to the debate over the utility of different approaches to institutional design in divided societies. For a better appreciation of what distinguishes the theory of power dividing from that of (consociational) power sharing and centripetalism, I shall focus in the following primarily on the conceptual chapters in Roeder and Rothchild's volume as the so far most comprehensive treatment of power dividing.

Roeder and Rothchild's main finding is that power sharing is a useful short-term mechanism to overcome commitment problems that may prevent conflict parties in the immediate aftermath of civil wars to agree to and stick with a peace settlement, but that it is detrimental to peace and stability in the long term. Instead, Roeder and Rothchild recommend power dividing as an alternative strategy to manage conflict in ethnically (or otherwise) divided societies. Predicated on the distinction of three types of democracy – Westminster majoritarianism, consociational super-majoritarianism, and power-dividing multiple majoritarianism – power dividing is seen as 'an overlooked alternative to majoritarian democracy and power sharing' as institutional options in ethnically divided societies (ibid, p. 6). Three strategies that are said to be central to power dividing – civil liberties, multiple majorities, and checks and balances – in practice result in an allocation of power between government and civil society such that 'strong, enforceable civil liberties . . . take many responsibilities out of the hands of government', while those that are left there are distributed 'among separate, independent organs that represent alternative, cross-cutting majorities', thus 'balanc[ing] one decisionmaking centre against another so as to check each majority . . . [f]or the most important issues that divide ethnic groups, but must be decided by a government common to all ethnic groups' (ibid., p. 15).

The key institutional instruments by which power dividing is meant to be realized are, first, extensive human rights bills that are meant to leave 'key decisions to the private sphere and civil society' (ibid., p. 6). Second, separation of powers between the branches of government and a range of specialized agencies dealing with specific, and clearly delimited, policy areas are to create multiple and changing majorities, thus 'increas[ing] the likelihood that members of ethnic minorities will be parts of political majorities on some issues and members of any ethnic majority will be members of political minorities on some issues' (ibid., p. 17). Third, checks and balances are needed 'to keep each of these decisionmaking centres that represents a specific majority from overreaching its authority' (ibid., p. 17). Thus, the power-dividing approach favours presidential over parliamentary systems, bicameral over unicameral legislatures, and independent judiciaries with powers of judicial review extending to acts of both legislative and executive branches. As a general rule, power dividing as a strategy to keep the peace in ethnically divided societies requires 'decisions [that] can threaten the stability of the constitutional order, such as amendments to peace settlements' be made by 'concurrent approval by multiple organs empowering different majorities' (ibid., p. 17).

Rejecting the classic options of majoritarian democracy, power sharing, protectorates and partition as long-term solutions that can provide stable democracy after civil wars, Roeder and Rothchild advocate the power-dividing arrangements associated with the US constitution: civil liberties, multiple majorities, and checks and balances. In order to substantiate this assertion, Roeder and Rothchild and their contributors address five different sets of issues in their volume: the suitability of different power-sharing regimes to lead to peace and democracy; their likely success at different stages in the transition from civil war to stable democracy; different factors that condition the success of power-sharing arrangements and institutions; whether alternative options are more likely to lead to stability and lasting peace; and whether a comprehensive strategy of intervention with phased institutions appropriate at different stages of the transition from civil war to democracy is possible.

Conceptually based primarily on the Madisonian model of federalism and the American presidential system (and thus perhaps somewhat overstated in its novelty), power dividing is a theoretically interesting alternative to power sharing and centripetalism. While it accepts key premises of the former as necessary to initiate a transition from war to peace, it shares many of the normative assumptions of centripetalism. Empirically, however, power dividing is less convincing as the panacea to ethnic conflict settlement than it is deemed to be, and this is evident already from Roeder and Rothchild's own volume. For example, Matthew Hoddie and Caroline Hartzell find that '[i]n particular . . . both military and territorial power sharing have a positive role to play in fostering post-war peace' and that '[t]hese provisions have the demonstrated capacity to set the stage for the period of transition by enhancing a sense of confidence among former enemies that their interests will not be jeopardised in the context of the postwar state' (Hoddie and Hartzell 2005, p. 103, see also Chapter 17, this volume). They also note the importance to think beyond power sharing at the level of central government and to include other mechanisms, such as military, territorial and economic power sharing all of which prove important in combination rather than in isolation. A very different set of findings regarding the utility of territorial decentralization (for example, territorial power sharing in Hoddie and Hartzell's terms) is presented by David Lake and Donald Rothchild (2005). They argue that three strategic problems – governance, the incompleteness of constitutions, and transient majorities – make it difficult for institutional arrangements of territorial decentralization to provide long-term peace and stability. The only circumstance in which they are optimistic about territorial decentralization is 'when there are multiple regions with numerous crosscutting political cleavages and relatively balanced capabilities' (ibid., p. 130). Additionally, they note that decentralization is likely not to have unintended negative consequences in the face of 'general fatigue with war, the development of a commitment to resolve disputes through bargaining and reciprocity, and the emergence of respect and good will among the parties' (p. 132).

This emphasis on considering conflict resolution mechanisms as a package rather than individually, unsurprisingly, is also one of the conclusions drawn by Valerie Bunce and Stephen Watts in their chapter on the post-communist states of Eurasia. While they also favour a unitary state approach, they find that '[i]ts success depends on whether it is combined with some other key characteristics, such as guarantees of minority rights and cultural autonomy, and separation of powers and proportionality in electoral systems' (Bunce and Watts 2005, p. 139). This proportionality claim, however, is disputed by Reilly, whose examination of nine stable democracies in divided societies finds that only four use PR, and further suggests that '[t]here are no examples of an ethnically plural long-term democracy outside the developed world using PR' (Reilly 2005, p. 171). As Reilly also emphasizes the impact of other factors on what is essentially a question of how well election outcomes reflect the diversity of a given society, such as the geographical distribution of ethnic groups in a country, the question of PR versus majoritarian/plurality electoral systems seems less relevant anyway. What matters is, again, the right package of institutions, which, as Reilly notes, can in some cases mean a 'combination of plurality elections and federalism' (ibid., p. 171).

The individual case studies of Lebanon, India, Ethiopia and South Africa in Roeder and Rothchild's volume all have some good things to say about power sharing but remain largely sceptical of its overall and long-term value. Marie-Joëlle Zahar (2005) uses Lebanon to make the point that power sharing there depended on external guarantors and as such did bring long periods of peace to the country but in the long run inhibited the country's transition to democracy. Edmond Keller and Lahra Smith (2005) in their study of Ethiopia have to deal with a rather different experiment in federalization, one that largely failed in its implementation because of a lack of state capacity (limited funds, insufficient qualified personnel, and material scarcity) and the emergence of new conflicts following federalization.

Amit Ahuja and Ashutosh Varshney (2005) describe the success of federalism in India to provide peace and stability in ethnically diverse societies, focusing on a number of factors that facilitate its success, including the technical and structural aspects of the design of the Indian federation and its political process. Yet perhaps most crucially, Ahuja and Varshney emphasize the importance of India being a nation, that is, the country as a whole and its constituent groups having a clear sense of their joint nationhood. The argument then is that where belonging to the nation (and by extension, the state) is by and large not disputed, mechanisms can be found to manage diversity effectively and peacefully. Put more trivially, if people want to live together, they can find ways to do so.

Finally, Roeder and Rothchild offer their conclusions and policy recommendations. This 'nation-state stewardship' seeks to limit 'power sharing to two tactical roles in the initiation phase', that is, the early period in the transition from civil war to peace. These two roles, according to Roeder and Rothchild, are an 'offer by a majority to reassure minorities about the peace implementation process' and 'a principle of proportionality for one-time, pump-priming decisions, such as the initial staffing of new bureaucracies and the armed forces' (Roeder and Rothchild 2005a, p. 320). They also reiterate an earlier point made in their introduction, and in a similar way by Lake and Rothchild in their chapter on territorial decentralization, namely that for power sharing to work after civil wars, extraordinary, and thus highly unlikely, circumstances need to be in place, primarily a shared national identity and an abundance of resources. As a consequence, they find that power sharing is likely to lead to 'institutional instability, the escalation of conflict, and blocked transitions to democracy' (Roeder and Rothchild 2005a, p. 325). They are equally critical of outside intervention, which they claim 'exacerbates many of the dilemmas of power sharing' and, in fact, introduces additional problems in itself (ibid., p. 328).

Instead of endorsing power sharing beyond the initiation phase of peace and democracy, Roeder and Rothchild offer nine policy recommendations for the strategy of nation-state stewardship: creating or holding together only those states in which constituent groups share a sense of nationhood and agree to live together; limiting government to minimize contentious issues that are decided centrally; delaying intervention until a clear victor emerges; lengthening protectorates to give moderates a chance to emerge; building institutions from the ground up so that local institutions of self-governance can emerge before central ones; phasing withdrawal in accordance with the build-up of local capacity; dividing power between different institutions and arenas such that ethnic stakes in politics are lowered; broadening negotiations for long-term arrangements to include other than just ethnically defined interest groups in the decision-making process; and limiting power sharing in favour of direct rule by the international community.

The main problem with this set of recommendations, however, is that, while they may be normatively appealing to proponents of liberalism, they are based on controversial empirical evidence presented (the conclusions reached by Roeder and Rothchild are not fully and unambiguously substantiated in the findings offered by their contributing authors) and they draw on a model of political system that contextually bears very little resemblance to the situation in conflict-torn societies (the success of the US model of democracy advocated remains context dependent: just because it works in the US does not mean that it can be successfully replicated elsewhere).

29.3.4 The Different Theories Compared

The preceding overview of three main theories of conflict resolution illustrates two important aspects of current academic and policy debates about how to establish sustainable institutional settlements in cases of ethnic conflicts: while there are fundamental differences in the underlying assumptions about how such settlements can succeed, certain institutional arrangements that complement the basic prescriptions of each approach are largely similar, if not identical (see Table 29.1).

29.4 THEORY MEETS PRACTICE: THE EMERGING STRATEGY OF COMPLEX POWER SHARING

While there is a degree of overlap across the three principal schools of conflict resolution discussed above, they differ significantly and intentionally in their principal recommendations. At the same time, they all represent Weberian ideal types of supposedly successful conflict settlements and are as such not empirically observable, much to the disappointment of their proponents. Horowitz (2008, p. 1226), for example, laments that comprehensively designed institutions to reduce conflict are very rare: 'partial adoptions are the rule, and coherent packages are the exception'. However, this can be hardly surprising. Conflict settlement negotiations, on the one hand, are often merely attempts to reform existing institutions, and such institutions have benefited some of the people participating in these negotiations who consequently have incentives to defend them. On the other hand, even where negotiations on a new set of institutions start from a clean slate, they are never free of competing preferences either. The negotiated settlements that result, thus, present compromises acceptable to the parties (and their various advisers) involved rather than a consistent application of existing theories of conflict resolution.

A striking feature of contemporary conflict resolution practice is that a large number of actual and proposed settlements involve a broad range of different conflict settlement mechanisms. This reflects the assumption that a combination of consociational, power dividing, centripetal mechanisms can indeed provide institutional solutions that are both acceptable to negotiators and conducive to accommodating conflict parties in an institutional framework in which they can settle their disputes by peaceful means. The need to combine a range of different mechanisms has been increasingly understood by practitioners of conflict resolution and has led to an emerging practice of conflict settlement that can be referred to as 'complex power sharing'.

Complex power sharing, in the way it is understood here, refers to a practice of conflict settlement that has a form of self-governance regime at its heart, but whose overall institutional design includes a range of further mechanisms for the accommodation of ethnic diversity in divided

Table 29.1 *Main institutional arrangements recommended by different theories of conflict resolution*

		Centripetalism	Liberal consociational power sharing	Power dividing
Principal recommendation		Inter-ethnic cooperation and moderation induced by electoral system design encouraging vote pooling	Inter-ethnic cooperation at elite level induced by institutional structure requiring jointness of executive decision making	Cooperation between different, changing coalitions of interest induced by separation of powers
State construction	Heterogeneity vs. homogeneity of federal units (if any)	Preference for heterogeneous units	Preference for units based on self-determining communities	Preference for heterogeneous units
	Number of units relative to number of groups	Preference for more units than groups	Preference for units equal to numbers of groups	No explicit connection between number of groups and units
Institutions of government	Government system	Presidential	Parliamentary or collective/rotating presidential system	Presidential
	Executive power sharing	Yes: voluntary	Yes: guaranteed	No, except in initial transition phase after civil wars
	Electoral system	Plurality preferential	List-PR or PR preferential	Plurality
	Judicial branch	Independent	Independent and representative	Independent
	Legal entrenchment	Yes	Yes	Yes
Rights and identities	Individual vs. group rights	Emphasis on individual rights	Emphasis on combination of individual and group rights	Emphasis on individual rights
	Recognition of distinct identities	Yes, but primarily as private matter	Yes, but as private and public matter	Yes, but primarily as private matter

societies, including those recommended by advocates of consociationalism, centripetalism and power dividing. Complex power sharing thus describes a practice of conflict settlement that requires a relatively complex institutional structures across different layers of authority from the centre down to local government units and that cannot be reduced to autonomy/(ethno)federation, (traditional) models of power sharing, centripetalism or power dividing, but rather represents a combination of them.

None of the three theories of conflict resolution discussed above fully captures this current practice of complex power sharing. Having said that, liberal consociationalism emerges as the one theory that is most open to incorporation of elements of centripetalism and power dividing. Within a liberal consociational framework, there is room (and a recognized need) for a range of power-dividing strategies, including a strong role for judicial entrenchment and enforcement mechanisms, and universally applicable and enforceable human rights legislation. Liberal consociationalism is also open to a vertical division of power on the basis of non-ascriptive, that is, non-ethnic criteria, but in contrast to power dividing and centripetalism does not rule it out either, should self-determined entities on that basis emerge and desire territorial or corporate self-governance. Liberal consociationalists and centripetalists share some common ground in terms of the principle of preferential electoral systems, even though they disagree about whether preferential PR or majoritarian systems are better suited to achieve outcomes conducive to stable settlements in the long term.

Yet, liberal consociationalism is not synonymous with complex power sharing, even though it offers a promising point of departure for a new research agenda on conflict resolution theory. In order to make a significant contribution to existing debates, a theory of complex power sharing would need to accomplish several tasks. First, most existing theories of conflict resolution are consequence focused, that is, they seek to explain why certain institutional designs offer the prospect of sustainable peace and stability, while others do not. They do this by offering normative and pragmatic accounts of the desirability and feasibility of particular institutions in divided societies, but these are not always, let alone successfully, grounded in theories of conflict, nor are the assumptions made about the drivers of conflict always fully spelt out. Yet, it is essential to understand the causes of conflict before viable prescriptions for its resolution can be offered. This is not to suggest that any single theory of conflict will be able to explain every distinct conflict, but rather that more reflection is needed about what institutions can address what causes. Fear requires a different response from deprivation, and people driven to violence by their desire for power need to be dealt with in a different way from those who fear the loss of their culture.

In other words, a theory of complex power sharing would need to explain why we find empirically a greater mix of institutions than existing theories recommend. Factoring in causes of conflict is one aspect of this, but two others are equally important. The first one has been examined at some length already and relates to the process of settlement, that is the structure of negotiations and the nature of the different actors participating in them (Horowitz 2002, 2008). The second one is a more careful consideration of 'objective' factors that might privilege certain institutions in their presence. For example, as O'Leary and McGarry illustrate in the case of Northern Ireland, the fact that this region is territorially distinct and clearly delineated, ethnically mixed, and that its two major groups have strong preferences for links with different actors outside their region, created a path towards a regional consociation embedded in two cross-border arrangements – the North–South Ministerial Council and the Council of the British Isles (McGarry and O'Leary 2004b).

Apart from the question why do complex power-sharing settlements emerge, a proper theory of conflict resolution also needs to be able to explain why they fail or succeed, that is, it needs to identify the conditions under which they can provide long-term peace and stability in divided societies. Ultimately, this can only be done empirically and thus requires a definition of what can be considered complex power-sharing settlements, the identification of relevant cases, and their analysis against standards of success and failure. On the basis of such a comprehensive theory of complex power sharing that enables us to understand why they emerge and why they succeed or fail, sensible policy recommendations for conflict settlement can be made, recommendations that most likely will integrate existing theories rather than reinforce the divisions between them.

References

Abouharb, M. Rodwan and David Cingranelli. 2007. *Human Rights and Structural Adjustment*. Cambridge: Cambridge University Press.

Acemoglu, Daron and James A. Robinson. 2006. *Economic Origins of Dictatorship and Democracy: Economic and Political Origins*. Cambridge: Cambridge University Press.

Adamson, Fiona B. 2000. 'International norms meet local structures: the dilemmas of democracy promotion in post-Soviet Central Asia.' Paper presented at the American Political Science Association, Washington, DC, 30 August–3 September.

Addison, Tony. 2004. 'Conflicts', in B. Lomborg (ed.), *Global Crises, Global Solutions*. Cambridge: Cambridge University Press: 167–174.

Addison, Tony. 2003. 'Africa's recovery from conflict: making peace work for the poor.' World Institute for Development Economics Research (WIDER), Helsinki, available at: http://www.wider.unu.edu/publications/policy-briefs/en_GB/pb6/.

Addison, Tony. 2009. 'The political economy of the transition from authoritarianism.' In *Transitional Justice and Development*, edited by P. De Grieff and R. Duthie. New York: Social Science Research Council and International Center for Transitional Justice.

Addison, Tony and M. Baliamoune-Lutz. 2006. 'Economic reform when institutional quality is weak: the case of the Maghreb.' *Journal of Policy Modeling* **28**:1029–43.

Addison, Tony, A. Geda, Philippe Le Billon and S. Mansoob Murshed. 2005. 'Reconstructing and reforming the financial system in conflict and "post-conflict" economies.' *Journal of Development Studies* **41**:703–18.

Addison, Tony, David Hulme and Ravi Kanbur. 2009. *Poverty Dynamics: Interdisciplinary Perspectives*. Oxford: Oxford University Press.

Addison, Tony, Philippe Le Billon and S. Mansoob Murshed. 2002. 'Conflict in Africa: the cost of peaceful behaviour.' *Journal of African Economies* **11**(3):365–86.

Addison, Tony and S. Mansoob Murshed. 2002. 'From conflict to reconstruction: reviving the social contract.' World Institute for Development Economics Research (WIDER), Helsinki.

Addison, Tony and S. Mansoob Murshed. 2003a. 'Debt relief and civil war.' *Journal of Peace Research* **40**:159–76.

Addison, Tony and S. Mansoob Murshed. 2003b. 'Explaining Violent

Conflict: Going Beyond Greed versus Grievance.' Special issue of the *Journal of International Development*: **15**(4).

Addison, Tony and S. Mansoob Murshed. 2005. 'Post-conflict reconstruction in Africa: some analytical issues.' In *Post-Conflict Economies in Africa*, edited by A.K. Fosu and P. Collier. Basingstoke: Palgrave Macmillan.

Addison, Tony and S. Mansoob Murshed. 2006. 'The social contract and violent conflict.' In *Civil War, Civil Peace*, edited by H. Yanacopoulos and J. Hanlon. Oxford: Currey, pp. 137–63.

Addison, Tony and A. Roe. 2004. *Fiscal Policy for Development: Poverty, Reconstruction, and Growth*. Basingstoke: Palgrave Macmillan.

Adebajo, A. 2002. 'Sierra Leone: a feast for the Sobels.' In *Building Peace in West Africa: Liberia, Sierra Leone, and Guinea Bissau*, edited by A. Adebajo. Boulder, CO: Lynne Rienner.

Adeney, Katharine. 2002. 'Constitutional centring: nation formation and consociational federalism in India and Pakistan.' *Journal of Commonwealth and Comparative Politics* **40**:8–33.

Adepoju, A., A. Boulton and M. Levin. 2007. 'Promoting integration through mobility: free movement and the ECOWAS Protocol.' UNHCR, Geneva.

Aguilar, P. and G. Retamal. 1998. 'Rapid educational response in complex emergencies: a discussion document.' International Bureau of Education, Geneva.

Aguilar, R. 2003. 'Angola's incomplete transition.' In *From Conflict to Recovery in Africa*, edited by T. Addison. Oxford: Oxford University Press.

Ahmed, M. 2008. 'The next frontier.' *Finance and Development* **45**:9–16.

Ahuja, A. and Ashutosh Varshney. 2005. 'Antecedent nationhood, subsequent statehood: explaining the relative success of Indian federalism.' In *Sustainable Peace: Power and Democracy after Civil Wars*, edited by P. G. Roeder and D. Rothchild. Ithaca, NY: Cornell University Press.

Akbulut-Yuksel, M. 2009. 'Children of war: the long-run effects of large-scale physical destruction and warfare on children.' IZA Discussion Paper 4407, Institute for the Study of Labor, Bonn.

Akerlof, G.A. and R.E. Kranton. 2000. 'Economics and identity.' *Quarterly Journal of Economics* **115**:715–53.

Akresh, R. and D. de Walque. 2008. 'Armed conflict and schooling: evidence from the 1994 Rwandan genocide.' HiCN Working Paper 47, Households in Conflict Network, Brighton.

Al-Ali, N. 2007. 'Gender, diasporas and post-Cold War conflict.' In *Diasporas in Conflict. Peace-makers or Peace-wreckers*, edited by

H. Smith and P. Stares. Tokyo: United Nations University Press, pp. 36–62.

Al-Ali, N. and N. Pratt. 2009. *Women and War in the Middle East*. London and New York: Zed Books.

Alao, A. and F. Olonisakin. 2001. 'Economic fragility and political fluidity: explaining natural resources and conflicts.' In *Managing Armed Conflicts in the 21st Century*, edited by A. Adebajo and C. Lekha Sriram. London: Frank Cass.

Alderman, H., J. Hoddinott and B. Kinsey. 2006. 'Long term consequences of early childhood malnutrition.' *Oxford Economic Papers* **58**:450–74.

Alemán, Eduardo and Daniel Treisman. 2005. 'Fiscal politics in "ethnically mined" developing federal states: central strategies and secessionist violence.' In *Sustainable Peace: Power and Democracy after Civil War*, edited by P.G. Roeder and D. Rothchild. Ithaca, NY: Cornell University Press, pp. 173–216.

Alesina, Alberto and Enrico Spolare. 2003. *The Size of Nations*. Cambridge, MA: MIT Press.

Ali, Ali Abdel Gadir, Ibrahim A. Elbadawi and Atta El-Batahani. 2005. 'The Sudan's civil war: why has it prevailed for so long?' In *Understanding Civil War: Evidence and Analysis*, vol. I: *Africa*, edited by P. Collier and N. Sambanis. Washington, DC: World Bank.

Allahar, A. 1996. 'Primordialism and ethnic political mobilisation in modern society.' *New Community* **22**:5–21.

Amenta, E., N. Caren, E. Chiarello and Y. Su. 2010. 'The political consequences of social movements.' *Annual Review of Sociology* **36**:287–307.

Amnesty International. 1996. 'Tanzania/Rwanda: international cooperation in forcing Rwandese refugees back from Tanzania.' Amnesty International, London.

Amnesty International. 2002. 'Rwanda-*Gacaca*: a question of justice.' Amnesty International, London.

Amnesty International. 2003. 'Iraq: forcible return of refugees and asylum-seekers is contrary to international law.' Amnesty International, London.

Amnesty International. 2007. 'Colombia: killings, arbitrary detentions, and death threats – the reality of trade unionism in Colombia.' Amnesty International, London.

Amnesty International. 2008a. 'Government cannot negotiate away International Criminal Court arrest warrants for LRA.' Amnesty International, London.

Amnesty International. 2008b. 'Uganda: agreement and annex on accountability and reconciliation falls short of a comprehensive plan to end impunity.' Amnesty International, London.

Anderson, Mary B. 1991. *Do No Harm: How Aid Can Support Peace – or War*. Boulder, CO: Lynne Rienner.

Andersson, A. 2000. 'Democracies and UN peacekeeping operations, 1990–1996.' *International Peacekeeping* **7**(2):1–22.

Anderson-Levitt, Kathryn. 2003. *Local Meanings, Global Schooling. Anthropology and World Culture Theory*. New York: Palgrave Macmillan.

Andreas, P. 2004. 'The clandestine political economy of war and peace in Bosnia.' *International Studies Quarterly* **48**:29–51.

Angell, D.J.R. 2004. 'The Angola Sanctions Committee.' In *The UN Security Council: From the Cold War to the 21st Century*, edited by D.M. Malone. Boulder, CO: Lynne Rienner.

Angrist, Joshua and Adriana Kugler. 2008. 'Rural windfall or resource curse? Coca, income and civil conflict in Colombia.' *Review of Economics and Statistics* **90**:191–215.

Annan, J., C. Blattman, D. Mazurana and K. Carlson. 2009. 'Women and girls at war: "Wives", mothers and fighters in the Lord's Resistance Army.' Households in Conflict Network, Brighton, available at: http://www.hicn.org/.

Annan, K. 1999. 'Report of the Secretary-General pursuant to General Assembly Resolution 53/35: the fall of Srebrenica. A/4/549, 15 November.' New York: United Nations.

Annan, Kofi. 2000. 'Secretary-General salutes International Workshop on Human Security in Mongolia.' Ulaanbaatar, May 8–10.

Apter, David. 1963. *Old Societies and New States*. New York: Free Press of Glencoe.

Arendt, Hannah. 1958. *The Human Condition*. Chicago, IL: University of Chicago Press.

Arendt, Hannah. 1967. *The Origins of Totalitarianism*, 2nd edn. New York: Harvest.

Arezki, Rabah and Frederick van der Ploeg. 2007. 'Can the natural resource curse be turned into a blessing? The role of trade policies and institutions.' IMF Working Paper WP/05/55, International Monetary Fund, Washington, DC.

Arjona, Ana and Stathis N. Kalyvas. 2006. 'Preliminary results of a survey of demobilized combatants in Colombia.' Working Paper, Yale University, New Haven, CT.

Arora, B. and D.V. Verney. 1995. *Multiple Identities in a Single State: Indian Federalism in Comparative Perspective*. New Delhi: Konark.

Ascher, W. 1999. *Why Governments Waste Natural Resources: Policy Failure in Developing Countries*. Baltimore, MD: Johns Hopkins University Press.

Aspinall, Ed. 2007. 'The construction of grievance: natural resources and identity in a separatist conflict.' *Journal of Conflict Resolution* **51**:950–70.

Atanassove-Cornelis, Elena. 2006. 'Defining and implementing human security: the case of Japan.' In *Human Security on Foreign Policy Agendas*, edited by T. Debiel and S. Werthes: Institute for Development and Peace, University of Duisburg-Essen.

Atlas, Pierre and Roy Licklider. 1999. 'Conflict among former allies after civil war settlement in Sudan, Zimbabwe, Chad, and Lebanon.' *Journal of Peace Research* **36**:35–54.

Auty, Richard M. 1993. *Sustaining Development in Mineral Economies: The Resource Curse Thesis*. London: Routledge.

Auty, Richard M. and Philippe Le Billon. 2007. 'Managing revenues from national resources and aid.' In *Trade, Aid, and Security: An Agenda for Peace and Development*, edited by O. Brown, M. Halle, S. Peña Moreno and S. Winkler. London: Earthscan.

Ayoob, Mohammed. 1996. 'State making, state breaking, and state failure.' In *Managing Global Chaos: Sources of and Responses to International Conflict*, edited by C.A. Crocker and F.O. Hampson. Washington, DC: United States Institute of Peace (USIP).

Ayres, R. William. 2000. 'A world flying apart? Violent nationalist conflicts and the end of the Cold War.' *Journal of Peace Research* **37**:105–17.

Baechler, Günther. 1999. *Violence through Environmental Discrimination*. Dordrecht: Kluwer.

Bahgat, Hossam and Soha Abdelaty. 2011. 'What Mubarak must do before stepping down.' *Washington Post*, February 5.

Bailey, S. 1994. 'Intervention: article 2.7 versus articles 55–56.' *International Relations* **12**(2):1–10.

Bajpai, Kanti. 2003. 'The idea of human security.' *International Studies* **40**:195–228.

Baker, Pauline H. 2001. 'Conflict resolution versus democratic governance: divergent paths to peace?' In *Turbulent Peace: The Challenges of Managing International Conflict*, edited by C. Crocker, F.O. Hampson and P. Aall. Washington, DC: United States Institute of Peace (USIP), pp. 753–64.

Bakewell, O. 2008. 'Keeping them in their place: the ambivalent relationship between development and migration in Africa.' *Third World Quarterly* **29**:1341–58.

Bakwena, Malebogo, Philip Bodman, Thanh Le and Kam Ki Tang. 2010. 'Avoiding the resource curse: the role of institutions.' Macroeconomics Research Group Working Paper, School of Economics, University of Queensland, Brisbane.

Baland, Jean-Marie and Patrick Francois. 2000. 'Rent-seeking and resource booms.' *Journal of Development Economics* **61**:527–42.

Ball, Nicole. 1996. 'Demobilizing and reintegrating soldiers: lessons from Africa.' In *Rebuilding Societies after Civil War: Critical Roles for International Assistance*, edited by K. Kumar. Boulder, CO: Lynne Rienner, pp. 85–105.

Ball, N. and D. Hendrickson. 2005. 'Review of international financing arrangements for disarmament, demobilization and reintegration, phase 2 report to working group 2 of the Stockholm initiative.' Stockholm Initiative on Disarmament, Demobilization and Reintegration (SIDDR), Stockholm.

Ballentine, Karen. 2003. 'Beyond greed and grievance: reconsidering the economic dynamics of armed conflict.' In *The Political Economy of Armed Conflict: Beyond Greed and Grievance*, edited by K. Ballentine and J. Sherman. Boulder, CO: Lynne Rienner.

Ballentine, Karen. 2004. 'Program on Economic Agendas in Civil Wars: Principal Research Findings and Policy Recommendations.' Final Project Report. International Peace Academy, New York.

Ballentine, Karen. 2007. 'Promoting conflict-sensitive business in fragile states: redressing skewed incentives.' In *Trade, Aid, and Security: An Agenda for Peace and Development*, edited by O. Brown, M. Halle, S. Peña Moreno and S. Winkler. London: Earthscan.

Ballentine, Karen and H. Nitzschke. 2003. 'Beyond greed and grievance: policy lessons from studies in the political economy of armed conflict.' International Peace Academy, New York.

Ballentine, Karen and H. Nitzschke. 2004. 'Business in armed conflict: an assessment of issues and options.' *Die Friedens-Warte: Journal of International Peace and Security* **79**:35–56.

Ballentine, Karen and H. Nitzschke. 2005. *Profiting from Peace: Managing the Resource Dimension of Civil Wars*. Boulder, CO: Lynne Rienner.

Ballentine, Karen and J. Sherman. 2003a. 'Introduction.' In *The Political Economy of Armed Conflict: Beyond Greed and Grievance*, edited by K. Ballentine and J. Sherman. Boulder, CO: Lynne Rienner.

Ballentine, Karen and J. Sherman. 2003b. *The Political Economy of Armed Conflict: Beyond Greed and Grievance*. Boulder, CO: Lynne Rienner.

Banerjee, Abhijit, Lakshhmi Iyer and Rohini Somanathan. 2005. 'History, social divisions, and public goods in rural India.' *Journal of the European Economic Association* **3**:639–47.

Banfield, J., V. Haufler and D. Lilly. 2003. 'Transnational corporations in conflict prone zones: public policy responses and a framework for action.' International Alert, London.

Bangura, Yusuf. 2006. *Ethnic Inequalities and Public Sector Governance.* Basingstoke: Palgrave Macmillan.

Banks, Glenn. 2005. 'Resources and conflict in the Asia-Pacific region: linking resources and conflict the Melanesian way.' *Pacific Economic Bulletin* **20**:185–91.

Bannon, Ian and Paul Collier. 2004. *Natural Resources and Violent Conflict: Options and Actions.* Washington, DC: World Bank.

Barnett, Jon and Neil Adger. 2007. 'Climate change, human security, and violent conflict.' *Political Geography* **26**:639–55.

Barnett, M. 2002. *Eyewitness to a Genocide: The United Nations and Rwanda.* Ithaca, NY: Cornell University Press.

Barron, Patrick. 2009. 'The limits of DDR: reintegration lessons from Aceh.' In *Small Arms Survey 2009.* Geneva: Small Arms Survey.

Barron, Patrick, Kai Kaiser and Menno Pradhan. 2009. 'Understanding variations in local conflict: evidence and implications from Indonesia.' *World Development* **37**:698–713.

Barrows, W.L. 1976. 'Ethnic diversity and political instability in Black Africa.' *Comparative Political Studies* **9**:139–70.

Barth, Fredrik (ed.). 1969. *Ethnic Groups and Boundaries: The Social Organization of Culture Difference.* London: Allen & Unwin.

Barth, F. 1994. 'Enduring and emerging issues in the analysis of ethnicity.' In *The Anthropology of Ethnicity: Beyond Ethnic Groups and Boundaries*, edited by H. Vermeulen and C. Govers. Amsterdam: Het Spinhuis.

Basu, Kaushik and Pham Hoang Van. 1998. 'The economics of child labor.' *American Economic Review* **88**:412–27.

Bates, Robert H. 1976. *Rural Responses to Industrialization.* New Haven, CT and London: Yale University Press.

Bates, Robert H. 2008. *When Things Fall Apart: State Failure in Late-Century Africa.* New York: Cambridge University Press.

Bates, Robert H. and Irene Yackolev. 2002. 'Ethnicity in Africa.' In *The Role of Social Capital In Development*, edited by C. Grootaert and T. van Bastelaer. New York: Cambridge University Press.

Bauer, O. 2000. *The Question of Nationalities and Social Democracy.* Translated by J. O'Donnell. Minneapolis, MN: University of Minnesota Press.

Baumgartner, F.R. and C. Mahoney. 2005. 'Social movements, the rise of new issues, and the public agenda.' In *Routing the Opposition: Social Movements, Public Policy, and Democracy*, edited by D.S. Meyer, V. Jenness and H. Ingram. Minneapolis, MN: University of Minneapolis Press.

Bayer, Resat and Matthew C. Rupert. 2004. 'Effects of civil wars on international trade, 1950–92.' *Journal of Peace Research* **41**:699–713.

Beardsley, K. 2004. 'UN involvement in international crises: selection, endogeneity, and authority.' Paper presented at the 45th Annual Meeting of the International Studies Association, Montreal.

Beber, B. and C. Blattman. 2010. 'The industrial organization of rebellion; the logic of forced labor and child soldiering.' Department of Political Science, Yale University, New Haven, CT.

Beck, Nathaniel, Kristian Skrede Gleditsch and Kyle Beardsley. 2006. 'Space is more than geography: using spatial econometrics in the study of civil war.' *International Studies Quarterly* **50**:27–44.

Becker, G.S. 1962. 'Investment in human capital: a theoretical analysis.' *Journal of Political Economy* **70**:9–49.

Becker, G.S. 1968. 'Crime and punishment: an economic approach.' *Journal of Political Economy* **76**:169–217.

Beebe, Shannon D. and Mary Kaldor. 2010. *The Ultimate Weapon Is No Weapon: Human Security and the New Rules of War and Peace.* New York: Public Affairs, Perseus Books.

Bell, D. 1975. 'Ethnicity and social change.' In *Ethnicity: Theory and Experience*, edited by N. Glazer and D. Moynihan. Cambridge, MA: Harvard University Press.

Bekerman, Zwi. 2005. 'Are Children to Educate for Peace in Conflict-Ridden Areas? A Critical Essay on Peace and Coexistence Education', *Intercultural Education* **16**(3):235–45.

Bellamy, A.J. 2004. 'The "next stage" in peace operations theory?' *International Peacekeeping* **11**(1):17–38.

Bellamy, A.J. and P.D. Williams. 2005. 'Who's keeping the peace? Regionalization and contemporary peace operations.' *International Security* **29**(4):157–95.

Belmont, Katharine, Scott Mainwaring and Andrew Reynolds. 2002. 'Introduction: institutional design, conflict management, and democracy in divided societies.' In *The Architecture of Democracy: Institutional Design, Conflict Management, and Democracy in the Late Twentieth Century*, edited by Andrew Reynolds. Oxford: Oxford University Press, pp. 1–11.

Bendix, D. and R. Stanley. 2008. 'Security sector reform in Africa: the promise and practice of a new donor approach.' African Centre for the Constructive Resolution of Disputes (ACCORD), Durban, South Africa.

Bénéï, Véronique (ed.). 2005. *Manufacturing Citizenship: Education and Nationalism in Europe, South Asia and China.* London: Routledge.

Benford, R.D. and D.A. Snow. 2000. 'Framing processes and social movements: an overview and assessment.' *Annual Review of Sociology* **26**:611–39.

Bercovitch, J. 1986. 'International mediation: a study of incidence, strategies and conditions for successful outcomes.' *Cooperation and Conflict* **21**(2):155–69.

Bercovitch, J. 2003. 'Managing ethnic conflicts: the role and relevance of mediation.' *World Affairs* **166**:56–69.

Bercovitch, J. 2011. *Theory and Practice of International Mediation: Selected Essays.* Abingdon: Taylor & Francis.

Bercovitch, J., J.T. Anagnoson and D.L. Willie. 1991. 'Some contextual issues and empirical trends in the study of successful mediation in international relations.' *Journal of Peace Research* **28**(1):7–17.

Bercovitch, J. and A. Houston. 1996. 'The study of international mediation: theoretical issues and empirical evidence.' In *Resolving International Conflicts*, edited by J. Bercovitch. Boulder, CO: Lynne Rienner, pp. 11–35.

Bercovitch, J. and R. Jackson. 1997. *International conflict: 1945–1995.* Washington, DC: Congressional Quarterly.

Bercovitch, J., V. Kremenyuk and I.W. Zartman. 2009. 'Introduction: the nature of conflict and conflict resolution.' In *The Sage Handbook of Conflict Resolution*, edited by J. Bercovitch, V. Kremenyuk and I.W. Zartman. London: Sage.

Bercovitch, J. and C. Lutmar. 2010. 'Beyond negotiation deadlocks: the importance of mediation and leadership change in breaking the deadlock.' In *Breaking Deadlocks in Multilateral Settings*, edited by A. Narliker. Cambridge: Cambridge University Press.

Berdal, Mats R. 1996. *Disarmament and Demobilisation after Civil Wars: Arms, Soldiers and the Termination of Armed Conflict.* Oxford: Oxford University Press.

Berdal, Mats. 2003. 'How "new" are "new wars"? Global economic change and the study of civil war.' *Global Governance* **9**:477–502.

Berdal, Mats. 2005. 'Beyond greed and grievance – and none too soon.' *Review of International Studies* **31**(4):687–98.

Berdal, Mats and David Keen. 1997. 'Violence and economic agendas in civil wars: some policy implications.' *Millennium: Journal of International Studies* **26**:795–818.

Berdal, Mats and David M. Malone. 2000. *Greed and Grievance: Economic Agendas in Civil Wars.* Boulder, CO: Lynne Rienner.

Berdal, Mats and M. Ucko. 2009. *Reintegrating Armed Groups after Conflict: Politics, Violence, and Transition.* London: Routledge.

Berejikian, Jeffrey. 1992. 'Revolutionary collective action and the agent-structure problem.' *American Political Science Review* **86**:647–57.

Berman, Eli and David D. Laitin. 2008. 'Religion, terrorism, and public goods: testing the club model.' *Journal of Public Economics* **92**:1942–67.

Bertram, Eva. 1995. 'Reinventing governments: the promise and perils of United Nations peacekeeping.' *Journal of Conflict Resolution* **39**:387–418.

Betts, R. 2009. 'The three faces of NATO.' *The National Interest* **100**:31–8.

Bevan, David L., Paul Collier and Jan Willem Gunning. 1999. *The Politics Economy of Poverty, Equity, and Growth: Nigeria and Indonesia*. New York: Oxford University Press.

BICC. 2001. 'The demobilization and reintegration of women combatants, wives of male soldiers, and war widows.' Bonn International Center for Conversion (BICC), Bonn.

Bickerton, C.P. 2007. 'State-building: exporting state-failure.' In *Politics without Sovereignty: A Critique of International Relations*, edited by C.P. Bickerton, P. Cunliffe and A. Gourevitch. London: Routledge.

Biermann, W. and M. Vadset. 1999. *UN Peacekeeping in Trouble: Lessons from the Former Yugoslavia*. Aldershot, UK and Brookfield, VT, USA: Ashgate.

Bigombe, Betty, Paul Collier and Nicholas Sambanis. 2000. 'Policies for building post-conflict peace.' *Journal of African Economies* **9**:322–47.

Binningsbø, Helga Malmin, Indra de Soysa and Nils Petter Gleditsch. 2007. 'Green giant, or straw man? Environmental pressure and civil conflict.' *Population and Environment* **28**:337–53.

Bitzinger, Richard and Barry Desker. 2011. 'Southeast Asia and its evolving security architecture.' In *Rewiring National Security*, edited by C. Crocker, F.O. Hampson and P. Aall. Washington, DC: US Institute of Peace Press.

Black, R. and S. Gent. 2004. 'Defining, measuring, and influencing sustainable return: the case of the Balkans.' Development Research Centre on Migration, Globalization and Poverty, University of Sussex, Brighton, available at: http://www.migrationdrc.org/publications/wor king_papers/WP-T7.pdf.

Blake, J. 2009. *Where Does the International Community Disarm, Demobilize, and Reintegrate Ex-Combatants? The Determinants of DDR after Civil Wars*. New York: Columbia University Press.

Blake, R. and M. Mouton. 1961. 'Reactions to intergroup competition under win–lose conditions.' *Management Science* **7**(4):420–35.

Blattman, C. and J. Annan. 2007. 'The consequences of child soldiering.' Households in Conflict Network, Brighton, available at: http://www. hicn.org/.

Blattman, C. and J. Annan. 2009. 'Child combatants in northern Uganda: reintegration myths and realities.' In *Security and Post-Conflict*

Reconstruction: Dealing with Fighters in the Aftermath of War, edited by R. Muggah. New York: Routledge.

Blattman, C. and E. Miguel. 2010. 'Civil war.' *Journal of Economic Literature* **48**:3–57.

Blauner, R. 1969. 'Internal colonialism and ghetto revolt.' *Social Problems* **16**:393–408.

Blimes, Randall J. 2006. 'The indirect effect of ethnic heterogeneity on the likelihood of civil war onset.' *Journal of Conflict Resolution* **50**:536–47.

Blomberg, S.B. and G.D. Hess. 2002. 'The temporal links between conflict and economic activity.' *Journal of Conflict Resolution* **46**:74–90.

Bloomfield, D., C. Nupen and P. Harris. 1998. 'Negotiation processes.' In *Democracy and Deep-Rooted Conflict: Options for Negotiators* edited by P. Harris and B. Reilly, Stockholm: International IDEA, pp. 59–113.

Bloomfield, L.P. 1964. *International Military Forces: The Question of Peacekeeping in an Armed and Disarming World*. Boston, MA: Little, Brown.

Bogaards, M. 1998. 'The favourable factors for consociational democracy: a review.' *European Journal of Political Research* **33**:475–96.

Bogaards, M. 2000. 'The uneasy relationship between empirical and normative types in consociational theory.' *Journal of Theoretical Politics* **12**:395–423.

Bogaards, M. 2003. 'Electoral choices for divided societies: multiethnic parties and constituency pooling in Africa.' *Journal of Commonwealth and Comparative Politics* **41**:59–80.

Boix, Carles. 2003. *Democracy and Redistribution*. Cambridge: Cambridge University Press.

Bonacich, E. 1972. 'A theory of ethnic antagonism: the split labor market.' *American Sociological Review* **37**:547–59.

Bornhorst, F., S. Gupta and J. Thornton. 2009. 'Natural resource endowments and the domestic revenue effect.' *European Journal of Political Economy* **25**:439–46.

Boschini, A.D., J. Pettersson and J. Roine. 2007. 'Resource curse or not: a question of appropriability.' *Scandinavian Journal of Economics* **109**:593–617.

Bosco, A. 1992. *The Federal Idea: The History of Federalism since 1945*. London: Lothian Foundation Press.

Boserup, Ester and T. Paul Schultz. 1990. *Economic and Demographic Relationships in Development*. Baltimore, MD: Johns Hopkins University Press.

Boucher, J. and V.K. Holt. 2009. 'Targeting spoilers: the role of United Nations Panels of Experts.' Henry L. Stimson Center, New York.

Boulden, J. 2001. *Peace Enforcement: The United Nations Experience in Congo, Somalia, and Bosnia*. Westport, CT: Praeger.

Bourdieu, Pierre and Jean-Claude Passeron. 1990 [1997]. *Reproduction in Education, Society, and Culture*. London: Sage.

Boussetta, H. 2001. 'Immigration, post-immigration politics, and the political mobilisation of ethnic minorities: a comparative case-study of Moroccans in four European cities.' KU Brussel, Brussels.

Bouta, T., G. Frerks and I. Bannon. 2005. *Gender, Conflict and Development*. Washington, DC: World Bank.

Boutros-Ghali, B. 1992. *An Agenda for Peace*. New York: United Nations.

Boutros-Ghali, B. 1999. *Unvanquished: A U.S.–U.N. Saga*. New York: Random House.

Boyce, James and Madelene O'Donnell. 2007. *Peace and the Public Purse: Economic Policies for Postwar Statebuilding*. Boulder, CO: Lynne Rienner.

Boyden, Jo. 2007. 'Children, war and world disorder in the 21st century: a review of theories and the literature on children's contributions to armed violence', *Conflict, Security and Development* 7(2):255–79.

Boyden, Jo and Joanna de Berry. 2004. 'Introduction', In *Children and Youth on the Front Line. Ethnography, Armed Conflict and Displacement*, edited by Jo Boyden and J. de Berry. New York: Berghahn Books.

Bozzoli, Carlos, Tilman Brück and Simon Sottsas. 2010. 'A survey of the global economic costs of conflict.' *Defence and Peace Economics* 21:165–76.

Brakman, Steven, Harry Garretsen and Marc Schramm. 2004. 'The strategic bombing of German cities during World War II and its impact on city growth.' *Journal of Economic Geography* 4:201–18.

Brams, Steven J. 2006. 'Fair division.' In *Oxford Handbook of Political Economy*, edited by Donald Wittman and Barry Weingast. Oxford: Oxford University Press, pp.425–37.

Brancati, Dawn. 2006. 'Decentralization: fueling the fire or dampening the flames of ethnic conflict and secessionism.' *International Organization* 60:651–85.

Brancati, Dawn. 2007. 'Political aftershocks: the impact of earthquakes on intrastate conflict.' *Journal of Conflict Resolution* 51:715–43.

Brass, Paul R. 1990. *The Politics of India since Independence*. New Delhi: Cambridge University Press.

Brass, Paul R. 1991. *Ethnicity and Nationalism: Theory and Comparison*. Newbury Park, CA: Sage.

Brass, Paul R. 2006. *Forms of Collective Violence: Riots, Pogroms and Genocide in Modern India*. New Delhi: Three Essays Collective.

Braungart, Richard G. 1984. 'Historical and generational patterns of youth movements: a global perspective.' *Comparative Social Research* 7:3–62.

Brautigam, Deborah, Odd-Helge Fjeldstad and Mick Moore. 2008. *Taxation and State-Building in Developing Countries: Capacity and Consent.* Cambridge: Cambridge University Press.

Brömmelhörster, J. and W.-C. Paes. 2003. *The Military as an Economic Actor: Soldiers in Business.* Basingstoke: Palgrave Macmillan.

Bronkhorst, D. 1995. *Truth and Reconciliation: Obstacles and Opportunities for Human Rights.* Amsterdam: Amnesty International (Dutch Section).

Brookings Institution-SAIS. 2003. 'Project on internal displacement. Conference on Internal Displacement in the IGAD sub-region: Report of the Experts Meeting.' Khartoum, Sudan, 20 August–2 September.

Brown, Graham K. 2008. 'Horizontal inequalities and separatism in Southeast Asia: a comparative perspective.' In *Horizontal Inequalities and Conflict: Understanding Group Violence in Multiethnic Societies,* edited by F. Stewart. London: Palgrave, pp. 252–84.

Brown, Graham K. 2010. 'The political economy of secessionism: identity, inequality and the state.' Centre for Development Studies, University of Bath, Bath.

Brown, Graham K. and Arnim Langer. 2010. 'Conceptualizing and measuring ethnicity.' *Oxford Development Studies* 38:409–34.

Brown, Graham K. and Arnim Langer. 2011. 'Riding the ever-rolling stream: time and econometric study of violent conflict.' *World Development* 39:188–98.

Brown, Graham K., Arnim Langer and Frances Stewart. 2011. 'A typology of post-conflict environments.' Centre for Research on Peace and Development (CRPD), University of Leuven, Leuven.

Brown, M.E. (ed.). 1996a. *The International Dimensions of Internal Conflict.* Cambridge, MA: MIT.

Brown, Michael E. 1996b. 'The causes and regional dimensions of internal conflict.' In *The International Dimensions of Internal Conflict,* edited by M.E. Brown. Cambridge, MA: MIT Press.

Browning, C.R. 2010. *Remembering Survival: Inside a Nazi Slave-Labor Camp.* New York: Norton.

Brubaker, Rogers. 1996. *Nationalism Reframed.* Cambridge: Cambridge University Press.

Brubaker, Rogers and David D. Laitin. 1998. 'Ethnic and nationalist violence.' *Annual Review of Sociology* 24:423–52.

Brück, Tilman. 2001. 'Mozambique: the economic effects of war.' In *War and Underdevelopment,* Vol. 2: Country Experiences, edited by

F. Stewart, V. Fitzgerald and Associates. Oxford: Oxford University Press.

Brück, Tilman. 2004. 'The welfare effect of farm household activity choices in post-war Mozambique.' Households in Conflict Network, Brighton and New Haven, available at: http://www.hicn.org/.

Brunnschweiler, Christa N. and Erwin H. Bulte. 2008. 'The resource curse revisited and revised: a tale of paradoxes and red herrings.' *Journal of Environmental Economics and Management* **55**:248–64.

Brunnschweiler, Christa N. and Erwin H. Bulte. 2009. 'Natural resources and violent conflict: resource abundance, dependence, and the onset of civil wars.' *Oxford Economic Papers* **61**:651–74.

Bryden, A. 2007. 'The linkage between DDR and SSR.' Governance and Social Development Resource Centre, University of Birmingham.

Buchanan, C. and M. Widmer. 2006. 'Negotiating disarmament: reflections on guns, fighters, and armed violence in peace processes.' Geneva Centre for Humanitarian Dialogue, Geneva.

Buckland, P. 1979. *The Factory of Grievances: Devolved Government in Northern Ireland, 1921–1939*. Dublin: Gill & Macmillan.

Bueno de Mesquita, B. and G.W. Downs. 2006. 'Intervention and democracy'. *International Organization* **60**(3):627–49.

Buhaug, Halvard. 2007. 'The future is more than scale: a reply to Diehl and O'Lear.' *Geopolitics* **12**:192–9.

Buhaug, Halvard. 2010. 'Climate not to blame for African civil wars.' *Proceedings of the National Academy of Sciences* **107**:16477–82.

Buhaug, Halvard et al. 2011. 'It's the Local Economy, Stupid! Geographic Wealth Dispersion and Conflict Outbreak Location,' *Journal of Conflict Resolution* **55**(5):814–40.

Buhaug, Halvard, Lars-Erik Cederman and Jan Ketil Rød. 2008a. 'Disaggregating ethno-nationalist civil wars: a dyadic test of exclusion theory.' *International Organization* **62**:531–51.

Buhaug, Halvard and Scott Gates. 2002. 'The geography of civil war.' *Journal of Peace Research* **39**:417–33.

Buhaug, Halvard and Kristian Skrede Gleditsch. 2008. 'Contagion or confusion? Why conflicts cluster in space.' *International Studies Quarterly* **52**:215–33.

Buhaug, Halvard, Nils Petter Gleditsch and Ole Magnus Theisen. 2008b. 'Implications of climate change for armed conflict.' Social Development Department, World Bank, Washington, DC, available at: http://site resources.worldbank.org/INTRANETSOCIALDEVELOPMENT/Re sources/SDCCWorkingPaper_Conflict.pdf.

Buhaug, Halvard, Nils Petter Gleditsch and Ole Magnus Theisen. 2010. 'Implications of climate change for armed conflict.' In *Social*

Dimensions of Climate Change: Equity and Vulnerability in a Warming World, edited by R. Mearns and A. Norton. Washington, DC: World Bank, pp. 75–101.

Buhaug, Halvard and Päivi Lujala. 2005. 'Accounting for scale: measuring geography in quantitative studies of civil war.' *Political Geography* **24**:399–418.

Buhaug, Halvard and Jan Ketil Rød. 2006. 'Local determinants of African civil wars, 1970–2001.' *Political Geography* **25**:315–35.

Buhaug, Halvard and Ole Magnus Theisen. 2010. 'On environmental change and armed conflict.' Under review.

Bunce, Valerie. 1999. *Subversive Institutions: The Design and the Destruction of Socialism and the State*. Cambridge: Cambridge University Press.

Bunce, Valerie and S. Watts. 2005. 'Managing diversity and sustaining democracy: ethnofederal versus unitary states in the post-Communist world.' In *Sustainable Peace: Power and Democracy after Civil Wars*, edited by P.G. Roeder and D. Rothchild. Ithaca, NY: Cornell University Press.

Bundervoet, T., P. Verwimp and R. Akresh. 2007. 'Health and civil war in rural Burundi.' IZA Discussion Paper 2951, Institute for the Study of Labor (IZA), Bonn.

Burke, Marshall B., Edward Miguel, Shanker Satyanath, John A. Dykema and David B. Lobell. 2009. 'Warming increases the risk of civil war in Africa.' *Proceedings of the National Academy of Sciences* **106**:20670–74.

Burnell, Peter. 2006. 'The coherence of democratic peacebuilding.' Research Paper 2006/147, UNU-WIDER, Helsinki.

Burnett, V. 2003. 'Afghanistan's blooming poppy trade fuelling instability and the Taliban.' *Financial Times* 30 October.

Burns, A.L. and N. Heathcote. 1963. *Peace-keeping by U.N. Forces: From Suez to the Congo*. New York: Praeger.

Bush, Kenneth and Diana Saltarelli. 2000. *The Two Faces of Education in Ethnic Conflict: Towards a Peacebuilding Education for Children*. Florence: UNICEF Innocenti Research Center.

Call, C. and M. Barnett. 1999. 'Looking for a few good cops: peacekeeping, peacebuilding and CIVPOL.' *International Peacekeeping* 6(4):43–68.

Call, Charles and John Schmitt. 2009. 'Explaining civil war recurrence.'

Carbonnier, G. 1998. 'Conflict, postwar rebuilding, and the economy.' United Nations Research Institute for Social Development (UNRISD), Geneva.

Carey, Sabine C. 2010. 'The use of repression as a response to domestic dissent.' *Political Studies* **58**:167–86.

Carlsson, I., H. Sung-Joo and R. Kupolati. 1999. 'Report of the independent inquiry into the actions of the United Nations during the

1994 genocide in Rwanda.' S/1257, 16 December. New York: United Nations.

Carment, David. 1993. 'The international dimensions of ethnic conflicts: concepts, indicators, and theory.' *Journal of Peace Research* **30**:137–50.

Carment, David and Frank Harvey. 2000. *Using Force to Prevent Ethnic Violence: An Evaluation of Theory and Evidence.* Westport, CT: Praeger.

Carment, David and A. Schnabel. 2003. *Conflict Prevention: Path to Peace or Grand Illusion?*. Tokyo: United Nations University Press.

Caron, D.D. 1993. 'The legitimacy of the collective authority of the Security Council.' *American Journal of International Law* **87**(2):552–99.

Carothers, Tom. 2009. 'Democracy assistance: political vs. developmental.' *Journal of Democracy* **20**:5–19.

Carter, T.A. 2007. 'United Nations intervention decisions: a strategic examination.' Working paper, Department of Political Science, Wayne State University, Detroit, MI.

Case, Anne and Christina Paxson. 2006. 'Stature and status: height, ability, and labor market outcomes.' *Journal of Political Economy* **16**:499–532.

Cassidy, R. 2004. *Peacekeeping in the Abyss: British and American Peacekeeping Doctrine and Practice after the Cold War.* Westport, CT: Praeger.

Cater, C. 2003. 'The political economy of conflict and UN intervention: rethinking the critical cases of Africa.' In *The Political Economy of Armed Conflict: Beyond Green and Grievance*, edited by K. Ballentine and J. Sherman. Boulder, CO: Lynne Rienner.

Caumartin, Corinne, George Gray Molina and Rosemary Thorp. 2008. 'Inequality, ethnicity and political violence in Latin America: the cases of Bolivia, Guatemala and Peru.' In *Horizontal Inequalities and Conflict: Understanding Group Violence in Multiethnic Societies*, edited by F. Stewart. London: Palgrave, pp. 227–47.

Cederman, Lars-Eric and Luc Girardin. 2007. 'Beyond fractionalization: mapping ethnicity onto nationalist insurgencies.' *American Political Science Review* **101**:173–85.

Cederman, Lars-Eric, Luc Girardin and Kristian Skrede Gleditsch. 2009. 'Ethnonationalist triads: assessing the influence of kin groups on civil wars.' *World Politics* **61**:403–37.

Cederman, Lars-Eric, Andreas Wimmer and Brian Min. 2010. 'Why do ethnic groups rebel? New data and analysis.' *World Politics* **62**:87–119.

Cerra, V. and S.C. Saxena. 2008. 'Growth dynamics: the myth of economic recovery.' *American Economic Review* **98**:439–57.

Chabal, P. and J.-P. Daloz. 1999. *Africa Works: Disorder as Political Instrument.* London: James Currey.

Chamarbagwala, R. and H. Morán. 2008. 'The human capital consequences of civil war: evidence from Guatemala.' Households in Conflict Network, available at: http://www.hicn.org/.

Chandler, David. 2006. *Empire in Denial: The Politics of State-Building*. London: Pluto.

Chandler, David. 2008. 'Human security: the dog that didn't bark.' *Security Dialogue* **39**:427–38.

Chauveau, J.P. and Paul Richards. 2008. 'West African insurgencies in agrarian perspective: Côte d'Ivoire and Sierra Leone compared.' *Journal of Agrarian Change* **8**:515–52.

Chen, Lincoln and V. Narasimhan. 2003. 'Human security and global health.' *Journal of Human Development* **4**:181–90.

Chen, S., N.V. Loayza and Marta Reynal-Querol. 2008. 'The aftermath of civil war.' *World Bank Economic Review* **22**:63–85.

Chenery, H., M.S. Ahluwalia, C.L.G. Bell, J. Duloy and Richard Jolly. 1974. *Redistribution with Growth: Policies to Improve Income Distribution in Developing Countries in the Context of Economic Growth*. Oxford: Oxford University Press.

Chesterman, S. 2004. *You, the People: The United Nations, Transitional Administration, and State Building*. Oxford: Oxford University Press.

Chopra, J. 1999. *Peace-Maintenance: The Evolution of International Political Authority*. London: Routledge.

Chopra, J. 2000. 'The UN's kingdom in East Timor.' *Survival* **42**(3):27–39.

Chopra, Radhika and P. Jeffery (eds). 2005. *Educational Regimes in Contemporary India*. New Delhi: Sage.

Chorbajian, Levon and George Shirinian. 1999. *Studies in Comparative Genocide*. New York: St Martin's Press.

Choucri, Nazli. 1974. *Population Dynamics Violence: Propositions, Insights, and Evidence.* Lexington, MA: Lexington Books.

Christensen, M. and M. Utas. 2008. 'Mercenaries of democracy: the "politricks" of remobilized combatants in the 2007 general elections, Sierra Leone.' *African Affairs* **107**:515–39.

Chua, Amy. 2003. *World on Fire*. New York: Doubleday.

Ciccone, Antonio. 2010. 'Transitory economic shocks and civil conflict'. Typescript, ICREA-Universitat Pompeu Fabra. URL: http://www.antoniociccone.eu/.

Ciccone, Antonio. 2011. 'Economic shocks and civil conflict: a comment.' *American Economic Review: Applied Economics* **3**(4):215–27.

CIFP. 2006. 'Fragile states: monitoring and assessment: the way forward.' Country Indicators for Foreign Policy, Carleton University, Ottawa.

Cilliers, J. 2000. 'Resource wars: a new type of insurgency.' In *Angola's*

War Economy: The Role of Oil and Diamonds, edited by J. Cilliers and C. Dietrich. Pretoria: Institute for Strategic Studies.

Cincotta, Richard P., Robert Engelman and Daniele Anastasion. 2003. *The Security Demographic: Population and Civil Conflict after the Cold War*. Washington, DC: Population Action International.

Clapham C. 1998. 'Being peacekept.' In *Peacekeeping in Africa*, edited by O. Furley and R. May. Aldershot: Ashgate, pp. 303–19.

Clark, Phil. 2007. 'Hybridity, holism, and "traditional" justice: the case of the Gacaca Community Courts in post-genocide Rwanda.' *George Washington International Law Review* **39**:765–837.

Clarke, W. and J. Herbst (eds). 1997. *Learning from Somalia: The Lessons of Armed Humanitarian Intervention*. Boulder, CO: Westview.

Claude, Iris L., Jr. 2006. 'Collective security as an approach to peace.' In *Classic Readings and Contemporary Debates in International Relations*, edited by D.M. Goldstein, P. Williams and J.M. Shafritz. Belmont, CA: Thomson Wadsworth.

Coate, R.A. (ed.). 1994. *U.S. Policy and the Future of the United Nations*. New York: Twentieth Century Fund.

Cohen, Abner. 1996. 'Ethnicity and politics.' In *Ethnicity*, edited by J. Hutchinson and A.D. Smith. Oxford: Oxford University Press.

Cohen, Jean L. and Andrew Arato. 1995. *Civil Society and Political Theory*. Cambridge, MA: MIT Press.

Cohen, Youssef, Brian R. Brown and A.F.K. Organski. 1981. 'The paradoxical nature of state-making: the violent creation of order.' *American Political Science Review* **75**:901–10.

Colleta, Nat. 1995. 'From warriors to workers: the World Bank's role in post-conflict reconstruction.' Report, World Bank, Washington, DC.

Colleta, Nat., M. Kostner and I. Wiederhofer. 1996. 'The transition from war to peace in Sub-Saharan Africa.' Report World Bank, Washington, DC.

Colleta, Nat. and Robert Muggah. 2009. 'Post-conflict security promotion.' *Journal of Security Sector Management* Winter: 1–25.

Collier, Paul. 1994. 'Demobilization and insecurity: a study in the economics of the transition from war to peace.' *Journal of International Development* **6**:343–51.

Collier, Paul. 1999. 'On the economic consequences of civil war.' *Oxford Economic Papers* **51**:168–83.

Collier, Paul. 2000a. 'Doing well out of war: an economic perspective.' In *Greed and Grievance: Economic Agendas in Civil Wars*, edited by M. Berdal and D.M. Malone. Boulder, CO: Lynne Rienner, pp. 91–111.

Collier, Paul. 2000b. 'Policy for post-conflict societies: reducing the risks of renewed conflict.' paper presented at the Economics of Political

Violence Conference, Princeton University, Princeton NJ, March 18–19.

Collier, Paul. 2000c. 'Rebellion as a quasi-criminal activity.' *Journal of Conflict Resolution* **44**:839–53.

Collier, Paul. 2006. 'Is aid oil? An analysis of whether Africa can absorb more aid.' *World Development* **34**:563–73.

Collier, Paul. 2009. *War, Guns, and Votes: Democracy in Dangerous Places*. New York: HarperCollins.

Collier, Paul and Robert Bates. 2008. 'Endogenizing syndromes.' In *The Political Economy of Economic Growth in Africa, 1960–2000*, edited by B.J. Ndulu, S. O'Connell, R.H. Bates, P. Collier and C. Saludo. Cambridge: Cambridge University Press.

Collier, Paul, Lisa Chauvet and Håvard Hegre. 2009. 'Conflicts: the security challenges in conflict-prone countries.' In *Global Crises, Global Solutions*, 2nd edn, edited by B. Lomborg. Cambridge: Cambridge University Press.

Collier, Paul, V.L. Elliott, Håvard Hegre, Anke Hoeffler, Marta Reynal-Querol and Nicholas Sambanis. 2003. *Breaking the Conflict Trap: Civil War and Development Policy*. Washington, DC: World Bank.

Collier, Paul and Anke Hoeffler. 1998. 'On economic causes of civil war.' *Oxford Economic Papers* **50**:563–73.

Collier, Paul and Anke Hoeffler. 2000. 'Greed and grievance in civil war.' World Bank, Washington, DC.

Collier, Paul and Anke Hoeffler. 2004a. 'Aid, policy and growth in post-conflict societies.' *European Economic Review* **48**:1125–45.

Collier, Paul and Anke Hoeffler. 2004b. 'Greed and grievance in civil war.' *Oxford Economic Papers* **56**:563–95.

Collier, Paul, Anke Hoeffler and Mans Söderbom. 2004. 'On the duration of civil war.' *Journal of Peace Research* **41**:253–73.

Collinson, S. 2003. *Power, Livelihoods, and Conflict: Case Studies in Political Economy Analysis for Humanitarian Action*. London: ODI.

Comisión de Esclarecimiento Histórico (CEH). 1999. 'Guatemala: Memoria del Silencio. Tomo I: Mandato y procedimiento de trabajo; causas y origineses del enfrantamiento armado interno.' Oficina de Servicios para Proyectosde las Naciones Unidas.

Commission on Human Security. 2003. 'Human Security Now: Protecting and Empowering People.' New York, available at: http://www. humansecurity-chs.org/finalreport/index.html.

Connor, Walker. 1984. *The National Question in Marxist–Leninist Theory and Strategy*. Princeton, NJ: Princeton University Press.

Cooke, Jacob E. 1961. *The Federalist Papers (1787–88)*. Middletown, CT: Wesleyan University Press.

Cooper, N. 2002. 'State collapse as business: the role of conflict trade and the emerging control agenda.' *Development and Change* **33**:935–55.

Cooper, N. 2006. 'Chimeric governance and the extension of resource regulation.' *Conflict, Security and Development* **6**:315–35.

Cooper, N., M. Pugh and J. Goodhand. 2004. *War Economies in a Regional Context: Challenges of Transformation.* Boulder, CO: Lynne Rienner.

Cordell, Keith and Stefan Wolff. 2010. *Ethnic Conflict: Causes, Consequences, Responses.* Cambridge: Polity Press.

Cornes, Richard and Todd Sandler. 1996. *The Theory of Externalities, Public Goods, and Club Goods.* Cambridge: Cambridge University Press.

Cortright, David. 1997. *The Price of Peace: Incentives and International Conflict Prevention.* Lanham, MD: Rowman & Littlefield.

Coughlan, R. and S.W.R.d.A. Samarasinghe. 1991. *Economic Dimensions of Ethnic Conflict: International Perspectives.* New York: St. Martin's Press.

Coulby, David; Robert Cowen and Crispin Jones (eds). 2000. *Education in Times of Transition.* London: Kogan Page Ltd.

Coulon, J. 1998. *Soldiers of Diplomacy: The United Nations, Peacekeeping, and the New World Order.* Toronto/Buffalo: University of Toronto Press.

Coulter, Chris. 2006. 'Being a bush wife. Women's lives through war and peace in Northern Sierra Leone.' PhD dissertation. Uppsala University.

Cousens, E.M., C. Kumar and K. Wermester (eds). 2001. *Peacebuilding as Politics: Cultivating Peace in Fragile Societies.* Boulder, CO: Lynne Rienner.

Cox, A.M. 1967. *Prospects for Peacekeeping.* Washington, DC: Brookings Institute.

CPRC. 2008. *Chronic Poverty Report: 2008–2009.* London: Chronic Poverty Research Centre.

Cramer, Chris. 2002. 'Homo economicus goes to war: methodological individualism, rational choice, and the political economy of war.' *World Development* **30**:1845–64.

Cramer, Chris. 2003. 'Does inequality cause conflict?' *Journal of International Development* **15**:397–412.

Cramer, Chris. 2006. *Civil War is Not a Stupid Thing: Accounting for Violence in Developing Countries.* London: C. Hurst.

CRED. 2009. *Annual Disaster Statistical Review: The Numbers and Trends 2008.* Brussels: Centre for Research on the Epidemiology of Disasters, available at: http://www.cred.be/sites/default/files/ADSR_2008.pdf.

CRED. 2010. 'CRED Crunch Issue no. 19 (February).' Centre for Research on the Epidemiology of Disasters, Brussels, available at: http://cred.be/sites/default/files/CredCrunch19.pdf.

Crisp, J. 1999. 'Policy challenges of the new diasporas: migrant networks and their impact on asylum flows and regimes.' Working Paper 99-05, Policy Research Unit, UNHCR, Geneva.

Crisp, J., J. Janz and J. Riera. 2009. 'Surviving in the city: a review of UNHCR's operation for Iraqi refugees in urban areas of Jordan, Lebanon, and Syria.' UNHCR New Issues in Refugee Research Working Paper 7, UNHCR, Geneva.

Crisp, Jeff; Christopher Talbot and Daiana B. Cipollone (eds). 2001. *Learning for a Future: Refugee Education in Developing Countries.* Geneva: UNHCR.

Crocker, C., F.O. Hampson and P. Aall. (eds) 1999a. *Herding Cats: Multiparty Mediation in a Complex World.* Washington, DC: US Institute of Peace Press.

Crocker, Chester, Fen Osler Hampson and Pamela Aall. 1999b. 'Rising to the challenge of multiparty mediation.' In *Herding Cats: Multiparty Mediation in a Complex World*, edited by C. Crocker, F.O. Hampson and P. Aall. Washington, DC: US Institute of Peace Press.

Crocker, C., F.O. Hampson and P. Aall. (eds). 2005. *Grasping the Nettle: Analyzing Cases of Intractable Conflict.* Washington, DC: US Institute of Peace Press.

Crocker, Chester, Fen Osler Hampson and Pamela Aall. 2011a. *Rewiring Regional Security in a Fragmented World.* Washington, DC: US Institute of Peace Press.

Crocker, Chester, Fen Osler Hampson and Pamela Aall. 2011b. 'Towards a concept of collective security management.' In *Rewiring Regional Security in a Fragmented World*, edited by C. Crocker, F.O. Hampson and P. Aall. Washington, DC: US Institute of Peace Press.

Crocker, D. 2000. 'Truth commissions, transitional justice, and civil society.' In *Truth v. Justice: The Morality of Truth Commissions*, edited by R. Rotberg and D. Thompson. Princeton, NJ: Princeton University Press.

Cronin, J. 1999. 'A Luta Dis-Continue: The TRC final report and the nation building project.' Johannesburg.

Crook, Richard Charles. 1997. 'Winning coalitions and ethno-regional politics: the failure of the opposition in the 1990 and 1995 elections in Côte d'Ivoire.' *African Affairs* **96**:215–42.

Crowley, J. 2001. 'The political participation of ethnic minorities.' *International Political Science Review* **22**:99–121.

Dadrian, Vahakn N. 1997. *The History of the Armenian Genocide: Ethnic*

Conflict from the Balkans to Anatolia to the Caucasus. Providence, RI: Berghahn.

Daalder, I.H. 1994. *The Clinton Administration and Multilateral Peace Operations.* Washington, DC: Institute of Studies Diplomacy Publications, Georgetown University.

Daniel, D.C.F., B.C. Hayes and C. de Jonge Oudraat. 1999. *Coercive Inducement and the Containment of International Crises.* Washington, DC: US Institute of Peace Press.

Danspeckgruber, W. 2005. 'Self-governance plus regional integration: a possible solution to self-determination claims.' In *Autonomy, Self-Governance, and Conflict Resolution: Innovative Approaches to Institutional Design in Divided Societies,* edited by M. Weller and S. Wolff. London: Routledge.

Darby, John. 1999. 'Northern Ireland: beyond the time of troubles.' In *The Accommodation of Cultural Diversity,* edited by C. Young. London: Macmillan.

Dasgupta, P. 1993. *An Enquiry into Well-Being and Destitution.* Oxford: Oxford University Press.

Date-Bah, E. 2003. *Jobs after War: A Critical Challenge in the Peace and Reconstruction Puzzle.* Geneva: International Labour Organisation (ILO).

Daun, H. (ed.). 2002. *Educational Restructuring in the Context of Globalization and Local Demands.* New York: Routledge/Falmer.

Davies, Lynn. 2004a. *Education and Conflict: Complexity and Chaos.* London: Routledge.

Davies, Lynn. 2004b. 'Building a Civic Culture Post-Conflict', *London Review of Education* 2(3):229–44.

Davies, Lynn. 2006. 'Education for Positive Conflict and Interruptive Democracy.' In *Education, Globalization and Social Change,* edited by Hugh Lauder et al. Oxford: Oxford University Press.

Davis, D.R. and D.E. Weinstein. 2002. 'Bones, bombs, and break points: the geography of economic activity.' *American Economic Review* **92**:1269–89.

de Ferranti, D., G.E. Perry, F. Ferreira and M. Walton. 2004. *Inequality in Latin America and the Caribbean: Breaking with History?* Washington, DC: World Bank.

De Groot, Olaf J. 2010. 'The spillover effects of conflict on economic growth in neighbouring countries in Africa.' *Defence and Peace Economics* **21**:149–64.

de Haas, H., O. Bakewell, S. Castles, G. Jonsson and S. Vezzoli. 2009. 'Mobility and human development.' UNDP, New York.

de Jonge Oudraat C. 1996. 'The United Nations and internal conflict.'

In M.E. Brown (ed.), *The International Dimensions of Internal Conflict*. Cambridge, MA: MIT, pp. 489–535.

De Jonge Oudraat, C. 2011. 'Play it again, Uncle Sam: NATO, the EU, and transatlantic relations.' In *Rewiring National Security*, edited by C. Crocker, F.O. Hampson and P. Aall. Washington, DC: US Institute of Peace Press.

De Mel, Neloufer. 2007. *Militarizing Sri Lanka. Popular Culture, Memory and Narrative in the Armed Conflict*. New Delhi: Sage.

de Soto, A. and G. del Castillo. 1994. 'Obstacles to peacebuilding.' *Foreign Policy* **94**:69–83.

de Soysa, Indra. 2002. 'Paradise is a bazaar? Greed, creed, and governance in civil war, 1989–1999.' *Journal of Peace Research* **39**:395–416.

de Vries, H. 2009. 'Economic provisions in peace agreements.' Clingendael Institute, The Hague.

de Waal, Alex. 2007. 'Sudan: what kind of state? What kind of crisis?' Crisis States Research Centre, London School of Economics and Political Science, available at: www.crisisstates.com/download/op/op2. DeWaal.pdf.

de Waal, Thomas. 2010. 'Remaking the Nagorno-Karabakh peace process.' *Survival* **52**:159–76.

de Walque, D. 2006. 'The long-term legacy of the Khmer Rouge period in Cambodia.' Paper presented at the First Annual Workshop, Households in Conflict Network, Berlin, 15–16 January.

Debiel, Tobias and Sascha Werthes. 2006. 'Human security on foreign policy agendas.' In *INEF Report 80/2006*. Essen: Institute for Development and Peace, University of Duisburg-Essen.

Debos, M. 2008. 'Fluid loyalties in a regional crisis: Chadian combatants in the Central African Republic.' *African Affairs* **107**:225–41.

Debrix, F. 1999. *Re-envisioning Peacekeeping: The United Nations and the Mobilization of Ideology*. Minneapolis, MN: University of Minnesota Press.

Degomme, Olivier and Debarati Guha-Sapir. 2010. 'Patterns of mortality rates in the Darfur conflict.' *The Lancet* **375**:294–300.

della Porta, Diana and Mario Diani. 1999. *Social Movements: An Introduction*. Oxford: Blackwell.

Department of Foreign Affairs and International Trade. 1999. 'Human Security: Safety for People in a Changing World.' Department of Foreign Affairs and International Trade, Government of Canada, Ottawa.

Dercon, Stefan. 2006. 'Economic reform, growth and the poor: evidence from rural Ethiopia.' *Journal of Development Economics* **81**:1–24.

Des Forges, A. and K. Roth. 2002. 'Justice or therapy? A discussion on

Helena Cobban's essay on Crime and Punishment in Rwanda.' *Boston Review* **27**. Available at: http://www.bostonreview.net/BR27.3/roth desforges.html.

Deutsch, M. 1973. *The Resolution of Conflict: Constructive and Destructive Processes*. New Haven, CT: Yale University Press.

DFID. 2005. 'Why we need to work more effectively in fragile states.' Department for International Development, UK Government, London.

DFID. 2007. 'Moving out of poverty: making migration work better for poor people.' Department for International Development, UK Government, London.

Diehl, P.F. 1993. *International Peacekeeping*. Baltimore, MD: Johns Hopkins University Press.

Diehl, Paul F. and J. Lepgold. 2003. *Regional Conflict Management*. Lanham, MD: Rowman & Littlefield.

Diehl, Paul F., J. Reifschneider and P.R. Hensel. 1996. 'United Nations intervention and recurring conflict.' *International Organization* **50**:683–700.

Dietrich Ortega, L.M. 2011. 'Gendered patterns of mobilisation and recruitment for political violence: experiences from three Latin American countries.' In *Understanding Collective Political Violence*, edited by Y. Guichaoua. Basingstoke: Palgrave Macmillan.

Dixon, J. 2009. 'Emerging consensus: results from the second wave of statistical studies on civil war termination.' *Civil Wars* **11**(2):121–36.

Dixon, Jeffrey. 2009. 'What causes civil wars? Integrating quantitative research findings.' *International Studies Review* **11**(4):707–35.

Djankov, Simeon and Marta Reynal-Querol. 2010. 'Poverty and civil war: revisiting the evidence.' *Review of Economics and Statistics* **92**:1035–41.

Do, Quy-Toan and Lakshmi Iyer. 2005. 'An empirical analysis of civil conflict in Nepal.' Harvard Business School, Boston, MA.

Dobbins, J., J.G. McGinn, K. Crane, S. Jones and R. Lal. 2003. *America's Role in Nation-Building: From Germany to Iraq*. Santa Monica/Arlington/Pittsburg: RAND Corp.

Donnelly, Thomas, Margaret Roth and Caleb Baker. 1991. *Operation Just Cause: The Storming of Panama*. New York: Lexington Books.

Dorussen, Han. 2005a. 'Economic coercion in civil conflict'. Paper presented at the Meeting of the Working Group on 'Governance and Peace', Center for the Study of Civil War (CSCW), Oslo, 14–15 May.

Dorussen, Han. 2005: 'Governance, Development, and State Building.' *European Journal of Development Research* **17**: 411–22.

Dorussen, Han. 2009. 'Ökonomische und Politische Zwangsmassnahmen in Ethnopolitischen Konflikt', In *Identität, Institutionen und*

Ökonomie: Ursachen Innenpolitischer Gewalt, edited by Margit Bussmann, Andreas Hasenclever and Gerald Schneider. PVS – Politische Vierteljahresschrift, Sonderheft 43 / 2009. Wiesbaden: GWV Fachverlage, pp. 417–44.

Douglas, I., C. Gleichmann, M. Odenwald, K. Steenken and A. Wilkinson. 2004. 'Disarmament, demobilization and reintegration: a practical field and classroom guide.' Druckerei Hassmuller and GTZ, Hamburg.

Douma, P. 2008. 'Reintegration in Burindi: between happy cows and lost investments.' Clingendael Institute, The Hague.

Downs, G. and Stephen John Stedman. 2003. 'Evaluation issues in peace implementation.' In *Ending Civil Wars: The Implementation of Peace Agreements*, edited by S.J. Stedman, D. Rothchild and E.M. Cousens. Boulder, CO: Lynne Rienner.

Doyle, M.W. 1995. *UN Peacekeeping in Cambodia: UNTAC's Civil Mandate*. Boulder, CO: Lynne Rienner.

Doyle, M.W., I. Johnstone and R.C. Orr (eds). 1997. *Keeping the Peace: Multidimensional UN Operations in Cambodia and El Salvador*. Cambridge: Cambridge University Press.

Doyle, Michael W. and Nicholas Sambanis. 2000. 'International peace-building: a theoretical and quantitative analysis.' *American Political Science Review* **94**:779–801.

Doyle, Michael W. and Nicholas Sambanis. 2006. *Making War and Building Peace: United Nations Peace Operations*. Princeton, NJ: Princeton University Press.

Drury, Alfred C. and Richard S. Olson. 1998. 'Disasters and political unrest: a quantitative investigation.' *Journal of Contingencies and Crisis Management* **6**:155–61.

Drury, B. 1994. 'Ethnic mobilisation: some theoretical considerations.' In *Ethnic Mobilisation in a Multi-Cultural Europe*, edited by J. Rex and B. Drury. Aldershot: Avebury.

Dubey, A. 2002. 'Domestic institutions and the duration of civil war settlements.' Paper presented at the 48th Annual Meeting of the International Studies Association, New Orleans.

Duffield, Mark. 1999. 'Globalization and war economies: promoting order or the return of history?' *The Fletcher Forum on World Affairs* **23**:779–801.

Duffield, Mark. 2001. *Global Governance and the New Wars: The Merging of Development and Security*. London: Zed Books.

Duffield, Mark. 2007. *Development, Security, and Unending War: Governing the World of Peoples*. Cambridge: Polity Press.

Duffield, Mark, K. Diagne and V. Tennant. 2009. 'Evaluation of UNHCR's returnee reintegration programme in Southern Sudan.'

UNHCR, Geneva, available at: http://www.unhcr.org/publ/RESEA RCH/48e47f972.pdf.

Dukuly, Abdullah. 2004. 'Education Liberia: civil war leaves school system in tatters.' In *InterPress Service*, 16 June, available at: http://ww2.aegis.org/news/ips/2004/ip040614.htm.

Durch, W.J. (ed.). 1993. *The Evolution of UN Peacekeeping.* New York: St. Martin's Press.

Durch, W.J. (ed.). 1996. *UN Peacekeeping, American Policy and the Uncivil Wars of the 1990s.* New York: St. Martin's Press.

Durch, W.J. and T.C. Berkman. 2006. *Who Should Keep the Peace? Providing Security for Twenty-First Century Peace Operations.* Washington, DC: Henry L. Stimson Center.

Durch, W.J., V.K. Holt, Caroline R. Earle and Moira K. Shanahan. 2003. 'The Brahimi Report and the future of UN peace operations.' The Henry L. Stimson Center, Washington, DC.

Duryea, Suzanne, David Lam and Deborah Levinson. 2007. 'Effects of economic shocks on children's employment and schooling in Brazil.' *Journal of Development Economics* **84**:188–214.

Eastmond, M. and J. Öjendal. 1999. 'Revisiting a repatriation success: the case of Cambodia.' In *The End of the Refugee Cycle? Refugee Repatriation and Reconstruction*, edited by R. Black and K. Koser. Oxford: Berghahn.

Eck, Kristine. 2010. 'Raising rebels: participation and recruitment in civil war.' Department of Peace and Conflict Research, Uppsala University, Uppsala.

Eckert, S. 2004. 'Lessons from the counter terrorism committee.' In *Profiting from Peace: Managing the Resource Dimension of Civil Wars*, edited by K. Ballentine and H. Nitzschke. Boulder, CO: Lynne Rienner.

ECP. 2007. 'Analysis of the disarmament, demobilization and reintegration programmes existing in the world during 2006.' Escola de Cultura de Paz, Madrid.

Edelman, M. 2001. 'Social movements: changing paradigms and forms of politics.' *Annual Review of Anthropology* **30**:285–317.

Edelstein, D.M. 2008. *Occupational Hazards: Success and Failure in Military Occupation.* Ithaca, NY: Cornell University Press.

Edmead, F. 1971. *Analysis and Prediction in International Mediation.* London: Unitar.

Egnell, R. and P. Haldén. 2009. 'Laudable, ahistorical, and overambitious: security sector reform meets state formation theory.' *Conflict, Security and Development* **9**:27–54.

Ehrlich, Paul R. 1968. *The Population Bomb.* New York: Ballantine.

Eisinger, P.K. 1973. 'The conditions of protest behavior in American cities.' *American Political Science Review* **67**:11–28.

Elazar, D. 1987. *Exploring Federalism*. Tuscaloosa, AL: University of Alabama.

Elazar, D. 1994. *Federalism and the Way to Peace*. Kingston, Ont.: Queen's Institute of Intergovernmental Relations.

Elbadawi, Ibrahim A. and Nicholas Sambanis. 2002. 'How much war will we see? Explaining the prevalence of civil war.' *Journal of Conflict Resolution* **46**:307–34.

Ellis, S. 1999. *The Mask of Anarchy: The Roots of Liberia's War*. New York: New York University Press.

Enloe, C. 2000. *Maneuvers: The International Politics of Militarizing Women's Lives*. Berkeley, CA: University of California Press.

Esteban, Joan and Debraj Ray. 2008. 'Polarization, fractionalization, and conflict.' *Journal of Peace Research* **45**:163–82.

Esty, Daniel C., Jack A. Goldstone, Ted Robert Gurr, Barbara Harff, Marc Levy, Geoffrey D. Dabelko, Pamela Surko and Alan N. Unger. 1998. *State Failure Task Force Report: Phase II Findings*. McLean, VA: Science Applications International, for State Failure Task Force.

European Council. 2003. 'A secure Europe in a better world: the European security strategy.' European Council, Brussels, available at: http://www.consilium.europa.eu/showPage.aspx?id=266&lang=EN (accessed December 14, 2010).

European Report on Development. 2009. 'Overcoming Fragility in Africa: Forging a New European Approach.' European Union, Brussels.

European Union. 2006. 'EU concept for support to disarmament, demobilization, and reintegration (DDR).' European Union (EU), Brussels.

Evans, D.K. and E. Miguel. 2004. 'Orphans and schooling in Africa: a longitudinal analysis.' Bureau for Research and Economic Analysis of Development, Harvard University, Cambridge MA.

Fabian, L.L. 1971. *Soldiers Without Enemies: Preparing the United Nations for Peacekeeping*. Washington, DC: Brookings Institution.

Fagen, P. 2006. 'Remittances in conflict and crises: how remittances sustain livelihoods in war, crises, and transitions to peace.' *AccessFinance* **11**:1–18.

Farah, D. 2004. *Blood from Stones: The Secret Financial Network of Terror*. New York: Broadway Books.

Farer, Tom. 2011. 'Human security: defining the elephant and imagining its tasks.' *Asian Journal of International Law* **1**:43–55.

Farr, V., H. Myrtinen and A. Schnabel (eds). 2009. *Sexed Pistols: The Gendered Impacts of Small Arms and Light Weapons*. Tokyo: United Nations University Press.

Fearon, James D. 1995. 'Rationalist explanations for war.' *International Organization* **49**:379–414.
Fearon, James D. 1998. 'Commitment problems and the spread of ethnic conflict.' In *The International Spread of Ethnic Conflict*, edited by D. Lake and D. Rothchild. Princeton, NJ: Princeton University Press.
Fearon, James D. 2004. 'Ethnic mobilization and ethnic violence.' Available at: http://www.seminario2005.unal.edu.co/Trabajos/Fearon/Ethnic%20mobilization%20and%20ethnic%20violence.pdf.
Fearon, James D. 2005. 'Primary commodities exports and civil war.' *Journal of Conflict Resolution* **49**:483–507.
Fearon, James D., Kimuli Kasara and David D. Laitin. 2007. 'Ethnic minority rule and civil war onset.' *American Political Science Review* **101**:187–93.
Fearon, James D. and David D. Laitin. 1996. 'Explaining interethnic cooperation.' *American Political Science Review* **90**:715–35.
Fearon, James D. and David D. Laitin. 2003. 'Ethnicity, insurgency, and civil war.' *American Political Science Review* **97**(1):75–90.
Ferenczi, T. 2004. 'The republic: a French myth.' In *The Shifting Foundations of Modern Nation-States*, edited by S. Godfrey and F. Unger. Toronto: University of Toronto Press, pp. 100–108.
Feuer, Lewis S. 1969. *The Conflict of Generations: The Character and Significance of Student Movements*. London: Heinemann.
Findlay, T. 2002. *The Use of Force in UN Peace Operations*. Oxford: SIPRI and Oxford University Press.
Finnemore, M. 2003. *The Purpose of Intervention: Changing Beliefs About the Use of Force*. Ithaca, NY: Cornell University Press.
Fisher, R.J. 1995. 'Pacific, impartial third party intervention in international conflict: a review and an analysis.' In *Beyond Confrontation: Learning Conflict Resolution in the Post-Cold War Era*, edited by J.A. Vasquez, S.M. Jaffe, J.T. Johnson and L. Stameto. Ann Arbor, MI: University of Michigan Press, pp. 39–59.
Fisher, R.J. 2006. 'Coordination between track two and track one diplomacy in successful cases of prenegotiation.' *International Negotiation* **11**:65–89.
Fisher, R.J. and L. Keashly. 1991. 'The potential complementarity of mediation and consultation within a contingency model of third party intervention.' *Journal of Peace Research* **28**(1):29–42.
Fjelde, Hanne and Indra de Soysa. 2009. 'Coercion, co-optation, or cooperation? State capacity and the risk of civil war, 1961–2004.' *Conflict Management and Peace Science* **26**:5–25.
Fleitz, F.H. 2002. *Peacekeeping Fiascoes of the 1990s: Causes, Solutions, and U.S. Interests*. Westport, CT: Praeger.

Flores, Thomas Edward and Irfan Nooruddin. 2009. 'Democracy under the gun: understanding postconflict economic recovery.' *Journal of Conflict Resolution* **53**:3–29.

Fofana, M. 2009. 'Les raisons de l'enrôlement des jeunes combattants de la rébellion du Nord de la Côte d'Ivoire.' Paper presented at the CRISE Workshop on Mobilisation for Political Violence: What Do We Know? Centre for Research on Inequality, Human Security, and Ethnicity (CRISE), University of Oxford, 17–18 March.

Forman, Shepard and Patrick Stewart. 2000. *Good Intentions: Pledges of Aid for Postconflict Recovery*. Boulder, CO: Lynne Rienner.

Forsyth, M. 1989. *Federalism and Nationalism*. Leicester: Leicester University Press.

Fortna, V.P. 2003. 'Inside and out: peacekeeping and the duration of peace after civil and interstate wars.' *International Studies Review* **5**(4):97–114.

Fortna, V.P. 2004a. 'Interstate peacekeeping: causal mechanisms and empirical effects.' *World Politics* **56**(4):481–519.

Fortna, Virginia Page. 2004b. 'Does peacekeeping keep peace? International intervention and the duration of peace after civil war.' *International Studies Quarterly* **48**:269–92.

Fortna, V.P. 2004c. *Peace Time: Cease-Fire Agreements and the Durability of Peace*. Princeton, NJ: Princeton University Press.

Fortna, Virginia Page. 2008a. *Does Peacekeeping Work? Shaping Belligerents' Choices after Civil War*. Princeton, NJ: Princeton University Press.

Fortna, V.P. 2008b. 'Peacekeeping and democratization.' In *From War to Democracy: Dilemmas of Peacebuilding*, edited by A. Jarstad and T. Sisk. Cambridge: Cambridge University Press, pp. 39–79.

Fortna, Virginia Page. 2009. 'Where have all the victories gone? Peacekeeping and war outcomes.' Working Paper, Columbia University, available at: http://www.columbia.edu/~vpf4/victories%20Sept%2020 09.pdf.

Fraenkel, J. and B. Grofman. 2004. 'A neo-Downsian model of the alternative vote as a mechanism for mitigating ethnic conflict in plural societies.' *Public Choice* **121**:487–506.

Fraenkel, J. and B. Grofman. 2006. 'Does the alternative vote foster moderation in ethnically divided societies? The case of Fiji.' *Comparative Political Studies* **39**:623–51.

Franke, K. 2006. 'Gendered subjects of transitional justice.' *Columbia Journal of Gender and Law* **15**:813–28.

Frankel, Jeffrey A. and David Romer. 1999. 'Does trade affect growth?' *American Economic Review* **89**:379–99.

Franklin, M.N. 2004. *Voter Turnout and the Dynamics of Electoral Competition in Established Democracies since 1945.* Cambridge: Cambridge University Press.

Franzese, Robert J. and Jude C. Hays. 2008. 'Interdependence in comparative politics: substance, theory, empirics.' *Comparative Political Studies* **41**:742–80.

Frechette, Louise. 1999. 'Statement by the United Nations Deputy Secretary-General'.

Friman, Henrik. 2009. 'WikiForce: global cooperation in new security structures.' In *Crosscutting Issues in International Transformation*, edited by D. Neal, H. Friman, R. Doughty and L. Wells, II. Washington, DC: National Defense University Press.

Fukuda-Parr, S. 2012. 'Correcting horizontal inequality as a development priority: poverty reduction strategy papers (PRSPs) in Haiti, Liberia and Nepal.' In *Horizontal Inequalities and Post-conflict Development*, edited by Arnim Langer, Frances Stewart and Rajesh Venugopal. Basingstoke: Palgrave.

Fukuyama, Francis. 1989. 'The end of history.' *National Interest* **16**:3–18.

Fuller, Bruce. 1991. *Growing Up Modern. The Western State Builds Third World Schools.* London: Routledge.

Gaddis, John Lewis. 1986. 'The long peace: elements of stability in the postwar international system.' *International Security* **10**:99–142.

Galor, O. and D. Weil. 2000. 'Population, technology, and growth: from Malthusian stagnation to the demographic transition and beyond.' *American Economic Review* **90**:806–28.

Galtung, J. 2001. 'After violence, reconstruction, reconciliation, and resolution: coping with visible and invisible effects of war and violence.' In *Reconciliation, Justice, and Coexistence: Theory and Practice*, edited by M. Abu-Nimer. Lanham, MD: Lexington Books.

Ganguly, R. and R. Taras. 1998. *Understanding Ethnic Conflict.* New York: Longman.

Garcia-Rodicio, A. 2001. 'Restoration of life: a new theoretical approach to voluntary repatriation based on a Cambodian experience of return.' *International Journal of Refugee Law* **13**:123–40.

Gardner Feldman, Lily. 1984. *The Special Relationship between West Germany and Israel.* Boston, MA: Allen & Unwin.

Gary, I. and Terry L. Karl. 2003. *Bottom of the Barrel: Africa's Oil and the Poor.* Washington, DC: Catholic Relief Services.

Gasper, Des. 2010a. 'Climate change and the language of human security.' Institute for Social Studies (ISS), The Hague.

Gasper, Des. 2010b. 'The idea of human security.' In *Climate Change,*

Ethics and Human Security, edited by K. O'Brien, A.L. St. Clair and B. Kristofferson. Cambridge: Cambridge University Press.

Gates, Scott. 2002. 'Recruitment and allegiance: the microfoundations of rebellion.' *Journal of Conflict Resolution* **46**:111–30.

Gates, Scott, Håvard Hegre, Håvard Mokleiv Nygård and Håvard Strand. 2012. 'Development consequences of armed conflict'. World Development **40**(9): 1713–1722. http://dx.doi.org/10.1016/j.worlddev.2012.04.031.

Gates, Scott, Håvard Hegre, Håvard Mokleiv Nygård and Håvard Strand. 2010b. 'Consequences of conflict in the MENA region.' Background Paper for World Bank Flagship Report on the Middle East and North Africa. World Bank, Washington, DC.

Gates, Scott; Håvard Hegre, Håvard Mokleiv Nygård and Håvard Strand. 2010a. 'Consequences of civil conflict'. WB Report 62027. Background Paper for World Development Report 2011. http://wdr2011.worldbank.org/PRIO.

Gaubatz, K.T. 1991. 'Elections cycles and war.' *Journal of Conflict Resolution* **35**(2):212–44.

Geffray, C. 1990. *La Cause des Armes au Mozambique: Anthropologie d'une Guerre Civile*. Paris: Karthala.

Gelb, Alan and Associates. 1988. *Oil Windfalls: Blessing or Curse?* New York: Oxford University Press.

Gellner, Ernest. 1983. *Nations and Nationalism*. Ithaca, NY: Cornell University Press.

Geneva Declaration Secretariat. 2008. 'Global burden of armed conflict.' Geneva Declaration, Geneva.

Ghani, Ashraf and Clare Lockhart. 2008. *Fixing Failed States: A Framework for Rebuilding a Fractured World*. Oxford: Oxford University Press.

Ghani, Ashraf, Clare Lockhart and M. Carnahan. 2005. 'Closing the sovereignty gap: an approach to state-building.' Overseas Development Institute, London.

Ghobarah, Hazem Adam, Paul Huth and Bruce Russett. 2003. 'Civil wars kill and main people long after the shooting stops.' *American Political Science Review* **97**(2):189–202.

Gibbs, D.N. 1997. 'Is peacekeeping a new form of imperialism?' *International Peacekeeping* **4**(1):122–8.

Gilligan, M.J. and E. Sergenti. 2007. 'Does peacekeeping keep peace? Using matching to improve causal inference.' Working Paper, Department of Politics, New York University and Harvard University.

Gilligan, Michael and Stephen J. Stedman. 2003. 'Where do the peacekeepers go?' *International Studies Review* **5**(4):37–54.

Ginifer, J. (ed.). 1997. *Beyond the Emergency: Development within UN Peace Missions*. London: Frank Cass.

Giustozzi, A. 2009. 'Bureaucratic façade and political realities of disarmament and demobilisation in Afghanistan.' *Conflict, Security and Development* **8**:169–92.

Glasius, Marlies and Mary Kaldor. 2006. *A Human Security Doctrine for Europe: Project, Principles, Practicalities*. London: Routledge.

Glassmyer, Katherine and Nicholas Sambanis. 2008. 'Rebel military integration and civil war termination.' *Journal of Peace Research* **45**:365–84.

Glazer, Nathan. 1983. 'Federalism and ethnicity: the American solution.' In *Ethnic Dilemmas, 1964–1982*, edited by N. Glazer. Cambridge, MA: Harvard University Press.

Glazer, Nathan. 2000. 'Disaggregating culture.' In *Culture Matters*, edited by L. Harrison and S.P. Huntington. New York: Basic Books.

Glazer, Nathan and D.P. Moynihan. 1974. 'Why ethnicity?' *Commentary* **58**:33–9.

Gleditsch, Kristian Skrede. 2007. 'Transnational dimensions of civil war.' *Journal of Peace Research* **44**:293–309.

Gleditsch, Kristian Skrede and Kyle Beardsley. 2004. 'Nosy neighbours.' *Journal of Conflict Resolution* **48**:379–402.

Gleditsch, Kristian Skrede, Idean Salehyan and Kenneth Schultz. 2008. 'Fighting at home, fighting abroad.' *Journal of Conflict Resolution* **52**:479–506.

Gleditsch, Kristian Skrede and Michael D. Ward. 2006. 'Diffusion and the international context of democratization.' *International Organization* **60**:911–33.

Gleditsch, Nils Petter. 2012. 'Whither the weather? Climate change and conflict.' *Journal of Peace Research* **49**(1):3–11.

Gleditsch, Nils Petter. 1998. 'Armed conflict and the environment: a critique of the literature.' *Journal of Peace Research* **35**:381–400.

Gleditsch, Nils Petter, Olav Bjerkholt, Ådne Cappelen, Ron P. Smith and J. Paul Dunne. 1996. *The Peace Dividend*. Amsterdam: Elsevier.

Gleditsch, Nils Petter, Håvard Hegre and Håvard Strand. 2009. 'Democracy and civil war.' In *Handbook of War Studies III*, edited by M. Midlarsky. Ann Arbor, MI: University of Michigan Press, pp. 155–92.

Gleditsch, Nils Petter and Ole Magnus Theisen. 2010. 'Resources, the environment, and conflict.' In *Handbook of Security Studies*, edited by M.D. Cavelty and V. Mauer. London: Routledge, pp. 221–31.

Gleditsch, Nils Petter and Henrik Urdal. 2002. 'Ecoviolence? Links between population growth, environmental scarcity and violent conflict in Thomas Homer-Dixon's work.' *Journal of International Affairs* **56**:283–302.

Gleditsch, Nils Petter, Peter Wallensteen, Mikael Eriksson, Margareta Sollenberg and Håvard Strand. 2002. 'Armed conflict 1946–2001: a new dataset.' *Journal of Peace Research* **39**:615–37.

Global Witness. 1998. 'A rough trade: the role of companies and governments in the Angolan conflict.' Global Witness, London.

Global Witness. 2002. 'Logs of war: the timber trade and armed conflict.' Fafo Institute, Oslo.

Global Witness. 2003. 'For a few dollars more: how al Qaida moved into the diamond trade.' Global Witness, London.

Global Witness. 2010a. 'Diamonds, Sierra Leone, a war criminal, and a super model.' Global Witness, London.

Global Witness. 2010b. 'Lessons UN-learned: How the UN and member states must do more to end national-resource fueled conflicts.' Global Witness, London.

Global Witness. 2010c. 'Simply criminal: targeting rogue companies in violent conflict.' Global Witness, London.

Goffman, E. 1975. *Frame Analysis: An Essay on the Organization of Experience*. Harmondsworth: Penguin.

Goldstone, Jack A. 1991. *Revolution and Rebellion in the Early Modern World*. Berkeley, CA: University of California Press.

Goldstone, Jack A. 2001. 'Demography, environment, and security.' In *Environmental Conflict*, edited by P.F. Diehl and N.P. Gleditsch. Boulder, CO: Westview, pp. 84–108.

Goodhand, J. 2004. 'Afghanistan, in Central Asia.' In *War Economies in a Regional Context: Challenges of Transformation*, edited by M. Pugh and N. Cooper, with J. Goodhand. Boulder, CO: Lynne Rienner, pp. 45–89.

Goodwin, Jeff. 2011. *No Other Way Out: States and Revolutionary Movements, 1945–1991*. Cambridge: Cambridge University Press.

Gordon, M. 1964. *Assimilation in American Life*. New York: Oxford University Press.

Goulding, M. 2002. *Peacemonger*. London: John Murray.

Graham, George. 2007. 'People's war? Self-interest, coercion and ideology in Nepal's Maoist insurgency.' *Small Wars and Insurgencies* **18**:231–48.

Grant, J.A. and I. Taylor. 2004. 'Global governance and conflict diamonds: the Kimberley process and the quest for clean gems.' *The Round Table* **93**:385–401.

Greene, Owen, Duncan Hiscock and Catherine Flew. 2008. 'Integration and co-ordination of DDR and SALW control programming: issues, experience and priorities.' Centre for International Cooperation and Security (CICS), University of Bradford, Bradford.

Greig, J.M. and Paul F. Diehl. 2005. 'The peacekeeping–peacemaking dilemma.' *International Studies Quarterly* **49**(4):621–45.

Greig, Michael. 2005. 'Stepping into the fray: when do mediators mediate?' *American Journal of Political Science* **49**:249–66.

Grignon, F. 2006. 'Economic agendas in the Congolese peace process.' In *The Democratic Republic of Congo: Economic Dimensions of War and Peace*, edited by M. Nest, F. Grignon and E.F. Kisangani. Boulder, CO: Lynne Rienner.

Grodsky, Brian. 2009. 'Re-ordering justice: towards a new methodological approach to studying transitional justice.' *Journal of Peace Research* **46**:819–37.

Grossmann, Herschel I. 1991. 'A general equilibrium model of insurrections.' *American Economic Review* **81**:912–21.

Grossmann, Herschel I. 2002. 'Make us a king: anarchy, predation, and the state.' *European Journal of Political Economy* **18**:31–46.

Guaqueta, A. 2002. 'Economic agendas in armed conflict: defining and developing the role of the UN.' International Peace Academy, New York.

Guichaoua, Yvan. 2009. 'Circumstantial alliances and loose loyalties in rebellion making.' MICROCON, Institute for Development Studies, University of Sussex, Brighton.

Guichaoua, Yvan. 2010. 'How do ethnic militias perpetuate in Nigeria? A micro-level perspective on the Oodua People's Congress.' *World Development* **38**:1657–66.

Gupta, Sanjeev, Benedict Clements, Rina Bhattacharya and Shamit Chakravarti. 2004. 'Fiscal consequences of armed conflict and terrorism in low- and middle-income countries.' *European Journal of Political Economy* **20**:403–21.

Gurr, Ted Robert. 1970. *Why Men Rebel*. Princeton, NJ: Princeton University Press.

Gurr, Ted Robert. 1993. *Minorities at Risk: A Global View of Ethnopolitical Conflicts*. Washington, DC: Institute of Peace Press.

Gurr, Ted Robert. 2000a. 'Ethnic warfare on the wane.' *Foreign Affairs* **79**:52–64.

Gurr, Ted Robert. 2000b. *People Versus States: Minorities at Risk in the New Century*. Washington, DC: United States Institute for Peace Press.

Gurses, M. and T.D. Mason. 2006. 'Democracy out of anarchy: how do features of a civil war influence the likelihood of post-civil war democracy?' Paper presented at the 47th Annual Meeting of the International Studies Association, San Diego, CA.

Guterres, A. 2006. 'Statement by Mr Antonio Guterres, United Nations High Commissioner for Refugees, to the United Nations Security Council, New York, 24 January 2006.' UNHCR, Geneva.

Guterres, A. 2008. 'Opening statement of High Commissioner Mr Antonio Guterres.' UNHCR, Geneva, 10 December, available at: http://www. reliefweb.int/rw/rwb.nsf/db900SID/ASAZ-7M7JAR?OpenDocument& RSS20=02-P.

Gutierrez Sanin, F. 2004. 'Criminal rebels? A discussion of civil war and criminality from the Colombian experience.' *Politics and Society* **32**:257–85.

Gutierrez Sanin, F. 2011. 'The dilemmas of recruitment: the Colombian case.' In *Understanding Collective Political Violence*, edited by Y. Guichaoua. Basingstoke: Palgrave Macmillan.

Gutmann, A. and D. Thompson. 2000. 'The moral foundations of truth commissions.' In *Truth v. Justice: The Morality of Truth Commissions*, edited by R. Rotberg and D. Thompson. Princeton, NJ: Princeton University Press.

Haacke, Jürgen and Paul D. Williams. 2009. 'Regional arrangements and security challenges: a comparative analysis.' London School of Economics and Political Science, London.

Haas, E.B. 1986. *Why We Still Need the United Nations: The Collective Management of International Conflict, 1945–1984*. Berkeley, CA: Institute of International Studies, University of California, Berkeley, CA.

Haas, E.B. 1993. 'Collective conflict management: evidence for a new world order?' In *Collective Security in a Changing World*, edited by T.G. Weiss. Boulder, CO: Lynne Rienner.

Haas, E.B., R.L. Butterworth and J.S. Nye. 1972. *Conflict Management by International Organizations*. Morristown, NJ: General Learning.

Habyarimana, J., Macartan Humphreys, Daniel Posner and Jeremy M. Weinstein. 2008. 'Better institutions, not partition.' *Foreign Affairs* **87**:138–41.

Habyarimana, J., Macartan Humphreys, Daniel Posner and Jeremy M. Weinstein. 2009. *Coethnicity: Diversty and the Dilemmas of Collectve Action*. New York: Russell Sage Foundation.

Hallberg, Johan Dittrich. 2012. 'PRIO Conflict Site 1989–2008: a geo-referenced dataset on armed conflict.' *Conflict Management and Peace Science* **29**(2): 219–232.

Hamber, B. 2009. *Transforming Societies after Political Violence: Truth, Reconciliation, and Mental Health*. New York: Springer.

Hammond, L. 2004. 'Tigrayan returnees' notion of home: five variations on a theme.' In *Homecomings: Unsettling Paths of Return*, edited by L. Long and E. Oxfeld. Oxford: Lexington Books.

Hampson, Fen Osler. 1996. *Nurturing Peace: Why Peace Settlements Succeed or Fail.* Washington, DC: United States Institute of Peace (USIP).

Hampson, Fen Osler. 2008. 'Human security and international relations.' In *Security Studies: An Introduction*, edited by P. Williams. London: Routledge.

Hanf, Theodor. 1991. 'Reducing conflict through cultural autonomy: Karl Renner's contribution.' In *State and Nation in Multi-Ethnic Societies: The Breakup of Multi-National States*, edited by U. Ra'anan, M. Mesner, K. Armes and K. Martin. Manchester: Manchester University Press.

Hanna, William. 2008. *Urban Dynamics in Black Africa.* New York: Aldine Transaction.

Harbom, L. and Peter Wallensteen. 2009. 'Armed conflicts, 1946–2008.' *Journal of Peace Research* **46**:577–87.

Harbom, Lotta and Peter Wallensteen. 2010. 'Armed conflicts, 1946–2009.' *Journal of Peace Research* **47**:501–9.

Harff, Barbara. 2003. 'No lessons learned from the Holocaust? Assessing risks of genocide and political mass murder since 1955.' *American Political Science Review* **97**(1):57–73.

Harper, K. 1994. 'Does the United Nations Security Council have the competence to act as court and legislature?' *NYU Journal of International Law and Politics* **27**(1):103–57.

Harpviken, Kristian Berg. 2008. 'From "Refugee Warriors" to "Returnee Warriors": militant homecoming in Afghanistan and beyond.' Centre for Global Studies, George Mason University, Fairfax, VA.

Harrison, L. and Samuel P. Huntington. 2000. *Culture Matters.* New York: Basic Books.

Harrison, S. and M. Nishihara (eds). 1995. *UN Peacekeeping: Japanese and American Perspectives.* Washington, DC: Carnegie Endowment for Interntional Peace.

Hart, Jason. 2011. 'The mobilisation of children: what's the difference?' In *Understanding Collective Political Violence*, edited by Y. Guichaoua. Basingstoke: Palgrave Macmillan.

Hartlyn, Jonathan. 1993. 'Civil violence and conflict resolution: the case of Colombia.' In *Stopping the Killing: How Civil Wars End*, edited by R. Licklider. New York: New York University Press, pp. 37–61.

Hartmann, Betsy. 2001. 'Will the circle be unbroken? A critique of the project on environment, population, and security.' In *Violent Environments*, edited by N.L. Peluso and M. Watts. Ithaca, NY: Cornell University Press, pp. 39–62.

Hartzell, Caroline A. 1999. 'Explaining the stability of negotiated settlements to intrastate wars.' *Journal of Conflict Resolution* **43**:3–22.

Hartzell, Caroline A. 2009a. 'Civil war settlements and post-conflict economic growth.' Paper presented at the Peace Science Society (International) annual meeting, Chapel Hill, NC, November 20–22.

Hartzell, Caroline A. 2009b. 'Settling civil wars: armed opponents' fates and the duration of the peace.' *Conflict Management and Peace Science* **26**:347–65.

Hartzell, Caroline A. and Matthew Hoddie. 2003a. 'Civil war settlements and the implementation of military power-sharing arrangements.' *Journal of Peace Research* **40**(3):303–20.

Hartzell, Caroline A. and Matthew Hoddie. 2003b. 'Institutionalizing peace: power sharing and post-civil war conflict management.' *American Journal of Political Science* **47**:318–32.

Hartzell, Caroline A. and Matthew Hoddie. 2007. *Crafting Peace: Power-Sharing Institutions and the Negotiated Settlement of Civil Wars.* University Park, PA: Pennsylvania State University Press.

Hartzell, Caroline A., Matthew Hoddie and Molly Bauer. 2010. 'Economic liberalization via IMF structural adjustment: sowing the seeds of civil war.' *International Organization* **64**:339–56.

Hartzell, Caroline A., Matthew Hoddie and Donald Rothchild. 2001. 'Stabilizing the peace after civil war: an investigation of some key variables.' *International Organization* **55**(1):183–208.

Hauge, Wenche. 2009. 'Group identity – a neglected asset: determinants of social and political participation among female ex-fighters in Guatemala.' *Conflict, Security and Development* **8**:295–316.

Hauge, Wenche and Tanja Ellingsen. 1998. 'Beyond environmental scarcity: causal pathways to conflict.' *Journal of Peace Research* **35**:299–317.

Hawk, K.H. 2002. *Constructing the Stable State: Goals for Intervention and Peacebuilding.* Westport, CT: Praeger.

Hawkins, L. and M. Hudson. 1990. *The Art of Effective Negotiation.* Melbourne: Business Library.

Hayden, Robert M. 1992. 'Constitutional nationalism in the formerly Yugoslav republics.' *Slavic Review* **51**:654–73.

Hayner, P. 1994. 'Fifteen truth commissions 1974–1994: a comparative study.' *Human Rights Quarterly* **16**:613–55.

Hayner, P. 2007. 'Negotiating peace in Liberia: preserving the possibility for justice.' Centre for Humanitarian Dialogue, Geneva.

Hechter, Michael. 1975. *Internal Colonialism: The Celtic Fringe in British National Development, 1536–1966.* London: Routledge & Kegan Paul.

Hechter, Michael. 2000. *Containing Nationalism.* Oxford: Oxford University Press.

Hegre, Håvard, Tanja Ellingsen, Scott Gates and Nils Petter Gleditsch. 2001. 'Towards a democratic civil peace? Democracy, political change, and civil war, 1816–1992.' *American Political Science Review* **95**(1):33–48.

Hegre, Håvard, Ranveig Gissinger and Nils Petter Gleditsch. 2003. 'Globalization and internal conflict.' In *Globalization and Conflict*, edited by K. Barbieri. Lanham, MD: Rowman & Littlefield, pp. 251–75.

Hegre, Håvard and Nicholas Sambanis. 2006. 'Sensitivity analysis of empirical results on civil war onset.' *Journal of Conflict Resolution* **50**(4):508–35.

Heinbecker, Paul and Patricia Goff. 2005. *Irrelevant or Indispensible? The United Nations in the 21st Century*. Waterloo, Ont.: Wilfred Laurier University Press.

Heldt, B. 2001/2002. 'Are intrastate peacekeeping operations less likely to succeed? Some statistical evidence.' *IRI Review* **6**(1):111–35.

Heldt, B. 2004. 'UN-led or non-UN-led peacekeeping operations?' *IRI Review* **9**:113–38.

Heldt, B. 2007. 'The impact of peacekeeping operations on post-conflict transitions to democracy.' Paper presented at the 48th Annual Meeting of the International Studies Association, Chicago, IL.

Henderson, D.A. 1996. 'Mediation success: an empirical analysis.' *Ohio State Journal of Dispute Resolution* **11**(1):105–48.

Hendrickson, D. and N. Ball. 2002. 'Off-budget military expenditure and revenue: issues and policy perspectives for donors.' King's College, London.

Hendrix, Cullen S. and Sarah M. Glaser. 2007. 'Trends and triggers: climate change and civil conflict in Sub-Saharan Africa.' *Political Geography* **26**:695–715.

Hepburn, A.C. 1983. 'Employment and religion in Belfast, 1901–1951.' In *Religion, Education and Employment: Aspects of Equal Opportunity in Northern Ireland*, edited by R.J. Cormack and R.D. Osborne. Belfast: Appletree.

Herbst, Jeffrey. 2000a. 'Economic incentives, natural resources, and conflict in Africa.' *Journal of African Economies* **9**:270–94.

Herbst, Jeffrey. 2000b. *State and Power in Africa: Comparative Lessons in Authority and Control*. Princeton, NJ: Princeton University Press.

Herbst, Jeffrey. 2001. 'The politics of revenue sharing in resource-dependent states.' World Institute for Development Economics Research (WIDER), Helsinki.

Hershfield, A.F. 1969. 'Ibo sons abroad: a window on the world.' Paper presented at the Annual Meetings of the African Studies Association, Montreal.

Herz, M. 2011. 'Institutional mechanisms for conflict resolution in South America.' In *Rewiring National Security*, edited by C. Crocker,

F.O. Hampson and P. Aall. Washington, DC: US Institute of Peace Press.

Heston, Alan, Robert Summers and Bettina Aten. 2002. 'Penn World Table Version 6.2.' Centre for International Comparisons, University of Pennsylvania, Philadelphia, PA, available at: http://pwt.econ. upenn.edu/php_site/pwt_index.php.

Hettne, B. 2010. 'Development and security: origins and future.' *Security Dialogue* **41**:31–52.

Hewitt, Joseph J., Jonathan Wilkenfeld and T.R. Gurr. 2010. 'Peace and conflict 2010.' Center for International Development and Conflict Management, University of Maryland, College Park, MD.

Higgins, R. 1969–81. *United Nations Peacekeeping: Documents and Commentary*. Oxford: Oxford University Press.

Hillen, J. 1998. *Blue Helmets: The Strategy of UN Military Operations*. London: Brassey's UK.

Hirsch, John L. and Robert B. Oakley. 1995. *Somalia and Operation Restore Hope: Reflections on Peacemaking and Peacekeeping*. Washington, DC: United States Institute of Peace (USIP).

Hobbes, Thomas. 1651 [1968]. *Leviathan*. London: Penguin.

Hoddie, Matthew and Caroline A. Hartzell. 2005. 'Power shaing in peace settlements: initiating the transition from civil war.' In *Sustainable Peace: Power and Democracy after Civil Wars*, edited by P.G. Roeder and D. Rothchild. Ithaca, NY: Cornell University Press.

Hoffmann, S. 1996. *The Ethics and Politics of Humanitarian Intervention*. Notre Dame, IN: University of Notre Dame Press.

Holbrooke, Richard. 1998. *To End a War*. New York: Random House.

Holsti, Kalevi J. 2000. 'The political sources of humanitarian disasters.' In *War, Hunger and Displacement: The Origin of Humanitarian Emergencies*, edited by E.W. Nafziger, F. Stewart and R. Väyrynen. Oxford: Oxford University Press.

Homer-Dixon, Thomas F. 1999. *Environment, Scarcity, and Violence*. Princeton, NJ: Princeton University Press.

Homer-Dixon, Thomas F. 2000. *The Ingenuity Gap*. New York: Knopf.

Homer-Dixon, Thomas F. and Jessica Blitt. 1998. *Ecoviolence: Links among Environment, Population, and Security*. Lanham, MD: Rowman & Littlefield.

Hooghe, Liesbet. 2003. 'Belgium: from regionalism to federalism.' In *The Territorial Management of Ethnic Conflict*, edited by J. Coakley. London: Frank Cass.

Horowitz, Donald L. 1985. *Ethnic Groups in Conflict*. Berkeley, CA: University of California Press.

Horowitz, Donald L. 1990. 'Ethnic conflict management for policymakers.' In *Conflict and Peacemaking in Multiethnic Societies*, edited by J. Montville. Lexington, MA: Lexington Books.

Horowitz, Donald L. 1991. *A Democratic South Africa? Constitutional Engineering in a Divided Society*. Berkeley, CA: University of California Press.

Horowitz, Donald L. 1993. 'Democracy in divided societies.' *Journal of Democracy* 4:18–38.

Horowitz, Donald L. 1998. 'Self-determination: politics, philosophy, and law.' In *National Self-Determination and Secession*, edited by M. Moore. Oxford: Oxford University Press.

Horowitz, Donald L. 2002. 'Constitutional design: proposals versus processes.' In *The Architecture of Democracy*, edited by A. Reynolds. Oxford: Oxford University Press.

Horowitz, Donald L. 2003. 'Electoral systems and their goals: a primer for decision-makers.' *Journal of Democracy* 14:115–27.

Horowitz, Donald L. 2004. 'The alternative vote and interethnic moderation: a reply to Fraenkel and Grofman.' *Public Choice* 121:507–17.

Horowitz, Donald L. 2006. 'Strategy takes a holiday: Fraenkel and Grofman on the alternative vote.' *Comparative Political Studies* 39:652–62.

Horowitz, Donald L. 2007. 'The many uses of federalism.' *Drake Law Review* 55:953–66.

Horowitz, Donald L. 2008. 'Conciliatory institutions and constitutional processes in post-conflict states.' *William and Mary Law Review* 49:1213–48.

Hovannisian, Richard G. 1999. *Remembrance and Denial: The Case of the Armenian Genocide*. Detroit, MI: Wayne State University Press.

Howard, L.M. 2002. 'UN peace implementation in Namibia: the causes of success.' *International Peacekeeping* 9(1):99–132.

Howard, L.M. 2008. *UN Peacekeeping in Civil Wars*. Cambridge: Cambridge University Press.

Huband, Mark. 2003. *The Skull Beneath the Skin: Africa After the Cold War*. Boulder, CO: Westview.

Human Rights Watch. 2005. 'Youth, poverty, and blood: the lethal legacy of West Africa's regional warriors.' Human Rights Watch, Washington, DC.

Human Rights Watch. 2008. 'Politics as war.' Human Rights Watch, Washington, DC.

Human Security Centre. 2005. *Human Security Report 2005: War and Peace in the 21st Century*. New York: Oxford University Press, available at: http://www.hsrgroup.org/human-security-reports/2005/text.aspx (accessed October 19, 2010).

Humphreys, Macartan. 2005. 'Natural resources, conflict and conflict resolution: uncovering the mechanisms.' *Journal of Conflict Resolution*, **49**:508–37.

Humphreys, Macartan, Jeffred D. Sachs and Joseph E. Stiglitz. 2007. *Escaping the Resource Curse*. New York: Columbia University Press.

Humphreys, Macartan and Jeremy M. Weinstein. 2004. 'What the fighters say: a survey of ex-combatants in Sierra Leone, June–August 2003.' The Earth Institute, New York.

Humphreys, Macartan and Jeremy M. Weinstein. 2007. 'Demobilization and reintegration.' *Journal of Conflict Resolution* **51**(4):531–67.

Humphreys, Macartan and Jeremy M. Weinstein. 2008. 'Who fights? The determinants of participation in civil war.' *American Journal of Political Science* **52**:436–55.

Huntington, Samuel P. 1996. *The Clash of Civilizations and the Remaking of World Order*. New York: Simon & Schuster.

Hutchful, E. and K. Aning. 2004. 'The political economy of conflict.' In *West Africa's Security Challenges: Building Peace in a Troubled Region*, edited by A. Adebajo and I. Rashid. Boulder, CO: Lynne Rienner.

Iannaccone, L.R. and E. Berman. 2006. 'Religious extremism: the good, the bad, and the deadly.' *Public Choice* **128**(1):109–29.

Ichino, A. and R. Winter-Ebner. 2004. 'The long-run educational cost of World War II.' *Journal of Labor Economics* **22**:57–86.

ICISS. 2001. *The Responsibility to Protect: Report of the International Commission on Intervention and State Sovereignty*. Ottawa: International Development Research Center.

ICWAC. 2000. 'Caught in the crossfire no more: a framework for commitment to war-affected children – Summary by the Chairs of the Experts.' International Conference on War-Affected Children (ICWAC), Winnipeg, 13–15 September.

IDA and IMF. 2006. 'Heavily Indebted Poor Countries (HIPC) initiative: statistical update.' IMF and World Bank, Washington, DC.

IDB. 2005. 'IDB country strategy with El Salvador.' Inter-American Development Bank, Washington, DC.

Ikelegbe, Augustine. 2006. 'The economy of conflict in the oil rich Niger Delta region of Nigeria.' *African and Asian Studies* **5**:23–56.

Iklé, Fred Charles. 1991. *Every War Must End*. New York: Columbia University Press.

IMF. 2007. *Kenya: Third Review under the Poverty Reduction and Growth Facility*. Washington, DC: International Monetary Fund.

International Commission on Intervention and State Sovereignty. 2001. *Responsibility to Protect*. Ottawa: International Development Research Centre.

International Crisis Group. 2002a. 'God, oil, and country: changing the logic of war in Sudan.' International Crisis Group, Brussels.

International Crisis Group. 2002b. 'Indonesia: Resources and conflict in Papua.' ICG, Jakarta/Brussels.

International Crisis Group. 2006. 'Moldova's uncertain future.' ICG, Brussels.

International Crisis Group. 2009. 'Afghanistan: What now for refugees?' International Crisis Group, Brussels, available at: http://www.crisis group.org/~/media/Files/asia/south-asia/afghanistan/175_afghanistan ___what_now_for_refugees.pdf.

International Peace Academy. 1984. *Peacekeeper's Handbook*. New York: Pergamon Press.

IPA/Fafo. 2005. 'Business and international crimes: assessing the liability of business entities for grave violations of international law.' Fafo Institute and the International Peace Academy, Oslo.

IPCC. 2007. *Climate Change, 2007: Impacts, Adaptation and Vulnerability. Contributions of Working Group II to the Fourth Assessment Report of the Intergovernmental Panel on Climate Change*. Cambridge: Cambridge University Press.

Iqbal, Zaryab. 2010. *War and the Health of Nations*. Stanford, CA: Stanford University Press.

Ireland, P. 1994. *The Policy Challenge of Ethnic Diversity: Immigrant Politics in France and Switzerland*. Cambridge, MA: Harvard University Press.

Ireland, P. 2000. 'Reaping what they sow: institutions and immigrant political participation in Western Europe.' In *Challenging Immigration and Ethnic Relations Politics: Comparative European Perspectives*, edited by R. Koopmans and P. Statham. Oxford: Oxford University Press.

IRIN. 2004. 'Our bodies, their battleground: gender-based violence in conflict zones.' Integrated Regional Information Networks (IRIN), September.

IRIN. 2009. 'Global: does emergency education save lives?' Integrated Regional Information Networks (IRIN) Global, Dakar. Available at: www.irinnews.org/Report.aspx?ReportId=82272.

Jackson, J. 1994. 'Repatriation and reconstruction in Zimbabwe during the 1980s.' In *When Refugees Go Home*, edited by T. Allen and H. Morsink. London: James Currey.

Jackson, Philip W. 1990 (orig. 1968). *Life In Classrooms*. New York: Teachers College Press,

Jackson, S. 2005. 'Protecting livelihoods in violent economies.' In *Profiting from Peace: Managing the Resource Dimension of Civil Wars*, edited by K. Ballentine and H. Nitzschke. Boulder, CO: Lynne Rienner.

Jackson, T.F. 2006. *From Civil Rights to Human Rights: Martin Luther King Jr. and the Struggle for Economic Justice*. Philadelphia, PA: University of Pennsylvania Press.

Jacoby, Hanan G. and Emmanuel Skoufias. 1997. 'Risk, financial markets, and human capital in a developing country.' *Review of Economic Studies* **64**:311–35.

Jakobsen, P.V. 1996. 'National interest, humanitarianism or CNN: what triggers UN peace enforcement after the Cold War?' *Journal of Peace Research* **33**(2):205–15.

James, A. 1969. *The Politics of Peace-Keeping*. New York: Praeger.

James, A. 1990. *Peacekeeping in International Politics*. New York: St. Martin's Press.

Jarstad, Anna. 2006. 'The logic of power sharing after civil war.' Paper presented at the PRIO Workshop on Power-Sharing and Democratic Governance, Oslo, 21–22 August.

Jarstad, Anna and Timothy Sisk. 2008. *From War to Democracy: Dilemmas of Peacebuilding*. Cambridge: Cambridge University Press.

Jean, F. and J.-C. Rufin. 1996. *Économies des Guerres Civiles*. Paris: Hachette.

Jeffrey, Craig et al. 2008. *Degrees without Freedom? Education, Masculinities and Unemployment in North India*. Stanford: Stanford University Press.

Jenne, E. 2007. *Ethnic Bargaining: The Paradox of Minority Empowerment*. Ithaca, NY: Cornell University Press.

Jensen, Stig and F. Stepputat. 2001. 'Demobilising armed civilians.' Centre for Development Research (CDR), Copenhagen.

Jenson, J. 1998. 'Social movement naming practices and the political opportunity structure.' Instituto Juan March de Estudios e Investigaciones, Madrid.

Jett, D.C. 1999. *Why Peacekeeping Fails*. New York: St. Martin's Press.

Jockel, J.T. 1994. *Canada and International Peacekeeping*. Toronto: Canadian Institute of Strategic Studies.

Johnston, D. and S. Mydans. 2008. 'Russia charged with trying to sell arms.' *New York Times* 7 March.

Johnston, H. 1995. 'A methodology for frame analysis: from discourse to cognitive schemata.' In *Social Movements and Cultures*, edited by H. Johnston and B. Klandermans. London: UCL Press.

Johnston, H. 2007. 'Mobilization.' In *Blackwell Encyclopedia of Sociology*, edited by G. Ritzer. Oxford: Blackwell.

Johnstone, I. 1995. *Rights and Reconciliation: UN Strategies in El Salvador*. Boulder, CO: Lynne Rienner.

Jolly, Richard, Louis Emmerij and Thomas G. Weiss. 2009. *UN Ideas that Changed the World*. Bloomington, IN: Indiana University Press.

Jomo, K.S. 1990. 'Whither Malaysia's New Economic Policy?' *Pacific Affairs* **63**:469–99.

Judt, Tony. 2000. 'The past is another country.' In *The Politics of Retribution in Europe: World War II and its Aftermath*, edited by I. Deák, J.T. Gross and T. Judt. Princeton, NJ: Princeton University Press, pp. 293–23.

Justino, Patricia. 2009. 'Poverty and violent conflict: a micro-level perspective on the causes and duration of warfare.' *Journal of Peace Research* **46**:315–33.

Justino, Patricia. 2010. 'War and poverty.' In *Handbook of the Economics of Peace and Security*, edited by M. Garfinkel and S. Skaperdas. Oxford: Oxford University Press.

Justino, Patricia and P. Verwimp. 2006. 'Poverty dynamics, violent conflict, and convergence in Rwanda.' Households in Conflict Network, available at: http://www.hicn.org/.

Kahl, Colin H. 1998. 'Population growth, environmental degradation, and state-sponsored violence: the case of Kenya 1991–93.' *International Security* **23**:80–119.

Kahl, Colin C. 2006. *States, Scarcity, and Civil Strife in the Developing World*. Princeton, NJ: Princeton University Press.

Kaldor, Mary. 1999. *New and Old Wars: Organized Violence in a Global Era*. Stanford, CA: Stanford University Press.

Kaldor, Mary. 2007. *Human Security: Reflections on Globalization and Intervention*. Cambridge: Polity Press.

Kalyvas, Stathis N. 2001. '"New" and "old" civil wars: a valid distinction?' *World Politics* **54**:99–118.

Kalyvas, Stathis N. 2003. 'The ontology of "political violence": action and identity in civil wars.' *Perspectives on Politics* **1**:475–94.

Kalyvas, Stathis N. 2006. *The Logic of Violence in Civil War*. Cambridge: Cambridge University Press.

Kalyvas, Stathis N. and M.A. Kocher. 2007. 'How "free" is free riding in civil wars? Violence, insurgency, and the collective action problem.' *World Politics* **59**:177–216.

Kaplan, Robert D. 1994. 'The coming anarchy: how scarcity, crime, overpopulation and disease are threatening the social fabric of our planet.' *Atlantic Monthly*:44–74.

Kaplan, Robert D. 2000. *The Coming Anarchy: Shattering the Dreams of the Post Cold War*. New York: Random House.

Karl, Terry L. 1997. *The Paradox of Plenty: Oil Booms and Petro States*. Berkeley, CA: University of California Press.

Katayanagi, M. 2002. *Human Rights Functions of United Nations Peacekeeping Operations*. The Hague: Martinus Nijhoff.

Kaufman, C. 1996. 'Possible and impossible solutions to ethnic civil wars.' *International Security* **20**(4):136–75.

Kaufman, J.P. and K.P. Williams. 2007. *Women, the State and War: A Comparative Perspective on Citizenship and Nationalism*. Lanham, MD: Rowman & Littlefield.

Keating, M. 2001. *Plurinational Democracy: Stateless Nations in a Post-Sovereignty Era*. Oxford: Oxford University Press.

Kecskemeti, Paul. 1958. *Strategic Surrender: The Politics of Victory and Defeat*. Stanford, CA: Stanford University Press.

Keefer, Philip. 2007. 'Clientelism, credibility, and the polity choices of young democracies.' *American Journal of Political Science* **51**:804–21.

Keen, David. 1998. *The Economic Functions of Violence in Civil Wars*. Oxford: Oxford University Press for the International Institute for Strategic Studies.

Keen, David. 2001. 'War and peace: what's the difference?' In *Managing Armed Conflict in the 21st Century*, edited by A. Adebajo and C. Lekha Sriram. London: Frank Cass.

Keen, David. 2005. *Conflict and Collusion in Sierra Leone*. Oxford: James Currey.

Keller, E.J. and L. Smith. 2005. 'Obstacles to implementing territorial decentralization: the first decade of Ethiopian federalism.' In *Sustainable Peace: Power and Democracy after Civil Wars*, edited by P.G. Roeder and D. Rothchild. Ithaca, NY: Cornell University Press.

Kelley, Allen C. and Robert M. Schmidt. 2001. 'Economic and demographic change: a synthesis of models, findings, and perspectives.' In *Population Matters: Demographic Change, Economic Growth, and Poverty in the Developing World*, edited by N. Birdsall, A.C. Kelley and S.W. Sinding. New York: Oxford University Press, pp. 67–105.

Kennedy, Paul. 2006. *The Parliament of Man: The Past, Present, and Future of the United Nations*. New York: Random House.

Kilroy, Walt. 2008. 'Disarmament, demobilisation and reintegration as a participatory process: involving communities and beneficiaries in post-conflict disarmament programmes.' Dublin City University, Dublin.

King, Gary and Christopher J.L. Murray. 2001. 'Rethinking human security.' *Political Science Quarterly* **116**:585–610.

King, P. 1982. *Federalism and Federation*. London: Croom Helm.

Kingma, K. 2000. *Demobilization in Sub-Saharan Africa: The Development and Security Impacts*. Basingstoke: Macmillan.

Kingma, K. and V. Sayers. 1994. 'Demobilization in the Horn of Africa.' BICC, Addis Ababa.

Kirwin, M. and W. Cho. 2009. 'Weak states and political violence in Sub-Saharan Africa.' AfroBarometer Working Paper no. 111.

Klare, Michael T. 2001. *Resource Wars: The New Landscape of Global Conflict*. New York: Metropolitan Books.

Knight, Malcom, Norma Loayza and Delano Villaneuva. 1996. 'The peace dividend: military spending cuts and economic growth.' *IMF Staff Papers* **43**:1–37.

Knight, Mark. 2008. 'Expanding the DDR model: politics and organisations.' *Journal of Security Sector Management* **6**:1–19.

Kolb, D. 1983. *The Mediators*. Cambridge, MA: MIT Press.

Kolstad, Ivar. 2009. 'The resource curse: which institutions matter?' *Applied Economics Letters* **16**(4):439–42.

Kornhauser, William. 1959. *The Politics of Mass Society*. New York: Free Press.

Koser, K. and N. Van Hear. 2003. 'Asylum, migration, and implications for countries of origin.' World Institute for Development Economics Research (WIDER), Helsinki.

Krain, Matthew. 1997. 'State sponsored mass murder: the onset and severity of genocides and politicides.' *Journal of Conflict Resolution* **41**(3):331–60.

Krain, Matthew. 2000. *Repression and Accommodation in Post-Revolutionary States*. New York: St Martin's Press.

Krasno, J., B. Hayes and D. Daniel (eds). 2003. *Leveraging for Success in United Nations Peace Operations*. Westport, CT: Praeger.

Kreisberg, Louis. 2007. 'Contemporary conflict resolution applications.' In *Leashing the Dogs of War: Conflict Management in a Divided World*, edited by C. Crocker, F.O. Hampson and P. Aall. Washington, DC: US Institute of Peace Press.

Kriesi, H. and M.G. Giugni. 1995. 'Introduction.' In *New Social Movements in Western Europe: A Comparative Analysis*, edited by H. Kriesi, R. Koopmans and J.W. Duyyendak. London: UCL Press.

Kriger, Norma J. 1992. *Zimbabwe's Guerrilla War: Peasant Voices*. Cambridge: Cambridge University Press.

Kritz, Neil. 1995. *Transitional Justice: How Emerging Democracies Reckon with Former Regimes*. Washington, DC: United States Institute of Peace (USIP).

Krueger, A.B. and J. Maleckova. 2003. 'Education, poverty, and terrorism: is there a causal connection?' *Journal of Economic Perspectives* **17**:119–44.

Krugman, Paul. 1987. 'The narrow moving band, the Dutch disease and the competitive consequences of Mrs Thatcher: notes on trade in the presence of dynamic scale economies.' *Journal of Development Economics* **27**:41–55.

Kull, Steven and Clay Ramsay. 2000. 'Challenging US policymakers' image of an isolated public.' *International Studies Perspectives* **1**:105–17.

Kumar, Krishna. 1997. 'The nature and focus of international assistance for rebuilding war torn societies.' In *Rebuilding Societies after Civil War: Critical Roles for International Assistance*, edited by K. Kumar. Boulder, CO: Lynne Rienner, pp. 1–39.

Kumar, K. (ed.). 1998. *Postconflict Elections, Democratization, and International Assistance*. Boulder, CO: Lynne Rienner.

Kumar, Krishna and Marina Ottaway. 1998. 'General conclusions and priorities for policy research.' In *Postconflict Elections, Democratization, and International Assistance*, edited by K. Kumar. Boulder, CO: Lynne Rienner, pp. 229–37.

Kymlicka, Will. 1995. *Multicultural Citizenship*. Oxford: Oxford University Press.

Kymlicka, Will. 2000. 'Nation-building and minority rights: comparing West and East.' *Journal of Ethnic and Migration Studies* **26**:183–212.

Kymlicka, Will. 2001. *Politics in the Vernacular*. Oxford: Oxford University Press.

Lacina, Bethany and Nils Petter Gleditsch. 2005. 'Monitoring trends in global combat: a new dataset of battle deaths.' *European Journal of Population* **21**:145–66.

Lake, David A. 2010. 'Building legitimate states after civil war.' In *Strengthening Peace in Post-Civil War States: Transforming Spoilers into Stakeholders*, edited by M. Hoddie and C.A. Hartzell. Chicago, IL: University of Chicago Press.

Lake, David A. and Donald Rothchild. 1996. 'Containing fear: the origins and management of ethnic conflicts.' *International Security* **21**(1):41–75.

Lake, David A. and Donald Rothchild. 2005. 'Territorial decentralization and civil war settlements.' In *Sustainable Peace: Power and Democracy after Civil Wars*, edited by P.G. Roeder and D. Rothchild. Ithaca, NY: Cornell University Press.

Lambourne, Wendy. 1999. 'The pursuit of justice and reconciliation: responding to genocide in Cambodia and Rwanda.' Paper presented at the 40th Annual International Studies Association Convention, Washington, DC, 16–20 February.

Landesman, P. 2003. 'Arms and the man.' *New York Times Magazine* 17 August.

Lane, Philip and Aaron Tornell. 1996. 'Power, growth and the voracity effect.' *Journal of Economic Growth* 1:213–41.

Langer, Arnim. 2005. 'Horizontal inequalities and violent group mobilisation in Côte d'Ivoire.' *Oxford Development Studies* 33:25–45.

Langer, Arnim, Frances Stewart and Rajesh Venugopal. 2012. 'Horizontal inequalities and post-conflict development: laying the foundations for durable peace.' In *Horizontal Inequalities and Post-conflict Development*, edited by Arnim Langer, Frances Stewart and Rajesh Venugopal. Basingstoke: Palgrave.

Lapidoth, Ruth. 1996. *Autonomy: Flexible Solutions to Ethnic Conflicts*. Washington, DC: United States Institute of Peace (USIP).

Lauder, Hugh et al. (eds). 2006. *Education, Globalization & Social Change*. Oxford: Oxford University Press.

Lavy, George. 1996. *Germany and Israel: Moral Debt and National Interest*. London: Frank Cass.

Lawson, D., A. McKay and J. Okidi. 2003. 'Poverty persistence and transitions in Uganda: a combined qualitative and quantitative analysis.' Chronic Poverty Research Centre, Manchester.

Lazar, Sian. 2010. 'Schooling and critical citizenship: pedagogies of political agencies in El Alto, Bolivia.' *Anthropology and Education Quarterly* 31:181–205.

Le Billon, Philippe. 2000a. 'The political ecology of transition in Cambodia 1989–1999: war, peace, and forest exploitation.' *Development and Change* 31:785–805.

Le Billon, Philippe. 2000b. 'The political economy of war: what relief agencies need to know.' Overseas Development Institute, London.

Le Billon, Philippe. 2001a. 'The political ecology of war: natural resources and armed conflict.' *Political Geography* 10:561–84.

Le Billon, Philippe. 2001b. 'Thriving on war: the Angolan conflict and private business.' *Review of African Political Economy* 28:629–35.

Le Billon, Philippe. 2003. 'Buying peace or fuelling war? The role of corruption in armed conflicts.' *Journal of International Development* 15:413–26.

Le Billon, Philippe. 2007. 'Geographies of war: perspectives on the "resource wars".' *Geography Compass* 1:163–82.

Le Billon, Philippe, J. Sherman and M. Hartwell. 2002. 'Policies and practices for regulating resource flows to armed conflicts.' International Peace Academy, Washington, DC.

Leaning, Jennifer and Sam Arie. 2000. 'Human Security: a framework for assessment in conflict and transition.' Tulane University, New Orleans, LA.

Lecocq, B. 2004. 'Unemployed intellectuals in the Sahara: the Teshumara

Nationalist Movement and the revolutions in Tuareg society.' *International Review of Social History* **49**:87–109.

Lederach, J.-P. 1997. *Building Peace: Sustainable Reconciliation in Divided Societies*. Washington, DC: United States Institute of Peace (USIP).

Lederman, Daniel and William F. Maloney (eds). 2007. *Natural Resources: Neither Curse Nor Destiny*. Stanford, CA: Stanford University Press.

Lee, W.O. et al. (eds). 2004. *Citizenship Education in Asia and the Pacific. Concepts and Issues*. Hong Kong: Kluwer Academic Publishers.

Leff, C.S. 1998. *The Czech and Slovak Republics: Nation versus State*. Boulder, CO: Westview.

Lehmann, I.A. 1999. *Peacekeeping and Public Information: Caught in the Crossfire*. London: Frank Cass.

Leighley, J.E. 2001. *Strength in Numbers: The Political Mobilization of Ethnic and Racial Minorities*. Princeton, NJ: Princeton University Press.

Leite, C. and J. Weidmann. 1999. 'Does mother nature corrupt? Natural resources, corruption, and economic growth.' International Monetary Fund, Washington, DC.

Leites, Nathan and Charles Wolf. 1970. *Rebellion and Authority: An Analytic Essay on Insurgent Conflicts*. Chicago, IL: Markham.

Lentin, R. (ed.). 1997. *Gender and Catastrophe*. London and New York: Zed Books.

Lepgold, J. and Thomas G. Weiss. 1998. *Collective Conflict Management and Changing World Politics*. Albany, NY: State University of New York Press.

Levi, Primo. 1988. *The Drowned and the Saved*. New York: Summit Books.

Lewicki, R. and J. Litterer. 1985. *Negotiation*. Homewood, IL: R.D. Irwin.

Li, K. 2007. 'Minister of Education urges international support for recovery in post-conflict Liberia.' United Nations Children's Fund (UNICEF), New York, available at: http://www.unicef.org/info bycountry/liberia_38362.html.

Lichbach, Mark Irving. 1995. *The Rebel's Dilemma*. Ann Arbor, MI: University of Michigan Press.

Licklider, Roy. 1995. 'The consequences of negotiated settlements in civil wars, 1945–1993.' *American Political Science Review* **89**(3):681–90.

Licklider, Roy. 1999. 'State-building after invasion: Germany, Japan, Panama, and Somalia.' *Small Wars and Insurgencies* **10**:82–116.

Licklider, Roy. 2000. 'False hopes? Democracy and the resumption of civil war.' Political Science Department, Rutgers University, New Brunswick, NJ.

Lieven, D. and John McGarry. 1993. 'Ethnic conflict in the Soviet Union and its successor states.' In *The Politics of Ethnic Conflict Regulation*, edited by J. McGarry and B. O'Leary. London: Routledge.

Lijphart, A. 1968. *The Politics of Accommodation: Pluralism and Democracy in the Netherlands*. Berkeley, CA: University of California Press.

Lijphart, Arend. 1977. *Democracy in Plural Societies: A Comparative Exploration*. New Haven, CT: Yale University Press.

Lijphart, Arend. 1979. 'Consociation and federation: conceptual and political links.' *Canadian Journal of Political Science* **12**:499–515.

Lijphart, Arend. 1985. *Power Sharing in South Africa*. Berkeley, CA: University of California Press.

Lijphart, A. 1986. 'Proportionality by non-PR methods: ethnic representation in Belgium, Cyprus, Lebanon, New Zealand, West Germany, and Zimbabwe.' In *Electoral Laws and Their Political Consequences*, edited by A. Lijphart and B. Grofman. New York, Agathon Press, pp. 113–23.

Lijphart, Arend. 1995. 'Self-determination versus pre-determination of ethnic minorities in power-sharing systems.' In *The Rights of Minority Cultures*, edited by W. Kymlicka. Oxford: Oxford University Press.

Lijphart, Arend. 1996. 'The puzzle of Indian democracy: a consociational interpretation.' *American Political Science Review* **90**:682–93.

Lijphart, Arend. 1999. *Patterns of Democracy: Government Forms and Performances in Thirty-Six Countries*. New Haven, CT: Yale University Press.

Lijphart, Arend. 2002. 'The wave of power-sharing democracy.' In *The Architecture of Democracy: Constitutional Design, Conflict Management and Democracy*, edited by A. Reynolds. Oxford: Oxford University Press.

Lijphart, Arend. 2004. 'Constitutional design for divided societies.' *Journal of Democracy* **15**:96–109.

Lilly, D. and Philippe le Billon. 2002. 'Regulating business in conflict zones: a synthesis of strategies.' Overseas Development Institute, London.

Lindley, A. 2007. 'Protracted displacement and remittances: the view from Eastleigh, Nairobi.' UNHCR, Geneva.

Lindley, A. 2009. 'The early morning phonecall: remittances from a refugee diaspora perspective.' *Journal of Ethnic and Migration Studies* **35**:1315–34.

Linnett, Jack. 2009. 'Grievances in Bougainville: analysing the impact of natural resources in conflict.' *POLIS Journal* **1**:1–36.

Linz, Juan J. 1999. 'Democracy, multinationalism, and federalism.' In

Demokratie in Ost und West, edited by A. Busch and W. Merkel. Frankfurt am Main: Suhrkamp.

Linz, Juan J. and Alfred Stepan. 1992. 'Political identities and electoral sequences: Spain, the Soviet Union, and Yugoslavia.' *Daedalus* **121**:123–39.

Liotta, P.H. 2002. 'The boomerang effect: the convergence of national and human security.' *Security Dialogue* **33**:473–88.

Liotta, P.H. and Taylor Owen. 2006. 'Why human security?' *Whitehead Journal of Diplomacy and International Relations* **7**:37–54.

Lippmann, B. and S. Malik. 2004. 'The 4Rs: The way ahead?' *Forced Migration Review* **12**:9–12.

Lipset, S.M. 1959. 'Some social requisites of democracy: economic development and political legitimacy.' *American Political Science Review* **53**:69–105.

Lipset, S.M. 1960. *Political Man: The Social Bases of Politics*. Garden City, NY: Doubleday.

Lipset, S.M. 1985. 'The revolt against modernity.' In *Consensus and Conflict: Essays in Political Sociology*, edited by S.M. Lipset. New Brunswick, NJ: Transaction.

Lister, Ruth. 1997 [2003]. *Citizenship: Feminist Perspectives*. New York: Palgrave Macmillan.

Loescher, G. 2001. *UNHCR and World Politics*. Oxford: Oxford University Press.

Loescher, G., A. Betts and J. Millner. 2008. *United Nations High Commissioner for Refugees*. London: Taylor & Francis.

Lomborg, Bjørn. 2001. *The Skeptical Environmentalist: Measuring the Real State of the World*. Cambridge: Cambridge University Press.

Lomborg, Bjørn. 2007. *Cool It: The Skeptical Environmentalist's Guide to Global Warming*. London: Cyan & Marshall Cavendish.

Long, Andrew G. 2008. 'Bilateral trade in the shadow of conflict.' *International Studies Quarterly* **52**:81–101.

Long, K. 2012. *The Point of No Return: Refugees, Rights and Repatriation*. Oxford: Oxford University Press.

Lorentzen, L.A. and J. Turpin (eds). 1998. *The Women and War Reader*. New York: New York University Press.

Lorwin, V.R. 1971. 'Segmented pluralism: ideological cleavages and political cohesion in the smaller European democracies.' *Comparative Politics* **3**(2):141–75.

Lucas, R.E., Jr. 1988. 'On the mechanics of economic development.' *Journal of Monetary Economics* **22**:3–42.

Lucas, R.E. Jr. 2002. *Lectures on Economics Growth*. Cambridge, MA: Harvard University Press.

Lujala, Päivi, Nils Petter Gleditsch and Elisabeth Gilmore. 2005. 'A diamond curse? Civil war and a lootable resource.' *Journal of Conflict Resolution* **49**:538–62.

Lujala, Päivi, Jan Ketil Rød and Nadja Thieme. 2007. 'Fighting over oil: introducing a new dataset.' *Conflict Management and Peace Science* **24**:239–56.

Lumsden, Malvern. 1997. 'Breaking the cycle of violence.' *Journal of Peace Research* **34**:377–83.

Luttwak, Edward N. 1999. 'Give war a chance.' *Foreign Affairs* **78**(4):36–44.

Lyall, Jason. 2009. 'Does indiscriminate violence incite insurgent attacks? Evidence from Chechnya.' *Journal of Conflict Resolution* **53**:331–62.

Maccini, Sharon and Dean Young. 2009. 'Under the weather: health, schooling, and economic consequences of early-life rainfall.' *American Economic Review* **99**(3):1006–26.

MacFarlane, S. Neil and Yuen Foong Khong. 2006. *Human Security and the UN: A Critical History*. Indianapolis, IN: Indiana University Press.

Mack, Andrew. 2002. 'Human security in the new millennium.' *Work in Progress: A Review of Research of the United Nations University* **16**(3):4–6.

Mack, Andrew. 2008. 'Human Security Brief 2007.' Simon Fraser University, Vancouver, available at: http://www.humansecuritybrief. info/HSR_Brief_2007.pdf.

Mackinlay, J. 1989. *The Peacekeepers: An Assessment of Peacekeeping Operations at the Arab–Israel Interface*. London: Unwin Hyman.

MacKinnon, M.G. 2000. *The Evolution of U.S. Peacekeeping Policy Under Clinton: A Fairweather Friend?* London: Frank Cass.

MacLean, George. 2006. 'Human security and the globalization of international security.' *Whitehead Journal of Diplomacy and International Relations* **7**:89–99.

MacRae, J. 1999. 'Aiding peace . . . and war: UNHCR, returnee reintegration, and the relief-development debate.' UNHCR, Geneva.

Maddox, John. 1972. *The Doomsday Syndrome*. New York: McGraw-Hill.

Madison, J., A. Hamilton and J. Jay. 1788 [1987]. *The Federalist Papers, edited and with an introduction by Isaac Kramnick*. Harmondsworth: Penguin.

Magdalena, Federico V. 1977. 'Intergroup conflict in the Southern Philippines: an empirical analysis.' *Journal of Peace Research* **14**:299–313.

Majocchi, L.V. 1991. 'Nationalism and federalism in 19th century Europe.' In *The Federal Idea: The History of Federalism from Enlightenment to 1945*, edited by A. Bosco. London: Lothian Foundation Press.

Malkki, L. 1995. 'Refugees and exile: from "refugee studies" to the national order of things.' *Annual Review of Anthropology* **24**:495–523.

Mamdani, M. 2001. *When Victims Become Killers: Colonialism, Nativism, and the Genocide in Rwanda*. Princeton, NJ: Princeton University Press.

Mancini, Luca. 2008. 'Horizontal inequality and communal violence: evidence from Indonesian districts.' In *Horizontal Inequalities and Conflict: Understanding Group Violence in Multiethnic Societies*, edited by F. Stewart. Basingstoke: Palgrave.

Mann, M. 2005. *The Dark Side of Democracy: Explaining Ethnic Cleansing*. Cambridge: Cambridge University Press.

Mansley, M. 2005. 'Private financial markets and corporate responsibility in conflict zones.' In *Profiting from Peace: Managing the Resource Dimension of Civil Wars*, edited by K. Ballentine and H. Nitzschke. Boulder, CO: Lynne Rienner.

Maranto, Robert and Paula S. Tuchman. 1992. 'Knowing the rational peasant: the creation of rival incentive structures in Vietnam.' *Journal of Peace Research* **29**:249–64.

March, J.G. and J.P. Olsen. 1989. *Rediscovering Institutions: The Organizational Basis of Politics*. New York: Free Press.

Mariot, N. 2003. 'Faut-il être motivé pour tuer? Sur quelques explications aux violences de guerre.' *Genèses, Science Sociales, et Histoire* **53**:154–77.

Marschall, Melissa, Paru Shah and Anirudh Ruhil. 2011. 'The study of local elections.' *PS: Political Science and Politics* **44**:97–100.

Marshall-Fratani, R. 2006. 'The war of "who is who": autochthony, nationalism, and citizenship in the Ivorian crisis.' *African Studies Review* **49**:9–43.

Marten, K.Z. 2004. *Enforcing the Peace: Learning from the Imperial Past*. New York: Columbia University Press.

Martin, Adrian. 2005. 'Environmental conflict between refugee and host communities.' *Journal of Peace Research* **42**:329–46.

Martiniello, M. and P. Statham. 1999. 'Introduction.' *Journal of Ethnic and Migration Studies* **25**:565–73.

Mason, T. David. 2004. *Caught in the Crossfire: Revolution, Repression, and the Rational Peasant*. Lanham, MD: Rowman & Littlefield.

Mason, T. David and Patrick J. Fett. 1996. 'How civil wars end: a rational choice approach.' *Journal of Conflict Resolution* **40**(4):546–68.

Mason, T. David and Dale A. Krane. 1989. 'The political-economy of death squads: towards a theory of the impact of state-sanctioned terror.' *International Studies Quarterly* **33**:175–98.

Mason, T. David, Joseph P. Weingarten, Jr and Patrick J. Fett. 1999.

'Win, lose or draw: predicting the outcome of civil wars.' *Political Research Quarterly* **52**:239–68.

Matovu, John Mary and Frances Stewart. 2001. 'Uganda: the social and economic costs of conflict.' In *War and Underdevelopment, Vol. 2: Country Experiences*, edited by F. Stewart, V. Fitzgerald and Associates. Oxford: Oxford University Press.

Mattes, Michaela and Burcu Savun. 2000. 'Fostering peace after civil war: commitment problems and agreement design.' *International Studies Quarterly* **53**:737–59.

Matthews, Bruce. 1995. 'University education in Sri Lanka in context: consequences of deteriorating standards', *Pacific Affairs* **68**(1):77–94.

Mavrotas, George, S. Mansoob Murshed and Sebastian Torres. 2011. 'Natural resource dependence and economic performance in the 1970–2000 period.' *Review of Development Economics* **15**:124–38.

Mayall, J. 1996. *The New Interventionism: 1991–1994*. Cambridge: Cambridge University Press.

Maybee, Bryan. 2009. *The Globalization of Security: State Power, Security Provision, and Legitimacy*. Basingstoke: Macmillan.

Maynard, Kimberly. 1999. *Healing Communities in Conflict: International Assistance in Complex Emergencies*. New York: Columbia University Press.

Mazurana, D.E. and S.R. Kay. 1999. *Women and Peacebuilding*. Montreal: International Centre for Human Rights and Democratic Development.

McAdam, Doug. 1982. *Political Process and the Development of Black Insurgency, 1930–1970*. Chicago, IL: University of Chicago Press.

McAdam, Doug. 1996. 'Conceptual origins, current problems, future directions.' In *Comparative Perspectives on Social Movements: Political Opportunities, Mobilizing Structures, and Cultural Framings*, edited by D. McAdam, J.D. McCarthy and M.N. Zald. Cambridge: Cambridge University Press.

McAdam, Doug, J.D. McCarthy and M.N. Zald. 1996. *Comparative Perspectives on Social Movements: Political Opportunities, Mobilizing Structures, and Cultural Framings*. Cambridge: Cambridge University Press.

McCoy, S. and J.E. van Dunem. 2009. 'Institutional design.' In *Taxation in a Developing Country: The Case of Mozambique*, edited by C. Arndt and F. Tarp. London: Routledge.

McGarry, John. 2001. 'Northern Ireland and the shortcomings of civic nationalism.' In *Northern Ireland and the Divided World*, edited by J. McGarry. Oxford: Oxford University Press.

McGarry, John. 2006. 'Iraq: Liberal consociation and conflict management.' Draft working paper.

McGarry, John. 2007. 'Asymmetrical federal systems.' *Ethnopolitics* **6**:105–16.

McGarry, John and Brendan O'Leary. 1993. 'The macro-political regulation of ethnic conflict.' In *The Politics of Ethnic Conflict Regulation*, edited by J. McGarry and B. O'Leary. London: Routledge.

McGarry, John and Brendan O'Leary. 2007. 'Iraq's constitution of 2005: liberal consociation as political prescription.' International Journal of Constitutional Law **5**(4): 670–98.

McGarry, John and Brendan O'Leary. 2004a. 'Introduction: consociational theory and Northern Ireland.' In *The Northern Ireland Conflict: Consociational Engagements*, edited by J. McGarry and B. O'Leary. Oxford: Oxford University Press.

McGarry, John and Brendan O'Leary. 2004b. *The Northern Ireland Conflict: Consociational Engagements.* Oxford: Oxford University Press.

McGarry, John and Brendan O'Leary. 2006a. 'Consociational theory, Northern Ireland's conflict, and its agreement: Part 1. What consociationalists can learn from Northern Ireland.' *Government and Opposition* **41**:43–63.

McGarry, John and Brendan O'Leary. 2006b. 'Consociational theory, Northern Ireland's conflict, and its agreement: Part 2. What critics of consociation can learn from Northern Ireland.' *Government and Opposition* **41**:249–77.

McGuire, M.C. and M. Olson. 1996. 'The economics of autocracy and majority rule: the invisible hand and the use of force.' *Journal of Economic Literature* **34**:72–96.

McLeod, Darryl and Maria Dávalos. 2007. 'Post-conflict employment and poverty reduction.' United Nations Development Programme (UNDP), New York.

McNamara, D. 1998. 'The future of protection and the responsibility of the state: statement to the 48th Session of the UNHCR Executive Committee.' *International Journal of Refugee Law* **10**:230–35.

McNeish, John-Andrew. 2010. 'Rethinking resource conflict.' Background paper for World Development Report 2011, Washington, DC, World Bank.

Mehlum, Halvor, Karl Moene and Ragnar Torvik. 2006a. 'Cursed by resources or by institutions?' *The World Economy* **29**:1117–31.

Mehlum, Halvor, Karl Moene and Ragnar Torvik. 2006b. 'Institutions and the resource curse.' *Economic Journal* **116**:1–20.

Meier, Patrick, Doug Bond and Joe Bond. 2007. 'Environmental influences on pastoral conflict in the Horn of Africa.' *Political Geography* **26**:716–35.

Meinert, Lotte. 2009. *Hopes in Friction. Schooling, Health and Everyday Life in Uganda*. Charlotte: Information Age Publishing, Inc.

Mendelson, S.E. 2005. *Barracks and Brothels: Peacekeepers and Human Trafficking in the Balkans*. Washington, DC: Center for Strategic and International Studies.

Mendelson-Forman, Johanna. 2002. 'Achieving socio-economic well-being in post-conflict settings.' *The Washington Quarterly* **25**:125–38.

Merrouche, O. 2006. 'The human capital cost of landmine contamination in Cambodia.' Households in Conflict Network, Brighton, available at: http://www.hicn.org/.

Metelits, C. 2009. 'The logic of change: pushing the boundaries of insurgent behavior theory.' *Defense and Security Analysis* **25**:105–18.

Meyer, D.S. 1995. 'Framing national security: elite public discourse on nuclear weapons during the Cold War.' *Political Communication* **12**:173–92.

Mgbeafulu, Mathias Chinonyere 2003. *Migration and the Economy: Igbo Migrants and the Nigerian Economy 1900 to 1970*. Toronto: iUniverse.

Miall, Hugh. 1992. *The Peacemakers: Peaceful Settlement of Disputes since 1945*. New York: St. Martin's Press.

Miguel, E. and G. Roland. 2006. 'The long run impact of bombing Vietnam.' National Bureau of Economic Research (NBER), Washington, DC.

Miguel, Edward, Shanker Satyanath and E. Sergenti. 2004. 'Economic shocks and civil conflict: an instrumental variables approach.' *Journal of Political Economy* **112**:725–53.

Mikell, G. 1997. *African Feminism. The Politics of Survival in Sub-Saharan Africa*. Philadelphia, PA: University of Pennsylvania Press.

Mill, John Stuart. 1861 [1962]. *Considerations on Representative Government*. Chicago, IL: Henry Regnery.

Mill, John Stuart. 1848 [1998]. *Principles of Political Economy*. Oxford: Oxford University Press.

Miller, Byron. 1994. 'Political empowerment, local–central state relations, and geographically shifting political opportunity structures: strategies of the Cambridge Massachusetts peace movement.' *Political Geography* **13**:393–406.

Miller, R. 1983. 'Religion and occupational mobility.' In *Religion, Education and Employment: Aspects of Equal Opportunity in Northern Ireland*, edited by R.J. Cormack and R.D. Osborne. Belfast: Appletree.

Milner, J. 2009. 'Refugees and the regional dynamics of peacebuilding.' *Refugee Survey Quarterly* **28**:13–30.

Mincer, J. 1974. *Schooling, Experience, and Earnings*. New York: National Bureau of Economic Research (NBER).

Minear, L., C. Scott and T.G. Weiss. 1996. *The News Media, Civil War, and Humanitarian Action*. Boulder, CO: Lynne Rienner.

Mitton, Kieron. 2008. 'Engaging disengagement: the political reintegration of Sierra Leone's Revolutionary United Front.' *Conflict, Security and Development* **8**:193–222.

Moller, Herbert. 1968. 'Youth as a force in the modern world.' *Comparative Studies in Society and History* **10**:238–60.

Monsutti, A. 2008. 'Afghan migratory strategies and the three solutions to the refugee problem.' *Refugee Survey Quarterly* **27**:558–73.

Montalvo, José G. and Marta Reynal-Querol. 2005. 'Ethnic polarization, potential conflict, and civil wars.' *American Economic Review* **95**:796–816.

Mooney, E. and C. French. 2005. 'Barriers and bridges: access to education for internally displaced children.' Brookings Institute–University of Bern.

Moore, M. 2001. *The Ethics of Nationalism*. Oxford: Oxford University Press.

Moore, Will H. 1998. 'Repression and dissent: substitution, context, and timing.' *American Journal of Political Science* **42**:851–73.

Moore, Will H. 2000. 'A substitution model of government coercion.' *Journal of Conflict Resolution* **44**(1):107–27.

Moore, Will H. and S. Shellman. 2004. 'Fear of persecution: forced migration, 1952–1995.' *Journal of Conflict Resolution* **48**(5):723–45.

Morcos, K. 2005. 'Chair's summary.' OECD Development Assistance Committee, London, available at: http://www.oecd.org/dataoecd/60/37/34401185.

Morgenstein, J. 2008. 'Consolidating disarmament: lessons from Colombia's reintegration program for demobilized paramilitaries.' United States Institute of Peace (USIP), Washington, DC.

Morgenthau, Hans J. 1985. *Politics among Nations: The Struggle for Power and Peace*. New York: Knopf.

Morrison, A. and J. Kiras. 1996. *UN Peace Operations and the Role of Japan*. Clementsport, NS: Canadian Peacekeeping.

Morselli, C. 2009. *Inside Criminal Networks*. New York: Springer Science and Business Media.

Moser, C. and F. Clark (eds). 2001. *Victims, Perpetrators or Actors? Gender, Armed Conflict and Political Violence*. London and New York: Zed Books.

Most, Benjamin and Harvey Starr. 1984. 'International relations theory, foreign policy substitutability, and "nice" laws.' *World Politics* **36**(3):383–406.

Most, Benjamin A. and Harvey Starr. 1989. *Inquiry, Logic and International Politics*. Columbia, SC: University of South Carolina Press.

Moxon-Browne, E (ed.). 1998. *A Future for Peacekeeping?* New York: St. Martin's Press.

Moynihan, D. 1993. *Pandaemonium: Ethnicity in International Politics*. Oxford: Oxford University Press.

Muggah, Robert. 2005. 'No magic bullet: a critical perspective on disarmament, demobilization and reintegration (DDR) and weapons reduction in post-conflict contexts.' *The Round Table* **94**:239–52.

Muggah, Robert. 2009a. 'Introduction: the emperor's clothes?' In *Security and Post-Conflict Reconstruction: Dealing with Fighters in the Aftermath of War*, edited by R. Muggah. New York: Routledge.

Muggah, Robert. 2009b. 'Once we were warriors: critical reflections on refugee and IDP militarisation and human security.' In *Human Security and Non-Citizens: Law, Policy, and International Affairs*, edited by A. Edwards and C. Fersteman. Cambridge: Cambridge University Press.

Muggah, Robert. 2009c. *Security and Post-Conflict Reconstruction: Dealing with Fighters in the Aftermath of War*. New York: Routledge.

Muggah, Robert and K. Krause. 2009. 'Closing the gap between peace operations and post-conflict insecurity: towards a violence reduction agenda.' *International Peacekeeping* **16**:136–50.

Mukherjee, Bumba. 2006. 'Why political power-sharing agreements lead to enduring peaceful resolution of some civil wars, but not others?' *International Studies Quarterly* **50**:479–504.

Mulkeen, A. 2007. 'Recruiting, retraining, and retaining secondary school teachers in Sub-Saharan Africa.' World Bank Working Paper 99, World Bank, Washington, DC.

Mullenbach, M.J. 2005. 'Deciding to keep peace: an analysis of international influences on the establishment of third-party peacekeeping missions.' *International Studies Quarterly* **49**(3):529–55.

Murdoch, J. and T. Sandler. 2002. 'Economic growth, civil wars and spatial spillovers.' *Journal of Conflict Resolution*, **46**:91–110.

Murdoch, James C. and Todd Sandler. 2004. 'Civil wars and economic growth: spatial dispersion.' *American Journal of Political Science* **48**:138–51.

Murphy, Kevin, Andrei Shleifer and Robert Vishny. 1991. 'The allocation of talent: implications for growth.' *Quarterly Journal of Economics* **106**:503–30.

Murphy, S.D. 1996. *Humanitarian intervention: The United Nations in an Evolving World Order*. Philadelphia, PA: University of Pennsylvania Press.

Murshed, S. Mansoob. 2010. *Explaining Civil War: A Rational Choice Approach*. Cheltenham, UK and Northampton, MA, USA: Edward Elgar.

Murshed, S. Mansoob and Scott Gates. 2005. 'Spatial-horizontal inequality and the Maoist insurgency in Nepal.' *Review of Development Economics* **9**:121–34.

Murshed, S. Mansoob and M. Zulfan Tadjoeddin. 2009. 'Revisiting the greed and grievance explanations for violent internal conflict.' *Journal of International Development* **21**:87–111.

Murshed, S. Mansoob, M. Zulfan Tadjoeddin and Anis Chowdhury. 2009. 'Is fiscal decentralization conflict abating? Routine violence and district level government in Java, Indonesia.' *Oxford Development Studies* **37**:397–441.

Mvukiyehe, E., C. Samii and G. Taylor. 2007. 'Wartime and post-conflict experiences in Burundi: an individual level survey.' Department of Political Science, Columbia University and New York University.

Mwanasali, M. 2000. 'The view from below.' In *Greed and Grievance: Economic Agendas in Civil Wars*, edited by M. Berdal and D.M. Malone. Boulder, CO: Lynne Rienner.

Nafziger, E. Wayne and Juha Auvinen. 2000. 'The economic causes of humanitarian emergencies.' In *War, Hunger and Displacement: The Origin of Humanitarian Emergencies*, edited by E.W. Nafziger, S. Frances and R. Väyrynen. Oxford: Oxford University Press.

Nafziger, E. Wayne and Juha Auvinen. 2002. 'Economic development, inequality, war, and state violence.' *World Development* **30**:153–63.

Nafziger, E. Wayne and Juha Auvinen. 2003. *Economic Development, Inequality, and War: Humanitarian Emergencies in Developing Countries*. Basingstoke: Palgrave Macmillan.

Nafziger, E. Wayne, Frances Stewart and R. Väyrynen. 2000. *War, Hunger, and Displacement: The Origins of Humanitarian Emergencies*. Vol. I: *The Origins of Humanitarian Emergencies: War and Displacement in Developing Countries*. Oxford: Oxford University Press.

Nagel, J. 1996. *American Indian Ethnic Renewal: Red Power and the Resurgence of Identity and Culture*. New York: Oxford University Press.

Nasr, V. 2001. 'The negotiable state: borders and power-struggles in Pakistan.' In *Right-Sizing the State: The Politics of Moving Borders*, edited by B. O'Leary, I.S. Lustick and T. Callaghy. Oxford: Oxford University Press.

Neary, Peter J. and Sweder van Wijnbergen. 1986. *Natural Resources and the Macroeconomy*. Oxford: Blackwell.

Nef, Jorge. 2006. 'Human security, mutual vulnerability, and sustainable development: a critical review.' *The Whitehead Journal of Diplomacy and International Relations* 7:55–73.

Nel, Philip R. and Marjolein Righarts. 2008. 'Natural disasters and the risk of violent civil conflict.' *International Studies Quarterly* 51:159–84.

Nest, M., F. Grignon and E.F. Kisangani. 2006. *The Democratic Republic of Congo: Economic Dimensions of War and Peace*. Boulder, CO: Lynne Rienner.

Ng, Eric. 2006. 'Is natural resource abundance beneficial or detrimental to income and growth?'. Paper presented at the 40th Annual Meeting of the Canadian Economics Association, Montreal, May.

Ngaruko, F. and Janvier Nkurunziza. 2000. 'An economic interpretation of conflict in Burundi.' *Journal of African Economies* 9:370–409.

Nielsen, Richard A., Michael G. Findley, Zachary S. Davis, Tara Candland and Daniel L. Nielson. 2010. 'Foreign aid shocks as a cause of violent armed conflict.' Department of Political Science, Brigham Young University, Provo, UT.

Nitzschke, H. 2003. 'Transforming war economics: challenge for peacemaking and peacebuilding .' International Peace Academy, New York.

Nitzschke, H. and K. Studdard. 2005. 'The legacies of war economies: challenges and options for peacemaking and peacebuilding.' *International Peacekeeping* 12:222–39.

Nkurunziza, Janvier. 2011. 'Inequality and post-conflict fiscal policies in Burundi.' In *Horizontal Inequalities in a Post-conflict Context* edited by A. Langer, F. Stewart and R. Venugopal. London: Palgrave.

Noel, S. 1993. 'Canadian responses to ethnic conflict: consociationalism, federalism, and control.' In *The Politics of Ethnic Conflict Regulation*, edited by J. McGarry and B. O'Leary. London: Routledge.

Nolte, Insa. 2008. '"Without women, nothing can succeed": Yoruba women in the Oodua People's Congress, Nigeria.' *Africa* 78:84–106.

Nordås, Ragnhild and Nils Petter Gleditsch. 2007. 'Climate change and conflict. Introduction to special issue on climate change and conflict.' *Political Geography* 26:627–38.

Nordlinger, Eric. 1972. *Conflict Regulation in Divided Societies*. Cambridge, MA: Harvard Center for International Affairs.

North, Douglass C., John Joseph Wallis and Barry R. Weingast. 2009. *Violence and Social Orders: A Conceptual Framework for Interpreting Recorded Human History*. Cambridge: Cambridge University Press.

Northedge, F.S. and M.D. Donelan. 1971. *International Disputes*. New York: St Martin's Press.

Norwegian Refugee Council. 1999. Available at: www.db.idpproject.org.

Novelli, M. 2008. *Colombia's Classroom Wars: Political Violence against Education Sector Trade Unions in Colombia.* Amsterdam: Education International.

Nugent, Jeffrey B. and R. Thomas Gillaspy. 1983. 'Old age pension and fertility in rural areas of less developed countries: some evidence from Mexico.' *Economic Development and Cultural Change* 31:809–29.

Nwokolo, Ndubuisi N. 2009. 'From grievance to greed: an analysis of violent conflicts in oil bearing communities in Nigeria.' Paper presented at the ERD Conference on 'New Faces for African Development', Accra, 21–23 May.

Nyberg-Sorensen, N. 2004. 'Opportunities and pitfalls in the migration–development nexus: Somaliland and beyond.' Danish Institute for International Studies, Copenhagen.

Nyberg-Sorensen, N., N. van Hear and P. Engberg-Pedersen. 2002. *The Migration–Development Nexus: Evidence and Policy Options.* Geneva: International Organization for Migration (IOM).

O'Brien, Karen, Asuncion Lera St. Clair and Berit Kristofferson. 2010. *Climate Change, Ethics and Human Security.* Cambridge: Cambridge University Press.

O'Hanlon, M.E. 2003. *Expanding Global Military Capacity for Humanitarian Intervention.* Washington, DC: Brookings Institution.

O'Lear, Shannon and Paul F. Diehl. 2007. 'Not drawn to scale: research on resource and environmental conflict.' *Geopolitics* 12:166–82.

O'Leary, Brendan. 2001. 'An iron law of nationalism and federation? A (neo-Diceyian) theory of the necessity of a federal Staatsvolk and of consociational rescue.' *Nations and Nationalism* 7:273–96.

O'Leary, Brendan. 2005a. 'Debating consociational politics: normative and explanatory arguments.' In *From Powersharing to Democracy*, edited by S. Noel. Montreal and Kingston, Ont.: McGill-Queen's University Press.

O'Leary, Brendan. 2005b. 'Powersharing, pluralist federation, and federacy.' In *The Future of Kurdistan in Iraq*, edited by B. O'Leary, J. McGarry and K. Salih. Philadelphia, PA: University of Pennsylvania Press.

O'Leary, Brendan. 2012. 'The federalization of Iraq and the break-up of Sudan: the Leonard Schapiro Lecture.' *Government and Opposition* 47(4): 481–516.

O'Malley, B. 2007. 'Education under attack: a global study on targeted political and military violence against education staff, teachers, union and government officials, and institutions.' UNESCO, Paris.

Oakley, R., M. Dziedzic and E. Goldberg. 1998. *Policing the New World*

Disorder: Peace Operations and Public Security. Washington, DC: National Defense University Press.

Obama, Barack H. 2009. 'The Nobel lecture.' Oslo, 10 December, available at: http://nobelpeaceprize.org/en_GB/laureates/laureates-2009/obama-lecture/.

Oberschall, A. 1973. *Social Conflict and Social Movements*. Englewood Cliffs, NJ: Prentice-Hall.

Oberschall, A. 2000. 'The manipulation of ethnicity: from ethnic cooperation to violence and war in Yugoslavia.' *Ethnic and Racial Studies* **23**:982–1001.

OECD. 2007. 'Principles for good international engagement in fragile states and situations.' OECD Development Assistance Committee, Paris; available at: http://www.oecd.org/dataoecd/61/45/38368714.pdf.

OECD. 2009. 'Conflict and fragility: armed violence reduction – enabling development.' OECD Development Co-operation Directorate, Paris.

Ogata, Sadako. 1998. 'Inclusion or exclusion: social development challenges for Asia and Europe.' Asian Development Bank, Manila, 27 April, available at: http://www.unhcr.ch/refworld/unhcr/hcspeech/27ap1998.htm (accessed August 22, 2010).

OHCHR. 1996. 'The administration of justice in post-genocide Rwanda.' Office of the High Commissioner for Human Rights (OHCHR), United Nations, Geneva.

Ohlsson, Leif. 2003. 'The risk of livelihood conflicts and the nature of policy measures required.' In *The Future of Peace in the Twenty-first Century*, edited by N.N. Kittrie, R. Carazo and J.R. Mancham. Washington, DC: Carolina Academic Press, pp. 305–21.

Olick, Jeffrey K. and David Levy. 1997. 'Collective memory and cultural constraint: holocaust myth and rationality in German politics.' *American Sociological Review* **62**:921–36.

Olivier, Pamela. 1980. 'Rewards and punishments as selective incentives for collective action: theoretical investigations.' *American Journal of Sociology* **85**:1356–75.

Ong, Aihwa. 1996. 'Cultural citizenship as subject-making: immigrants negotiating racial and cultural boundaries in the United States.' *Current Anthropology* **37**:737–62.

Orentlicher, D. 1991. 'Settling accounts: the duty to prosecute human rights violations of a prior regime.' *New York Law Journal* **100**:2562–8.

Organski, A.F.K. and J. Kugler. 1977. 'The cost of major wars: the Phoenix factor.' *American Political Science Review* **71**:1347–66.

Organski, A.F.K. and J. Kugler. 1980. *The War Ledger*. Chicago, IL: Chicago University Press.

OSCE. 2010. 'Caucasus and Moldova.' Organization for Security and Cooperation in Europe, Paris.

Osorio, Rafel Guerreiro. 2008. 'Is all socioeconomic inequality among racial groups in Brazil caused by racial discrimination?' International Poverty Centre, Brasilia.

Østby, Gudrun. 2008a. 'Horizontal inequalities, political environment and civil conflict: evidence from 55 developing countries.' In *Horizontal Inequalities and Conflict: Understanding Group Violence in Multiethnic Countries*, edited by F. Stewart. London: Palgrave.

Østby, Gudrun. 2008b. 'Polarization, horizontal inequalities, and violent civil conflict.' *Journal of Peace Research* **45**:143–82.

Østby, Gudrun, Ragnhild Nordås and Jan Ketil Rød. 2009. 'Regional inequalities and civil conflict in Sub-Saharan Africa.' *International Studies Quarterly* **53**:301–24.

Østby, Gudrun, Henrik Urdal, M. Zulfan Tadjoeddin, S. Mansoob Murshed and Håvard Strand. 2011. 'Population pressure, horizontal inequality, and political violence: a disaggregated study of Indonesian provinces, 1990–2003.' *Journal of Development Studies* **47**(3):377–98.

Ott, C.M. 1972. 'Mediation as a method of conflict resolution: two cases.' *International Organization*, **26**(4):595–618.

Ottaway, M. 2002. 'Rebuilding state institutions in collapsed states.' *Development and Change* **33**(5):1001–23.

Ottaway, Marina. 2003. 'Promoting democracy after conflict: the difficult choices.' *International Studies Perspectives* **4**:314–22.

Otunnu, O.A. and Michael W. Doyle. 1998. *Peacemaking and Peacekeeping for the New Century*. Lanham, MD: Rowman & Littlefield.

Ozerdem, Alpaslan. 2003. 'Vocational training of former Kosovo Liberation Army combatants: for what purpose and end?' *Conflict, Security and Development* **3**:393–405.

Ozerdem, Alpaslan and Sukanya Podder. 2011. *Child Soldiers: From Recruitment to Reintegration*. London: Palgrave.

Palmer, G. and A. Bhandari. 2000. 'The investigation of substitutability in foreign policy.' *Journal of Conflict Resolution* **44**(1):3–10.

Pantuliano, S., M. Buchana-Smith, P. Murphy and I. Mosel. 2008. 'The long road home: opportunities and obstacles to the reintegration of IDPs and refugees returning to Southern Sudan and the Three Areas.' Overseas Development Institute, London.

Parente, S.L. and E.C. Prescott. 2000. *Barriers to Riches*. Cambridge, MA: MIT Press.

Paris, Roland. 2001. 'Human security: paradigm shift or hot air?' *International Security* **26**:87–102.

Paris, Roland. 2004. *At War's End: Building Peace after Civil Conflict*. Cambridge: Cambridge University Press.

Paul, James. 2004. 'Working with nongovernmental organizations.' In *The UN Security Council: From the Cold War to the 21st Century*, edited by D.M. Malone. Boulder, CO: Lynne Rienner, pp. 373–87.

Peake, Gordon. 2008. 'What the veterans say: unpacking DDR programmes in Timor Leste.' Centre for International Cooperation and Security (CICS), University of Bradford, Bradford.

Pelcovits, N.A. 1984. *Peacekeeping on Arab-Israeli Fronts: Lessons from the Sinai and Lebanon*. SAIS Paper 3. Boulder, CO: Westview.

Peluso, Nancy Lee and Michael Watts. 2001a. *Violent Environments*. Ithaca, NY: Cornell University Press.

Peluso, Nancy Lee and Michael Watts. 2001b. 'Violent environments.' In *Violent Environments*, edited by N.L. Peluso and M. Watts. Ithaca, NY: Cornell University Press, pp. 3–38.

Pérez de Cuéllar J. 1997. *Pilgrimage for Peace: A Secretary-General's Memoir*. New York: St. Martin's Press.

Peskin, V. 2005. 'Courting Rwanda: the promises and pitfalls of the ICTR Outreach Programme.' *Journal of International Criminal Justice* 3:950–61.

Petersen, Roger Dale. 1993. 'A community-based theory of rebellion.' *European Journal of Sociology* 34:41–78.

Petersen, Roger Dale. 2001. *Resistance and Rebellion: Lessons from Eastern Europe*. Cambridge: Cambridge University Press.

Petersen, Roger Dale. 2002. *Understanding Ethnic Violence: Fear, Hatred, and Resentment in Twentieth Century Eastern Europe*. Cambridge: Cambridge University Press.

Pfabigan, A. 1991. 'The political feasibility of the Austro-Marxist proposal for the solution of the nationality problem of the Danubian monarchy.' In *State and Nation in Multi-Ethnic Societies: The Breakup of Multi-National States*, edited by U. Ra'anan, M. Mesner, K. Armes and K. Martin. Manchester: Manchester University Press.

Pickering, J. and M. Peceny. 2006. 'Forging democracy at gunpoint.' *International Studies Quarterly* 50(3):539–5.

Piguet, Etienne. 2010. 'Linking climate change, environmental degradation, and migration: a methodological overview.' *Wiley Interdisciplinary Reviews-Climate Change* 1(4):517–24.

Pillar, P. 1983. *Negotiating Peace: War Termination as a Bargaining Process*. Princeton, NJ: Princeton University Press.

Piven, F.F. and R.A. Cloward. 1995. 'Collective protest: a critique of resource-mobilization theory.' In *Social Movements: Critiques, Concepts, Case-Studies*, edited by S.M. Lyman. London: Macmillan.

Popkin, Samuel L. 1988. 'Political entrepreneurs and peasant movements in Vietnam.' In *Rationality and Revolution*, edited by M. Taylor. Cambridge: Cambridge University Press.

Porto, J.G. 2002. 'Contemporary conflict analysis in perspective.' In *Security and Surfeit: The Ecology of African Conflicts*, edited by J. Lind and K. Sturman. Pretoria: Institute of Security Studies.

Posen, Barry. 1993. 'The security dilemma and ethnic conflict.' In *Ethnic Conflict and International Security*, edited by M.E. Brown. Princeton, NJ: Princeton University Press.

Pouligny, B. 2006. *Peace Operations Seen from Below: UN Missions and Local People*. Bloomfield, CT: Kumarian Press.

Pouligny, B., S. Chesterman and A. Schnabel (eds). 2007. *After Mass Crime: Rebuilding States and Communities*. Tokyo/New York: United Nations University Press.

Premdas, R.R. 1998. *Secession and Self-Determination in the Caribbean: Nevis and Tobago*. St Augustine, Trinidad: University of the West Indies.

Pruitt, D.G. 1981. *Negotiation Behavior*. New York: Academic Press.

Pruitt, D.G. and P. Carnevale. 1993. *Negotiation of Social Conflict*. Buckingham: Open University Press.

Prunier, Gerard. 2007. *Darfur: The Ambiguous Genocide*. Ithaca, NY: Cornell University Press.

Przeworski, A., M.E. Alvarez, J.A. Cheibub and F. Limongi. 2000. *Democracy and Development: Political Institutions and Wellbeing in the World, 1950–1990*. Cambridge: Cambridge University Press.

Pugel, James. 2009. 'Measuring reintegration in Liberia: assessing the gap between outputs and outcomes.' In *Security and Post-Conflict Reconstruction: Dealing with Fighters in the Aftermath of War*, edited by R. Muggah. New York: Routledge.

Pugh, M. 2002. 'Postwar political economy in Bosnia and Herzegovina: the spoils of peace.' *Global Governance* **8**:467–82.

Pugh, M. 2004. 'Peacekeeping and critical theory.' *International Peacekeeping* **11**(1):39–58.

Pugh, M. and W.P. Singh Sidhu. 2003. *The United Nations and Regional Security: Europe and Beyond*. Boulder, CO: Lynne Rienner.

Quinn, J. Michael, T. David Mason and Mehmet Gurses. 2007. 'Sustaining the peace: determinants of civil war recurrence.' *International Interactions* **33**:167–93.

Raeymaekers, T. and J. Cuvalier. 2002. 'Contributing to the war economy in the DRC: European companies and the coltan trade.' International Peace Information Service, Brussels.

Ragin, Charles C. 1987. *The Comparative Method: Moving Beyond*

Qualitative and Quantitative Strategies. Berkeley, CA: University of California Press.

RAID. 2004. 'Unanswered questions: companies, conflict, and the Democratic Republic of Congo.' Rights and Accountability in Development (RAID), London.

Raleigh, Clionadh and Lisa Jordan. 2010. 'Climate change and migration.' In *Social Dimensions of Climate Change: Equity and Vulnerability in a Warming World*, edited by R. Mearns and A. Norton. Washington, DC: World Bank, pp. 103–31.

Raleigh, Clionadh and Henrik Urdal. 2007. 'Climate change, environmental degradation and armed conflict.' *Political Geography* **26**:674–94.

Ramsbotham, O., T. Woodhouse and H. Miall. 2010. *Contemporary Conflict Resolution: The Prevention, Management, and Transformation of Deadly Conflicts*. Cambridge: Polity Press.

Rapoport, A. 1960. *Fights, Games, and Debates*. Ann Arbor, MI: University of Michigan Press.

Ratha, D. 2003. 'Workers' remittances: an important and stable source of external development finance.' In *Global Development Finance 2003*, edited by World Bank. Washington, DC: World Bank.

Ratha, D. and W. Shaw. 2007. 'South–south migration and remittances.' World Bank, Washington, DC.

Ratner, S. 1995. *The New UN Peacekeeping: Building Peace in the Lands of Conflict after the Cold War*. New York: St. Martin's Press.

Regan, A.J. 2003. 'The Bougainville conflict: political and economic agendas.' In *The Political Economy of Armed Conflict: Beyond Greed and Grievance*, edited by K. Ballentine and J. Sherman. Boulder, CO: Lynne Rienner.

Regan, Patrick M. 2000. *Civil Wars and Foreign Powers: Outside Intervention in Intrastate Conflict*. Ann Arbor, MI: University of Michigan Press.

Reilly, B. 1997. 'Preferential voting and political engineering: a comparative study.' *Journal of Commonwealth and Comparative Politics* **35**:1–19.

Reilly, B. 2001. *Democracy in Divided Societies: Electoral Engineering for Conflict Management*. Cambridge: Cambridge University Press.

Reilly, B. 2005. 'Does the choice of electoral system promote democracy? The gap between theory and practice.' In *Sustainable Peace: Power and Democracy after Civil Wars*, edited by P.G. Roeder and D. Rothchild. Ithaca, NY: Cornell University Press.

Reilly, B. 2006. *Democracy and Diversity: Political Engineering in the Asia–Pacific*. Oxford: Oxford University Press.

Reiter, Dan. 2003. 'Exploring the bargaining model of war.' *Perspectives on Politics* **1**:27–43.

Renner, M. 2002. 'The anatomy of war resources.' Worldwatch Institute, Washington, DC.

Reno, W. 1995. *Corruption and State Politics in Sierra Leone*. New York: Cambridge University Press.

Reno, W. 1998. *Warlord Politics and the African State*. Boulder, CO: Lynne Rienner.

Reno, W. 2000. 'Shadow states and the political economy of civil wars.' In *Greed and Grievance: Economic Agendas in Civil Wars*, edited by M. Berdal and D.M. Malone. Boulder, CO: Lynne Rienner.

Reno, W. 2002. 'The politics of insurgency in collapsing states.' *Development and Change* **33**:838–58.

Restrepo, J. and Robert Muggah. 2009. 'Colombia's quiet demobilization: a security dividend.' In *Security and Post-Conflict Reconstruction: Dealing with Fighters in the Aftermath of War*, edited by R. Muggah. New York: Routledge.

Reuveny, Rafael. 2007. 'Climate change-induced migration and conflict.' *Political Geography* **26**:656–73.

Reynal-Querol, Marta. 2002. 'Ethnicity, political systems, and civil wars.' *Journal of Conflict Resolution* **46**:29–54.

Richani, N. 2002. *Systems of Violence: The Political Economy of War and Peace in Colombia*. Albany, NY: State University of New York.

Richards, Paul. 2005. 'To fight or to farm? Agrarian dimensions of the Mano River conflicts (Liberia and Sierra Leone).' *African Affairs* **104**:571–90.

Richardson, John M., Jr and Jianxin Wang. 1993. 'Peace accords: seeking conflict resolution in deeply divided societies.' In *Peace Accords and Ethnic Conflict*, edited by K.M. da Silva and S.W.R.d.A. Samarasinghe. London: Pinter, pp. 173–98.

Rigterink, Anouk. 2010. 'The wrong suspect: an enquiry into the endogeneity of natural resource measures to civil war.' Paper presented at the CSAE Conference on 'Economic Development in Africa', Centre for the Study of African Economies, University of Oxford, 21–23 March.

Riker, William. 1964. *Federalism: Origin, Operation, Significane*. Boston, MA: Little, Brown.

Rikhye, I.J. 1984. *The Theory and Practice of Peacekeeping*. London: C. Hurst.

Ring, L. Zenana. 2006. *Everyday Peace in a Karachi Apartment Building*. Bloomington, IN: Indiana University Press.

Rodriguez, Catherine and Fabio José Sanchez Torrez. 2009. 'Armed conflict exposure, human capital investments, and child labor: evidence from Colombia.' Households in Conflict Network, Brighton, available at: http://www.hicn.org/.

Rodrik, Dani. 2002. 'After neoliberalism, what?' Paper presented at the Conference on 'Alternatives to Neo-Liberalism', Washington, DC, 23 May.

Rodrik, Dani. 2007. *One Economics, Many Recipes: Globalization, Institutions and Economic Growth*. Princeton, NJ: Princeton University Press.

Roeder, Philip G. 1991. 'Soviet federalism and ethnic mobilization.' *World Politics* **43**:196–232.

Roeder, Philip G. 2005. 'Power dividing as an alternative to ethnic power sharing.' In *Sustainable Peace: Power and Democracy after Civil War*, edited by P.G. Roeder and D. Rothchild. Ithaca, NY: Cornell University Press, pp. 51–82.

Roeder, Philip G. and Donald Rothchild. 2005a. 'Conclusion: nation-state stewardship and the alternatives to power sharing.' In *Sustainable Peace: Power and Democracy after Civil Wars*, edited by P.G. Roeder and D. Rothchild. Ithaca, NY: Cornell University Press.

Roeder, Philip G. and Donald Rothchild (eds) 2005b. *Sustainable Peace: Power and Democracy after Civil Wars*. Ithaca, NY: Cornell University Press.

Rone, J. 2003. 'Sudan, oil, and human rights.' Human Rights Watch, New York.

Rosecrance, Richard. 1986. *The Rise of Trading States: Commerce and Conquest in the Modern World*. New York: Basic Books.

Rosenstone, Steven J. and John Mark Hansen. 1993. *Mobilization, Participation, and Democracy in America*. New York: Macmillan.

Ross, Michael L. 1999. 'The political economy of the resource curse.' *World Politics* **51**:297–322.

Ross, Michael L. 2001a. 'Does oil hinder democracy?' *World Politics* **53**:325–61.

Ross, Michael L. 2001b. *Timber Booms and Institutional Breakdown in Southeast Asia*. Cambridge: Cambridge University Press.

Ross, Michael L. 2003. 'Oil, drugs, and diamonds: the varying roles of natural resources in civil war.' In *The Political Economy of Armed Conflict: Beyond Greed and Grievance*, edited by K. Ballentine and J. Sherman. Boulder, CO: Lynne Rienner.

Ross, Michael L. 2004a. 'How does natural resource wealth influence civil wars? Evidence from 13 cases.' *International Organization* **58**:35–67.

Ross, Michael L. 2004b. 'Does taxation lead to representation?' *British Journal of Political Science* **34**:229–49.

Ross, Michael L. 2004c. 'What do we know about natural resources and civil wars?' *Journal of Peace Research* **41**:337–56.

Ross, Michael L. 2006. 'A closer look at oil, diamonds, and civil war.' *Annual Review of Political Science* **9**:265–300.

Ross, Michael L. 2009. 'Oil and democracy revisited.' University of California Los Angeles (UCLA), Los Angeles.

Rosser, Andrew. 2006. 'The political economy of the resource curse: a literature survey.' Institute of Development Studies (IDS), University of Sussex, Brighton.

Rotberg, R. 2000. 'Truth commissions and the provision of truth, jsutice, and reconciliation.' In *Truth v. Justice: The Morality of Truth Commissions*, edited by R. Rotberg and D. Thompson. Princeton, NJ: Princeton University Press.

Rotberg, R. 2003. *When States Fail: Causes and Consequences*. Princeton, NJ: Princeton University Press.

Rothchild, Donald. 1997. *Managing Ethnic Conflict in Africa: Pressures and Incentives for Cooperation*. Washington, DC: Brookings Institute.

Rothchild, Donald. 2008. 'Africa's power sharing institutions as a response to insecurity: assurance without deterrence.' In *Intra-State Conflict, Governments, and Security: Dilemmas of Deterrence and Assurance*, edited by S.M. Saideman and M.-J.J. Zahar. London: Routledge, pp. 138–60.

Rothchild, Donald and Michael W. Foley. 1988. 'African states and the politics of inclusive coalitions.' In *The Precarious Balance: State and Society in Africa*, edited by D. Rothchild and N. Chazan. Boulder, CO: Lynne Rienner, pp. 233–63.

Rothchild, Donald and Philip G. Roeder. 2005. 'Dilemmas of state-building in divided societies.' In *Sustainable Peace: Power and Democracy after Civil War*, edited by P.G. Roeder and D. Rothchild. Ithaca, NY: Cornell University Press, pp. 1–25.

Rothschild, Emma. 1995. 'What is security?' *Daedalus* **124**:53–98.

Rothstein, B. 2000. 'Political institutions: an overview.' In *A New Handbook of Political Science*, edited by R. Goodin and H.-D. Klingemann. Oxford: Oxford University Press.

Ruane, Joseph and Jennifer Todd. 2010. 'Ethnicity and religion, redefining the research agenda.' *Ethnopolitics* **9**(1):1–8.

Rubin, B.R. 2004. 'Road to ruin: Afghanistan's booming opium industry.' Center on International Cooperation, New York.

Rubin, B.R., A. Armstrong and G.R. Ntegeye. 2001. *Regional Conflict Formation in the Great Lakes Region of Africa: Structure, Dynamics, and Challenges for Policy*. New York: Center on International Cooperation.

Rubin, J. and B. Brown. 1975. *The Social Psychology of Bargaining and Negotiation*. New York: Academic Press.

Ruggie, J.G. 1994. 'Peacekeeping and U.S. interests.' *Washington Quarterly* **17**(4):175–84.

Rustad, Siri Aas, Halvard Buhaug, Åshild Falch and Scott Gates. 2011. 'All conflict is local: modeling sub-national variation in civil conflict risk.' *Conflict Management and Peace Science* **28**:15–40.

Sabine, George H. 1961. *A History of Political Theory*. New York: Holt, Rinehart & Winston.

Sachs, Jeffrey and Andrew Warner. 1995. 'Natural resource abundance and economic growth.' National Bureau of Economic Research (NBER), Cambridge, MA.

Sachs, Jeffrey and Andrew Warner. 1999. 'The big push, natural resource booms, and growth.' *Journal of Development Economics* **59**:43–76.

Sachs, Jeffrey and Andrew Warner. 2001. 'The curse of natural resources.' *European Economic Review* **45**:827–38.

Sala-i-Martin, Xavier and Arvind Subramanian. 2003. 'Addressing the natural resource curse: an illustration from Nigeria.' National Bureau of Economic Research (NBER), Cambridge, MA.

Salehyan, Idean. 2007. 'Transnational rebels: neighboring states and sanctuaries for rebel groups.' *World Politics* **59**:217–42.

Salehyan, Idean. 2008. 'From climate change to conflict? No consensus yet.' *Journal of Peace Research* **45**:315–26.

Salehyan, Idean. 2009. *Rebels Without Borders: Transnational Insurgencies in World Politics*. Ithaca, NY: Cornell University Press.

Salehyan, Idean. 2010. 'The delegation of war to rebel organizations.' *Journal of Conflict Resolution* **54**:493–515.

Salehyan, Idean and Kristian Skrede Gleditsch. 2007. 'Refugees and the spread of civil war.' *International Organization* **60**:335–66.

Salehyan, Idean, Kristian Skrede Gleditsch and David Cunningham. 2011. 'Explaining external support for insurgent groups.' *International Organization* **66**(4):709–44.

Sambanis, Nicholas. 2000. 'Partition as a solution to ethnic war: an empirical critique of the theoretical literature.' *World Politics* **52**:437–83.

Sambanis, Nicholas. 2002. 'A review of recent advances and future directions in the quantitative literature on civil war.' *Defence and Peace Economics* **13**:215–43.

Sambanis, N. 2004a. 'Using case studies to expand economic models of civil war.' *Perspectives on Political Science* **2**(2):259–79.

Sambanis, Nicholas. 2004b. 'What is civil war? Conceptual and empirical complexities of an operational definition.' *Journal of Conflict Resolution* **48**:814–58.

Sambanis, N. and J. Schulhofer-Wohl. 2007. 'Evaluating multilateral interventions in civil wars: a comparison of UN and non-UN peace operations.' In *Multilateralism and Security Institutions in an Era of Globalization*, edited by D. Bourantonis, K. Ifantis and P. Tsakonis, London: Routledge, pp. 252–87.

Sarkin, J. 1996. 'The trials and tribulations of South Africa's Truth and Reconciliation Commission.' *South Africa Journal on Human Rights* **12**:617–40.

Save the Children UK. 2005. 'Forgotten casualties of war: girls in armed conflict.' Save the Children UK, London.

Scacco, A. 2010. 'Who riots? Explaining individual participation in ethnic violence.' Working paper, Columbia University, New York, available at: https://files.nyu.edu/als8/public/files/Scacco__Who__Riots.pdf.

Schabas, W. 2005. 'War economies, economic actors, and international law.' In *Profiting from Peace: Managing the Resource Dimension of Civil Wars*, edited by K. Ballentine and H. Nitzschke. Boulder, CO: Lynne Rienner.

Scheper-Hughes, Nancy. 2007. 'The gray zone: small wars, peacetime crimes, and invisible genocides.' In *The Shadow Side of Fieldwork: Exploring the Blurred Borders between Ethnography and Life*, edited by A. McLean and A. Leibing. Oxford: Blackwell.

Schirch, L. 2001. 'Ritual reconciliation: transforming identity/reframing conflict.' In *Reconciliation, Justice, and Coexistence: Theory and Practice*, edited by M. Abu-Nimer. Lanham, MD: Lexington Books.

Schmeidl, S. 1997. 'Exploring the causes of forced migration: a pooled analysis, 1971–1990.' *Social Science Quarterly* **78**:284–308.

Schultz, T.W. 1961. 'Investment in human capital.' *American Economic Review* **51**:1–17.

Sen, Amartya. 1999. *Development as Freedom*, Oxford: Oxford University Press.

Sewell, W.H. 2005. *Logics of History: Social Theory and Social Transformation*. Chicago, IL: University of Chicago Press.

Shanto, I. and A.F. Simon. 2000. 'New perspectives and evidence on political communication and campaign effects.' *Annual Review of Psychology* **51**:149–69.

Shemyakina, O. 2007. 'The effect of armed conflict on the accumulation of schooling: results from Tajikistan.' Households in Conflict Network, Brighton, available at: http://www.hicn.org/.

Sherman, J. 2002. 'Policies and practices for regulating resource flows to armed conflict.' International Peace Academy, New York.

Sherman, J. 2003. 'Burma: lessons from the ceasefires.' In *The Political*

Economy of Armed Conflict: Beyond Greed and Grievance, edited by K. Ballentine and J. Sherman. Boulder, CO: Lynne Rienner.

Shleifer, Andrei and Robert W. Vishny. 1993. 'Corruption.' *Quarterly Journal of Economics* **108**:599–617.

Simmons, Beth A., Frank Dobbin and Geoffrey Garrett. 2006. 'Introduction: the international diffusion of liberalism.' *International Organization* **60**:781–810.

Simon, Julian L. 1989. 'Lebensraum: paradoxically, population growth may eventually end wars.' *Journal of Conflict Resolution* **33**:164–80.

Sisk, Timothy D. 1996. *Power Sharing and International Mediation in Ethnic Conflict*. Washington, DC: United States Institute of Peace (USIP).

Sivard, R.L. 1996. *World Military and Social Expenditure 1996*. Washington, DC: World Priorities.

Skocpol, Theda. 1982. 'Review: what makes peasants revolutionary?' *Comparative Politics* **14**:351–75.

Skocpol, Theda. 2003. *Diminished Democracy: From Membership to Management in American Civic Life*. Norman, OK: Oklahoma University Press.

Skran, C. 1995. *Refugees in Inter-War Europe*. Oxford: Oxford University Press.

Slantchev, Branislav L. 2003. 'The principle of convergence in wartime negotiations.' *American Political Science Review* **97**:621–32.

Slettebak, Rune T. 2012. Don't blame the weather! Climate-related natural disasters and civil conflict.' *Journal of Peace Research* **49**(1):163–76.

Smelser, Neil. 1963. *Theory of Collective Behavior*. New York: Free Press.

Smillie, I. 2005. 'What lessons from the Kimberley Process certification regime?' In *Profiting from Peace: Managing the Resource Dimension of Civil Wars*, edited by K. Ballentine and H. Nitzschke. Boulder, CO: Lynne Rienner.

Smillie, I., L. Gberie and R. Hazleton. 2000. *The Heart of the Matter: Sierra Leone, Diamonds, and Human Security*. Ottawa: Partnership Africa Canada.

Smith, Alistair and Allan C. Stam. 2004. 'Bargaining and the nature of war.' *Journal of Conflict Resolution* **48**:783–813.

Smith, Alan and Tony Vaux. 2003. 'Education, conflict and international development.' Department for International Development, UK Government, London.

Snow, D.A. and R.D. Benford. 1998. 'Ideology, frame resonance, and participant mobilization.' *International Social Movement Research* 1:197–218.

Snyder, Jack. 2000. *From Voting to Violence: Democratization and Nationalist Conflict*. New York: W.W. Norton.

Snyder, R. 2006. 'Does lootable wealth breed disorder? A political economy of extraction framework.' *Comparative Political Studies* 39:943–68.

Soares, F.V. and T. Britto. 2007. 'Confronting capacity constraints on conditional cash transfers in Latin America: the cases of El Salvador and Paraguay.' International Poverty Centre, Brasilia.

Soderberg, Mimmi and Thomas Ohlson. 2003. 'Democratisation and armed conflicts.' Swedish International Development Cooperation Agency (SIDA), Stockholm.

Sollenberg, Margareta and Peter Wallensteen. 2001. 'Major armed conflicts.' *Journal of Peace Research* 38(5):629–44.

Sommers, Marc. 2002. Children, Education and War: Reaching Education for All (EFA) Objectives in Countries Affected by Conflict. Working Paper, No.1, Conflict prevention and Reconstruction Unit. Washington, D.C.: The World Bank.

Sørensen, Birgitte Refslund. 2011. 'Entanglements of politics and education in Sri Lanka.' 215–38, In *Trysts with Democracy. Political Practice in South Asia*. Edited by Stig Toft Madsen et al. Anthem South Asian Studies. London: Anthem Press.

Sørensen, B. 2008. 'The politics of citizenship and difference in Sri Lankan schools.' *Anthropology and Education Quarterly* 39(4):423–43.

Spear, J. 2006. 'From political economies of war to political economies of peace: the contribution of disarmament, demobilization, and reintegration after wars of predation.' *Contemporary Security Policy* 21:168–89.

Specker, L. 2008. 'The R phase of DDR processes: an overview of key lessons learned and practical experiences.' Clingendael Institute, The Hague.

Sphere Project and INEE. 2009. 'Integrating quality education with humanitarian response for humanitarian accountability: the Sphere–INEE Companionship.' Inter-Agencies Network for Education in Emergencies (INEE) and the Sphere Project, New York.

Sriskandarajah, D. 2002. 'The migration–development nexus: Sri Lankan case study.' *International Migration* 40:283–305.

Stanley Foundation. 2000. 'Creating the International Legal Assistance Consortium.' Muscatine, IA.

Stanley, William and Charles T. Call. 1997. 'Building a new civilian police force in El Salvador.' In *Rebuilding Societies after Civil War: Critical*

Roles for International Assistance, edited by K. Kumar. Boulder, CO: Lynne Rienner, pp. 107–34.

Stark, Odet and David Bloom. 1985. 'The new economics of labor migration.' *American Economic Review* **75**:173–85.

Stedman, Stephen John. 1991. *Peacemaking in Civil War: International Mediation in Zimbabwe, 1974–1980*. Boulder, CO: Lynne Rienner.

Stedman, Stephen John. 1993. 'The end of the Zimbabwean civil war.' In *Stopping the Killing: How Civil Wars End*, edited by R. Licklider. New York: New York University Press.

Stedman, Stephen John. 1996. 'Negotiation and mediation in internal conflicts.' In *The International Dimension of Internal Conflict*, edited by M.E. Brown. Cambridge, MA: MIT Press.

Stedman, Stephen John. 1997. 'Spoiler problems in peace processes.' *International Security* **22**:5–53.

Stedman, Stephen John. 1998. 'Conflict prevention as strategic interaction: the spoiler problem and the case of Rwanda.' In *Preventing Violent Conflicts: Past Record and Future Challenges*, edited by P. Wallensteen. Uppsala, Sweden: Department of Peace and Conflict Research, Uppsala University.

Stedman, Stephen John. 2007. 'UN transformation in an era of soft balancing.' *International Affairs* **83**:933–44.

Stedman, Stephen John, Donald Rothchild and Elizabeth M. Cousens (eds). 2002. *Ending Civil Wars: the Implementation of Peace Agreements*. Boulder, CO: Lynne Rienner.

Steinberger, Michael. 2001. 'So, are civilizations at war? Interview with Samuel P. Huntington.' In *The Observer*. 21 October, available at: http://www.guardian.co.uk/world/2001/oct/21/afghanistan.religion2.

Steiner, J. 1989. 'Power-sharing: another Swiss export product?' In *Conflict and Peacemaking in Multiethnic Societies*, edited by J. Montville. Lexington, MA: Lexington Books.

Stepan, Alfred. 1999. 'Federalism and democracy: beyond the US model.' *Journal of Democracy* **10**:19–34.

Stepan, Alfred. 2001. *Arguing Comparative Politics*. Oxford: Oxford University Press.

Stepputat, F. 2004. 'Dynamics of return and sustainable reintegration in a "Mobile Livelihoods" framework.' Danish Institute for International Studies, Copenhagen.

Stern Review. 2006. 'The economics of climate change.' HM Treasury, London.

Stevick, E. Doyle and Bradley Levinson. 2007. *Reimagining Civic Education: How Diverse Societies Form Democratic Citizens*. Plymouth, UK: Rowman & Littlefield.

Stewart, Frances. 2000. 'Crisis prevention: tackling horizontal inequalities.' *Oxford Development Studies* **28**:245–62.

Stewart, Frances. 2002a. 'Horizontal inequalities as a source of conflict.' In *From Reaction to Conflict Prevention: Opportunities for the UN System*, edited by F. Osler Hampson and D.M. Malone. Boulder, CO: Lynne Rienner.

Stewart, Frances. 2002b. 'Horizontal inequality: a neglected dimension of development.' WIDER Annual Development Lecture, Helsinki, 14 December.

Stewart, Frances. 2008a. *Horizontal Inequalities and Conflict: Understanding Group Violence in Multiethnic Societies.* London: Palgrave.

Stewart, Frances. 2008b. 'Policies towards horizontal inequalities in post-conflict reconstruction.' In *Making Peace Work: The Challenges of Social and Economic Reconstruction*, edited by T. Addison and T. Brück. Basingstoke: Palgrave Macmillan.

Stewart, Frances and Graham K. Brown. 2009. 'Fragile states.' Centre for Research on Inequality, Human Security, and Ethnicity (CRISE), University of Oxford, Oxford.

Stewart, Frances, Graham K. Brown and Arnim Langer. 2008. 'Policies towards horizontal inequalities.' In *Horizontal Inequalities and Conflict: Understanding Group Violence in Multiethnic Societies*, edited by F. Stewart. London: Palgrave, pp. 301–26.

Stewart, Frances, Valpy Fitzgerald and Associates. 2001. *War and Underdevelopment: The Economic and Social Consequences of Conflict*, Vol. 1. Oxford: Oxford University Press.

Stewart, Frances, C. Huang and M. Wang. 2001. 'Internal wars in developing countries: an empirical overview of economic and social consequences.' In *War and Underdevelopment*, Vol. 1, edited by F. Stewart, V. Fitzgerald and Associates. Oxford: Oxford University Press.

Stoll, David. 1993. *Between Two Armies in the Ixil Towns of Guatemala.* New York: Columbia University Press.

Straus, Scott. 2006. *The Order of Genocide: Race, Power, and War in Rwanda* Ithaca, NY: Cornell University Press.

Strimling, Andrea. 2006. 'Stepping out of the tracks: cooperation between official diplomats and private facilitators.' *International Negotiation* **11**:91–127.

Studdard, K. 2004. 'War economies in a regional context: overcoming the challenges of transformation.' IPA Policy Report, International Peace Academy, New York.

Study Group on Europe's Security Capabilities. 2004. 'A human security doctrine for Europe: the Barcelona report.'

Suberu, Rotimi. 2001. *Federalism and Ethnic Conflict in Nigeria.* Washington, DC: United States Institute of Peace (USIP).

Suberu, Rotimi. 2009. 'Religion and institutions: federalism and the management of conflicts over Sharia in Nigeria.' *Journal of International Development* **21**:547–60.

Suberu, Rotimi and Larry Diamond. 2000. 'Institutional design, ethnic conflict management, and democracy in Nigeria.' In *The Architecture of Democracy: Institutional Design, Conflict Management and Democracy,* edited by A. Reynolds. Oxford: Oxford University Press.

Suhrke, Astri. 1999. 'Human security and the interest of states.' *Security Dialogue* **30**:265–76.

Suhrke, Astri. 2004. 'A stalled initiative.' *Security Dialogue* **35**:365.

Suliman, Mohamed. 1997. 'Ethnicity from perception to cause of violent conflicts: the case of the Fur and Nuba conflicts in Western Sudan.' Paper presented to the CONTICI International Workshop, Bern, 8–11 July.

Suliman, Mohamed. 1999a. 'Conflict resolution among the Borana and the Fur: similar features, different outcomes.' In *Ecology, Politics, and Violent Conflict*, edited by M. Suliman. London: Zed, pp. 286–9.

Suliman, Mohamed. 1999b. 'The rationality and irrationality of violence in Sub-Saharan Africa.' In *Ecology, Politics, and Violent Conflict*, edited by M. Suliman. London: Zed, pp. 27–43.

Swanson, P. 2002. 'Fuelling conflicts: the oil industry and armed conflict.' Fafo Institute, Oslo.

Swee, E. 2009. 'On war and schooling attainment: the case of Bosnia and Herzegovina.' Households in Conflict Network, Brighton, available at: http://www.hicn.org/.

Tadjbakhsh, Shahrbanou and Anuradha Chenoy. 2007. *Human Security: Concepts and Implications.* London: Routledge.

Tadjoeddin, M. Zulfan. 2011. 'The Economic Origins of Indonesia's Secessionist Conflicts', *Civil Wars* **13**(3):312–32.

Tadjoeddin, M. Zulfan. 2010. 'Political economy of conflict during Indonesia's democratic transition.' PhD thesis, University of Western Sydney, Sydney.

Tadjoeddin, M. Zulfan and Anis Chowdhury. 2009. 'Socioeconomic perspectives on violent conflict in Indonesia.' *The Economics of Peace and Security Journal* **4**:38–47.

Tadjoeddin, M. Zulfan, I. Suharyo Widjajanti and Satish Mishra. 2001. 'Regional disparity and vertical conflict in Indonesia.' *Journal of the Asia Pacific Economy* **6**:283–304.

Talbott, Strobe. 2008. *The Great Experiment: The Story of Ancient*

Empires, Modern States, and the Quest for a Global Nation. New York: Simon & Schuster.

Talentino, A.K. 2007. 'Perceptions of peacebuilding: the dynamic of imposer and imposed upon.' *International Studies Perspective* **8**(2):152–71.

Tarrow, S. 1983. *Struggling to Reform: Social Movements and Policy Change During Cycles of Protest*. Ithaca, NY: Cornell University Press.

Tarrow, S. 1994. *Power in Movement: Social Movements, Collective Action, and Politics*. Ithaca, NY: Cornell University Press.

Tawil, Sobhi & Alexander and Harvey (eds). 2004. *Education, Conflict and Social Cohesion*. Geneva: UNESCO, International Bureau of Education.

Taylor, Mark. 2002. 'Emerging conclusions, March 2002.' Fafo Project on the Economies of Conflict: Private Sector Activity in Armed Conflict. Fafo Institute, Oslo.

Taylor, Michael. 1988. 'Rationality and revolutionary collective action.' In *Rationality and Revolution*, edited by M. Taylor. Cambridge: Cambridge University Press.

Taylor, Reepert. 1996. 'Political science encounters "race" and "ethnicity".' *Ethnic and Racial Studies* **19**:884–95.

Teiwes, Frederick C. 1987. 'Establishment and consolidation of the new regime.' In *The Cambridge History of China. Vol. 14, The People's Republic, Part I: The Emergence of Revolutionary China, 1949–1965*, edited by J.K. Fairbank and D. Twitchett. Cambridge: Cambridge University Press.

Tellnes, J.F. 2005. 'Dealing with petroleum issues in civil war negotiations: the case of Sudan.' Paper presented at the 13th Annual National Political Science Conference, Hurdalssjøen.

Thakur, Ramesh. 1997. 'From national to human security.' In *Asia-Pacific Security: The Economics-Politics Nexus*, edited by S. Harris and A. Mack. Sydney: Allen & Unwin.

Thakur, R. 2002. 'Outlook: intervention, sovereignty and the responsibility to protect: experiences from ICISS.' *Security Dialogue* **33**(3):323–40.

Thakur, Ramesh and A. Schnabel. 2001. *United Nations Peacekeeping Operations: Ad Hoc Missions, Permanent Engagement*. Tokyo: United Nations University Press.

Thakur, R. and C.A. Thayer (eds). 1995. *A Crisis of Expectations: UN Peacekeeping in the 1990s*. Boulder, CO: Westview.

Tharoor, S. 1995–96. 'Should UN peacekeeping go "back to basics"?' *Survival* **37**(4):52–64.

Theisen, Ole Magnus. 2008. 'Blood and soil? Resource scarcity and internal armed conflict revisited.' *Journal of Peace Research* **45**:801–18.

Theisen, Ole Magnus, Helge Holtermann and Halvard Buhaug. 2012. 'Draught, political exclusion, and civil war.' *International Security* **36**(3):79–106.

Thiruchandran, S. 1999. *Women, Narration and Nation: Collective Images and Multiple Identities*. New Delhi: Vikas.

Tjosvold, D. 1974. 'Threat as a low power person's strategy in bargaining: social face and tangible outcomes.' *International Journal of Group Tensions* **4**:494–510.

Thomas, Caroline. 2000. *Global Governance, Development and Human Security*. London: Pluto.

Thomas, D., K. Beegle, E. Frankenberg, B. Sikoki, J. Strauss and G. Teruel. 2004. 'Education in a crisis.' *Journal of Development Economics* **74**:53–85.

Thoms, O., J. Ron and Roland Paris. 2008. 'The effects of transitional justice mechanisms: a summary of emirical research findings and implications for analysts and practitioners.' Centre for International Policy Studies, University of Ottawa, Ottawa.

Tikly, Leon. 2001. 'Globalisation and Education in the Postcolonial World: Towards a Conceptual Framework', *Comparative Education* **37**(2):151–71.

Tikly, Leon. 2009. 'Education and the New Imperialism', 23–45, In Roland Sintos Coloma (ed.) *Postcolonial Challenges in Education*. New York: Peter Lang.

Tilly, Charles. 1978. *From Mobilization to Revolution*. New York: McGraw-Hill.

Tilly, Charles. 1990. *Coercion, Capital, and European States, AD 990–1990*. Oxford: Blackwell.

Tilly, Charles. 1998. *Durable Inequality*. Berkeley, CA: University of California Press.

Tilly, Charles. 2003. *The Politics of Collective Violence*. Cambridge: Cambridge University Press.

Tobler, Waldo. 1970. 'A computer movie simulation of urban growth in the Detroit region.' *Economic Geography* **46**:234–40.

Toft, Monica Duffy. 2010. 'Ending civil wars: a case for rebel victory?' *International Security* **34**:7–36.

Tol, Richard S.J. and Sebastian Wagner. 2010. 'Climate change and violent conflict in Europe over the last millennium.' *Climatic Change* **99**:65–79.

Tölöyan, Khachig. 1987. 'Cultural narrative and the motivation of the terrorist.' *Journal of Strategic Studies* **10**:217–33.

Torjesen, Stina. 2006. 'The political economy of disarmament, demobilisation and reintegration.' Norwegian Institute of International Affairs (NUPI), Oslo.

Torvik, Ragnar. 2002. 'Natural resources, rent seeking, and welfare.' *Journal of Development Economics* **67**:455–70.

Touval, S. 1982. *The Peace Brokers: Mediators in the Arab-Israeli Conflict 1948–1979.* Princeton, NJ: Princeton University Press.

TraCCC. 2001. 'Transnational crime and peacekeeping: Comparative perspectives.' Transnational Crime and Corruption Center (TraCCC), Washington, DC.

Tranchant, Jean-Pierre. 2007. 'Decentralization and ethnic conflict: the role of empowerment.' MPRA Paper no. 3713, available at: http://mpra.ub.uni-muenchen.de/3713/.

Tranchant, Jean-Pierre. 2008. 'Fiscal decentralisation, institutional quality, and ethnic conflict: a panel data analysis, 1985–2001.' *Conflict, Security and Development* **8**:419–514.

Treisman, Daniel. 2000. 'The causes of corruption: a cross national study.' *Journal of Public Economics* **76**:399–457.

Truong, Thanh-Dam and Des Gasper. 2010. *Transnational Migration and Human Security.* New York: Springer.

Turshen, M. and C. Twagiramariya (eds). 1998. *What Women Do in Wartime.* London and New York: Zed Books.

Turton, David. 1997. 'War and ethnicity: global connections and local violence in North East Africa and Former Yugoslavia.' *Oxford Development Studies* **25**:77–94.

Turton, David and P. Marsden. 2002. 'Taking refugees for a ride? The politics of refugee return to Afghanistan.' Afghanistan Research and Evaluation Unit (AREU), Kabul.

Tutu, Desmond. 1999. *No Future without Forgiveness.* New York: Doubleday.

UCDP. 2011. 'UCDP/PRIO Armed Conflict Dataset v.4-2011, 1946–2010.' Uppsala Conflict Data Program (UCDP)/Peace Research Institute of Oslo (PRIO).

Uchendu, Victor C. 1965. *The Igbo of Southeast Nigeria.* New York: Holt, Rinehart, & Winston.

Ucko, D. 2008. 'Militias, tribes, and insurgents: the challenge of political reintegration in Iraq.' *Conflict, Security and Development* **3**:341–73.

Ukiwo, Ukoha. 2008. 'Horizontal inequalities and ethnic violence: evidence from Calabar and Warri, Nigeria.' In *Horizontal Inequalites and Conflict: Understanding Group Violence in Multiethnic Societies*, edited by F. Stewart. London: Palgrave, pp. 190–204.

ul-Haq, Mahbub. 1995. *Reflections on Human Development*. New York: Oxford University Press.

Underdaal, A. 1983. 'Causes of negotiation failure.' *European Journal of Political Research* 11(2):183–95.

UNDP. 1994. *Human Development Report 1994*. New York: Oxford University Press.

UNDP. 1999. *Human Development Report 1999*. New York: Oxford University Press.

UNDP. 2005. 'Sustaining post-conflict economic recovery: lessons and challenges.' Bureau of Crisis Prevention and Recovery, United Nations Development Programme (UNDP), New York.

UNDP. 2008. *Post-Conflict Economic Recovery: Enabling Local Ingenuity*. New York: United Nations Development Programme (UNDP).

UNDP Liberia. 2006. *Liberia National Human Development Report*. Monrovia: United Nations Development Programme Liberia.

UNEP. 2007a. 'Environmental degradation triggering tensions and conflict in Sudan.' United Nations Environment Programme, Nairobi, available at: http://www.unep.org/Documents.Multilingual/Default.asp?DocumentID=512&ArticleID=5621&l=en.

UNEP. 2007b. 'Sudan: post-conflict environmental assessment.' United Nations Environment Programme, Nairobi.

UNESCO. 2010. *Education Under Attack 2010*. Paris: United Nations Educational, Scientific and Cultural Organization.

UNHCR. 1993. 'Information note on the development of UNHCR's Guidelines on the Protection Aspects of Voluntary Repatriation.' UNHCR, Geneva, available at: http://www.unhcr.org/refworld/docid/3ae68cbd4.html.

UNHCR. 1994. 'UNHCR's operation experience with interally displaced persons.' United Nations High Commission for Refugees (UNHCR), Geneva.

UNHCR. 2007a. 'Discussion paper: Refugee protection and durable solutions in the context of international migration.' UNHCR, Geneva.

UNHCR. 2007b. 'Refugee Protection and Mixed Migration: A 10-Point Plan of Action.' UNHCR, Geneva.

UNHCR. 2009a. 'Refugee Protection and Mixed Migration: The 10-Point Plan in Action.' UNHCR, Geneva.

UNHCR. 2009b. 'Report of the Extraordinary Meeting of 8 December 2009 of the sixty-first session of the Executive Committee of the Programme of the United Nations High Commissioner for Refugees.' UNHCR, Geneva.

UNHCR. 2009c. 'UNHCR policy on refugee protection and solutions in urban areas.' UNHCR, Geneva.

UNHCR/OSCE. 2002. 'Ninth assessment of the situation of ethnic minorities in Kosovo.' United Nations High Commission for Refugees (UNHCR) and the Organization for Security and Cooperation in Europe (OSCE), Geneva.

UNIDIR. 1995–98. *Managing Arms in Peace Processes*. New York and Geneva: United Nations.

United Nations. 1990. *The Blue Helmets: A Review of United Nations Peace-Keeping* 2nd edn. New York: United Nations.

United Nations. 1992. 'An agenda for peace: preventive diplomacy, peace-making and peacekeeping.' Available at: http://www.un.org/Docs/SG/agpeace.html.

United Nations. 1996. *The Blue Helmets: A Review of United Nations Peace-Keeping* 3rd edn. New York: United Nations.

United Nations. 1997. 'Office of the United Nations High Commissioner for Refugees.' United Nations, New York.

United Nations. 1998. 'Office of the United Nations High Commissioner for Refugees.' United Nations, New York.

United Nations. 2000a. 'Report of the panel of experts on violations of the Security Council sanctions against UNITA.' United Nations, New York.

United Nations. 2000b. 'Report of the panel on United Nations peace operations.' Available at: http://www.un.org/peace/reports/peace operations/.

United Nations. 2001. 'Report of the Panel of Experts on the Illegal Exploitation of Resources and Other Forms of Wealth in the Democratic Republic of Congo.' United Nations, New York.

United Nations. 2004a. 'A more secure world: our shared responsibility.' United Nations, New York.

United Nations. 2004b. 'Role of business in conflict prevention, peace-keeping, and post-conflict reconstruction.' United Nations, New York.

United Nations. 2004c. 'Report of the Secretary-General's high-level panel on threats, challenges, and change. A more secure world: our shared responsibility.' Available at: http://www.un.org/secureworld/.

United Nations. 2005. 'World Summit Outcome Document.' United Nations, New York, available at: http://www.who.int/hiv/universal access2010/worldsummit.pdf (accessed January 10, 2011).

United Nations. 2006a. 'Integrated Disarmament, Demobilization and Reintegration Standards.' United Nations, New York.

United Nations. 2006b. 'Resolution 1674, 28 April. The Protection of Civilians in Armed Conflict.' Available at: http://www.secur itycouncilreport.org/atf/cf/%7B65BFCF9B-6D27-4E9C-8CD3-CF6E4 FF96FF9%7D/Civilians%20SRES1674.pdf.

United Nations. 2007. 'Maintenance of international peace and security: natural resources and conflict.' United Nations, New York.

United Nations. 2008a. 'Policies for post-conflict employment creation, income generation, and reintegration.' International Labour Organisation (ILO) and UNDP Bureau for Crisis Prevention and Recovery, Geneva and New York.

United Nations. 2008b. 'Protect, respect, and remedy: a framework for business and human rights.' United Nations, New York.

United Nations. 2009a. 'Report of the Secreatary-General on peacebuilding in the immediate aftermath of conflict.' United Nations, New York, available at: http://daccess-ods.un.org/TMP/9737302.06489563.html.

United Nations. 2009b. 'World Population Prospects: the 2008 Revision. Executive Summary.' United Nations, New York, available at: http://esa.un.org/unpd/wpp2008/pdf/WPP2008_Executive-Summary_Edited_6-Oct-2009.pdf.

United Nations. 2010a. 'Business and human rights: further steps toward the operationalization of the "protect, respect, and remedy" framework.' United Nations, New York.

United Nations. 2010b. 'Report of the Secretary-General to the Sixty-Fourth Session of the United Nations General Assembly.' United Nations, New York, available at: http://hdr.undp.org/en/media/SG_Human_Security_Report_12_04_10.pdf (accessed February 2, 2011).

United States Department of State. 2010. 'Leading through civilian power: 2010 quadrennial diplomacy and development review.' United States Department of State, Washington, DC, available at: http://www.state.gov/s/dmr/qddr/ (accessed January 17, 2011).

University of Illinois Office of International Criminal Justice. 1990. 'Panama City Citizen Survey: Panama's Public Force.' University of Illinois, Chicago, IL.

Urdal, Henrik. 2005. 'People vs. Malthus: population pressure, environmental degradation and armed conflict revisited.' *Journal of Peace Research* **42**:417–34.

Urdal, Henrik. 2006. 'A clash of generations? Youth bulges and political violence.' *International Studies Quarterly* **50**:607–29.

Urdal, Henrik. 2008. 'Population, resources and political violence: a sub-national study of India 1956–2002.' *Journal of Conflict Resolution* **52**:590–617.

Urquhart, B. 1972. *Hammarskjold*. New York: Knopf.

Urquhart, B. 1987. *A Life in Peace and War*. London: Weidenfeld & Nicholson.

Ury, W. 1991. *Getting Past No: Negotiating in Difficult Situations*. New York. Bantam Dell.

USAID. 2005a. 'Community focused reintegration.' United States Agency for International Development (USAID), Washington, DC.

USAID. 2005b. 'Fragile states strategy.' United States Agency for International Development (USAID), Washington, DC, available at: http://www.usaid.gov/policy/2005_fragile_states_strategy.

USAID. 2007. 'Role of education and the demobilization of child soldiers.' United States Agency for International Development (USAID), Washington, DC.

Utas, M. 2005. 'Victimcy, girlfriending, soldiering: tactic agency in a young woman's social navigation of the Liberian war zone.' *Anthropological Quarterly* **78**:403–30.

Valentin, Karen. 2005. *Schooled for the Future? Educational Policy and Everyday Life Among Urban Squatters in Nepal*. Greenwich, CT: Information Age Publishing, Inc.

Van Hear, N. 2004. '"I went as far as my money would take me": conflict, forced migration, and class.' COMPAS, University of Oxford, Oxford.

van Houten, P. and Stefan Wolff. 2007. 'The stability of autonomy arrangements: the role of external agents.' Paper presented at the 48th Annual Convention of the International Studies Association, Chicago, IL, February 28, available at: http://www.allacademic.com/meta/p179305_index.html.

Varshney, Ashutosh. 2003. *Ethnic Conflict and Civil Life: Hindus and Muslims in India*. New Haven, CT: Yale University Press.

Vermeersch, Peter. 2010. 'Political mobilization.' In *The International Encyclopedia of Political Science*, edited by G.T. Kurian. Washington, DC: CQ Press.

Verwimp, Philip, Patricia Justino and Tilman Brück. 2009. 'The analysis of conflict: a micro-level perspective.' *Journal of Peace Research* **46**(3):307–14.

Vigh, H. 2006. *Navigating Terrains of War: Youth and Soldiering in Guinea-Bissau*. New York: Berghahn.

Vines, Alex. 2004. 'Monitoring UN sanctions in Africa: the role of panels of experts'. In *Verification Yearbook 2003*. London: VERTIC.

Vines, Alex and Bereni Oruitemeka. 2008. 'Bullets to ballots: the reintegration of UNITA in Angola.' *Conflict, Security and Development* **8**:241–63.

Virtanen, P. and D. Ehrenpreis. 2007. 'Growth, poverty, and inequality in Mozambique.' International Poverty Centre, Brasilia.

Viterna, Jocelyn S. 2006. 'Pulled, pushed, and persuaded: explaining women's mobilization into the Salvadoran guerrilla army.' *American Journal of Sociology* **112**:1–45.

von Beyme, K. 1985. *Political Parties in Western Democracies*. Aldershot: Gower.

von Hippel, K. 2000a. *Democracy by Force: US Military Intervention in the Post-Cold War World*. Cambridge: Cambridge University Press.

von Hippel, Karin. 2000b. 'Democracy by force: a renewed commitment to nation building.' *Washington Quarterly* **23**:95–112.

Vreeland, James Raymond. 2008. 'The effect of political regime on civil war: unpacking anocracy.' *Journal of Conflict Resolution* **52**:401–25.

Waddell, N. and Phil Clark. 2009. 'Introduction.' In *Courting Conflict? Justice, Peace and the ICC in Africa*, edited by N. Waddell and P. Clark. London: Royal African Society.

Wagner, Robert Harrison. 1993. 'The causes of peace.' In *Stopping the Killing: How Civil Wars End*, edited by R. Licklider. New York: New York University Press.

Wainhouse, D.W. 1966. *International Peace Observation: A History and Forecast*. Baltimore, MD: Johns Hopkins University Press.

Wainhouse, D.W. 1973. *International Peacekeeping at the Crossroads: National Support – Experience and Prospects*. Baltimore, MD: Johns Hopkins University Press.

Waldmeir, Patti. 1997. *Anatomy of a Miracle: The End of Apartheid and the Birth of the New South Africa*. New York: W.W. Norton.

Wall, J.A. Jr, J.B. Stark and R.L. Standifer. 2001. 'Mediation: current review and theory development.' *Journal of Conflict Resolution* **45**(3):370–91.

Wallensteen, Peter and Margareta Sollenberg. 1998. 'Armed conflict and regional conflict complexes.' *Journal of Peace Research* **35**:621–34.

Wallensteen, Peter, C. Staibano and Mikael Eriksson. 2003. 'Making targeted sanctions effective: guidelines for the implementation of UN policy options.' Department of Peace and Conflict Research, Uppsala University, Uppsala.

Walter, Barbara. 1997. 'The critical barrier to civil war settlement.' *International Organization* **51**(3):335–64.

Walter, Barbara F. 1999. 'Designing transitions from civil war.' *International Security* **24**:127–55.

Walter, Barbara. 2001. *Committing to Peace: The Successful Settlement of Civil Wars*. Princeton, NJ: Princeton University Press.

Walter, B. 2002. *Committing to Peace: The Successful Settlement of Civil Wars*. Princeton, NJ: Princeton University Press.

Walter, Barbara. 2004. 'Does conflict beget conflict? Explaining recurring civil war.' *Journal of Peace Research* **41**:371–88.

Walter, Barbara and Jack Snyder. 1999. *Civil Wars, Insecurity and Intervention*. New York: Columbia University Press.

Waltz, Kenneth A. 2000. 'Structural realism after the Cold War.' *International Security* **25**:5–41.

Wantchekon, L. 2004. 'The paradox of "warlord" democracy: a theoretical investigation.' *American Political Science Review* **98**(1):17–33.

Wantchekon, L. and Z. Neeman. 2002. 'A theory of post-civil war democratization.' *Journal of Theoretical Politics* **14**(4):439–64.

Wantchekon, Leonard and David Nickerson. 1999. 'Multilateral intervention facilitates post-civil war democratization.' Political Science Department, Yale University, New Haven, CT.

Warner, D. 1994. 'Voluntary repatriation and the meaning of Return to Home: a critique of liberal mathematics.' *Journal of Refugee Studies* **7**:160–74.

Waterman, Harvey. 1993. 'Political order and the "settlement" of civil wars.' In *Stopping the Killing: How Civil Wars End*, edited by R. Licklider. New York: New York University Press, pp. 292–302.

Watts, Jonathan. 2007. 'Riots and hunger feared as demand for gran sends food costs soaring.' *The Guardian* 4 December, available at: http://www.guardian.co.uk/world/2007/dec/04/china.business.

Watts, R. 1987. 'Federalism.' In *The Blackwell Encyclopaedia of Political Institutions*, edited by V. Bogdanor. Oxford: Basil Blackwell.

Watts, R. 1998. 'Federalism, federal political systems, and federations.' *Annual Review of Political Science* **1**:117–37.

Watts, R. 2001. 'Models of federal power-sharing.' *International Social Science Journal* **53**:23–32.

Weiner, Myron. 1978. *Sons of the Soil: Migration and Ethnic Conflict in India*. Princeton, NJ: Princeton University Press.

Weinstein, J.M. 2005. 'Autonomous recovery and international intervention in comparative perspective.' Working paper, Department of Political Science, Stanford University, Stanford, CA.

Weinstein, Jeremy M. 2006. *Inside Rebellion: The Politics of Insurgent Violence*. Cambridge: Cambridge University Press.

Weiss, T.G. (ed.). 1995. *The United Nations and Civil Wars*. Boulder, CO: Lynne Rienner.

Weiss, Thomas G. 1999. *Military–Civilian Interactions: Intervening in Humanitarian Crises*. Lanham, MD: Rowman & Littlefield.

Weller, Marc. 1992. 'The international response to the dissolution of the Social Federal Republic of Yugoslavia.' *American Journal of International Law* **86**:569–607.

Wells, Linton, II and Walter Christman. 2009. 'Transformational initiatives in civil military operations: STAR-TIDES and maritime environments.' In *Crosscutting Issues in International Transformation*, edited by D. Neal, H. Friman, R. Doughty and L. Wells, II. Washington, DC: National Defense University Press.

Welsch, H. 2008. 'Resource abundance and internal armed conflict: types of natural resources and the incidence of "new wars".' *Ecological Economics* **67**:503–13.

Wennmann, A. 2007a. 'Money matters: the economic dimensions of peace mediation.' Graduate Institute of International Studies, Geneva.

Wennmann, A. 2007b. 'The political economy of conflict financing: a comprehensive approach beyond natural resources.' *Global Governance* **13**:427–44.

Wennmann, A. 2008. *Economic Dimensions of Peace Mediation.* Geneva: Graduate Institute of International Studies, University of Geneva.

Wennmann, A. 2010. 'Income sharing from natural resources.' Center on Conflict, Development, and Peacebuilding (CCDP), Graduate Institute of International Studies, Geneva.

Werner, Suzanne. 1999. 'The precarious nature of peace: resolving the issues, enforcing the settlement, and renegotiating the terms.' *American Journal of Political Science* **43**(3):912–34.

Werner, Suzanne and Amy Yuen. 2005. 'Making and keeping peace.' *International Organization* **59**(2):261–92.

Werthes, Sascha and David Bosold. 2006. 'Caught between pretension and substantiveness: ambiguities of human security as a political leitmotif.' In *Human Security on Foreign Policy Agendas*, edited by T. Debiel and S. Werthes. Essen: Institute for Development and Peace, University of Duisburg-Essen, available at: http://www.inef.uni-duisburg.de/page/documents/Report80.pdf (accessed February 1, 2011).

White, N.D. 1990. *The United Nations and the Maintenance of International Peace and Security.* Manchester: Manchester University Press.

Whitworth, S. 2004. *Men, Militarism, and UN Peacekeeping: A Gendered Analysis.* Boulder, CO: Lynne Rienner.

Whyte, John. 1983. 'How much discrimination was there under the unionist regime, 1921–68?' In *Contemporary Irish Studies*, edited by T. Gallagher and J. O'Connell. Manchester: Manchester University Press.

Wilkenfeld, J. and M. Brecher. 1984. 'International crises, 1945–1975: the UN dimension.' *International Studies Quarterly* **28**:45–67.

Wilkinson, Steven I. 2004. *Votes and Violence.* New York: Cambridge University Press.

Williams, Michael C. 1998. *Civil–Military Relations and Peacekeeping.* Oxford: Oxford University Press.

Williams, P. and J. Picarelli. 2005. 'Combating organized crime in conflict.' In *Profiting from Peace: Managing the Resource Dimension of Civil Wars*, edited by K. Ballentine and H. Nitzschke. Boulder, CO: Lynne Rienner.

Willibald, S. 2006. 'Does money work? Cash transfers to ex-combatants in disarmament, demobilization and reintegration processes.' *Disasters* **30**:316–39.

Wimmer, Andreas. 2003. 'Democracy and ethno-religious conflict in Iraq.' *Survival* **45**:111–34.

Wimmer, Andreas, Lars-Erik Cederman and Brian Min. 2009. 'Ethnic politics and armed conflict: a configurational analysis of a new global dataset.' *American Sociological Review* **74**:316–37.

Winer, J. 2005. 'Tracking conflict commodities and finance.' In *Profiting from Peace: Managing the Resource Dimension of Civil Wars*, edited by K. Ballentine and H. Nitzschke. Boulder, CO: Lynne Rienner.

Wiseman, H. (ed.). 1983. *Peacekeeping: Appraisals and Proposals*. New York: Pergamon and International Peace Academy.

Witsenburg, Karen and Wario R. Adano. 2009. 'Of rain and raids: violent livestock raiding in northern Kenya.' *Civil Wars* **11**:514–38.

Wlodarczyk, N. 2009. *Magic and Warfare: Appearance and Reality in Contemporary African Conflict and Beyond*. Basingstoke: Palgrave Macmillan.

Wohlforth, William C. 1998. 'Reality check: revising theories of international politics in response to the end of the Cold War.' *World Politics* **50**:650–80.

Wolff, Stefan. 2003. *Disputed Territories: The Transnational Dynamics of Ethnic Conflict Settlement*. New York and Oxford: Berghahn.

Wolff, Stefan. 2005. 'Electoral systems design and power sharing regimes.' In *Powersharing: New Challenges for Divided Societies*, edited by I. O'Flynn and D. Russell. Ann Arbor, MI: University of Michigan Press.

Wolff, Stefan. 2007. *Ethnic Conflict: A Global Perspective*. Oxford: Oxford University Press.

Wolff, Stefan and Marc Weller. 2008. *Institutions for the Management of Ethnopolitical Conflicts in Central and Eastern Europe*. Strasbourg: Council of Europe Publishing.

Wolffsohn, Michael. 1993. *Eternal Guilt? Forty Years of German–Jewish–Israeli Relations*. New York: Columbia University Press.

Wood, Elisabeth Jean. 2000. *Forging Democracy from Below: Insurgent Transitions in South Africa and El Salvador*. New York: Cambridge University Press.

Wood, Elisabeth Jean. 2003. *Insurgent Collective Action and Civil War in El Salvador*. Cambridge: Cambridge University Press.

Woodward, Susan. 1995. *Balkan Tragedy*. New York: Brookings Institute.
Woodward, Susan. 2002. 'Economic priorities for successful peace implementation.' In *Ending Civil Wars: The Implementation of Peace Agreements*, edited by S.J. Stedman, D. Rothchild and E.M. Cousens. Boulder, CO: Lynne Rienner.
Woodward, Susan. 2010. 'Post-Cold War debates on international security.' The New School GPIA Workshop: The Practices of Human Rights – Human Security, New York, October 8.
Worby, P. 1999. 'Lessons learned from the UNHCR involvement in the Guatemalan Refugee Repatriation and Reintegration Programme.' UNHCR, Geneva, available at: http://www.unhcr.org/research/RESEARCH/3ae6bd4f0.pdf.
World Bank. 1998. *Post-conflict Reconstruction: the Role of the World Bank*. Washington, DC: World Bank, Conflict Prevention and Reconstruction Unit, available at: http://siteresources.worldbank.org/INTLICUS/Resources/pcr-role-of-bank.pdf.
World Bank. 2000. *El Salvador Post-Conflict Reconstruction*. Washington, DC: World Bank, Operations Evaluation Department.
World Bank. 2005a. *Fragile States: Good Practice in Country Assistance Strategies*. Washington, DC: World Bank.
World Bank. 2005b. 'Reshaping the Future: Education and Postconflict Reconstruction.' Board Report no. 34790, World Bank, Washington, DC.
World Bank. 2009a. 'Madagascar: Country brief.' Report, World Bank, Washington, DC.
World Bank. 2009b. *Migration and Remittances at a Glance*. Washington, DC: World Bank.
Ylönen, A. 2005. 'Grievances and the roots of insurgencies: Southern Sudan and Darfur.' *Peace, Conflict and Development* 7:59–98.
Young, John. 1998. 'The Tigray People's Liberation Front.' In *African Guerrillas*, edited by C.S. Clapham. Bloomington, IN: Indiana University Press.
Young, O. 1968. *The Politics of Force*. Princeton, NJ: Princeton University Press.
Youngs, G. 2009. 'Private pain/public peace: women's rights as human rights and Amnesty International's report on violence against women'. In A.G. Jónasdóttir and K.B. Jones (eds), *The Political Interests of Gender Revisited: Redoing Theory and Research with a Feminist Face*. Tokyo: United Nations University Press, pp. 275–95.
Zahar, Marie-Joëlle. 1999. 'Mercenaries, brigands . . . and politicians: militia decision-making and civil conflict resolution.' Department of Political Science, McGill University, Montreal.

Zahar, Marie-Joelle J. 2003. 'Reframing the spoiler debate in peace processes.' In *Progressing Towards Settlement: Contemporary Peace Processes*, edited by J. Darby and R. Mac Ginty. Basingstoke: Palgrave Macmillan.

Zahar, Marie-Joelle J. 2005. 'Power sharing in Lebanon: foreign protectors, domestic peace, and democratic failure.' In *Sustainable Peace: Power and Democracy after Civil Wars*, edited by P.G. Roeder and D. Rothchild. Ithaca, NY: Cornell University Press.

Zakaria, Fareed. 2001. 'The roots of rage.' *Newsweek* 138.

Zald, M.N. and R. Ash. 1966. 'Social movement organizations: growth, decay, and change.' *Social Forces* **44**:327–41.

Zanger, Sabine C. 2000. 'A global analysis of the effect of political regime changes on life integrity violations, 1977–1993.' *Journal of Peace Research* **37**:213–33.

Zartman, I. William. 1989. *Ripe for Resolution: Conflict and Intervention in Africa*. New York: Oxford University Press.

Zartman, I. William. 1993. 'The unfinished agenda: negotiating internal conflicts.' In *Stopping the Killing: How Civil Wars End*, edited by R. Licklider. New York: New York University Press.

Zartman, I. William. 1995. *Elusive Peace: Negotiating an End to Civil Conflicts*. Washington, DC: Brookings Institute.

Zimmerman, S. 2009. 'Irregular secondary movements to Europe: seeking asylum beyond refuge.' *Journal of Refugee Studies* **22**:74–96.

Zyck, S. 2009. 'Former combatant reintegration and fragmentation in contemporary Afghanistan.' *Conflict, Security and Development* **9**:111–31.

Index